Financial Reporting and Analysis

CFA® PROGRAM CURRICULUM • VOLUME 3

LEVEL I
2010

CFA
INSTITUTE

Custom Publishing

New York   Boston   San Francisco
London   Toronto   Sydney   Tokyo   Singapore   Madrid
Mexico City   Munich   Paris   Cape Town   Hong Kong   Montreal

10 9 8 7 6 5

2008160751

AG/RH

Please visit our website at *www.pearsoncustom.com*

**Pearson
Custom Publishing**
is a division of

www.pearsonhighered.com

ISBN 10: 0-558-16019-0
ISBN 13: 978-0-558-16019-7

CONTENTS

iii

HOW TO USE THE CFA PROGRAM CURRICULUM

Congratulations on your decision to enter the Chartered Financial Analyst (CFA®) Program. This exciting and rewarding program of study reflects your desire to become a serious investment professional. You are embarking on a program noted for its high ethical standards and the breadth of knowledge, skills, and abilities it develops. Your commitment to the CFA Program should be educationally and professionally rewarding.

The credential you seek is respected around the world as a mark of accomplishment and dedication. Each level of the program represents a distinct achievement in professional development. Successful completion of the program is rewarded with membership in a prestigious global community of investment professionals. CFA charterholders are dedicated to life-long learning and maintaining currency with the ever-changing dynamics of a challenging profession. The CFA Program represents the first step towards a career-long commitment to professional education.

The CFA examination measures your degree of mastery of the assigned CFA Program curriculum. Effective study and preparation based on that curriculum are keys to your success on the examination.

Curriculum Development

The CFA Program curriculum is grounded in the practice of the investment profession. Utilizing a collaborative website, CFA Institute performs a continuous practice analysis with investment professionals around the world to determine the knowledge, skills, and abilities that are relevant to the profession. Regional panels and targeted surveys are also conducted annually to verify and reinforce the continuous feedback. The practice analysis process ultimately defines the Candidate Body of Knowledge (CBOK™) an inventory of knowledge and responsibilities expected of the investment management professional at the level of a new CFA charterholder. The process also determines how much emphasis each of the major topic areas receives on the CFA examinations.

A committee made up of practicing charterholders, in conjunction with CFA Institute staff, designs the CFA Program curriculum to deliver the CBOK to candidates. The examinations, also written by practicing charterholders, are designed to allow you to demonstrate your mastery of the CBOK as set forth in the CFA Program curriculum. As you structure your personal study program, you should emphasize mastery of the CBOK and the practical application of that knowledge. For more information on the practice analysis, CBOK, and development of the CFA Program curriculum, please visit www.cfainstitute.org/toolkit.

Organization

The Level I CFA Program curriculum is organized into 10 topic areas. Each topic area begins with a brief statement of the material and the depth of knowledge expected.

Each topic area is then divided into one or more study sessions. These study sessions—18 sessions in the Level I curriculum—should form the basic structure of your reading and preparation.

Each study session includes a statement of its structure and objective, and is further divided into specific reading assignments. The outline on the inside front cover of each volume illustrates the organization of these 18 study sessions.

The reading assignments are the basis for all examination questions, and are selected or developed specifically to teach the CBOK. These readings are drawn from CFA Program-commissioned content, textbook chapters, professional journal articles, research analyst reports, and cases. Many readings include problems and solutions as well as appendices to help you learn.

Reading-specific Learning Outcome Statements (LOS) are listed in the pages introducing each study session as well as at the beginning of each reading. These LOS indicate what you should be able to accomplish after studying the reading. We encourage you to review how to properly use LOS, and the descriptions of commonly used LOS "command words," at www.cfainstitute.org/toolkit. The command words signal the depth of learning you are expected to achieve from the reading. You should use the LOS to guide and focus your study, as each examination question is based on an assigned reading and one or more LOS. However, the readings provide context for the LOS and enable you to apply a principle or concept in a variety of scenarios. The candidate is responsible for the entirety of all of the required material in a study session, the assigned readings as well as the end-of-reading questions and problems.

Features of the Curriculum

▶ **Required vs. Optional Segments** - You should read all of the pages for an assigned reading. In some cases, however, we have reprinted an entire chapter or article and marked those parts of the reading that are not required as "optional." The CFA examination is based only on the required segments, and the optional segments are included only when they might help you to better understand the required segments (by seeing the required material in its full context). When an optional segment begins, you will see an icon and a solid vertical bar in the outside margin that will continue until the optional segment ends, accompanied by another icon. *Unless the material is specifically marked as optional, you should assume it is required.* Keep in mind that the optional material is provided strictly for your convenience and will not be tested. You should rely on the required segments and the reading-specific LOS in preparing for the examination.

▶ **Problems/Solutions** - *All questions and problems in the readings as well as their solutions (which are provided directly following the problems) are required material.* When appropriate, we have included problems within and after the readings to demonstrate practical application and reinforce your understanding of the concepts presented. The questions and problems are designed to help you learn these concepts and may serve as a basis for exam questions. Many of the questions are adapted from past CFA examinations.

▶ **Margins** - The wide margins in each volume provide space for your note-taking.

▶ **Two-Color Format** - To enrich the visual appeal and clarity of the exhibits, tables, and text, the curriculum is printed in a two-color format.

▶ **Six-Volume Structure** - For portability of the curriculum, the material is spread over six volumes.

▶ **Glossary and Index** - For your convenience, we have printed a comprehensive glossary and index in each volume. Throughout the curriculum, a **bolded blue** word in a reading denotes a term defined in the glossary.

▶ **Source Material -** The authorship, publisher, and copyright owners are given for each reading for your reference. We recommend that you use this CFA Institute curriculum rather than the original source materials because the curriculum may include only selected pages from outside readings, updated sections within the readings, and may have problems and solutions tailored to the CFA Program.

▶ **LOS Self-Check -** We have inserted checkboxes next to each LOS that you can use to track your progress in mastering the concepts in each reading.

Designing Your Personal Study Program

Create a Schedule - An orderly, systematic approach to examination preparation is critical. You should dedicate a consistent block of time every week to reading and studying. Complete all reading assignments and the associated problems and solutions in each study session. Review the LOS both before and after you study each reading to ensure that you have mastered the applicable content and can demonstrate the knowledge, skill, or ability described by the LOS and the assigned reading. Use the new LOS self-check to track your progress and highlight areas of weakness for later review.

You will receive periodic e-mail communications that contain important study tips and preparation strategies. Be sure to read these carefully.

CFA Institute estimates that you will need to devote a minimum of 10–15 hours per week for 18 weeks to study the assigned readings. Allow a minimum of one week for each study session, and plan to complete them all at least 30–45 days prior to the examination. This schedule will allow you to spend the final four to six weeks before the examination reviewing the assigned material and taking online sample and mock examinations.

At CFA Institute, we believe that candidates need to commit to a *minimum* of 270–300 hours reading and reviewing the curriculum and end-of-reading questions and problems. Many candidates have also incorporated the online sample examinations into their preparations during the final weeks before the exam. This recommendation, however, may substantially underestimate the hours needed for appropriate examination preparation depending on your individual circumstances, relevant experience, and academic background. You will undoubtedly adjust your study time to conform to your own strengths and weaknesses, and your educational and professional background.

You will probably spend more time on some study sessions than on others, but on average you should plan on devoting 15 hours per study session. You should allow ample time for both in-depth study of all topic areas and additional concentration on those topic areas for which you feel least prepared.

Preliminary Readings - The reading assignments in Economics assume candidates already have a basic mastery of the concepts typically presented in introductory university-level economics courses. Information on suggested readings to improve your knowledge of these topics precedes the relevant study sessions.

Candidate Preparation Toolkit - We have created the online toolkit to provide a single comprehensive location with resources and guidance for candidate preparation. In addition to in-depth information on study program planning, the CFA Program curriculum, and the online sample and mock examinations, the toolkit also contains curriculum errata, printable study session outlines, sample examination questions, and more. Errata that we have identified in the curriculum are corrected and listed periodically in the errata listing in the toolkit. We encourage you to use the toolkit as your central preparation resource during your tenure as a candidate. Visit the toolkit at www.cfainstitute.org/toolkit.

Online Sample Examinations - As part of your study of the assigned curriculum, use the CFA Institute online sample examinations to assess your exam preparation as you progress toward the end of your study. After each question, you will receive immediate feedback noting the correct response and indicating the relevant assigned reading, so you'll be able to identify areas of weakness for further study. The 120-minute sample examinations reflect the question formats, topics, and level of difficulty of the actual CFA examinations. Aggregate data indicate that the CFA examination pass rate was higher among candidates who took one or more online sample examinations than among candidates who did not take the online sample examinations. For more information on the online sample examinations, please visit www.cfainstitute.org/toolkit.

Online Mock Examinations - In response to candidate requests, CFA Institute has developed mock examinations that mimic the actual CFA examinations not only in question format and level of difficulty, but also in length. The three-hour online mock exams simulate the morning and afternoon sessions of the actual CFA exam, and are intended to be taken after you complete your study of the full curriculum, so you can test your understanding of the CBOK and your readiness for the exam. To further differentiate, feedback is provided at the end of the exam, rather than after each question as with the sample exams. CFA Institute recommends that you take these mock exams at the final stage of your preparation toward the actual CFA examination. For more information on the online mock examinations, please visit www.cfainstitute.org/toolkit.

Tools to Measure Your Comprehension of the Curriculum

With the addition of the online mock exams, CFA Institute now provides three distinct ways you can practice for the actual CFA exam. The full descriptions are above, but below is a brief summary of each:

End-of-Reading Questions and Problems - These are found at the end of each reading in the printed curriculum, and should be used to test your understanding of the concepts.

Online Sample Exams - Typically available two months before the CFA exam, online sample exams are designed to assess your exam preparation, and can help you target areas of weakness for further study.

Online Mock Exams - In contrast to the sample exams, mock exams are not available until closer to the actual exam date itself. Mock exams are designed to replicate the exam day experience, and should be taken near the end of your study period to prepare for exam day.

Preparatory Providers - After you enroll in the CFA Program, you may receive numerous solicitations for preparatory courses and review materials. Although preparatory courses and notes may be helpful to some candidates, you should view these resources as *supplements* to the assigned CFA Program curriculum. The CFA examinations reference only the CFA Institute assigned curriculum—no preparatory course or review course materials are consulted or referenced. Before you decide on a supplementary prep course, do some research. Determine the experience and expertise of the instructors, the accuracy and currency of their content, the delivery method for their materials, and the provider's claims of success. Most importantly, make sure the provider is in compliance with the CFA Institute Prep Provider Guidelines Program. Three years of prep course products can be a significant investment, so make sure you're getting a sufficient return. Just remember, there are no shortcuts to success on the CFA examinations. Prep products can enhance your learning experience, but the CFA curriculum is the key to success. For more information on the Prep Provider Guidelines Program, visit www.cfainstitute.org/cfaprog/resources/prepcourse.html.

SUMMARY

Every question on the CFA examination is based on specific pages in the required readings and on one or more LOS. Frequently, an examination question is also tied to a specific example highlighted within a reading or to a specific end-of-reading question and/or problem and its solution. To make effective use of the curriculum, please remember these key points:

1. All pages printed in the Custom Curriculum are required reading for the examination except for occasional sections marked as optional. You may read optional pages as background, but you will not be tested on them.

2. All questions, problems, and their solutions - printed at the end of readings - are required study material for the examination.

3. You should make appropriate use of the CFA Candidate Toolkit, the online sample/mock examinations, and preparatory courses and review materials.

4. You should schedule and commit sufficient study time to cover the 18 study sessions, review the materials, and take sample/mock examinations.

5. **Note:** Some of the concepts in the study sessions may be superseded by updated rulings and/or pronouncements issued after a reading was published. Candidates are expected to be familiar with the overall analytical framework contained in the assigned readings. Candidates are not responsible for changes that occur after the material was written.

Feedback

At CFA Institute, we are committed to delivering a comprehensive and rigorous curriculum for the development of competent, ethically grounded investment professionals. We rely on candidate and member feedback as we work to incorporate content, design, and packaging improvements. You can be assured that we will continue to listen to your suggestions. Please send any comments or feedback to curriculum@cfainstitute.org. Ongoing improvements in the curriculum will help you prepare for success on the upcoming examinations, and for a lifetime of learning as a serious investment professional.

4⅝ 4¹¹/₁₆ — ⅜
5½ 5½ —
5½ 21³/₁₆ — ¹/₁₆
20⅝ 21³/₁₆ — ¹/₁₆
17⅜ 18⅛ + ⅞
6½ 6½ — ½
7¼ 31/₃₂ — ⅛
15/₁₆
9/₁₆ ⅝
1¹/₃₂
7¹⁵/₁₆ 7¹³/₁₆ 7¹⁵/₁₆
2⅝ 2¹¹/₃₂ 2½ +
2¾ 2¼ 2¼
12¹/₁₆ 11⅜ 11¾ +
87 33¾ 33 33¹/₁₆ —
602 25⅝ 24⁹/₁₆ 25⅝ +
833 12 11⅝ 11⅝ +
16 10½ 10½ 10½ —
78 15⅝ 15¹³/₁₆ 15⅝ —
4508 9¹/₁₆ 8¼ 8¼ +
430 11¼ 10⅛ 10⅛ —

FINANCIAL REPORTING AND ANALYSIS

TOPIC LEVEL LEARNING OUTCOME

The candidate should be able to demonstrate a thorough knowledge
of financial accounting procedures and the rules that govern
disclosure. Emphasis is on basic financial statements and how
alternative accounting methods affect those statements and the
analysis of financial statement relationships.

$4\frac{5}{8}$ $4\frac{7}{16}$ $\frac{5}{8}$

$5\frac{1}{2}$ $5\frac{1}{2}$ $-$ $\frac{5}{8}$

$5\frac{1}{2}$ $21\frac{3}{16}$ $-$ $\frac{1}{16}$

$20\frac{5}{8}$ $21\frac{3}{16}$ $-$ $\frac{1}{16}$

$17\frac{3}{8}$ $18\frac{1}{8}$ $+$ $\frac{7}{8}$

$18\frac{1}{2}$ $6\frac{1}{2}$ $-$

$6\frac{1}{2}$ $6\frac{1}{2}$ $-$ $\frac{1}{2}$

$7\frac{1}{4}$ $31\frac{31}{32}$ $-$ $\frac{1}{8}$

$\frac{15}{16}$ $\frac{9}{16}$

$\frac{9}{16}$

$\frac{15}{32}$

$7\frac{13}{16}$ $7\frac{15}{16}$

$7\frac{15}{16}$ $7\frac{13}{16}$ $7\frac{15}{16}$

$2\frac{11}{32}$ $2\frac{1}{2}$ $+$

$2\frac{5}{8}$ $2\frac{11}{32}$ $2\frac{1}{4}$

$2\frac{3}{4}$ $2\frac{1}{4}$ $2\frac{1}{4}$

$11\frac{3}{8}$ $11\frac{3}{4}$ $+$

$6\frac{1}{6}$ $12\frac{1}{16}$ $11\frac{3}{8}$ $11\frac{3}{4}$ $+$

$33\frac{1}{16}$ $-$

87 $33\frac{3}{4}$ 33 $33\frac{1}{16}$ $-$

$24\frac{9}{16}$ $25\frac{7}{8}$ $+$

602 $25\frac{5}{8}$ $24\frac{9}{16}$ $25\frac{7}{8}$ $+$

$11\frac{5}{8}$ $11\frac{7}{8}$ $+$

833 12 $11\frac{5}{8}$ $11\frac{7}{8}$ $+$

16 $10\frac{1}{2}$ $10\frac{1}{2}$ $10\frac{1}{2}$ $-$

78 $15\frac{7}{8}$ $15\frac{13}{16}$ $15\frac{7}{8}$ $-$

$8\frac{1}{2}$ $+$

508 $9\frac{1}{16}$ $8\frac{1}{4}$ $8\frac{1}{2}$ $+$

430 $11\frac{1}{4}$ $10\frac{1}{8}$ $10\frac{1}{8}$

STUDY SESSION 7
FINANCIAL REPORTING AND ANALYSIS:
An Introduction

The readings in this study session discuss the general principles of the financial reporting system, underscoring the critical role of the analysis of financial reports in investment decision making.

The first reading introduces the range of information that an analyst may use in analyzing the financial performance of a company, including the principal financial statements (the income statement, balance sheet, statement of cash flows, and statement of changes in owners' equity), notes to those statements, and management's discussion and analysis of results. A general framework for addressing most financial statement analysis tasks is also presented.

A company's financial statements are the end-products of a process for recording the business transactions of the company. The second reading illustrates this process, introducing such basic concepts as the accounting equation and accounting accruals.

The presentation of financial information to the public by a company must conform to applicable financial reporting standards based on factors such as the jurisdiction in which the information is released. The final reading in this study explores the role of financial reporting standard-setting bodies worldwide and the International Financial Reporting Standards framework promulgated by one key body, the International Accounting Standards Board. The movement towards worldwide convergence of financial reporting standards is also introduced.

Note:
New rulings and/or pronouncements issued after the publication of the readings in Study Sessions 7 through 10 in financial statement analysis may cause some of the information in these readings to become dated. Candidates are expected to be familiar with the overall analytical framework contained in the study session readings, as well as the implications of alternative accounting methods for financial analysis and valuation, as provided in the assigned readings.

For the purpose of Level I questions on financial statement analysis, when a ratio is defined and calculated differently in various texts, candidates should use the definitions given in the CFA Institute copyrighted readings by Robinson, et al. Variations in ratio definitions are part of the nature of practical financial analysis.

READING ASSIGNMENTS

Reading 29   Financial Statement Analysis: An Introduction
International Financial Statement Analysis, by Thomas R.
Robinson, CFA, Jan Hendrik van Greuning, CFA, R. Elaine Henry,
CFA, and Michael A. Broihahn, CFA

Reading 30   Financial Reporting Mechanics
International Financial Statement Analysis, by Thomas R.
Robinson, CFA, Jan Hendrik van Greuning, CFA, R. Elaine Henry,
CFA, and Michael A. Broihahn, CFA

Reading 31   Financial Reporting Standards
International Financial Statement Analysis, by Thomas R.
Robinson, CFA, Jan Hendrik van Greuning, CFA, R. Elaine Henry,
CFA, and Michael A. Broihahn, CFA

FINANCIAL STATEMENT ANALYSIS: AN INTRODUCTION

by Thomas R. Robinson, CFA, Jan Hendrik van Greuning, CFA, R. Elaine Henry, CFA, and Michael A. Broihahn, CFA

LEARNING OUTCOMES

The candidate should be able to:	Mastery
a. discuss the roles of financial reporting and financial statement analysis;	☐
b. discuss the role of key financial statements (income statement, balance sheet, statement of cash flows, and statement of changes in owners' equity) in evaluating a company's performance and financial position;	☐
c. discuss the importance of financial statement notes and supplementary information, including disclosures of accounting methods, estimates, and assumptions, and management's discussion and analysis;	☐
d. discuss the objective of audits of financial statements, the types of audit reports, and the importance of effective internal controls;	☐
e. identify and explain information sources other than annual financial statements and supplementary information that analysts use in financial statement analysis;	☐
f. describe the steps in the financial statement analysis framework.	☐

THEME

The information presented in financial reports, including the financial statements, financial notes, and management's discussion and analysis, allows the financial analyst to assess a company's performance and financial position. An analyst may be called upon to perform a financial analysis for a variety of reasons, including the valuation of equity securities, the assessment of credit risk, the performance of due diligence in an acquisition, and the evaluation of a subsidiary's performance relative to other business units. Major considerations in both equity analysis and credit analysis are evaluating a company's financial position, ability to generate profits and cash flow, and ability to generate future growth in profits and cash flow.

International Financial Statement Analysis, by Thomas R. Robinson, CFA, Jan Hendrik van Greuning, CFA, R. Elaine Henry, CFA, and Michael A. Broihahn, CFA. Copyright © 2007 by CFA Institute. Reprinted with permission.

INTRODUCTION

Analysts are employed in a number of functional areas. Commonly, analysts evaluate an investment in some type of security that has characteristics of equity (representing an ownership position) or debt (representing a lending position). In arriving at investment decisions or recommendations, analysts need to evaluate the performance, financial position, and value of the company issuing the securities. Company financial reports, which include financial statements and other data, provide the information necessary to evaluate the company and its securities. Consequently, the analyst must have a firm understanding of the information provided in each company's financial reports, including the financial notes and other forms of supplementary information.

This reading is organized as follows: Section 2 discusses the scope of financial statement analysis. Section 3 describes the sources of information used in financial statement analysis, including the primary financial statements (income statement, balance sheet, and statement of cash flows). Section 4 provides a framework for guiding the financial statement analysis process. A summary of the key points and practice problems in the CFA Institute multiple-choice format conclude the reading.

SCOPE OF FINANCIAL STATEMENT ANALYSIS

The role of financial reporting by companies is to provide information about their performance, financial position, and changes in financial position that is useful to a wide range of users in making economic decisions.[1] The role of financial statement analysis is to take financial reports prepared by companies, combined with other information, to evaluate the past, current, and prospective performance and financial position of a company for the purpose of making investment, credit, and other economic decisions.

In evaluating financial reports, analysts typically have an economic decision in mind. Examples include the following:

▶ Evaluating an equity investment for inclusion in a portfolio.
▶ Evaluating a merger or acquisition candidate.
▶ Evaluating a subsidiary or operating division of a parent company.
▶ Deciding whether to make a venture capital or other private equity investment.
▶ Determining the credit-worthiness of a company that has made a loan request.
▶ Extending credit to a customer.

---

[1] See paragraph 12 of the "Framework for the Preparation and Presentation of Financial Statements," originally published by the International Accounting Standards Committee in 1989 and then adopted by the International Accounting Standards Board in 2001.

► Examining compliance with debt covenants or other contractual arrangements.

► Assigning a debt rating to a company or bond issue.

► Valuing a security for making an investment recommendation to others.

► Forecasting future net income and cash flow.

There are certain themes in financial analysis. In general, analysts seek to examine the performance and financial position of companies as well as forecast future performance and financial position. Analysts are also concerned about factors that affect risks to the company's future performance and financial position. An examination of performance can include an assessment of a company's profitability (the ability to earn a profit from delivering goods and services) and its cash flow generating ability (the ability to produce cash receipts in excess of cash disbursements). Profit and cash flow are not equivalent. Profit represents the excess of the prices at which goods or services are sold over all the costs of providing those goods and services (regardless of when cash is received or paid). Example 1 illustrates the distinction between profit and cash flow.

EXAMPLE 1

Profit versus Cash Flow

Sennett Designs (SD) sells imported furniture on a retail basis. SD began operations during December 2006 and sold furniture for cash of €250,000. The furniture that was sold by SD was delivered by the supplier during December, but the supplier has granted SD credit terms according to which payment is not due until January 2007. SD is obligated to pay €220,000 in January for the furniture it sold during December.

1. How much is SD's profit for December 2006 if no other transactions occurred?

2. How much is SD's cash flow for December 2006?

Solution to 1: SD's profit for December 2006 is the excess of the sales price (€250,000) over the cost of the goods that were sold (€220,000), or €30,000.

Solution to 2: The December 2006 cash flow is €250,000.

Although profitability is important, so is the ability to generate positive cash flow. Cash flow is important because, ultimately, cash is needed to pay employees, suppliers, and others to continue as a going concern. A company that generates positive cash flow from operations has more flexibility in funding needed investments and taking advantage of attractive business opportunities than an otherwise comparable company without positive cash flow. Additionally, cash flow is the source of returns to providers of capital. Therefore, the expected magnitude of future cash flows is important in valuing corporate securities and in determining the company's ability to meet its obligations. The ability to meet short-term obligations is generally referred to as **liquidity**, and the ability to meet long-term obligations is generally referred to as **solvency**. However, as shown in Example 1, cash flow in a given period is not a complete measure of performance in that period; for example, a company may be obligated to make future cash payments as a result of a transaction generating positive cash flow in the current period.

As noted earlier, profits reflect the ability of a company to deliver goods and services at prices in excess of the costs of delivering the goods and services. Profits also provide useful information about future (and past) cash flows. If the transaction of Example 1 were repeated year after year, the long-term average annual cash flow of SD would be €30,000, its annual profit. Many analysts not only evaluate past profitability but also forecast future profitability.

Exhibit 1 shows how news media coverage of corporate earnings announcements places corporate results in the context of analysts' expectations. Furthermore, analysts frequently use earnings in valuation, for example, when they

---

EXHIBIT 1　　An Earnings Release and Analyst Reaction

Panel A. Excerpt from Apple Earnings Release

Apple Reports Third Quarter Results
Posts Second Highest Quarterly Revenue and Earnings in Company's History

CUPERTINO, California—July 19, 2006—Apple® today announced financial results for its fiscal 2006 third quarter ended July 1, 2006. The Company posted revenue of $4.37 billion and a net quarterly profit of $472 million, or $.54 per diluted share. These results compare to revenue of $3.52 billion and a net profit of $320 million, or $.37 per diluted share, in the year-ago quarter. Gross margin was 30.3 percent, up from 29.7 percent in the year-ago quarter. International sales accounted for 39 percent of the quarter's revenue.

Apple shipped 1,327,000 Macintosh® computers and 8,111,000 iPods during the quarter, representing 12 percent growth in Macs and 32 percent growth in iPods over the year-ago quarter. . . .

Panel B. Excerpt from CNET News.com Report

"Mac Sales Up 12 Percent as Apple Profits Soar" by Tom Krazit

Apple Computer's third-quarter revenue fell a little short of expectations, but profitability was far higher than expected and Mac sales increased at a healthy clip.

. . . Net income was $472 million, or 54 cents per share, an improvement of 48 percent compared with last year's results of $320 million in net income and 37 cents per share. Analysts surveyed by Thomson First Call had been expecting Apple to report $4.4 billion in revenue and earn 44 cents per share.

. . . The outlook for the next period will probably disappoint some investors. The company predicted fourth-quarter revenue would be about $4.5 billion to $4.6 billion, less than the $4.9 billion analysts had been expecting. Apple executives will hold a conference call later Wednesday to discuss results.

Sources: www.apple.com/pr/library/2006/jul/19results.html and http://news.com.com/Mac+sales+up+12+percent+as+Apple+profits+soar/2100-1047_3-6096116.html.

value shares of a company on the basis of the price-to-earnings ratio (P/E) in relation to peer companies' P/Es or when they use a present value model of valuation that is based on forecasted future earnings.

Analysts are also interested in the current financial position of a company. The financial position can be measured by comparing the resources controlled by the company in relation to the claims against those resources. An example of a resource is cash. In Example 1, if no other transactions occur, the company should have cash at 31 December 2006 of €250,000. This cash can be used by the company to pay the obligation to the supplier (a claim against the company) and may also be used to make distributions to the owner (who also has a claim against the company for any profits that have been earned). Financial position is particularly important in credit analysis, as depicted in Exhibit 2.

EXHIBIT 2	Grupo Imsa Press Release Dated 18 January 2005

Standard & Poor's and Fitch Upgrade Grupo Imsa's Credit Rating

MONTERREY, Mexico: Grupo Imsa (NYSE:IMY) (BMV:IMSA) announces that Standard & Poor's has recently upgraded the Company's local currency corporate credit rating from BBB− to BBB and its national scale rating from mxAA to mxAA+. Fitch Mexico also increased Grupo Imsa's domestic rating from AA(mex) to AA+(mex). These rating upgrades reflect the positive results of Grupo Imsa's main businesses and the strengthening of its financial position, combined with the Company's geographic diversification, market leadership, state-of-the-art technology and high operational efficiency.

Mr. Marcelo Canales, Grupo Imsa's CFO, explained: "Grupo Imsa follows a policy of maintaining a solid financial position that ensures the Company's continuity for the benefit of our employees, shareholders and creditors. We take our financial commitments very seriously, as can be seen from the fact that during our 70 years of existence we have always complied with our financial obligations. The change in rating also reflects the strength of our business model and its capacity to generate cash." Mr. Canales added: "These upgrades in credit rating should translate into a better valuation of our debt to reflect Grupo Imsa's new financial reality."

Grupo Imsa, a holding company, dates back to 1936 and is today one of Mexico's leading diversified industrial companies, operating in three core businesses: steel processed products; steel and plastic construction products; and aluminum and other related products. With manufacturing and distribution facilities in Mexico, the United States, Europe and throughout Central and South America, Grupo Imsa currently exports to all five continents. Grupo Imsa's shares trade on the Mexican Stock Exchange (IMSA) and, in the United States, on the NYSE (IMY).

This document contains forward-looking statements relating to Grupo Imsa's future performance or its current expectations or beliefs, including statements regarding the intent, belief or current expectations of the Company and its management. Investors are cautioned that any such forward-looking statements are not guarantees of future performance and involve a number of risks and uncertainties pertaining to the industries in which the Company participates. Grupo Imsa does not intend, and does not assume any obligation, to update these forward-looking statements.

Source: Business Wire, 18 January 2005.

In conducting a financial analysis of a company, the analyst will regularly refer to the company's financial statements, financial notes and supplementary schedules, and a variety of other information sources. The next section introduces the major financial statements and most commonly used information sources.

3   MAJOR FINANCIAL STATEMENTS AND OTHER INFORMATION SOURCES

In order to perform an equity or credit analysis of a company, an analyst must collect a great deal of information. The nature of the information will vary based on the individual task but will typically include information about the economy, industry, and company as well as information about comparable peer companies. Much of this information will come from outside the company, such as economic statistics, industry reports, trade publications, and databases containing information on competitors. The company itself provides some of the core information for analysis in its financial reports, press releases, and conference calls and webcasts.

Companies prepare financial reports to report to investors and creditors on financial performance and financial strength at regular intervals (annually, semi-annually, and/or quarterly). Financial reports include financial statements and supplemental information necessary to assess the performance and financial position of the company. Financial statements are the end results of an accounting recordkeeping process that records the economic activities of a company. They summarize this information for use by investors, creditors, analysts, and others interested in a company's performance and financial position. In order to provide some assurances as to the information provided in the financial statements and related notes, the financial statements are audited by independent accountants who express an opinion on whether the financial statements fairly portray the company's performance and financial position.

3.1 Financial Statements and Supplementary Information

The key financial statements that are the focus of analysis are the income statement, balance sheet, statement of cash flows, and statement of changes in owners' equity. The income statement and statement of cash flows portray different aspects of a company's performance over a period of time. The balance sheet portrays the company's financial position at a given point in time. The statement of changes in owners' equity provides additional information regarding the changes in a company's financial position. In addition to the financial statements, a company provides other information in its financial reports that is useful to the financial analyst. As part of his or her analysis, the financial analyst should read and assess this additional information, which includes:

▶ notes to the financial statements (also known as footnotes) and supplementary schedules;

▶ management's discussion and analysis (MD&A); and

▶ the external auditor's report(s).

The following sections illustrate the major financial statements.

3.1.1 Income Statement

The income statement presents information on the financial results of a company's business activities over a period of time. The income statement communicates how much revenue the company generated during a period and what costs it incurred in connection with generating that revenue. Net income (revenue minus all costs) on the income statement is often referred to as the "bottom line" because of its proximity to the bottom of the income statement.[2] Income statements are reported on a consolidated basis, meaning that they include the revenues and expenses of affiliated companies under the control of the parent (reporting) company. The income statement is sometimes referred to as a **statement of operations** or **profit and loss** (P&L) **statement**. The basic equation underlying the income statement is Revenue − Expenses = Net income.

In Exhibit 3, the income statement is presented with the most recent year in the first column and the earliest year in the last column. Although this is a common presentation, analysts should be careful when reading an income statement because in other cases, the years may be listed from most distant to most recent.

Exhibit 3 shows that Wal-Mart's total revenue for the fiscal year ended 31 January 2005 was (in millions) $287,989. Wal-Mart then subtracted its operating costs and expenses to arrive at an operating income (profit) of $17,091. Operating income reflects a company's profits from its usual business activities, before deducting interest expense or taxes. Operating income is thus often referred to as EBIT, or earnings before interest and taxes. Operating income reflects the company's underlying performance independent of the use of financial leverage. Wal-Mart's total interest cost (net of the interest income that was earned from investments) for 2005 was $986; its earnings before taxes were, therefore, $16,105. Total income tax expense for 2005 was $5,589, and the minority interest expense (income earned by the minority shareholders from Wal-Mart subsidiary companies) was $249. After deducting these final expenses, Wal-Mart's net income for fiscal 2005 was $10,267.

Companies present their basic and diluted earnings per share on the face of the income statement. Earnings per share represents the net income divided by the number of shares of stock outstanding during the period. Basic earnings per share uses the weighted-average number of common shares that were actually outstanding during the period, whereas diluted earnings per share uses diluted shares—the number of shares that would be outstanding if potentially dilutive claims on common shares (e.g., stock options) were exercised by their holders. Wal-Mart's basic earning per share for 2005 was $2.41 ($10,267 net income ÷ 4,259 basic shares outstanding). Likewise, Wal-Mart's diluted earnings per share for 2005 was also $2.41 ($10,267 net income ÷ 4,266 diluted shares).

An analyst examining the income statement might note that Wal-Mart was profitable in each year and that revenue, operating income, net income, and earnings per share—all measures of profitability—increased over the three-year period. The analyst might formulate questions related to profitability, such as the following:

▶ Is the growth in revenue related to an increase in units sold, an increase in prices, or some combination?

▶ After adjusting for growth in the number of stores, is the company still more profitable over time?

▶ How does the company compare with other companies in the industry?

---

[2] "Net income" is also referred to as "net earnings" or "net profit." In the event that costs exceed revenues, it is referred to as "net loss."

EXHIBIT 3	Wal-Mart Consolidated Statements of Income (in Millions except per Share Data)		
Fiscal Years Ended 31 January	**2005**	**2004**	**2003**
Revenues:			
Net sales	$285,222	$256,329	$229,616
Other income, net	2,767	2,352	1,961
	287,989	258,681	231,577
Costs and expenses:			
Cost of sales	219,793	198,747	178,299
Operating, selling, general, and administrative expenses	51,105	44,909	39,983
Operating income	17,091	15,025	13,295
Interest:			
Debt	934	729	799
Capital lease	253	267	260
Interest income	(201)	(164)	(132)
Interest, net	986	832	927
Income from continuing operations before income taxes and minority interest	16,105	14,193	12,368
Provision for income taxes:			
Current	5,326	4,941	3,883
Deferred	263	177	474
Total	5,589	5,118	4,357
Income from continuing operations before minority interest	10,516	9,075	8,011
Minority interest	(249)	(214)	(193)
Income from continuing operations	10,267	8,861	7,818
Income from discontinued operations, net of tax	–	193	137
Net income	$ 10,267	$ 9,054	$ 7,955
Basic net income per common share:			
Income from continuing operations	$ 2.41	$ 2.03	$ 1.77
Income from discontinued operations	–	0.05	0.03
Basic net income per common share	$ 2.41	$ 2.08	$ 1.80
Diluted net income per common share:			
Income from continuing operations	$ 2.41	$ 2.03	$ 1.76
Income from discontinued operations	–	0.04	0.03
Diluted net income per common share	$ 2.41	$ 2.07	$ 1.79
Weighted-average number of common shares:			
Basic	4,259	4,363	4,430
Diluted	4,266	4,373	4,446
Dividends per common share	$ 0.52	$ 0.36	$ 0.30

Answering such questions requires the analyst to gather, analyze, and interpret facts from a number of sources, including the income statement. The reading on understanding the income statement will explain the income statement in greater detail. The next section illustrates the balance sheet, the second major financial statement.

3.1.2 *Balance Sheet*

The **balance sheet** (also known as the **statement of financial position** or **statement of financial condition**) presents a company's current financial position by disclosing resources the company controls (assets) and what it owes (liabilities) at a specific point in time. **Owners' equity** represents the excess of assets over liabilities. This amount is attributable to the owners or shareholders of the business; it is the residual interest in the assets of an entity after deducting its liabilities. The three parts of the balance sheet are formulated in an accounting relationship known as the accounting equation: Assets = Liabilities + Owners' equity (that is, the total amount for assets must *balance* to the combined total amounts for liabilities and owners' equity). Alternatively, the three parts of the balance sheet of the accounting relationship may be formulated as Assets − Liabilities = Owners' equity. Depending on the form of the organization, owners' equity also goes by several alternative titles, such as "partners' capital" or "shareholders' equity."

Exhibit 4 presents Wal-Mart's consolidated balance sheets for the fiscal years ended 31 January 2004 and 2005.

EXHIBIT 4	Wal-Mart Consolidated Balance Sheets (in Millions except per Share Data)	
Fiscal Years Ended 31 January	**2005**	**2004**
Assets		
Current assets:		
Cash and cash equivalents	$ 5,488	$ 5,199
Receivables	1,715	1,254
Inventories	29,447	26,612
Prepaid expenses and other	1,841	1,356
Total current assets	38,491	34,421
Property and equipment, at cost:		
Land	14,472	12,699
Buildings and improvements	46,582	40,192
Fixtures and equipment	21,461	17,934
Transportation equipment	1,530	1,269
Property and equipment, at cost	84,045	72,094
Less accumulated depreciation	18,637	15,684
Property and equipment, net	65,408	56,410

(Exhibit continued on next page . . .)

EXHIBIT 4	(continued)		

Property under capital lease:

Property under capital lease		4,997	4,286
Less accumulated amortization		1,838	1,673
Property under capital lease, net		3,159	2,613
Goodwill		10,803	9,882
Other assets and deferred charges		2,362	2,079
Total assets		**$120,223**	**$105,405**

Liabilities and shareholders' equity

Current liabilities:

Commercial paper		$ 3,812	$ 3,267
Accounts payable		21,671	19,425
Accrued liabilities		12,155	10,671
Accrued income taxes		1,281	1,377
Long-term debt due within one year		3,759	2,904
Obligations under capital leases due within one year		210	196
Total current liabilities		42,888	37,840
Long-term debt		20,087	17,102
Long-term obligations under capital leases		3,582	2,997
Deferred income taxes and other		2,947	2,359
Minority interest		1,323	1,484

Shareholders' equity:

Preferred stock ($0.10 par value; 100 shares authorized, none issued)		–	–
Common stock ($0.10 par value; 11,000 shares authorized, 4,234 and 4,311 issued and outstanding in 2005 and 2004, respectively)		423	431
Capital in excess of par value		2,425	2,135
Other accumulated comprehensive income		2,694	851
Retained earnings		43,854	40,206
Total shareholders' equity		49,396	43,623
Total liabilities and shareholders' equity		**$120,223**	**$105,405**

At 31 January 2005, Wal-Mart's total resources or assets were $120,223 (in millions). Shareholders' equity (in millions) was $49,396. Although Wal-Mart does not give a total amount for all the balance sheet liabilities, it may be determined from the accounting relationship as Total assets − Total shareholders' equity or $120,223 − $49,396 = $70,827.[3] Using the balance sheet and applying financial statement analysis, the analyst will be able to answer such questions as:

---

[3] Note that this computation includes an amount labeled "minority interest in liabilities." Minority interest represents ownership in a subsidiary company by others (not the parent company). Accounting rulemakers are currently considering reclassifying this amount as part of owners' equity.

▶ Has the company's liquidity (ability to meet short-term obligations) improved?

▶ Is the company solvent (does it have sufficient resources to cover its obligations)?

▶ What is the company's financial position relative to the industry?

The reading on understanding the balance sheet will cover the analysis of the balance sheet in more depth. The next section illustrates the statement of cash flows.

3.1.3 Statement of Cash Flows

Although the income statement and balance sheet provide a measure of a company's success in terms of performance and financial position, cash flow is also vital to a company's long-term success. Disclosing the sources and uses of cash helps creditors, investors, and other statement users evaluate the company's liquidity, solvency, and financial flexibility. **Financial flexibility** is the ability to react and adapt to financial adversities and opportunities. The statement of cash flows classifies all company cash flows into operating, investing, and financing activity cash flows. **Operating activities** involve transactions that enter into the determination of net income and are primarily activities that comprise the day-to-day business functions of a company. **Investing activities** are those activities associated with the acquisition and disposal of long-term assets, such as equipment. **Financing activities** are those activities related to obtaining or repaying capital to be used in the business.

Exhibit 5 presents Wal-Mart's consolidated statement of cash flows for the fiscal years ended 31 January 2003, 2004, and 2005.

EXHIBIT 5	Wal-Mart Consolidated Statements of Cash Flows (in Millions)		
Fiscal Years Ended 31 January	**2005**	**2004**	**2003**
Cash flows from operating activities:			
Income from continuing operations	$ 10,267	$ 8,861	$ 7,818
Adjustments to reconcile net income to net cash provided by operating activities:			
Depreciation and amortization	4,405	3,852	3,364
Deferred income taxes	263	177	474
Other operating activities	378	173	685
Changes in certain assets and liabilities, net of effects of acquisitions:			
Decrease (increase) in accounts receivable	(304)	373	(159)
Increase in inventories	(2,635)	(1,973)	(2,219)
Increase in accounts payable	1,694	2,587	1,748
Increase in accrued liabilities	976	1,896	1,212
Net cash provided by operating activities of continuing operations	15,044	15,946	12,923
Net cash provided by operating activities of discontinued operations	–	50	82
Net cash provided by operating activities	15,044	15,996	13,005

(Exhibit continued on next page . . .)

EXHIBIT 5	(continued)

Cash flows from investing activities:

Payments for property and equipment	(12,893)	(10,308)	(9,245)
Investment in international operations	(315)	(38)	(749)
Proceeds from the disposal of fixed assets	953	481	311
Proceeds from the sale of McLane	–	1,500	–
Other investing activities	(96)	78	(73)
Net cash used in investing activities of continuing operations	(12,351)	(8,287)	(9,756)
Net cash used in investing activities of discontinued operations	–	(25)	(83)
Net cash used in investing activities	(12,351)	(8,312)	(9,839)

Cash flows from financing activities:

Increase in commercial paper	544	688	1,836
Proceeds from issuance of long-term debt	5,832	4,099	2,044
Purchase of company stock	(4,549)	(5,046)	(3,383)
Dividends paid	(2,214)	(1,569)	(1,328)
Payment of long-term debt	(2,131)	(3,541)	(1,261)
Payment of capital lease obligations	(204)	(305)	(216)
Other financing activities	113	111	(62)
Net cash used in financing activities	(2,609)	(5,563)	(2,370)
Effect of exchange rate changes on cash	205	320	(199)
Net increase in cash and cash equivalents	289	2,441	597
Cash and cash equivalents at beginning of year	5,199	2,758	2,161
Cash and cash equivalents at end of year	$ 5,488	$ 5,199	$ 2,758

Supplemental disclosure of cash flow information:

Income tax paid	$ 5,593	$ 4,358	$ 4,539
Interest paid	1,163	1,024	1,085
Capital lease obligations incurred	377	252	381

In the cash flows from operating activities section of Wal-Mart's statement of cash flows, the company reconciles its net income to net cash provided by operating activities. This emphasizes the different perspectives of the income statement and statement of cash flows. Income is reported when earned, not necessarily when cash is received. The statement of cash flows presents another aspect of performance: the ability of a company to generate cash flow from running its business. Ideally, the analyst would like to see that the primary source of cash flow is from operating activities (as opposed to investing or financing activities). Note that Wal-Mart had a large amount of operating cash flow, which increased from 2003 to 2004 but decreased slightly in 2005. Although operating cash flow was high, an analyst might question why net income increased but operating cash flow decreased in 2005.

The summation of the net cash flows from operating, investing, and financing activities and the effect of exchange rates on cash equals the net change in cash during the fiscal year. For Wal-Mart, the summation of these four cash flow activities in 2005 was $289, which thus increased the company's cash from $5,199 at 31 January 2004 (beginning cash balance) to $5,488 at 31 January 2005 (ending cash balance). Note that these beginning and ending cash balances agree with the cash reported on Wal-Mart's balance sheets in Exhibit 4.

The statement of cash flows will be treated in more depth in the reading on understanding the statement of cash flows.

3.1.4 Statement of Changes in Owners' Equity

The income statement, balance sheet, and statement of cash flows represent the primary financial statements used to assess a company's performance and financial position. A fourth financial statement is also available; this can be a "statement of changes in owners' equity," "statement of shareholders' equity," or "statement of retained earnings." This fourth statement, regardless of format chosen, primarily serves to report changes in the owners' investment in the business over time and assists the analyst in understanding the changes in financial position reflected on the balance sheet.

3.1.5 Financial Notes and Supplementary Schedules

Financial notes and supplementary schedules are an integral part of the financial statements. By way of example, the financial notes and supplemental schedules provide explanatory information about the following:

▶ business acquisitions and disposals;

▶ commitments and contingencies;

▶ legal proceedings;

▶ stock option and other employee benefit plans;

▶ related-party transactions;

▶ significant customers;

▶ subsequent events;

▶ business and geographic segments; and

▶ quarterly financial data.

Additionally, the footnotes contain information about the methods and assumptions used to prepare the financial statements. Comparability of financial statements is a critical requirement for objective financial analysis. Financial statement comparability occurs when information is measured and reported in a similar manner over time and for different companies. Comparability allows the analyst to identify and analyze the real economic substance differences and similarities between companies. The International Accounting Standards Board based in London sets forth standards under which international financial statements should be prepared. These are referred to as international financial reporting standards (IFRS). Similarly, the Financial Accounting Standards Board (FASB) in the United States sets forth standards (called statements of financial accounting standards) that constitute the key part of the body of principles known as generally accepted accounting principles (U.S. GAAP). These two organizations are working to make their standards similar, but there are key differences. When comparing a U.S. company with a European company, an analyst must understand differences in these standards, which can relate, for example, to the period in which to report revenue.

Even within each of these sets of standards there can be choices for management to make that can reduce comparability between companies. Both IFRS and U.S. GAAP allow the use of alternative accounting methods to measure company financial performance and financial condition where there are differences in economic environments between companies. Additionally, some principles require the use of estimates and assumptions in measuring performance and financial condition. This flexibility is necessary because, ideally, a company will select those methods, estimates, and assumptions within the principles that fairly reflect the unique economic environment of the company's business and industry. Although this flexibility in accounting principles ostensibly meets the divergent needs of many businesses, it creates a problem for the analyst because comparability is lost when flexibility occurs. For example, if a company acquires a piece of equipment to use in its operations, accounting standards require that the cost of the asset be reported as an expense in a systematic manner over the life of the equipment (estimating the process of the equipment wearing out). This allocation of the cost is known as **depreciation**. The standards permit a great deal of flexibility, however, in determining the manner in which each year's expense is determined. Two companies may acquire similar equipment but use different methods and assumptions to record the expense over time. Comparing the companies' performance directly is then impaired by this difference.

A company's accounting policies (methods, estimates, and assumptions) are generally presented in the notes to the financial statements. A note containing a summary of significant accounting policies reveals, for example, how the company recognizes its revenues and depreciates its capital assets. Analysts must be aware of the methods, estimates, and assumptions used by a company to determine if they are similar to those of other companies that are being used as benchmarks. If they are not similar, the analyst who understands accounting techniques can make adjustments to make the financial statements more comparable.

3.1.6 Management's Discussion and Analysis

Publicly held companies are often required to include in their financial reports a section called management's discussion and analysis (MD&A). In it, management must highlight any favorable or unfavorable trends and identify significant events and uncertainties that affect the company's liquidity, capital resources, and results of operations. The MD&A must also provide information about the effects of inflation, changing prices, or other material events and uncertainties that may cause the future operating results and financial condition to materially depart from the current reported financial information. Companies should also provide disclosure in the MD&A that discusses the critical accounting policies that require management to make subjective judgments and that have a significant impact on reported financial results. The MD&A section of a company's report provides a good starting place for understanding what is going on in the financial statements. Nevertheless, it is only one input for the analyst in seeking an objective and independent perspective on a company's performance and prospects.

3.1.7 Auditor's Reports

Financial statements presented in company annual financial reports are often required to be audited (examined) by an independent accounting firm that then expresses an opinion on the financial statements. Audits may be required by contractual arrangement, law, or regulation. Just as there are standards for preparing financial statements, there are standards for auditing and for expressing the resulting auditor's opinion. International standards for auditing have been developed by the International Auditing and Assurance Standards Board of the International Federation of Accountants. These standards have been adopted by many countries. Other countries, such as the United States, have developed their own standards. With the enactment of the Sarbanes–Oxley Act in the United States, auditing standards are being promulgated by the Public Company Accounting Oversight Board (PCAOB). Under International Standard on Auditing 200:

> The objective of an audit of financial statements is to enable the auditor to express an opinion whether the financial statements are prepared, in all material respects, in accordance with an applicable financial reporting framework.[4]

Publicly traded companies may also have requirements set by regulators or stock exchanges, such as appointing an independent audit committee of the board of directors to oversee the audit process. The audit process provides a basis for the independent auditor to express an audit opinion on the fairness of the financial statements that were audited. Because audits are designed and conducted by using audit sampling techniques, independent auditors cannot express an opinion that provides absolute assurance about the accuracy or precision of the financial statements. Instead, the independent audit report provides *reasonable assurance* that the financial statements are *fairly presented*, meaning that there is a high degree of probability that the audited financial statements are free from *material* error, fraud, or illegal acts that have a direct effect on the financial statements.

The standard independent audit report for a publicly traded company normally has several paragraphs under both the international and U.S. auditing standards. The first or "introductory" paragraph describes the financial statements that were audited and the responsibilities of both management and the independent auditor. The second or "scope" paragraph describes the nature of the audit process and provides the basis for the auditor's expression about reasonable assurance on the fairness of the financial statements. The third or "opinion" paragraph expresses the auditor's opinion on the fairness of the audited financial statements. An *unqualified* audit opinion states that the financial statements give a "true and fair view" (international) or are "fairly presented" (international and U.S.) in accordance with applicable accounting standards. This is often referred to as a "clean" opinion and is the one that analysts would like to see in a financial report. There are several other types of opinions. A *qualified* audit opinion is one in which there is some limitation or exception to accounting standards. Exceptions are described in the audit report with additional explanatory paragraphs so that the analyst can determine the importance of the exception. An *adverse* audit opinion occurs when the financial statements materially depart from accounting standards and are not fairly presented. An adverse opinion makes analysis of the financial statements easy: Don't bother, because the company's financial statements cannot be relied upon. Finally, a *disclaimer of opinion* occurs when, for some reason, the auditors are unable to issue an opinion. Exhibit 6 presents the independent auditor's report for Wal-Mart. Note that Wal-Mart received a "clean" or unqualified audit opinion from Ernst & Young LLP for the company's fiscal year ended 31 January 2005.

---

[4] International Federation of Accountants, *Handbook of International Auditing, Assurance, and Ethics Pronouncements*, 2006 edition, p. 230, available at www.ifac.org.

EXHIBIT 6	Wal-Mart's Independent Audit Report

Report of Independent Registered Accounting Firm
WAL-MART

The Board of Directors and Shareholders,
Wal-Mart Stores, Inc.

We have audited the accompanying consolidated balance sheets of Wal-Mart Stores, Inc. as of January 31, 2005 and 2004, and the related consolidated statements of income, shareholders' equity and cash flows for each of the three years in the period ended January 31, 2005. These financial statements are the responsibility of the company's management. Our responsibility is to express an opinion on these financial statements based on our audits.

We conducted our audits in accordance with the standards of the Public Company Accounting Oversight Board (United States). Those standards require that we plan and perform the audit to obtain reasonable assurance about whether the financial statements are free of material misstatement. An audit includes examining on a test basis, evidence supporting the amounts and disclosures in the financial statements. An audit also includes assessing the accounting principles used and significant estimates made by management, as well as evaluating the overall financial statement presentation. We believe that our audits provide a reasonable basis for our opinion.

In our opinion, the financial statements referred to above present fairly, in all material respects, the consolidated financial position of Wal-Mart Stores, Inc. at January 31, 2005 and 2004, and the consolidated results of its operations and its cash flows for each of the three years in the period ended January 31, 2005, in conformity with U.S. generally accepted accounting principles.

We also have audited, in accordance with the standards of the Public Accounting Oversight Board (United States), the effectiveness of Wal-Mart Stores, Inc.'s internal control over financial reporting as of January 31, 2005, based on criteria established in *Internal Control—Integrated Framework* issued by the Committee of Sponsoring Organizations of the Treadway Committee and our report dated March 25, 2005 expressed an unqualified opinion thereon.

Ernst & Young LLP
Rogers, Arkansas
March 25, 2005

Source: 2005 Wal-Mart Stores, Inc., Annual Report.

In the United States, under the Sarbanes–Oxley Act, the auditors must also express an opinion on the company's internal control systems. This information may be provided in a separate opinion or incorporated as a fourth paragraph in the opinion related to the financial statements. The internal control system is the company's internal system that is designed, among other things, to ensure that the company's process for generating financial reports is sound.

Although management has always been responsible for maintaining effective internal control, the Sarbanes–Oxley Act greatly increases management's responsibility for demonstrating that the company's internal controls are effective. Publicly traded companies in the United States are now required by securities regulators to:

▶ accept responsibility for the effectiveness of internal control;

▶ evaluate the effectiveness of internal control using suitable control criteria;

▶ support the evaluation with sufficient competent evidence; and

▶ provide a report on internal control.

The Sarbanes–Oxley Act specifically requires management's report on internal control to:

▶ state that it is management's responsibility to establish and maintain adequate internal control;

▶ identify management's framework for evaluating internal control;

▶ include management's assessment of the effectiveness of the company's internal control over financial reporting as of the end of the most recent year, including a statement as to whether internal control over financial reporting is effective;

▶ include a statement that the company's auditors have issued an attestation report on management's assessment; and

▶ certify that the company's financial statements are fairly presented.

Exhibit 7 presents Wal-Mart management's report on internal control to its company's shareholders. Note that Wal-Mart has fully complied with each of the reporting criterion that were discussed in the preceding paragraph.

EXHIBIT 7	Wal-Mart's Report to Shareholders on Corporate Governance and Internal Control

Management's Report to Our Shareholders
WAL-MART

Management of Wal-Mart Stores, Inc. ("Wal-Mart") is responsible for the preparation, integrity and objectivity of Wal-Mart's consolidated financial statements and other financial information contained in this Annual Report to Shareholders. Those consolidated financial statements were prepared in conformity with accounting principles generally accepted in the United States. In preparing those consolidated financial statements, Management was required to make certain estimates and judgments, which are based upon currently available information and Management's view of current conditions and circumstances.

The Audit Committee of the Board of Directors, which consists solely of independent directors, oversees our process of reporting financial information and the audit of our consolidated financial statements. The Audit Committee stays informed of the financial condition of Wal-Mart and regularly reviews Management's financial policies and procedures, the independence of our independent auditors, our internal control and the objectivity of our financial reporting. Both the independent financial auditors and the internal auditors have free access to the Audit Committee and meet with the Audit Committee periodically, both with and without Management present.

(Exhibit continued on next page . . .)

EXHIBIT 7   (continued)

We have retained Ernst & Young LLP, an independent registered public accounting firm, to audit our consolidated financial statements found in this annual report. We have made available to Ernst & Young LLP all of our financial records and related data in connection with their audit of our consolidated financial statements.

We have filed with the Securities and Exchange Commission the required certifications related to our consolidated financial statements as of and for the year ended January 31, 2005. These certifications are attached as exhibits to our Annual Report on Form 10-K for the year ended January 31, 2005. Additionally, we have also provided to the New York Stock Exchange the required annual certification of our Chief Executive Officer regarding our compliance with the New York Stock Exchange's corporate governance listing standards.

Report on Internal Control over Financial Reporting

Management has responsibility for establishing and maintaining adequate internal control over financial reporting. Internal control over financial reporting is a process designed to provide reasonable assurance regarding the reliability of financial reporting and the preparation of financial statements for external reporting purposes in accordance with accounting principles generally accepted in the United States. Because of its inherent limitations, internal control over financial reporting may not prevent or detect misstatements. Management has assessed the effectiveness of the company's internal control over financial reporting as of January 31, 2005. In making its assessment, Management has utilized the criteria set forth by the Committee of Sponsoring Organizations ("COSO") of the Treadway Commission in *Internal Control – Integrated Framework*. Management concluded that based on its assessment, Wal-Mart's internal control over financial reporting was effective as of January 31, 2005. Management's assessment of the effectiveness of the company's internal control over financial reporting as of January 31, 2005 has been audited by Ernst & Young LLP, an independent registered public accounting firm, as stated in their report which appears in this Annual Report to Shareholders.

Evaluation of Disclosure Controls and Procedures

We maintain disclosure controls and procedures designed to provide reasonable assurance that information, which is required to be timely disclosed, is accumulated and communicated to Management in a timely fashion. Management has assessed the effectiveness of these disclosure controls and procedures as of January 31, 2005 and determined that they were effective as of that date to provide reasonable assurance that information required to be disclosed by us in the reports we file or submit under the Securities Exchange Act of 1934, as amended, is accumulated and communicated to Management, as appropriate, to allow timely decisions regarding required disclosure and are effective to provide reasonable assurance that such information is recorded, processed, summarized and reported within the time periods specified by the SEC's rules and forms.

Report on Ethical Standards

Our company was founded on the belief that open communications and the highest standard of ethics are necessary to be successful. Our long-standing "Open Door" communication policy helps Management be aware of and address issues in a timely and effective manner. Through the open door policy all associates are encouraged to inform Management at the appropriate level when they are concerned about any matter pertaining to Wal-Mart.

Wal-Mart has adopted a Statement of Ethics to guide our associates in the continued observance of high ethical standards such as honesty, integrity and compliance with the law in the conduct of Wal-Mart's business. Familiarity and compliance with the Statement of Ethics is required of all associates who are part of Management. The company also maintains a separate Code of Ethics for our senior financial officers. Wal-Mart also has in

(Exhibit continued on next page . . .)

EXHIBIT 7 **(continued)**

place a Related-Party Transaction Policy. This policy applies to all of Wal-Mart's Officers and Directors and requires material related-party transactions to be reviewed by the Audit Committee. The Officers and Directors are required to report material related-party transactions to Wal-Mart. We maintain an ethics office which oversees and administers an ethics hotline. The ethics hotline provides a channel for associates to make confidential and anonymous complaints regarding potential violations of our statement of ethics, including violations related to financial or accounting matters.

H. Lee Scott
President and Chief Executive Officer

Thomas M. Schoewe
Executive Vice President and Chief Financial Officer

Source: 2005 Wal-Mart Stores, Inc., Annual Report.

Although these reports provide some assurances to analysts, they are not infallible. The analyst must always use a degree of healthy skepticism when analyzing financial statements.

3.2 Other Sources of Information

The information described in the previous section is generally provided to shareholders on an annual basis. Interim reports are also provided by the company either semiannually or quarterly. Interim reports generally present the four key financial statements and footnotes but are not audited. These interim reports provide updated information on a company's performance and financial position since the last annual period. Companies also prepare proxy statements for distribution to shareholders on matters that are to be put to a vote at the company's annual (or special) meeting of shareholders. The proxy statement typically provides useful information regarding management and director compensation and company stock performance and discloses any potential conflicts of interest that may exist between management, the board, and shareholders. Companies also provide relevant current information on their websites and in press releases and as part of conference calls. When performing financial statement analysis, analysts should review all these company sources of information as well as information from external sources regarding the economy, the industry, the company, and peer (comparable) companies. Information on the economy, industry, and peer companies is useful in putting the company's financial performance and position in perspective and in assessing the company's future. The next section presents a framework for using all this information in financial statement analysis.

4   FINANCIAL STATEMENT ANALYSIS FRAMEWORK

Analysts work in a variety of positions. Some are equity analysts whose main objective is to evaluate potential equity (share) investments to determine whether a prospective investment is attractive and what an appropriate purchase price might be. Others are credit analysts who evaluate the credit-worthiness of a company to decide whether (and with what terms) a loan should be made or what credit rating should be assigned. Analysts may also be involved in a variety of other tasks, such as evaluating the performance of a subsidiary company, evaluating a private equity investment, or finding stocks that are overvalued for purposes of taking a short position. This section presents a generic framework for financial statement analysis that can be used in these various tasks. The framework is summarized in Exhibit 8.[5]

The following sections discuss the individual phases of financial statement analysis.

4.1 Articulate the Purpose and Context of Analysis

Prior to undertaking any analysis, it is essential to understand the purpose of the analysis. An understanding of the purpose is particularly important in financial statement analysis because of the numerous available techniques and the substantial amount of data.

Some analytical tasks are well defined, in which case articulating the purpose of the analysis requires little decision making by the analyst. For example, a periodic credit review of an investment-grade debt portfolio or an equity analyst's report on a particular company may be guided by institutional norms such that the purpose of the analysis is given. Furthermore, the format, procedures, and/or sources of information may also be given.

For other analytical tasks, articulating the purpose of the analysis requires the analyst to make decisions. The purpose of an analysis guides further decisions about the approach, the tools, the data sources, the format in which to report results of the analysis, and the relative importance of different aspects of the analysis.

When facing a substantial amount of data, a less experienced analyst may be tempted to just start crunching numbers and creating output. It is generally advisable to resist the temptation and thus avoid the black hole of pointless number crunching. Consider the questions: If you could wave a magic wand and have all the numbers crunched, what conclusion would you be able to draw? What question would you be able to answer? What decision would your answer support?

The analyst should also define the context at this stage. Who is the intended audience? What is the end product—for example, a final report explaining conclusions and recommendations? What is the time frame (i.e., when is the report due)? What resources and resource constraints are relevant to completion of the analysis? Again, the context may be predefined (i.e., standard and guided by institutional norms).

Having clarified the purpose and context of the financial statement analysis, the analyst should next compile the specific questions to be answered by the

---

[5] Components of this framework have been adapted from van Greuning and Bratanovic (2003, p. 300) and from Benninga and Sarig (1997, pp. 134–156).

EXHIBIT 8	Financial Statement Analysis Framework	
Phase	**Sources of Information**	**Output**
1. Articulate the purpose and context of the analysis.	► The nature of the analyst's function, such as evaluating an equity or debt investment or issuing a credit rating. ► Communication with client or supervisor on needs and concerns. ► Institutional guidelines related to developing specific work product.	► Statement of the purpose or objective of analysis. ► A list (written or unwritten) of specific questions to be answered by the analysis. ► Nature and content of report to be provided. ► Timetable and budgeted resources for completion.
2. Collect data.	► Financial statements, other financial data, questionnaires, and industry/economic data. ► Discussions with management, suppliers, customers, and competitors. ► Company site visits (e.g., to production facilities or retail stores).	► Organized financial statements. ► Financial data tables. ► Completed questionnaires, if applicable.
3. Process data.	► Data from the previous phase.	► Adjusted financial statements. ► Common-size statements. ► Ratios and graphs. ► Forecasts.
4. Analyze/interpret the processed data.	► Input data as well as processed data.	► Analytical results.
5. Develop and communicate conclusions and recommendations (e.g., with an analysis report).	► Analytical results and previous reports. ► Institutional guidelines for published reports.	► Analytical report answering questions posed in Phase 1. ► Recommendation regarding the purpose of the analysis, such as whether to make an investment or grant credit.
6. Follow up.	► Information gathered by periodically repeating above steps as necessary to determine whether changes to holdings or recommendations are necessary.	► Updated reports and recommendations.

analysis. For example, if the purpose of the financial statement analysis (or, more likely, the particular stage of a larger analysis) is to compare the historical performance of three companies operating in a particular industry, specific questions would include: What has been the relative growth rate of the companies and what has been the relative profitability of the companies?

4.2 Collect Data

Next, the analyst obtains the data required to answer the specific questions. A key part of this step is obtaining an understanding of the company's business, financial performance, and financial position (including trends over time and in comparison with peer companies). For historical analyses, financial statement data alone are adequate in some cases. For example, to screen a large number of alternative companies for those with a minimum level of profitability, financial statement data alone would be adequate. But to address more in-depth questions, such as why and how one company performed better or worse than its competitors, additional information would be required. As another example, to compare the historical performance of two companies in a particular industry, the historical financial statements would be sufficient to determine which had faster growing sales or earnings and which was more profitable; however, a broader comparison with overall industry growth and profitability would obviously require industry data.

Furthermore, information on the economy and industry is necessary to understand the environment in which the company operates. Analysts often take a top-down approach whereby they 1) gain an understanding of the macroeconomic environment, such as prospects for growth in the economy and inflation, 2) analyze the prospects of the industry in which the subject company operates based on the expected macroeconomic environment, and 3) determine the prospects for the company in the expected industry and macroeconomic environments. For example, an analyst may need to forecast future growth in earnings for a company. To project future growth, past company data provide one basis for statistical forecasting; however, an understanding of economic and industry conditions can improve the analyst's ability to forecast a company's earnings based on forecasts of overall economic and industry activity.

4.3 Process Data

After obtaining the requisite financial statement and other information, the analyst processes this data using appropriate analytical tools. For example, processing the data may involve computing ratios or growth rates; preparing common-size financial statements; creating charts; performing statistical analyses, such as regressions or Monte Carlo simulations; performing equity valuation; performing sensitivity analyses; or using any other analytical tools or combination of tools that are available and appropriate to the task. A comprehensive financial analysis at this stage would include the following:

▶ Reading and evaluating financial statements for each company subject to analysis. This includes reading the footnotes and understanding what accounting standards have been used (for example, IFRS or U.S. GAAP), what accounting choices have been made (for example, when to report revenue on the income statement), and what operating decisions have been made that affect reported financial statements (for example, leasing versus purchasing equipment).

▶ Making any needed adjustments to the financial statements to facilitate comparison, when the unadjusted statements of the subject companies reflect differences in accounting standards, accounting choices, or operating decisions. Note that commonly used databases do not make such analyst adjustments.

► Preparing or collecting common-size financial statement data [which scale data to directly reflect percentages (e.g., of sales) or changes (e.g., from the prior year)] and financial ratios (which are measures of various aspects of corporate performance based on financial statement elements). On the basis of common-size financial statements and financial ratios, analysts can evaluate a company's relative profitability, liquidity, leverage, efficiency, and valuation in relation to past results and/or peers' results.

4.4 Analyze/Interpret the Processed Data

Once the data have been processed, the next step—critical to any analysis—is to interpret the output. The answer to a specific financial analysis question is seldom the numerical answer alone; the answer to the analytical question relies on the interpretation of the output and the use of this interpreted output to support a conclusion or recommendation. The answers to the specific analytical questions may themselves achieve the underlying purpose of the analysis, but usually, a conclusion or recommendation is required. For example, an equity analysis may require a buy, hold, or sell decision or a conclusion about the value of a share of stock. In support of the decision, the analysis would cite such information as target value, relative performance, expected future performance given a company's strategic position, quality of management, and whatever other information was important in reaching the decision.

4.5 Develop and Communicate Conclusions/Recommendations

Communicating the conclusion or recommendation in an appropriate format is the next step in an analysis. The appropriate format will vary by analytical task, by institution, and/or by audience. For example, an equity analyst report would typically include the following components:[6]

► summary and investment conclusion;
► business summary;
► risks;
► valuation; and
► historical and pro forma tables.

The contents of reports may also be specified by regulatory agencies or professional standards. For example, the CFA Institute *Standards of Practice Handbook* (SOPH) dictates standards that must be followed in communicating recommendations. The SOPH provides, in part:

> Standard V(B) states the responsibility of members and candidates to include in their communications those key factors that are instrumental to the investment recommendation presented. A critical part of this requirement is to distinguish clearly between opinions and facts. In preparing a research report, the member or candidate must present the basic characteristics of the security being analyzed, which will allow the reader to evaluate the report and incorporate information the reader deems relevant to his or her investment decision making process.[7]

---

[6] Stowe, Robinson, Pinto, and McLeavey (2002, p. 27).

[7] *Standards of Practice Handbook* (2006, p. 105).

The SOPH requires that limitations to the analysis and any risks inherent to the investment be disclosed. Furthermore, the SOPH requires that any report include elements important to the analysis and conclusions so that readers can evaluate the conclusions themselves.

4.6 Follow Up

The process does not end with the report. If an equity investment is made or a credit rating assigned, periodic review is required to determine if the original conclusions and recommendations are still valid. In the case of a rejected investment, follow up may not be necessary but may be appropriate to determine if the analysis process should be refined (for example, if a rejected investment turns out to be successful in the market). Follow up may involve repeating all the above steps in the process on a periodic basis.

SUMMARY

This reading has presented an overview of financial statement analysis. Among the major points covered are the following:

▶ The primary purpose of financial reports is to provide information and data about a company's financial position and performance, including profitability and cash flows. The information presented in financial reports—including the financial statements, financial notes, and management's discussion and analysis—allows the financial analyst to assess a company's financial position and performance and trends in that performance.

▶ Key financial statements that are a primary focus of analysis include the income statement, balance sheet, statement of cash flows, and statement of owners' equity.

▶ The income statement presents information on the financial results of a company's business activities over a period of time. The income statement communicates how much revenue the company generated during a period and what costs it incurred in connection with generating that revenue. The basic equation underlying the income statement is Revenue − Expense = Net income.

▶ The balance sheet discloses what a company owns (assets) and what it owes (liabilities) at a specific point in time. Owners' equity represents the portion belonging to the owners or shareholders of the business; it is the residual interest in the assets of an entity after deducting its liabilities. The three parts of the balance sheet are formulated in the accounting relationship of Assets = Liabilities + Owners' equity.

▶ Although the income statement and balance sheet provide a measure of a company's success, cash and cash flow are also vital to a company's long-term success. Disclosing the sources and uses of cash in the statement of cash flows helps creditors, investors, and other statement users evaluate the company's liquidity, solvency, and financial flexibility.

▶ The statement of changes in owners' equity reflects information about the increases or decreases to a company's owners' equity.

▶ In addition to the financial statements, a company provides other sources of financial information that are useful to the financial analyst. As part of his or her analysis, the financial analyst should read and assess the information presented in the company's financial note disclosures and supplementary schedules as well as the information contained in the management's discussion and analysis (MD&A). Analysts must also evaluate footnote disclosures regarding the use of alternative accounting methods, estimates, and assumptions.

▶ A publicly traded company must have an independent audit performed on its year-end financial statements. The auditor's opinion provides some assurance about whether the financial statements fairly reflect a company's performance and financial position. In addition, for U.S. publicly traded companies, management must demonstrate that the company's internal controls are effective.

▶ The financial statement analysis framework provides steps that can be followed in any financial statement analysis project, including the following:

  ▶ articulate the purpose and context of the analysis;

  ▶ collect input data;

  ▶ process data;

  ▶ analyze/interpret the processed data;

  ▶ develop and communicate conclusions and recommendations; and

  ▶ follow up.

PRACTICE PROBLEMS FOR READING 29

1. Providing information about the performance and financial position of companies so that users can make economic decisions best describes the role of:

    A. auditing.

    B. financial reporting.

    C. financial statement analysis.

2. A company's current financial position would *best* be evaluated using the:

    A. balance sheet.

    B. income statement.

    C. statement of cash flows.

3. A company's profitability for a period would *best* be evaluated using the:

    A. balance sheet.

    B. income statement.

    C. statement of cash flows.

4. Accounting methods, estimates, and assumptions used in preparing financial statements are found in:

    A. footnotes.

    B. the auditor's report.

    C. the proxy statement.

5. Information about management and director compensation would *best* be found in:

    A. footnotes.

    B. the auditor's report.

    C. the proxy statement.

6. Information about material events and uncertainties would *best* be found in:

    A. footnotes.

    B. the proxy statement.

    C. management's discussion and analysis.

7. What type of audit opinion is preferred when analyzing financial statements?

    A. Qualified.

    B. Adverse.

    C. Unqualified.

8. Ratios are an input into which step in the financial analysis framework?

    A. Process data.

    B. Collect input data.

    C. Analyze/interpret the processed data.

SOLUTIONS FOR READING 29

1. B is correct. This is the role of financial reporting. The role of financial statement analysis is to evaluate the financial reports.

2. A is correct. The balance sheet portrays the current financial position. The income statement and statement of cash flows present different aspects of performance.

3. B is correct. Profitability is the performance aspect measured by the income statement. The balance sheet portrays the current financial position. The statement of cash flows presents a different aspect of performance.

4. A is correct. The footnotes disclose choices in accounting methods, estimates, and assumptions.

5. C is correct. Although some aspects of management compensation would be found in the footnotes, this is a required disclosure in the proxy statement.

6. C is correct. This is a component of management's discussion and analysis.

7. C is correct. An unqualified opinion is a "clean" opinion and indicates that the financial statements present the company's performance and financial position fairly.

8. C is correct. Ratios are an output of the process data step but are an input into the analyze/interpret data step.

FINANCIAL REPORTING MECHANICS

by Thomas R. Robinson, CFA, Jan Hendrik van Greuning, CFA,
Karen O'Connor Rubsam, CFA, R. Elaine Henry, CFA, and
Michael A. Broihahn, CFA

LEARNING OUTCOMES

The candidate should be able to:	Mastery
a. explain the relationship of financial statement elements and accounts, and classify accounts into the financial statement elements;	☐
b. explain the accounting equation in its basic and expanded forms;	☐
c. explain the process of recording business transactions using an accounting system based on the accounting equations;	☐
d. explain the need for accruals and other adjustments in preparing financial statements;	☐
e. explain the relationships among the income statement, balance sheet, statement of cash flows, and statement of owners' equity;	☐
f. describe the flow of information in an accounting system;	☐
g. explain the use of the results of the accounting process in security analysis.	☐

THEME

The mechanics of the accounting process is the foundation for financial reporting. Understanding those mechanics enables an analyst to understand the interrelationships of financial accounts and statements and, therefore, to better assess a company's financial performance.

International Financial Statement Analysis, by Thomas R. Robinson, CFA, Jan Hendrik van Greuning, CFA, R. Elaine Henry, CFA, and Michael A. Broihahn, CFA. Copyright © 2007 by CFA Institute. Reprinted with permission.

1

INTRODUCTION

The financial statements of a company are end-products of a process for recording transactions of the company related to operations, financing, and investment. The structures of financial statements themselves reflect the system of recording and organizing transactions. To be an informed user of financial statements, the analyst must be knowledgeable about the principles of this system. This reading will supply that essential knowledge, taking the perspective of the user rather than the preparer. Learning the process from this perspective will enable an analyst to grasp the critical concepts without being overwhelmed by the detailed technical skills required by the accountants who prepare financial statements that are a major component of financial reports.

This reading is organized as follows: Section 2 describes the three groups into which business activities are classified for financial reporting purposes. Any transaction affects one or more of these groups. Section 3 describes how the elements of financial statements relate to accounts, the basic content unit of classifying transactions. The section is also an introduction to the linkages among the financial statements. Section 4 provides a step-by-step illustration of the accounting process. Section 5 explains the consequences of timing differences between the elements of a transaction. Section 6 provides an overview of how information flows through a business's accounting system. Section 7 introduces the use of financial reporting in security analysis. A summary of the key points and practice problems in the CFA Institute multiple-choice format conclude the reading.

2   THE CLASSIFICATION OF BUSINESS ACTIVITIES

Accountants give similar accounting treatment to similar types of business transactions. Therefore, a first step in understanding financial reporting mechanics is to understand how business activities are classified for financial reporting purposes.

Business activities may be classified into three groups for financial reporting purposes: operating, investing, and financing activities.

▶ **Operating activities** are those activities that are part of the day-to-day business functioning of an entity. Examples include the sale of meals by a restaurant, the sale of services by a consulting firm, the manufacture and sale of ovens by an oven-manufacturing company, and taking deposits and making loans by a bank.

▶ **Investing activities** are those activities associated with acquisition and disposal of long-term assets. Examples include the purchase of equipment or sale of surplus equipment (such as an oven) by a restaurant (contrast this to the sale of an oven by an oven manufacturer, which would be an operating activity), and the purchase or sale of an office building, a retail store, or a factory.

▶ **Financing activities** are those activities related to obtaining or repaying capital. The two primary sources for such funds are owners (shareholders) or creditors. Examples include issuing common shares, taking out a bank loan, and issuing bonds.

Understanding the nature of activities helps the analyst understand where the company is doing well and where it is not doing so well. Ideally, an analyst would prefer that most of a company's profits (and cash flow) come from its operating activities. Exhibit 1 provides examples of typical business activities and how these activities relate to the elements of financial statements described in the following section.

EXHIBIT 1	Typical Business Activities and Financial Statement Elements Affected
Operating activities	▶ Sales of goods and services to customers: (R) ▶ Costs of providing the goods and services: (X) ▶ Income tax expense: (X) ▶ Holding short-term assets or incurring short-term liabilities directly related to operating activities: (A), (L)
Investing activities	▶ Purchase or sale of assets, such as property, plant, and equipment: (A) ▶ Purchase or sale of other entities' equity and debt securities: (A)
Financing activities	▶ Issuance or repurchase of the company's own preferred or common stock: (E) ▶ Issuance or repayment of debt: (L) ▶ Payment of distributions (i.e., dividends to preferred or common stockholders): (E)

Assets (A), Liabilities (L), Owners' Equity (E), Revenue (R), and Expenses (X).

Not all transactions fit neatly in this framework for purposes of financial statement presentation. For example, interest received by a bank on one of its loans would be considered part of operating activities because a bank is in the business of lending money. In contrast, interest received on a bond investment by a restaurant may be more appropriately classified as an investing activity because the restaurant is not in the business of lending money.

The next section discusses how transactions resulting from these business activities are reflected in a company's financial records.

ACCOUNTS AND FINANCIAL STATEMENTS   3

Business activities resulting in transactions are reflected in the broad groupings of financial statement elements: Assets, Liabilities, Owners' Equity, Revenue, and Expenses.[1] In general terms, these elements can be defined as follows: **assets** are

---

[1] International Financial Reporting Standards use the term "income" to include revenue and gains. Gains are similar to revenue; however, they arise from secondary or peripheral activities rather than from a company's primary business activities. For example, for a restaurant, the sale of surplus restaurant equipment for more than its cost is referred to as a gain rather than revenue. Similarly, a loss is like an expense but arises from secondary activities. Gains and losses may be considered part of operations on the income statement (for example, a loss due to a decline in value of inventory) or may be part of nonoperating activities (for example, the sale of nontrading investments). Under U.S. GAAP, financial statement elements are defined to include assets, liabilities, owners' equity, revenue, expenses, gains, and losses. To illustrate business transactions in this reading, we will use the simple classification of revenues and expenses. All gains and revenue will be aggregated in revenue, and all losses and expenses will be aggregated in expenses.

the economic resources of a company; **liabilities** are the creditors' claims on the resources of a company; **owners' equity** is the residual claim on those resources; **revenues** are inflows of economic resources to the company; and **expenses** are outflows of economic resources or increases in liabilities.[2]

Accounts provide individual records of increases and decreases in a *specific* asset, liability, component of owners' equity, revenue, or expense. The financial statements are constructed using these elements.

3.1 Financial Statement Elements and Accounts

Within the financial statement elements, accounts are subclassifications. **Accounts** are individual records of increases and decreases in a specific asset, liability, component of owners' equity, revenue, or expense. For financial statements, amounts recorded in every individual account are summarized and grouped appropriately within a financial statement element. Exhibit 2 provides a listing of common accounts. These accounts will be described throughout this reading or in following readings. Unlike the financial statement elements, there is no standard set of accounts applicable to all companies. Although almost every company has certain accounts, such as cash, each company specifies the accounts in its accounting system based on its particular needs and circumstances. For example, a company in the restaurant business may not be involved in trading securities and, therefore, may not need an account to record such an activity. Furthermore, each company names its accounts based on its business. A company in the restaurant business might have an asset account for each of its ovens, with the accounts named "Oven-1" and "Oven-2." In its financial statements, these accounts would likely be grouped within long-term assets as a single line item called "Property, plant, and equipment."

A company's challenge is to establish accounts and account groupings that provide meaningful summarization of voluminous data but retain enough detail to facilitate decision making and preparation of the financial statements. The actual accounts used in a company's accounting system will be set forth in a **chart of accounts**. Generally, the chart of accounts is far more detailed than the information presented in financial statements.

Certain accounts are used to offset other accounts. For example, a common asset account is accounts receivable, also known as "trade accounts receivable" or "trade receivables." A company uses this account to record the amounts it is owed by its customers. In other words, sales made on credit are reflected in accounts receivable. In connection with its receivables, a company often expects some amount of uncollectible accounts and, therefore, records an estimate of the amount that may not be collected. The estimated uncollectible amount is recorded in an account called **allowance for bad debts**. Because the effect of the allowance for bad debts account is to reduce the balance of the company's accounts receivable, it is known as a "contra asset account." Any account that is offset or deducted from another account is called a "**contra account**." Common contra asset accounts include allowance for bad debts (an offset to accounts receivable for the amount of accounts receivable that are estimated to be uncollectible), **accumulated depreciation** (an offset to property, plant, and equipment reflecting the amount of the cost of property, plant, and equipment that has

---

[2] The authoritative accounting standards provide significantly more detailed definitions of the accounting elements. Also note that "owners' equity" is a generic term and more specific titles are often used such as "shareholders' equity," "stockholders' equity," or "partners' capital." The broader terms "equity" and "capital" are also used on occasion.

been allocated to current and previous accounting periods), and **sales returns and allowances** (an offset to revenue reflecting any cash refunds, credits on account, and discounts from sales prices given to customers who purchased defective or unsatisfactory items).

EXHIBIT 2	Common Accounts
Assets	▶ Cash and cash equivalents
	▶ Accounts receivable, trade receivables
	▶ Prepaid expenses
	▶ Inventory
	▶ Property, plant, and equipment
	▶ Investment property
	▶ Intangible assets (patents, trademarks, licenses, copyright, goodwill)
	▶ Financial assets, trading securities, investment securities
	▶ Investments accounted for by the equity method
	▶ Current and deferred tax assets
	▶ [for banks, Loans (receivable)]
Liabilities	▶ Accounts payable, trade payables
	▶ Provisions or accrued liabilities
	▶ Financial liabilities
	▶ Current and deferred tax liabilities
	▶ Reserves
	▶ Minority interest
	▶ Unearned revenue
	▶ Debt payable
	▶ Bonds (payable)
	▶ [for banks, Deposits]
Owners' equity	▶ Capital, such as common stock par value
	▶ Additional paid-in capital
	▶ Retained earnings
	▶ Other comprehensive income
Revenue	▶ Revenue, sales
	▶ Gains
	▶ Investment income (e.g., interest and dividends)
Expense	▶ Cost of goods sold
	▶ Selling, general, and administrative expenses "SG&A" (e.g., rent, utilities, salaries, advertising)
	▶ Depreciation and amortization
	▶ Interest expense
	▶ Tax expense
	▶ Losses

For presentation purposes, assets are sometimes categorized as "current" or "noncurrent." For example, Tesco (a large European retailer) presents the following major asset accounts in its 2006 financial reports:

Noncurrent assets:

▶ Intangible assets including goodwill;

▶ Property, plant, and equipment;

▶ Investment property;

▶ Investments in joint ventures and associates.

Current assets:

▶ Inventories;

▶ Trade and other receivables;

▶ Cash and cash equivalents.

Noncurrent assets are assets that are expected to benefit the company over an extended period of time (usually more than one year). For Tesco, these include the following: intangible assets, such as goodwill;[3] property, plant, and equipment used in operations (e.g., land and buildings); other property held for investment, and investments in the securities of other companies.

Current assets are those that are expected to be consumed or converted into cash in the near future, typically one year or less. **Inventories** are the unsold units of product on hand (sometimes referred to as inventory stock). **Trade receivables** (also referred to as **commercial receivables**, or simply **accounts receivable**) are amounts customers owe the company for products that have been sold as well as amounts that may be due from suppliers (such as for returns of merchandise). **Other receivables** represent amounts owed to the company from parties other than customers. **Cash** refers to cash on hand (e.g., petty cash and cash not yet deposited to the bank) and in the bank. **Cash equivalents** are very liquid short-term investments, usually maturing in 90 days or less. The presentation of assets as current or noncurrent will vary from industry to industry and from country to country. Some industries present current assets first, whereas others list noncurrent assets first. This is discussed further in later readings.

3.2 Accounting Equations

The five financial statement elements noted previously serve as the inputs for equations that underlie the financial statements. This section describes the equations for three of the financial statements: balance sheet, income statement, and statement of retained earnings. A statement of retained earnings can be viewed as a component of the statement of stockholders' equity, which shows *all* changes to owners' equity, both changes resulting from retained earnings and changes resulting from share issuance or repurchase. The fourth basic financial statement, the statement of cash flows, will be discussed in a later section.

The **balance sheet** presents a company's financial position at a *particular point in time*. It provides a listing of a company's assets and the claims on those assets (liabilities and equity claims). The equation that underlies the balance

---

[3] **Goodwill** is an intangible asset that represents the excess of the purchase price of an acquired company over the value of the net assets acquired.

sheet is also known as the "basic accounting equation." A company's financial position is reflected using the following equation:

$$\text{Assets} = \text{Liabilities} + \text{Owners' equity} \tag{1a}$$

Presented in this form, it is clear that claims on assets are from two sources: liabilities or owners' equity. Owners' equity is the **residual claim** of the owners (i.e., the owners' remaining claim on the company's assets after the liabilities are deducted). The concept of the owners' residual claim is well illustrated by the slightly rearranged balance sheet equation, roughly equivalent to the structure commonly seen in the balance sheets of U.K. companies:

$$\text{Assets} - \text{Liabilities} = \text{Owners' equity} \tag{1b}$$

Other terms are used to denote owners' equity, including shareholders' equity, stockholders' equity, net assets, equity, net worth, net book value, and partners' capital. The exact titles depend upon the type of entity, but the equation remains the same. Owners' equity at a given date can be further classified by its origin: capital contributed by owners, and earnings retained in the business up to that date: [4]

$$\text{Owners' equity} = \text{Contributed capital} + \text{Retained earnings} \tag{2}$$

The **income statement** presents the performance of a business for a *specific period of time.* The equation reflected in the income statement is the following:

$$\text{Revenue} - \text{Expenses} = \text{Net income (loss)} \tag{3}$$

Note that **net income (loss)** is the difference between two of the elements: revenue and expenses. When a company's revenue exceeds its expenses, it reports net income; when a company's revenues are less than its expenses, it reports a net loss. Other terms are used synonymously with revenue, including sales and turnover (in the United Kingdom). Other terms used synonymously with net income include net profit and net earnings.

Also, as noted earlier, revenue and expenses generally relate to providing goods or services in a company's primary business activities. In contrast, gains (losses) relate to increases (decreases) in resources that are not part of a company's primary business activities. Distinguishing a company's primary business activities from other business activities is important in financial analysis; however, for purposes of the accounting equation, gains are included in revenue and losses are included in expenses.

The balance sheet and income statement are two of the primary financial statements. Although these are the common terms for these statements, some variations in the names occur. A balance sheet can be referred to as a "statement of financial position" or some similar term that indicates it contains balances at a point in time. Income statements can be titled "statement of operations,"

---

[4] This formula reflects the fundamental origins of owners' equity and reflects the basic principles of accounting. The presentation is somewhat simplified. In practice, the owners' equity section of a company's balance sheet may include other items, such as treasury stock (which arises when a company repurchases and holds its own stock) or other comprehensive income. **Comprehensive income** includes all income of the company. Some items of comprehensive income are not reported on the income statement. These items as a group are called **other comprehensive income**; such items arise, for example, when there are changes in the value of assets or liabilities that are not reflected in the income statement.

"statement of income," "statement of profit and loss," or some other similar term showing that it reflects the company's operating activity for a period of time. A simplified balance sheet and income statement are shown in Exhibit 3.

EXHIBIT 3	Simplified Balance Sheet and Income Statement

ABC Company, Inc. Balance Sheet As of 31 December 20X1		ABC Company, Inc. Income Statement For the Year Ended 31 December 20X1	
Assets	2,000	Revenue	250
Liabilities	500	Expense	50
Owners' equity	1,500	Net income	200
	2,000		

The balance sheet represents a company's financial position at a point in time, and the income statement represents a company's activity over a period of time. The two statements are linked together through the retained earnings component of owners' equity. Beginning retained earnings is the balance in this account at the beginning of the accounting period, and ending retained earnings is the balance at the end of the period. A company's ending retained earnings is composed of the beginning balance (if any), plus net income, less any distributions to owners (dividends). Accordingly, the equation underlying retained earnings is:

$$\text{Ending retained earnings} = \text{Beginning retained earnings} + \text{Net income} - \text{Dividends} \qquad \textbf{(4a)}$$

Or, substituting Equation 3 for Net income, equivalently:

$$\text{Ending retained earnings} = \text{Beginning retained earnings} + \text{Revenues} - \text{Expenses} - \text{Dividends} \qquad \textbf{(4b)}$$

As its name suggests, retained earnings represent the earnings (i.e., net income) that are retained by the company—in other words, the amount not distributed as dividends to owners. Retained earnings is a component of owners' equity and links the "as of" balance sheet equation with the "activity" equation of the income statement. To provide a combined representation of the balance sheet and income statement, we can substitute Equation 2 into Equation 1a. This becomes the expanded accounting equation:

$$\text{Assets} = \text{Liabilities} + \text{Contributed capital} + \text{Ending retained earnings} \qquad \textbf{(5a)}$$

Or equivalently, substituting Equation 4b into Equation 5a, we can write:

$$\text{Assets} = \text{Liabilities} + \text{Contributed capital} + \text{Beginning retained earnings} + \text{Revenue} - \text{Expenses} - \text{Dividends} \qquad \textbf{(5b)}$$

The last five items, beginning with contributed capital, are components of owners' equity.

The **statement of retained earnings** shows the linkage between the balance sheet and income statement. Exhibit 4 shows a simplified example of financial statements for a company that began the year with retained earnings of $250 and recognized $200 of net income during the period. The example assumes the company paid no dividends and, therefore, had ending retained earnings of $450.

The basic accounting equation reflected in the balance sheet (Assets = Liabilities + Owners' equity) implies that every recorded transaction affects at least two accounts in order to keep the equation in balance, hence the term **double-entry accounting** that is sometimes used to describe the accounting process. For example, the use of cash to purchase equipment affects two accounts (both asset accounts): cash decreases and equipment increases. As another example, the use of cash to pay off a liability also affects two accounts (one asset account and one liability account): cash decreases and the liability decreases. With each transaction, the accounting equation remains in balance, which is a fundamental accounting concept. Example 1 presents a partial balance sheet for an actual company and an application of the accounting equation. Examples 2 and 3 provide further practice for applying the accounting equations.

EXHIBIT 4	Simplified Balance Sheet, Income Statement, and Statement of Retained Earnings

Point in Time: Beginning of Period Balance Sheet	Change over Time: Income Statement *and* Changes in Retained Earnings	Point in Time: End of Period Balance Sheet

ABC Company, Inc. (Beginning) Balance Sheet As of 31 December 20X0		**ABC Company, Inc. Income Statement Year Ended 31 December 20X1**		**ABC Company, Inc. (Ending) Balance Sheet As of 31 December 20X1**	
Assets	2,000	Revenue	250	Assets	2,200
		Expense	50		
Liabilities	500	Net income	200	Liabilities	500
Contributed equity	1,250			Contributed equity	1,250
Retained earnings	**250**			**Retained earnings**	**450**
Owners' equity	1,500			Owners' equity	1,700
	2,000				2,200

ABC Company, Inc.
Statement of Retained Earnings
Year Ended 31 December 20X1

Beginning retained earnings	250
Plus net income	200
Minus dividends	0
Ending retained earnings	**450**

EXAMPLE 1

Using Accounting Equations (1)

Canon is a manufacturer of copy machines and other electronic equipment. Abbreviated balance sheets as of 31 December 2004 and 2005 are presented below.

Canon and Subsidiaries
Consolidated Balance Sheets
(Millions of Yen)

	31 Dec 2005	31 Dec 2004
Assets		
Total assets	¥4,043,553	¥3,587,021
Liabilities and stockholders' equity		
Total liabilities	1,238,535	1,190,331
Total stockholders' equity	?	2,396,690
Total liabilities and stockholders' equity	¥4,043,553	¥3,587,021

Using Equation 1a, address the following:

1. Determine the amount of stockholders' equity as of 31 December 2005.
2. **A.** Calculate and contrast the absolute change in total assets in 2005 with the absolute change in total stockholders' equity in 2005.
   B. Based on your answer to 2A, state and justify the relative importance of growth in stockholders' equity and growth in liabilities in financing the growth of assets over the two years.

Solution to 1: Total stockholders' equity is equal to assets minus liabilities; in other words, it is the residual claim to the company's assets after deducting liabilities. For 2005, the amount of Canon's total stockholders' equity was thus ¥4,043,553 million − ¥1,238,535 million = ¥2,805,018 million in 2005.

Solution to 2:

A. Total assets increased by ¥4,043,553 million − ¥3,587,021 million = ¥456,532 million. Total stockholders' equity increased by ¥2,805,018 million − ¥2,396,690 million = ¥408,328 million. Thus, in 2005, total assets grew by more than total stockholders' equity (¥456,532 million is larger than ¥408,328 million).

B. Using the relationship Assets = Liabilities + Owners' equity, the solution to 2A implies that total liabilities increased by the difference between the increase in total assets and the increase in total stockholders' equity, that is, by ¥456,532 million − ¥408,328 million = ¥48,204 million. (If liabilities had not increased by ¥48,204 million, the accounting equation would not be in balance.) Contrasting the growth in total stockholders' equity (¥408,328 million) with the growth in total liabilities (¥48,204 million), we see that the growth in stockholders' equity was relatively much more important than the growth in liabilities in financing total asset growth in 2005.

EXAMPLE 2

Using Accounting Equations (2)

An analyst has collected the following information regarding a company in advance of its year-end earnings announcement (amounts in millions):

Estimated net income	$ 150
Beginning retained earnings	$2,000
Estimated distributions to owners	$ 50

The analyst's estimate of ending retained earnings (in millions) should be closest to:

A. $2,000.
B. $2,100.
C. $2,150.
D. $2,200.

Solution: B is correct. Beginning retained earnings is increased by net income and reduced by distributions to owners: $2,000 + $150 − $50 = $2,100.

EXAMPLE 3

Using Accounting Equations (3)

An analyst has compiled the following information regarding RDZ, Inc.

Liabilities at year-end	€1,000
Contributed capital at year-end	€1,000
Beginning retained earnings	€500
Revenue during the year	€4,000
Expenses during the year	€3,800

There have been no distributions to owners. The analyst's estimate of total assets at year-end should be closest to:

A. €2,000.
B. €2,300.
C. €2,500.
D. €2,700.

Solution: D is correct. Ending retained earnings is first determined by adding revenue minus expenses to beginning retained earnings to obtain €700. Total assets would be equal to the sum of liabilities, contributed capital, and ending retained earnings: €1,000 + €1,000 + €700 = €2,700.

Having described the components and linkages of financial statements in abstract terms, we now examine more concretely how business activities are recorded. The next section illustrates the accounting process with a simple step-by-step example.

4 THE ACCOUNTING PROCESS

The accounting process involves recording business transactions such that periodic financial statements can be prepared. This section illustrates how business transactions are recorded in a simplified accounting system.

4.1 An Illustration

Key concepts of the accounting process can be more easily explained using a simple illustration. We look at an illustration in which three friends decide to start a business, Investment Advisers, Ltd. (IAL). They plan to issue a monthly newsletter of securities trading advice and to sell investment books. Although they do not plan to manage any clients' funds, they will manage a trading portfolio of the owners' funds to demonstrate the success of the recommended strategies from the newsletter. Because this illustration is meant to present accounting concepts, any regulatory implications will not be addressed. Additionally, for this illustration, we will assume that the entity will not be subject to income taxes; any income or loss will be passed through to the owners and be subject to tax on their personal income tax returns.

As the business commences, various business activities occur. Exhibit 5 provides a listing of the business activities that have taken place in the early stages of operations. Note that these activities encompass the types of operating, investing, and financing business activities discussed above.

4.2 The Accounting Records

If the owners want to evaluate the business at the end of January 2006, Exhibit 5 does not provide a sufficiently meaningful report of what transpired or where the company currently stands. It is clear that a system is needed to track this information and to address three objectives:

▶ Identify those activities requiring further action (e.g., collection of outstanding receivable balances).

▶ Assess the profitability of the operations over the month.

▶ Evaluate the current financial position of the company (such as cash on hand).

EXHIBIT 5	Business Activities for Investment Advisers, Ltd.

#	Date	Business Activity
1	31 December 2005	▶ File documents with regulatory authorities to establish a separate legal entity. Initially capitalize the company through deposit of $150,000 from the three owners.
2	2 January 2006	▶ Set up a $100,000 investment account and purchase a portfolio of equities and fixed-income securities.
3	2 January 2006	▶ Pay $3,000 to landlord for office/warehouse. $2,000 represents a refundable deposit, and $1,000 represents the first month's rent.
4	3 January 2006	▶ Purchase office equipment for $6,000. The equipment has an estimated life of two years with no salvage value.[5]
5	3 January 2006	▶ Receive $1,200 cash for a one-year subscription to the monthly newsletter.
6	10 January 2006	▶ Purchase and receive 500 books at a cost of $20 per book for a total of $10,000. Invoice terms are that payment from IAL is due in 30 days. No cash changes hands. These books are intended for resale.
7	10 January 2006	▶ Spend $600 on newspaper and trade magazine advertising for the month.
8	15 January 2006	▶ Borrow $12,000 from a bank for working capital. Interest is payable annually at 10 percent. The principal is due in two years.
9	15 January 2006	▶ Ship first order to a customer consisting of five books at $25 per book. Invoice terms are that payment is due in 30 days. No cash changes hands.
10	15 January 2006	▶ Sell for cash 10 books at $25 per book at an investment conference.
11	30 January 2006	▶ Hire a part-time clerk. The clerk is hired through an agency that also handles all payroll taxes. The company is to pay $15 per hour to the agency. The clerk works six hours prior to 31 January, but no cash will be paid until February.
12	31 January 2006	▶ Mail out the first month's newsletter to customer. This subscription had been sold on 3 January. See item 5.
13	31 January 2006	▶ Review of the investment portfolio shows that $100 of interest income was earned and the market value of the portfolio has increased by $2,000. The balance in the investment account is now $102,100. The securities are classified as "trading" securities.

An accounting system will translate the company's business activities into usable financial records. The basic system for recording transactions in this illustration is a spreadsheet with each of the different types of accounts represented by a column. The accounting equation provides a basis for setting up this system. Recall the accounting Equation 5b:

$$\text{Assets} = \text{Liabilities} + \text{Contributed capital} + \text{Beginning retained earnings} + \text{Revenue} - \text{Expenses} - \text{Dividends}$$

---

[5] **Salvage value** is the amount the company estimates that it can sell the asset for at the end of its useful life.

The specific accounts to be used for IAL's system include the following:

► Asset Accounts:

Cash

Investments

Prepaid rent (cash paid for rent in advance of recognizing the expense)

Rent deposit (cash deposited with the landlord, but returnable to the company)

Office equipment

Inventory

Accounts receivable

► Liability Accounts:

Unearned fees (fees that have not been earned yet, even though cash has been received)

Accounts payable (amounts owed to suppliers)

Bank debt

► Equity Accounts:

Contributed capital

Retained earnings

    Income

        Revenue

        Expenses

    Dividends

Exhibit 6 presents the spreadsheet representing IAL's accounting system for the first 10 transactions. Each event is entered on a new row of the spreadsheet as it occurs. To record events in the spreadsheet, the financial impact of each needs to be assessed and the activity expressed as an accounting transaction. In assessing the financial impact of each event and converting these events into accounting transactions, the following steps are taken:

1. Identify which accounts are affected, by what amount, and whether the accounts are increased or decreased.

2. Determine the element type for each account identified in Step 1 (e.g., cash is an asset) and where it fits in the basic accounting equation. Rely on the economic characteristics of the account and the basic definitions of the elements to make this determination.

3. Using the information from Steps 1 and 2, enter the amounts in the appropriate column of the spreadsheet.

4. Verify that the accounting equation is still in balance.

At any point in time, basic financial statements can be prepared based on the subtotals in each column.

EXHIBIT 6   Accounting System for Investment Advisers, Ltd.

#	Assets =			Liabilities		+	Owners' Equity				
	Cash	Other Assets	Account	Amount	Account		Contributed Capital	Beginning Retained Earnings	Revenue	Expense	Dividends
Beg. Balance	0	0		0			0	0	0	0	0
1 Capitalize	150,000						150,000				
2 Investments	(100,000)	100,000	Investments								
3 Pay landlord	(3,000)	1,000	Prepaid rent								
		2,000	Rent deposit								
4 Buy equipment	(6,000)	6,000	Office equipment								
5 Sell subscription	1,200			1,200	Unearned fees						
6 Buy books		10,000	Inventory	10,000	Accounts payable						
7 Advertise	(600)									(600)	
8 Borrow	12,000			12,000	Bank debt						
9 Sell books on account		125	Accounts receivable						125	(100)	
		(100)	Inventory								
10 Cash sale	250	(200)	Inventory						250	(200)	
Subtotal	53,850	118,825		23,200			150,000		375	(900)	

The following discussion identifies the accounts affected and the related element (Steps 1 and 2) for the first 10 events listed in Exhibit 5. The accounting treatment shows the account affected in bold and the related element in brackets. The recording of these entries into a basic accounting system (Steps 3 and 4) is depicted on the spreadsheet in Exhibit 6.

Because this is a new business, the accounting equation begins at zero on both sides. There is a zero beginning balance in all accounts.

---

31 December 2005

#	Business Activity	Accounting Treatment
1	▶ File documents with regulatory authorities to establish a separate legal entity. Initially capitalize the company through deposit of $150,000 from the three owners.	▶ **Cash [A]** is increased by $150,000, and **contributed capital [E]**[6] is increased by $150,000.

Accounting elements: Assets (A), Liabilities (L), Equity (E), Revenue (R), and Expenses (X).

This transaction affects two elements: assets and equity. Exhibit 6 demonstrates this effect on the accounting equation. The company's balance sheet at this point in time would be presented by subtotaling the columns in Exhibit 6:

Investment Advisers, Ltd.
Balance Sheet
As of 31 December 2005

Assets	
Cash	$150,000
Total assets	$150,000
Liabilities and owners' equity	
Contributed capital	$150,000
Total liabilities and owners' equity	$150,000

The company has assets (resources) of $150,000, and the owners' claim on the resources equals $150,000 (their contributed capital) as there are no liabilities at this point.

---

[6] The account title will vary depending upon the type of entity (incorporated or not) and jurisdiction. Alternative account titles are "common shares," "common stock," "members' capital," "partners' capital," etc.

For this illustration, we present an unclassified balance sheet. An **unclassified balance sheet** is one that does not show subtotals for current assets and current liabilities. Assets are simply listed in order of liquidity (how quickly they are expected to be converted into cash). Similarly, liabilities are listed in the order in which they are expected to be satisfied (or paid off).

2 January 2006

#	Business Activity	Accounting Treatment
2	▶ Set up a $100,000 investment account and purchase a portfolio of equities and fixed-income securities.	▶ **Investments [A]** were increased by $100,000, and **cash [A]** was decreased by $100,000.

Accounting elements: Assets (A), Liabilities (L), Equity (E), Revenue (R), and Expenses (X).

This transaction affects two accounts, but only one element (assets) and one side of the accounting equation, as depicted in Exhibit 6. Cash is reduced when the securities are purchased. Another type of asset, investments, increases. We examine the other transaction from 2 January before taking another look at the company's balance sheet.

2 January 2006

#	Business Activity	Accounting Treatment
3	▶ Pay $3,000 to landlord for office/warehouse. $2,000 represents a refundable deposit, and $1,000 represents the first month's rent.	▶ **Cash [A]** was decreased by $3,000, **deposits [A]** were increased by $2,000, and **prepaid rent [A]** was increased by $1,000.

Accounting elements: Assets (A), Liabilities (L), Equity (E), Revenue (R), and Expenses (X).

Once again, this transaction affects only asset accounts. Note that the first month's rent is initially recorded as an asset, prepaid rent. As time passes, the company will incur rent expense, so a portion of this prepaid asset will be transferred to expenses and thus will appear on the income statement as an expense.[7] This will require a later adjustment in our accounting system. Note that the

---

[7] An argument can be made for treating this $1,000 as an immediate expense. We adopt the approach of recording a prepaid asset in order to illustrate accrual accounting. A situation in which a company prepays rent (or insurance or any similar expense) for a time span covering multiple accounting periods more clearly requires the use of accrual accounting.

transactions so far have had no impact on the income statement. At this point in time, the company's balance sheet would be:

Investment Advisers, Ltd.
Balance Sheet
As of 2 January 2006

Assets	
Cash	$ 47,000
Investments	100,000
Prepaid rent	1,000
Deposits	2,000
Total assets	$150,000
Liabilities and owners' equity	
Contributed capital	$150,000
Total liabilities and owners' equity	$150,000

Note that the items in the balance sheet have changed, but it remains in balance; the amount of total assets equals total liabilities plus owners' equity. The company still has $150,000 in resources, but the assets now comprise cash, investments, prepaid rent, and deposits. Each asset is listed separately because they are different in terms of their ability to be used by the company. Note also that the owners' equity claim on these assets remains $150,000 because the company still has no liabilities.

3 January 2006

#	Business Activity	Accounting Treatment
4	▶ Purchase office equipment for $6,000 in cash. The equipment has an estimated life of two years with no salvage value.	▶ **Cash [A]** was decreased by $6,000, and **office equipment [A]** was increased by $6,000.

Accounting elements: Assets (A), Liabilities (L), Equity (E), Revenue (R), and Expenses (X).

The company has once again exchanged one asset for another. Cash has decreased while office equipment has increased. Office equipment is a resource that will provide benefits over multiple future periods and, therefore, its cost must also be spread over multiple future periods. This will require adjustments to our accounting records as time passes. **Depreciation** is the term for the process of spreading this cost over multiple periods.

3 January 2006

#	Business Activity	Accounting Treatment
5	▶ Receive $1,200 cash for a one-year subscription to the monthly newsletter.	▶ **Cash [A]** was increased by $1,200, and **unearned fees [L]** was increased by $1,200.

Accounting elements: Assets (A), Liabilities (L), Equity (E), Revenue (R), and Expenses (X).

In this transaction, the company has received cash related to the sale of subscriptions. However, the company has not yet actually earned the subscription fees because it has an obligation to deliver newsletters in the future. So, this amount is recorded as a liability called **unearned fees** (or **unearned revenue**). In the future, as the company delivers the newsletters and thus fulfills its obligation, this amount will be transferred to revenue. If the company fails to deliver the newsletters, the fees will need to be returned to the customer. As of 3 January 2006, the company's balance sheet would appear as

Investment Advisers, Ltd.
Balance Sheet
As of 3 January 2006

Assets	
Cash	$ 42,200
Investments	100,000
Prepaid rent	1,000
Deposits	2,000
Office equipment	6,000
Total assets	$151,200
Liabilities and owners' equity	
Liabilities	
Unearned fees	$ 1,200
Equity	
Contributed capital	$150,000
Total liabilities and owners' equity	$151,200

The company now has $151,200 of resources, against which there is a claim by the subscription customer of $1,200 and a residual claim by the owners of $150,000. Again, the balance sheet remains in balance, with total assets equal to total liabilities plus equity.

10 January 2006

#	Business Activity	Accounting Treatment
6	▶ Purchase and receive 500 books at a cost of $20 per book for a total of $10,000. Invoice terms are that payment from IAL is due in 30 days. No cash changes hands. These books are intended for resale.	▶ **Inventory [A]** is increased by $10,000, and **accounts payable [L]** is increased by $10,000.

Accounting elements: Assets (A), Liabilities (L), Equity (E), Revenue (R), and Expenses (X).

The company has obtained an asset, inventory, which can be sold to customers at a later date. Rather than paying cash to the supplier currently, the company has incurred an obligation to do so in 30 days. This represents a liability to the supplier that is termed accounts payable.

10 January 2006

#	Business Activity	Accounting Treatment
7	▶ Spend $600 on newspaper and trade magazine advertising for the month.	▶ **Cash [A]** was decreased by $600, and **advertising expense [X]** was increased by $600.

Accounting elements: Assets (A), Liabilities (L), Equity (E), Revenue (R), and Expenses (X).

Unlike the previous expenditures, advertising is an expense, not an asset. Its benefits relate to the current period. Expenditures such as advertising are recorded as an expense when they are incurred. Contrast this expenditure with that for equipment, which is expected to be useful over multiple periods and thus is initially recorded as an asset, and then reflected as an expense over time. Also, contrast this treatment with that for rent expense, which was paid in advance and can be clearly allocated over time, and thus is initially recorded as a prepaid asset and then reflected as an expense over time. The advertising expenditure in this example relates to the current period. If the company had paid in advance for several years worth of advertising, then a portion would be capitalized (i.e., recorded as an asset), similar to the treatment of equipment or prepaid rent and expensed in future periods. We can now prepare a partial income statement for the company reflecting this expense:

Investment Advisers, Ltd.
Income Statement
For the Period 1 January through 10 January 2006

Total revenue		$ 0
Expenses		
Advertising	600	
Total expense		600
Net income (loss)		$ (600)

Because the company has incurred a $600 expense but has not recorded any revenue (the subscription revenue has not been earned yet), an income statement for Transactions 1 through 7 would show net income of minus $600 (i.e., a net loss). To prepare a balance sheet for the company, we need to update the retained earnings account. Beginning retained earnings was $0 (zero). Adding the net loss of $600 (made up of $0 revenue minus $600 expense) and deducting any dividend ($0 in this illustration) gives ending retained earnings of minus $600. The ending retained earnings covering Transactions 1–7 is included in the interim balance sheet:

Investment Advisers, Ltd.
Balance Sheet
As of 10 January 2006

Assets	
Cash	$ 41,600
Investments	100,000
Inventory	10,000
Prepaid rent	1,000
Deposits	2,000
Office equipment	6,000
Total assets	$160,600
Liabilities and owners' equity	
Liabilities	
Accounts payable	$ 10,000
Unearned fees	1,200
Total liabilities	11,200
Equity	
Contributed capital	150,000
Retained earnings	(600)
Total equity	149,400
Total liabilities and owners' equity	$160,600

As with all balance sheets, the amount of total assets equals total liabilities plus owners' equity—both are $160,600. The owners' claim on the business has been reduced to $149,400. This is due to the negative retained earnings (sometimes referred to as a retained "deficit"). As noted, the company has a net loss after the first seven transactions, a result of incurring $600 of advertising expenses but not yet producing any revenue.

15 January 2006

#	Business Activity	Accounting Treatment
8	▶ Borrow $12,000 from a bank for working capital. Interest is payable annually at 10 percent. The principal is due in two years.	▶ **Cash [A]** is increased by $12,000, and **bank debt [L]** is increased by $12,000.

Accounting elements: Assets (A), Liabilities (L), Equity (E), Revenue (R), and Expenses (X).

Cash is increased, and a corresponding liability is recorded to reflect the amount owed to the bank. Initially, no entry is made for interest that is expected to be paid on the loan. In the future, interest will be recorded as time passes and interest accrues (accumulates) on the loan.

15 January 2006

#	Business Activity	Accounting Treatment
9	▶ Ship first order to a customer consisting of five books at $25 per book. Invoice terms are that payment is due in 30 days. No cash changes hands.	▶ **Accounts receivable [A]** increased by $125, and **revenue [R]** increased by $125. Additionally, **inventory [A]** decreased by $100, and **cost of goods sold [X]** increased by $100.

Accounting elements: Assets (A), Liabilities (L), Equity (E), Revenue (R), and Expenses (X).

The company has now made a sale. Sale transaction records have two parts. One part represents the $125 revenue to be received from the customer, and the other part represents the $100 cost of the goods that have been sold. Although payment has not yet been received from the customer in payment for the goods, the company has delivered the goods (five books) and so revenue is recorded. A corresponding asset, accounts receivable, is recorded to reflect amounts due from the customer. Simultaneously, the company reduces its inventory balance by the cost of the five books sold and also records this amount as an expense termed **cost of goods sold**.

15 January 2006

#	Business Activity	Accounting Treatment
10	▶ Sell for cash 10 books at $25 per book at an investment conference.	▶ **Cash [A]** is increased by $250, and **revenue [R]** is increased by $250. Additionally, **inventory [A]** is decreased by $200, and **cost of goods sold [X]** is increased by $200.

Accounting elements: Assets (A), Liabilities (L), Equity (E), Revenue (R), and Expenses (X).

Similar to the previous sale transaction, both the $250 sales proceeds and the $200 cost of the goods sold must be recorded. In contrast with the previous sale, however, the sales proceeds are received in cash. Subtotals from Exhibit 6 can once again be used to prepare a preliminary income statement and balance sheet to evaluate the business to date:

Investment Advisers, Ltd.
Income Statement
For the Period 1 January through 15 January 2006

Total revenue		$ 375
Expenses		
Cost of goods sold	300	
Advertising	600	
Total expenses		900
Net income (loss)		$ (525)

Investment Advisers, Ltd.
Balance Sheet
As of 15 January 2006

Assets	
Cash	$ 53,850
Accounts receivable	125
Investments	100,000
Inventory	9,700
Prepaid rent	1,000
Deposits	2,000
Office equipment	6,000
Total assets	$172,675

(Continued on next page . . .)

(continued)

Liabilities and owners' equity	
Liabilities	
Accounts payable	$ 10,000
Unearned fees	1,200
Bank debt	12,000
Total liabilities	23,200
Equity	
Contributed capital	150,000
Retained earnings	(525)
Total equity	149,475
Total liabilities and owners' equity	$172,675

An income statement covering Transactions 1–10 would reflect revenue to date of $375 for the sale of books minus the $300 cost of those books and minus the $600 advertising expense. The net loss is $525, which is shown in the income statement as $(525) using the accounting convention that indicates a negative number using parentheses. This net loss is also reflected on the balance sheet in retained earnings. The amount in retained earnings at this point equals the net loss of $525 because retained earnings had $0 beginning balance and no dividends have been distributed. The balance sheet reflects total assets of $172,675 and claims on the assets of $23,200 in liabilities and $149,475 owners' equity. Within assets, the inventory balance represents the cost of the 485 remaining books (a total of 15 have been sold) at $20 each.

Transactions 1–10 occurred throughout the month and involved cash, accounts receivable, or accounts payable; accordingly, these transactions clearly required an entry into the accounting system. The other transactions, items 11–13, have also occurred and need to be reflected in the financial statements, but these transactions may not be so obvious. In order to prepare complete financial statements at the end of a reporting period, an entity needs to review its operations to determine whether any accruals or other adjustments are required. A more complete discussion of accruals and adjustments is set forth in the next section, but generally speaking, such entries serve to allocate revenue and expense items into the correct accounting period. In practice, companies may also make adjustments to correct erroneous entries or to update inventory balances to reflect a physical count.

In this illustration, adjustments are needed for a number of transactions in order to allocate amounts across accounting periods. The accounting treatment for these transactions is shown in Exhibit 7. Transactions are numbered sequentially, and an "a" is added to a transaction number to denote an adjustment relating to a previous transaction. Exhibit 8 presents the completed spreadsheet reflecting these additional entries in the accounting system.

EXHIBIT 7	Investment Advisers, Ltd., Accruals and Other Adjusting Entries on 31 January 2006

#	Business Activity	Accounting Treatment
11	▸ Hire a part-time clerk. The clerk is hired through an agency that also handles all payroll taxes. The company is to pay $15 per hour to the agency. The clerk works six hours prior to 31 January, but no cash will be paid until February.	▸ The company owes $90 for wages at month end. Under accrual accounting, expenses are recorded when incurred, not when paid. ▸ **Accrued wages [L]** is increased by $90, and **payroll expense [X]** is increased by $90. The accrued wage liability will be eliminated when the wages are paid.
12	▸ Mail out the first month's newsletter to customer. This subscription had been sold on 3 January.	▸ One month (or 1/12) of the $1,200 subscription has been satisfied, so $100 can be recognized as revenue. ▸ **Unearned fees [L]** is decreased by $100, and **fee revenue [R]** is increased by $100.
13	▸ Review of the investment portfolio shows that $100 of interest income was earned and the market value of the portfolio has increased by $2,000. The balance in the investment account is now $102,100. The securities are classified as "trading" securities.	▸ **Interest income [R]** is increased by $100, and the **investments** account **[A]** is increased by $100. ▸ The $2,000 increase in the value of the portfolio represents unrealized gains that are part of income for traded securities. The **investments** account **[A]** is increased by $2,000, and **unrealized gains [R]** is increased by $2,000.
3a	▸ In item 3, $3,000 was paid to the landlord for office/warehouse, including a $2,000 refundable deposit and $1,000 for the first month's rent. ▸ Now, the first month has ended, so this rent has become a cost of doing business.	▸ To reflect the full amount of the first month's rent as a cost of doing business, **prepaid rent [A]** is decreased by $1,000, and **rent expense [X]** is increased by $1,000.
4a	▸ In item 4, office equipment was purchased for $6,000 in cash. The equipment has an estimated life of two years with no salvage value. ▸ Now, one month (or 1/24) of the useful life of the equipment has ended, so a portion of the equipment cost has become a cost of doing business.	▸ A portion (1/24) of the total $6,000 cost of the office equipment is allocated to the current period's cost of doing business. ▸ **Depreciation expense [X]** is increased by $250, and **accumulated depreciation [A]** (a contra asset account) is increased by $250. ▸ Accumulated depreciation is a contra asset account to office equipment.
8a	▸ The company borrowed $12,000 from a bank on 15 January, with interest payable annually at 10 percent and the principal due in two years. ▸ Now, one-half of one month has passed since the borrowing.	▸ One-half of one month of interest expense has become a cost of doing business. $12,000 × 10% = $1,200 of annual interest, equivalent to $100 per month or $50 for one-half month. ▸ **Interest expense [X]** is increased by $50, and **interest payable [L]** is increased by $50.

Accounting elements: Assets (A), Liabilities (L), Equity (E), Revenue (R), and Expenses (X).
Notes: Items 11–13 are repeated from Exhibit 5. Items 3a, 4a, and 8a reflect adjustments relating to items 3, 4, and 8 from Exhibit 5.

EXHIBIT 8   Accounting System for Investment Advisers, Ltd.

	Assets =			Liabilities		Owners' Equity				
#	Cash	Other Assets	Account	Amount	Account	Contributed Capital	Beginning Retained Earnings	Revenue	Expense (Enter as Negative)	Dividends (Enter as Negative)
Beg. Bal	0	0		0		0	0	0	0	0
1 Capitalize	150,000					150,000				
2 Investments	(100,000)	100,000	Investments							
3 Pay landlord	(3,000)	1,000	Prepaid rent							
		2,000	Rent deposit							
4 Buy equipment	(6,000)	6,000	Office equipment							
5 Sell subscript.	1,200			1,200	Unearned fees					
6 Buy books		10,000	Inventory	10,000	Accounts payable					
7 Advertise	(600)								(600)	
8 Borrow	12,000			12,000	Bank debt					
9 Sell books on account		(100)	Inventory					125	(100)	
		125	Accounts receivable							
10 Cash sale	250	(200)	Inventory					250	(200)	
11 Accrue wages				90	Accrued wages				(90)	
12 Earn subscription fees				(100)	Unearned fees			100		
13 Investment income		100	Investments					100		
		2,000	Investments					2,000		
3a Rent expense		(1,000)	Prepaid rent						(1,000)	
4a Depreciate equipment		(250)	Accumulated depreciation (equipment)						(250)	
8a Accrue interest				50	Interest payable				(50)	
Subtotal	53,850	119,675		23,240		150,000		2,575	(2,290)	

A final income statement and balance sheet can now be prepared reflecting all transactions and adjustments.

Investment Advisers, Ltd.
Income Statement
For the Period 1 January through 31 January 2006

Revenues	
Fee revenue	$ 100
Book sales	375
Investment income	2,100
Total revenues	$ 2,575
Expenses	
Cost of goods sold	$ 300
Advertising	600
Wage	90
Rent	1,000
Depreciation	250
Interest	50
Total expenses	2,290
Net income (loss)	$ 285

Investment Advisers, Ltd.
Balance Sheet
As of 31 January 2006

Assets	
Cash	$ 53,850
Accounts receivable	125
Investments	102,100
Inventory	9,700
Prepaid rent	0
Office equipment, net	5,750
Deposits	2,000
Total assets	$173,525
Liabilities and owners' equity	
Liabilities	
Accounts payable	$ 10,000
Accrued wages	90
Interest payable	50
Unearned fees	1,100
Bank debt	12,000

(Continued on next page . . .)

(continued)		
Total liabilities		23,240
Equity		
Contributed capital		150,000
Retained earnings		285
Total equity		150,285
Total liabilities and owners' equity		$173,525

From the income statement, we can determine that the business was profitable for the month. The business earned $285 after expenses. The balance sheet presents the financial position. The company has assets of $173,525, and claims against those assets included liabilities of $23,240 and an owners' claim of $150,285. The owners' claim reflects their initial investment plus reinvested earnings. These statements are explored further in the next section.

4.3 Financial Statements

The spreadsheet in Exhibit 8 is an organized presentation of the company's transactions and can help in preparing the income statement and balance sheet presented above. Exhibit 9 presents all financial statements and demonstrates their relationships. Note that the data for the income statement come from the revenue and expense columns of the spreadsheet (which include gains and losses). The net income of $285 (revenue of $2,575 minus expenses of $2,290) was retained in the business rather than distributed to the owners as dividends. The net income, therefore, becomes part of ending retained earnings on the balance sheet. The detail of retained earnings is shown in the statement of owners' equity.

The balance sheet presents the financial position of the company using the assets, liabilities, and equity accounts from the accounting system spreadsheet. The statement of cash flows summarizes the data from the cash column of the accounting system spreadsheet to enable the owners and others to assess the sources and uses of cash. These sources and uses of cash are categorized according to group of business activity: operating, investing, or financing. The format of the statement of cash flows presented here is known as the **direct format**, which refers to the operating cash section appearing simply as operating cash receipts less operating cash disbursements. An alternative format for the operating cash section, which begins with net income and shows adjustments to derive operating cash flow, is known as the **indirect format**. The alternative formats and detailed rules are discussed in the reading on understanding the statement of cash flows.

EXHIBIT 9   **Investment Advisers, Ltd., Financial Statements**

Investment Advisers, Ltd.
Balance Sheet
As of

	12/31/2005	1/31/2006
Assets		
Cash	150,000	53,850
Accounts receivable	0	125
Investments	0	102,100
Inventory		9,700
Office equipment, net		5,750
Deposits		2,000
Total assets	150,000	173,525
Liabilities		
Accounts payable	0	10,000
Accrued expenses		140
Unearned fees		1,100
Bank debt		12,000
Total liabilities		23,240
Owners' equity		
Contributed capital	150,000	150,000
Retained earnings	0	285
Total equity	150,000	150,285
Total liabilities and equity	150,000	173,525

Investment Advisers, Ltd.
Income Statement
For the Month Ended 1/31/2006

Fee revenue	100
Book sales revenue	375
Investment income	2,100
Total revenue	2,575
Cost of goods sold	300
Other expense	1,990
Total expense	2,290
Net income (loss)	285

Investment Advisers, Ltd.
Statement of Cash Flows
For the Month Ended 1/31/2006

Cash received from customers	1,450
Cash paid to landlord	(3,000)
Cash paid for advertising	(600)
Investments in trading securities	(100,000)
Operating cash flows	(102,150)
Capital expenditures	(6,000)
Investing cash flows	(6,000)
Borrowing	12,000
Financing cash flows	12,000
Net decrease in cash	(96,150)
Cash at 12/31/05	150,000
Cash at 1/31/06	53,850

Investment Advisers, Ltd.
Statement of Owners' Equity
31 January 2006

	Contributed Capital	Retained Earnings	Total
Balance at 12/31/05	150,000	0	150,000
Issuance of stock			
Net income (loss)		285	285
Distributions			
Balance at 1/31/06	150,000	285	150,285

Financial statements use the financial data reported in the accounting system and present this data in a more meaningful manner. Each statement reports on critical areas. Specifically, a review of the financial statements for the IAL illustration provides the following information:

▶ **Balance Sheet**. This statement provides information about a company's financial position at a point in time. It shows an entity's assets, liabilities, and owners' equity at a particular date. Two years are usually presented so that comparisons can be made. Less significant accounts can be grouped into a single line item. One observation from the IAL illustration is that although total assets have increased significantly (about 16 percent), equity has increased less than 0.2 percent—most of the increase in total assets is due to the increase in liabilities.

▶ **Income Statement**. This statement provides information about a company's profitability over a period of time. It shows the amount of revenue, expense, and resulting net income or loss for a company during a period of time. Again, less significant accounts can be grouped into a single line item—in this illustration, expenses other than cost of goods sold are grouped into a single line item. The statement shows that IAL has three sources of revenue and made a small profit in its first month of operations. Significantly, most of the revenue came from investments rather than subscriptions or book sales.

▶ **Statement of Cash Flows**. This statement provides information about a company's cash flows over a period of time. It shows a company's cash inflows (receipts) and outflows (payments) during the period. These flows are categorized according to the three groups of business activities: operating, financing, and investing. In the illustration, IAL reported a large negative cash flow from operations ($102,150), primarily because its trading activities involved the purchase of a portfolio of securities but no sales were made from the portfolio. (Note that the purchase of investments for IAL appears in its operating section because the company is in the business of trading securities. In contrast, for a nontrading company, investment activity would be shown as investing cash flows rather than operating cash flows.) IAL's negative operating and investing cash flows were funded by $12,000 bank borrowing and a $96,150 reduction in the cash balance.

▶ **Statement of Owners' Equity**. This statement provides information about the composition and changes in owners' equity during a period of time. In this illustration, the only change in equity resulted from the net income of $285. A **Statement of Retained Earnings** (not shown) would report the changes in a company's retained earnings during a period of time.

These statements again illustrate the interrelationships among financial statements. On the balance sheet, we see beginning and ending amounts for assets, liabilities, and owners' equity. Owners' equity increased from $150,000 to $150,285. The statement of owners' equity presents a breakdown of this $285 change. The arrow from the statement of owners' equity to the owners' equity section of the balance sheet explains that section of the balance sheet. In the

IAL illustration, the entire $285 change resulted from an increase in retained earnings. In turn, the increase in retained earnings resulted from $285 net income. The income statement presents a breakdown of the revenues and expenses resulting in this $285. The arrow from the income statement to the net income figure in the owners' equity section explains how reported net income came about.

Also on the balance sheet, we see that cash decreased from $150,000 at the beginning of the month to $53,850 at the end of the month. The statement of cash flows provides information on the increases and decreases in cash by group of business activity. The arrow from the statement of cash flows to the ending cash figure shows that the statement of cash flows explains in detail the ending cash amount.

In summary, the balance sheet provides information at a point in time (financial position), whereas the other statements provide useful information regarding the activity during a period of time (profitability, cash flow, and changes in owners' equity).

ACCRUALS AND VALUATION ADJUSTMENTS 5

In a simple business model such as the investment company discussed in the illustration above, many transactions are handled in cash and settled in a relatively short time frame. Furthermore, assets and liabilities have a fixed and determinable value. Translating business transactions into the accounting system is fairly easy. Difficulty usually arises when a cash receipt or disbursement occurs in a different period than the related revenue or expense, or when the reportable values of assets vary. This section will address the accounting treatment for these situations—namely, accruals and valuation adjustments.

5.1 Accruals

Accrual accounting requires that revenue be recorded when earned and that expenses be recorded when incurred, irrespective of when the related cash movements occur. The purpose of accrual entries is to report revenue and expense in the proper accounting period. Because accrual entries occur due to timing differences between cash movements and accounting recognition of revenue or expense, it follows that there are only a few possibilities. First, cash movement and accounting recognition can occur at the same time, in which case there is no need for accruals. Second, cash movement may occur before or after accounting recognition, in which case accruals are required. The possible situations requiring accrual entries are summarized into four types of accrual entries shown in Exhibit 10 and discussed below. Each type of accrual involves an originating entry and at least one adjusting entry at a later date or dates.

EXHIBIT 10	Accruals		

	Cash Movement prior to Accounting Recognition	**Cash Movement in the Same Period as Accounting Recognition**	**Cash Movement after Accounting Recognition**
Revenue	**UNEARNED (DEFERRED) REVENUE** ▶ **Originating entry**–record cash receipt and establish a liability (such as unearned revenue) ▶ **Adjusting entry**–reduce the liability while recording revenue	Settled transaction –no accrual entry needed	**UNBILLED (ACCRUED) REVENUE** ▶ **Originating entry**–record revenue and establish an asset (such as unbilled revenue) ▶ **Adjusting entry**–When billing occurs, reduce unbilled revenue and increase accounts receivable. When cash is collected, eliminate the receivable.
Expense	**PREPAID EXPENSE** ▶ **Originating entry**–record cash payment and establish an asset (such as prepaid expense) ▶ **Adjusting entry**–reduce the asset while recording expense		**ACCRUED EXPENSES** ▶ **Originating entry**–establish a liability (such as accrued expenses) and record an expense ▶ **Adjusting entry**–reduce the liability as cash is paid

Unearned (or **deferred**) **revenue** arises when a company receives cash prior to earning the revenue. In the IAL illustration, in Transaction 5, the company received $1,200 for a 12-month subscription to a monthly newsletter. At the time the cash was received, the company had an obligation to deliver 12 newsletters and thus had not yet earned the revenue. Each month, as a newsletter is delivered, this obligation will decrease by 1/12th (i.e., $100). And at the same time, $100 of revenue will be earned. The accounting treatment involves an originating entry (the initial recording of the cash received and the corresponding liability to deliver newsletters) and, subsequently, 12 future adjusting entries, the first one of which was illustrated as Transaction 12. Each adjusting entry reduces the liability and records revenue.

In practice, a large amount of unearned revenue may cause some concern about a company's ability to deliver on this future commitment. Conversely, a positive aspect is that increases in unearned revenue are an indicator of future revenues. For example, a large liability on the balance sheet of an airline relates to cash received for future airline travel. Revenue will be recognized as the travel occurs, so an increase in this liability is an indicator of future increases in revenue.

Unbilled (or **accrued**) **revenue** arises when a company earns revenue prior to receiving cash but has not yet recognized the revenue at the end of an accounting period. In such cases, the accounting treatment involves an originating entry to record the revenue earned through the end of the accounting period and a related receivable reflecting amounts due from customers. When the company receives payment (or if goods are returned), an adjusting entry eliminates the receivable.

Accrued revenue specifically relates to end-of-period accruals; however, the concept is similar to any sale involving deferred receipt of cash. In the IAL illustration, in Transaction 9, the company sold books on account, so the revenue was recognized prior to cash receipt. The accounting treatment involved an entry to record the revenue and the associated receivable. In the future, when the company receives payment, an adjusting entry (not shown) would eliminate the receivable. In practice, it is important to understand the quality of a company's receivables (i.e., the likelihood of collection).

Prepaid expense arises when a company makes a cash payment prior to recognizing an expense. In the illustration, in Transaction 3, the company prepaid one month's rent. The accounting treatment involves an originating entry to record the payment of cash and the prepaid asset reflecting future benefits, and a subsequent adjusting entry to record the expense and eliminate the prepaid asset. (See the boxes showing the accounting treatment of Transaction 3, which refers to the originating entry, and Transaction 3a, which refers to the adjusting entry.) In other words, prepaid expenses are assets that will be subsequently expensed. In practice, particularly in a valuation, one consideration is that prepaid assets typically have future value only as future operations transpire, unless they are refundable.

Accrued expenses arise when a company incurs expenses that have not yet been paid as of the end of an accounting period. Accrued expenses result in liabilities that usually require future cash payments. In the IAL illustration, the company had incurred wage expenses at month end, but the payment would not be made until after the end of the month (Transaction 11). To reflect the company's position at the end of the month, the accounting treatment involved an originating entry to record wage expense and the corresponding liability for wages payable, and a future adjusting entry to eliminate the liability when cash is paid (not shown because wages will be paid only in February). Similarly, the IAL illustration included interest accrual on the company's bank borrowing. (See the boxes showing the accounting treatment of Transaction 8, where Transaction 8 refers to the originating entry, and Transaction 8a, which refers to the adjusting entry.)

As with accrued revenues, accrued expenses specifically relate to end-of-period accruals. Accounts payable are similar to accrued expenses in that they involve a transaction that occurs now but the cash payment is made later. Accounts payable is also a liability but often relates to the receipt of inventory (or perhaps services) as opposed to recording an immediate expense. Accounts payable should be listed separately from other accrued expenses on the balance sheet because of their different nature.

Overall, in practice, complex businesses require additional accruals that are theoretically similar to the four categories of accruals discussed above but which require considerably more judgment. For example, there may be significant lags between a transaction and cash settlement. In such cases, accruals can span many accounting periods (even 10–20 years!), and it is not always clear when revenue has been earned or an expense has been incurred. Considerable judgment is required to determine how to allocate/distribute amounts across periods. An example of such a complex accrual would be the estimated annual revenue for a contractor on a long-term construction project, such as building a nuclear power plant. In general, however, accruals fall under the four general types and follow essentially the same pattern of originating and adjusting entries as the basic accruals described.

5.2 Valuation Adjustments

In contrast to accrual entries that allocate revenue and expenses into the appropriate accounting periods, valuation adjustments are made to a company's assets or liabilities—only where required by accounting standards—so that the accounting records reflect the current market value rather than the historical cost. In this discussion, we focus on valuation adjustments to assets. For example, in the IAL illustration, Transaction 13 adjusted the value of the company's investment portfolio to its current market value. The income statement reflects the $2,100 increase (including interest), and the ending balance sheets report the investment portfolio at its current market value of $102,100. In contrast, the equipment in the IAL illustration was not reported at its current market value and no valuation adjustment was required.

As this illustration demonstrates, accounting regulations do not require all types of assets to be reported at their current market value. Some assets (e.g., trading securities) are shown on the balance sheet at their current market value, and changes in that market value are reported in the income statement. Some assets are shown at their historical cost (e.g., specific classes of investment securities being held to maturity). Other assets (e.g., a particular class of investment securities) are shown on the balance sheet at their current market value, but changes in market value bypass the income statement and are recorded directly into shareholders' equity under a component referred to as "other comprehensive income." This topic will be discussed in more detail in later readings.

In summary, where valuation adjustment entries are required for assets, the basic pattern is the following for increases in assets: An asset is increased with the other side of the equation being a gain on the income statement or an increase to other comprehensive income. Conversely for decreases: An asset is decreased with the other side of the equation being a loss on the income statement or a decrease to other comprehensive income.

6   ACCOUNTING SYSTEMS

The accounting system set forth for the IAL illustration involved a very simple business, a single month of activity, and a small number of transactions. In practice, most businesses are more complicated and have many more transactions. Accordingly, actual accounting systems, although using essentially the same logic as discussed in the illustration, are both more efficient than a spreadsheet and more complex.

6.1 Flow of Information in an Accounting System

Accounting texts typically discuss accounting systems in detail because accountants need to understand each step in the process. While analysts do not need to know the same details, they should be familiar with the flow of information through a financial reporting system. This flow and the key related documents are described in Exhibit 11.

EXHIBIT 11	**Accounting System Flow and Related Documents**

| Journal entries and adjusting entries | A journal is a document or computer file in which business transactions are recorded in the order in which they occur (chronological order). The general journal is the collection of all business transactions in an accounting system sorted by date. All accounting systems have a general journal to record all transactions. Some accounting systems also include special journals. For example, there may be one journal for recording sales transactions and another for recording inventory purchases.

Journal entries—recorded in journals—are dated, show the accounts affected, and the amounts. If necessary, the entry will include an explanation of the transaction and documented authorization to record the entry. As the initial step in converting business transactions into financial information, the journal entry is useful for obtaining detailed information regarding a particular transaction.

Adjusting journal entries, a subset of journal entries, are typically made at the end of an accounting period to record items such as accruals that are not yet reflected in the accounting system. |

| General ledger and T-accounts | A ledger is a document or computer file that shows all business transactions by account. Note that the general ledger, the core of every accounting system, contains all of the same entries as that posted to the general journal—the only difference is that the data are sorted by date in a journal and by account in the ledger. The general ledger is useful for reviewing all of the activity related to a single account. T-accounts, explained in Appendix 30A, are representations of ledger accounts and are frequently used to describe or analyze accounting transactions. |

| Trial balance and adjusted trial balance | A trial balance is a document that lists account balances at a particular point in time. Trial balances are typically prepared at the end of an accounting period as a first step in producing financial statements. A key difference between a trial balance and a ledger is that the trial balance shows only total ending balances. An initial trial balance assists in the identification of any adjusting entries that may be required. Once these adjusting entries are made, an adjusted trial balance can be prepared. |

| Financial statements | The financial statements, a final product of the accounting system, are prepared based on the account totals from an adjusted trial balance. |

6.2 Debits and Credits

Reviewing the example of IAL, it is clear that the accounting treatment of every transaction involved at least two accounts and the transaction either increased or decreased the value of any affected account. Traditionally, accounting systems have used the terms **debit** and **credit** to describe changes in an account resulting from the accounting processing of a transaction. The correct usage of "debit" and "credit" in an accounting context differs from how these terms are used in everyday language.[8] The accounting definitions of debit and credit ensure that, in processing a transaction, the sum of the debits equals the sum of the credits, which is consistent with the accounting equation always remaining in balance.

Although mastering the usage of the terms "debit" and "credit" is essential for an accountant, an analyst can still understand financial reporting mechanics without speaking in terms of debits and credits. In general, this text avoids the use of debit/credit presentation; however, for reference, Appendix 30A presents the IAL illustration in a debit and credit system.

The following section broadly describes some considerations for using financial statements in security analysis.

7   USING FINANCIAL STATEMENTS IN SECURITY ANALYSIS

Financial statements serve as a foundation for credit and equity analysis, including security valuation. Analysts may need to make adjustments to reflect items not reported in the statements (certain assets/liabilities and future earnings). Analysts may also need to assess the reasonableness of management judgment (e.g., in accruals and valuations). Because analysts typically will not have access to the accounting system or individual entries, they will need to infer what transactions were recorded by examining the financial statements.

7.1 The Use of Judgment in Accounts and Entries

Quite apart from deliberate misrepresentations, even efforts to faithfully represent the economic performance and position of a company require judgments and estimates. Financial reporting systems need to accommodate complex business models by recording accruals and changes in valuations of balance sheet accounts. Accruals and valuation entries require considerable judgment and thus create many of the limitations of the accounting model. Judgments could prove wrong or, worse, be used for deliberate earnings manipulation. An important first step in analyzing financial statements is identifying the types of accruals and valuation entries in an entity's financial statements. Most of these items will be noted in the critical accounting policies/estimates section of management's discussion and analysis (MD&A) and in the significant accounting policies footnote, both found in the annual report. Analysts should use this disclosure to identify the key accruals and valuations for a company. The analyst needs to be aware, as Example 4 shows, that the manipulation of earnings and assets can take place within the context of satisfying the mechanical rules governing the recording of transactions.

---

[8] In accounting, debits record increases of asset and expense accounts or decreases in liability and owners' equity accounts. Credits record increases in liability, owners' equity, and revenue accounts or decreases in asset accounts. Appendix 30A provides more details.

EXAMPLE 4

The Manipulation of Accounting Earnings

As discussed in this reading, the accounting equation can be expressed as Assets = Liabilities + Contributed capital + Ending retained earnings (Equation 5a). Although the equation must remain in balance with each transaction, management can improperly record a transaction to achieve a desired result. For example, when a company spends cash and records an expense, assets are reduced on the left side of the equation and expenses are recorded, which lowers retained earnings on the right side. The balance is maintained. If, however, a company spent cash but did not want to record an expense in order to achieve higher net income, the company could manipulate the system by reducing cash and increasing another asset. The equation would remain in balance and the right-hand side of the equation would not be affected at all. This was one of the techniques used by managers at WorldCom to manipulate financial reports, as summarized in a U.S. Securities and Exchange Commission complaint against the company (emphasis added):

> In general, WorldCom manipulated its financial results in two ways. First, WorldCom reduced its operating expenses by improperly releasing certain reserves held against operating expenses. Second, **WorldCom improperly reduced its operating expenses by recharacterizing certain expenses as capital assets.** Neither practice was in conformity with generally accepted accounting principles ("GAAP"). Neither practice was disclosed to WorldCom's investors, despite the fact that both practices constituted changes from WorldCom's previous accounting practices. Both practices falsely reduced WorldCom's expenses and, accordingly, had the effect of artificially inflating the income WorldCom reported to the public in its financial statements from 1999 through the first quarter of 2002.[9]

In 2005, the former CEO of WorldCom was sentenced to 25 years in prison for his role in the fraud.[10] The analyst should be aware of the possibility of manipulation of earnings and be on the lookout for large increases in existing assets, new unusual assets, and unexplained changes in financial ratios.

7.2 Misrepresentations

It is rare in this age of computers that the mechanics of an accounting system do not work. Most computer accounting systems will not allow a company to make one-sided entries. It is important to note, however, that just because the mechanics work does not necessarily mean that the judgments underlying the financial statements are correct. An unscrupulous accountant could structure entries to achieve a desired result. For example, if a manager wanted to record fictitious

---

[9] SEC vs. WorldCom, 5 November 2002: www.sec.gov/litigation/complaints/comp17829.htm.

[10] "Ebbers Is Sentenced to 25 Years For $11 Billion WorldCom Fraud," *Wall Street Journal*, 14 July 2005, A1.

revenue, a fictitious asset (a receivable) could be created to keep the accounting equation in balance. If the manager paid for something but did not want to record an expense, the transaction could be recorded in a prepaid asset account. If cash is received but the manager does not want to record revenue, a liability could be created. Understanding that there has to be another side to every entry is key in detecting inappropriate accounting because—usually in the course of "fixing" one account—there will be another account with a balance that does not make sense. In the case of recording fictitious revenue, there is likely to be a growing receivable whose collectibility is in doubt. Ratio analysis, which is discussed further in later readings, can assist in detecting suspect amounts in these accounts. Furthermore, the accounting equation can be used to detect likely accounts where aggressive or even fraudulent accounting may have occurred.

SUMMARY

The accounting process is a key component of financial reporting. The mechanics of this process convert business transactions into records necessary to create periodic reports on a company. An understanding of these mechanics is useful in evaluating financial statements for credit and equity analysis purposes and in forecasting future financial statements. Key concepts are as follows:

► Business activities can be classified into three groups: operating activities, investing activities, and financing activities.

► Companies classify transactions into common accounts that are components of the five financial statement elements: assets, liabilities, equity, revenue, and expense.

► The core of the accounting process is the basic accounting equation: Assets = Liabilities + Owners' equity.

► The expanded accounting equation is Assets = Liabilities + Contributed capital + Beginning retained earnings + Revenue − Expenses − Dividends.

► Business transactions are recorded in an accounting system that is based on the basic and expanded accounting equations.

► The accounting system tracks and summarizes data used to create financial statements: the balance sheet, income statement, statement of cash flows, and statement of owners' equity. The statement of retained earnings is a component of the statement of owners' equity.

► Accruals are a necessary part of the accounting process and are designed to allocate activity to the proper period for financial reporting purposes.

► The results of the accounting process are financial reports that are used by managers, investors, creditors, analysts, and others in making business decisions.

► An analyst uses the financial statements to make judgments on the financial health of a company.

► Company management can manipulate financial statements, and a perceptive analyst can use his or her understanding of financial statements to detect misrepresentations.

APPENDIX 30A

A DEBIT/CREDIT ACCOUNTING SYSTEM

The main section of this reading presented a basic accounting system represented as a spreadsheet. An alternative system that underlies most manual and electronic accounting systems uses debits and credits. Both a spreadsheet and a debit/credit system are based on the basic accounting equation:

Assets = Liabilities + Owners' equity

Early generations of accountants desired a system for recording transactions that maintained the balance of the accounting equation and avoided the use of negative numbers (which could lead to errors in recording). The system can be illustrated with T-accounts for every account involved in recording transactions. The T-account is so named for its shape:

T-Account

Debit	Credit

The left-hand side of the T-account is called a "debit," and the right-hand side is termed a "credit." The names should not be construed as denoting value. A debit is not better than a credit and vice versa. Debit simply means the left side of the T-account, and credit simply means the right side. Traditionally, debit is abbreviated as "DR," whereas credit is abbreviated "CR." The T-account is also related to the balance sheet and accounting equation as follows:

Balance Sheet

Assets	Liabilities
	Owners' Equity

Assets are referred to as the left side of the balance sheet (and accounting equation) and hence are on the left side of the T-account. Assets are, therefore, recorded with a debit balance. In other words, to record an increase in an asset, an entry is made to the left-hand side of a T-account. A decrease to an asset is recorded on the right side of a T-account. Liabilities and owners' equity are referred to as the right side of the balance sheet (and accounting equation). Increases to liabilities and owners' equity are recorded on the right side of a T-account; decreases to liabilities and owners' equity are recorded on the left side.

At any point in time, the balance in an account is determined by summing all the amounts on the left side of the account, summing all the amounts on the right side of the account, and calculating the difference. If the sum of amounts on the left side of the account is greater than the sum of amounts on the right side of the account, the account has a debit balance equal to the difference. If the sum of amounts on the right side of the account is greater than the sum of amounts on the left side of the account, the account has a credit balance.

EXHIBIT A-1	Balance Sheet T-Accounts for Investment Advisers, Ltd.

Cash	Accounts Receivable	Inventory

Investments	Office Equipment	Accumulated Depreciation

Deposits	Prepaid Rent	Accounts Payable

Accrued Wages	Unearned Fees	Bank Debt

Accrued Interest	Contributed Capital	Retained Earnings

A T-account is created for each asset account, liability account, and owners' equity account. The collection of these T-accounts at the beginning of the year for a fictitious company, Investment Advisers, Ltd. (IAL), is presented in Exhibit A-1. Each balance sheet T-account is termed a "permanent" or "real" account because the balance in the account carries over from year-to-year.

T-accounts are also set up for each income statement account. These T-accounts are referred to as "temporary" or "nominal" accounts because they are transferred at the end of each fiscal year by transferring any net income or loss to the balance sheet account, Retained Earnings. Income statement T-accounts for IAL are presented in Exhibit A-2.

EXHIBIT A-2   Income Statement T-Accounts for Investment Advisers, Ltd.

Fee Revenue	Book Sales Revenue	Investment Income

Cost of Goods Sold	Advertising Expense	Rent Expense

Depreciation Expense	Wage Expense	Interest Expense

The collection of all business transactions sorted by account, real and temporary, for a company comprise the general ledger. The general ledger is the core of every accounting system, where all transactions are ultimately entered. To illustrate the use of T-accounts, we will use the transactions for IAL summarized in Exhibit A-3. We will first enter each transaction into the general ledger T-accounts, then use the information to prepare financial statements.

EXHIBIT A-3   Business Transactions for Investment Advisers, Ltd.

#	Date	Business Activity
1	31 December 2005	▶ File documents with regulatory authorities to establish a separate legal entity. Initially capitalize the company through deposit of $150,000 from the three owners.
2	2 January 2006	▶ Set up a $100,000 investment account and purchase a portfolio of equities and fixed-income securities.
3	2 January 2006	▶ Pay $3,000 to landlord for office/warehouse. $2,000 represents a refundable deposit, and $1,000 represents the first month's rent.
4	3 January 2006	▶ Purchase office equipment for $6,000. The equipment has an estimated life of two years with no salvage value.
5	3 January 2006	▶ Receive $1,200 cash for a one-year subscription to the monthly newsletter.

(Exhibit continued on next page . . .)

EXHIBIT A-3	(continued)

6	10 January 2006	▶ Purchase and receive 500 books at a cost of $20 per book for a total of $10,000. Invoice terms are that payment from IAL is due in 30 days. No cash changes hands. These books are intended for resale.
7	10 January 2006	▶ Spend $600 on newspaper and trade magazine advertising for the month.
8	15 January 2006	▶ Borrow $12,000 from a bank for working capital. Interest is payable annually at 10 percent. The principal is due in two years.
9	15 January 2006	▶ Ship first order to a customer consisting of five books at $25 per book. Invoice terms are that payment is due in 30 days. No cash changes hands.
10	15 January 2006	▶ Sell for cash 10 books at $25 per book at an investment conference.
11	30 January 2006	▶ Hire a part-time clerk. The clerk is hired through an agency that also handles all payroll taxes. The company is to pay $15 per hour to the agency. The clerk works six hours prior to 31 January, but no cash will be paid until February.
12	31 January 2006	▶ Mail out the first month's newsletter to customer. This subscription had been sold on 3 January. See item 5.
13	31 January 2006	▶ Review of the investment portfolio shows that $100 of interest income was earned and the market value of the portfolio has increased by $2,000. The balance in the investment account is now $102,100. Securities are classified as "trading" securities.

Because this is a new business, the company's general ledger T-accounts initially have a zero balance.

31 December 2005 (excerpt from Exhibit A-3)

#	Business Activity	Accounting Treatment
1	▶ File documents with regulatory authorities to establish a separate legal entity. Initially capitalize the company through deposit of $150,000 from the three owners.	▶ **Cash [A]** is increased by $150,000, and **contributed capital [E]**[1] is increased by $150,000.

Accounting elements: Assets (A), Liabilities (L), Equity (E), Revenue (R), and Expenses (X).

[1] The account title will vary depending upon the type of entity (incorporated or not) and jurisdiction. Alternative account titles are "common shares," "common stock," "members' capital," "partners' capital," etc.

This transaction affects two accounts: cash and contributed capital. (Cash is an asset, and contributed capital is part of equity.) The transaction is entered into the T-accounts as shown below. The number in parenthesis references the transaction number.

Cash		Contributed Capital	
150,000 (1)			150,000 (1)

Cash is an asset account, and assets are on the left-hand side of the balance sheet (and basic accounting equation); therefore, cash is increased by recording the $150,000 on the debit (left) side of the T-account. Contributed capital is an equity account, and equity accounts are on the right-hand side of the balance sheet; therefore, contributed capital is increased by recording $150,000 on the credit (right) side of the T-account. Note that the sum of the debits for this transaction equals the sum of the credits:

DR = $150,000

CR = $150,000

DR = CR

Each transaction must always maintain this equality. This ensures that the accounting system (and accounting equation) is kept in balance. At this point in time, the company has assets (resources) of $150,000, and the owners' claim on the resources equals $150,000 (their contributed capital) because there are no liabilities at this point.

Transactions are recorded in a journal, which is then "posted to" (recorded in) the general ledger. When a transaction is recorded in a journal, it takes the form:

Date	Account	DR	CR
13 Dec 2005	Cash	150,000	
	Contributed Capital		150,000

This kind of entry is referred to as a "journal entry," and it is a summary of the information that will be posted in the general ledger T-accounts.

2 January 2006 (excerpt from Exhibit A-3)

#	Business Activity	Accounting Treatment
2	▶ Set up a $100,000 investment account and purchase a portfolio of equities and fixed-income securities.	▶ **Investments [A]** were increased by $100,000, and **cash [A]** was decreased by $100,000.

Accounting elements: Assets (A), Liabilities (L), Equity (E), Revenue (R), and Expenses (X).

This transaction affects two accounts but only one side of the accounting equation. Cash is reduced when the investments are purchased. Another type of asset, investments, increases. The T-account entries are shown below:

Cash		Investment	
150,000 (1)	100,000 (2)	100,000 (2)	

The cash account started with a $150,000 debit balance from the previous transaction. Assets are reduced by credit entries, so the reduction in cash is recorded by entering the $100,000 on the credit (right) side of the cash T-account. The investment account is also an asset, and the increase in investments is recorded by entering $100,000 on the debit side of the investments T-account. Transaction 2 balances because Transaction 2 debits equal Transaction 2 credits.

Going forward, we will use the traditional accounting terms of debit (debiting, debited) to indicate the action of entering a number in the debit side of an account, and credit (crediting, credited) to indicate the action of entering an amount on the credit side of an account.

2 January 2006 (excerpt from Exhibit A-3)

#	Business Activity	Accounting Treatment
3	▶ Pay $3,000 to landlord for office/warehouse. $2,000 represents a refundable deposit, and $1,000 represents the first month's rent.	▶ **Cash [A]** was decreased by $3,000, **deposits [A]** were increased by $2,000, and **prepaid rent [A]** was increased by $1,000.

Accounting elements: Assets (A), Liabilities (L), Equity (E), Revenue (R), and Expenses (X).

Cash is reduced once again by crediting the account by $3,000. On the other side of the transaction, two asset accounts increase. Deposits are increased by debiting the account for $2,000, while prepaid rent is increased by debiting that account for $1,000:

Cash		Deposits	Prepaid Rent	
150,000 (1)	100,000 (2)	2,000 (3)	1,000 (3)	
	3,000 (3)			

The sum of the debits for Transaction 3 equals the sum of the credits (i.e., $3,000).

3 January 2006 (excerpt from Exhibit A-3)

#	Business Activity	Accounting Treatment
4	▶ Purchase office equipment for $6,000 in cash. The equipment has an estimated life of two years with no salvage value.	▶ **Cash [A]** was decreased by $6,000, and **office equipment [A]** was increased by $6,000.

Accounting elements: Assets (A), Liabilities (L), Equity (E), Revenue (R), and Expenses (X).

Cash is credited for $6,000, while office equipment is debited for $6,000. Both are asset accounts, so these entries reflect a reduction in cash and an increase in office equipment.

Cash		**Office Equipment**
150,000 (1)	100,000 (2)	6,000 (4)
	3,000 (3)	
	6,000 (4)	

3 January 2006 (excerpt from Exhibit A-3)

#	Business Activity	Accounting Treatment
5	▶ Receive $1,200 cash for a one-year subscription to the monthly newsletter.	▶ **Cash [A]** was increased by $1,200, and **unearned fees [L]** was increased by $1,200.

Accounting elements: Assets (A), Liabilities (L), Equity (E), Revenue (R), and Expenses (X).

In this transaction, the company has received cash related to the sale of subscriptions. However, the company has not yet actually earned the subscription fees because it has an obligation to deliver newsletters in the future. So, this amount is recorded as a liability called "unearned fees" (or "unearned revenue"). In the future, as the company delivers the newsletters and thus fulfills its obligation, this amount will be transferred to revenue. If they fail to deliver the newsletters, the fees will need to be returned to the customer. To record the transaction, cash is debited (increased), while a liability account, unearned fees, is credited. Liabilities are on the right-hand side of the balance sheet and are, therefore, increased by crediting the T-account.

Cash		Unearned Fees	
150,000 (1)	100,000 (2)		1,200 (5)
1,200 (5)	3,000 (3)		
	6,000 (4)		

The sum of Transaction 5 debits and credits each equal $1,200.

10 January 2006 (excerpt from Exhibit A-3)

#	Business Activity	Accounting Treatment
6	▶ Purchase and receive 500 books at a cost of $20 per book for a total of $10,000. Invoice terms are that payment from IAL is due in 30 days. No cash changes hands. These books are intended for resale.	▶ **Inventory [A]** is increased by $10,000, and **accounts payable [L]** is increased by $10,000.

Accounting elements: Assets (A), Liabilities (L), Equity (E), Revenue (R), and Expenses (X).

The company has obtained an asset, inventory, which can be sold to customers at a later date. Rather than paying cash to the supplier currently, the company has an obligation to do so in 30 days. This represents a liability ("accounts payable") to the supplier. Inventory is debited for $10,000, while the liability, accounts payable, is credited for $10,000. Note that there is no impact on the cash account.

Inventory		Accounts Payable	
10,000 (6)			10,000 (6)

10 January 2006 (excerpt from Exhibit A-3)

#	Business Activity	Accounting Treatment
7	▶ Spend $600 on newspaper and trade magazine advertising for the month.	▶ **Cash [A]** was decreased by $600, and **advertising expense [X]** was increased by $600.

Accounting elements: Assets (A), Liabilities (L), Equity (E), Revenue (R), and Expenses (X).

Unlike the previous expenditures, advertising is not an asset. Its future economic benefits are unclear, unlike equipment, which is expected to be useful over multiple periods. Expenditures such as advertising are recorded as an expense when they are incurred. To record the advertising expense, cash is credited for $600, and advertising expense is debited for $600. Expenses reduce net income, and thus reduce retained earnings. Decreases in retained earnings, as with any equity account, are recorded as debits. The entries with respect to retained earnings will be presented later in this section after the income statement.

Cash		Advertising Expense	
150,000 (1)	100,000 (2)	600 (7)	
1,200 (5)	3,000 (3)		
	6,000 (4)		
	600 (7)		

15 January 2006 (excerpt from Exhibit A-3)

#	Business Activity	Accounting Treatment
8	▶ Borrow $12,000 from a bank for working capital. Interest is payable annually at 10 percent. The principal is due in two years.	▶ **Cash [A]** is increased by $12,000, and **Bank debt [L]** is increased by $12,000.

Accounting elements: Assets (A), Liabilities (L), Equity (E), Revenue (R), and Expenses (X).

Cash is debited, and a corresponding liability is credited. Initially, no entry is made for interest that is expected to be paid on the loan. Interest will be recorded in the future as time passes and interest accrues (accumulates) on the loan.

Cash		Bank Debt	
150,000 (1)	100,000 (2)	12,000 (8)	
1,200 (5)	3,000 (3)		
12,000 (8)	6,000 (4)		
	600 (7)		

The debits and credits of Transaction 8 each total $12,000.

15 January 2006 (excerpt from Exhibit A-3)

#	Business Activity	Accounting Treatment
9	▶ Ship first order to a customer consisting of five books at $25 per book. Invoice terms are that payment is due in 30 days. No cash changes hands.	▶ **Accounts receivable [A]** increased by $125, and **book sales revenue [R]** increased by $125. Additionally, **inventory [A]** decreased by $100, and **cost of goods sold [X]** increased by $100.

Accounting elements: Assets (A), Liabilities (L), Equity (E), Revenue (R), and Expenses (X).

The company has now made a sale. Sale transaction records have two parts. One part records the $125 revenue to be received from the customer, and the other part records the $100 cost of the goods that have been sold. For the first part, accounts receivable is debited (increased) for $125, and a revenue account is credited for $125.

Accounts Receivable		Book Sales Revenue	
125 (9)			125 (9)

For the second part, inventory is credited (reduced) for $100, and an expense, cost of goods sold, is debited (increased) to reflect the cost of inventory sold.

Inventory		Cost of Goods Sold	
10,000 (6)	100 (9)	100 (9)	

Note that the sum of debits and the sum of credits for Transaction 9 both equal $225. The $225 is not meaningful by itself. What is important is that the debits and credits balance.

15 January 2006 (excerpt from Exhibit A-3)

#	Business Activity	Accounting Treatment
10	▶ Sell for cash 10 books at $25 per book at an investment conference.	▶ **Cash [A]** is increased by $250, and **book sales revenue [R]** is increased by $250. Additionally, **inventory [A]** is decreased by $200, and **cost of goods sold [X]** is increased by $200.

Accounting elements: Assets (A), Liabilities (L), Equity (E), Revenue (R), and Expenses (X).

Similar to the previous transaction, both the sales proceeds and cost of the goods sold must be recorded. In this case, however, the sales proceeds are received in cash. To record the sale proceeds, the entries include a debit to cash for $250 and a corresponding credit to book sales revenue for $250. To record cost of goods sold, the entries include a debit to cost of goods sold and a credit to inventory.

Cash		Book Sales Revenue	
150,000 (1)	100,000 (2)		125 (9)
1,200 (5)	3,000 (3)		250 (10)
12,000 (8)	6,000 (4)		
250 (10)	600 (7)		

Inventory		Cost of Goods Sold	
10,000 (6)	100 (9)	100 (9)	
	200 (10)	200 (10)	

Transaction 10's debits and credits are equal, maintaining the accounting system's balance.

---

30 January 2006 (excerpt from Exhibit A-3)

#	Business Activity	Accounting Treatment
11	▶ Hire a part-time clerk. The clerk is hired through an agency that also handles all payroll taxes. The company is to pay $15 per hour to the agency. The clerk works six hours prior to 31 January, but no cash will be paid until February.	▶ The company owes $90 for wages at month-end. Under accrual accounting, expenses are recorded when incurred, not when paid. ▶ **Accrued wages [L]** is increased by $90, and **wage expense [X]** is increased by $90. The accrued wage liability will be eliminated when the wages are paid.

Accounting elements: Assets (A), Liabilities (L), Equity (E), Revenue (R), and Expenses (X).

Accrued wages is a liability that is increased by crediting that account, whereas payroll is an expense account that is increased with a debit.

Accrued Wages		Wage Expense	
	90 (11)	90 (11)	

31 January 2006 (excerpt from Exhibit A-3)

#	Business Activity	Accounting Treatment
12	▶ Mail out the first month's newsletter to customer. This subscription had been sold on 3 January.	▶ One month (or 1/12) of the $1,200 subscription has been satisfied, and thus $100 can be recognized as revenue. ▶ **Unearned fees [L]** is decreased by $100, and **fee revenue [R]** is increased by $100.

Accounting elements: Assets (A), Liabilities (L), Equity (E), Revenue (R), and Expenses (X).

To record the recognition of one month of the subscription fee, the account fee revenue is credited (increased) by $100, and the related liability is debited (decreased) by $100.

Fee Revenue		Unearned Fees	
	100 (12)	100 (12)	1,200 (5)

31 January 2006 (excerpt from Exhibit A-3)

#	Business Activity	Accounting Treatment
13	▶ Review of the investment portfolio shows that $100 of interest income was earned and the market value of the portfolio has increased by $2,000. The balance in the investment account is now $102,100. The securities are classified as "trading" securities.	▶ **Investment income [R]** is increased by $100, and the **investments** account **[A]** is increased by $100. ▶ The $2,000 increase in the value of the portfolio represents unrealized gains that are part of income for traded securities. The **investments** account **[A]** is increased by $2,000, and **investment income [R]** is increased by $2,000.

Accounting elements: Assets (A), Liabilities (L), Equity (E), Revenue (R), and Expenses (X).

The investments account is an asset account that is debited (increased) for $2,100, and investment income is a revenue account that is credited (increased) by $2,100.

Investments		Investment Income	
100,000 (2)			2,100 (13)
2,100 (13)			

These entries complete the recording of the first 13 transactions. In this illustration, there are three adjustments. An adjustment must be made related to Transaction 3 to account for the fact that a month has passed and rent expense has been incurred. We refer to this as Transaction 3a. Adjustments must also be made for an estimate of the depreciation of the office equipment (Transaction 4a) and for interest that has accrued on the loan (Transaction 8a).

31 January 2006

#	Business Activity	Accounting Treatment
3a	▶ In item 3, $3,000 was paid to the landlord for office/warehouse, including a $2,000 refundable deposit and $1,000 for the first month's rent. ▶ Now, the first month has ended, so this rent has become a cost of doing business.	▶ To reflect the full amount of the first month's rent as a cost of doing business, **prepaid rent [A]** is decreased by $1,000, and **rent expense [X]** is increased by $1,000.

Accounting elements: Assets (A), Liabilities (L), Equity (E), Revenue (R), and Expenses (X).

Prepaid rent (an asset) is credited for $1,000 to reduce the balance, and rent expense is debited for the same amount to record the fact that the expense has now been incurred. After this entry, the balance of the prepaid rent asset account is $0.

Prepaid Rent		Rent Expense	
1,000 (3)	1,000 (3a)	1,000 (3a)	

31 January 2006

#	Business Activity	Accounting Treatment
4a	▶ In item 4, office equipment was purchased for $6,000 in cash. The equipment has an estimated life of two years with no salvage value. ▶ Now, one month (or 1/24) of the useful life of the equipment has ended so a portion of the equipment cost has become a cost of doing business.	▶ A portion (1/24) of the total $6,000 cost of the office equipment is allocated to the current period's cost of doing business. ▶ **Depreciation expense [X]** is increased by $250, and **accumulated depreciation** is increased by $250. ▶ Accumulated depreciation is a contra asset account to office equipment.

Accounting elements: Assets (A), Liabilities (L), Equity (E), Revenue (R), and Expenses (X).

Because some time has passed, accounting principles require that the estimated depreciation of the equipment be recorded. In this case, one could directly credit office equipment for $250; however, a preferred method is to credit an account called "accumulated depreciation," which is associated with the office equipment account. This accumulated depreciation account "holds" the cumulative amount of the depreciation related to the office equipment. When financial reports are prepared, a user is able to see both the original cost of the equipment as well as the accumulated depreciation. The user, therefore, has insight into the age of the asset, and perhaps how much time remains before it is likely to be replaced. Accumulated depreciation is termed a "contra" asset account and is credited for $250, while depreciation expense is debited (increased) for $250.

Accumulated Depreciation		Depreciation Expense	
	250 (4a)	250 (4a)	

31 January 2006

#	Business Activity	Accounting Treatment
8a	▶ The company borrowed $12,000 from a bank on 15 January, with interest payable annually at 10 percent and the principal due in two years. ▶ Now, one-half of one month has passed since the borrowing.	▶ One-half of one month of interest expense has become a cost of doing business. $12,000 times 10% equals $1,200 of annual interest, equivalent to $100 per month and $50 for one-half month. ▶ **Interest expense [X]** is increased by $50, and **accrued interest [L]** is increased by $50.

Accounting elements: Assets (A), Liabilities (L), Equity (E), Revenue (R), and Expenses (X).

Accrued interest is a liability that is credited (increased) for $50, and interest expense is debited (increased) for $50. Accrued interest is also sometimes referred to as "interest payable."

Accrued Interest		Interest Expense	
	50 (8a)	50 (8a)	

Exhibit A-4 summarizes the general ledger T-accounts for IAL at this point in time. For accounts with multiple entries, a line is drawn and the debit and credit columns are summed and netted to determine the current balance in the account. The balance is entered below the line. These individual account totals are then summarized in a trial balance as depicted in Exhibit A-5. A trial balance is a summary of the account balances at a point in time. An accountant can prepare a trial balance at any time to ensure that the system is in balance and to review current amounts in the accounts. Note that the debit and credit columns each total $176,065, confirming that the system is in balance. Any difference in the column totals would indicate an error had been made. The trial balance totals have no particular significance and are not used in preparing financial statements. These totals are simply the sum of debits and credits in the accounting system at that point in time.

EXHIBIT A-4	General Ledger T-Accounts for Investment Advisers, Ltd.

Cash

150,000 (1)	100,000 (2)
1,200 (5)	3,000 (3)
12,000 (8)	6,000 (4)
250 (10)	600 (7)
53,850	

Accounts Receivable

125 (9)	

Inventory

10,000 (6)	100 (9)
	200 (10)
9,700	

Investments

100,000 (2)	
2,100 (13)	
102,100	

Office Equipment

6,000 (4)	

Accumulated Depreciation

	250 (4a)

Deposits

2,000 (3)	

Prepaid Rent

1,000 (3)	1,000 (3a)
0	

Accounts Payable

	10,000 (6)

Accrued Wages

	90 (11)

Unearned Fees

100 (12)	1,200 (5)
	1,100

Bank Debt

	12,000 (8)

Accrued Interest

	50 (8a)

Contributed Capital

	150,000 (1)

Retained Earnings

Fee Revenue

	100 (12)

Book Sales Revenue

	125 (9)
	250 (10)
	375

Investment Income

	2,100 (13)

Cost of Goods Sold

100 (9)	
200 (10)	
300	

Advertising Expense

600 (7)	

Rent Expense

1,000 (3a)	

Depreciation Expense

250 (4a)	

Wage Expense

90 (11)	

Interest Expense

50 (8a)	

EXHIBIT A-5	Investment Advisers, Ltd., Trial Balance		
		DR	**CR**
Cash		53,850	
Accounts receivable		125	
Inventory		9,700	
Investments		102,100	
Office equipment		6,000	
Accumulated depreciation			250
Deposits		2,000	
Prepaid rent		0	
Accounts payable			10,000
Accrued wages			90
Unearned fees			1,100
Bank debt			12,000
Accrued interest			50
Contributed capital			150,000
Retained earnings			
Fee revenue			100
Book sales revenue			375
Investment income			2,100
Cost of goods sold		300	
Advertising expense		600	
Rent expense		1,000	
Depreciation expense		250	
Wage expense		90	
Interest expense		50	
Total		**176,065**	**176,065**

After ensuring that the balances in the trial balance are correct (if there are errors, they are corrected and an adjusted trial balance is prepared), we prepare the financial statements. The trial balance provides the information necessary to prepare the balance sheet and the income statement. The detail in the general ledger must be reviewed to prepare the statement of cash flows and statement of owners' equity. After the income statement is prepared, the temporary accounts are closed out (i.e., taken to a zero balance) by transferring each of their balances to retained earnings. This typically occurs at year-end and is termed the "closing process." Exhibits A-6 and A-7 show the post-closing general ledger and trial balance, respectively.

EXHIBIT A-6   Post-Closing General Ledger T-Accounts for Investment Advisers, Ltd.

Cash		Accounts Receivable		Inventory	
150,000 (1)	100,000 (2)	125 (9)		10,000 (6)	100 (9)
1,200 (5)	3,000 (3)				200 (10)
12,000 (8)	6,000 (4)			9,700	
250 (10)	600 (7)				
53,850					

Investments		Office Equipment		Accumulated Depreciation	
100,000 (2)		6,000 (4)			250 (4a)
2,100 (13)					
102,100					

Deposits		Prepaid Rent		Accounts Payable	
2,000 (3)		1,000 (3)	1,000 (3a)		10,000 (6)
		0			

Accrued Wages		Unearned Fees		Bank Debt	
	90 (11)	100 (12)	1,200 (5)		12,000 (8)
			1,100		

Accrued Interest		Contributed Capital		Retained Earnings	
	50 (8a)		150,000 (1)		285

Fee Revenue		Book Sales Revenue		Investment Income	
	0		0		0

Cost of Goods Sold		Advertising Expense		Rent Expense	
0		0		0	

Depreciation Expense		Wage Expense		Interest Expense	
0		0		0	

EXHIBIT A-7	Investment Advisers, Ltd., Post-Closing Trial Balance	
	DR	CR
Cash	53,850	
Accounts receivable	125	
Inventory	9,700	
Investments	102,100	
Office equipment	6,000	
Accumulated depreciation		250
Deposits	2,000	
Prepaid rent	0	
Accounts payable		10,000
Accrued wages		90
Unearned fees		1,100
Bank debt		12,000
Accrued interest		50
Contributed capital		150,000
Retained earnings		285
Fee revenue		0
Book sales revenue		0
Investment income		0
Cost of goods sold	0	
Advertising expense	0	
Rent expense	0	
Depreciation expense	0	
Wage expense	0	
Interest expense	0	
Total	**173,775**	**173,775**

Financial statements are identical whether using a spreadsheet approach or a debit/credit approach. Accordingly, the financial statements for IAL that would be prepared using the trial balances are identical to those presented in the main body of the reading as Exhibit 9.

OPTIONAL SEGMENT

ENDS

PRACTICE PROBLEMS FOR READING 30

1. Which of the following items would most likely be classified as an operating activity?

   A. Issuance of debt.

   B. Acquisition of a competitor.

   C. Sale of automobiles by an automobile dealer.

2. Which of the following items would most likely be classified as a financing activity?

   A. Issuance of debt.

   B. Payment of income taxes.

   C. Investments in the stock of a supplier.

3. Which of the following elements represents an economic resource?

   A. Asset.

   B. Liability.

   C. Owners' equity.

4. Which of the following elements represents a residual claim?

   A. Asset.

   B. Liability.

   C. Owners' equity.

5. An analyst has projected that a company will have assets of €2,000 at year-end and liabilities of €1,200. The analyst's projection of total owners' equity should be closest to:

   A. €800.

   B. €2,000.

   C. €3,200.

6. An analyst has collected the following information regarding a company in advance of its year-end earnings announcement (in millions):

Estimated net income	$ 200
Beginning retained earnings	$1,400
Estimated distributions to owners	$ 100

   The analyst's estimate of ending retained earnings (in millions) should be closest to:

   A. $1,300.

   B. $1,500.

   C. $1,700.

7. An analyst has compiled the following information regarding Rubsam, Inc.

Liabilities at year-end	€1,000
Contributed capital at year-end	€500
Beginning retained earnings	€600
Revenue during the year	€5,000
Expenses during the year	€4,300

There have been no distributions to owners. The analyst's most likely estimate of total assets at year-end should be closest to:

A. €2,100.

B. €2,300.

C. €2,800.

8. A group of individuals formed a new company with an investment of $500,000. The most likely effect of this transaction on the company's accounting equation at the time of the formation is an increase in cash and:

A. an increase in revenue.

B. an increase in liabilities.

C. an increase in contributed capital.

9. HVG, LLC paid $12,000 of cash to a real estate company upon signing a lease on 31 December 2005. The payment represents a $4,000 security deposit and $4,000 of rent for each of January 2006 and February 2006. Assuming that the correct accounting is to reflect both January and February rent as prepaid, the most likely effect on HVG's accounting equation in December 2005 is:

A. no net change in assets.

B. a decrease in assets of $8,000.

C. a decrease in assets of $12,000.

10. TRR Enterprises sold products to customers on 30 June 2006 for a total price of €10,000. The terms of the sale are that payment is due in 30 days. The cost of the products was €8,000. The most likely net change in TRR's total assets on 30 June 2006 related to this transaction is:

A. €0.

B. €2,000.

C. €10,000.

11. On 30 April 2006, Pinto Products received a cash payment of $30,000 as a deposit on production of a custom machine to be delivered in August 2006. This transaction would most likely result in which of the following on 30 April 2006?

A. No effect on liabilities.

B. A decrease in assets of $30,000.

C. An increase in liabilities of $30,000.

12. Squires & Johnson, Ltd., recorded €250,000 of depreciation expense in December 2005. The most likely effect on the company's accounting equation is:

A. no effect on assets.

B. a decrease in assets of €250,000.

C. an increase in liabilities of €250,000.

13. An analyst who is interested in assessing a company's financial position is most likely to focus on which financial statement?

    A. Balance sheet.

    B. Income statement.

    C. Statement of cash flows.

14. The statement of cash flows presents the flows into which three groups of business activities?

    A. Operating, Nonoperating, and Financing.

    B. Operating, Investing, and Financing.

    C. Operating, Nonoperating, and Investing.

15. Which of the following statements about cash received prior to the recognition of revenue in the financial statements is *most* accurate? The cash is recorded as:

    A. deferred revenue, an asset.

    B. accrued revenue, a liability.

    C. deferred revenue, a liability.

16. When, at the end of an accounting period, a revenue has been recognized in the financial statements but no billing has occurred and no cash has been received, the accrual is to:

    A. unbilled (accrued) revenue, an asset.

    B. deferred revenue, an asset.

    C. unbilled (accrued) revenue, a liability.

17. When, at the end of an accounting period, cash has been paid with respect to an expense incurred but not yet recognized in the financial statements, the business should then record:

    A. an accrued expense, an asset.

    B. a prepaid expense, an asset.

    C. an accrued expense, a liability.

18. When, at the end of an accounting period, cash has not been paid with respect to an expense that has been incurred, the business should then record:

    A. an accrued expense, an asset.

    B. a prepaid expense, an asset.

    C. an accrued expense, a liability.

19. The collection of all business transactions sorted by account in an accounting system is referred to as:

    A. a trial balance.

    B. a general ledger.

    C. a general journal.

20. If a company reported fictitious revenue, it could try to cover up its fraud by:

    A. decreasing assets.

    B. increasing liabilities.

    C. creating a fictitious asset.

SOLUTIONS FOR READING 30

1. C is correct. Sales of products, a primary business activity, are classified as an operating activity. Issuance of debt would be a financing activity. Acquisition of a competitor and the sale of surplus equipment would both be classified as investing activities.

2. A is correct. Issuance of debt would be classified as a financing activity. B is incorrect because payment of income taxes would be classified as an operating activity. C is incorrect because the investments in common stock would be generally classified as investing activities.

3. A is correct. An asset is an economic resource of an entity that will either be converted into cash or consumed.

4. C is correct. Owners' equity is a residual claim on the resources of a business.

5. A is correct. Assets must equal liabilities plus owners' equity and, therefore, €2,000 = €1,200 + Owners' equity. Owners' equity must be €800.

6. B is correct.

Beginning retained earnings	$1,400
+ Net income	200
− Distributions to owners	(100)
= Ending retained earnings	$1,500

7. C is correct.

Assets = Liabilities + Contributed capital + Beginning retained earnings − Distributions to owners + Revenues − Expenses

Liabilities	$1,000
+ Contributed capital	500
+ Beginning retained earnings	600
− Distributions to owners	(0)
+ Revenues	5,000
− Expenses	(4,300)
= Assets	$2,800

8. C is correct. This is a contribution of capital by the owners. Assets would increase by $500,000 and contributed capital would increase by $500,000, maintaining the balance of the accounting equation.

9. A is correct. The payment of January rent represents prepaid rent (an asset), which will be adjusted at the end of January to record rent expense. Cash (an asset) decreases by $12,000. Deposits (an asset) increase by $4,000. Prepaid rent (an asset) increases by $8,000. There is no net change in assets.

10. B is correct. The sale of products without receipt of cash results in an increase in accounts receivable (an asset) of €10,000. The balance in inventory (an asset) decreases by €8,000. The net increase in assets is €2,000. This would be balanced by an increase in revenue of €10,000 and an increase in expenses (costs of goods sold) of €8,000.

11. C is correct. The receipt of cash in advance of delivering goods or services results in unearned revenue, which is a liability. The company has an obligation to deliver $30,000 in goods in the future. This balances the increase in cash (an asset) of $30,000.

12. B is correct. Depreciation is an expense and increases accumulated depreciation. Accumulated depreciation is a contra account which reduces property, plant, and equipment (an asset) by €250,000. Assets decrease by €250,000, and expenses increase by €250,000.

13. A is correct. The balance sheet shows the financial position of a company at a particular point in time. The balance sheet is also known as a "statement of financial position."

14. B is correct. The three sections of the statement of cash flows are operating, investing, and financing activities.

15. C is correct. Cash received prior to revenue recognition increases cash and deferred or unearned revenue. This is a liability until the company provides the promised goods or services.

16. A is correct. When cash is to be received after revenue has been recognized but no billing has actually occurred, an unbilled (accrued) revenue is recorded. Such accruals would usually occur when an accounting period ends prior to a company billing its customer. This type of accrual can be contrasted with a simple credit sale, which is reflected as an increase in revenue and an increase in accounts receivable. No accrual is necessary.

17. B is correct. Payment of expenses in advance is called a prepaid expense, which is classified as an asset.

18. C is correct. When an expense is incurred and no cash has been paid, expenses are increased and a liability ("accrued expense") is established for the same amount.

19. B is correct. The general ledger is the collection of all business transactions sorted by account in an accounting system. The general journal is the collection of all business activities sorted by date.

20. C is correct. In order to balance the accounting equation, the company would either need to increase assets or decrease liabilities. Creating a fictitious asset would be one way of attempting to cover up the fraud.

FINANCIAL REPORTING STANDARDS

by Thomas R. Robinson, CFA, Jan Hendrik van Greuning, CFA, Karen O'Connor Rubsam, CFA, R. Elaine Henry, CFA, and Michael A. Broihahn, CFA

LEARNING OUTCOMES

The candidate should be able to:	Mastery
a. explain the objective of financial statements and the importance of reporting standards in security analysis and valuation;	☐
b. explain the role of standard-setting bodies, such as the International Accounting Standards Board and the U.S. Financial Accounting Standards Board, and regulatory authorities such as the International Organization of Securities Commissions, the U.K. Financial Services Authority, and the U.S. Securities and Exchange Commission in establishing and enforcing financial reporting standards;	☐
c. discuss the ongoing barriers to developing one universally accepted set of financial reporting standards;	☐
d. describe the International Financial Reporting Standards (IFRS) framework, including the qualitative characteristics of financial statements, the required reporting elements, and the constraints and assumptions in preparing financial statements;	☐
e. explain the general requirements for financial statements;	☐
f. compare and contrast key concepts of financial reporting standards under IFRS and alternative reporting systems, and discuss the implications for financial analysis of differing financial reporting systems;	☐
g. identify the characteristics of a coherent financial reporting framework and barriers to creating a coherent financial reporting network;	☐
h. discuss the importance of monitoring developments in financial reporting standards and of evaluating company disclosures of significant accounting policies.	☐

THEME

Financial statements are created based on a conceptual framework established by standard-setting bodies and regulatory authorities. Understanding the principles underlying this financial reporting framework will allow an analyst to assess the securities valuation implications of any financial statement element or transaction.

1   INTRODUCTION

Financial reporting standards determine the types and amounts of information that must be provided to investors and creditors so that they may make informed decisions. This reading focuses on the broad framework within which these standards are created. An understanding of the underlying framework of financial reporting standards, which is broader than knowledge of specific accounting rules, will allow an analyst to assess the valuation implications of *any* financial statement element or transaction—including newly developed transactions that are not specifically addressed by the standards.

Section 2 of this reading discusses the objective of financial statements and the importance of financial standards in security analysis and valuation. Section 3 describes the financial reporting standard-setting bodies and regulatory authorities that establish financial reporting standards. Section 4 examines the trend toward convergence of global financial reporting standards. The International Financial Reporting Standards (IFRS) framework is presented in Section 5, and Section 6 compares IFRS with alternative reporting systems.[1] Section 7 discusses the characteristics of an effective financial reporting framework. Section 8 discusses the importance of monitoring developments in financial reporting standards. A summary of the key points and practice problems in the CFA Institute multiple-choice format conclude the reading.

2   THE OBJECTIVE OF FINANCIAL REPORTING

Financial reporting begins with a simple enough premise. The International Accounting Standards Board (IASB), which is the international accounting standard-setting body, expresses it as follows in its *Framework for the Preparation and Presentation of Financial Statements*:

> The objective of financial statements is to provide information about the financial position, performance, and changes in financial position of an entity; this information should be useful to a wide range of users for the purpose of making economic decisions.[2]

---

[1] The body of standards issued by the IASB is referred to as "International Financial Reporting Standards," which include previously issued International Accounting Standards (IAS). "Financial reporting" is a broad term including reporting on accounting, financial statements, and other information found in company financial reports.

[2] *Framework for the Preparation and Presentation of Financial Statements*, International Accounting Standards Committee, 1989, adopted by IASB 2001, paragraph 12.

Until recently, financial reporting standards were developed mostly independently by each country's standard-setting body. This has created a wide range of standards, some of which are quite comprehensive and complex, and others more general. Recent accounting scandals have raised awareness of the need for more uniform global financial reporting standards and provided the impetus for stronger coordination among the major standard-setting bodies. Such coordination is also a natural outgrowth of the increased globalization of capital markets.

Developing financial reporting standards is complicated because the underlying economic reality is complicated. The financial transactions and organizations that financial statements purport to represent are complicated. There is often uncertainty about transactions, resulting in the need for accruals and estimates. These accruals and estimates necessitate judgment. Judgment varies from one preparer to the next. Accordingly, standards are needed to achieve some type of consistency in these judgments. Even with such standards there will be no one right answer. Nevertheless, financial reporting standards try to limit the range of acceptable answers to ensure some measure of consistency in financial statements.

EXAMPLE 1

Estimates in Financial Reporting

In order to make comparisons across companies (cross-sectional analysis) and over time for a single company (time-series analysis), it is important that accounting methods are comparable and consistently applied. However, accounting standards must be flexible enough to recognize that there are differences in the underlying economics between businesses.

Suppose two companies buy the same model of machinery to be used in their respective businesses. The machine is expected to last for several years. Financial reporting standards should require that both companies account for this equipment by initially recording the cost of the machinery as an asset. Without such a standard, the companies could report the purchase of the equipment differently. For example, one company might record the purchase as an asset and the other might record the purchase as an expense. An accounting standard ensures that both companies would be required to record the transaction in a similar manner.

Accounting standards typically would require the cost of the machine to be apportioned over the estimated useful life of an asset as an expense called depreciation. Because the two companies may be operating the machinery differently, financial reporting standards must retain some flexibility. One company might operate the machinery only a few days per week, whereas the other company operates the equipment continuously throughout the week. Given the difference in usage, it would not be appropriate for the two companies to report an identical amount of depreciation expense each period. Financial reporting standards must allow for some discretion such that management can match their financial reporting choices to the underlying economics of their business while ensuring that similar transactions are recorded in a similar manner between companies.

The IASB and the U.S. Financial Accounting Standards Board (FASB) have developed similar financial reporting frameworks, both of which specify the overall objective and qualities of information to be provided. Financial reports are intended to provide information to many users, including investors, creditors, employees, customers, and others. As a result of this multipurpose nature, financial reports are *not* designed with only asset valuation in mind. However, financial reports provide important inputs into the process of valuing a company or the securities a company issues. Understanding the financial reporting framework—including how and when judgments and estimates can affect the numbers reported—enables an analyst to evaluate the information reported and to use the information appropriately when assessing a company's financial performance. Clearly, such an understanding is also important in assessing the financial impact of business decisions and in making comparisons across entities.

3   FINANCIAL REPORTING STANDARD-SETTING BODIES AND REGULATORY AUTHORITIES

A distinction needs to be made between standard-setting bodies and regulatory authorities. Standard-setting bodies, such as the IASB and FASB, are typically private sector organizations consisting of experienced accountants, auditors, users of financial statements, and academics. Regulatory authorities, such as the SEC in the United States and the FSA in the United Kingdom, are governmental entities that have the legal authority to enforce financial reporting requirements and exert other controls over entities that participate in the capital markets within their jurisdiction.

In other words, *generally*, standard-setting bodies make the rules and regulatory authorities enforce the rules. Note, however, that regulators often retain the legal authority to establish financial reporting standards in their jurisdiction and can overrule the private sector standard-setting bodies.

EXAMPLE 2

Industry-Specific Regulation

In certain cases, there exist multiple regulatory bodies that affect a company's financial reporting requirements. For example, in almost all jurisdictions around the world, banking-specific regulatory bodies establish requirements related to risk-based capital measurement, minimum capital adequacy, provisions for doubtful loans, and minimum monetary reserves. An awareness of such regulations provides an analyst with the context to understand a bank's business, including the objectives and scope of allowed activities.

In the United States, the Office of the Comptroller of the Currency charters and regulates all national banks. In the United Kingdom, the FSA regulates the financial services industry. In some countries, a single entity serves both as the central bank and as the regulatory body for the country's financial institutions.

This section provides a brief overview of the most important international standard-setting body, the IASB, followed by a description of the International Organization of Securities Commissions (IOSCO), capital markets regulation in the European Union (EU), and an overview of the U.S. Securities and Exchange Commission (SEC).

3.1 International Accounting Standards Board

The IASB is the standard-setting body responsible for developing international financial reporting and accounting standards. The four goals of the IASB are:

(a) to develop, in the public interest, a single set of high quality, understandable and enforceable global accounting standards that require high quality, transparent and comparable information in financial statements and other financial reporting to help participants in the world's capital markets and other users make economic decisions;

(b) to promote the use and rigorous application of those standards;

(c) in fulfilling the objectives associated with (a) and (b), to take account of, as appropriate, the special needs of small and medium-sized entities and emerging economies; and

(d) to bring about convergence of national accounting standards and International Accounting Standards and International Financial Reporting Standards to high quality solutions.[3]

The predecessor of the IASB, the International Accounting Standards Committee (IASC), was founded in June 1973 as a result of an agreement by accountancy bodies in Australia, Canada, France, Germany, Japan, Mexico, the Netherlands, the United Kingdom and Ireland, and the United States. By 1998, the IASC had expanded membership to 140 accountancy bodies in 101 countries. In 2001, the IASC was reconstituted into the IASB. The IASB has 14 full-time board members who deliberate new financial reporting standards.[4]

The IASB is overseen by the International Accounting Standards Committee Foundation, which has 19 trustees who appoint the members of the IASB, establish the budget, and monitor the IASB's progress. The IASB is advised by the Standards Advisory Council, which is composed of about 50 members representing organizations and individuals with an interest in international financial reporting.

3.2 International Organization of Securities Commissions

The IOSCO, formed in 1983 as the successor organization of an inter-American regional association (created in 1974), has 181 members that regulate more than 90 percent of the world's financial capital markets.

---

[3] *International Accounting Standards Committee Foundation Constitution*, IASCF, July 2005, part A, paragraph 2.

[4] Although the name of the IASB incorporates "Accounting Standards" and early standards were titled International Accounting Standards (IAS), the term "International Financial Reporting Standards" is being used for new standards. The use of the words "financial reporting" recognizes the importance of disclosures outside of the core financial statements, such as management discussion of the business, risks, and future plans.

In 1998, IOSCO adopted a comprehensive set of *Objectives and Principles of Securities Regulation*, which is recognized as international benchmarks for all markets. IOSCO sets out three core objectives of securities regulation:

▶ protecting investors;

▶ ensuring that markets are fair, efficient, and transparent; and

▶ reducing systematic risk.

Standards related to financial reporting, including accounting and auditing standards, are key components in achieving these objectives. The IOSCO's *Objectives and Principles of Securities Regulation* states:

> Full disclosure of information material to investors' decisions is the most important means for ensuring investor protection. Investors are, thereby, better able to assess the potential risks and rewards of their investments and, thus, to protect their own interests. As key components of disclosure requirements, accounting and auditing standards should be in place and they should be of a high and internationally acceptable quality.[5]

Historically, regulation and related financial reporting standards were developed within individual countries and were often based on the cultural, economic, and political norms of each country. As financial markets have become more global, it has become desirable to establish comparable financial reporting standards internationally. Ultimately, laws and regulations are established by individual jurisdictions, so this also requires cooperation among regulators. In order to ensure adherence to international financial standards, it is important to have uniform regulation across national boundaries. The IOSCO aims to assist in attaining this goal of uniform regulation.

3.3 Capital Markets Regulation in Europe

Each individual member state of the EU regulates capital markets in its jurisdiction. There are, however, certain regulations that have been adopted at the EU level. These include standards and directives related to enforcement of IFRS, a proposed directive to adopt International Standards on Auditing, and proposed directives concerning the board of directors' responsibility for a company's financial statements. The EU, under its Accounting Regulation, will likely serve a role similar to the SEC in the United States as it must endorse each international standard for use in Europe.

In 2001, the European Commission established two committees related to securities regulation: the European Securities Committee (ESC) and the Committee of European Securities Regulators (CESR). The ESC consists of high-level representatives of member states and advises the European Commission on securities policy issues. The CESR is an independent advisory body composed of representatives of regulatory authorities of the member states.

As noted earlier, regulation still rests with the individual member states and, therefore, requirements for registering shares and filing periodic financial reports vary from country to country. Over time, this process is expected to become more uniform in the EU.

---

[5] *Objectives and Principles of Securities Regulation*, IOSCO, May 2003, section 4.2.1.

3.4 Capital Markets Regulation in the United States

Any company issuing securities within the United States, or otherwise involved in U.S. capital markets, is subject to the rules and regulations of the U.S. SEC. The SEC, one of the oldest and most developed regulatory authorities, originated as a result of reform efforts made after the great stock market crash of 1929, sometimes referred to as simply the "Great Crash."

3.4.1 Significant Securities-Related Legislation

There are numerous SEC rules and regulations affecting reporting companies, broker/dealers, and other market participants. From a financial reporting and analysis perspective, the most significant of these acts are the Securities Acts of 1933 and 1934 and the Sarbanes–Oxley Act of 2002.

▶ **Securities Act of 1933 (The 1933 Act)**—This act specifies the financial and other significant information that investors must receive when securities are sold, prohibits misrepresentations, and requires initial registration of all public issuances of securities.

▶ **Securities Exchange Act of 1934 (The 1934 Act)**—This act created the SEC, gave the SEC authority over all aspects of the securities industry, and empowered the SEC to require periodic reporting by companies with publicly traded securities.

▶ **Sarbanes–Oxley Act of 2002**—The Sarbanes–Oxley Act of 2002 created the Public Company Accounting Oversight Board (PCAOB) to oversee auditors. The SEC is responsible for carrying out the requirements of the act and overseeing the PCAOB. The act addresses auditor independence; for example, it prohibits auditors from providing certain nonaudit services to the companies they audit. The act strengthens corporate responsibility for financial reports; for example, it requires the chief executive officer and the chief financial officer to certify that the company's financial reports fairly present the company's condition. Furthermore, Section 404 of the Sarbanes–Oxley Act requires management to report on the effectiveness of the company's internal control over financial reporting and to obtain a report from its external auditor attesting to management's assertion about the effectiveness of the company's internal control.

3.4.2 SEC Filings: Key Sources of Information for Analysts

Companies satisfy compliance with these acts principally through the completion and submission (i.e., filing) of standardized forms issued by the SEC. There are more than 50 different types of SEC forms that are used to satisfy reporting requirements; the discussion herein will be limited to those forms most relevant for financial analysts.

In 1993, the SEC began to mandate electronic filings of the required forms through its Electronic Data Gathering, Analysis, and Retrieval (EDGAR) system. As of 2005, most SEC filings are required to be made electronically. EDGAR has made corporate and financial information more readily available to investors and the financial community. Most of the SEC filings that an analyst would be interested in can be retrieved from the internet from one of many websites, including the SEC's own website. Some filings are required upon the initial offering of securities, whereas others are required on a periodic basis thereafter. The following are some of the more common information sources used by analysts.

▶ **Securities Offerings Registration Statement**—The 1933 Act requires companies offering securities to file a registration statement. New issuers as well as previously registered companies that are issuing new securities are required to file these statements. Required information and the precise form vary depending upon the size and nature of the offering. Typically, required information includes: 1) disclosures about the securities being offered for sale, 2) the relationship of these new securities to the issuer's other capital securities, 3) the information typically provided in the annual filings, 4) recent audited financial statements, and 5) risk factors involved in the business.

EXAMPLE 3

Initial Registration Statement

In 2004, Google filed a Form S-1 registration statement with the U.S. SEC to register its initial public offering of securities (Class A Common Stock). In addition to copious amounts of financial and business information, the registration statement provided a 20-page discussion of risks related to Google's business and industry. This type of qualitative information is helpful, if not essential, in making an assessment of a company's credit or investment risk.

▶ **Forms 10-K, 20-F, and 40-F**—These are forms that companies are required to file *annually*. Form 10-K is for U.S. registrants, Form 40-F is for certain Canadian registrants, and Form 20-F is for all other non-U.S. registrants. These forms require a comprehensive overview, including information concerning a company's business, financial disclosures, legal proceedings, and information related to management. The financial disclosures include a historical summary of financial data (usually 10 years), management's discussion and analysis (MD&A) of the company's financial condition and results of operations, and audited financial statements.

▶ **Annual Report**—In addition to the SEC's annual filings (e.g., form 10-K), most companies prepare an annual report to shareholders. This is not a requirement of the SEC. The annual report is usually viewed as one of the most significant opportunities for a company to present itself to shareholders and other external parties; accordingly, it is often a highly polished marketing document with photographs, an opening letter from the chief executive officer, financial data, market segment information, research and development activities, and future corporate goals. In contrast, the Form 10-K is a more legal type of document with minimal marketing emphasis. Although the perspectives vary, there is considerable overlap between a company's annual report and its Form 10-K. Some companies elect to prepare just the Form 10-K or a document that integrates both the 10-K and annual report.

▶ **Proxy Statement/Form DEF-14A**—The SEC requires that shareholders of a company receive a proxy statement prior to a shareholder meeting. A proxy is an authorization from the shareholder giving another party the right to cast its vote. Shareholder meetings are held at least once a year, but any special meetings also require a proxy statement. Proxies, especially annual meeting proxies, contain information that is often useful to financial analysts. Such information typically includes proposals that require a shareholder vote, details of security ownership by management and principal owners, biographical information on directors, and disclosure of executive compensation. Proxy statement information is filed with the SEC as Form DEF-14A.

▶ **Forms 10-Q and 6-K**—These are forms that companies are required to submit for interim periods (quarterly for U.S. companies on Form 10-Q, semiannually for many non-U.S. companies on Form 6-K). The filing requires certain financial information, including unaudited financial statements and an MD&A for the interim period covered by the report. Additionally, if certain types of nonrecurring events—such as the adoption of a significant accounting policy, commencement of significant litigation, or a material limitation on the rights of any holders of any class of registered securities— take place during the period covered by the report, these events must be included in the Form 10-Q report. Companies may provide the 10-Q report to shareholders or may prepare a separate, abbreviated, quarterly report to shareholders.

3.4.3 Other Filings

There are other SEC filings that a company or its officers make—either periodically, or, if significant events or transactions have occurred, in between the periodic reports noted above. By their nature, these forms sometimes contain the most interesting and timely information and may have significant valuation implications.

▶ **Form 8-K**—In addition to filing annual and interim reports, SEC registrants must report material corporate events on a more current basis. Form 8-K (6-K for non-U.S. registrants) is the "current report" companies must file with the SEC to announce such major events as acquisitions or disposals of corporate assets, changes in securities and trading markets, matters related to accountants and financial statements, corporate governance and management changes, and Regulation FD disclosures.[6]

▶ **Form 144**—This form must be filed with the SEC as notice of the proposed sale of restricted securities or securities held by an affiliate of the issuer in reliance on Rule 144. Rule 144 permits limited sales of restricted securities without registration.

▶ **Forms 3, 4, and 5**—These forms are required to report beneficial ownership of securities. These filings are required for any director or officer of a registered company as well as beneficial owners of greater than 10 percent of a class of registered equity securities. Form 3 is the initial statement, Form 4 reports changes, and Form 5 is the annual report. These forms, along with Form 144, can be used to examine purchases and sales of securities by officers, directors, and other affiliates of the company.

---

[6] Regulation FD provides that when an issuer discloses material nonpublic information to certain individuals or entities—generally, securities market professionals such as stock analysts or holders of the issuer's securities who may trade on the basis of the information—the issuer must make public disclosure of that information. In this way, the rule aims to promote full and fair disclosure.

▶ **Form 11-K**—This is the annual report of employee stock purchase, savings, and similar plans. It might be of interest to analysts for companies with significant employee benefit plans because it contains more information than that disclosed in the company's financial statements.

4   CONVERGENCE OF GLOBAL FINANCIAL REPORTING STANDARDS

Recent activities have moved the goal of one set of universally accepted financial reporting standards out of the theoretical sphere into the realm of reality.

In 2002, the IASB and FASB each acknowledged their commitment to the development of high-quality, compatible accounting standards that could be used for both domestic and cross-border financial reporting (in an agreement referred to as "The Norwalk Agreement"). Both the IASB and FASB pledged to use their best efforts to 1) make their existing financial reporting standards fully compatible as soon as practicable, and 2) to coordinate their future work programs to ensure that, once achieved, compatibility is maintained. The Norwalk Agreement was certainly an important milestone, and both bodies are working toward convergence through an ongoing short-term convergence project, a convergence research project, and joint projects such as revenue recognition and business combinations.

In 2004, the IASB and FASB agreed that, in principle, any significant accounting standard would be developed cooperatively. It is likely to take considerable time to work out differences on existing IFRS and U.S. generally accepted accounting principles (GAAP) because of other pressing priorities and honest differences in principles. Development of one universally accepted financial reporting framework is a major undertaking and is expected to take a number of years. Exhibit 1 provides a summary of the worldwide adoption status of IFRS.

In some ways, the move toward one global set of financial reporting standards has made the barriers to full convergence more apparent. Standard-setting bodies and regulators can have differing views. In addition, they may be influenced by strong industry lobbying groups and others that will be subject to these reporting standards. For example, the FASB faced strong opposition when it first attempted to adopt standards requiring companies to expense employee stock compensation plans.[7] The IASB has experienced similar political pressures. The issue of political pressure is compounded when international standards are involved, simply because there are many more interested parties and many more divergent views and objectives. The integrity of the financial reporting framework depends on the standard setter's ability to balance various points of view.

5   THE INTERNATIONAL FINANCIAL REPORTING STANDARDS FRAMEWORK

The IFRS *Framework for the Preparation and Presentation of Financial Statements* (referred to here as the "Framework") sets forth the concepts that underlie the preparation and presentation of financial statements for external uses. The *Framework* is designed to assist the IASB in developing standards and to instruct preparers of financial statements on the principles of financial statement

---

[7] The second attempt was successful and FASB Statement 123R now requires the expensing of stock options.

EXHIBIT 1	International Adoption Status of IFRS as of December 2006
Europe	▶ The EU requires companies listed in EU countries to adopt IFRS for the 2005 financial statements. ▶ The IASB decides in late 2006 that it will not require the application of new IFRS or major amendments to existing standards before 1 January 2009. ▶ Switzerland requires that multinational main board companies must choose either U.S. GAAP or IFRS.
United States	▶ The SEC accepts IFRS for non-U.S. registrants but currently requires a reconciliation to U.S. GAAP. It has indicated that it will revisit this requirement after the filing of 2005 financial statements. ▶ The FASB is engaged in numerous projects with the IASB to achieve convergence of U.S. GAAP to IFRS. Full convergence, however, is not expected to be completed in the foreseeable future.
Canada	▶ In 2006, Canada's Accounting Standards Board decided to converge Canadian GAAP with IFRS.
Central and South America	▶ Guatemala, Costa Rica, Ecuador, Nicaragua, Panama, Peru, and Honduras require IFRS for all domestic listed companies. ▶ Venezuela required adoption of IFRS beginning in 2006 for listed companies and 2007 for others. ▶ El Salvador permits IFRS for domestic listed companies.
Caribbean	▶ Bahamas, Barbados, Jamaica, Trinidad and Tobago, Dominican Republic, and Haiti require IFRS for all domestic listed companies.
Asia Pacific countries	▶ Bangladesh requires the use of IFRS, and Australia and New Zealand have adopted IFRS "equivalent" standards for the 2005 and 2007, respectively, financial statements. ▶ Japan has launched a joint project with the IASB to reduce differences between Japanese accounting standards and IFRS. ▶ China requires IFRS for some domestic listed companies. ▶ Hong Kong and Philippines have adopted national standards that are equivalent to IFRS except for some effective dates and transition. ▶ Singapore has adopted many IFRS. ▶ Myanmar and Sri Lanka permit the use of IFRS for domestic listed companies.
Africa and the Middle East	▶ South Africa, Tanzania, Kenya, Egypt, and Malawi require IFRS for all domestic listed companies.
Russian Federation and former Soviet Union	▶ The Russian Federation requires IFRS for banks and has proposed phasing in requiring all domestic listed companies to use IFRS beginning in 2006.

Sources: Based on data from www.iasb.org and www.iasplus.com.

construction. Importantly, the *Framework* is also designed to assist users of financial statements—including financial analysts—in interpreting the information
contained therein.

The *Framework* is diagrammed in Exhibit 2. The top part shows how the
objective of financial statements determines the characteristics that the reporting elements (relating to performance and financial position) should embody.
In practice, decisions in financial statement preparation must satisfy a number of
constraints, such as cost–benefit trade-offs. Finally, underlying financial statement preparation, and, therefore, placed at the bottom of the exhibit, are certain important assumptions.

EXHIBIT 2   IFRS Framework for the Preparation and Presentation of Financial Statements

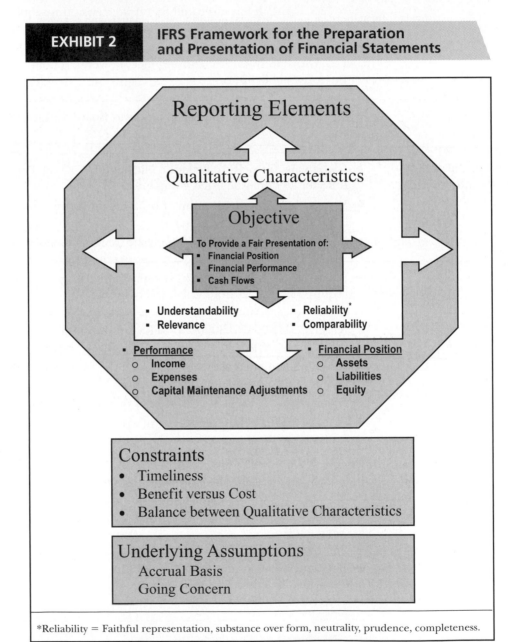

*Reliability = Faithful representation, substance over form, neutrality, prudence, completeness.

In the following, we discuss the *Framework* starting at the center: the objective of financial statements.

5.1 Objective of Financial Statements

At the center of the *Framework* is the objective: fair presentation of the company's financial position, its financial performance, and its cash flows. All other aspects of the *Framework* flow from that central objective.

Fair presentation to whom? And for what purpose? The introduction to the *Framework* states that the objective of financial statements is:

> . . . to provide information about the financial position, performance, and changes in financial position of an entity; this information should be useful to a wide range of users for the purpose of making economic decisions.[8]

The range of users includes investors, employees, lenders, suppliers, other creditors, customers, government agencies, the public, and analysts. The purpose of all this information is to be useful in making economic decisions. The types of economic decisions differ by users, so the specific information needed differs as well. However, although these users may have unique information needs, there are some information needs that are common across all users. One common need is for information about the company's financial position: its resources and its financial obligations. Information about a company's financial performance explains how and why the company's financial position changed in the past and can be useful in evaluating potential changes in the future. The third common information need reflected in the *Framework* diagram is the need for information about a company's cash. How did the company obtain cash? By selling its products and services, borrowing, other? How did the company use cash? Paying expenses, investing in new equipment, paying dividends, other?

5.2 Qualitative Characteristics of Financial Statements

Flowing from the central objective of providing a *fair presentation* of information that is *useful* to decision makers, the *Framework* elaborates on what constitutes usefulness. The *Framework* identifies four principal qualitative characteristics that make financial information useful: understandability, relevance, reliability, and comparability.[9]

1. *Understandability.* Understandability of information is defined in terms of who should be able to understand it. The *Framework* specifies that the information should be readily understandable by users who have a basic knowledge of business, economic activities, and accounting, and who have a willingness to study the information with reasonable diligence.

2. *Relevance.* Relevance of information is defined in terms of whether the information influences economic decisions of users, helping them to evaluate past, present, and future events, or to confirm or correct their past evaluations. Relevant information is typically timely, rather than dated. Relevant information is detailed enough to help users assess the risks and opportunities of a company (e.g., information on business segments or

---

[8] *Framework for the Preparation and Presentation of Financial Statements*, IASC, 1989, adopted by IASB 2001, paragraph 12.

[9] Ibid., paragraphs 24–42.

geographical segments). In choosing the level of detail to present, a criterion of materiality is applied. **Materiality** means that omission or misstatement of the information could make a difference to users' decisions.

3. *Reliability.* Reliable information is free from material error and bias. It is information that a user can depend upon to represent a company's financial situation faithfully and completely (within the bounds of materiality and cost). Reliable information also reflects economic reality, not just the legal form of a transaction or event. The following factors contribute to reliability:

   ▶ *Faithful representation.* Information must represent faithfully the transactions and other events it either purports to represent or could reasonably be expected to represent.

   ▶ *Substance over form.* It is necessary that transactions and other events be accounted for and represented in accordance with their substance and economic reality and not merely their legal form.

   ▶ *Neutrality.* Information contained in the financial statements must be neutral—that is, free from bias.

   ▶ *Prudence.* Prudence is the inclusion of a degree of caution in making the estimates required under conditions of uncertainty. It does not, however, allow the deliberate misstatement of elements in the financial statements in an attempt to be conservative by providing for hidden reserves or excessive provisions.

   ▶ *Completeness.* Financial statements must be complete within the bounds of materiality and cost.

4. *Comparability.* Information should be presented in a consistent manner over time and in a consistent manner between entities to enable users to make significant comparisons.

Financial information exhibiting these principal qualitative characteristics normally results in fair presentation (sometimes termed a "true and fair view").

5.3 Constraints on Financial Statements

Although it would be ideal for financial statements to exhibit all of these qualitative characteristics and thus to achieve maximal usefulness, there are several constraints in achieving this goal.[10]

One constraint is the necessity for trade-offs across the desirable characteristics. For example, to be relevant, information must be timely; however, it may take considerable time to ensure the information is error-free (i.e., reliable). The aim is a balance between relevance and reliability.

Another constraint on useful financial information is the cost of providing this information. Optimally, benefits derived from information should exceed the cost of providing it. Again, the aim is a balance between costs and benefits.

A further constraint involves what financial statements omit. Financial statements, by necessity, omit information that is nonquantifiable. For example, the creativity, innovation, and competence of a company's work force are not directly captured in the financial statements. Similarly, customer loyalty, a positive corporate culture, environmental respectfulness, and many other nonquantifiable aspects about a company are not directly reflected in the financial

---

[10] Ibid., paragraphs 43–45.

statements. Of course, to the extent that these nonquantifiable items result in superior financial performance, a company's financial reports will reflect the results.

EXAMPLE 4

Balancing Qualitative Characteristics of Useful Information

A trade-off between qualitative characteristics often occurs. For example, when a company records sales revenue, it is required to simultaneously estimate and record an expense for potential bad debts (uncollectible accounts). This is considered to provide relevant information about the net profits for the accounting period. However, because bad debts may not be known with certainty until a later period, there is a sacrifice of reliability. The bad debt expense is simply an estimate. It is apparent that it is not always possible to simultaneously fulfill all qualitative characteristics.

5.4 The Elements of Financial Statements

Financial statements portray the financial effects of transactions and other events by grouping them into broad classes (elements) according to their economic characteristics.

Three elements of financial statements are directly related to the measurement of the financial position: assets, liabilities, and equity.[11]

▶ **Assets**. Resources controlled by the enterprise as a result of past events and from which future economic benefits are expected to flow to the enterprise. Assets are what a company owns (e.g., inventory and equipment).

▶ **Liabilities**. Present obligations of an enterprise arising from past events, the settlement of which is expected to result in an outflow of resources embodying economic benefits. Liabilities are what a company owes (e.g., bank borrowings).

▶ **Equity** (commonly known as "shareholders' equity"). Assets less liabilities. Equity is the residual interest in the assets after subtracting the liabilities.

The elements of financial statements directly related to the measurement of performance are income and expenses.[12]

▶ **Income**. Increases in economic benefits in the form of inflows or enhancements of assets, or decreases of liabilities that result in an increase in equity (other than increases resulting from contributions by owners). Income includes both revenues and gains. Revenues represent income from the ordinary activities of the enterprise (e.g., the sale of products). Gains may result from ordinary activities or other activities (the sale of surplus equipment).

---

[11] Ibid., paragraph 49.

[12] Ibid., paragraph 70.

▶ **Expenses**. Decreases in economic benefits in the form of outflows or depletions of assets, or increases in liabilities that result in decreases in equity (other than decreases because of distributions to owners). Expenses include losses, as well as those items normally thought of as expenses, such as the cost of goods sold or wages.

5.4.1 Underlying Assumptions in Financial Statements

At the base of the *Framework*, two important assumptions underlying financial statements are shown: accrual basis and going concern. These assumptions determine how financial statement elements are recognized and measured.[13]

"Accrual basis" refers to the underlying assumption that financial statements aim to reflect transactions when they actually occur, not necessarily when cash movements occur. For example, accrual accounting specifies that a company reports revenues *when they are earned*, regardless of whether the company received cash before delivering the product, after delivering the product, or at the time of delivery.

"Going concern" refers to the assumption that the company will continue in business for the foreseeable future. To illustrate, consider the value of a company's inventory if it is assumed that the inventory can be sold over a normal period of time versus the value of that same inventory if it is assumed that the inventory must all be sold in a day (or a week). Companies with the intent to liquidate or materially curtail operations would require different information for a fair presentation.

EXAMPLE 5

Going Concern

In reporting the financial position of a company that is assumed to be a going concern, it may be appropriate to list assets at some measure of a current value based upon normal market conditions. However, if a company is expected to cease operations and be liquidated, it may be more appropriate to list such assets at an appropriate liquidation value, namely, a value that would be obtained in a forced sale.

5.4.2 Recognition of Financial Statement Elements

Recognition is the process of incorporating in the balance sheet or income statement an item that meets the definition of an element and satisfies the criteria for recognition. A financial statement element (assets, liabilities, equity, income, and expenses) should be recognized in the financial statements if:[14]

▶ it is *probable* that any future economic benefit associated with the item will flow to or from the enterprise, and

▶ the item has a cost or value that can be *measured with reliability*.

---

[13] Ibid., paragraphs 22 and 23.

[14] Ibid., paragraph 83.

5.4.3 Measurement of Financial Statement Elements

Measurement is the process of determining the monetary amounts at which the elements of the financial statements are to be recognized and carried in the balance sheet and income statement. The following alternative bases of measurement are used to different degrees and in varying combinations to measure assets and liabilities:

▶ **Historical cost.** Historical cost is simply the amount of cash or cash equivalents paid to purchase an asset, including any costs of acquisition and/or preparation. If the asset was not bought for cash, historical cost is the fair value of whatever was given in order to buy the asset. When referring to liabilities, the historical cost basis of measurement means the amount of proceeds received in exchange for the obligation.

▶ **Current cost.** In reference to assets, current cost is the amount of cash or cash equivalents that would have to be paid to buy the same or an equivalent asset today. In reference to liabilities, the current cost basis of measurement means the undiscounted amount of cash or cash equivalents that would be required to settle the obligation today.

▶ **Realizable (settlement) value.** In reference to assets, realizable value is the amount of cash or cash equivalents that could currently be obtained by selling the asset in an orderly disposal. For liabilities, the equivalent to realizable value is called "settlement value"—that is, settlement value is the undiscounted amount of cash or cash equivalents expected to be paid to satisfy the liabilities in the normal course of business.

▶ **Present value.** For assets, present value is the present discounted value of the future net cash inflows that the asset is expected to generate in the normal course of business. For liabilities, present value is the present discounted value of the future net cash outflows that are expected to be required to settle the liabilities in the normal course of business.

▶ **Fair value.** Fair value is the amount at which an asset could be exchanged, or a liability settled, between knowledgeable, willing parties in an arm's-length transaction, which may involve either market measures or present value measures.

5.5 General Requirements for Financial Statements

The *Framework* provides a basis for establishing standards and the elements of financial statements, but it does not address the contents of the financial statements. Having discussed the *Framework*, we now need to address the general requirements for financial statements.

The required financial statements, the fundamental principles underlying their presentation, and the principles of presentation are provided by International Accounting Standard (IAS) No. 1, *Presentation of Financial Statements*. These general requirements are illustrated in Exhibit 3 and described in the following subsections.

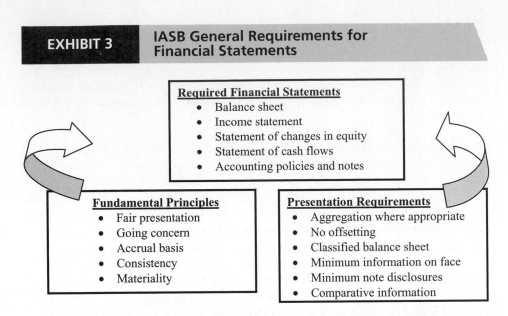

EXHIBIT 3   **IASB General Requirements for Financial Statements**

Required Financial Statements
- Balance sheet
- Income statement
- Statement of changes in equity
- Statement of cash flows
- Accounting policies and notes

Fundamental Principles
- Fair presentation
- Going concern
- Accrual basis
- Consistency
- Materiality

Presentation Requirements
- Aggregation where appropriate
- No offsetting
- Classified balance sheet
- Minimum information on face
- Minimum note disclosures
- Comparative information

In the following, we discuss required financial statements, the fundamental principles underlying the preparation of financial statements, and the principles of presentation in greater detail.

5.5.1 Required Financial Statements

Under IAS No. 1, a complete set of financial statements includes:[15]

- ▶ a balance sheet;
- ▶ an income statement;
- ▶ a statement of changes in equity showing either:
  - ▶ all changes in equity, or
  - ▶ changes in equity other than those arising from transactions with equityholders acting in their capacity as equityholders;[16]
- ▶ a statement of cash flows; and
- ▶ notes comprising a summary of significant accounting policies and other explanatory notes.

Entities are encouraged to furnish other related financial and nonfinancial information in addition to the financial statements. Financial statements need to present fairly the financial position, financial performance, and cash flows of an entity.

---

[15] IAS No. 1, *Presentation of Financial Statements*, paragraph 8.

[16] Examples of transactions with equityholders acting in their capacity as equityholders include sale of equity securities to investors, distributions of earnings to investors, and repurchases of equity securities from investors.

5.5.2 Fundamental Principles Underlying the Preparation of Financial Statements

A company that applies the IFRS states explicitly in the notes to its financial statements that it is in compliance with the standards. Except in extremely rare circumstances, such a statement is only made when a company is in compliance with *all* requirements of IFRS.

IAS No. 1 specifies a number of fundamental principles underlying the preparation of financial statements. These principles clearly reflect the *Framework*.

- *Fair presentation.* The application of IFRS is presumed to result in financial statements that achieve a fair presentation. The IAS describes fair presentation as follows:

  > Fair presentation requires faithful representation of the effects of transactions, events and conditions in accordance with the definitions and recognition criteria for assets, liabilities, income and expenses set out in the Framework.[17]

- *Going concern.* Financial statements are prepared on a going concern basis unless management either intends to liquidate the entity or to cease trading, or has no realistic alternative but to do so. If not presented on a going concern basis, the fact and rationale should be disclosed.

- *Accrual basis.* Financial statements (except for cash flow information) are to be prepared using the accrual basis of accounting.

- *Consistency.* The presentation and classification of items in the financial statements are usually retained from one period to the next. Comparative information of prior periods is disclosed for all amounts reported in the financial statements, unless an IFRS requires or permits otherwise.

- *Materiality.* Omissions or misstatements of items are material if they could, individually or collectively, influence the economic decisions of users taken on the basis of the financial statements. Any material item shall be presented separately.

5.5.3 Presentation Requirements

IAS No. 1 also specifies a number of principles that guide the presentation of financial statements. These principles include the following:

- *Aggregation.* Each material class of similar items is presented separately. Dissimilar items are presented separately unless they are immaterial.

- *No offsetting.* Assets and liabilities, and income and expenses, are not offset unless required or permitted by an IFRS.

- *Classified balance sheet.* The balance sheet should distinguish between current and noncurrent assets, and between current and noncurrent liabilities unless a presentation based on liquidity provides more relevant and reliable information (e.g., in the case of a bank or similar financial institution).

---

[17] IAS No. 1, *Presentation of Financial Statements*, paragraph 13.

▶ *Minimum information on the face of the financial statements.* IAS No. 1 specifies the minimum line item disclosures on the face of, or in the notes to, the balance sheet, the income statement, and the statement of changes in equity. For example, companies are specifically required to disclose the amount of their plant, property, and equipment as a line item on the face of the balance sheet. The specific requirements are listed in Exhibit 4.

▶ *Minimum information in the notes* (or on face of financial statements). IAS No. 1 specifies disclosures about information to be presented in the financial statements. This information must be provided in a systematic manner and cross-referenced from the face of the financial statements to the notes. The required information is summarized in Exhibit 5.

▶ *Comparative information.* For all amounts reported in a financial statement, comparative information should be provided for the previous period unless another standard requires or permits otherwise. Such comparative information allows users to better understand reported amounts.

EXHIBIT 4	**IAS No. 1: Minimum Required Line Items in Financial Statements**

On the face of the balance sheet

▶ Plant, property, and equipment
▶ Investment property
▶ Intangible assets
▶ Financial assets (not listed in other line items)
▶ Investments accounted for using the equity method
▶ Biological assets
▶ Inventories
▶ Trade and other receivables
▶ Cash and cash equivalents
▶ Trade and other payables
▶ Provisions
▶ Financial liabilities (not listed in other line items)
▶ Liabilities and assets for current tax
▶ Deferred tax liabilities and deferred tax assets
▶ Minority interest, presented within equity
▶ Issued capital and reserves attributable to equityholders of the parent

On the face of the income statement

▶ Revenue
▶ Finance costs
▶ Share of the profit or loss of associates and joint ventures accounted for using the equity method
▶ Pretax gain or loss recognized on the disposal of assets or settlement of liabilities attributable to discontinuing operations
▶ Tax expense
▶ Profit or loss
▶ Profit or loss attributable to minority interest
▶ Profit or loss attributable to equityholders of the parent

(Exhibit continued on next page . . .)

EXHIBIT 4	(continued)
On the face of the statement of changes in equity	▶ Profit or loss for the period ▶ Each item of income and expense for the period that, as required by other Standards or by Interpretations, is recognized directly in equity, and the total of these items ▶ Total income and expense for the period, showing separately the total amounts attributable to equityholders of the parent and to minority interest ▶ For each component of equity, the effects of changes in accounting policies and corrections of errors recognized in accordance with IAS No. 8

EXHIBIT 5	Summary of IFRS Required Disclosures in the Notes to the Financial Statements
Disclosure of accounting policies	▶ Measurement bases used in preparing financial statements ▶ Each accounting policy used even if not covered by the IFRS ▶ Judgments made in applying accounting policies that have the most significant effect on the amounts recognized in the financial statements
Estimation uncertainty	▶ Key assumptions about the future and other key sources of estimation uncertainty that have a significant risk of causing material adjustment to the carrying amount of assets and liabilities within the next year
Other disclosures	▶ Description of the entity, including its domicile, legal form, country of incorporation, and registered office or business address ▶ Nature of operations or principal activities, or both ▶ Name of parent and ultimate parent

COMPARISON OF IFRS WITH ALTERNATIVE REPORTING SYSTEMS

6

The recent adoption of IFRS as the required financial reporting standard by the EU and other countries has advanced the goal of global convergence. Nevertheless, there are still significant differences in financial reporting in the global capital markets. Arguably, the most critical are the differences that exist between IFRS and U.S. GAAP. After the EU adoption of IFRS in 2005, these two reporting standards account for a significant number of the world's listed companies.

This section will discuss the differences between IFRS and U.S. GAAP that affect the framework and general financial reporting requirements. The readings on individual financial statements will review in more detail the differences in these financial reporting standards as they apply to specific financial statements. The reading on the convergence of international standards also makes relevant points.

6.1 U.S. GAAP

The FASB or its predecessor organizations have been issuing financial reporting standards in the United States since the 1930s. Currently, the FASB is the primary body setting these standards. There are, however, several other organizations that have issued guidance in the past. These include the American Institute of Certified Public Accountants' (AICPA) Accounting Standards Executive Committee (AcSEC), the Emerging Issues Task Force (EITF), and the FASB staff. Since the introduction of the Sarbanes–Oxley Act, changes have been made that essentially limit these other bodies from providing any new guidance unless it is directly under the direction of the FASB. The EITF has come under the more formal oversight of the FASB, and the AICPA AcSEC will no longer issue new standards applicable to public companies.

6.1.1 U.S. GAAP Authoritative Guidance

Together, the standards and interpretations issued by these bodies comprise U.S. GAAP. A "GAAP hierarchy" was established to provide guidance as to the order of authority of the various sources of accounting pronouncements. In other words, the GAAP hierarchy defines the sources of accounting principles and a framework for selecting the right principle. This hierarchy is especially important for new transactions and those policies where there is no explicit authoritative guidance. The GAAP hierarchy was originally established in the auditing area rather than the accounting area, but it is currently being re-examined by the FASB. The FASB is also working on a project to bring all authoritative guidance from these various sources into one set of authoritative literature called the "Codification."

The top level of the hierarchy includes standards issued by the FASB. If an answer is not found at that level, preparers and auditors consider other sources of GAAP. The literature referred to in the GAAP hierarchy that comprises U.S. GAAP is extensive. The FASB has stated that there are more than 2,000 pronouncements comprising U.S. GAAP. The FASB alone has issued 7 Concept Statements, 153 Standards, 47 Interpretations, and numerous Technical Bulletins. Recently, the FASB began issuing FASB Staff Positions, which provide still another source of U.S. GAAP.

As these standards have been developed over many years and by various bodies, they are more a patchwork than a cohesive framework. Although U.S. GAAP does have an explicit conceptual framework that was developed in the late 1970s/early 1980s, not all of the standards adhere completely to the framework. Some standards were developed prior to the framework and certain of the more recent standards are rule based as preparers and auditors request detailed rules and clear-cut do's and don'ts in an effort to reduce the need for judgment.

6.1.2 Role of the SEC in U.S. GAAP

U.S. GAAP, as established by the standard-setting bodies noted above, is officially recognized as authoritative by the SEC (Financial Reporting Release No. 1, Section 101, and reaffirmed in the April 2003 Policy Statement). However, the SEC retains the authority to establish standards. Although it has rarely overruled the FASB, the SEC does issue Staff Accounting Bulletins (SABs). SABs reflect the SEC's views regarding accounting-related disclosure practices and can be found on the SEC website.

6.1.3 Convergence of the U.S. GAAP and IASB Framework

A joint IASB–FASB project was begun in October 2004 to develop a common conceptual framework. The project, which currently has a five-year timetable, is divided into seven phases. The initial focus is on achieving the convergence of the frameworks and improving particular aspects of the framework dealing with objectives, qualitative characteristics, elements recognition, and measurement. A December 2004 discussion paper presented the broad differences between the two frameworks. These differences are summarized in Exhibit 6. Additionally, under U.S. GAAP, there is not a single standard like IAS No. 1 that specifies the presentation of financial statements; instead, standards for presentation of financial statements are dispersed in many different FASB pronouncements and SEC regulations.

EXHIBIT 6	Summary of Differences between IFRS and U.S. GAAP Frameworks
	U.S. GAAP (FASB) Framework
Purpose of the framework	The FASB framework is similar to the IASB framework in its purpose to assist in developing and revising standards, but it resides at a lower level in the hierarchy—a very important difference. Under IFRS, management is expressly required to consider the framework if there is no standard or interpretation for that issue. The FASB framework does not have a similar provision.
Objectives of financial statements	There is general agreement on the objectives of financial statements: Both frameworks have a broad focus to provide relevant information to a wide range of users. The principal difference is that the U.S. GAAP framework provides separate objectives for business entities versus nonbusiness entities rather than one objective as in the IASB framework.
Underlying assumptions	Although the U.S. GAAP framework recognizes the importance of the accrual and going concern assumptions, these are not given as much prominence as in the IASB framework. In particular, the going concern assumption is not well developed in the FASB framework.
Qualitative characteristics	The U.S. GAAP framework identifies the same qualitative characteristics but also establishes a hierarchy of those characteristics. Relevance and reliability are considered primary qualities, whereas comparability is deemed to be a secondary quality under the FASB framework. The fourth qualitative characteristic, understandability, is treated as a user-specific quality in the U.S. GAAP framework and is seen as a link between the characteristics of individual users and decision-specific qualities of information. The FASB framework indicates that it cannot base its decisions on the specific circumstances of individual users.
Constraints	There is similar discussion of the constraints in both frameworks.

(Exhibit continued on next page . . .)

EXHIBIT 6   **(continued)**

Financial statement elements (definition, recognition, and measurement)

▶ *Performance elements.* The FASB framework includes three elements relating to financial performance in addition to revenue and expenses: gains, losses, and comprehensive income. Comprehensive income is a more encompassing concept than net income, as it includes all changes in equity during a period except those resulting from investments by and distributions to owners.

▶ *Financial position elements.* The FASB framework defines an asset as "a future economic benefit" rather than the "resource" from which future economic benefits are expected to flow to the entity as in the IASB framework. It also includes the term "probable" to define the assets and liabilities elements. As discussed below, the term "probable" is part of the IASB framework recognition criteria. Additionally, the frameworks have different meanings of probable.

▶ *Recognition of elements.* The FASB framework does not discuss the term "probable" in its recognition criteria, whereas the IASB framework requires that it is probable that any future economic benefit flow to/from the entity. The FASB framework also has a separate recognition criterion of relevance.

▶ *Measurement of elements.* Measurement attributes (historical cost, current cost, settlement value, current market value, and present value) are broadly consistent, and both frameworks lack fully developed measurement concepts. Furthermore, the FASB framework prohibits revaluations except for certain categories of financial instruments, which have to be carried at fair value.

6.2 Implications of Other Reporting Systems

As more countries adopt IFRS, the need to examine other financial reporting systems will be minimized. Additionally, the IASB and FASB are considering frameworks from other jurisdictions in developing their joint framework. Nevertheless, analysts are likely to encounter financial statements that are prepared on a basis other than IFRS. Although the number and relevance of different local GAAP reporting systems are likely to decline, industry-specific financial reports—such as those required for banking or insurance companies—will continue to exist.

6.3 Reconciliation of Financials Prepared According to Different Standards

When analyzing financial statements created under different frameworks, reconciliation schedules and disclosures regarding the significant differences between the reporting bases are usually available. For example, the SEC currently requires reconciliation for foreign private issuers that do not prepare financial statements in accordance with U.S. GAAP. The EU is currently considering requiring reconciliations for companies trading on European markets that do not prepare financial statements using IFRS. Such reconciliations can reveal additional information related to the more judgmental components of the financial statements and can have important implications for security valuation.

A first look at the disclosure related to any such differences can sometimes be daunting, particularly if the reconciliation is lengthy. For example, Syngenta's 2005 U.S. SEC Form 20-F filing discusses these differences in Note 33, "Significant Differences between IFRS and United States Generally Accepted Accounting Principles." This note is longer than 15 pages!

Given the length of reconciliation disclosure, a systematic method to quickly digest the information can be helpful. A good starting point is the chart that provides the numerical reconciliation of net income and shareholders' equity (see Exhibit 7). These reconciliations can be reviewed to identify the significant items; large amounts should be examined in more detail. The Syngenta disclosure indicates that the company's 2005 net income based on U.S. GAAP was $556 million, compared with the $622 million of net income reported under IFRS. The reconciliation indicates that most significant differences relate to accounting for acquisitions (purchase accounting adjustments include a $7 million decrease and an $80 million decrease), accounting for pension provisions ($15 million), and accounting for various tax-related items. In some instances, further analysis would be undertaken to determine the implications of each significant difference based on disclosures in the indicated notes.

EXHIBIT 7	Reconciliation of GAAP Income—Syngenta (US$ in millions)		
	2005	**2004**	**2003 (adjusted)**
Net income (loss) reported under IFRS attributable to Syngenta AG shareholders	622	460	248
U.S. GAAP adjustments:			
Purchase accounting: Zaneca agrochemicals business	(7)	62	43
Purchase accounting: other acquisitions	(80)	(62)	(67)
Restructuring charges	(9)	47	32
Pension provisions (including post-retirement benefits)	(15)	43	2
Deferred taxes on stock-based compensation	3	(3)	2
Deferred taxes on unrealized profit in inventory	(33)	(61)	36
Impairment losses	(7)	(1)	
Other items	28	(17)	(4)
Valuation allowance against deferred tax assets	26	(34)	–
Tax on undistributed earnings of subsidiaries	1	(27)	–
Deferred tax effect of U.S. GAAP adjustments	27	(55)	(42)
Net income/(loss) reported under U.S. GAAP	556	352	250

Source: 2005 U.S. SEC Form 20-F.

7   EFFECTIVE FINANCIAL REPORTING

A discussion of the characteristics of an effective framework and the barriers to the creation of such a framework offer additional perspective on the financial reporting frameworks reviewed above.

7.1 Characteristics of an Effective Financial Reporting Framework

Any effective financial reporting system needs to be a coherent one (i.e., a framework in which all the pieces fit together according to an underlying logic). Such frameworks have several characteristics:

▶ *Transparency*. A framework should enhance the transparency of a company's financial statements. Transparency means that users should be able to see the underlying economics of the business reflected clearly in the company's financial statements. Full disclosure and fair presentation create transparency.

▶ *Comprehensiveness*. To be comprehensive, a framework should encompass the full spectrum of transactions that have financial consequences. This spectrum includes not only transactions currently occurring but also new types of transactions as they are developed. So, an effective financial reporting framework is based on principles that are universal enough to provide guidance for recording both existing and newly developed transactions.

▶ *Consistency*. An effective framework should ensure reasonable consistency across companies and time periods. In other words, similar transactions should be measured and presented in a similar manner regardless of industry, company size, geography, or other characteristics. Balanced against this need for consistency, however, is the need for sufficient flexibility to allow companies sufficient discretion to report results in accordance with underlying economic activity.

7.2 Barriers to a Single Coherent Framework

Although effective frameworks all share the characteristics of transparency, comprehensiveness, and consistency, there are some conflicts that create inherent limitations in any financial reporting standards framework. Specifically, it is difficult to completely satisfy all these characteristics concurrently, so any framework represents an attempt to balance the relative importance of these characteristics. Three areas of conflict include valuation, standard-setting approach, and measurement.

▶ *Valuation*. As discussed, various bases for measuring the value of assets and liabilities exist, such as historical cost, current cost, realizable value, and present value. Historical cost valuation, under which an asset's value is its initial cost, requires minimal judgment. In contrast, other valuation approaches require considerable judgment. Over time, both the IASB and FASB have recognized that it may be more appropriate to measure certain elements of financial statements using some fair value method in spite of the judgment required.[18] Fair value is the amount at which an asset could

---

[18] The FASB is currently developing a Fair Value Measurement standard that will also be reviewed by the IASB. This standard is expected to be effective for fiscal years beginning after 15 November 2007 in the United States.

be exchanged, or a liability settled, between knowledgeable willing parties in an arm's-length transaction; clearly, in many cases, determining fair value requires considerable judgment. Fair value may be more relevant, whereas historical cost may be more reliable.

▶ *Standard-setting approach.* Financial reporting standards can be established based on 1) principles, 2) rules, or 3) a combination of principles and rules (sometimes referred to as "objectives oriented"). A principles-based approach provides a broad financial reporting framework with little specific guidance on how to report a particular element or transaction. Such principles-based approaches require the preparers of financial reports and auditors to exercise considerable judgment in financial reporting. In contrast, a rules-based approach establishes specific rules for each element or transaction. Rules-based approaches are characterized by a list of yes-or-no rules, specific numerical tests for classifying certain transactions (known as "bright-line tests"), exceptions, and alternative treatments. The third alternative, an objectives-oriented approach, combines the other two approaches by including both a framework of principles and appropriate levels of implementation guidance.

IFRS has been referred to as a "principles-based approach." The FASB, which has been criticized for having a rules-based approach in the past, has explicitly stated that it is moving to adopt a more objectives-oriented approach to standard setting. There is a joint project underway to develop a common conceptual framework, and this is likely to be more objectives oriented.

▶ *Measurement.* The balance sheet presents elements at a point in time, whereas the income statement reflects changes during a period of time. Because these statements are related, standards regarding one of the statements have an effect on the other statement. Financial reporting standards can be established taking an "asset/liability" approach, which gives preference to proper valuation of the balance sheet, or a "revenue/expense" approach that focuses more on the income statement. This conflict can result in one statement being reported in a theoretically sound manner, but the other statement reflecting less relevant information. In recent years, standard setters have predominantly used an asset/liability approach.

EXAMPLE 6

Conflicts between Measurement Approaches

Prime Retailers (PR), a U.S.-based distributor of men's shirts, has a policy of marking its merchandise up by $5 per unit. At the beginning of 2005, PR had 10,000 units of inventory on hand, which cost $15 per unit. During 2006, PR purchased 100,000 units of inventory at a cost of $22 per unit. Also during 2006, PR sold 100,000 units of inventory at $27 per unit. How shall PR reflect the cost of the inventory sold: $15 or $22?

In order to match current costs with current revenues, PR (which does not operate in an IFRS jurisdiction) may decide that it is appropriate to use a method of inventory costing that assumes that the most recently purchased inventory is sold first. So, the assumption is that the

100,000 units of sales had a cost of $22. A partial income statement for PR would be:

Sales	$2,700,000
Cost of sales	$2,200,000
Gross profit	$500,000

The **gross profit** reflected in this manner reflects the current cost of goods matched with the current level of revenues.

But PR still has 10,000 units of inventory on hand. The assumption must be that the 10,000 remaining units had a cost of $15 per unit. Therefore, the value of the inventory reflected on the balance sheet would be $150,000.

Although the income statement reflects current costs, the remaining inventory on the balance sheet does not reflect current information. The inventory is reflected at the older cost of $15 per unit. An analyst would likely find this older cost less relevant than the current cost of that inventory.

8   MONITORING DEVELOPMENTS IN FINANCIAL REPORTING STANDARDS

In studying financial reporting and financial statement analysis in general, the analyst needs to be aware that reporting standards are evolving rapidly. Analysts need to monitor ongoing developments in financial reporting and assess their implications for security analysis and valuation. The need to monitor developments in financial reporting standards does not mean that analysts should be accountants. An accountant monitors these developments from a preparer's perspective; an analyst needs to monitor from a user's perspective. More specifically, analysts need to know how these developments will affect financial reports.

Analysts can remain aware of developments in financial reporting standards by monitoring three areas: new products or transactions, actions of standard setters and other groups representing users of financial statements (such as CFA Institute), and company disclosures regarding critical accounting policies and estimates.

8.1 New Products or Types of Transactions

New products and new types of transactions can have unusual or unique elements to them such that no explicit guidance in the financial reporting standards exists. New products or transactions typically arise from economic events, such as new businesses (e.g., the internet), or from a newly developed financial instrument or financial structure. Financial instruments, exchange traded or not, are typically designed to enhance a company's business or to mitigate inherent risks. However, at times, financial instruments or structured transactions have been developed primarily for purposes of financial report "window dressing."

Although companies might discuss new products and transactions in their financial reports, the analyst can also monitor business journals and the capital markets to identify such items. Additionally, when one company in an industry develops a new product or transaction, other companies in the industry often do the same. Once new products, financial instruments, or structured transactions are identified, it is helpful to gain an understanding of the business purpose. If necessary, an analyst can obtain further information from a company's management, which should be able to describe the economic purpose, the financial statement reporting, significant estimates, judgments applied in determining the reporting, and future cash flow implications for these items. The financial reporting framework presented here is useful in evaluating the potential effect on financial statements even though a standard may not have been issued as to how to report a particular transaction.

8.2 Evolving Standards and the Role of CFA Institute

Although the actions of standard setters and regulators are unlikely to be helpful in identifying new products and transactions given the lag between new product development and regulatory action, monitoring the actions of these authorities is, nonetheless, important for another reason: Changes in regulations can affect companies' financial reports and, thus, valuations. This is particularly true if the financial reporting standards change to require more explicit identification of matters affecting asset/liability valuation or financial performance. For example, a recent regulatory change requires companies to report the value of employee stock options as an expense in the income statement. Prior to the required expensing, an analyst could assess the impact of stock options on a company's performance and the dilutive effect to shareholders by reviewing information disclosed in the notes to the financial statements. To the extent that some market participants do not examine financial statement details and thus ignore this expense when valuing a company's securities, more explicit identification could affect the value of the company's securities.

The IASB and FASB have numerous major projects underway that will most likely result in new standards. It is important to keep up to date on these evolving standards. The IASB (www.iasb.org) and FASB (www.fasb.org) provide a great deal of information on their websites regarding new standards and proposals for future changes in standards. In addition, the IASB and FASB seek input from the financial analyst community—those who regularly use financial statements in making investment and credit decisions. When a new standard is proposed, an exposure draft is made available and users of financial statements can draft comment letters and position papers for submission to the IASB and FASB in order to evaluate the proposal.

CFA Institute is active through its CFA Centre for Financial Market Integrity in advocating improvements to financial reporting. Volunteer members of CFA Institute serve on several liaison committees that meet regularly to make recommendations to the IASB and FASB on proposed standards and to draft comment letters and position papers. You can view the CFA Centre's positions on financial reporting issues at www.cfainstitute.org/cfacentre/.

In October 2005, the CFA Centre issued a position paper titled *A Comprehensive Business Reporting Model: Financial Reporting for Investors*, which provides a suggested model for significantly improving financial reporting. The position paper states:

> Corporate financial statements and their related disclosures are critical to sound investment decision making. The well being of the world's financial markets, and of the millions of investors who entrust their financial present and future to those markets, depends directly on the quality of the information financial statements and disclosures provide. Consequently, the quality of the information drives global financial markets. The quality, in turn, depends directly on the quality of the

principles and standards by which managers recognize and measure the economic activities and events affecting their companies' operations. To succeed, a partnership is needed among standard setters, common shareowners, and other investors to bring full transparency and the highest integrity to the standards and the processes by which those standards are developed. CFA Institute and the CFA Centre for Financial Market Integrity are committed to join in a partnership to improve financial market integrity in the 21st century.[19]

Among other principles, the proposed model stresses the importance of information regarding the current fair value of assets and liabilities, of neutrality in financial reporting, and of providing detailed information on cash flows to investors through the choice of the so-called direct format for the statement of cash flows.[20]

In summary, analysts can improve their investment decision making by keeping current on financial reporting standards, and various web-based sources provide the means to do so. In addition, analysts can contribute to improving financial reporting by sharing their users' perspective with standard-setting bodies, which typically invite comments concerning proposed changes.

8.3 Company Disclosures

A good source for obtaining information regarding the effect of financial reporting standards on a company's financial statements is typically the company itself. This information is provided in the footnotes to the financial statements and accompanying discussion.

8.3.1 Disclosures Relating to Critical and Significant Accounting Policies

As noted earlier, financial reporting standards need to restrict alternatives but retain flexibility in allowing enterprises to match their accounting methods with underlying economics. As a result, companies choose among alternative accounting policies (e.g., depreciation methods) and use estimates (e.g., depreciable lives of assets). Under both IFRS and U.S. GAAP, companies are required to disclose their accounting policies and estimates in the footnotes to the financial statements. Public companies must discuss their accounting policies and estimates in management's discussion and analysis (MD&A). This disclosure indicates the policies that management deems most important. Although many of the policies are discussed in both the MD&A and the footnotes to the financial statements, there is typically a distinction between the two discussions. The MD&A disclosure relates to those policies that require significant judgments and estimates, whereas the footnote discusses all accounting policies, irrespective of whether judgment was required. Each disclosure has value.

In analyzing financial reporting disclosures, the following questions should be addressed:

▶ What policies have been discussed?

▶ Do these policies appear to cover all of the significant balances on the financial statements?

---

[19] *A Comprehensive Business Reporting Model: Financial Reporting for Investors*, CFA Institute Centre for Financial Market Integrity, 24 October 2005, p. 3.

[20] See the reading on the statement of cash flows for further information on the direct format.

▶ Which policies are identified as requiring significant estimates?

▶ Have there been any changes in these disclosures from one year to the next?

Example 7 summarizes the accounting policies discussed in Disney's 2004 annual report MD&A and Note 2, "Summary of Significant Accounting Policy."

Two items usually requiring significant judgment include revenue recognition and timing of reporting the related expenses. As a result, the types of judgments and estimates in revenue recognition and expense reporting are usually discussed in both the MD&A and in the footnotes.

8.3.2 Disclosures Regarding the Impact of Recently Issued Accounting Standards

Internationally, public companies face disclosure requirements related to recently issued accounting standards. In the United States, the SEC (in its SABs) also requires public companies to provide information regarding the likely future impact of recently issued accounting standards. Under IFRS, IAS No. 8

EXAMPLE 7

List of Significant Accounting Policy Disclosures: Disney MD&A Notes

▶ Film and television revenue and costs

▶ Revenue recognition

▶ Pension and post-retirement benefit plan actuarial assumptions

▶ Goodwill, intangible assets, long-lived assets, and investments

▶ Contingencies and litigation

▶ Income tax audit

▶ Principles of consolidation

▶ Accounting changes

▶ Use of estimates

▶ Advertising expenses

▶ Cash and cash equivalents

▶ Investments

▶ Translation policy

▶ Inventories

▶ Film and television costs

▶ Capitalized software costs

▶ Parks, resorts, and other property

▶ Goodwill and other intangible assets

▶ Risk management contracts

▶ Earnings per share

▶ Stock options

▶ Reclassifications

---

similarly requires discussion about pending implementations of new standards and the known or estimable information relevant to assessing the impact of the new standards. These disclosures can alert an analyst to significant changes in reported financial statement amounts that could affect security valuation. Although each discussion will be different, the conclusions that a company can reach about a new standard include:

1. the standard does not apply;
2. the standard will have no material impact;
3. management is still evaluating the impact; or
4. the impact of adoption is discussed.

Exhibit 8 provides some of the disclosures provided by Syngenta in its 2004 Form 20-F relating to recently issued accounting standards. In the exhibit, "IFRIC" refers to the International Financial Reporting Interpretations Committee—formerly known as the "Standing Interpretations Committee" or "SIC"—which is responsible for interpreting IAS and IFRS.

Clearly, disclosures indicating the expected impact provide the most meaningful information. In addition, disclosures indicating that the standard does not apply or will not have a material effect are also helpful. However, disclosures indicating that management is still evaluating the impact of a new standard create some uncertainty about whether the change might materially affect the company.

EXHIBIT 8	**Impact of Recently Issued Accounting Standards: Syngenta**
Standard does not apply	IFRIC amendment to SIC-12, "Special Purpose Entities," was published in October 2004 and requires employee share trusts and similar entities established under share participation plans to be consolidated with effect from 1 January 2005. *Syngenta operates its employee share participation plans without using entities of this type, and the amendment will have no effect on the consolidated financial statements.*
No material impact	Amendment to IAS No. 39, "Transition and Initial Recognition of Financial Assets and Financial Liabilities," was issued in December 2004. It will be effective from Syngenta as from 1 January 2005. The amendment changes the transitional requirements on adoption of IAS No. 39 (revised December 2003). *Syngenta does not expect the amendment to have a material effect on its consolidated financial statements.*
Evaluating the impact	IFRIC 4, "Determining Whether an Arrangement Contains a Lease," was issued in December 2004 and requires contracts for the supply of goods or services that depend upon the use of a specific asset to be treated in certain circumstances as containing a lease of that asset in addition to a supply contract. IFRIC 4 will be mandatory for Syngenta with effect from 1 January 2006. *During 2005, Syngenta will assess the impact on its consolidated financial statements from adopting IFRIC 4.*
Impact described	As stated in Note 2 above, Syngenta will apply IFRS 3, "Business Combinations," and the related revisions to IAS No. 36 and IAS No. 38, to all previous business combinations with effect from 1 January 2005. *Goodwill amortization expense will no longer be recorded. Goodwill amortization expense on these acquisitions in 2004 was US$56 million. The related tax credit was US$2 million because in most cases the amortization is not tax deductible. Syngenta will test goodwill for impairment annually.*

Note: Emphasis added.

SUMMARY

An awareness of the reporting framework underlying financial reports can assist in security valuation and other financial analysis. The framework describes the objectives of financial reporting, desirable characteristics for financial reports, the elements of financial reports, and the underlying assumptions and constraints of financial reporting. An understanding of the framework, broader than knowledge of a particular set of rules, offers an analyst a basis from which to infer the proper financial reporting, and thus security valuation implications, of *any* financial statement element or transaction.

We have discussed how financial reporting systems are developed, the conceptual objectives of financial reporting standards, the parties involved in standard-setting processes, and how financial reporting standards are converging into one global set of standards. A summary of the key points for each section is noted below:

▶ *The objective of financial reporting*:
  ▶ The objective of financial statements is to provide information about the financial position, performance, and changes in financial position of an entity; this information should be useful to a wide range of users for the purpose of making economic decisions.[21]

  ▶ Financial reporting requires policy choices and estimates. These choices and estimates require judgment, which can vary from one preparer to the next. Accordingly, standards are needed to attempt to ensure some type of consistency in these judgments.

▶ *Financial reporting standard-setting bodies and regulatory authorities*. Private sector standard-setting bodies and regulatory authorities play significant but different roles in the standard-setting process. In general, standard-setting bodies make the rules, and regulatory authorities enforce the rules. However, regulators typically retain legal authority to establish financial reporting standards in their jurisdiction.

▶ *Convergence of global financial reporting standards*. The IASB and FASB, along with other standard setters, are working to achieve convergence of financial reporting standards. Listed companies in many countries are adopting IFRS. Barriers to full convergence still exist.

▶ *The IFRS Framework*. The IFRS *Framework* sets forth the concepts that underlie the preparation and presentation of financial statements for external users, provides further guidance on the elements from which financial statements are constructed, and discusses concepts of capital and capital maintenance.
  ▶ The objective of fair presentation of useful information is the center of the *Framework*. The qualitative characteristics of useful information include understandability, relevance, reliability, and comparability.

  ▶ The IFRS *Framework* identifies the following elements of financial statements: assets, liabilities, equity, income, expense, and capital maintenance adjustments.

---

[21] *Framework for the Preparation and Presentation of Financial Statements*, IASC, 1989, adopted by IASB 2001, paragraph 12.

▶ The *Framework* is constructed based on the underlying assumptions of accrual basis and going concern but acknowledges three inherent constraints: timeliness, benefit versus cost, and balance between qualitative characteristics.

▶ *IFRS financial statements.* IAS No. 1 prescribes that a complete set of financial statements includes a balance sheet, an income statement, a statement of changes in equity, a statement of cash flows, and notes. The notes include a summary of significant accounting policies and other explanatory information.

  ▶ Financial statements need to adhere to the fundamental principles of fair presentation, going concern, accrual basis, consistency, and materiality.

  ▶ Financial statements must also satisfy the presentation requirements of appropriate aggregation, no offsetting, and a classified balance sheet. Statements must provide the required minimum information on the face of the financial statements and note disclosures.

▶ *Comparison of IFRS with alternative reporting systems.* A significant number of the world's listed companies report under either IFRS or U.S. GAAP. Although these standards are moving toward convergence, there are still significant differences in the framework and individual standards. Frequently, companies provide reconciliations and disclosures regarding the significant differences between reporting bases. These reconciliations can be reviewed to identify significant items that could affect security valuation.

▶ *Characteristics of a coherent financial reporting framework.* Effective frameworks share three characteristics: transparency, comprehensiveness, and consistency. Effective standards can, however, have conflicting approaches on valuation, the bases for standard setting (principle or rules based), and resolution of conflicts between balance sheet and income statement focus.

▶ *Monitoring developments.* Analysts can remain aware of ongoing developments in financial reporting by monitoring three areas: new products or transactions, standard setters' and regulators' actions, and company disclosures regarding critical accounting policies and estimates.

PRACTICE PROBLEMS FOR READING 31

1. Which of the following is *not* an objective of financial statements as expressed by the International Accounting Standards Board?

   A. To provide information about the performance of an entity.

   B. To provide information about the financial position of an entity.

   C. To provide information about the users of an entity's financial statements.

2. International accounting standards are currently developed by which entity?

   A. The Financial Services Authority.

   B. The International Accounting Standards Board.

   C. The International Accounting Standards Committee.

3. U.S. Financial Accounting Standards are currently developed by which entity?

   A. The United States Congress.

   B. The Financial Services Authority.

   C. The Financial Accounting Standards Board.

4. The SEC requires which of the following be issued to shareholders before a shareholder meeting?

   A. Form 10-K.

   B. Statement of cash flow.

   C. Proxy statement.

5. According to the *Framework for the Preparation and Presentation of Financial Statements*, which of the following is a qualitative characteristic of information in financial statements?

   A. Accuracy.

   B. Timeliness.

   C. Comparability.

6. Which of the following is *not* a constraint on the financial statements according to the IFRS *Framework*?

   A. Timeliness.

   B. Understandability.

   C. Benefit versus cost.

7. The assumption that an entity will continue to operate for the foreseeable future is called:

   A. accrual basis.

   B. comparability.

   C. going concern.

8. The assumption that the effects of transactions and other events are recognized when they occur, not necessarily when cash movements occur, is called:

   A. accrual basis.

   B. going concern.

   C. relevance.

9. Neutrality of information in the financial statements most closely contributes to which qualitative characteristic?
   A. Relevance.
   B. Reliability
   C. Comparability.

10. Does fair presentation entail full disclosure and transparency?

	Full Disclosure	Transparency
A.	No	Yes
B.	Yes	No
C.	Yes	Yes

11. Valuing assets at the amount of cash or equivalents paid or the fair value of the consideration given to acquire them at the time of acquisition most closely describes which measurement of financial statement elements?
   A. Current cost.
   B. Realizable cost.
   C. Historical cost.

12. The valuation technique under which assets are recorded at the amount that would be received in an orderly disposal is:
   A. current cost.
   B. present value.
   C. realizable value.

13. Which of the following is *not* a required financial statement according to IAS No. 1?
   A. Income statement.
   B. Statement of changes in equity.
   C. Statement of changes in income.

14. Which of the following elements of financial statements is most closely related to measurement of performance?
   A. Assets.
   B. Expenses.
   C. Liabilities.

15. Which of the following elements of financial statements is most closely related to measurement of financial position?
   A. Equity.
   B. Income.
   C. Expenses.

16. Which of the following is *not* a characteristic of a coherent financial reporting framework?

    A. Timeliness.

    B. Consistency.

    C. Transparency.

17. In the past, the Financial Accounting Standards Board has been criticized as having:

    A. a rules-based approach to standards.

    B. a principles-based approach to standards.

    C. an objectives-oriented approach to standards.

18. Which of the following types of discussions regarding new accounting standards in management's discussion would provide the most meaningful information to an analyst?

    A. The standard does not apply.

    B. The impact of adoption is discussed.

    C. The standard will have no material impact.

SOLUTIONS FOR READING 31

1. C is correct. Providing information about users is not an objective of financial statements. The objectives are to provide information about the entity's financial position, performance, and changes in financial position.

2. B is correct. The IASB is currently charged with developing International Accounting Standards. The IASC was the predecessor organization to the IASB.

3. C is correct. U.S. Financial Accounting Standards are developed by the FASB.

4. C is correct. The SEC requires that shareholders of a company receive a proxy statement prior to a shareholder meeting. Such meetings are held at least once a year, but any special meetings would also require a proxy.

5. C is correct. The qualitative characteristics of financial statements according to the IFRS *Framework* are understandability, relevance, reliability, and comparability.

6. B is correct. The *Framework* recognizes the following constraints on providing relevant, reliable information: timeliness, benefit versus cost, and balancing of the qualitative characteristics.

7. C is correct. The IFRS *Framework* identifies two important underlying assumptions of financial statements: accrual basis and going concern. Going concern is the assumption that the entity will continue to operate for the foreseeable future. Enterprises with the intent to liquidate or materially curtail operations would require different information for a fair presentation.

8. A is correct. The IFRS *Framework* identifies two important underlying assumptions of financial statements: accrual basis and going concern. Accrual basis reflects the effects of transactions and other events being recognized when they occur, not necessarily when cash movements occur. These effects are recorded and reported in the financial statements of the periods to which they relate.

9. B is correct. The qualitative characteristic of reliability is contributed to by faithful representation, substance over form, neutrality, prudence, and completeness.

10. C is correct. Fair presentation involves both full disclosure and transparency.

11. C is correct. Historical cost is the consideration paid to acquire an asset.

12. C is correct. The amount that would be received in an orderly disposal is realizable value.

13. C is correct. Under IAS No. 1, a complete set of financial statements includes: a balance sheet, an income statement, a statement of changes in equity, a statement of cash flows, and notes comprising a summary of significant accounting policies and other explanatory notes.

14. B is correct. The elements of financial statements related to the measure of performance are income and expenses.

15. A is correct. The elements of financial statements related to the measurement of financial position are assets, liabilities, and equity.

16. A is correct. Timeliness is not a characteristic of a coherent financial reporting framework. Consistency, transparency, and comprehensiveness are characteristics of a coherent financial reporting framework.

17. A is correct. The FASB has been criticized in the past as having a rules-based approach; however, it has indicated that it is moving toward an objectives-oriented approach.

18. B is correct. A discussion of the impact would be the most meaningful, although A and C would also be useful.

STUDY SESSION 8
FINANCIAL REPORTING AND ANALYSIS:
The Income Statement, Balance Sheet, and Cash Flow Statement

Each reading in this study session focuses on one of the three major financial statements: the balance sheet, the income statement, and the statement of cash flows. For each financial statement, the chapter details its purpose, construction, pertinent ratios, and common-size analysis. Understanding these concepts allows a financial analyst to evaluate trends in performance for several measurement periods and to compare the performance of different companies during the same period(s). Additional analyst tools, such as the earnings per share calculation, are also described.

READING ASSIGNMENTS

Reading 32	Understanding the Income Statement *International Financial Statement Analysis,* by Thomas R. Robinson, CFA, Jan Hendrik van Greuning, CFA, R. Elaine Henry, CFA, and Michael A. Broihahn, CFA
Reading 33	Understanding the Balance Sheet *International Financial Statement Analysis,* by Thomas R. Robinson, CFA, Jan Hendrik van Greuning, CFA, R. Elaine Henry, CFA, and Michael A. Broihahn, CFA
Reading 34	Understanding the Cash Flow Statement *International Financial Statement Analysis,* by Thomas R. Robinson, CFA, Jan Hendrik van Greuning, CFA, R. Elaine Henry, CFA, and Michael A. Broihahn, CFA
Reading 35	Financial Analysis Techniques *International Financial Statement Analysis,* by Thomas R. Robinson, CFA, Jan Hendrik van Greuning, CFA, R. Elaine Henry, CFA, and Michael A. Broihahn, CFA

23⅝ 24
4⅝ 4¹¹/₁₆ — ⅜
5½ 5½ —
5½ 21³/₁₆ — ⅛
20⅝ 21³/₁₆ — ⅛
17⅜ 18⅛ + ⅞
6½ 6½ — ½
7¼ 3¹/₃₂ — ⅛
15/₁₆ ⁹/₁₆
9/₁₆
1¹/₃₂ 7¹⁵/₁₆
7¹¹/₁₆ 7¹³/₁₆ 7¹⁵/₁₆
2⅝ 2¹¹/₃₂ 2½ +
2¾ 2¼ 2¼
6¼ 12¹/₁₆ 11⅜ 11¾ +
87 33¾ 33 33⅛ —
602 25⅝ 24⁹/₁₆ 25⅝ +
833 12 11⅝ 11⅛ +
16 10½ 10½ 10⅛ —
78 15⅝ 15¹³/₁₆ 15⅛ —
4508 9¹/₁₆ 8¼ 8⅛ +
11¼ 10⅛

UNDERSTANDING THE INCOME STATEMENT

by Thomas R. Robinson, CFA, Jan Hendrik van Greuning, CFA,
R. Elaine Henry, CFA, and Michael A. Broihahn, CFA

LEARNING OUTCOMES

The candidate should be able to:

Mastery

a. describe the components of the income statement, and construct an income statement using the alternative presentation formats of that statement; ☐

b. explain the general principles of revenue recognition and accrual accounting, demonstrate specific revenue recognition applications (including accounting for long-term contracts, installment sales, barter transactions, and gross and net reporting of revenue), and discuss the implications of revenue recognition principles for financial analysis; ☐

c. discuss the general principles of expense recognition, such as the matching principle, specific expense recognition applications (including depreciation of long-term assets and inventory methods), and the implications of expense recognition principles for financial analysis; ☐

d. demonstrate the appropriate method of depreciating long-term assets, accounting for inventory, or amortizing intangibles, based on facts that might influence the decision; ☐

e. distinguish between the operating and nonoperating components of the income statement; ☐

f. discuss the financial reporting treatment and analysis of nonrecurring items (including discontinued operations, extraordinary items, and unusual or infrequent items) and changes in accounting standards; ☐

g. describe the components of earnings per share and calculate a company's earnings per share (both basic and diluted earnings per share) for both a simple and complex capital structure; ☐

h. differentiate between dilutive and antidilutive securities, and discuss the implications of each for the earnings per share calculation; ☐

137

i.	describe and calculate comprehensive income;	☐
j.	state the accounting classification for items that are excluded from the income statement but affect owners' equity, and list the major types of items receiving that treatment.	☐

THEME

The income statement presents results of a company's performance during a period of time. Recognizing income in the period earned is a basic objective of accrual accounting. Accrual accounting, therefore, requires companies to choose appropriate revenue and expense recognition policies and to estimate certain related parameters. Understanding a company's accounting choices and estimates enables an analyst to assess a company's performance, to evaluate trends in performance, and to compare different companies' performance.

1   INTRODUCTION

The income statement presents information on the financial results of a company's business activities over a period of time. The income statement communicates how much revenue the company generated during a period and what costs it incurred in connection with generating that revenue. The basic equation underlying the income statement is Revenue minus Expense equals Net income. The income statement is also called the "statement of operations" or "statement of earnings," or, sometimes, in business jargon, it is called the "P&L" for profit and loss.

Investment analysts intensely scrutinize companies' income statements. Equity analysts are interested in them because equity markets often reward relatively high- or low-earnings growth companies with above-average or below-average valuations, respectively. Fixed-income analysts examine the components of income statements, past and projected, for information on companies' abilities to make promised payments on their debt over the course of the business cycle. Corporate financial announcements frequently emphasize income statements more than the other financial statements.

This reading is organized as follows. Section 2 describes the components of the income statement and its format. Section 3 describes basic principles and selected applications related to the recognition of revenue, and Section 4 describes basic principles and selected applications related to the recognition of expenses. Section 5 covers nonrecurring items and nonoperating items. Section 6 explains the calculation of earnings per share. Section 7 introduces income statement analysis. Section 8 explains comprehensive income and its reporting. A summary of the key points and practice problems in the CFA Institute multiple-choice format complete the reading.

COMPONENTS AND FORMAT OF THE INCOME STATEMENT

2

On the top line of the income statement, companies typically report revenue. **Revenue** refers to amounts charged for the delivery of goods or services in the ordinary activities of a business. The term **net revenue** means that the revenue number is shown after adjustments (e.g., for estimated returns or for amounts unlikely to be collected). "Revenue" is often used synonymously with "sales."[1] Exhibits 1 and 2 show the income statements for Groupe Danone, a French food

EXHIBIT 1	Groupe Danone Consolidated Statements of Income (in Millions of Euros)		
	Year Ended 31 December		
	2002	**2003**	**2004**
Net sales	13,555	13,131	13,700
Cost of goods sold	(6,442)	(5,983)	(6,369)
Selling expenses	(4,170)	(4,176)	(4,294)
General and administrative expenses	(964)	(977)	(997)
Research and development expenses	(133)	(130)	(131)
Other (expense) income	(256)	(261)	(204)
Operating income	1,590	1,604	1,705
Nonrecurring items	458	(60)	(105)
Interest expense, net	(110)	(70)	(73)
Income before provision for income taxes and minority interests	1,938	1,474	1,527
Provision for income taxes	(490)	(488)	(457)
Income before minority interests	1,448	986	1,070
Minority interests	(182)	(184)	(189)
Share in net income of affiliates	17	37	(564)
Net income	1,283	839	317

---

[1] **Sales** is sometimes understood to refer to the sale of goods, whereas "revenue" can include the sale of goods or services; however, the terms are often used interchangeably. In some countries, turnover is used in place of "revenue."

manufacturer, and Kraft Foods, a U.S. food manufacturer. For the year ended 31 December 2004, Danone reports €13.7 billion of net sales, whereas Kraft reports $32.2 billion of net revenues.[2]

EXHIBIT 2	Kraft Foods and Subsidiaries Consolidated Statements of Earnings (in Millions of Dollars, except per-Share Data)		

	Year Ended 31 December		
	2004	**2003**	**2002**
Net revenues	$32,168	$30,498	$29,248
Cost of sales	20,281	18,531	17,463
Gross profit	11,887	11,967	11,785
Marketing, administration, and research costs	6,658	6,136	5,644
Integration costs and a loss on sale of a food factory		(13)	111
Asset impairment and exit costs	603	6	142
Losses (gains) on sales of businesses	3	(31)	(80)
Amortization of intangibles	11	9	7
Operating income	4,612	5,860	5,961
Interest and other debt expense, net	666	665	847
Earnings from continuing operations before income taxes and minority interest	3,946	5,195	5,114
Provision for income taxes	1,274	1,812	1,813
Earnings from continuing operations before minority interest	2,672	3,383	3,301
Minority interest in earnings from continuing operations, net	3	4	4
Earnings from continuing operations	2,669	3,379	3,297
(Loss) earnings from discontinued operations, net of income taxes	(4)	97	97
Net earnings	$2,665	$3,476	$3,394

Note that Groupe Danone lists the years in increasing order from left to right with the most recent year in the last column, whereas Kraft lists the years in decreasing order with the most recent year listed in the first column. These alternative formats are common. There are also differences in presentations of items, such as expenses. Groupe Danone shows expenses such as cost of goods sold in parenthesis to explicitly show that these are subtracted from revenue. Kraft, on

[2] Following net income, the income statement will also present **earnings per share**, the amount of earnings per common share of the company. Earnings per share will be discussed in detail later in this reading, and the per-share display has been omitted from these exhibits to focus on the core income statement.

the other hand, does not place cost of sales in parenthesis. Rather, it is implicitly understood that this is an expense and is subtracted in arriving at subtotals and totals. The analyst should always verify the order of years and presentation of negative items before analysis is begun because there is flexibility in how companies may present the income statement.

At the bottom of the income statement, companies report net income (or, essentially synonymously, net earnings or profit). For 2004, Danone reports €317 million of net income and Kraft reports $2,665 million of net earnings. Net income is often referred to as "the bottom line." The basis for this expression is that net income is the final—or bottom—line in an income statement. Because net income is often viewed as the single most relevant number to describe a company's performance over a period of time, the term "bottom line" sometimes is used in general business jargon to mean any final or most relevant result.

Net income also includes **gains** and **losses**, which are asset inflows and outflows, respectively, not directly related to the ordinary activities of the business. For example, if a company sells products, these are reported as revenue and the costs are listed separately. However, if a company sells surplus land that is not needed, the cost of the land is subtracted from the sales price and the net result is reported as a gain or a loss.

In addition to presenting the net income, income statements also present subtotals that are significant to users of financial statements. Some of the subtotals are specified by international financial reporting standards (IFRS), particularly nonrecurring items, but other subtotals are not specified.[3] International Accounting Standard (IAS) No. 1, *Presentation of Financial Statements*, requires that certain items, such as revenue, finance costs, and tax expense, be separately stated on the face of the income statement. IAS No. 1 also requires that headings and subtotals should also "be presented on the face of the income statement when such presentation is relevant to an understanding of the entity's financial performance."[4] IAS No. 1 states that expenses may be grouped together either by their nature or function. For example, grouping together expenses such as depreciation on manufacturing equipment and depreciation on administrative facilities into a single line item called "depreciation" represents a **grouping by nature** of the expense. An example of **grouping by function** would be grouping together expenses into a category such as cost of goods sold, which would include some salaries (e.g., salespeople's), material costs, depreciation, and other direct sales-related expenses.

One subtotal often shown in an income statement is **gross profit** (or, synonymously, **gross margin**). When an income statement shows a gross profit subtotal, it is said to use a **multi-step format** rather than a **single-step format**. The Kraft Foods income statement is an example of the multi-step format, whereas the Danone income statement is a single step. For manufacturing and merchandising companies, for whom gross profit is most relevant, gross profit is calculated as revenue minus the cost of the goods that were sold.[5] For service companies, gross profit is calculated as revenue minus the cost of services that were

---

[3] The body of standards issued by the International Accounting Standards Board is now referred to as International Financial Reporting Standards, which include previously issued International Accounting Standards. "Financial reporting" is a broad term including reporting on accounting, financial statements, and other information found in company financial reports.

[4] IAS No. 1, *Presentation of Financial Statements*, paragraph 83.

[5] Later readings will provide additional information about alternative methods to calculate cost of goods sold.

provided. In summary, gross profit is the amount of revenue available after subtracting the costs of delivering goods or services such as material and labor. Other expenses related to running the business are subtracted after gross profit.

Another important subtotal shown on the income statement is **operating profit** (or, synonymously, operating income). Operating profit further deducts operating expenses such as selling, general, administrative, and research and development expenses. Operating profit reflects a company's profits on its usual business activities before deducting taxes. For financial firms, interest expense would be included in operating expenses and subtracted in arriving at operating profit. For nonfinancial companies, interest expense would not be included in operating expenses and would be subtracted after operating profit because it relates to nonoperating activities for such companies. For some companies composed of a number of separate business segments, operating profit can be useful in evaluating the performance of the individual businesses, reflecting the reality that interest and tax expenses are more relevant at the level of the overall company rather than an individual segment level. For example, in its Investor Relations information, DaimlerChrysler notes, "Especially on the pre-tax level, Operating Profit is the principal earnings indicator for the Segments, Divisions and Business Units."[6] The specific calculations of gross margin and operating profit may vary by company, and a reader of financial statements can consult the notes to the statements to identify significant variations across companies.

Note that both Groupe Danone and Kraft Foods include a line item on their income statements referring to minority interest. Danone and Kraft both consolidate subsidiaries over which they have control. Consolidation means that they include all of the revenues and expenses of those subsidiaries even if they own less than 100 percent. Minority interest represents the portion of income that belongs to minority shareholders of these consolidated subsidiaries, as opposed to the parent company.

Exhibit 3 shows the income statement for CRA International (then known as Charles River Associates), a company providing management consulting services. These examples illustrate basic points about the income statement, including variations across the statements—some of which depend on the industry, whereas others reflect differences in accounting policies and practices of a particular company. In addition, some differences within an industry are primarily differences in terminology, whereas others are more fundamental accounting differences. Footnotes to the financial statements are helpful in identifying such differences.

Having introduced the components and format of an income statement, the next objective is to understand the actual reported numbers in it. To accurately interpret reported numbers, the analyst needs to be familiar with the principles of revenue and expense recognition—that is, how revenue and expenses are measured and attributed to a given accounting reporting period. Revenue and expense recognition are our next topics.

---

[6] DaimlerChrysler/Investor Relations/Basic Information/Controlling systems at www.daimlerchrysler.com.

EXHIBIT 3	Charles River Associates Incorporated Consolidated Statements of Income (in Thousands, except per-Share Data)		
	Year Ended		
	27 Nov. 2004 (52 weeks)	**29 Nov. 2003 (52 weeks)**	**30 Nov. 2002 (53 weeks)**
Revenues	$216,735	$163,458	$130,690
Cost of services	127,716	100,168	80,659
Gross profit	89,019	63,290	50,031
Selling, general, and administrative expenses	57,286	43,055	36,600
Income from operations	31,733	20,235	13,431
Interest income	904	429	486
Interest expense	(1,751)	(38)	(120)
Other expense	(260)	(306)	(29)
Income before provision for income taxes and minority interest	30,626	20,320	13,768
Provision for income taxes	(13,947)	(8,737)	(5,879)
Income before minority interest	16,679	11,583	7,889
Minority interest	(335)	(154)	547
Net income	$16,344	$11,429	$8,436

REVENUE RECOGNITION　　3

Revenue is the top line in an income statement, so we begin the discussion with revenue recognition. A first task is to explain some relevant accounting terminology.

The terms "revenue," "sales," "gains," "losses," and "net income" ("profit," "net earnings") have been previously briefly defined. The IFRS *Framework for the Preparation and Presentation of Financial Statements* (referred to here as "the Framework" for short) provides further relevant details. The *Framework* provides that profit is a frequently used measure of performance that is composed of income and expenses.[7] It defines **income** as follows:

> Income is increases in economic benefits during the accounting period in the form of inflows or enhancements of assets or decreases of liabilities that result in increases in equity, other than those relating to contributions from equity participants.[8]

International Financial Reporting Standards use the term "income" to include revenue and gains. Gains are similar to revenue; however, they arise from secondary or peripheral activities rather than from a company's primary business activities. For example, for a restaurant, the sale of surplus restaurant equipment for more than its cost is referred to as a gain rather than as revenue. Similarly, a

---

[7] IASB, *International Framework for the Preparation and Presentation of Financial Statements*, paragraph 69.
[8] Ibid., paragraph 70.

loss is like an expense but arises from secondary activities. Gains and losses may be considered part of operating activities (e.g., a loss due to a decline in the value of inventory) or may be considered part of nonoperating activities (e.g., the sale of nontrading investments).

In a simple hypothetical scenario, revenue recognition would not be an issue. For instance, a company sells goods to a buyer for cash with no returns allowed: When should the company recognize revenue? In this instance, it is clear that revenue should be recognized when the exchange of goods for cash takes place. In practice, however, determining when revenue should be recognized can be somewhat more complex for a number of reasons discussed in the following sections.

3.1 General Principles

An important concept concerning revenue recognition is that it can occur independently of cash movements. For example, assume a company sells goods to a buyer on credit and so does not actually receive cash until some later time. A fundamental principle of accrual accounting is that revenue is recognized when it is earned, so the company's financial records reflect the sale when it is made and a related accounts receivable is created. Later, when cash changes hands, the company's financial records simply reflect that cash has been received to settle an account receivable. Similarly, there are situations when a company receives cash up front and actually delivers the product or service later, perhaps over a period of time. In this case, the company would record **unearned revenue**, which is then recognized as being earned over time. (One example would be a subscription payment received up front for a publication that is to be delivered periodically over time, the accounting for which was illustrated earlier.)

The basic revenue recognition principles promulgated by accounting regulators deal with the definition of "earned." The International Accounting Standards Board (IASB) provides that revenue for the sale of goods is to be recognized (reported on the income statement) when the following conditions are satisfied:[9]

► the entity has transferred to the buyer the significant risks and rewards of ownership of the goods;

► the entity retains neither continuing managerial involvement to the degree usually associated with ownership nor effective control over the goods sold;

► the amount of revenue can be measured reliably;

► it is probable that the economic benefits associated with the transaction will flow to the entity; and

► the costs incurred or to be incurred in respect of the transaction can be measured reliably.

The IASB notes that the transfer of the risks and rewards of ownership normally occurs when goods are delivered to the buyer or when legal title to goods transfers. However, as noted by the above remaining conditions, transfer of goods will not always result in the recognition of revenue. For example, if goods are delivered to a retail store to be sold on consignment and title is not transferred, the revenue would not yet be recognized.[10]

---

[9] IASB, IAS No. 18, *Revenue*, paragraph 14.

[10] IAS No. 18 describes a "consignment sale" as one in which the recipient undertakes to sell the goods for the shipper. Revenue is recognized when the recipient sells the goods to a third party. IAS No. 18, Appendix, paragraph 2.

The Financial Accounting Standards Board (FASB)[11] specifies that revenue should be recognized when it is "realized or realizable and earned." The U.S. Securities and Exchange Commission (SEC),[12] motivated in part because of the frequency with which overstating revenue occurs in connection with fraud and/or misstatements, provides guidance on how to apply the accounting principles. This guidance names four criteria to determine when revenue is realized or realizable and earned:

1. There is evidence of an arrangement between buyer and seller. For instance, this would disallow the practice of recognizing revenue in a period by delivering the product just before the end of an accounting period and then completing a sales contract *after* the period end.

2. The product has been delivered, or the service has been rendered. For instance, this would preclude revenue recognition when the product has been shipped but the *risks and rewards of ownership have not actually passed* to the buyer.

3. The price is determined, or determinable. For instance, this would preclude a company from recognizing revenue that is based on some *contingency*.

4. The seller is reasonably sure of collecting money. For instance, this would preclude a company from recognizing revenue when the customer is *unlikely to pay*.

The IASB standards separately deal with the recognition of revenue for services:[13]

► When the outcome of a transaction involving the rendering of services can be estimated reliably, revenue associated with the transaction shall be recognized by reference to the stage of completion of the transaction at the balance sheet date.

► The outcome of a transaction can be estimated reliably when all the following conditions are satisfied:

  ► the amount of revenue can be measured reliably;

  ► it is probable that the economic benefits associated with the transaction will flow to the entity;

  ► the stage of completion of the transaction at the balance sheet date can be measured reliably; and

  ► the costs incurred for the transaction and the costs to complete the transaction can be measured reliably.

Companies must disclose their revenue recognition policies in the footnotes to their financial statements. Analysts should review these policies carefully to understand how and when a company recognizes revenue, which may differ depending upon the types of product sold and services rendered. Exhibit 4 presents a portion of the revenue recognition footnote for DaimlerChrysler from its 2005 annual report prepared under IFRS.

---

[11] See Statement of Financial Accounting Concepts No. 5, paragraph 83(b).

[12] See SEC Staff Accounting Bulletin 101.

[13] IASB, IAS No. 18, paragraph 20.

EXHIBIT 4	Partial Revenue Recognition Footnote for DaimlerChrysler

Revenue for sales of vehicles, service parts and other related products is recognized when persuasive evidence of an arrangement exists, delivery has occurred or services have been rendered, the price of the transaction is fixed and determinable, and collectibility is reasonably assured.

Revenues are recognized net of discounts, cash sales incentives, customer bonuses and rebates granted. Non-cash sales incentives that do not reduce the transaction price to the customer are classified within cost of sales. Shipping and handling costs are recorded as cost of sales in the period incurred.

DaimlerChrysler uses price discounts to adjust market pricing in response to a number of market and product factors, including: pricing actions and incentives offered by competitors, economic conditions, the amount of excess industry production capacity, the intensity of market competition, and consumer demand for the product. The Group may offer a variety of sales incentive programs at any point in time, including: cash offers to dealers and consumers, lease subsidies which reduce the consumer's monthly lease payment, or reduced financing rate programs offered to consumers.

The Group records as a reduction to revenue at the time of sale to the dealer the estimated impact of sales incentives programs offered to dealers and consumers. This estimated impact represents the incentive programs offered to dealers and consumers as well as the expected modifications to these programs in order for the dealers to sell their inventory.

The topic of revenue recognition remains important, and new challenges have evolved, particularly in areas of e-commerce and services such as software development. Standard setters continue to evaluate current revenue recognition standards and issue new guidance periodically to deal with new types of transactions. Additionally, there are occasional special cases for revenue recognition, as discussed in the next section.

3.2 Revenue Recognition in Special Cases

The general principles discussed above are helpful for dealing with most revenue recognition issues. There are some areas where revenue recognition is more difficult to determine. For example, in limited circumstances, revenue may be recognized before or after goods are delivered or services are rendered, as summarized in Exhibit 5.

The following sections discuss revenue recognition in the case of long-term contracts, installment sales, and barter.

3.2.1 Long-Term Contracts

A **long-term contract** is one that spans a number of accounting periods. Such contracts raise issues in determining when the earnings process has been completed. How should a company apportion the revenue earned under a long-term

EXHIBIT 5	Revenue Recognition in Special Cases	
Before Goods Are Delivered or Services Rendered	**At the Time** Goods Are Delivered or Services Rendered	**After** Goods Are Delivered or Services Rendered
For example, with long-term contracts where the outcome can be reliably measured, the percentage-of-completion method is used.	Recognize revenues using normal revenue recognition criteria (IAS, FAS, SEC).	For example, with real estate sales where there is doubt about the buyer's ability to complete payments, the installment method and cost recovery method are appropriate.

contract to each accounting period? If, for example, the contract is a service contract or a licensing arrangement, the company may recognize the revenue ratably over the period of time of the contract rather than at the end of the contract term. As stated in IAS No. 18 regarding the rendering of services:

> The recognition of revenue by reference to the stage of completion of a transaction is often referred to as the percentage-of-completion method. Under this method, revenue is recognized in the accounting periods in which the services are rendered. The recognition of revenue on this basis provides useful information on the extent of service activity and performance during a period. IAS 11 *Construction Contracts* also requires the recognition of revenue on this basis. The requirements of that Standard are generally applicable to the recognition of revenue and the associated expenses for a transaction involving the rendering of services.[14]

As noted in IAS No. 18, construction contracts are another example of contracts that may span a number of accounting periods. IAS No. 11 provides that when the outcome of a construction contract can be measured reliably, revenue and expenses should be recognized in reference to the stage of completion. U.S. generally accepted accounting principles (U.S. GAAP) have a similar requirement. In both cases, the percentage-of-completion method of accounting is used. Under the **percentage-of-completion** method, in each accounting period, the company estimates what percentage of the contract is complete and then reports that percentage of the total contract revenue in its income statement. Contract costs for the period are expensed against the revenue. Therefore, net income or profit is reported each year as work is performed.

Under IAS No. 11, if the outcome of the contract cannot be measured reliably, then revenue is only reported to the extent of contract costs incurred (if it is probable the costs will be recovered). Costs are expensed in the period incurred. Under this method, no profit would be reported until completion of the contract. Under U.S. GAAP, a different method is used when the outcome cannot be measured reliably, termed the "completed contract method." Under the **completed contract** method, the company does not report any revenue until the contract is finished. Under U.S. GAAP, the completed contract method is also appropriate when the contract is not a long-term contract. Note, however, that when a contract is started and completed in the same period, there is no difference between the percentage-of-completion and completed contract methods.

---

[14] IAS No. 18, paragraph 21.

Examples 1, 2, and 3 provide illustrations of these revenue recognition methods. As shown, the percentage-of-completion method results in revenue recognition sooner than the completed contract method and thus may be considered a less conservative approach. In addition, the percentage-of-completion method relies on management estimates and is thus not as objective as the completed contract method. However, an advantage of the percentage-of-completion method is that it results in better matching of revenue recognition with the accounting period in which it was earned. Because of better matching with the periods in which work is performed, the percentage-of-completion method is the preferred method of revenue recognition for long-term contracts and is required when the outcome can be measured reliably under both IFRS and U.S. GAAP. Under both IFRS and U.S. GAAP, if a loss is expected on the contract, the loss is reported immediately, not upon completion of the contract, regardless of the method used (e.g., percentage-of-completion or completed contract).

EXAMPLE 1

Revenue Recognition for Long-Term Contracts: Recognizing Revenue Ratably

New Era Network Associates has a five-year license to provide networking support services to a customer. The total amount of the license fee to be received by New Era is $1 million. New Era recognizes license revenue ratably regardless of the time at which cash is received. How much revenue will New Era recognize for this license?

Solution: For this license, New Era Network Associates will recognize $200,000 each year for five years (calculated as $1 million divided by 5).

EXAMPLE 2

Revenue Recognition for Long-Term Contracts: Percentage-of-Completion Method

Stelle Technology has a contract to build a network for a customer for a total sales price of $10 million. The network will take an estimated three years to build, and total building costs are estimated to be $6 million. Stelle recognizes long-term contract revenue using the percentage-of-completion method and estimates percentage complete based on expenditure incurred as a percentage of total estimated expenditures.

1. At the end of Year 1, the company has spent $3 million. Total costs to complete are estimated to be another $3 million. How much revenue will Stelle recognize in Year 1?

2. At the end of Year 2, the company has spent $5.4 million. Total costs to complete are estimated to be another $0.6 million. How much revenue will Stelle recognize in Year 2?

3. At the end of Year 3, the contract is complete. The company spent a total of $6 million. How much revenue will Stelle recognize in Year 3?

Solution to 1: Stelle has spent 50 percent of the total project costs ($3 million divided by $6 million), so in Year 1, the company will recognize 50 percent of the total contract revenue (i.e., $5 million).

Solution to 2: Because Stelle has spent 90 percent of the total project costs ($5.4 million divided by $6 million), by the end of Year 2, it will need to have recognized 90 percent of the total contract revenue (i.e., $9 million). Stelle has already recognized $5 million of revenue in Year 1, so in Year 2, the company will recognize $4 million revenue ($9 million minus $5 million).

Solution to 3: Because Stelle has spent 100 percent of the total project costs, by the end of Year 3, it will need to have recognized 100 percent of the total contract revenue (i.e., $10 million). Stelle had already recognized $9 million of revenue by the end of Year 2, so in Year 3, the company will recognize $1 million revenue ($10 million minus $9 million).

	Year 1	Year 2	Year 3	Total
Revenue	$5 million	$4 million	$1 million	$10 million

EXAMPLE 3

Revenue Recognition for Long-Term Contracts: Completed Contract Method

Kolenda Technology Group has a contract to build a network for a customer for a total sales price of $10 million. This network will take an estimated three years to build, but considerable uncertainty surrounds total building costs because new technologies are involved. Kolenda recognizes contract revenue using the completed contract method.

1. At the end of Year 1, Kolenda has spent $3 million. How much revenue will the company recognize in Year 1?
2. At the end of Year 2, Kolenda has spent $5.4 million. How much revenue will the company recognize in Year 2?
3. At the end of Year 3, the contract is complete. Kolenda spent a total of $6 million. How much revenue will the company recognize in Year 3?

Solution to 1: No revenue will be recognized until the contract is complete. In Year 1, Kolenda will recognize $0.

Solution to 2: No revenue will be recognized until the contract is complete. In Year 2, Kolenda will recognize $0.

Solution to 3: Because the contract is complete, Kolenda will recognize the total contract revenue (i.e., $10 million).

	Year 1	Year 2	Year 3	Total
Revenue	$0 million	$0 million	$10 million	$10 million

3.2.2 Installment Sales

As noted above, revenue is normally reported when goods are delivered or services are rendered, independent of the period in which cash payments for those goods or services are received. This principle applies even to **installment** sales—sales in which proceeds are to be paid in installments over an extended period. Under limited circumstances, recognition of revenue or profit may be required to be deferred for some installment sales.

An example of such deferral arises for certain sales of real estate on an installment basis. Revenue recognition for sales of real estate[15] varies depending on specific aspects of the sale transaction. Under normal conditions, sales of real estate are reported at the time of sale using the normal revenue recognition conditions. International standards note that in the case of real estate sales, the time at which legal title transfers may differ from the time at which the buyer acquires a vested interest. Continuing involvement in the real estate by the seller may also indicate that risks and rewards of ownership of the property have not been transferred. There may also be significant doubt of the ability of the buyer to complete payment for a real estate sales contract. IAS No. 18 provides that in the case of real estate where the down payment and payments received do not provide sufficient evidence of the commitment of the buyer, revenue should only be reported to the extent cash is received. This is a conservative treatment because the reporting of revenue is deferred. Similar provisions exist under U.S. GAAP except that under U.S. GAAP the full revenue is shown in the year of sale but some of the profit is deferred.

Two methods may be appropriate in these limited circumstances and relate to the amount of profit to be recognized each year from the transaction: the **installment method** and the **cost recovery method**. Under the installment method, the portion of the total profit of the sale that is recognized in each period is determined by the percentage of the total sales price for which the seller has received cash. Exhibit 6 presents an example of a disclosure of an installment sale of real estate under U.S. GAAP where a portion of the profit was recognized and the remainder was deferred.

---

[15] IAS No. 18, Appendix, paragraph 9, and FASB Statement No. 66, *Accounting for Sales of Real Estate.*

EXHIBIT 6	Installment Sale Disclosure for First Bancshares

On June 22, 2004, an agreement was entered into to sell the property and equipment of South Central Missouri Title Company, Inc., for $252,000. In addition, South Central entered into a covenant not to compete agreement with the purchaser. Expense related to the sale totaled $61,512. As of the date of the sale, the assets sold had a net book value of $100,166. The majority of the sales price was in the form of a promissory note to South Central with a five year maturity. The transaction closed on July 16, 2004. As a result of this sale, the subsidiary will no longer offer sales of title insurance or real estate closing services. The company accounted for this sale on the installment method because the initial investment by the buyer was not substantial enough to warrant full recognition of the gain. However, the recovery of the cost of the property is reasonably assured if the buyer defaults. The following schedule summarizes certain information for the transaction:

Revenue	$252,000
Cost of sale	161,678
Deferred gain	90,322
Deferred gain recognized during FY 2005	8,026
Deferred gain at June 30, 2005	$82,296

Source: First Bancshares Form 10K, filed 11/1/2005.

The cost recovery method of revenue recognition is an appropriate alternative for many of the same situations as the installment method. Under the cost recovery method, the seller does not report any profit until the cash amounts paid by the buyer—including principal and interest on any financing from the seller—are greater than all the seller's costs of the property. Example 4 below provides an example of the differences between the installment method and the cost recovery method.

Installment sales and cost recovery treatment of revenue recognition are rare for financial reporting purposes, especially for assets other than real estate. IAS No. 18 provides that installment sales other than real estate generally require revenue to be recognized at the time of sale; however, it further provides that the guidance found in IAS No. 18 must be considered in light of local laws regarding the sale of goods in a particular country.

EXAMPLE 4

The Installment and Cost Recovery Methods of Revenue Recognition

Assume the total sales price and cost of a property are $2,000,000 and $1,100,000, respectively, so that the total profit to be recognized is $900,000. The amount of cash received by the seller as a down payment is $300,000, with the remainder of the sales price to be received over a 10-year period. It has been determined that there is significant doubt about the ability and commitment of the buyer to complete all payments. How much profit will be recognized attributable to the down payment if:

1. The installment method is used?

2. The cost recovery method is used?

Solution to 1: The installment method apportions the cash receipt between cost recovered and profit using the ratio of profit to sales value; here, this ratio equals $900,000/$2,000,000 = 0.45 or 45 percent. Therefore, the seller will recognize the following profit attributable to the down payment: 45 percent of $300,000 = $135,000.

Solution to 2: Under the cost recovery method of revenue recognition, the company would not recognize any profit attributable to the down payment because the cash amounts paid by the buyer still do not exceed the cost of $1,100,000.

3.2.3 Barter

Revenue recognition issues related to barter transactions became particularly important as e-commerce developed. As an example, if Company A exchanges advertising space for computer equipment from Company B but no cash changes hands, can Company A and B both report revenue? Such an exchange is referred to as a "barter transaction."

An even more challenging revenue recognition issue evolved from barter transactions—round-trip transactions. As an example, if Company A sells advertising services (or energy contracts, or commodities) to Company B and almost simultaneously buys an almost identical product from Company B, can Company A report revenue at the fair value of the product sold? Because the company's revenue would be approximately equal to its expense, the net effect of the transaction would have no impact on net income or cash flow. However, the amount of revenue reported would be higher, and the amount of revenue can be important to a company's valuation. In the earlier stages of e-commerce, for example, some equity valuations were based on sales (because many early internet companies reported no net income).

Under IFRS, revenue from barter transactions must be measured based on the fair value of revenue from similar nonbarter transactions with unrelated parties (parties other than the barter partner).[16] Similarly, the FASB states that revenue can be recognized at fair value only if a company has historically received cash payments for such services and can thus use this historical experience as a basis for determining fair value.[17]

3.2.4 Gross versus Net Reporting

Another revenue recognition issue that became particularly important with the emergence of e-commerce is the issue of gross versus net reporting. Merchandising companies typically sell products that they purchased from a supplier. In

---

[16] IASB, SIC Interpretation 31, Revenue—Barter Transactions Involving Advertising Services, paragraph 5.

[17] See Emerging Issues Task Force EITF 99-17, "Accounting for Advertising Barter Transactions."

accounting for their sales, the company records the amount of the sale proceeds as sales revenue and their cost of the products as the cost of goods sold. As internet-based merchandising companies developed, many sold products that they had never held in inventory; they simply arranged for the supplier to ship the products directly to the end customer. In effect, many such companies were agents of the supplier company, and the net difference between their sales proceeds and their costs was equivalent to a sales commission. What amount should these companies record as their revenues—the gross amount of sales proceeds received from their customers, or the net difference between sales proceeds and their cost?

U.S. GAAP indicates that the approach should be based on the specific situation and provides guidance for determining when revenue should be reported gross versus net.[18] To report gross revenues, the following criteria are relevant: The company is the primary obligor under the contract, bears inventory risk and credit risk, can choose its supplier, and has reasonable latitude to establish price. If these criteria are not met, the company should report revenues net. Example 5 provides an illustration.

EXAMPLE 5

Gross versus Net Reporting of Revenues

Flyalot has agreements with several major airlines to obtain airline tickets at reduced rates. The company pays only for tickets it sells to customers. In the most recent period, Flyalot sold airline tickets to customers over the internet for a total of $1.1 million. The cost of these tickets to Flyalot was $1 million. The company's direct selling costs were $2,000. Once the customers receive their ticket, the airline is responsible for providing all services associated with the customers' flight.

1. Demonstrate the reporting of revenues under:
   A. gross reporting.
   B. net reporting.
2. Determine and justify the appropriate method for reporting revenues.

Solution to 1: The table below shows how reporting would appear on a gross and a net basis.

	A. Gross Reporting	B. Net Reporting
Revenues	$1,100,000	$100,000
Cost of sales	1,002,000	2,000
Gross margin	$98,000	$98,000

---

[18] See Emerging Issues Task Force EITF 99-19, "Reporting Revenue Gross as a Principal versus Net as an Agent."

Solution to 2: Flyalot should report revenue on a net basis. Flyalot pays only for tickets it sells to customers and thus did not bear inventory risk. In addition, the airline—not Flyalot—is the primary obligor under the contract. Revenues should be reported as $100,000.

3.3 Implications for Financial Analysis

As we have seen, companies use a variety of revenue recognition methods. Furthermore, a single company may use different revenue recognition policies for different businesses. Companies disclose their revenue recognition policies in the footnotes to their financial statement, often in the first note.

The following aspects of a company's revenue recognition policy are particularly relevant to financial analysis: whether a policy results in recognition of revenue sooner rather than later (sooner is less conservative), and to what extent a policy requires the company to make estimates. In order to analyze a company's financial statements, and particularly to compare one company's financial statements with those of another company, it is helpful to understand any differences in their revenue recognition policies. Although it may not be possible to calculate the monetary effect of differences between particular companies' revenue recognition policies and estimates, it is generally possible to characterize the relative conservatism of a company's policies and to qualitatively assess how differences in policies might affect financial ratios.

With familiarity of the basic principles of revenue recognition in hand, the next section begins a discussion of expense recognition.

EXAMPLE 6

Revenue Recognition Policy for Motorola

As disclosed in the footnotes to the financial statements shown below (emphasis added), Motorola (NYSE:MOT) uses different revenue recognition policies depending on the type of revenue-producing activity, including product sales, long-term contracts, contracts involving unproven technology, revenue for services, and revenue for licensing agreements.

> **Revenue Recognition:** The Company recognizes revenue for *product sales* when title transfers, the risks and rewards of ownership have been transferred to the customer, the fee is fixed and determinable, and collection of the related receivable is probable, which is generally at the time of shipment. Accruals are established, with the related reduction to revenue, for allowances for discounts and price protection, product returns and incentive programs for distributors and end customers related to these sales based on actual historical exposure at the time the related revenues are recognized. For *long-term contracts*, the Company uses the percentage-of-completion method to recognize revenues and costs based on the percentage of costs incurred to date compared to the total estimated contract costs. For *contracts involving new unproven technologies*, revenues and profits are deferred until technological feasibility is established, customer acceptance is obtained and other contract-specific terms have been completed. Provisions for losses are

recognized during the period in which the loss first becomes apparent. *Revenue for services* is recognized ratably over the contract term or as services are being performed. *Revenue related to licensing agreements* is recognized over the licensing period or at the time the Company has fulfilled its obligations and the fee to be received is fixed and determinable.

Source: Motorola 10-K financial statement footnotes for the year ended 31 December 2004, as filed with the SEC. Emphasis added.

EXAMPLE 7

Revenue Recognition of i2 Technologies

On 9 June 2004, the SEC announced it had settled a securities fraud case against i2 Technologies (NASDAQ: ITWO) involving the misstatement of approximately $1 billion in revenues. The SEC announcement explains that the company recognized revenue up front on its software licenses, which was inappropriate because some of the software lacked complete functionality either for general use or for use by a particular customer.

Source: SEC Accounting and Auditing Enforcement Release No. 2034.

EXPENSE RECOGNITION   4

Expenses are deducted against revenue to arrive at a company's net profit or loss. Under the IASB *Framework*, **expenses** are "decreases in economic benefits during the accounting period in the form of outflows or depletions of assets or incurrences of liabilities that result in decreases in equity, other than those relating to distributions to equity participants."[19]

The IASB *Framework* also states:

The definition of expenses encompasses losses as well as those expenses that arise in the course of the ordinary activities of the enterprise. Expenses that arise in the course of the ordinary activities of the enterprise include, for example, cost of sales, wages and depreciation. They usually take the form of an outflow or depletion of assets such as cash and cash equivalents, inventory, property, plant and equipment.

Losses represent other items that meet the definition of expenses and may, or may not, arise in the course of the ordinary activities of the enterprise. Losses represent decreases in economic benefits and as such they are no different in nature from other expenses. Hence, they are not regarded as a separate element in this Framework.

Losses include, for example, those resulting from disasters such as fire and flood.[20]

---

[19] IASB *Framework for the Preparation and Presentation of Financial Statements*, paragraph 70.
[20] Ibid., paragraphs 78–80.

Similar to the issues with revenue recognition, in a simple hypothetical scenario, expense recognition would not be an issue. For instance, assume a company purchased inventory for cash and sold the entire inventory in the same period. When the company paid for the inventory, absent indications to the contrary, it is clear that the inventory cost has been incurred and should be recognized as an expense (cost of goods sold) in the financial records. Assume also that the company paid all operating and administrative expenses in cash within each accounting period. In such a simple hypothetical scenario, no issues of expense recognition would arise. In practice, however, as with revenue recognition, determining when expenses should be recognized can be somewhat more complex.

4.1 General Principles

In general, a company recognizes expenses in the period that it consumes (i.e., uses up) the economic benefits associated with the expenditure, or loses some previously recognized economic benefit.[21]

A general principle of expense recognition is the **matching principle**, also known as the "matching of costs with revenues."[22] Under the matching principle, a company directly matches some expenses (e.g., cost of goods sold) with associated revenues. Unlike the simple scenario in which a company purchases inventory and sells all of the inventory within the same accounting period, in practice, it is more likely that some of the current period's sales are made from inventory purchased in a previous period. It is also more likely that some of the inventory purchased in the current period will remain unsold at the end of the current period and so will be sold in the following period. The matching principle requires that the company match the cost of goods sold with the revenues of the period.

Period costs, expenditures that less directly match the timing of revenues, are reflected in the period when a company makes the expenditure or incurs the liability to pay. Administrative expenses are an example of period costs. Other expenditures that also less directly match the timing of revenues relate more directly to future expected benefits; in this case, the expenditures are allocated systematically with the passage of time. An example is depreciation expense (discussed below).

Examples 8 and 9 demonstrate the matching principle applied to inventory and cost of goods sold.

---

[21] Ibid., paragraph 94.
[22] Ibid., paragraph 95.

EXAMPLE 8

The Matching of Inventory Costs with Revenues

Kahn Distribution Limited (KDL) purchases inventory items for resale. During 2006, Kahn had the following transactions:

Quarter Inventory Purchases

First quarter	2,000 units at $40 per unit
Second quarter	1,500 units at $41 per unit
Third quarter	2,200 units at $43 per unit
Fourth quarter	1,900 units at $45 per unit
Total	7,600 units at a total cost of $321,600

Inventory sales during the year were 5,600 units at $50 per unit. KDL determines that there were 2,000 remaining units of inventory and specifically identifies that 1,900 were those purchased in the fourth quarter and 100 were purchased in the third quarter. What are the revenue and expense associated with these transactions during 2006?

Solution: The revenue for 2006 would be $280,000 (5,600 units × $50 per unit). Initially, the total cost of the goods purchased would be recorded as inventory (an asset) in the amount of $321,600. During 2006, the cost of the 5,600 units sold would be expensed (matched against the revenue) while the cost of the 2,000 remaining unsold units would remain in inventory as follows:

Cost of Goods Sold

From the first quarter	2,000 units at $40 per unit =	$ 80,000
From the second quarter	1,500 units at $41 per unit =	$ 61,500
From the third quarter	2,100 units at $43 per unit =	$ 90,300
Total cost of goods sold		$231,800

Cost of Goods Remaining in Inventory

From the third quarter	100 units at $43 per unit =	$ 4,300
From the fourth quarter	1,900 units at $45 per unit =	$85,500
Total remaining (or ending) inventory cost		$89,800

To confirm that total costs are accounted for:
$231,800 + $89,800 = $321,600
The cost of the goods sold would be expensed against the revenue of $280,000 as follows:

Revenue	$280,000
Cost of goods sold	231,800
Gross profit	$ 48,200

The remaining inventory amount of $89,800 will be matched against revenue in a future year when the inventory items are sold.

EXAMPLE 9

Alternative Inventory Costing Methods

In Example 8, KDL was able to specifically identify which inventory items were sold and which remained in inventory to be carried over to later periods. That method is called the **specific identification method**. It is not always possible to specifically identify which items were sold, so the accounting standards permit the assignment of inventory costs to costs of goods sold and to ending inventory using cost flow assumptions. Under both IFRS and U.S. GAAP, companies may use either of two methods to assign costs: the First In, First Out (FIFO) method, or the weighted average cost method. Under the **FIFO method**, it is simply assumed that the earliest items purchased were sold first. Ending inventory would, therefore, include only the latest purchases. It turns out that those items specifically identified as sold in Example 8 were also the first items purchased, so in this example, under FIFO, the cost of goods sold would also be $231,800, calculated as above. The **weighted average cost method** simply averages the total available costs over the total available units.

For KDL, the weighted average cost would be

$321,600/7,600 units = $42.3158 per unit

Cost of goods sold using the weighted average cost method would be

5,600 units at $42.3158 = $236,968

Ending inventory using the weighted average cost method would be

2,000 units at $42.3158 = $ 84,632

Another method is available under U.S. GAAP but is not permitted under IFRS. This method is the Last In, First Out (LIFO) method. Under the **LIFO method**, it is assumed that the most recent items purchased were sold first. Although this may seem contrary to common sense, it is logical in certain circumstances. For example, lumber in a lumberyard may be stacked up with the oldest lumber on the bottom. As lumber is sold, it is sold from the top of the stack, so the last lumber in is the first lumber out. Theoretically, a company should choose this method under U.S. GAAP if the physical inventory flows in this manner.[23] Under the LIFO method, in the KDL example, it would be assumed that the 2,000 units remaining in ending inventory would have come from the first quarter's purchases:[24]

Ending inventory 2,000 units at $40 per unit = $80,000

The remaining costs would be allocated to cost of goods sold under LIFO:

Total costs of $321,600 less $80,000 remaining
    in ending inventory = $241,600

---

[23] Practically, the reason some companies choose to use LIFO in the United States is to reduce taxes. When prices and inventory quantities are rising, LIFO will normally result in lower income and hence lower taxes. U.S. tax regulations require that if LIFO is used on a company's tax return, it must also be used on the company's GAAP financial statements.

[24] If data on the precise timing of quarterly sales were available, the answer would differ because the cost of goods sold would be determined during the quarter rather than at the end of the quarter.

Alternatively, the cost of the last 5,600 units purchased is allocated to cost of goods sold under LIFO:

1,900 units at $45 per unit + 2,200 units at $43 per unit + 1,500 units at $41 per unit = $241,600

Exhibit 7 summarizes and compares inventory costing methods.

EXHIBIT 7	Summary Table on Inventory Costing Methods		
Method	Description	Cost of Goods Sold When Prices Are Rising, Relative to Other Two Methods	Ending Inventory When Prices Are Rising, Relative to Other Two Methods
FIFO (first in, first out)	Assumes that earliest items purchased were sold first	Lowest	Highest
LIFO (last in, first out)	Assumes most recent items purchased were sold first	Highest[a]	Lowest[a]
Weighted average cost	Averages total costs over total units available	Middle	Middle

[a]Assumes no LIFO layer liquidation. **LIFO layer liquidation** occurs when the volume of sales rises above the volume of recent purchases so that some sales are made from existing, relatively low-priced inventory rather than from more recent purchases.

4.2 Issues in Expense Recognition

The following sections cover applications of the principles of expense recognition to certain common situations.

4.2.1 Doubtful Accounts

When a company sells its products or services on credit, it is likely that some customers will ultimately default on their obligations (i.e., fail to pay). At the time of the sale, it is not known which customer will default. (If it were known that a particular customer would ultimately default, presumably a company would not sell on credit to that customer.) One possible approach to recognizing credit losses on customer receivables would be for the company to wait until such time as a customer defaulted and only then recognize the loss (**direct write-off method**). Such an approach would usually not be consistent with generally accepted accounting principles.

Under the matching principle, at the time revenue is recognized on a sale, a company is required to record an estimate of how much of the revenue will ultimately be uncollectible. Companies make such estimates based on previous experience with uncollectible accounts. Such estimates may be expressed as a proportion of the overall amount of sales, the overall amount of receivables, or the amount of receivables overdue by a specific amount of time. The company records its estimate of uncollectible amounts as an expense on the income statement, not as a direct reduction of revenues.

4.2.2 Warranties

At times, companies offer warranties on the products they sell. If the product proves deficient in some respect that is covered under the terms of the warranty, the company will incur an expense to repair or replace the product. At the time of sale, the company does not know the amount of future expenses it will incur in connection with its warranties. One possible approach would be for a company to wait until actual expenses are incurred under the warranty and to reflect the expense at that time. However, this would not result in a matching of the expense with the associated revenue.

Under the matching principle, a company is required to estimate the amount of future expenses resulting from its warranties, to recognize an estimated warranty expense in the period of the sale, and to update the expense as indicated by experience over the life of the warranty.

4.2.3 Depreciation and Amortization

Companies commonly incur costs to obtain long-lived assets. **Long-lived assets** are assets expected to provide economic benefits over a future period of time greater than one year. Examples are land (property), plant, equipment, and **intangible assets** (assets lacking physical substance) such as trademarks. The costs of most long-lived assets are allocated over the period of time during which they provide economic benefits. The two main types of long-lived assets whose costs are *not* allocated over time are land and those intangible assets with indefinite useful lives.

Depreciation is the process of systematically allocating costs of long-lived assets over the period during which the assets are expected to provide economic benefits. "Depreciation" is the term commonly applied to this process for physical long-lived assets such as plant and equipment (land is not depreciated), and **amortization** is the term commonly applied to this process for intangible long-lived assets with a finite useful life.[25] Examples of intangible long-lived assets with a finite useful life include an acquired mailing list, an acquired patent with a set expiration date, and an acquired copyright with a set legal life. The term "amortization" is also commonly applied to the systematic allocation of a premium or discount relative to the face value of a fixed-income security over the life of the security.

IAS No. 16, *Property, Plant, and Equipment*, requires that the depreciable amount (cost less residual value) be allocated on a systematic basis over the remaining useful life of the asset. The method used to compute depreciation must reflect the pattern over which the economic benefits of the asset are expected to be consumed. IAS No. 16 does not prescribe a particular method for computing depreciation but notes that several methods are commonly used, such as the straight-line method, diminishing balance method (accelerated depreciation), and the units of production method (depreciation varies depending upon production or usage).

The **straight-line method** allocates evenly the cost of long-lived assets less estimated residual value over the estimated useful life of an asset. (The term

---

[25] Under SFAS No. 142, intangible assets with indefinite life are not amortized. Instead, they are tested at least annually for impairment (i.e., if the current value of an intangible asset is materially lower than its value in the company's books, the value of the asset is considered to be impaired and its value must be decreased).

"straight line" derives from the fact that the annual depreciation expense, if represented as a line graph over time, would be a straight line. In addition, a plot of the cost of the asset minus the cumulative amount of annual depreciation expense, if represented as a line graph over time, would be a straight line with a negative downward slope.) Calculating depreciation and amortization requires two significant estimates: the estimated useful life of an asset and the estimated residual value (also known as "salvage value") of an asset. Under IAS No. 16, the residual value is the amount that the company expects to receive upon sale of the asset at the end of its useful life. Example 10 assumes that an item of equipment is depreciated using the straight-line method and illustrates how the annual depreciation expense varies under different estimates of the useful life and estimated residual value of an asset. As shown, annual depreciation expense is sensitive to both the estimated useful life and to the estimated residual value.

EXAMPLE 10

Sensitivity of Annual Depreciation Expense to Varying Estimates of Useful Life and Residual Value

Using the straight-line method of depreciation, annual depreciation expense is calculated as

$$\frac{\text{Cost} - \text{Residual value}}{\text{Estimated useful life}}$$

Assume the cost of an asset is $10,000. If, for example, the residual value of the asset is estimated to be $0 and its useful life is estimated to be 5 years, the annual depreciation expense under the straight-line method would be ($10,000 − $0)/5 years = $2,000. In contrast, holding the estimated useful life of the asset constant at 5 years but increasing the estimated residual value of the asset to $4,000 would result in annual depreciation expense of only $1,200 [calculated as ($10,000 − $4,000)/5 years]. Alternatively, holding the estimated residual value at $0 but increasing the estimated useful life of the asset to 10 years would result in annual depreciation expense of only $1,000 [calculated as ($10,000 − $0)/10 years]. Exhibit 8 shows annual depreciation expense for various combinations of estimated useful life and residual value.

EXHIBIT 8 — Annual Depreciation Expense (in Dollars)

Estimated Useful Life (Years)	Estimated Residual Value					
	0	1,000	2,000	3,000	4,000	5,000
2	5,000	4,500	4,000	3,500	3,000	2,500
4	2,500	2,250	2,000	1,750	1,500	1,250
5	2,000	1,800	1,600	1,400	1,200	1,000
8	1,250	1,125	1,000	875	750	625
10	1,000	900	800	700	600	500

Generally, alternatives to the straight-line method of depreciation are called **accelerated methods of depreciation** because they accelerate (i.e., speed up) the timing of depreciation. Accelerated depreciation methods allocate a greater proportion of the cost to the early years of an asset's useful life. These methods are appropriate if the plant or equipment is expected to be used up faster in the early years (e.g., an automobile). A commonly used accelerated method is the **diminishing balance method**, as mentioned in IAS No. 16 (also known as the declining balance method). The diminishing balance method is demonstrated in Example 11.

EXAMPLE 11

An Illustration of Diminishing Balance Depreciation

Assume the cost of computer equipment was $11,000, the estimated residual value is $1,000, and the estimated useful life is five years. Under the diminishing or declining balance method, the first step is to determine the straight-line rate, the rate at which the asset would be depreciated under the straight-line method. This rate is measured as 100 percent divided by the useful life or 20 percent for a five-year useful life. Under the straight-line method, 1/5 or 20 percent of the depreciable cost of the asset (here, $11,000 − $1,000 = $10,000) would be expensed each year for five years: The depreciation expense would be $2,000 per year.

The next step is to determine an acceleration factor that approximates the pattern of the asset's wear. Common acceleration factors are 150 percent and 200 percent. The latter is known as **double declining balance depreciation** because it depreciates the asset at double the straight-line rate. Using the 200 percent acceleration factor, the diminishing balance rate would be 40 percent (20 percent × 2.0). This rate is then applied to the remaining undepreciated balance of the asset each period (known as the **net book value**).

At the beginning of the first year, the net book value is $11,000. Depreciation expense for the first full year of use of the asset would be 40 percent of $11,000, or $4,400. Under this method, the residual value, if any, is generally not used in the computation of the depreciation each period (the 40 percent is applied to $11,000 rather than to $11,000 minus residual value). However, the company will stop taking depreciation when the salvage value is reached.

At the beginning of Year 2, the net book value is measured as

Asset cost	$11,000
Less: Accumulated depreciation	(4,400)
Net book value	$ 6,600

For the second full year, depreciation expense would be $6,600 × 40 percent, or $2,640. At the end of the second year (i.e., beginning of the third year), a total of $7,040 ($4,400 + $2,640) of depreciation would have been recorded. So, the remaining net book value at the beginning of the third year would be

Asset cost	$11,000
Less: Accumulated depreciation	(7,040)
Net book value	$ 3,960

For the third full year, depreciation would be $3,960 × 40 percent, or $1,584. At the end of the third year, a total of $8,624 ($4,400 + $2,640 + $1,584) of depreciation would have been recorded. So, the remaining net book value at the beginning of the fourth year would be

Asset cost	$11,000
Less: Accumulated depreciation	(8,624)
Net book value	$ 2,376

For the fourth full year, depreciation would be $2,376 × 40 percent, or $950. At the end of the fourth year, a total of $9,574 ($4,400 + $2,640 + $1,584 + $950) of depreciation would have been recorded. So, the remaining net book value at the beginning of the fifth year would be

Asset cost	$11,000
Less: Accumulated depreciation	(9,574)
Net book value	$ 1,426

For the fifth year, if deprecation were determined as in previous years, it would amount to $570 ($1,426 × 40 percent). However, this would result in a remaining net book value of the asset below its estimated residual value of $1,000. So, instead, only $426 would be depreciated, leaving a $1,000 net book value at the end of the fifth year.

Asset cost	$11,000
Less: Accumulated depreciation	(10,000)
Net book value	$ 1,000

Companies often use a zero or small residual value, which creates problems for diminishing balance depreciation because the asset never fully depreciates. In order to fully depreciate the asset over the initially estimated useful life when a zero or small residual value is assumed, companies often adopt a depreciation policy that combines the diminishing balance and straight-line methods. An example would be a depreciation policy of using double-declining balance depreciation and switching to the straight-line method halfway through the useful life.

Under accelerated depreciation methods, there is a higher depreciation expense in early years relative to the straight-line method. This results in higher expenses and lower net income in the early depreciation years. In later years, there is a reversal with accelerated depreciation expense lower than straight-line depreciation. Accelerated depreciation is sometimes referred to as a "conservative" accounting choice because it results in lower net income in the early years of asset use.

For those intangible assets that must be amortized (those with an identifiable useful life), the process is the same as for depreciation; only the name of the expense is different. IAS No. 38, *Intangible Assets*, states that if a pattern cannot be determined over the useful life, then the straight-line method should be used. In most cases under international accounting standards and U.S. GAAP, amortizable intangible assets are amortized using the straight-line method with no residual value. **Goodwill**[26] and intangible assets with indefinite life are not amortized. Instead, they are tested at least annually for impairment (i.e., if the current value of an intangible asset or goodwill is materially lower than its value in the company's books, the value of the asset is considered to be impaired and its value in the company's books must be decreased).

In summary, to calculate depreciation and amortization, a company must choose a method, estimate the asset's useful life, and estimate residual value. Clearly, different choices have a differing effect on depreciation or amortization expense and, therefore, on reported net income.

4.3 Implications for Financial Analysis

A company's estimates for doubtful accounts and/or for warranty expenses can affect its reported net income. Similarly, a company's choice of depreciation or amortization method, estimates of assets' useful lives, and estimates of assets' residual values can affect reported net income. These are only a few of the choices and estimates that affect a company's reported net income.

As with revenue recognition policies, a company's choice of expense recognition can be characterized by its relative conservatism. A policy that results in recognition of expenses later rather than sooner is considered less conservative. In addition, many items of expense require the company to make estimates that can significantly affect net income. Analysis of a company's financial statements, and particularly comparison of one company's financial statements with those of another, requires an understanding of differences in these estimates and their potential impact.

If, for example, a company shows a significant year-to-year change in its estimates of uncollectible accounts as a percentage of sales, warranty expenses as percentage of sales, or estimated useful lives of assets, the analyst should seek to understand the underlying reasons. Do the changes reflect a change in business operations (e.g., lower estimated warranty expenses reflecting recent experience of fewer warranty claims because of improved product quality)? Or are the changes seemingly unrelated to changes in business operations and thus possibly a signal that a company is manipulating estimates in order to achieve a particular effect on its reported net income?

As another example, if two companies in the same industry have dramatically different estimates for uncollectible accounts as a percentage of their sales, warranty expenses as a percentage of sales, or estimated useful lives as a percentage of assets, it is important to understand the underlying reasons. Are the differences consistent with differences in the two companies' business operations (e.g., lower uncollectible accounts for one company reflecting a different, more creditworthy customer base or possibly stricter credit policies)? Another difference consistent with differences in business operations would be a difference in estimated useful lives of assets if one of the companies employs newer equipment. Or, alternatively, are the differences seemingly inconsistent with differences in the two companies' business operations, possibly signaling that a company is manipulating estimates?

Information about a company's accounting policies and significant estimates are described in the footnotes to the financial statements and in the management discussion and analysis section of a company's annual report.

---

[26] Goodwill is recorded in acquisitions and is the amount by which the price to purchase an entity exceeds the amount of net identifiable assets acquired (the total amount of identifiable assets acquired less liabilities assumed).

When possible, the monetary effect of differences in expense recognition policies and estimates can facilitate more meaningful comparisons with a single company's historical performance or across a number of companies. An analyst can use the monetary effect to adjust the reported expenses so that they are on a comparable basis.

Even when the monetary effects of differences in policies and estimates cannot be calculated, it is generally possible to characterize the relative conservatism of the policies and estimates and, therefore, to qualitatively assess how such differences might affect reported expenses and thus financial ratios.

NONRECURRING ITEMS AND NONOPERATING ITEMS

5

From a company's income statements, we can see its earnings from last year and in the previous year. Looking forward, the question is: What will the company earn next year and in the years after?

To assess a company's future earnings, it is helpful to separate those prior years' items of income and expense that are likely to continue in the future from those items that are less likely to continue.[27] Some items from prior years are clearly not expected to continue in the future periods and are separately disclosed on a company's income statement. Two such items are 1) discontinued operations, and 2) extraordinary items (the latter category is no longer permitted under IFRS). These two items, if applicable, must be reported separately from continuing operations.[28]

For other items on a company's income statement, such as unusual items, accounting changes, and nonoperating income, the likelihood of their continuing in the future is somewhat less clear and requires the analyst to make some judgments.

5.1 Discontinued Operations

When a company disposes of or establishes a plan to dispose of one of its component operations and will have no further involvement in the operation, the income statement reports separately the effect of this disposal as a "discontinued" operation under both IFRS and U.S. GAAP. Financial standards provide various criteria for reporting the effect separately, which are generally that the discontinued component must be separable both physically and operationally.[29]

Because the discontinued operation will no longer provide earnings (or cash flow) to the company, an analyst can eliminate discontinued operations in formulating expectations about a company's future financial performance.

In Exhibit 2, Kraft reported a loss from discontinued operations of $4 million in 2004 and earnings of $97 million in both 2003 and 2002. In Footnote 5 of its financial statements, Kraft explains that it sold substantially all of its sugar confectionary business (including brands such as Life Savers and Altoids). The $4 million loss and $97 million earnings refer to the amount of loss (earnings) of the sugar confectionary business in each of those years.

---

[27] In business writing, items expected to continue in the future are often described as "persistent" or "permanent," whereas those not expected to continue are described as "transitory."

[28] These requirements apply to material amounts.

[29] IFRS No. 5, *Non-Current Assets Held for Sale and Discontinued Operations*, paragraphs 31–33.

5.2 Extraordinary Items

IAS No. 1 prohibits classification of any income or expense items as being "extraordinary."[30] Under U.S. GAAP, an extraordinary item is one that is both unusual in nature and infrequent in occurrence. Extraordinary items are presented separately on the income statement and allow a reader of the statements to see that these items are not part of a company's operating activities and are not expected to occur on an ongoing basis. Extraordinary items are shown net of tax and appear on the income statement below discontinued operations. An example of an extraordinary item is provided in Example 12.

EXAMPLE 12

Extraordinary Gain: Purchase of a Business for Less than the Fair Value of the Identifiable Net Assets

Vicon Industries in its annual report made the following disclosure:

> On October 1, 2004, the Company entered into an agreement to purchase all of the operating assets of Videotronic Infosystems GmbH ("Videotronic"), a Germany based video system supplier which was operating under insolvency protection, for 700,000 Eurodollars [sic] (approximately $868,000)... During the year ended September 30, 2005, the Company recognized a $211,000 extraordinary gain on the recovery of Videotronic net assets in excess of their allocated purchase price. Such gain includes adjustments to assigned values of accounts receivable, inventories, trade payables and severance liabilities.

Source: Vicon Industries 10-K Report for fiscal year ended 30 September 2005, filed 29 December 2005: Note 15.

Companies apply judgment to determine whether an item is extraordinary based on guidance from accounting standards (Accounting Principles Board Opinion No. 30). Judgment on whether an item is unusual in nature requires consideration of the company's environment, including its industry and geography. Determining whether an item is infrequent in occurrence is based on expectations of whether it will occur again in the near future. Standard setters offer specific guidance in some cases. For example, following Hurricanes Katrina and Rita in 2005, the American Institute of Certified Public Accountants issued Technical Practice Aid 5400.05, which states (the material in square brackets has been added): "A natural disaster [such as a hurricane, tornado, fire, or earthquake] of a type that is reasonably expected to re-occur would not meet both conditions [for classification as an extraordinary item]."

Given the requirements for classification of an item as extraordinary—unusual and infrequent—an analyst can generally eliminate extraordinary items from expectations about a company's future financial performance unless there is some indication that such an extraordinary item may reoccur.

---

[30] IAS No. 1, *Presentation of Financial Statements*, paragraph 85, effective 2005. In prior years, classification of items as extraordinary was permitted.

5.3 Unusual or Infrequent Items

Items that do not meet the definition of extraordinary are shown as part of a company's continuing operations. Items that are unusual or infrequent—but not both—cannot be shown as extraordinary. For example, restructuring charges, such as costs to close plants and employee termination costs, are considered part of a company's ordinary activities. As another example, gains and losses arising when a company sells an asset or part of a business for more or less than its carrying value are also disclosed separately on the income statement but are not considered extraordinary because such sales are considered ordinary business activities.[31]

Highlighting the unusual or infrequent nature of these items assists an analyst in judging the likelihood that such items will reoccur.

In Exhibit 2, Kraft's income statement showed several such infrequent but not unusual items, all of which are included as part of operating income. The company reported a $111 million loss in 2002 from "integration costs and a loss on sale of a food factory," followed by a $13 million reduction of these costs in 2003. In Note 14 of its financial statements, the company explains that these costs arose from consolidating production lines in North America. Also, the company reported $142 million, $6 million, and $603 million in 2002, 2003, and 2004, respectively, for "asset impairment and exit costs" and explains in the footnotes that the large costs in 2004 are related to its restructuring program and reflect asset disposals, severance, and other implementation aspects.

Finally, Kraft reported an $80 million gain on the sale of businesses in 2002 and a $31 million gain in 2003, followed by a $3 million loss on the sale of businesses in 2004. In Note 14 of its financial statements, Kraft explains that the $80 million gain in 2002 arose from the sale of its Latin American bakery ingredient business and several small food businesses; the $31 million gain in 2003 arose from the sale of a European rice business and an Italian fresh cheese business; and the $3 million loss in 2004 arose from the sale of a Brazilian snack nuts business and Norwegian candy business trademarks. An analyst would seek to understand how these disposals fit with the company's strategy and what effect, if material, these disposals would have on the company's future operations.

Generally, in forecasting future operations, an analyst would assess whether the items reported are likely to reoccur and also possible implications for future earnings. It is generally not advisable simply to ignore all unusual items.

5.4 Changes in Accounting Standards

At times, standard setters issue new pronouncements that require companies to change accounting principles. In other cases, changes in accounting principles (e.g., from one acceptable inventory costing method to another) are made for other reasons, such as providing a better reflection of the company's performance. Changes in accounting principles are reported through retrospective application,[32] unless it is impractical to do so. *Retrospective application* means that the financial statements for all fiscal years shown in a company's financial report are presented as if the newly adopted accounting principle had been used

---

[31] In its financial statement footnotes, Groupe Danone provides a reconciliation between operating income under French GAAP, which excludes certain exceptional items (such as gains and losses on disposals), and U.S. GAAP.

[32] IAS No. 8, *Accounting Policies, Changes in Accounting Estimates and Errors*, and FASB Financial Accounting Statement No. 154, *Accounting Changes and Error Corrections*.

throughout the entire period. Footnotes to the financial statements describe the change and explain the justification for the change.

Because changes in accounting principles are retrospectively applied, the financial statements that appear within a financial report are comparable. So, if a company's annual report for 2006 includes its financial statements for fiscal years 2004, 2005, and 2006, all of these statements will be comparable.

In years prior to 2005, under both IFRS and U.S. GAAP, the cumulative effect of changes in accounting policies was typically shown at the bottom of the income statement in the year of change instead of using retrospective application. It is possible that future accounting standards may occasionally require a company to report the change differently than retrospective application. Footnote disclosures are required to explain how the transition from the old standard to the new one was handled. During the period when companies make the transition from the old standard to the new, an analyst would examine disclosures to ensure comparability across companies.

In contrast to changes in accounting policies (such as whether to expense the cost of employee stock options), companies sometimes make *changes in accounting estimates* (such as the useful life of a depreciable asset). Changes in accounting estimates are handled prospectively, with the change affecting the financial statements for the period of change and future periods.[33] No adjustments are made to prior statements, and the adjustment is not shown on the face of the income statement. Significant changes should be disclosed in the footnotes.

Another possible adjustment is a *correction of an error for a prior period* (e.g., in financial statements issued for an earlier year). This cannot be handled by simply adjusting the current period income statement. Correction of an error for a prior period is handled by restating the financial statements (including the balance sheet, statement of owners' equity, and statement of cash flows) for the prior periods presented in the current financial statements.[34] Footnote disclosures are required regarding the error. These disclosures should be examined carefully because they may reveal weaknesses in the company's accounting systems and financial controls.

5.5 Nonoperating Items: Investing and Financing Activities

Nonoperating items are reported separately from operating income. For example, if a nonfinancial service company invests in equity or debt securities issued by another company, any interest, dividends, or profits from sales of these securities will be shown as nonoperating income. In general, for nonfinancial services companies,[35] nonoperating income that is disclosed separately on the income statement (or in the notes) includes amounts earned through investing activities.

Among nonoperating items on the income statement (or accompanying notes), nonfinancial service companies also disclose the interest expense on their debt securities, including amortization of any discount or premium. The amount of interest expense is related to the amount of a company's borrowings and is generally described in the financial footnotes. For financial service companies, interest income and expense are likely components of operating activities.

---

[33] Ibid.

[34] Ibid.

[35] Examples of financial services firms are insurance companies, banks, brokers, dealers, and investment companies.

In practice, investing and financing activities may be disclosed on a net basis, with the components disclosed separately in the footnotes. In its income statement for 2004, Kraft, for example, disclosed net interest and other debt expense of $666 million. The financial statement footnotes (not shown) further disclose that Kraft's total interest expense was $679 million and interest income was $13 million, thus the net $666 million. Groupe Danone's footnotes provide similar disclosures.

For purposes of assessing a company's future performance, the amount of financing expense will depend on the company's financing policy (target capital structure) and borrowing costs. The amount of investing income will depend on the purpose and success of investing activities. For a nonfinancial company, a significant amount of financial income would typically warrant further exploration. What are the reasons underlying the company's investments in the securities of other companies? Is the company simply investing excess cash in short-term securities to generate income higher than cash deposits, or is the company purchasing securities issued by other companies for strategic reasons, such as access to raw material supply or research?

EARNINGS PER SHARE   6

One metric of particular importance to an equity investor is earnings per share (EPS). EPS is an input into ratios such as the price/earnings ratio. Additionally, each shareholder in a company owns a different number of shares. A presentation of EPS, therefore, enables each shareholder to compute his or her share of the company's earnings. Under IFRS, IAS No. 33, *Earnings Per Share*, requires the presentation of EPS on the face of the income statement for net profit or loss (net income) and profit or loss (income) from continuing operations. Similar presentation is required under U.S. GAAP by Financial Accounting Statement No. 128, *Earnings Per Share*. This section outlines the calculations for EPS and explains how the calculation differs for a simple versus complex capital structure.

6.1 Simple versus Complex Capital Structure

A company's capital is composed of its equity and debt. Some types of equity have preference over others, and some debt (and other instruments) may be converted into equity. Under IFRS, the type of equity for which EPS is presented are ordinary shares. **Ordinary shares** are those equity shares that are subordinate to all other types of equity. This is the basic ownership of the company—the equityholders who are paid last in a liquidation of the company and who benefit the most when the company does well. Under U.S. GAAP, this equity is referred to as **common stock** or **common shares**, reflecting U.S. language usage. The terms "ordinary shares," "common stock," and "common shares" are used equivalently in the remaining discussion.

When a company has any securities that are potentially convertible into common stock, it is said to have a complex capital structure. Specific examples of securities that are potentially convertible into common stock include convertible bonds, convertible preferred stock, employee stock options, and warrants.[36] If a

---

[36] A warrant is a call option typically attached to securities issued by a company, such as bonds. A warrant gives the holder the right to acquire the company's stock from the company at a specified price within a specified time period. IFRS and U.S. GAAP standards regarding earnings per share apply equally to call options, warrants, and equivalent instruments.

company's capital structure does not include securities that are potentially convertible into common stock, it is said to have a simple capital structure.

The distinction between simple versus complex capital structure is relevant to the calculation of EPS because any securities that are potentially convertible into common stock could, as a result of conversion, potentially dilute (i.e., decrease) EPS. Information about such a potential dilution is valuable to a company's current and potential shareholders; therefore, accounting standards require companies to disclose what their EPS would be if all dilutive securities were converted into common stock. The EPS that would result if all dilutive securities were converted is called **diluted EPS**. In contrast, **basic EPS** is calculated using the actual earnings available to common stock and the weighted average number of shares outstanding.

Companies are required to report both their basic EPS and their diluted EPS. Kraft reported basic EPS of $1.56 and diluted EPS of $1.55 for 2004, lower than EPS (from continuing operations) of $1.95 for 2003. Danone reported basic EPS of 1.26 and diluted EPS of 1.25 for 2004, much lower than 2003. An analyst would try to determine the causes underlying the changes in EPS, a topic we will address following an explanation of the calculations of both basic and diluted EPS.

6.2 Basic EPS

Basic EPS is the amount of income available to common shareholders divided by the weighted average number of common shares outstanding over a period. The amount of income available to common shareholders is the amount of net income remaining after preferred dividends (if any) have been paid. Thus, the formula to calculate basic EPS is:

$$\text{Basic EPS} = \frac{\text{Net income} - \text{Preferred dividends}}{\text{Weighted average number of shares outstanding}} \qquad \text{(1)}$$

The weighted average number of shares outstanding is a time weighting of common shares outstanding, and the methodology applies to calculating diluted EPS. As an example, assume a company began the year with 2,000,000 shares outstanding and repurchased 100,000 shares on 1 July. The weighted average number of shares outstanding would be the sum of 2,000,000 shares × 1/2 year + 1,900,000 shares × 1/2 year, or 1,950,000 shares. So, the company would use 1,950,000 shares in calculating its basic EPS.

If the number of shares of common stock increases as a result of a stock dividend, stock bonus, or a stock split (all three represent the receipt of additional shares by existing shareholders), the EPS calculation reflects the change retroactively to the beginning of the period.

Examples of a basic EPS computation are presented in Examples 13, 14, and 15.

EXAMPLE 13

A Basic EPS Calculation (1)

For the year ended 31 December 2006, Shopalot Company had net income of $1,950,000. The company had an average of 1,500,000 shares of common stock outstanding, no preferred stock, and no convertible securities. What was Shopalot's basic EPS?

Solution: Shopalot's basic EPS was $1.30, calculated as $1,950,000 divided by 1,500,000 shares.

EXAMPLE 14

A Basic EPS Calculation (2)

For the year ended 31 December 2006, Angler Products had net income of $2,500,000. The company declared and paid $200,000 of dividends on preferred stock. The company also had the following common stock share information:

Shares outstanding on 1 January 2006	1,000,000
Shares issued on 1 April 2006	200,000
Shares repurchased (treasury shares) on 1 October 2006	(100,000)
Shares outstanding on 31 December 2006	1,100,000

1. What is the company's weighted average number of shares outstanding?
2. What is the company's basic EPS?

Solution to 1: The weighted average number of shares outstanding is determined by the length of time each quantity of shares was outstanding:

$1,000,000 \times (3 \text{ months}/12 \text{ months}) =$	250,000
$1,200,000 \times (6 \text{ months}/12 \text{ months}) =$	600,000
$1,100,000 \times (3 \text{ months}/12 \text{ months}) =$	275,000
Weighted average number of shares outstanding	1,125,000

Solution to 2: Basic EPS is (Net income − Preferred dividends)/ Weighted average number of shares = ($2,500,000 − $200,000)/ 1,125,000 = $2.04

EXAMPLE 15

A Basic EPS Calculation (3)

Assume the same facts as in Example 14 except that on 1 December 2006, the company institutes a 2 for 1 stock split. Each shareholder receives two shares in exchange for each current share that he or she owns. What is the company's basic EPS?

Solution: For EPS calculation purposes, a stock split is treated as if it occurred at the beginning of the period. The weighted average number of shares would, therefore, be 2,250,000, and the basic EPS would be $1.02.

6.3 Diluted EPS

If a company has a simple capital structure (i.e., one with no potentially dilutive securities), then its basic EPS is equal to its diluted EPS. If, however, a company has dilutive securities, its diluted EPS is lower than its basic EPS. The sections below describe the effects of three types of potentially dilutive securities: convertible preferred, convertible debt, and employee stock options.

6.3.1 Diluted EPS when a Company Has Convertible Preferred Stock Outstanding

When a company has convertible preferred stock outstanding, diluted EPS is calculated using the **if-converted method** (i.e., what EPS would have been *if* the convertible preferred securities had been converted at the beginning of the period). What would have been the effect if the securities had been converted? If the convertible preferred securities had been converted, these securities would no longer be outstanding; instead, additional common stock would be outstanding. Therefore, if such a conversion had been taken place, the company would not have paid preferred dividends and would have had more shares of common stock.

The diluted EPS using the if-converted method for convertible preferred stock is equal to the amount of net income divided by the weighted average number of shares outstanding plus the new shares of common stock that would be issued upon conversion of the preferred. Thus, the formula to calculate diluted EPS using the if-converted method for preferred stock is:

$$\text{Diluted EPS} = \frac{(\text{Net income})}{\left(\begin{array}{c}\text{Weighted average number of shares}\\\text{outstanding} + \text{New common shares that}\\\text{would have been issued at conversion}\end{array}\right)} \qquad (2)$$

A diluted EPS calculation using the if-converted method for preferred stock is provided in Example 16.

EXAMPLE 16

A Diluted EPS Calculation Using the If-Converted Method for Preferred Stock

For the year ended 31 December 2006, Bright-Warm Utility Company had net income of $1,750,000. The company had an average of 500,000 shares of common stock outstanding, 20,000 shares of convertible preferred, and no other potentially dilutive securities. Each share of preferred pays a dividend of $10 per share, and each is convertible into five shares of the company's common stock. Calculate the company's basic and diluted EPS.

Solution: If the 20,000 shares of convertible preferred had each converted into 5 shares of the company's common stock, the company would have had an additional 100,000 shares of common stock (5 shares of common for each of the 20,000 shares of preferred). If the conversion had taken place, the company would not have paid preferred dividends of $200,000 ($10 per share for each of the 20,000 shares of preferred). As shown in Exhibit 9, the company's basic EPS was $3.10 and its diluted EPS was $2.92.

EXHIBIT 9	Calculation of Diluted EPS for Bright-Warm Utility Company Using the If-Converted Method: Case of Preferred Stock	
	Basic EPS	**Diluted EPS Using If-Converted Method**
Net income	$1,750,000	$1,750,000
Preferred dividend	−200,000	0
Numerator	$1,550,000	$1,750,000
Weighted average number of shares outstanding	500,000	500,000
If converted	0	100,000
Denominator	500,000	600,000
EPS	**$3.10**	**$2.92**

6.3.2 *Diluted EPS when a Company Has Convertible Debt Outstanding*

When a company has convertible debt outstanding, the diluted EPS calculation is similar to the calculation for convertible preferred: Diluted EPS is calculated using the if-converted method (i.e., what EPS would have been *if* the convertible debt had been converted at the beginning of the period). If the convertible debt had been converted, the debt securities would no longer be outstanding; instead, additional common stock would be outstanding. Therefore, if such a conversion had taken place, the company would not have paid interest on the convertible debt and would have had more shares of common stock.

To calculate diluted EPS using the if-converted method for convertible debt, the amount of net income available to common shareholders must be increased by the amount of after-tax interest related to the convertible debt. In addition, the weighted average number of shares in the denominator increases by the number of new shares of common stock that would be issued upon conversion of the convertible debt. Thus, the formula to calculate diluted EPS using the if-converted method for convertible debt is:

$$\text{Diluted EPS} = \frac{\begin{array}{c}(\text{Net income} + \text{After-tax interest on} \\ \text{convertible debt} - \text{Preferred dividends})\end{array}}{\begin{array}{c}(\text{Weighted average number of shares} \\ \text{outstanding} + \text{New common shares that} \\ \text{could have been issued at conversion})\end{array}} \qquad (3)$$

A diluted EPS calculation using the if-converted method for convertible debt is provided in Example 17.

EXAMPLE 17

A Diluted EPS Calculation Using the If-Converted Method for Convertible Debt

Oppnox Company reported net income of $750,000 for the year ended 31 December 2005. The company had an average of 690,000 shares of common stock outstanding. In addition, the company has only one potentially dilutive security: $50,000 of 6 percent convertible bonds, convertible into a total of 10,000 shares. Assuming a tax rate of 30 percent, calculate Oppnox's basic and diluted EPS.

Solution: If the convertible debt had been converted, the debt securities would no longer be outstanding; instead, an additional 10,000 shares of common stock would be outstanding. Also, if such a conversion had taken place, the company would not have paid interest on the convertible debt of $3,000, equivalent to $3,000(1 − 0.30) = $2,100 on an after-tax basis. To calculate diluted EPS using the if-converted method for convertible debt, the amount of net income available to common shareholders is increased by $2,100. Also, the weighted average number of shares in the denominator increases by 10,000 shares.

EXHIBIT 10	Calculation of Diluted EPS for Oppnox Company Using the If-Converted Method: Case of a Convertible Bond	
	Basic EPS	Diluted EPS Using If-Converted Method
Net income	$750,000	$750,000
After-tax cost of interest		2,100
Numerator	$750,000	$752,100
Weighted average number of shares outstanding	690,000	690,000
If converted	0	10,000
Denominator	690,000	700,000
EPS	**$1.09**	**$1.07**

6.3.3 Diluted EPS when a Company Has Stock Options, Warrants, or Their Equivalents Outstanding

Under U.S. GAAP, when a company has stock options, warrants, or their equivalents[37] outstanding, the diluted EPS is calculated using the **treasury stock method** (i.e., what EPS would have been *if* the options had been exercised and the company had used the proceeds to repurchase common stock). If the options had been exercised, the company would have received cash for the amount of the option exercise price. The options would no longer be outstanding; instead, additional common stock would be outstanding. Under the treasury stock method, a further calculation is made to adjust the number of shares outstanding by the number of shares that could have been purchased with the cash received upon exercise of the options.

To calculate diluted EPS using the treasury stock method for options, the weighted average number of shares in the denominator increases by the number of new shares of common stock that would be issued upon exercise of the options minus the number of shares that could have been purchased with the cash received upon exercise of the options. No change is made to the numerator. Thus, the formula to calculate diluted EPS using the treasury stock method for options is

$$\text{Diluted EPS} = \frac{(\text{Net income} - \text{Preferred dividends})}{\begin{array}{c}(\text{Weighted average number of shares} \\ \text{outstanding} + \text{New shares that could} \\ \text{have been issued at option exercise} - \\ \text{Shares that could have been purchased} \\ \text{with cash received upon exercise})\end{array}} \qquad (4)$$

---

[37] Hereafter, options, warrants, and their equivalents will be referred to simply as "options" because the accounting treatment is interchangeable for these instruments under IFRS and U.S. GAAP.

A diluted EPS calculation using the treasury stock method for options is provided in Example 18.

EXAMPLE 18

A Diluted EPS Calculation Using the Treasury Stock Method for Options

Hihotech Company reported net income of $2.3 million for the year ended 30 June 2005 and had an average of 800,000 common shares outstanding. The company has outstanding 30,000 options with an exercise price of $35 and no other potentially dilutive securities. Over the year, the company's market price has averaged $55 per share. Calculate the company's basic and diluted EPS.

Solution: Using the treasury stock method, we first calculate that the company would have received $1,050,000 ($35 for each of the 30,000 options exercised) if all the options had been exercised. The options would no longer be outstanding; instead, 30,000 new shares of common stock would be outstanding. Under the treasury stock method, we reduce the number of new shares by the number of shares that could have been purchased with the cash received upon exercise of the options. At an average market price of $55 per share, the $1,050,000 proceeds from option exercise could have purchased 19,091 shares of treasury stock. Therefore, the net new shares issued would have been 10,909 (calculated as 30,000 minus 19,091). No change is made to the numerator. As shown in Exhibit 11, the company's basic EPS was $2.88 and the diluted EPS was $2.84.

EXHIBIT 11	Calculation of Diluted EPS for Hihotech Company Using the Treasury Stock Method: Case of Stock Options	
	Basic EPS	**Diluted EPS Using Treasury Stock Method**
Net income	$2,300,000	$2,300,000
Numerator	$2,300,000	$2,300,000
Weighted average number of shares outstanding	800,000	800,000
If converted	0	10,909
Denominator	800,000	810,909
EPS	**$2.88**	**$2.84**

Under IFRS, IAS No. 33 requires a similar computation but does not refer to it as the "treasury stock method." The company is required to consider that any assumed proceeds are received from the issuance of new shares at the average market price for the period. These new "inferred" shares would be disregarded in the computation of diluted EPS, but the excess of the new shares issued under options contracts over the new "inferred" shares would be added into the weighted average number of shares outstanding. The results are similar to the treasury stock method, as shown in Example 19.

EXAMPLE 19

Diluted EPS for Options under IFRS

Assuming the same facts as in Example 18, calculate the weighted average number of shares outstanding for diluted EPS under IFRS.

Solution: If the options had been converted, the company would have received $1,050,000. If this amount had been received from the issuance of new shares at the average market price of $55 per share, the company would have sold 19,091 shares. The excess of the shares issued under options (30,000) over the shares the company could have sold at market prices (19,091) is 10,909. This amount is added to the weighted average number of shares outstanding of 800,000 to get diluted shares of 810,909. Note that this is the same result as that obtained under U.S. GAAP; it is just derived in a different manner.

6.3.4 Other Issues with Diluted EPS

It is possible that some potentially convertible securities could be **antidilutive** (i.e., their inclusion in the computation would result in an EPS higher than the company's basic EPS). Under accounting standards, antidilutive securities are not included in the calculation of diluted EPS. In general, diluted EPS reflects maximum potential dilution. Example 20 provides an illustration of an antidilutive security.

EXAMPLE 20

An Antidilutive Security

For the year ended 31 December 2006, Dim-Cool Utility Company had net income of $1,750,000. The company had an average of 500,000 shares of common stock outstanding, 20,000 shares of convertible preferred, and no other potentially dilutive securities. Each share of preferred pays a dividend of $10 per share, and each is convertible into three shares of the company's common stock. What was the company's basic and diluted EPS?

Solution: If the 20,000 shares of convertible preferred had each converted into 3 shares of the company's common stock, the company would have had an additional 60,000 shares of common stock (3 shares of common for each of the 20,000 shares of preferred). If the conversion had taken place, the company would not have paid preferred dividends of $200,000 ($10 per share for each of the 20,000 shares of preferred). The effect of using the if-converted method would be EPS of $3.13, as shown in Exhibit 12. Because this is greater than the company's basic EPS of $3.10, the securities are said to be antidilutive and the effect of their conversion would not be included in diluted EPS. Diluted EPS would be the same as basic EPS (i.e., $3.10).

EXHIBIT 12	Calculation for an Antidilutive Security	
	Basic EPS	**Diluted EPS Using If-Converted Method**
Net income	$1,750,000	$1,750,000
Preferred dividend	−200,000	0
Numerator	$1,550,000	$1,750,000
Weighted average number of shares outstanding	500,000	500,000
If converted	0	60,000
Denominator	500,000	560,000
EPS	$3.10	$3.13[a]

[a]Exceeds basic EPS; security is antidilutive and, therefore, not included.

7   ANALYSIS OF THE INCOME STATEMENT

In this section, we apply two analytical tools to analyze the income statement: common-size analysis and income statement ratios. In analyzing the income statement, the objective is to assess a company's performance over a period of time—compared with its own historical performance or to the performance of another company.

7.1 Common-Size Analysis of the Income Statement

Common-size analysis of the income statement can be performed by stating each line item on the income statement as a percentage of revenue.[38] Common-size statements facilitate comparison across time periods (time-series analysis) and across companies of different sizes (cross-sectional analysis).

To illustrate, Panel A of Exhibit 13 presents an income statement for three hypothetical companies. Company A and Company B, each with $10 million in sales, are larger (as measured by sales) than Company C, which has only $2 million in sales. In addition, Companies A and B both have higher operating profit: $2 million and $1.5 million, respectively, compared with Company C's operating profit of only $400,000.

EXHIBIT 13

Panel A: Income Statements for Companies A, B, and C ($)

	A	B	C
Sales	$10,000,000	$10,000,000	$2,000,000
Cost of sales	3,000,000	7,500,000	600,000
Gross profit	7,000,000	2,500,000	1,400,000
Selling, general, and administrative expenses	1,000,000	1,000,000	200,000
Research and development	2,000,000	–	400,000
Advertising	2,000,000	–	400,000
Operating profit	2,000,000	1,500,000	400,000

Panel B: Common-Size Income Statements for Companies A, B, and C (%)

	A	B	C
Sales	100%	100%	100%
Cost of sales	30	75	30
Gross profit	70	25	70
Selling, general, and administrative expenses	10	10	10
Research and development	20	0	20
Advertising	20	0	20
Operating profit	20	15	20

Note: Each line item is expressed as a percentage of the company's sales.

---

[38] This format can be distinguished as "vertical common-size analysis." As the reading on financial statement analysis discusses, there is another type of common-size analysis, known as "horizontal common-size analysis," that states items in relation to a selected base year value. Unless otherwise indicated, text references to "common-size analysis" refer to vertical analysis.

How can an analyst meaningfully compare the performance of these companies? By preparing a common-size income statement, as illustrated in Panel B, an analyst can readily see that the percentages of Company C's expenses and profit relative to its sales are exactly the same as for Company A. Furthermore, although Company C's operating profit is lower than Company B's in absolute dollars, it is higher in percentage terms (20 percent for Company C compared with only 15 percent for Company B). For each $100 of sales, Company C generates $5 more operating profit than Company B. In other words, Company C is more profitable than Company B based on this measure.

The common-size income statement also highlights differences in companies' strategies. Comparing the two larger companies, Company A reports significantly higher gross profit as a percentage of sales than does Company B (70 percent compared with 25 percent). Given that both companies operate in the same industry, why can Company A generate so much higher gross profit? One possible explanation is found by comparing the operating expenses of the two companies. Company A spends significantly more on research and development and on advertising than Company B. Expenditures on research and development likely result in products with superior technology. Expenditures on advertising likely result in greater brand awareness. So, based on these differences, it is likely that Company A is selling technologically superior products with a better brand image. Company B may be selling its products more cheaply (with a lower gross profit as a percentage of sales) but saving money by not investing in research and development or advertising. In practice, differences across companies are more subtle, but the concept is similar. An analyst, noting significant differences, would seek to understand the underlying reasons for the differences and their implications for the future performance of the companies.

For most expenses, comparison to the amount of sales is appropriate. However, in the case of taxes, it is more meaningful to compare the amount of taxes with the amount of pretax income. Using financial footnote disclosure, an analyst can then examine the causes for differences in effective tax rates. To project the companies' future net income, an analyst would project the companies' pretax income and apply an estimated effective tax rate determined in part by the historical tax rates.

Vertical common-size analysis of the income statement is particularly useful in cross-sectional analysis—comparing companies with each other for a particular time period or comparing a company with industry or sector data. The analyst could select individual peer companies for comparison, use industry data from published sources, or compile data from databases based on a selection of peer companies or broader industry data. For example, Exhibit 14 presents common-size income statement data compiled for the components of the Standard & Poor's 500 classified into the 10 S&P/MSCI Global Industrial Classification System (GICS) sectors using 2005 data. Note that when compiling aggregate data such as this, some level of aggregation is necessary and less detail may be available than from peer company financial statements. The performance of an individual company can be compared with industry or peer company data to evaluate its relative performance.

EXHIBIT 14 — Common-Size Income Statement Statistics for the S&P 500 Classified by S&P/MSCI GICS Sector Data for 2005

Panel A: Median Data

	Energy	Materials	Industrials	Consumer Discretionary	Consumer Staples	Health Care	Financials	Information Technology	Telecom. Services	Utilities
No. observations	29	30	49	85	36	52	87	73	9	31
Operating margin	17.24	11.85	11.94	11.15	12.53	16.73	34.62	12.59	22.85	13.52
Pretax margin	19.17	10.95	10.55	10.17	10.76	14.03	23.28	13.60	18.18	9.27
Taxes	5.63	2.87	2.94	3.59	3.26	4.69	6.51	4.06	4.27	3.12
Profit margin	13.97	7.68	7.28	6.87	6.74	9.35	16.09	11.60	10.91	6.93
Cost of goods sold	66.52	68.35	69.02	63.29	56.24	45.29	42.29	47.17	41.76	76.79
Selling, general, and administrative expenses	3.82	10.20	15.88	22.46	25.07	31.77	28.98	31.81	22.40	4.91

Panel B: Mean Data

	Energy	Materials	Industrials	Consumer Discretionary	Consumer Staples	Health Care	Financials	Information Technology	Telecom. Services	Utilities
No. observations	29	30	49	85	36	52	87	73	9	31
Operating margin	23.13	14.12	13.16	12.69	14.51	17.84	35.45	15.13	20.66	14.60
Pretax margin	23.96	12.58	11.09	10.38	12.03	15.83	23.42	15.25	15.19	8.00
Taxes	7.72	3.38	3.33	3.94	3.81	4.94	6.65	4.98	5.14	2.48
Profit margin	16.02	8.58	7.69	6.32	8.15	10.80	16.37	10.26	9.52	5.68
Cost of goods sold	62.36	67.87	68.92	62.41	56.62	49.20	51.47	46.65	40.61	76.51
Selling, general, and administrative expenses	5.44	13.05	17.45	22.82	25.88	30.48	27.68	33.06	22.81	4.91
Average tax rate computed on mean	32.22	26.89	30.04	37.98	31.65	31.21	28.40	32.66	33.82	30.99

Source: Based on data from Compustat.

7.2 Income Statement Ratios

One aspect of financial performance is profitability. One indicator of profitability is **net profit margin**, also known as **profit margin** and **return on sales**, which is calculated as net income divided by revenue (or sales).[39]

$$\text{Net profit margin} = \frac{\text{Net income}}{\text{Revenue}}$$

Net profit margin measures the amount of income that a company was able to generate for each dollar of revenue. A higher level of net profit margin indicates higher profitability and is thus more desirable. Net profit margin can also be found directly on the common-size income statements.

For Kraft Foods, net profit margin for 2004 was 8.3 percent (calculated as earnings from continuing operations of $2,669 million, divided by net revenues of $32,168 million). To judge this ratio, some comparison is needed. Kraft's profitability can be compared with that of another company or with its own previous performance. Compared with previous years, Kraft's profitability has declined. In 2003, net profit margin was 11.1 percent, and in 2002, it was 11.3 percent.

Another measure of profitability is the gross profit margin. Gross profit is calculated as revenue minus cost of goods sold, and the **gross profit margin** is calculated as the gross profit divided by revenue.

$$\text{Gross profit margin} = \frac{\text{Gross profit}}{\text{Revenue}}$$

The gross profit margin measures the amount of gross profit that a company generated for each dollar of revenue. A higher level of gross profit margin indicates higher profitability and thus is generally more desirable, although differences in gross profit margins across companies reflect differences in companies' strategies. For example, consider a company pursuing a strategy of selling a differentiated product (e.g., a product differentiated based on brand name, quality, superior technology, or patent protection). The company would likely be able to sell the differentiated product at a higher price than a similar, but undifferentiated, product and, therefore, would likely show a higher gross profit margin than a company selling an undifferentiated product. Although a company selling a differentiated product would likely show a higher gross profit margin, this may take time. In the initial stage of the strategy, the company would likely incur costs to create a differentiated product, such as advertising or research and development, which would not be reflected in the gross margin calculation.

Kraft's gross profit (shown in Exhibit 2) was $11,785 in 2002 and $11,887 in 2004. In other words, in absolute terms, Kraft's gross profit increased. However, expressing gross profit as a percentage of net revenues,[40] it is apparent that Kraft's gross profit margin declined, as Exhibit 15 illustrates. From over 40 percent in 2002, Kraft's profit margin declined to 36.95 percent in 2004.

---

[39] In the definition of margin ratios of this type, "sales" is often used interchangeably with "revenue." "Return on sales" has also been used to refer to a class of profitability ratios having revenue in the denominator.

[40] Some items disclosed separately in Kraft's actual income statement have been summarized as "other operating costs (income)" for this display.

EXHIBIT 15	Kraft's Gross Profit Margin					
	2004		**2003**		**2002**	
	$ Millions	**%**	**$ Millions**	**%**	**$ Millions**	**%**
Net revenues	32,168	100.00	30,498	100.00	29,248	100.00
Cost of sales	20,281	63.05	18,531	60.76	17,463	59.71
Gross profit	11,887	**36.95**	11,967	**39.24**	11,785	**40.29**

The net profit margin and gross profit margin are just two of the many subtotals that can be generated from common-size income statements. Other "margins" used by analysts include the **operating margin** (operating income divided by revenue) and **pretax margin** (earnings before taxes divided by revenue).

COMPREHENSIVE INCOME

8

The general expression for net income is revenue minus expenses. There are, however, certain items of revenue and expense that, by accounting convention, are excluded from the net income calculation. To understand how reported shareholders' equity of one period links with reported shareholders' equity of the next period, we must understand these excluded items, known as **other comprehensive income**.

Comprehensive income is defined as "the change in equity [net assets] of a business enterprise during a period from transactions and other events and circumstances from nonowner sources. It includes all changes in equity during a period except those resulting from investments by owners and distributions to owners."[41] So, comprehensive income includes *both* net income and other revenue and expense items that are excluded from the net income calculation (other comprehensive income). Assume, for example, a company's beginning shareholders' equity is €110 million, its net income for the year is €10 million, its cash dividends for the year are €2 million, and there was no issuance or repurchase of common stock. If the company's actual ending shareholders' equity is €123 million, then €5 million [€123 − (€110 + €10 − €2)] has bypassed the net income calculation by being classified as other comprehensive income. (If the company had no other comprehensive income, its ending shareholders' equity would have been €118 million [€110 + €10 − €2].)

In U.S. financial statements, according to U.S. GAAP, four types of items are treated as other comprehensive income.

▶ Foreign currency translation adjustments. In consolidating the financial statements of foreign subsidiaries, the effects of translating the subsidiaries' balance sheet assets and liabilities at current exchange rates are included as other comprehensive income.

---

[41] See SFAS No. 130, Concepts Statement 6, paragraph 70.

▶ Unrealized gains or losses on derivatives contracts accounted for as hedges. Changes in the fair value of derivatives are recorded each period, but these changes in value for certain derivatives (those considered hedges) are treated as other comprehensive income and thus bypass the income statement.

▶ Unrealized holding gains and losses on a certain category of investment securities, namely, available-for-sale securities.

▶ Changes in the funded status of a company's defined benefit post-retirement plans.

The third type of item is perhaps the simplest to illustrate. Holding gains on securities arise when a company owns securities over an accounting period, during which time the securities' value increases. Similarly, holding losses on securities arise when a company owns securities over a period during which time the securities' value decreases. If the company has not sold the securities (i.e., realized the gain or loss), its holding gain or loss is said to be unrealized. The question is: Should the company reflect these unrealized holding gains and losses in its income statement?

According to accounting standards, the answer depends on how the company has categorized the securities. Categorization depends on what the company intends to do with the securities. If the company intends to actively trade the securities, the answer is yes; the company should categorize the securities as **trading securities** and reflect unrealized holding gains and losses in its income statement. However, if the company does not intend to actively trade the securities, the securities may be categorized as available-for-sale securities. For available-for-sale securities, the company does not reflect unrealized holding gains and losses in its income statement. Instead, unrealized holding gains and losses on available-for-sale securities bypass the income statement and go directly to shareholders' equity.

Even though unrealized holding gains and losses on available-for-sale securities are excluded from a company's net income, they are *included* in a company's comprehensive income.

The fourth item, concerning defined benefit post-retirement plans, recently changed. Until recently, so-called minimum pension liability adjustments were treated as other comprehensive income; however, a new standard (SFAS No. 158, which is effective for public companies as of the end of fiscal years after 15 December 2006), will eliminate the need for minimum pension liability adjustments. The need for those adjustments resulted from pension accounting which often created a divergence between a pension plan's funded status and the amount reported on the balance sheet. Under the new standard, companies are required to recognize the overfunded or underfunded status of a defined benefit post-retirement plan as an asset or liability on their balance sheet.[42]

SFAS No. 130 allows companies to report comprehensive income at the bottom of the income statement, on a separate statement of comprehensive income, or as a column in the statement of shareholders' equity; however, presentation alternatives are currently being reviewed by both U.S. and non-U.S. standard setters.

Particularly in comparing financial statements of two companies, it is relevant to examine significant differences in comprehensive income.

---

[42]A defined benefit plan is said to be overfunded if the amount of assets in a trust fund for that plan exceeds that plan's obligations. If the amount of assets in a trust fund for that plan is less than the plan's obligations, it is underfunded.

EXAMPLE 21

Other Comprehensive Income

Assume a company's beginning shareholders' equity is €200 million, its net income for the year is €20 million, its cash dividends for the year are €3 million, and there was no issuance or repurchase of common stock. The company's actual ending shareholders' equity is €227 million.

1. What amount has bypassed the net income calculation by being classified as other comprehensive income?
   A. €0.
   B. €7 million.
   C. €10 million.
   D. €30 million.

2. Which of the following statements best describes other comprehensive income?
   A. Income earned from diverse geographic and segment activities.
   B. Income earned from activities that are not part of the company's ordinary business activities.
   C. Income related to the sale of goods and delivery of services.
   D. Income that increases stockholders' equity but is not reflected as part of net income.

Solution to 1: C is correct. If the company's actual ending shareholders' equity is €227 million, then €10 million [€227− (€200 + €20 − €3)] has bypassed the net income calculation by being classified as other comprehensive income.

Solution to 2: D is correct. Answers A and B are not correct because they do not specify whether such income is reported as part of net income and shown in the income statement. Answer C is not correct because such activities would typically be reported as part of net income on the income statement.

EXAMPLE 22

Other Comprehensive Income in Analysis

An analyst is looking at two comparable companies. Company A has a lower price/earnings (P/E) ratio than Company B, and the conclusion that has been suggested is that Company A is undervalued. As part of examining this conclusion, the analyst decides to explore the question: What would the company's P/E look like if total comprehensive income per share—rather than net income per share—were used as the relevant metric?

	Company A	Company B
Price	$35	$30
EPS	$1.60	$0.90
P/E ratio	21.9×	33.3×
Other comprehensive income (loss) $ million	$(16.272)	$(1.757)
Shares (millions)	22.6	25.1

Solution: As shown by the following table, part of the explanation for Company A's lower P/E ratio may be that its significant losses—accounted for as other comprehensive income (OCI)—are not included in the P/E ratio.

	Company A	Company B
Price	$35	$30
EPS	$1.60	$0.90
OCI (loss) $ million	($16.272)	$(1.757)
Shares (millions)	22.6	25.1
OCI (loss) per share	$(0.72)	$(0.07)
Comprehensive EPS = EPS + OCI per share	$0.88	$0.83
Price/Comprehensive EPS ratio	39.8×	36.1×

SUMMARY

This reading has presented the elements of income statement analysis. The income statement presents information on the financial results of a company's business activities over a period of time; it communicates how much revenue the company generated during a period and what costs it incurred in connection with generating that revenue. A company's net income and its components (e.g., gross margin, operating earnings, and pretax earnings) are critical inputs into both the equity and credit analysis processes. Equity analysts are interested in earnings because equity markets often reward relatively high- or low-earnings growth companies with above-average or below-average valuations, respectively. Fixed-income analysts examine the components of income statements, past and projected, for information on companies' abilities to make promised payments on their debt over the course of the business cycle. Corporate financial announcements frequently emphasize income statements more than the other financial statements. Key points to this reading include the following:

▶ The income statement presents revenue, expenses, and net income.

▶ The components of the income statement include: revenue; cost of sales; sales, general, and administrative expenses; other operating expenses; nonoperating income and expenses; gains and losses; nonrecurring items; net income; and EPS.

▶ An income statement that presents a subtotal for gross profit (revenue minus cost of goods sold) is said to be presented in a multi-step format. One that does not present this subtotal is said to be presented in a single-step format.

▶ Revenue is recognized in the period it is earned, which may or may not be in the same period as the related cash collection. Recognition of revenue when earned is a fundamental principle of accrual accounting.

▶ In limited circumstances, specific revenue recognition methods may be applicable, including percentage of completion, completed contract, installment sales, and cost recovery.

▶ An analyst should identify differences in companies' revenue recognition methods and adjust reported revenue where possible to facilitate comparability. Where the available information does not permit adjustment, an analyst can characterize the revenue recognition as more or less conservative and thus qualitatively assess how differences in policies might affect financial ratios and judgments about profitability.

▶ The general principles of expense recognition include the matching principle. Expenses are matched either to revenue or to the time period in which the expenditure occurs (period costs) or to the time period of expected benefits of the expenditures (e.g., depreciation).

▶ In expense recognition, choice of method (i.e., depreciation method and inventory cost method), as well as estimates (i.e., uncollectible accounts, warranty expenses, assets' useful life, and salvage value) affect a company's reported income. An analyst should identify differences in companies' expense recognition methods and adjust reported financial statements where possible to facilitate comparability. Where the available information does not permit adjustment, an analyst can characterize the policies and estimates as more or less conservative and thus qualitatively assess how differences in policies might affect financial ratios and judgments about companies' performance.

▶ To assess a company's future earnings, it is helpful to separate those prior years' items of income and expense that are likely to continue in the future from those items that are less likely to continue.

▶ Some items from prior years clearly are not expected to continue in future periods and are separately disclosed on a company's income statement. Two such items are 1) discontinued operations and 2) extraordinary items. Both of these items are required to be reported separately from continuing operations.

▶ For other items on a company's income statement, such as unusual items and accounting changes, the likelihood of their continuing in the future is somewhat less clear and requires the analyst to make some judgments.

▶ Nonoperating items are reported separately from operating items. For example, if a nonfinancial service company invests in equity or debt securities issued by another company, any interest, dividends, or profits from sales of these securities will be shown as nonoperating income.

▶ Basic EPS is the amount of income available to common shareholders divided by the weighted average number of common shares outstanding over a period. The amount of income available to common shareholders is the amount of net income remaining after preferred dividends (if any) have been paid.

▶ If a company has a simple capital structure (i.e., one with no potentially dilutive securities), then its basic EPS is equal to its diluted EPS. If, however, a company has dilutive securities, its diluted EPS is lower than its basic EPS.

▶ Diluted EPS is calculated using the if-converted method for convertible securities and the treasury stock method for options.

▶ Common-size analysis of the income statement involves stating each line item on the income statement as a percentage of sales. Common-size statements facilitate comparison across time periods and across companies of different sizes.

▶ Two income-statement-based indicators of profitability are net profit margin and gross profit margin.

▶ Comprehensive income includes *both* net income and other revenue and expense items that are excluded from the net income calculation.

PRACTICE PROBLEMS FOR READING 32

1. Expenses on the income statement may be grouped by:

   A. nature, but not by function.

   B. function, but not by nature.

   C. either function or nature.

2. An example of an expense classification by function is:

   A. tax expense.

   B. interest expense.

   C. cost of goods sold.

3. Denali Limited, a manufacturing company, had the following income statement information:

Revenue	$4,000,000
Cost of goods sold	$3,000,000
Other operating expenses	$ 500,000
Interest expense	$ 100,000
Tax expense	$ 120,000

Denali's gross profit is equal to:

   A. $280,000.

   B. $500,000.

   C. $1,000,000.

4. Under IFRS, income includes increases in economic benefits from:

   A. increases in owners' equity related to owners' contributions.

   B. increases in liabilities not related to owners' contributions.

   C. enhancements of assets not related to owners' contributions.

5. Fairplay had the following information related to the sale of its products during 2006, which was its first year of business:

Revenue	$1,000,000
Returns of goods sold	$ 100,000
Cash collected	$ 800,000
Cost of goods sold	$ 700,000

Under the accrual basis of accounting, how much net revenue would be reported on Fairplay's 2006 income statement?

   A. $200,000.

   B. $800,000.

   C. $900,000.

6. If the outcome of a long-term contract can be measured reliably, the preferred accounting method under both IFRS and U.S. GAAP is:

   A. the installment method.

   B. the completed contract method.

   C. the percentage-of-completion method.

7. At the beginning of 2006, Florida Road Construction entered into a contract to build a road for the government. Construction will take four years. The following information as of 31 December 2006 is available for the contract:

Total revenue according to contract	$10,000,000
Total expected cost	$ 8,000,000
Cost incurred during 2006	$ 1,200,000

Under the completed contract method, how much revenue will be reported in 2006?

   A. None.

   B. $300,000.

   C. $1,500,000.

8. During 2006, Argo Company sold 10 acres of prime commercial zoned land to a builder for $5,000,000. The builder gave Argo a $1,000,000 down payment and will pay the remaining balance of $4,000,000 to Argo in 2007. Argo purchased the land in 1999 for $2,000,000. Using the installment method, how much profit will Argo report for 2006?

   A. None.

   B. $600,000.

   C. $1,000,000.

9. Using the same information as in Question 8, how much profit will Argo report for 2006 by using the cost recovery method?

   A. None.

   B. $1,000,000.

   C. $3,000,000.

10. Under IFRS, revenue from barter transactions should be measured based on the fair value of revenue from:

   A. similar barter transactions with related parties.

   B. similar barter transactions with unrelated parties.

   C. similar nonbarter transactions with unrelated parties.

11. Apex Consignment sells items over the internet for individuals on a consignment basis. Apex receives the items from the owner, lists them for sale on the internet, and receives a 25 percent commission for any items sold. Apex collects the full amount from the buyer and pays the net amount after commission to the owner. Unsold items are returned to the owner after 90 days. During 2006, Apex had the following information:

   ▶ Total sales price of items sold during 2006 on consignment was €2,000,000.

   ▶ Total commissions retained by Apex during 2006 for these items was €500,000.

   How much revenue should Apex report on its 2006 income statement?

   A. €500,000.

   B. €2,000,000.

   C. €1,500,000.

12. During 2007, Accent Toys Plc., which began business in October of that year, purchased 10,000 units of its most popular toy at a cost of £10 per unit in October. In anticipation of heavy December sales, Accent purchased 5,000 additional units in November at a cost of £11 per unit. During 2007, Accent sold 12,000 units at a price of £15 per unit. Under the First In, First Out (FIFO) method, what is Accent's cost of goods sold for 2007?

   A. £105,000.

   B. £120,000.

   C. £122,000.

13. Using the same information as in Question 12, what would Accent's cost of goods sold be under the weighted average cost method?

   A. £120,000.

   B. £122,000.

   C. £124,000.

14. Which inventory method is least likely to be used under IFRS?

   A. First In, First Out (FIFO).

   B. Last In, First Out (LIFO).

   C. Weighted average.

15. At the beginning of 2007, Glass Manufacturing purchased a new machine for its assembly line at a cost of $600,000. The machine has an estimated useful life of 10 years and estimated residual value of $50,000. Under the straight-line method, how much depreciation would Glass take in 2008 for financial reporting purposes?

   A. None.

   B. $55,000.

   C. $60,000.

16. Using the same information as in Question 15, how much depreciation would Glass take in 2007 for financial reporting purposes under the double-declining balance method?

   A. $60,000.

   B. $110,000.

   C. $120,000.

17. Which combination of depreciation methods and useful lives is most conservative in the year a depreciable asset is acquired?

   A. Straight-line depreciation with a long useful life.

   B. Straight-line depreciation with a short useful life.

   C. Declining balance depreciation with a short useful life.

18. Under IFRS, a loss from the destruction of property in a fire would most likely be classified as:

   A. continuing operations.

   B. an extraordinary item.

   C. discontinued operations.

19. For 2007, Flamingo Products had net income of $1,000,000. At 1 January 2007, there were 1,000,000 shares outstanding. On 1 July 2007, the company issued 100,000 new shares for $20 per share. The company paid $200,000 in dividends to common shareholders. What is Flamingo's basic earnings per share for 2007?

   A. $0.73.

   B. $0.91.

   C. $0.95.

20. Cell Services (CSI) had 1,000,000 average shares outstanding during all of 2007. During 2007, CSI also had 10,000 options outstanding with exercise prices of $10 each. The average stock price of CSI during 2007 was $15. For purposes of computing diluted earnings per share, how many shares would be used in the denominator?

   A. 1,000,000.

   B. 1,003,333.

   C. 1,010,000.

SOLUTIONS FOR READING 32

1. C is correct. IAS No. 1 states that expenses may be categorized by either nature or function.

2. C is correct. Cost of goods sold is a classification by function. The other two expenses represent classifications by nature.

3. C is correct. Gross margin is revenue minus cost of goods sold. A represents net income and B represents operating income.

4. C is correct. Under IFRS, income includes increases in economic benefits from increases in assets, enhancement of assets, and decreases in liabilities.

5. C is correct. Net revenue is revenue for goods sold during the period less any returns and allowances, or $1,000,000 minus $100,000 = $900,000. A is incorrect; this represents gross profit. B is incorrect; this is the cash collected that is not used under the accrual basis.

6. C is correct. The preferred method is the percentage-of-completion method. The completed contract method should be used only when the outcome cannot be measured reliably.

7. A is correct. Under the completed contract method, no revenue would be reported until the project is completed. B is incorrect. This is the profit under the percentage-of-completion method. C is incorrect. This is the revenue under the percentage-of-completion method.

8. B is correct. The installment method apportions the cash receipt between cost recovered and profit using the ratio of profit to sales value (i.e., $3,000,000 ÷ $5,000,000 = 60 percent). Argo will, therefore, recognize $600,000 in profit for 2006 ($1,000,000 cash received × 60 percent). A uses the cost recovery method. C is the cash received.

9. A is correct. Under the cost recovery method, the company would not recognize any profit until the cash amounts paid by the buyer exceeded Argo's cost of $2,000,000.

10. C is correct. Revenue for barter transactions should be measured based on the fair value of revenue from similar nonbarter transactions with unrelated parties.

11. A is correct. Apex is not the owner of the goods and should only report its net commission as revenue. C is the amount paid to the owners. B is the total amount collected on behalf of the owners.

12. C is correct. Under the First In, First Out (FIFO) method, the first 10,000 units sold came from the October purchases at $10, and the next 2,000 units sold came from the November purchases at $11. A is incorrect; this is cost of goods sold under the Last In, First Out (LIFO) method. B is incorrect because it places a cost of $10 on all units.

13. C is correct. Under the weighted average cost method:

October purchases	10,000 units	£100,000
November purchases	5,000 units	£55,000
Total	15,000 units	£155,000

£155,000/15,000 units = £10.3333 × 12,000 units = £124,000.

14. B is correct. The Last In, First Out (LIFO) method is not permitted under IFRS. The other methods are permitted.

15. B is correct. Straight-line depreciation would be ($600,000 − $50,000)/10, or $55,000. A assumes the machine was totally expensed in 2007. C ignores the $50,000 residual value.

16. C is correct. Double-declining balance depreciation would be $600,000 × 20 percent (twice the straight-line rate). A uses 10 percent instead of 20 percent. B applies the depreciation percentage after the residual value has been subtracted from the initial book value.

17. C is correct. This would result in the highest amount of depreciation in the first year and hence the lowest amount of net income relative to the other choices.

18. A is correct. A fire may be infrequent, but it would still be part of continuing operations. IFRS does not permit classification of an item as extraordinary. Discontinued operations relate to a decision to dispose of an operating division.

19. C is correct. The weighted average number of shares outstanding for 2007 is 1,050,000. Basic earnings per share would be $1,000,000 divided by 1,050,000, or $0.95. A subtracts the common dividends from net income and uses 1,100,000 shares. B uses the proper net income but 1,100,000 shares.

20. B is correct. With stock options, the treasury stock method must be used. Under that method, the company would receive $100,000 (10,000 × $10) and would repurchase 6,667 shares ($100,000/$15). The shares for the denominator would be:

Shares outstanding	1,000,000
Options exercised	10,000
Treasury shares purchased	(6,667)
Denominator	1,003,333

UNDERSTANDING THE BALANCE SHEET

by Thomas R. Robinson, CFA, Jan Hendrik van Greuning, CFA,
R. Elaine Henry, CFA, and Michael A. Broihahn, CFA

READING

33

LEARNING OUTCOMES

The candidate should be able to:	Mastery
a. illustrate and interpret the components of the balance sheet and discuss the uses of the balance sheet in financial analysis;	☐
b. describe the various formats of balance sheet presentation;	☐
c. explain how assets and liabilities arise from the accrual process;	☐
d. compare and contrast current and noncurrent assets and liabilities;	☐
e. explain the measurement bases (e.g., historical cost and fair value) of assets and liabilities, including current assets, current liabilities, tangible assets, and intangible assets;	☐
f. demonstrate the appropriate classifications and related accounting treatments for marketable and nonmarketable financial instruments held as assets or owed by the company as liabilities;	☐
g. list and explain the components of owners' equity;	☐
h. interpret balance sheets and statements of changes in equity.	☐

THEME

The balance sheet presents the financial position of a company at a point in time. The information in a balance sheet allows the financial analyst to better assess a company's ability to meet debt obligations, generate future cash flows, and make distributions to owners. However, the balance sheet has limitations, especially as it relates to the measurement of assets and liabilities. The analyst must understand the measurement of assets and liabilities and the structure of the balance sheet in order to accurately assess the financial position of a company.

International Financial Statement Analysis, by Thomas R. Robinson, CFA, Jan Hendrik van Greuning, CFA, R. Elaine Henry, CFA, and Michael A. Broihahn, CFA. Copyright © 2007 by CFA Institute. Reprinted with permission.

195

1 INTRODUCTION

The starting place for analyzing a company's financial position is typically the balance sheet. Creditors, investors, and analysts recognize the value of the balance sheet and also its limitations. The balance sheet provides such users with information on a company's resources (assets) and its sources of capital (its equity and liabilities/debt). It normally also provides information about the future earnings capacity of a company's assets as well as an indication of cash flows that may come from receivables and inventories.

However, the balance sheet does have limitations, especially relating to how assets and liabilities are measured. Liabilities and, sometimes, assets may not be recognized in a timely manner. Furthermore, the use of historical costs rather than fair values to measure some items on the balance sheet means that the financial analyst may need to make adjustments to determine the real (economic) net worth of the company. By understanding how a balance sheet is constructed and how it may be analyzed, the reader should be able to make appropriate use of it.

This reading is organized as follows. In Section 2, we describe and illustrate the format, structure, and components of the balance sheet. Section 3 discusses the measurement bases for assets and liabilities. Section 4 describes the components of equity and illustrates the statement of changes in shareholders' equity. Section 5 introduces balance sheet analysis. A summary of the key points and practice problems in the CFA Institute multiple-choice format conclude the reading.

2 COMPONENTS AND FORMAT OF THE BALANCE SHEET

The **balance sheet** discloses what an entity owns and what it owes at a specific point in time; thus, it is also referred to as the **statement of financial position**.[1]

The financial position of an entity is described in terms of its assets, liabilities, and equity:

▶ **Assets (A)** are resources controlled by the company as a result of past events and from which future economic benefits are expected to flow to the entity.

▶ **Liabilities (L)** represent obligations of a company arising from past events, the settlement of which is expected to result in an outflow of economic benefits from the entity.

▶ **Equity (E)** Commonly known as shareholders' equity or **owners' equity**, equity is determined by subtracting the liabilities from the assets of a company, giving rise to the accounting equation: $A - L + E$ or $A - L = E$. Equity can be viewed as a residual or balancing amount, taking assets and liabilities into account.

---

[1] The balance sheet is also known as the *statement of financial condition*.

Assets and liabilities arise as a result of business transactions (e.g., the purchase of a building or issuing a bond.) The accounting equation is useful in assessing the impact of transactions on the balance sheet. For example, if a company borrows money in exchange for a note payable, assets and liabilities increase by the same amount. Assets and liabilities also arise from the accrual process. As noted in earlier readings, the income statement reflects revenue and expenses reported on an accrual basis regardless of the period in which cash is received and paid. Differences between accrued revenue and expenses and cash flows will result in assets and liabilities. Specifically:

► revenue reported on the income statement before cash is received; this results in accrued revenue or accounts receivable, which is an asset. This is ultimately reflected on the balance sheet as an increase in accounts receivable and an increase in retained earnings.

► cash received before revenue is to be reported on the income statement; this results in a deferred revenue or unearned revenue, which is a liability. For example, if a company pays in advance for delivery of custom equipment, the balance sheet reflects an increase in cash and an increase in liabilities.

► expense reported on the income statement before cash is paid; this results in an accrued expense, which is a liability. This is reflected on the balance sheet as an increase in liabilities and a decrease in retained earnings.

► cash paid before an expense is to be reported on the income statement; this results in a deferred expense, also known as a "prepaid expense," which is an asset. On the balance sheet, cash is reduced and prepaid assets are increased.

Exhibit 1 illustrates what an unformatted balance sheet might look like, providing examples of a selection of assets and liabilities. The account "trade creditors" (also known as "accounts payable") arises when goods are purchased on credit and received into inventory before their purchase price is paid in cash. Because an expense is recognized before cash is paid, it is an example of the type of accrual described in the third bullet point.

EXHIBIT 1	Listing of Assets, Liabilities, and Owners' Equity Funds			
Element	**20X9**	**20X8**	**Financial Statement Element**	**Equation**
Inventory	€20,000	€16,000	Asset	+ **A**
Property, plant, and equipment	53,000	27,000	Asset	
Subtotal	**73,000**	**43,000**		
Trade creditors	(14,000)	(7,000)	Liability	− **L**
Bond repayable in 5 years' time	(37,000)	(16,000)	Liability	
Owners' equity	**€22,000**	**€20,000**	**Equity** (balancing amount)	= **E**

2.1 Structure and Components of the Balance Sheet

As noted above, the balance sheet presents the financial position of a company. The financial position shows the relative amounts of assets, liabilities, and equity held by the enterprise at a particular point in time.

2.1.1 Assets

Assets are generated either through purchase (investing activities), or generated through business activities (operating activities), or financing activities, such as issuance of debt.

Through the analysis of the liabilities and equity of an entity, the analyst is able to determine *how* assets are acquired or funded. Funding for the purchase may come from shareholders (financing activities) or from creditors (either through direct financing activities, or indirectly through the surplus generated through operating activities that may be funded by current liabilities/trade finance).

The reading on financial reporting standards defined **assets** as "resources controlled by the enterprise as a result of past events and from which future economic benefits are expected to flow to the enterprise." This formal definition of an asset tells us that its essence lies in its capability to generate future benefits, which, therefore, alerts the reader of the financial statements about the future earnings capability of the entity's assets. A simpler definition of an asset is that it is a store of wealth (such as cash, marketable securities, and property).

Turning back to the official definition of assets, we note that financial statement elements (such as assets) should only be recognized in the financial statements if:

▶ it is probable that any future economic benefit associated with the item will flow to the entity, and

▶ the item has a cost or value that can be *measured* with reliability (this aspect will be discussed more fully in Section 3 of this reading).

Values that are typically included in assets will include amounts that have been spent but which have not been recorded as an expense on the income statement (as in the case of inventories) because of the matching principle, or amounts that have been reported as earned on an income statement but which have not been received (as in the case of accounts receivable).

Exhibit 1 included inventories as well as property, plant, and equipment as examples of assets. Exhibit 2 provides a more complete list of assets that may be found on the face of the balance sheet.

EXHIBIT 2	Typical Assets Disclosed on the Balance Sheet

Cash and cash equivalents

Inventories

Trade and other receivables

Prepaid expenses

Financial assets

Deferred tax assets

Property, plant, and equipment

Investment property

Intangible assets

Investments accounted for using the equity method

Natural resource assets

Assets held for sale

2.1.2 Liabilities

Liabilities (and equity capital) represent the ways in which the funds were raised to acquire the assets. **Liabilities** are technically defined as probable future sacrifices of economic benefits arising from present obligations of an entity to transfer assets or provide services to other entities in the future as a result of past transactions or events. Alternatively, a liability can be described as:

▶ Amounts received but which have not been reported as revenues or income on an income statement and/or will have to be repaid (e.g., notes payable).

▶ Amounts that have been reported as expenses on an income statement but which have not been paid (e.g., accounts payable, accruals, and taxes payable).

Exhibit 1 included trade creditors as well as a long-term bond payable as examples of liabilities. Exhibit 3 provides a more complete list of liabilities that may be found on the face of the balance sheet.

EXHIBIT 3	Typical Liabilities Disclosed on the Balance Sheet

Bank borrowings/notes payable

Trade and other payables

Provisions

Unearned revenues

Financial liabilities

Accrued liabilities

Deferred tax liabilities

2.1.3 Equity

Equity represents the portion belonging to the owners or shareholders of a business. **Equity** is the residual interest in the assets of an entity after deducting its liabilities, also referred to as net asset value:

$$\text{Equity} = \text{Assets} - \text{Liabilities}$$

Equity is increased by contributions by the owners or by profits (including gains) made during the year and is decreased by losses or withdrawals in the form of dividends.

Almost every aspect of a company is either directly or indirectly influenced by the availability and/or the cost of equity capital. The adequacy of equity capital is one of the key factors to be considered when the safety or soundness of a particular company is assessed. An adequate equity base serves as a safety net for a variety of risks to which any entity is exposed in the course of its business. Equity capital provides a cushion to absorb possible losses and thus provides a basis for maintaining creditor confidence in a company. Equity capital also is the ultimate determinant of a company's borrowing capacity. In practice, a company's balance sheet cannot be expanded beyond a level determined by its equity capital without increasing the risk of financial distress to an unacceptable level; the availability of equity capital consequently determines the maximum level of assets.

The cost and amount of capital affect a company's competitive position. Because shareholders expect a return on their equity, the obligation to earn such a return impacts the pricing of company products. There is also another important aspect to the level of capital, namely, the perspective of the market. The issuance of debt requires public confidence in a company, which, in turn, can best be established and maintained by an equity capital buffer. If a company faces a shortage of equity capital or if the cost of capital is high, a company stands to lose business to its competitors.

The key purposes of equity capital are to provide stability and to absorb losses, thereby providing a measure of protection to creditors in the event of liquidation. As such, the capital of a company should have three important characteristics:

▶ It should be permanent.

▶ It should not impose mandatory fixed charges against earnings (in the case of banks).

▶ It should allow for legal subordination to the rights of creditors.

Exhibit 4 provides a list of equity information that is disclosed on the balance sheet.

EXHIBIT 4	**Typical Equity Information Disclosed on the Balance Sheet**

Minority interest, presented within equity

Issued capital and paid-in capital attributable to equityholders of the parent

Earnings retained in the company

Parent shareholders' equity

Information that is usually disclosed for each class of equity on the face of the balance sheet or in notes to the financial statements includes:

▶ Number of shares authorized

▶ Number of shares issued and fully paid

▶ Number of shares issued and not fully paid

▶ Par (or stated) value per share, or a statement that it has no par (stated) value

▶ Reconciliation of shares at beginning and end of reporting period

▶ Rights, preferences, and restrictions attached to that class

▶ Shares in the entity held by entity, subsidiaries, or associates

▶ Shares reserved for issue under options and sales contracts

The total amount of equity capital is of fundamental importance. Also important is the nature of the company ownership—the identity of those owners who can directly influence the company's strategic direction and risk management policies. This is particularly critical for financial institutions, such as banks. For example, a bank's ownership structure must ensure the integrity of its capital, and owners must be able to supply more capital if and when needed.

2.2 Format of the Balance Sheet

As the balance sheet provides information about the financial position of the company, it should distinguish between major categories and classifications of assets and liabilities.

Detail and formats of balance sheets vary from company to company. The basic information contained in balance sheets is the same though, regardless of the format. When using the **report format**, assets, liabilities, and equity are listed in a single column. The **account format** follows the pattern of the traditional general ledger accounts, with assets at the left and liabilities and equity at the right of a central dividing line. The report format is most commonly preferred and used by financial statement preparers.

If a company were to have many assets and liabilities, the balance sheet might become quite difficult to read. Grouping together the various classes of assets and liabilities, therefore, results in a balance sheet format described as a **classified balance sheet**.

"Classification," in this case, is the term used to describe the grouping of accounts into subcategories—it helps readers to gain a quick perspective of the company's financial position. Classification assists in drawing attention to specific amounts and also to groups of accounts.

Classifications most often distinguish between current and noncurrent assets/liabilities, or by financial and nonfinancial categories—all in order to provide information related to the liquidity of such assets or liabilities (albeit indirectly in many cases).

2.2.1 Current and Noncurrent Distinction

The balance sheet should distinguish between current and noncurrent assets and between current and noncurrent liabilities unless a presentation based on liquidity provides more relevant and reliable information (e.g., in the case of a bank or similar financial institution).

From Exhibit 5, it should be clear that in essence, the current/noncurrent distinction is also an attempt at incorporating liquidity expectations into the structure of the balance sheet. Assets expected to be liquidated or used up within one year or one operating cycle of the business, whichever is greater, are classified as current assets. A company's operating cycle is the amount of time that elapses between spending cash for inventory and supplies and collecting the cash from its sales to customers. Assets not expected to be liquidated or used up within one year or one operating cycle of the business, whichever is greater, are classified as noncurrent (long-term) assets.

The excess of current assets over current liabilities is called **working capital**. The level of working capital tells analysts about the ability of an entity to meet liabilities as they fall due. Yet, working capital should not be too large because funds could be tied up that could be used more productively elsewhere.

EXHIBIT 5	Balance Sheet: Current versus Noncurrent Distinction	
Apex Corporation	20X9	20X8
Assets		
Current assets	€20,000	€16,000
Noncurrent assets	53,000	27,000
Total assets	**€73,000**	**€43,000**
Liabilities and equity		
Current liabilities	14,000	7,000
Noncurrent liabilities	37,000	16,000
Total liabilities	**51,000**	**23,000**
Equity	**22,000**	**20,000**
Total liabilities and equity	**€73,000**	**€43,000**

Some **current assets** are allocated to expenses immediately (e.g., inventory) when sales or cash transactions take place, whereas noncurrent assets are allocated over the useful lives of such assets. Current assets are maintained for operating purposes and represent cash or items expected to be converted into cash or used up (e.g., prepaid expenses) in the current period. Current assets, therefore, tell us more about the operating activities and the operating capability of the entity.

Noncurrent assets represent the infrastructure from which the entity operates and are not consumed or disposed in the current period. Such assets represent potentially less-liquid investments made from a strategic or longer-term perspective (e.g., to secure trading advantages, supply lines, or other synergies, such as equity securities held, investments in associates, or investments in subsidiaries).

A **current liability** is a liability that satisfies any of the following criteria:

▶ It is expected to be settled in the entity's normal operating cycle.

▶ It is held primarily for the purpose of being traded.

▶ It is due to be settled within one year after the balance sheet date.

▶ The entity does not have an unconditional right to defer settlement of the liability for at least one year after the balance sheet date.

Financial liabilities are classified as current if they are due to be settled within one year after the balance sheet date, even if the original term was for a period longer than one year. All other liabilities are classified as **noncurrent**.

International Accounting Standard (IAS) No. 1 specifies that some current liabilities, such as trade payables and some accruals for employee and other operating costs, are part of the working capital used in the entity's normal operating cycle. Such operating items are classified as current liabilities even if they will be settled more than one year after the balance sheet date. When the entity's normal operating cycle is not clearly identifiable, its duration is assumed to be one year.

Noncurrent liabilities include financial liabilities that provide financing on a long-term basis, and they are, therefore, not part of the working capital used in the entity's normal operating cycle; neither are they due for settlement within one year after the balance sheet date.

2.2.2 Liquidity-Based Presentation

Paragraph 51 of IAS No. 1 requires the use of the current/noncurrent format of presentation for the balance sheet, except when a presentation based on liquidity provides information that is reliable and is more relevant. When that exception applies, all assets and liabilities shall be presented broadly in order of liquidity.

Entities such as banks are clearly candidates for such a liquidity-based presentation in their balance sheets. Exhibit 6 shows how the asset side of a bank's balance sheet could be ordered using a liquidity-based presentation.

EXHIBIT 6	Bank Balance Sheet: Asset Side Order Using a Liquidity-Based Presentation

Assets

1. Cash and balances with the central bank
2. Trading securities
3. Securities held for stable liquidity portfolio purposes
4. Placements with and loans to banks and credit institutions (net of specific provisions)
5. Loans and advances to other customers
6. Investments—long-term interests in other entities
7. Property, plant, and equipment
8. Other assets (prepayments, etc.)

Total Assets

2.2.3 IFRS and U.S. GAAP Balance Sheet Illustrations

This section illustrates actual corporate balance sheets prepared under international financial reporting standards (IFRS) and generally accepted accounting principles (GAAP) via examples from Roche Group and Sony Corporation, respectively.

Roche is a leading international healthcare company based in Switzerland and prepares its financial statements in accordance with IFRS. Exhibit 7 presents the comparative balance sheets from the company's annual report for the fiscal years ended 31 December 2005 and 2004.

Roche prepares its balance sheets using the report format. The balance sheet also gives noncurrent assets before current assets and long-term liabilities before current liabilities, following common practice under IFRS. Note also that Roche shows the minority interest for its consolidated subsidiary companies in the shareholders' equity section as required under IFRS. **Minority interest** represents the portion of consolidated subsidiaries owned by others. For example, if a company owns 85 percent of a subsidiary, 100 percent of the subsidiary's assets and liabilities are included in the consolidated balance sheet. Minority interest represents the 15 percent of the net assets of the subsidiary not owned by the parent company.

EXHIBIT 7	Roche Group Consolidated Balance Sheets (CHF Millions)	
	31 December	
	2005	**2004**
Noncurrent assets		
Property, plant, and equipment	15,097	12,408
Goodwill	6,132	5,532
Intangible assets	6,256	6,340
Investments in associated companies	58	55
Financial long-term assets	2,190	1,227
Other long-term assets	660	484
Deferred income tax assets	1,724	1,144
Post-employment benefit assets	1,622	1,577
Total noncurrent assets	**33,739**	**28,767**
Current assets		
Inventories	5,041	4,614
Accounts receivables	7,698	7,014
Current income tax assets	299	159
Other current assets	1,703	2,007
Receivable from Bayer Group collected on 1 January 2005	—	2,886
Marketable securities	16,657	10,394
Cash and cash equivalents	4,228	2,605
Total current assets	**35,626**	**29,679**
Total assets	**69,365**	**58,446**
Noncurrent liabilities		
Long-term debt	(9,322)	(7,077)
Deferred income tax liabilities	(3,518)	(3,564)
Post-employment benefit liabilities	(2,937)	(2,744)
Provisions	(1,547)	(683)
Other noncurrent liabilities	(806)	(961)
Total noncurrent liabilities	**(18,130)**	**(15,029)**
Current liabilities		
Short-term debt	(348)	(2,013)
Current income tax liabilities	(811)	(947)
Provisions	(833)	(1,223)
Accounts payable	(2,373)	(1,844)

(Exhibit continued on next page . . .)

EXHIBIT 7	(continued)		
		31 December	
		2005	**2004**
Accrued and other current liabilities		(5,127)	(4,107)
Total current liabilities		**(9,492)**	**(10,134)**
Total liabilities		**(27,622)**	**(25,163)**
Total net assets		**41,743**	**33,283**
Equity			
Capital and reserves attributable to Roche shareholders		34,922	27,998
Equity attributable to minority interests		6,821	5,285
Total equity		**41,743**	**33,283**

Sony Corporation and its consolidated subsidiaries are engaged in the development, design, manufacture, and sale of various kinds of electronic equipment, instruments, and devices for consumer and industrial markets. Sony is also engaged in the development, production, and distribution of recorded music and image-based software. Sony Corporation has prepared a set of consolidated financial statements in accordance with U.S. GAAP. Exhibit 8 presents the comparative balance sheets from the company's U.S. GAAP annual report for the fiscal years ended 31 March 2005 and 2004.

Sony prepares its balance sheets using the report format. Under U.S. GAAP, current assets are presented before long-term assets, and current liabilities are presented before long-term liabilities. The current/long-term presentation rule is applicable for all manufacturing, merchandising, and service companies, although there are some regulated industry exceptions (e.g., utility companies) where the presentation is reversed (similar to the common IFRS practice of presenting long-term assets before current assets and long-term liabilities before current liabilities). Note also that Sony shows the minority interest for its consolidated subsidiary companies in an "in-between" or "mezzanine" section between the liabilities and shareholders' equity sections. This mezzanine presentation for minority interest is common under U.S. GAAP; however, minority interest may also be shown under either liabilities or shareholders' equity. By contrast, under IFRS, a minority interest is presented in the shareholders' equity section. The Financial Accounting Standards Board (FASB) is considering a change to U.S. GAAP to conform their standards to IFRS.

EXHIBIT 8	Sony Corporation Consolidated Balance Sheets (¥ Millions)		
		31 March	
		2005	**2004**
Assets			
Current assets:			
Cash and cash equivalents		779,103	849,211
Time deposits		1,492	4,662

(Exhibit continued on next page . . .)

EXHIBIT 8	(continued)		

| | | **31 March** | |
	2005		**2004**
Marketable securities	460,202		274,748
Notes and accounts receivable, trade	1,113,071		1,123,863
Allowance for doubtful accounts and sales returns	(87,709)		(112,674)
Inventories	631,349		666,507
Deferred income taxes	141,154		125,532
Prepaid expenses and other current assets	517,509		431,506
Total current assets	3,556,171		3,363,355
Film costs	278,961		256,740
Investments and advances:			
Affiliated companies	252,905		86,253
Securities investments and other	2,492,784		2,426,697
	2,745,689		2,512,950
Property, plant, and equipment:			
Land	182,900		189,785
Buildings	925,796		930,983
Machinery and equipment	2,192,038		2,053,085
Construction in progress	92,611		98,480
Less—Accumulated depreciation	(2,020,946)		(1,907,289)
	1,372,399		1,365,044
Other assets:			
Intangibles, net	187,024		248,010
Goodwill	283,923		277,870
Deferred insurance acquisition costs	374,805		349,194
Deferred income taxes	240,396		203,203
Other	459,732		514,296
	1,545,880		1,592,573
Total assets	9,499,100		9,090,662
Liabilities and Stockholders' Equity			
Current liabilities:			
Short-term borrowings	63,396		91,260
Current portion of long-term debt	166,870		383,757
Notes and accounts payable, trade	806,044		778,773
Accounts payable, other and accrued expenses	746,466		812,175
Accrued income and other taxes	55,651		57,913
Deposits from customers in the banking business	546,718		378,851
Other	424,223		479,486
Total current liabilities	2,809,368		2,982,215

(Exhibit continued on next page . . .)

EXHIBIT 8	**(continued)**		

| | | 31 March | |
		2005	**2004**
Long-term liabilities:			
Long-term debt		678,992	777,649
Accrued pension and severance costs		352,402	368,382
Deferred income taxes		72,227	96,193
Future insurance policy benefits and other		2,464,295	2,178,626
Other		227,631	286,737
		3,795,547	3,707,587
Minority interest in consolidated subsidiaries		23,847	22,858
Stockholders' equity:			
Subsidiary tracking stock, no par value—			
Authorized 100,000,000 shares, outstanding 3,072,000 shares		3,917	3,917
Common stock, no par value—			
2004-Authorized 3,500,000,000 shares,			
outstanding 926,418,280 shares			476,350
2005-Authorized 3,500,000,000 shares,			
outstanding 997,211,213 shares		617,792	
Additional paid-in capital		1,134,222	992,817
Retained earnings		1,506,082	1,367,060
Accumulated other comprehensive income—			
Unrealized gains on securities		62,669	69,950
Unrealized losses on derivative investments		(2,490)	(600)
Minimum pension liability adjustments		(90,030)	(89,261)
Foreign currency translation adjustments		(355,824)	(430,048)
		(385,675)	(449,959)
Treasury stock, at cost			
Subsidiary tracking stock (2004—0 shares, 2005—32 shares)		(0)	(0)
Common stock (2004—2,468,258 shares, 2005—1,118,984 shares)		(6,000)	(12,183)
		2,870,338	2,378,002
Total liabilities and stockholders' equity		9,499,100	9,090,662

MEASUREMENT BASES OF ASSETS AND LIABILITIES

3

In portraying an asset or liability on the balance sheet, the question arises as to how it should be measured. For example, an asset may have been acquired many years ago at a cost of $1,000,000 but may have a current value of $5,000,000. Should this asset be listed at its historic cost or its current value? On the one hand, historical cost provides a reliable and objectively determined measurement base—there would be no dispute regarding what the asset cost. On the other hand, users of financial statements (e.g., creditors) may prefer to know what the asset could be sold for currently if the company needed to raise cash. Some assets and liabilities can be more objectively valued in the marketplace than others (e.g., when an established market exists in which the asset or liability trades regularly, such as an investment in another publicly traded company). As a result, the balance sheet under current standards is a mixed model: Some assets and liabilities are reported based on historical cost, sometimes with adjustments, whereas other assets and liabilities are measured based upon a current value intended to represent the asset's fair value. Fair value and historical value can be defined as follows.

▶ **Fair value.** Fair value is the amount at which an asset could be exchanged, or a liability settled, between knowledgeable willing parties in an arm's length transaction. When the asset or liability trades regularly, its fair value is usually readily determinable from its market price (sometimes referred to as **fair market value**).

▶ **Historical cost.** The historical cost of an asset or liability is its cost or fair value at acquisition, including any costs of acquisition and/or preparation.

In limited circumstances other measurement bases are sometimes used, such as **current cost** (the cost to replace an asset) or **present value** (the present discounted value of future cash flows). The key question for analysts is how the reported measures of assets and liabilities on the balance sheet relate to economic reality and to each other. To answer this question, the analyst needs to understand the accounting policies applied in preparing the balance sheet and the measurement bases used. Analysts may need to make adjustments to balance sheet measures of assets and liabilities in assessing the investment potential or credit-worthiness of a company. For example, land is generally reported at historical cost on the balance sheet because this measure is objective and any measure of current value (other than an actual sale) would be very subjective. Through diligent research, an analyst may find companies that own valuable land that is not adequately reflected on the balance sheet.[2]

For all of these reasons, the balance sheet value of total assets should not be accepted as an accurate measure of the total value of a company. The value of a company is a function of many factors, including future cash flows expected to be generated by the company and current market conditions. The balance sheet provides important information about the value of some assets and information about future cash flows but does not represent the value of the company as a whole.

Once individual assets and liabilities are measured, additional decisions may be necessary as to how these measures are reflected on the balance sheet. Accounting standards generally prohibit the offsetting of assets and liabilities other than in limited circumstances. For example, if a building is purchased for $10,000,000 subject to a mortgage of $8,000,000, the building is reported as an asset for $10,000,000 while the mortgage is shown separately as a liability ($8,000,000). It is important that these assets and liabilities be reported separately. Offsetting in the balance sheet, except when offsetting reflects the substance of the transaction or other event, detracts from the ability of users to understand the transactions, events, and conditions that have occurred and to assess the entity's future cash flows. However, disclosing or measuring assets net of valuation allowances (e.g., obsolescence allowances on inventories and doubtful accounts allowances on receivables) is not considered to be offsetting. Offsetting is also permitted in limited circumstances where there are restrictions on the availability of assets (such as with pension plans).

---

[2] See, for example, "Beyond the Balance-Sheet: Land-Ho," *Forbes*, 4 September 2006, pp. 84–85, which examines a handful of stocks with valuable land holdings not reflected on the balance sheet.

According to IFRS, fair presentation requires the faithful representation on the balance sheet of the effects of transactions, other events, and conditions in accordance with the definitions and recognition criteria for assets, liabilities, income, and expenses set out in the IFRS *Framework*, as presented in the reading on financial reporting standards. The application of IFRS is presumed to result in fair presentation.

The financial statements should disclose the following information related to the measures used for assets and liabilities shown on the balance sheet:

▶ accounting policies, including the cost formulas used;

▶ total carrying amount of inventories and amount per category;

▶ amount of inventories carried at fair value less costs to sell;

▶ amount of any write-downs and reversals of any write-down;

▶ circumstances or events that led to the reversal of a write-down;

▶ inventories pledged as security for liabilities; and

▶ amount of inventories recognized as an expense.

The notes to financial statements and management's discussion and analysis are integral parts of the U.S. GAAP and IFRS financial reporting processes. They provide important required detailed disclosures, as well as other information provided voluntarily by management. This information can be invaluable when determining whether the measurement of assets is comparable to other entities being analyzed. The notes include information on such topics as the following:

▶ specific accounting policies that were used in compiling the financial statements;

▶ terms of debt agreements;

▶ lease information;

▶ off-balance sheet financing;

▶ breakdowns of operations by important segments;

▶ contingent assets and liabilities; and

▶ detailed pension plan disclosure.

The notes would also provide information in respect of:

Disclosure of accounting policies	▶ Measurement bases used in preparing financial statements. ▶ Each accounting policy used. ▶ Judgments made in applying accounting policies that have the most significant effect on the amounts recognized in the financial statements.
Estimation uncertainty	▶ Key assumptions about the future and other key sources of estimation uncertainty that have a significant risk of causing material adjustment to the carrying amount of assets and liabilities within the next year.
Other disclosures	▶ Description of the entity, including its domicile, legal form, country of incorporation, and registered office or business address. ▶ Nature of operations or principal activities, or both. ▶ Name of parent and ultimate parent.

EXAMPLE 1

Analysis of Off-Balance Sheet Disclosures

Hewitt Associates (NYSE: HEW) posted the following table on page 43 of its SEC Form 10K for the fiscal year ending 30 September 2005. The table was included in the Management Discussion and Analysis.

Contractual Obligations

(in Millions)

		Payments Due in Fiscal Year			
	Total	**2006**	**2007–08**	**2009–10**	**Thereafter**
Operating leases (1)	737	89	149	123	376
Capital leases:					
Principal	80	4	9	11	56
Interest	41	6	11	9	15
Total leases:	121	10	20	20	71
Debt:					
Principal	259	36	50	30	143
Interest	50	12	18	13	7
Total debt:	309	48	68	43	150
Purchase commitments	73	34	37	2	—
Other long-term liabilities	72	8	16	9	39
Total contractual obligations	$1,312	$189	$290	$197	$636

On pages 56–57 of the 10K, Hewitt posted the following balance sheet (abbreviated on the following pages). Of the obligations listed above, only the capital leases and other long-term liabilities are included explicitly on the balance sheet.

Hewitt Associates, Inc.
Consolidated Balance Sheets
(Dollars in Thousands except Share and per-Share Amounts)

	30 September	
	2005	**2004**
Assets		
Current assets:		
Cash and cash equivalents	$ 163,928	$ 129,481
Short-term investments	53,693	183,205
Client receivables and unbilled work in process	595,691	522,882
Refundable income taxes	23,100	—
Prepaid expenses and other current assets	60,662	50,546
Funds held for clients	97,907	14,693
Deferred income taxes, net	5,902	246
Total current assets	1,000,883	901,053
Noncurrent assets:		
Deferred contract costs	253,505	162,602
Property and equipment, net	302,875	236,099
Capitalized software, net	110,997	85,350
Other intangible assets, net	261,999	107,322
Goodwill	694,370	285,743
Other assets, net	32,711	29,805
Total noncurrent assets	1,656,457	906,921
Total assets	2,657,340	1,807,974
Liabilities		
Current liabilities:		
Accounts payable	57,412	20,909
Accrued expenses	156,575	83,226
Funds held for clients	97,907	14,693
Advanced billings to clients	156,257	106,934
Accrued compensation and benefits	141,350	181,812
Short-term debt and current portion of long-term debt	35,915	13,445
Current portion of capital lease obligations	3,989	5,373
Employee deferred compensation and accrued profit sharing	30,136	49,450
Total current liabilities	679,541	475,842
Long-term liabilities:		
Deferred contract revenues	140,474	118,025
Debt, less current portion	222,692	121,253
Capital lease obligations, less current portion	76,477	79,982

	30 September	
	2005	**2004**
Other long-term liabilities	127,376	83,063
Deferred income taxes, net	99,423	70,456
Total long-term liabilities	666,442	472,779
Total liabilities	1,345,983	948,621
Commitments and contingencies (Notes 12 and 17)		
Stockholders' Equity		
Total stockholders' equity	1,311,357	859,353
Total liabilities and stockholders' equity	$2,657,340	$1,807,974

Operating leases represent assets used by the company but for which accounting standards do not currently require the assets or related obligations to be reported on the company's balance sheet. Analysts, however, frequently prefer to adjust the balance sheet to determine how it would look if the assets had been purchased and financed. Credit analysts, such as Standard & Poor's, also make this adjustment to better reflect the credit-worthiness of the company. Ideally, the analyst would like to know the implied interest rate in the lease agreements and use this to determine the present value of the asset and related liability, because each lease payment effectively has an interest and a principal component. For this initial example, we will use a shortcut method. Assuming operating leases can be segregated into principal and interest components at approximately the same rate as the capital leases, they represent a liability worth nearly $500 million that is not recorded on the balance sheet. The analyst would adjust the balance sheet by adding that amount to fixed assets and liabilities to examine the current economic position. This information would not have been uncovered based solely upon a review of the balance sheet. Important disclosures about assets and liabilities can be found in the footnotes to the financial statements and in management's discussion of the financial statements.

3.1 Current Assets

Current assets are assets expected to be realized or intended for sale or consumption in the entity's normal operating cycle. Typical current assets that appear on the face of the balance sheet include:

▶ Assets held primarily for trading.

▶ Assets expected to be realized within 12 months after the balance sheet date.

▶ Cash or cash equivalents, unless restricted in use for at least 12 months.

▶ Marketable securities—Debt or equity securities that are owned by a business, traded in a public market, and whose value can be determined from price information in a public market. Examples of marketable securities include treasury bills, notes, bonds, and equity securities, such as common stocks and mutual fund shares.

▶ Trade receivables—Amounts owed to a business by its customers for products and services already delivered are included as trade receivables. Allowance has to be made for bad debt expenses, reducing the gross receivables amount.

▶ Inventories—Physical products on hand such as goods that will eventually be sold to an entity's customers, either in their current form (finished goods) or as inputs into a process to manufacture a final product (raw materials and work-in-process).

▶ Other current assets—Short-term items not easily classifiable into the above categories (e.g., prepaid expenses).

Exhibit 9 illustrates how the current asset amounts of €20,000 (20X9) and €16,000 (20X8) have been expanded from the one amount shown in Exhibit 5. In the sections below, some of the issues surrounding the measurement principles for inventories and prepaid expenses are discussed.

EXHIBIT 9	Apex Current Assets	
	20X9	**20X8**
Current assets	**€20,000**	**€16,000**
Cash and cash equivalents	3,000	2,000
Marketable securities	3,000	4,000
Trade receivables	5,000	3,000
Inventories	7,000	6,000
Other current assets—prepaid expenses	2,000	1,000

3.1.1 Inventories

Inventories should be measured at the lower of cost or net realizable value. The cost of inventories comprises all costs of purchase, costs of conversion, and other costs incurred in bringing the inventories to their present location and condition. The following amounts should be excluded in the determination of inventory costs:

▶ abnormal amounts of wasted materials, labor, and overheads;

▶ storage costs, unless they are necessary prior to a further production process;

▶ administrative overheads; and

▶ selling costs.

The net realizable value (NRV) is the estimated selling price less the estimated costs of completion and costs necessary to make the sale.

Accounting standards allow different valuation methods. For example, IAS No. 2 allows only the first-in, first-out (FIFO), weighted average cost (WAC), and specific identification methods. Some accounting standard setters (such as U.S. GAAP) also allow LIFO (last-in, first-out) as an additional inventory valuation method, whereas LIFO is not allowed under IFRS.

The following techniques can be used to measure the cost of inventories if the resulting valuation amount approximates cost:

▶ **Standard cost**, which should take into account the normal levels of materials, labor, and actual capacity. The standard cost should be reviewed regularly in order to ensure that it approximates actual costs.

▶ The **retail method** in which the sales value is reduced by the gross margin to calculate cost. An average gross margin percentage should be used for each homogeneous group of items. In addition, the impact of marked-down prices should be taken into consideration.

EXAMPLE 2

Analysis of Inventory

Cisco Systems is the world's leading provider of networking equipment. In its third quarter 2001 Form 10-Q filed with the U.S. Securities and Exchange Commission (U.S. SEC) on 1 June 2001, the company made the following disclosure:

> We recorded a provision for inventory, including purchase commitments, totaling $2.36 billion in the third quarter of fiscal 2001, of which $2.25 billion related to an additional excess inventory charge. Inventory purchases and commitments are based upon future sales forecasts. To mitigate the component supply constraints that have existed in the past, we built inventory levels for certain components with long lead times and entered into certain longer-term commitments for certain components. Due to the sudden and significant decrease in demand for our products, inventory levels exceeded our requirements based on current 12-month sales forecasts. This additional excess inventory charge was calculated based on the inventory levels in excess of 12-month demand for each specific product. We do not currently anticipate that the excess inventory subject to this provision will be used at a later date based on our current 12-month demand forecast.

Even after the inventory charge, Cisco held approximately $2 billion of inventory on the balance sheet, suggesting that the write-off amounted to half its inventory. In addition to the obvious concerns raised as to management's poor performance anticipating how much they would need, many analysts were concerned about how the write-off would affect Cisco's future reported earnings. When this inventory is sold in a future period, a "gain" could be reported based on a lower cost basis for the inventory. In this case, management indicated that the intent was to scrap the inventory. When the company subsequently released its annual earnings, the press release stated:[3]

> Net sales for fiscal 2001 were $22.29 billion, compared with $18.93 billion for fiscal 2000, an increase of 18%. Pro forma net income, which excludes the effects of acquisition charges, payroll tax on stock option exercises, restructuring costs and other special charges, excess inventory charge (benefit), and net gains realized on minority investments, was $3.09 billion or $0.41 per share for fiscal 2001, compared with pro forma net income of $3.91 billion or $0.53 per share for fiscal 2000, decreases of 21% and 23%, respectively.

---

[3] Cisco Press Release dated 7 August 2001 from www.cisco.com.

> Actual net loss for fiscal 2001 was $1.01 billion or $0.14 per share, compared with actual net income of $2.67 billion or $0.36 per share for fiscal 2000.
>
> Note that the company focused on "pro forma earnings" initially, which excluded the impact of many items, including the inventory write-off. The company only gave a brief mention of actual (U.S. GAAP) results.

3.1.2 Prepaid Expenses

Prepaid expenses are normal operating expenses that have been paid in advance. The advance payment creates an asset out of a transaction that would normally have resulted in an expense. Examples might include prepaid rent or prepaid insurance. Prepaid expenses will be expensed in future periods as they are used up. Generally, expenses are reported in the period in which they are incurred as opposed to when they are paid. If a company pays its insurance premium for the next calendar year on 31 December, the expense is not incurred at that date; the expense is incurred as time passes (in this example, 1/12 in each following month).

3.2 Current Liabilities

Current liabilities are those liabilities that are expected to be settled in the entity's normal operating cycle, held primarily for trading and due to be settled within 12 months after the balance sheet date.

Exhibit 10 illustrates how the current liabilities amounts of €14,000 (20X9) and €7,000 (20X8) have been expanded from the one amount shown in Exhibit 5. In the sections below, some of the issues surrounding the measurement principles for payables, accrued liabilities, and unearned revenue are discussed.

Noncurrent interest-bearing liabilities to be settled within 12 months after the balance sheet date can be classified as noncurrent liabilities if:

▶ the original term of the liability is greater than 12 months;

▶ it is the intention to refinance or reschedule the obligation; or

▶ the agreement to refinance or reschedule the obligation is completed on or before the balance sheet date.

EXHIBIT 10	Apex Current Liabilities	
	20X9	**20X8**
Current liabilities	**€14,000**	**€7,000**
Trade and other payables	5,000	2,000
Notes payable	3,000	1,000
Current portion of noncurrent borrowings	2,000	1,000
Current tax payable	2,000	2,000
Accrued liabilities	1,000	500
Unearned revenue	1,000	500

3.2.1 Trade and Other Payables (Accounts Payable)

Accounts payable are amounts that a business owes its vendors for goods and services that were purchased from them but which have not yet been paid.

3.2.2 Notes Payable

Notes payable are amounts owed by a business to creditors as a result of borrowings that are evidenced by a (short-term) loan agreement. Examples of notes payable include bank loans and other current borrowings other than those arising from trade credit. Notes payable may also appear in the long-term liability section of the balance sheet if they are due after one year or the operating cycle, whichever is longer.

3.2.3 Current Portion of Noncurrent Borrowings

By convention, liabilities expected to be repaid or liquidated within one year or one operating cycle of the business, whichever is greater, are classified as current liabilities. Other liabilities are classified as noncurrent. For example, Exhibit 10 shows that €2,000 of Apex's noncurrent borrowings will come due within a year; therefore, the €2,000 constitutes a current liability.

3.2.4 Current Tax Payable

Current taxes payable are tax expenses that have been determined and recorded on a company's income statement but which have not yet been paid.

3.2.5 Accrued Liabilities

Accrued liabilities (also known as **accrued expenses**) are expenses that have been reported on a company's income statement but which have not yet been paid because there is no legal obligation to pay them as of the balance sheet date. Common examples of accrued liabilities are accrued interest payable and accrued wages payable.

3.2.6 Unearned Revenue

Unearned revenue (also known as **deferred revenue**) is the collection of money in advance of delivery of the goods and services associated with the revenue. Examples include rental income received in advance, advance fees for servicing office equipment, and advance payments for magazine subscriptions received from customers.

3.3 Tangible Assets

Tangible assets are long-term assets with physical substance that are used in company operations. These noncurrent assets are carried at their historical cost less any accumulated depreciation or accumulated depletion. Historical cost generally consists of vendor invoice cost, freight cost, and any other additional costs incurred to

EXAMPLE 3

Analysis of Unearned Revenue

Germany's SAP AG is one of the world's leading providers of business software solutions and one of the world's three largest independent software companies based on market capitalization. At year-end 2005, SAP reported the following assets and liabilities on its balance sheet (in € thousands):[4]

	2005	**2004**
Assets		
Goodwill	€626,546	€456,707
Other intangible assets	139,697	68,186
Property, plant, and equipment	1,094,965	999,083
Financial assets	534,155	100,382
Fixed assets	2,395,363	1,624,358
Inventories	19,376	11,692
Accounts receivable, net	2,251,027	1,929,100
Other assets	635,554	537,645
Accounts receivable and other assets	2,886,581	2,466,745
Marketable securities	209,565	10,164
Liquid assets	3,213,572	3,196,542
Nonfixed assets	6,329,094	5,685,143
Deferred taxes	250,698	205,601
Prepaid expenses and deferred charges	87,587	70,370
Total assets	€9,062,742	€7,585,472
thereof total current assets	6,241,125	4,849,537
Shareholders' equity and liabilities		
Subscribed capital	316,458	316,004
Treasury stock	(775,318)	(569,166)
Additional paid-in capital	372,767	322,660
Retained earnings	5,986,186	4,830,156
Accumulated other comprehensive loss	(117,855)	(305,401)
Shareholders' equity	5,782,238	4,594,253
Minority interests	7,615	21,971
Pension liabilities and similar obligations	183,619	139,690
Other reserves and accrued liabilities	1,839,140	1,768,723
Reserves and accrued liabilities	2,022,759	1,908,413
Bonds	6,927	7,277
Other liabilities	838,778	728,838

---

[4] In its annual report, SAP AG chose to provide the subtotal of current assets and current liabilities at the bottom of the respective portions of the balance sheet rather than within the balance sheet to distinguish how much of its nonfixed assets are current. According to Footnote 1 of SAP AG's 2005 annual report: "Non-fixed assets are comprised of Inventories, Accounts receivable, Other assets, Marketable securities, and Liquid assets including amounts to be realized in excess of one year."

	2005	2004
Other liabilities	845,705	736,115
Deferred income	404,425	324,720
Total shareholders' equity and liabilities	€9,062,742	€7,585,472
thereof current liabilities	2,781,685	2,591,872

The final line shows that deferred income rose nearly 25 percent to end 2005 with a value of €404.4 million. SAP describes the line as follows:

> Deferred income consists mainly of prepayments for maintenance and deferred software license revenues. Such amounts will be recognized as software, maintenance, or service revenue, depending upon the reasons for the deferral when the basic criteria in SOP 97-2 have been met (see Note 3).

Although investors prefer to see many liabilities minimized, deferred revenue represents money the company has already been paid for services that will be delivered in the future. Because it will then be recognized as revenue, many investors monitor the deferred income line (when significant) as an indicator of future revenue growth.

make the asset operable. Examples of tangible assets include land, buildings, equipment, machinery, furniture, and natural resources owned by the company, such as copper mines, oil and gas properties, and timberlands. If any of these assets are not used in company operations, they must be classified as investment assets.

3.4 Intangible Assets

Intangible assets are amounts paid by a company to acquire certain rights that are not represented by the possession of physical assets. A distinction can be made between identifiable intangibles and unidentifiable intangibles. An **identifiable intangible** can be acquired singly and is typically linked to specific rights or privileges having finite benefit periods. Examples include patents and trademarks. An **unidentifiable intangible** cannot be acquired singly and typically possesses an indefinite benefit period. An example is accounting goodwill, discussed further in Section 3.4.2.

A company should assess whether the useful life of an intangible asset is finite or infinite and, if finite, the length of its life, or number of production or similar units constituting its useful life. Amortization and impairment principles apply as follows:

▶ An intangible asset with a finite useful life is amortized on a systematic basis over the best estimate of its useful life.

▶ An intangible asset with an infinite useful life should be tested for impairment annually but not amortized.

The balance sheet and notes should disclose the gross carrying amount (book value) less accumulated amortization for each class of asset at the beginning and the end of the period.

Companies may also have intangible assets that are not recorded on their balance sheets. These intangible assets might include management skill, valuable trademarks and name recognition, a good reputation, proprietary products, and so forth. Such assets are valuable and would fetch their worth if a company were to be sold.

Financial analysts have traditionally viewed the values assigned to intangible assets, particularly unidentifiable intangibles, with caution. Consequently, in assessing financial statements, they often exclude the book value assigned to intangibles, particularly unidentifiable intangibles, reducing net equity by an equal amount and increasing pretax income by any amortization expense or impairment associated with the intangibles. An arbitrary assignment of zero value to intangibles is not advisable. The analyst should examine each listed intangible and assess whether an adjustment should be made.

3.4.1 Specifically Identifiable Intangibles

Under IFRS, specifically identifiable intangible assets are nonfinancial assets without physical substance but which can be identified. Such assets are recognized on the balance sheet if it is probable that future economic benefits will flow to the company and the cost of the asset can be measured reliably. Examples of identifiable intangible assets include patents, trademarks, copyrights, franchises, and other rights. Identifiable intangible assets may have been created or purchased by a company. Determining the cost of internally created intangible assets can be difficult and subjective. For these reasons, internally created identifiable intangibles are less likely to be reported on the balance sheet under IFRS or U.S. GAAP. IAS No. 38 applies to all intangible assets that are not specifically dealt with in other international accounting standards. This standard determines that the intangible assets reported on a balance sheet are only those intangibles that have been *purchased* or *created* (in strictly limited instances).

IAS No. 38 provides that for internally created intangible assets, the company must identify the research phase and the development phase. The research phase includes activities that seek new knowledge or products. The development phase occurs after the research phase and includes design or testing of prototypes and models. IAS No. 38 prohibits the capitalization of costs as intangible assets during the research phase. Instead, these costs must be expensed on the income statement. Costs incurred in the development stage can be capitalized as intangible assets if certain criteria are met, including technological feasibility, the ability to use or sell the resulting asset, and the ability to complete the project.

All other expenses related to the following categories are **expensed**. They include:

► internally *generated* brands, mastheads, publishing titles, customer lists, etc.
► start-up costs
► training costs
► administrative and other general overhead costs
► advertising and promotion
► relocation and reorganization expenses
► redundancy and other termination costs

U.S. GAAP prohibits the capitalization as an asset of almost all research and development costs. All such costs usually must be expensed. Generally, under U.S. GAAP, acquired intangible assets are reported as separately identifiable intangibles (as opposed to goodwill) if they arise from contractual rights (such as a licensing agreement), other legal rights (such as patents), or have the ability to be separated and sold (such as a customer list).

EXAMPLE 4

Measuring Intangible Assets

Alpha, Inc., a motor vehicle manufacturer, has a research division that worked on the following projects during the year:

Project 1: Research aimed at finding a steering mechanism that does not operate like a conventional steering wheel but reacts to the impulses from a driver's fingers.

Project 2: The design of a prototype welding apparatus that is controlled electronically rather than mechanically, which has been determined to be technologically feasible.

The following is a summary of the expenses of the particular department (in thousands of euros):

	General	Project 1	Project 2
Material and services	€128	€935	€620
Labor			
Direct labor	—	620	320
Administrative personnel	720	—	—
Overhead			
Direct	—	340	410
Indirect	270	110	60

Five percent of administrative personnel costs can be attributed to each of Projects 1 and 2. Explain the capitalization of Alpha's development costs for Projects 1 and 2 under IFRS.

Solution: Under IFRS, the capitalization of development costs for Projects 1 and 2 would be as follows:

Project 1: Classified as research so all costs
                are recognized as expenses.   NIL
Project 2: (620 + 320 + 410 + 60)   €1,410

Note that Project 2 is in the development stage and costs related to the project should be capitalized under IFRS. However, under IAS No. 38, administrative personnel costs should be expensed.

3.4.2 Goodwill

In a purchase acquisition, the excess of the cost of acquisition over the acquirer's interest in the fair value of the identifiable assets and liabilities acquired is described as goodwill and is recognized as an asset.

The subject of recognizing goodwill in financial statements has found both proponents and opponents among professionals. The proponents of goodwill recognition assert that goodwill is the "present value of excess returns that a company is able to earn." This group claims that determining the present value of these excess returns is analogous to determining the present value of future cash flows associated with other assets and projects. Opponents of goodwill recognition claim that the prices paid for acquisitions often turn out to be based on unrealistic expectations, thereby leading to future write-offs of goodwill.

Analysts should distinguish between accounting goodwill and economic goodwill. Economic goodwill is based on the economic performance of the entity, whereas accounting goodwill is based on accounting standards and only reported for past acquisitions. Economic goodwill is what should concern analysts and investors, and it is often not reflected on the balance sheet. This economic goodwill should be reflected in the stock price. Many analysts believe that goodwill should not be listed on the balance sheet, as it cannot be sold separately from the entity. These analysts believe that only assets that can be separately identified and sold be reflected on the balance sheet. Other financial statement users may desire to analyze goodwill and any subsequent impairment charges to assess management's performance on prior acquisitions.

Under IFRS and U.S. GAAP, goodwill should be capitalized and tested for impairment annually. Goodwill is not amortized. Impairment of goodwill is a noncash expense. If goodwill is deemed to be impaired, it is charged against income in the current period. This charge reduces current earnings. Assets are also reduced, so some performance measures, such as return on assets (net income divided by average total assets), may actually increase in future periods.

Under IFRS No. 3, the purchase method of accounting can be summarized by the following steps:

▶ The cost of acquisition is determined.

▶ The fair value of the acquiree's assets is determined.

▶ The fair value of the acquiree's liabilities and contingent liabilities is determined.

▶ Calculate the goodwill arising from the purchase as follows:

  ▶ The book value of the acquirer's assets and liabilities should be combined with the fair value adjustments of the acquiree's assets, liabilities, and contingent liabilities.

  ▶ Any goodwill should be recognized as an asset in the combined entity's balance sheet.

Despite the clear guidance incorporated in IFRS No. 3, many analysts believe that the determination of fair values involves considerable management discretion. Values for intangible assets, such as computer software, might not be easily validated when analyzing purchase acquisitions.

Management judgment can be particularly apparent in the allocation of the excess purchase price (after all other allocations to assets and liabilities). If, for example, the remaining excess purchase price is allocated to goodwill, there will be no impact on the company's net income because goodwill is not amortized (but is tested for impairment). If the excess were to be allocated to fixed assets, depreciation would rise, thus reducing net income and producing incorrect financial statements. (**Depreciation** is the allocation of the costs of a long-term [tangible] asset over its useful life.)

Goodwill can significantly affect the comparability of financial statements between companies using different accounting methods. As such, an analyst should remove any distortion that the recognition, amortization, and impairment of goodwill might create by adjusting the company's financial statements. Adjustments should be made by:

▶ computing financial ratios using balance sheet data that exclude goodwill;

▶ reviewing operating trends using data that exclude the amortization of goodwill or impairment to goodwill charges; and

▶ evaluating future business acquisitions by taking into account the purchase price paid relative to the net assets and earnings prospects of the acquired company.

IFRS No. 3 requires disclosure of the factors that contributed to goodwill and a description of each intangible asset that was not recognized separately from goodwill.

EXAMPLE 5

Goodwill Impairment

Vodafone Group, PLC, is a leading international provider of mobile communications services. It entered many of its international markets by acquiring local carriers. On 27 February 2006, Vodafone issued a press release that included the following information:

Reflecting the increasingly competitive environment in the industry, Vodafone has incorporated into its latest ten year plan a lower view of growth prospects for a number of key operating companies, particularly in the medium to long term, than those it has used previously.

The result of these factors is that Vodafone expects to report:
▶ An impairment of the Group's goodwill in the range of GBP 23 billion to GBP 28 billion in respect of reductions in the aggregate goodwill for Vodafone Germany, Vodafone Italy and, potentially, Vodafone Japan. It is expected that most of the total will be attributable to Vodafone Germany.
▶ No impairment for any other subsidiary, joint venture or investment in associated undertakings.
▶ No impairment in respect of finite lived assets.

A summary of the Group's goodwill in respect of subsidiary undertakings and joint ventures as of 30 September 2005 follows.

GBP Billion	
Germany	35.5
Italy	19.7
Japan	9.0
Spain	10.3
U.K.	0.7
Other subsidiaries and joint ventures	6.3
	81.5

How significant is this goodwill impairment and, with reference to acquisition prices, what might it indicate?

Solution: Given that the goodwill impairment was approximately equal to one-third the total value of goodwill recorded, it would appear to be significant. According to the press release, the impairment has arisen due to a competitive environment and lower expected growth rates. The operations involved appear now to be worth less than the price that was paid for their acquisition.

3.5 Financial Instruments: Financial Assets and Financial Liabilities

International accounting standards define a financial instrument as a contract that gives rise to a financial asset of one entity, and a financial liability or equity instrument of another entity. Financial instruments, both assets and liabilities, come in a variety of forms. Financial assets include investments in stocks and bonds and similar instruments. Financial liabilities include bonds, notes payable, and similar instruments. Some financial instruments may be classified as either an asset or a liability depending upon the contractual terms and current market conditions. One example of such a complex financial instrument is a derivative. A **derivative** is a financial instrument for which the value is derived based on some underlying factor (interest rate, exchange rate, commodity price, security price, or credit rating) and for which little or no initial investment is required. Derivatives may be used to hedge business transactions or for speculation.

Mark-to-market (fair value adjustments to financial assets and liabilities) is the process whereby the value of most trading assets (e.g., those held for trading and that are available for sale) and trading liabilities are adjusted to reflect current fair value. Such adjustments are often made on a daily basis, and cumulative balances are reversed on the subsequent day, prior to recalculating a fresh cumulative mark-to-market adjustment.

All financial assets and financial liabilities (including derivatives) should be recognized when the entity becomes a party to the contractual provisions of an instrument. For the purchase or sale of financial assets where market convention determines a fixed period between trade and settlement dates, the trade or settlement date can be used for recognition. Interest is not normally accrued between trade and settlement dates, but mark-to-market adjustments are made regardless of whether the entity uses trade date or settlement date accounting. Although IAS No. 39 allows the use of either date, trade date accounting is preferred by most treasury accountants.

Exhibit 11 provides a summary of how various financial assets and liabilities are classified and measured.

From Exhibit 11, marketable securities such as stocks and bonds may be classified as trading, available for sale, and held to maturity. To illustrate the different accounting treatments of the gains and losses on marketable securities, consider an entity that invests €100,000,000 in a 5 percent coupon fixed-income security portfolio. After six months, the company receives the first coupon payment of €2,500,000. Additionally, interest rates have declined and the value of the fixed-income securities has increased by €2,000,000. Exhibit 12 illustrates how this situation will be portrayed in the balance sheet assets and equity, as well as the income statement of the entity concerned, under each of the following three accounting policies for marketable securities: assets held for trading purposes, assets available for sale, and held-to-maturity assets.

EXHIBIT 11　　　**Measurement of Financial Assets and Liabilities**

Measured at Fair Value

Financial Assets

Financial assets held for trading (e.g., stocks and bonds)

Available-for-sale financial assets (e.g., stocks and bonds)

Derivatives whether stand-alone or embedded in nonderivative instruments

Nonderivative instruments (including financial assets) with fair value exposures *hedged* by derivatives

Financial Liabilities

Derivatives

Financial liabilities held for trading

Nonderivative instruments (including financial liabilities) with fair value exposures *hedged* by derivatives

Measured at Cost or Amortized Cost

Financial Assets

Unlisted instruments (investments where the fair value is not reliably measurable)

Held-to-maturity investments (bonds intended to be held to maturity)

Loans and receivables

Financial Liabilities

All other liabilities (such as bonds payable or notes payable)

EXHIBIT 12	Accounting for Gains and Losses on Marketable Securities		

Balance Sheet As of 30 June 200X	Trading Portfolio	Available-for-Sale Portfolio	Held to Maturity
Assets			
Deposits	2,500,000	2,500,000	2,500,000
Cost of securities	100,000,000	100,000,000	100,000,000
Unrealized gains (losses) on securities	2,000,000	2,000,000	—
	104,500,000	104,500,000	102,500,000
Liabilities			
Equity			
Paid-in capital	100,000,000	100,000,000	100,000,000
Retained earnings	4,500,000	2,500,000	2,500,000
Other comprehensive income (losses)	—	2,000,000	—
	104,500,000	104,500,000	102,500,000

Income Statement For Period 1 January–30 June 200X

Interest income	2,500,000	2,500,000	2,500,000
Unrealized gains (losses)	2,000,000	—	—
	4,500,000	2,500,000	2,500,000

In the case of marketable securities classified as either trading or available for sale, the investments are listed under assets at fair market value. For exposition purposes, Exhibit 12 shows the unrealized gain on a separate line. Practically, the investments would be listed at their fair value of €102,000,000 on one line within assets. In the case of trading securities, the unrealized gain is included on the income statement and thus reflected in retained earnings. In the case of available-for-sale securities, the unrealized gain is not included on the income statement; rather, it is deferred as part of other comprehensive income within owners' equity. As noted in the reading on the income statement, other comprehensive income includes gains and losses that have not yet been reported on the income statement due to particular accounting standards. In the case of held-to-maturity securities, the unrealized gain is not reflected on either the balance sheet or income statement.

In the case of liabilities such as bonds issued by a company, these are normally reported at amortized cost on the balance sheet, as noted in Exhibit 11. For example, if a company issues bonds with a total par value of $10,000,000 at a price of $9,750,000 (issued at a discount), the bonds are reported as a liability of $9,750,000 (cost). As time passes, the discount of $250,000 is amortized such that the bond will be listed as a liability of $10,000,000 at maturity. Similarly, any bond premium would be amortized for bonds issued at a premium.

EQUITY

Equity is the residual claim on a company's assets after subtracting liabilities. It represents the claim of the owner against the company. Equity includes funds directly invested in the company by the owners, as well as earnings that have been reinvested over time. Equity can also include items of gain or loss that are not yet recognized on the company's income statement.

4.1 Components of Equity

IFRS and U.S. GAAP both define equity (or net assets) as the residual interest in the assets of an entity that remain after deducting its liabilities. There are five potential components that comprise the owners' equity section of the balance sheet:

1. *Capital contributed by owners.* Capital ownership in a corporation is evidenced through the issuance of common stock, although preferred stock (a hybrid security with some characteristics of debt) may be issued by some companies in addition to common stock. Preferred shares have rights that take precedence over the rights of common shareholders—rights that generally pertain to receipt of dividends (not always cumulative if omitted by the board of directors) and receipt of assets if the company is liquidated. Common and preferred shares may have a par value (or stated value) or may be issued as no par shares (depending on governmental requirements at the time of incorporation). Where par or stated value requirements exist, it must be disclosed in the stockholders' equity section of the balance sheet. In addition, the number of shares authorized, issued, and outstanding must be disclosed for each class of stock issued by the company. The number of authorized shares is the number of shares that may be sold by the company under its articles of incorporation. The number of issued shares is those shares that have been sold to investors while the number of outstanding shares consists of the issued shares less those shares repurchased (treasury stock) by the company.

2. *Minority interest (or noncontrolling interest).* The equity interests of minority shareholders in the subsidiary companies that have been consolidated by the parent (controlling) company but that are not wholly owned by the parent company.

3. *Retained earnings (or retained deficit).* Amounts that have been recognized as cumulatively earned in the company's income statements but which have not been paid to the owners of the company through dividends.

4. *Treasury stock (or own shares repurchased).* The repurchase of company shares may occur when management considers the shares undervalued or when it wants to limit the effects of dilution from various employee stock compensation plans. Treasury stock is a reduction of shareholders' equity and a reduction of total shares outstanding. Treasury shares are nonvoting and do not receive dividends if declared by the company.

5. *Accumulated comprehensive income (or other reserves).* Amounts that may either increase or decrease total shareholders' equity but are not derived from the income statement or through any company transactions in its own equity shares.

In June 1997, the FASB released Statement of Financial Accounting Standard (SFAS) No. 130, *Reporting of Comprehensive Income.* This statement established certain standards for reporting and presenting comprehensive income in the general-purpose financial statements. SFAS No. 130 was issued in response to users' concerns that certain changes in assets and liabilities were bypassing the income statement and appearing in the statement of changes in stockholders' equity. The purpose of SFAS No. 130 was to report all items that met the definition of "comprehensive income" in a prominent financial statement for the same period in which they were recognized. In accordance with the definition provided by Statement of Financial Accounting Concepts No. 6, **comprehensive income** was to include all changes in owners' equity that resulted from transactions of the business entity with non-owners. Comprehensive income can be defined as:

Comprehensive income = Net income + Other comprehensive income

According to SFAS No. 130, **other comprehensive income** (OCI) is part of total comprehensive income but generally excluded from net income. Prior to SFAS No. 130, these three items—foreign currency translation adjustments, minimum pension liability adjustments, and unrealized gains or losses on available-for-sale investments—were disclosed as separate components of stockholders' equity on the balance sheet. Under SFAS No. 130, they are to be reported as OCI. Furthermore, they must be reported separately, as the FASB decided that information about each component is more important than information about the aggregate. Later, under SFAS No. 133, net unrealized losses on derivatives were also included in the definition of OCI. The intent of SFAS No. 130 was that "if used with related disclosures and other information in financial statements, the information provided by reporting comprehensive income would assist investors, creditors, and other financial statement users in assessing an enterprise's economic activities and its timing and magnitude of future cash flows."

Although the FASB required that "an enterprise shall display total comprehensive income and its components in a financial statement that is displayed with the same prominence as other financial statements that constitute a full set of financial statements," it did not specify which format was required, except that net income should be shown as a component of comprehensive income in that financial statement. According to SFAS No. 130, three alternative formats are allowed for presenting OCI and total comprehensive income:

▶ below the line for net income in a traditional income statement (as a combined statement of net income and comprehensive income);

▶ in a separate statement of comprehensive income that begins with the amount of net income for the year; or

▶ in a statement of changes in stockholders' equity.

Under IFRS, the component changes are also reported in the statement of equity; however, it is not presently required that a comprehensive income amount be reported.

Exhibit 13 illustrates how the equity amounts of €22,000 (20X9) and €20,000 (20X8) have been expanded from the one amount shown in Exhibit 5.

EXHIBIT 13	Apex Stockholders' Equity	
	20X9	**20X8**
Equity	**€22,000**	**€20,000**
Share capital	10,000	10,000
Preferred shares	2,000	2,000
Share premium (paid-in capital)	—	—
Other reserves (unrealized gains and losses)	1,000	—
Retained earnings	9,000	8,000
Own shares repurchased (treasury shares)	—	—

4.2 Statement of Changes in Shareholders' Equity

The **statement of changes in shareholders' equity** reflects information about the increases or decreases to a company's net assets or wealth. With respect to comprehensive income, the following items, if present, must be disclosed:

- ▶ unrealized gains or losses on available-for-sale investments;
- ▶ gains or losses from derivatives that qualify as net investment hedges or cash flow hedges;
- ▶ minimum pension liability adjustments from underfunded defined-benefit plans; and
- ▶ foreign currency translation adjustments on foreign subsidiary companies.

Other information in the changes in equity statement or in notes includes the following:

- ▶ capital transactions with owners and distributions to owners;
- ▶ reconciliation of the balance of accumulated profit or loss (retained earnings) at the beginning and end of the year; and
- ▶ reconciliation of the carrying amount of each class of equity capital, share premium (paid-in capital), and accumulated comprehensive income (reserve) at the beginning and end of the period.

Exhibit 14 presents Sony Corporation's Consolidated Statement of Changes in Stockholders' Equity for the fiscal years ended 31 March 2004 and 2005. In this statement, Sony complies with the reconciliation and disclosure requirements that were discussed above.

EXHIBIT 14 **Sony Corporation and Consolidated Subsidiaries Consolidated Statement of Changes in Stockholders' Equity (¥ Millions)**

	Subsidiary Tracking Stock	Common Stock	Additional Paid-In Capital	Retained Earnings	Accumulated Other Comprehensive Income	Treasury Stock, at Cost	Total
Balance at 31 March 2003	3,917	472,361	984,196	1,301,740	(471,978)	(9,341)	2,280,895
Conversion of convertible bonds		3,989	3,988				7,977
Stock issued under exchange offering			5,409				5,409
Comprehensive income:							
Net income				88,511			88,511
Other comprehensive income, net of tax							
Unrealized gains on securities:							
Unrealized holding gains or losses arising during period					57,971		57,971
Less: Reclassification adjustment for gains or losses included in net income					(5,679)		(5,679)
Unrealized losses on derivative instruments:							
Unrealized holding gains or losses arising during period					7,537		7,537
Less: Reclassification adjustment for gains or losses included in net income					(3,344)		(3,344)
Minimum pension liability adjustment					93,415		93,415
Foreign currency translation adjustments:							
Translation adjustments arising during period					(129,113)		(129,113)
Less: Reclassification adjustment for losses included in net income					1,232		1,232
Total comprehensive income							110,530
Stock issue costs, net of tax				(53)			(53)
Dividends declared				(23,138)			(23,138)
Purchase of treasury stock						(8,523)	(8,523)
Reissuance of treasury stock			(776)			5,681	4,905
Balance at 31 March 2004	3,917	476,350	992,817	1,367,060	(449,959)	(12,183)	2,378,022

(Exhibit continued on next page . . .)

EXHIBIT 14   (continued)

	Subsidiary Tracking Stock	Common Stock	Additional Paid-In Capital	Retained Earnings	Accumulated Other Comprehensive Income	Treasury Stock, at Cost	Total
Balance at 31 March 2004	3,917	476,350	992,817	1,367,060	(449,959)	(12,183)	2,378,022
Exercise of stock acquisition rights		52	53				105
Conversion of convertible bonds		141,390	141,354				282,744
Stock-based compensation			340				340
Comprehensive income:							
Net income				163,838			163,838
Other comprehensive income, net of tax							
Unrealized gains on securities:							
Unrealized holding gains or losses arising during period					5,643		5,643
Less: Reclassification adjustment for gains or losses included in net income					(12,924)		(12,924)
Unrealized losses on derivative instruments:							
Unrealized holding gains or losses arising during period					(209)		(209)
Less: Reclassification adjustment for gains or losses included in net income					(1,681)		(1,681)
Minimum pension liability adjustment					(769)		(769)
Foreign currency translation adjustments:							
Translation adjustments arising during period					74,224		74,224
Total comprehensive income							228,122
Stock issue costs, net of tax				(541)			(541)
Dividends declared				(24,030)			(24,030)
Purchase of treasury stock						(416)	(416)
Reissuance of treasury stock			(342)	(245)		6,599	6,012
Balance at 31 March 2005	**3,917**	**617,792**	**1,134,222**	**1,506,082**	**(385,675)**	**(6,000)**	**2,870,338**

USES AND ANALYSIS OF THE BALANCE SHEET

The classified sections of Apex Corporation's balance sheets have been discussed and illustrated throughout this reading. Exhibit 15 now presents the complete detailed balance sheets for Apex, which we will use as the basis for a discussion of how to analyze a balance sheet.

EXHIBIT 15	Apex Detailed Balance Sheets	

Balance Sheet (000)	20X9	20X8
Assets		
Current assets	**€20,000**	**€16,000**
Cash and cash equivalents	3,000	2,000
Marketable securities: 3 types	3,000	4,000
Trade receivables	5,000	3,000
Inventories	7,000	6,000
Other current assets	2,000	1,000
Noncurrent assets	**53,000**	**27,000**
Property, plant, and equipment	35,000	20,000
Goodwill	5,000	1,000
Other intangible assets	3,000	1,000
Noncurrent investments (subsidiaries, associates, joint ventures)	10,000	5,000
Total assets	**€73,000**	**€43,000**
Liabilities and Equity		
Current liabilities	**14,000**	**7,000**
Trade and other payables	5,000	2,000
Current borrowings	3,000	1,000
Current portion of noncurrent borrowings	2,000	1,000
Current tax payable	2,000	2,000
Accrued liabilities	1,000	500
Unearned revenue	1,000	500
Noncurrent liabilities	**37,000**	**16,000**
Noncurrent borrowings	30,000	10,000
Deferred tax	6,000	5,000
Noncurrent provisions	1,000	1,000
Total liabilities	**51,000**	**23,000**
Equity	**22,000**	**20,000**
Share capital	10,000	10,000
Preference shares	2,000	2,000
Share premium (paid-in capital)	—	—
Other reserves (unrealized gains and losses)	1,000	—
Retained earnings	9,000	8,000
Own shares repurchased (treasury shares)	—	—
Total liabilities and shareholders' equity	**€73,000**	**€43,000**

If a company is growing or shrinking, comparing balance sheet amounts from year to year may not clearly show trends. Additionally, comparing companies is difficult unless adjustments are made for size. Two techniques used to analyze balance sheets adjusted for differences or changes are common-size analysis and ratio analysis.

5.1 Common-Size Analysis of the Balance Sheet

The first technique, common-size analysis, involves stating all balance sheet items as a percentage of total assets.[5] Vertical common-size statements are useful in comparing a company's current balance sheet with prior-year balance sheets or to other companies in the same industry. Horizontal common-size analysis provides a format to accomplish the former but not the latter. Exhibit 16 illustrates vertical common-size balance sheets for Apex Corporation. Horizontal common-size analysis is demonstrated in a later reading.

EXHIBIT 16	Apex Common-Size Balance Sheets		
Balance Sheet (Percent of Total Assets)		**20X9**	**20X8**
Assets			
Current assets		**27.4**	**37.2**
Cash and cash equivalents		4.1	4.7
Marketable securities: 3 types		4.1	9.3
Trade receivables		6.8	7.0
Inventories		9.6	14.0
Other current assets		2.7	2.3
Noncurrent assets		**72.6**	**62.8**
Property, plant, and equipment		47.9	46.5
Goodwill		6.8	2.3
Other intangible assets		4.1	2.3
Noncurrent investments (subsidiaries, associates, joint ventures)		13.7	11.6
Total assets		**100.0**	**100.0**

(Exhibit continued on next page . . .)

---

[5] This format can be distinguished as "vertical common-size analysis." As the reading on financial statement analysis will discuss, another type of common-size analysis, known as "horizontal common-size analysis," states quantities in terms of a selected base-year value. Unless otherwise indicated, text references to "common-size analysis" refer to vertical analysis.

EXHIBIT 16	(continued)		

Balance Sheet (Percent of Total Assets)	20X9	20X8
Liabilities and Equity		
Current liabilities	**19.2**	**16.3**
Trade and other payables	6.8	4.7
Current borrowings	4.1	2.3
Current portion of noncurrent borrowings	2.7	2.3
Current tax payable	2.7	4.7
Accrued liabilities	1.4	1.2
Unearned revenue	1.4	1.2
Noncurrent liabilities	**50.7**	**37.2**
Noncurrent borrowings	41.1	23.3
Deferred tax	8.2	11.6
Noncurrent provisions	1.4	2.3
Total liabilities	**69.9**	**53.5**
Shareholders' equity	**30.1**	**46.5**
Share capital	13.7	23.3
Preference shares	2.7	4.7
Share premium (paid-in capital)	—	—
Other reserves (unrealized gains and losses)	1.4	—
Retained earnings	12.3	18.6
Own shares repurchased (treasury shares)	—	—
Total liabilities and shareholders' equity	**100.0**	**100.0**

The common-size analysis for Apex clearly shows that for 20X9, the company is less liquid and is more leveraged than it was in 20X8. Regarding liquidity, current assets have decreased and current liabilities have increased when compared with the prior year. With respect to leverage, both noncurrent and total liabilities have increased when compared with the prior year.

EXAMPLE 6

Common-Size Analysis

Applying common-size analysis to the Roche Group balance sheets presented in Exhibit 7, which one of the following line items increased in 2005 relative to 2004?

A. Goodwill.
B. Inventories.
C. Long-term debt.
D. Accounts receivables.

Solution: C is correct. Long-term debt increased as a percentage of total assets from 12.1 percent of total assets in 2004 (CHF7,077 ÷ CHF58,446) to 13.4 percent in 2005 (CHF9,322 ÷ CHF69,365).

Although goodwill, inventories, and accounts receivables all increased in absolute Swiss franc amounts during 2005, they declined as a percentage of total assets when compared with the previous year.

Vertical common-size analysis of the balance sheet is particularly useful in cross-sectional analysis—comparing companies to each other for a particular time period or comparing a company with industry or sector data. The analyst could select individual peer companies for comparison, use industry data from published sources, or compile data from databases. Some common sources of published data are:

► *Annual Statement Studies*, published by the Risk Management Association (RMA). This volume provides abbreviated common-size (and ratio) data by industry. The source of data includes both public and nonpublic company data collected by financial institutions and may reflect non-GAAP, unaudited data.

► *Almanac of Business and Industrial Financial Ratios*, by Leo Troy. This is an annually revised publication, currently published by CCH.

When analyzing a company, many analysts prefer to select the peer companies for comparison or to compile their own industry statistics. For example, Exhibit 17 presents common-size balance sheet data compiled for the 10 sectors of Standard & Poor's 500 using 2005 data. The sector classification follows the S&P/MSCI Global Industrial Classification System (GICS). The exhibit presents mean and median common-size balance sheet data for those companies in the S&P 500 for which 2005 data was available in the Compustat database.[6]

---

[6] An entry of zero for an item (e.g., current assets) was excluded from the data, except in the case of preferred stock. Note that most financial institutions did not provide current asset or current liability data, so these are reported as not available in the database.

EXHIBIT 17　Common-Size Balance Sheet Statistics for the S&P 500 Grouped by S&P/MSCI GICS Sector (in Percent except No. of Observations; Data for 2005)

Panel A. Median Data

	Energy	Materials	Industrials	Consumer Discretionary	Consumer Staples	Health Care	Financials	Information Technology	Telecom Services	Utilities
No. observations	29	30	49	85	36	52	87	73	9	31
Cash	7.55	6.07	4.89	7.60	4.50	18.50	5.32	28.35	2.05	1.61
Receivables	11.16	13.56	16.50	9.60	9.92	11.91	28.95	10.64	4.71	5.49
Inventories	3.98	10.21	10.38	15.43	14.67	7.49	1.37	5.52	0.95	2.13
Other current	1.64	2.51	3.59	3.33	2.75	3.85	0.98	4.00	1.49	4.59
Current assets	27.29	35.65	36.58	43.92	33.18	41.61	NA	56.05	10.06	16.89
PPE	54.70	37.21	15.79	20.99	27.53	13.70	1.06	9.80	42.57	55.04
Accts payable	7.50	7.01	6.91	6.99	8.54	4.54	34.73	4.14	2.49	3.89
Current liabilities	17.94	20.18	24.48	27.13	29.55	23.87	NA	22.90	13.70	17.13
LT debt	14.77	19.86	17.43	17.81	21.39	11.43	11.98	8.01	23.13	29.35
Total liabilities	50.72	63.82	62.29	56.73	65.36	47.87	89.81	37.10	58.39	75.28
Preferred stock	0.00	0.00	0.00	0.00	0.00	0.00	0.00	0.00	0.00	0.28
Common equity	49.28	36.18	37.71	43.27	34.64	52.13	10.19	62.90	41.61	22.89
Total equity	49.28	36.18	37.71	43.27	34.64	52.13	10.19	62.90	41.61	24.72

(Exhibit continued on next page . . .)

LT = long term, PPE = property, plant, and equipment.

EXHIBIT 17   (continued)

Panel B. Mean Data

	Energy	Materials	Industrials	Consumer Discretionary	Consumer Staples	Health Care	Financials	Information Technology	Telecom Services	Utilities
No. observations	29	30	49	85	36	52	87	73	9	31
Cash	7.56	9.16	7.91	10.19	7.45	19.55	10.49	33.43	3.32	2.85
Receivables	11.83	14.30	17.92	12.46	9.92	12.96	34.02	12.78	5.16	6.78
Inventories	5.32	10.82	10.21	19.36	15.54	9.23	6.88	6.51	0.94	2.62
Other current	2.98	2.73	4.07	3.74	3.09	4.08	1.09	4.60	2.49	6.44
Current assets	27.14	36.82	36.41	40.18	36.35	44.62	NA	56.71	11.59	18.60
PPE	54.84	35.70	24.83	25.38	30.77	16.76	1.92	13.05	48.53	57.48
Accts payable	9.07	8.80	7.12	10.46	9.82	8.75	35.09	7.03	2.76	4.53
Current liabilities	19.00	21.02	25.48	27.71	28.66	25.50	NA	23.99	13.56	18.92
LT debt	17.84	20.18	18.78	19.05	23.51	14.83	18.16	10.60	31.00	31.94
Total liabilities	53.16	61.72	61.10	57.64	64.67	48.88	80.50	40.05	65.74	76.83
Preferred stock	0.50	0.76	0.14	0.11	0.01	0.18	0.93	0.06	0.04	0.60
Common equity	46.33	37.52	38.76	42.25	35.32	50.94	18.60	59.89	34.22	22.57
Total equity	46.84	38.28	38.90	42.36	35.33	51.12	19.50	59.95	34.26	23.17

LT = long term, PPE = property, plant, and equipment.

Source: Based on data from Compustat.

Some interesting general observations can be made from these data:

► Energy and utility companies have the largest amounts of property, plant, and equipment. Utilities also have the highest level of long-term debt and use some preferred stock.

► Financial companies have the greatest percentage of liabilities.

► Telecommunications services and utility companies have the lowest level of receivables.

► Inventory levels are highest for consumer discretionary and consumer staples companies.

► Information technology companies use the least amount of leverage as evidenced by the entries for long-term debt and total liabilities.

Example 7 shows an analyst using cross-sectional common-size balance sheet data.

EXAMPLE 7

Cross-Sectional Common-Size Analysis

Jason Lu is examining four companies in the computer industry to evaluate their relative financial position as reflected on their balance sheet. He has compiled the following vertical common-size data for Dell, Hewlett-Packard Co., Gateway, and Apple Computer.

Cross-Sectional Analysis

**Consolidated Balance Sheets
(in Percent of Total Assets)**

Company Fiscal Year	DELL 3 Feb 2006	HPQ 31 Oct 2005	GTW 31 Dec 2005	AAPL 30 Sep 2005
Assets				
Current assets:				
Cash and cash equivalents	30.47	17.99	21.99	30.22
Short-term investments	8.72	0.02	8.50	41.30
Accounts receivable, net	17.69	16.11	17.97	7.75
Financing receivables, net	5.90	n/a	n/a	n/a
Inventories	2.49	8.89	11.42	1.43
Other current assets	11.34	13.03	22.06	8.48
Total current assets	76.62	56.05	81.94	89.17
Property, plant, and equipment, net	8.68	8.34	4.33	7.07
Investments	11.64	9.70	0.00	0.00
Long-term financing receivables, net	1.41	n/a	n/a	n/a
Other assets	1.65	25.91	13.73	3.76
Total Assets	100.00	100.00	100.00	100.00

Company Fiscal Year	DELL 3 Feb 2006	HPQ 31 Oct 2005	GTW 31 Dec 2005	AAPL 30 Sep 2005
Liabilities and Stockholders' Equity				
Current liabilities:				
Accounts payable	42.58	13.22	39.66	15.40
Short-term debt	0.00	2.37	2.60	0.00
Accrued and other	26.34	25.10	23.60	14.76
Total current liabilities	68.92	40.69	65.86	30.16
Long-term debt	2.18	4.39	15.62	0.00
Other liabilities	11.03	6.84	2.98	5.20
Commitments and contingent liabilities	0.00	0.00	0.00	0.00
Total liabilities	82.13	51.92	84.46	35.36
Stockholders' equity				
Total stockholders' equity	17.87	48.08	15.54	64.64

HPQ = Hewlett-Packard Co., GTW = Gateway, AAPL = Apple Computer, n/a = not available.

Source: Based on data from Bloomberg.

From this data, Lu learns the following:

▶ All four companies have a high level of cash, consistent with the information technology sector. Dell and Apple have a much higher than normal balance in cash and investments combined. This may reflect their business models, which have generated large operating cash flows in recent years.

▶ Apple has the lowest level of accounts receivable. Further research is necessary to learn if this is related to Apple's cash sales through retail stores or if the company has been selling/factoring receivables to a greater degree than the other companies.

▶ Dell and Apple both have an extraordinarily low level of inventory. Both utilize a just-in-time inventory system and rely on suppliers to hold inventory until needed. Additional scrutiny of the footnotes accompanying their annual reports reveals that Dell includes some "in-transit" inventory in other current assets and that Apple regularly makes purchase commitments that are not currently recorded as inventory and uses contract manufacturers to assemble and test some finished products. Dell has a smaller relative amount of purchase commitments. Hewlett-Packard has similar purchase commitments to Apple, and all of the companies make some use of contract manufacturers, but no mention is made of them about the extent that inventory may be "understated" through such use. Overall, it appears that the inventory levels may be understated somewhat for Dell and Apple but that, all things considered, they have been more efficient at managing inventory than Hewlett-Packard or Gateway.

▶ All four companies have a level of property, plant, and equipment below that of the sector, with Gateway having the lowest level.

> ► Hewlett-Packard has a large amount of "other assets." Further analysis reveals that this represents purchased intangibles, particularly goodwill from acquisitions.
>
> ► Dell and Gateway have a large amount of accounts payable. Due to Dell's high level of cash and investments, this is likely not a problem for Dell; however, it could indicate that Gateway could have difficulty in paying suppliers. An analysis of Gateway's cash flows would be warranted.
>
> ► Consistent with the industry, Dell, Hewlett-Packard, and Apple have very low levels of long-term debt. Gateway has a high level relative to the industry, which warrants further examination to assess the company's financial risk.

5.2 Balance Sheet Ratios

The second technique permitting comparison across time (time-series analysis) and across companies (cross-sectional analysis) is ratio analysis. In ratio analysis, the analyst may examine the level and trend of a ratio in relation to past values of the ratio for the company, thereby providing information on changes in the financial position of a company over time. The analyst may also compare a ratio against the values of the ratio for comparable companies, thereby providing information on the financial position of a company in relation to that of its peer group. So-called **balance sheet ratios** are those involving balance sheet items only. Balance sheet ratios fall under the heading of **liquidity ratios** (measuring the company's ability to meet its short-term obligations) or **solvency ratios** (measuring the company's ability to meet long-term and other obligations). The use of these ratios along with other balance sheet ratios and ratios combining balance sheet data with other financial statement data are discussed in a later reading. Exhibit 18 summarizes the calculation and interpretation of selected balance sheet ratios.

EXHIBIT 18	Balance Sheet Ratios	
Liquidity Ratios	**Calculation**	**Measurement**
Current	Current assets ÷ Current liabilities	Ability to meet current liabilities
Quick (acid test)	(Cash + Marketable securities + Receivables) ÷ Current liabilities	Ability to meet current liabilities
Cash	(Cash + Marketable securities) ÷ Current liabilities	Ability to meet current liabilities
Solvency Ratios		
Long-term debt to equity	Total long-term debt ÷ Total equity	Financial risk and financial leverage
Debt to equity	Total debt ÷ Total equity	Financial risk and financial leverage
Total debt	Total debt ÷ Total assets	Financial risk and financial leverage
Financial leverage	Total assets ÷ Total equity	Financial risk and financial leverage

Some have questioned the usefulness of financial statement analysis in a world where capital markets are said to be efficient. After all, they say, an efficient market is forward looking, whereas the analysis of financial statements is a look at the past. However, the value of financial analysis is that it enables the analyst to gain insights that can assist in making forward-looking projections required by an efficient market. Financial ratios serve the following purposes:

► They provide insights into the microeconomic relationships within a company that help analysts project earnings and free cash flow (which is necessary to determine entity value and credit-worthiness).

► They provide insights into a company's financial flexibility, which is its ability to obtain the cash required to meet financial obligations or to make asset acquisitions, even if unexpected circumstances should develop. Financial flexibility requires a company to possess financial strength (a level and trend of financial ratios that meet or exceed industry norms), lines of credit, or assets that can be easily used as a means of obtaining cash, either by their outright sale or by using them as collateral.

► They provide a means of evaluating management's ability. Key performance ratios can serve as quantitative measures for ranking management's ability relative to a peer group.

EXAMPLE 8

Ratio Analysis

For the following ratio questions, refer to the balance sheet information for Roche Group presented in Exhibit 7.

1. The **current ratio** for Roche Group at 31 December 2005 is closest to:

   A. 1.29.
   B. 1.86.
   C. 1.97.
   D. 3.75.

2. Using the balance sheet information presented in Exhibit 7 for Roche Group, which one of the following ratios increased in 2005 relative to 2004?

   A. Current ratio.
   B. Total debt ratio.
   C. Debt-to-equity ratio.
   D. Financial leverage ratio.

Solution to 1: D is correct. The current ratio (current assets ÷ current liabilities) is 3.75 (CHF35,626 ÷ CHF9,492).

Solution to 2: A is correct. The current ratio (current assets ÷ current liabilities) increased from 2.93 (CHF29,679 ÷ CHF10,134) in 2004 to 3.75 (CHF35,626 ÷ CHF9,492) in 2005. The total debt ratio declined from 43.1 percent in 2004 to 39.8 percent in 2005; the **debt-to-equity ratio** declined from 75.6 percent in 2004 to 66.2 percent in 2005; and the **financial leverage ratio** declined from 1.756 in 2004 to 1.662 in 2005.

Financial ratio analysis is limited by:

▶ The use of alternative accounting methods. Accounting methods play an important role in the interpretation of financial ratios. It should be remembered that ratios are usually based on data taken from financial statements. Such data are generated via accounting procedures that might not be comparable among companies because companies have latitude in the choice of accounting methods. This lack of consistency across companies makes comparability difficult to analyze and limits the usefulness of ratio analysis. Some accounting alternatives currently found include the following:

   ▶ first-in-first-out (FIFO) or last-in-first-out (LIFO) inventory valuation methods;

   ▶ cost or equity methods of accounting for unconsolidated associates;

   ▶ straight-line or accelerated consumption pattern methods of depreciation; and

   ▶ capitalized or operating lease treatment.

▶ The homogeneity of a company's operating activities. Many companies are diversified with divisions operating in different industries. This makes it difficult to find comparable industry ratios to use for comparison purposes. It is better to examine industry-specific ratios by lines of business.

▶ The need to determine whether the results of the ratio analysis are mutually consistent. One set of ratios might show a problem and another set might indicate that this problem is short term in nature.

▶ The need to use judgment. The analyst must use judgment when performing ratio analysis. A key issue is whether a ratio for a company is within a reasonable range for an industry, with this range being determined by the analyst. Although financial ratios are used to help assess the growth potential and risk of a business, they cannot be used alone to directly value a company or determine its credit-worthiness. The entire operation of the business must be examined, and the external economic and industry setting in which it is operating must be considered when interpreting financial ratios.

SUMMARY

The starting place for analyzing a company is typically the balance sheet. It provides users such as creditors or investors with information regarding the sources of finance available for projects and infrastructure. At the same time, it normally provides information about the future earnings capacity of a company's assets as well as an indication of cash flows implicit in the receivables and inventories.

The balance sheet has many limitations, especially relating to the measurement of assets and liabilities. The lack of timely recognition of liabilities and, sometimes, assets, coupled with historical costs as opposed to fair value accounting for all items on the balance sheet, implies that the financial analyst must make numerous adjustments to determine the economic net worth of the company.

The balance sheet discloses what an entity owns (assets) and what it owes (liabilities) at a specific point in time, which is why it is also referred to as the statement of financial position. Equity represents the portion belonging to the owners or shareholders of a business. Equity is the residual interest in the assets of an entity after deducting its liabilities. The value of equity is increased by any generation of new assets by the business itself or by profits made during the year and is decreased by losses or withdrawals in the form of dividends.

The analyst must understand the structure and format of the balance sheet in order to evaluate the liquidity, solvency, and overall financial position of a company. Key points are:

▶ The "report format" of the balance sheet lists assets, liabilities, and equity in a single column. The "account format" follows the pattern of the traditional general ledger accounts, with assets at the left and liabilities and equity at the right of a central dividing line.

▶ The balance sheet should distinguish between current and noncurrent assets and between current and noncurrent liabilities unless a presentation based on liquidity provides more relevant and reliable information.

▶ Assets expected to be liquidated or used up within one year or one operating cycle of the business, whichever is greater, are classified as current assets. Assets not expected to be liquidated or used up within one year or one operating cycle of the business, whichever is greater, are classified as noncurrent assets.

▶ Liabilities expected to be settled or paid within one year or one operating cycle of the business, whichever is greater, are classified as current liabilities. Liabilities not expected to be settled or paid within one year or one operating cycle of the business, whichever is greater, are classified as noncurrent liabilities.

▶ Asset and liability values reported on a balance sheet may be measured on the basis of fair value or historical cost. Historical cost values may be quite different from economic values. Balance sheets must be evaluated critically in light of accounting policies applied in order to answer the question of how the values relate to economic reality and to each other.

▶ The notes to financial statements are an integral part of the U.S. GAAP and IFRS financial reporting processes. They provide important required detailed disclosures, as well as other information provided voluntarily by management. This information can be invaluable when determining whether the measurement of assets is comparable to other entities being analyzed.

► Tangible assets are long-term assets with physical substance that are used in company operations.

► Intangible assets are amounts paid by a company to acquire certain rights that are not represented by the possession of physical assets. A company should assess whether the useful life of an intangible asset is finite or infinite and, if finite, the length of its life.

► Under IFRS and U.S. GAAP, goodwill should be capitalized and tested for impairment annually. Goodwill is not amortized.

► Financial instruments are contracts that give rise to both a financial asset of one entity and a financial liability of another entity. Financial instruments come in a variety of instruments, including derivatives, hedges, and marketable securities.

► There are five potential components that comprise the owners' equity section of the balance sheet: contributed capital, minority interest, retained earnings, treasury stock, and accumulated comprehensive income.

► The statement of changes in equity reflects information about the increases or decreases to a company's net assets or wealth.

► Ratio analysis is used by analysts and managers to assess company performance and status. Another valuable analytical technique is common-size (relative) analysis, which is achieved through the conversion of all balance sheet items to a percentage of total assets.

PRACTICE PROBLEMS FOR READING 33

1. Resources controlled by a company as a result of past events are:
   A. equity.
   B. assets.
   C. liabilities.

2. Equity equals:
   A. Assets – Liabilities.
   B. Liabilities – Assets.
   C. Assets + Liabilities.

3. Distinguishing between current and noncurrent items on the balance sheet and presenting a subtotal for current assets and liabilities is referred to as:
   A. the report format.
   B. the account format.
   C. a classified balance sheet.

4. All of the following are current assets *except*:
   A. cash.
   B. goodwill.
   C. inventories.

5. Debt due within one year is considered:
   A. current.
   B. preferred.
   C. long term.

6. Money received from customers for products to be delivered in the future is recorded as:
   A. revenue and an asset.
   B. an asset and a liability.
   C. revenue and a liability.

7. The carrying value of inventories reflects:
   A. their original cost.
   B. their current value.
   C. the lower of original cost or net realizable value.

8. When a company pays its rent in advance, its balance sheet will reflect a reduction in:
   A. assets and liabilities.
   B. liabilities and shareholders' equity.
   C. one category of assets and an increase in another.

9. Accrued liabilities are:
   A. balanced against an asset.
   B. expenses that have been paid.
   C. expenses that have been reported on the income statement.

10. The initial measurement of goodwill is:

   A. not subject to management discretion.

   B. based on an acquisition's purchase price.

   C. based on the acquired company's book value.

11. Defining total asset turnover as revenue divided by average total assets, all else equal, impairment write-downs of long-lived assets owned by a company will most likely result in an increase for that company in:

   A. the debt-to-equity ratio but not the total asset turnover.

   B. the total asset turnover but not the debt-to-equity ratio.

   C. both the debt-to-equity ratio and the total asset turnover.

12. For financial assets classified as trading securities, how are unrealized gains and losses reflected in shareholders' equity?

   A. They are not recognized.

   B. As an adjustment to paid-in capital.

   C. They flow through income into retained earnings.

13. For financial assets classified as available for sale, how are unrealized gains and losses reflected in shareholders' equity?

   A. They are not recognized.

   B. They flow through retained earnings.

   C. As a separate line item (other comprehensive income).

14. For financial assets classified as held to maturity, how are unrealized gains and losses reflected in shareholders' equity?

   A. They are not recognized.

   B. They flow through retained earnings.

   C. As a separate line item (valuation gains/losses).

15. Under IFRS, the minority interest in consolidated subsidiaries is presented on the balance sheet as:

   A. a long-term liability.

   B. separately, but as a part of shareholders' equity.

   C. a mezzanine item between liabilities and shareholders' equity.

16. Retained earnings are a component of:

   A. liabilities.

   B. minority interest.

   C. owners' equity.

17. When a company buys shares of its own stock to be held in treasury, it records a reduction in:

   A. both assets and liabilities.

   B. both assets and shareholders' equity.

   C. assets and an increase in shareholders' equity.

18. A common-size analysis of the balance sheet is most likely to signal investors that the company:

   A. has increased sales.

   B. is using assets efficiently.

   C. is becoming more leveraged.

19. An investor concerned whether a company can meet its near-term obligations is most likely to calculate the:

    A. current ratio.

    B. debt-to-equity ratio.

    C. return on total capital.

20. The most stringent test of a company's liquidity is its:

    A. cash ratio.

    B. quick ratio.

    C. current ratio.

21. An investor worried that a company may go bankrupt would most likely examine its:

    A. current ratio.

    B. return on equity.

    C. debt-to-equity ratio.

22. Using the information presented in Exhibit 8, the quick ratio for Sony Corp. at 31 March 2005 is *closest* to:

    A. 0.44.

    B. 0.81.

    C. 0.84.

23. Applying common-size analysis to the Sony Corp. balance sheets presented in Exhibit 8, which one of the following line items increased in 2005 relative to 2004?

    A. Goodwill.

    B. Securities investments and other.

    C. Deferred insurance acquisition costs.

24. Using the information presented in Exhibit 8, the financial leverage ratio for Sony Corp. at 31 March 2005 is *closest* to:

    A. 2.30.

    B. 2.81.

    C. 3.31.

SOLUTIONS FOR READING 33

1. B is correct. Assets are resources controlled by a company as a result of past events.

2. A is correct. Assets = Liabilities + Equity and, therefore, Assets − Liabilities = Equity.

3. C is correct. A classified balance sheet is one that classifies assets and liabilities as current or noncurrent and provides a subtotal for current assets and current liabilities.

4. B is correct. Goodwill is a long-term asset, and the others are all current assets.

5. A is correct. Current liabilities are those liabilities, including debt, due within one year. Long-term liabilities are not due within the current year.

6. B is correct. The cash received from customers represents an asset. The obligation to provide a product in the future is a liability called "unearned income" or "unearned revenue." Once the product is delivered, the liability will be converted into revenue.

7. C is correct. Inventories are carried at historical cost, unless the current replacement cost of the inventory is less.

8. C is correct. Paying rent in advance will reduce cash and increase prepaid expenses, both of which are assets.

9. C is correct. Accrued liabilities are expenses that have been reported on a company's income statement but have not yet been paid.

10. B is correct. Initially, goodwill is measured as the difference between the purchase price paid for an acquisition and the fair value of the acquired company's net assets.

11. C is correct. Impairment write-downs reduce equity in the denominator of the debt-to-equity ratio but do not affect debt, so the debt-to-equity ratio is expected to increase. Impairment write-downs reduce total assets but do not affect revenue. Thus, total asset turnover is expected to increase.

12. C is correct. For financial assets classified as trading securities, unrealized gains and losses are reported on the income statement and flow to shareholders' equity as part of retained earnings.

13. C is correct. For financial assets classified as available for sale, unrealized gains and losses are not recorded on the income statement but do appear on the balance sheet. Shareholders' equity is adjusted through a separate line item for valuation gains and losses termed "other comprehensive income."

14. A is correct. When financial assets are classified as held to maturity, gains and losses are recognized only when realized.

15. B is correct. IFRS requires that minority interest in consolidated subsidiaries be classified as shareholders' equity.

16. C is correct. Retained earnings are a component of owners' equity.

17. B is correct. Share repurchases reduce the company's cash (an asset). Shareholders' equity is reduced because there are fewer shares outstanding and treasury stock is an offset to owners' equity.

18. C is correct. Common-size analysis (as presented in the reading) tells investors how the composition of assets is changing over time. As a result, it can signal when the company is becoming more leveraged.

19. A is correct. The current ratio compares assets that can quickly be turned into cash to liabilities that need to be paid within one year. The other ratios are more suited to longer-term concerns.

20. A is correct. The cash ratio determines how much of a company's near-term obligations can be settled with existing cash balances.

21. C is correct. The debt-to-equity ratio tells how much financial risk a company is exposed to.

22. B is correct. The quick ratio ([Cash + Marketable securities + Receivables] ÷ Current liabilities) is 0.81 ([¥779,103 + ¥1,492 + ¥460,202 + ¥1,113,071 − ¥87,709] ÷ ¥2,809,368).

23. C is correct. Deferred insurance acquisition costs increased as a percentage of total assets from 3.84 percent in 2004 (¥349,194 ÷ ¥9,090,662) to 3.95 percent in 2005 (¥374,805 ÷ ¥9,499,100). Although the accounts given in choices A and B increased in absolute Japanese yen terms during 2005, these accounts declined as a percentage of total assets in 2005.

24. C is correct. The financial leverage ratio (Total assets ÷ Total equity) is 3.31 (¥9,499,100 ÷ ¥2,870,338).

UNDERSTANDING THE CASH FLOW STATEMENT

by Thomas R. Robinson, CFA, Jan Hendrik van Greuning, CFA,
R. Elaine Henry, CFA, and Michael A. Broihahn, CFA

LEARNING OUTCOMES

The candidate should be able to:	Mastery
a. compare and contrast cash flows from operating, investing, and financing activities and classify cash flow items as relating to one of these three categories, given a description of the items;	☐
b. describe how noncash investing and financing activities are reported;	☐
c. compare and contrast the key differences in cash flow statements prepared under international financial reporting standards and U.S. generally accepted accounting principles;	☐
d. demonstrate the difference between the direct and indirect methods of presenting cash from operating activities and explain the arguments in favor of each;	☐
e. demonstrate the steps in the preparation of direct and indirect cash flow statements, including how cash flows can be computed using income statement and balance sheet data;	☐
f. describe the process of converting a cash flow statement from the indirect to the direct method of presentation;	☐
g. analyze and interpret a cash flow statement using both total currency amounts and common-size cash flow statements;	☐
h. explain and calculate free cash flow to the firm, free cash flow to equity, and other cash flow ratios.	☐

International Financial Statement Analysis, by Thomas R. Robinson, CFA, Jan Hendrik van Greuning, CFA, R. Elaine Henry, CFA, and Michael A. Broihahn, CFA. Copyright © 2007 by CFA Institute. Reprinted with permission.

249

THEME

The information in a cash flow statement helps financial analysts assess a company's historical ability to generate cash that can be invested in additional assets or distributed to its capital providers. The cash flow statement classifies all cash flows as being provided by (or used for) operating, investing, or financing activities and has two major presentation formats: indirect and direct. The analysis of a company's cash flow statements can provide useful information for understanding the company's business and reported earnings, and helps in uncovering relationships that can be useful in the prediction of future cash flows.

1 INTRODUCTION

The cash flow statement provides information about a company's *cash receipts* and *cash payments* during an accounting period, showing how these cash flows link the ending cash balance to the beginning balance shown on the company's balance sheet. The cash-based information provided by the cash flow statement contrasts with the accrual-based information from the income statement. For example, the income statement reflects revenues when earned rather than when cash is collected; in contrast, the cash flow statement reflects cash receipts when collected as opposed to when the revenue was earned. A reconciliation between reported income and cash flows from operating activities provides useful information about when, whether, and how a company is able to generate cash from its operating activities. Although income is an important measure of the results of a company's activities, cash flow is also essential. As an extreme illustration, a hypothetical company that makes all sales on account, without regard to whether it will ever collect its accounts receivable, would report healthy sales on its income statement and might well report significant income; however, with zero cash inflow, the company would not survive. The cash flow statement also provides a reconciliation of the beginning and ending cash on the balance sheet.

In addition to information about cash generated (or, alternatively, cash used) in operating activities, the cash flow statement provides information about cash provided (or used) in a company's investing and financing activities. This information allows the analyst to answer such questions as:

▶ Does the company generate enough cash from its operations to pay for its new investments, or is the company relying on new debt issuance to finance them?

▶ Does the company pay its dividends to common stockholders using cash generated from operations, from selling assets, or from issuing debt?

Answers to these questions are important because, in theory, generating cash from operations can continue indefinitely, but generating cash from selling assets, for example, is possible only as long as there are assets to sell. Similarly, generating cash from debt financing is possible only as long as lenders are willing to lend, and the lending decision depends on expectations that the company will ultimately have adequate cash to repay its obligations. In summary, information about the sources and uses of cash helps creditors, investors, and other statement users evaluate the company's liquidity, solvency, and financial flexibility.

This reading explains how cash flow activities are reflected in a company's cash flow statement. The reading is organized as follows. Section 2 describes the components and format of the cash flow statement, including the classification of cash flows under international financial reporting standards (IFRS) and U.S. generally accepted accounting principles (GAAP) and the direct and indirect formats for presenting the cash flow statement. Section 3 discusses the linkages of the cash flow statement with the income statement and balance sheet and the steps in the preparation of the cash flow statement. Section 4 demonstrates the analysis of cash flow statements, including the conversion of an indirect cash flow statement to the direct method and how to use common-size cash flow analysis, free cash flow measures, and cash flow ratios used in security analysis. A summary of the key points and practice problems in CFA Institute multiple-choice format conclude the reading.

COMPONENTS AND FORMAT OF THE CASH FLOW STATEMENT

2

The analyst needs to be able to extract and interpret information on cash flows from financial statements prepared according to any allowable format. The basic components and allowable formats of the cash flow statement are well established.

► The cash flow statement has subsections relating specific items to the operating, investing, and financing activities of the company.

► Two presentation formats are available: the direct and the indirect.

The following discussion presents these topics in greater detail.

2.1 Classification of Cash Flows and Noncash Activities

All companies engage in operating, investing, and financing activities. These activities are the classifications used in the cash flow statement under both IFRS and U.S. GAAP. Under IFRS, International Accounting Standard No. 7, (IAS No. 7), *Cash Flow Statements*, provides that cash flows are categorized as follows:[1]

► **Operating activities** include the company's day-to-day activities that create revenues, such as selling inventory and providing services. Cash inflows result from cash sales and from collection of accounts receivable. Examples

---

[1] IAS No. 7 became effective on 1 January 1994.

include cash receipts from the provision of services and royalties, commissions, and other revenue. To generate revenue, companies undertake activities such as manufacturing inventory, purchasing inventory from suppliers, and paying employees. Cash outflows result from cash payments for inventory, salaries, taxes, and other operating-related expenses and from paying accounts payable. Additionally, operating activities include cash receipts and payments related to securities held for dealing or trading purposes (as opposed to being held for investment, as discussed below).

▶ **Investing activities** include purchasing and selling investments. Investments include property, plant, and equipment; intangible assets; other long-term assets; and both long-term and short-term investments in the equity and debt (bonds and loans) issued by other companies. For this purpose, investments in equity and debt securities exclude: a) any securities considered cash equivalents (very short-term, highly liquid securities) and b) **dealing** or **trading securities** (held for trading), the purchase and sale of which are considered operating activities even for companies where this is not a primary business activity. Cash inflows in the investing category include cash receipts from the sale of nontrading securities (available-for-sale, held-to-maturity); property, plant, and equipment; intangibles; or other long-term assets. Cash outflows include cash payments for the purchase of these assets.

▶ **Financing activities** include obtaining or repaying capital, such as equity and long-term debt. The two primary sources of capital are shareholders and creditors. Cash inflows in this category include cash receipts from issuing stock (common or preferred) or bonds and cash receipts from borrowing. Cash outflows include cash payments to repurchase stock (e.g., treasury stock), to pay dividends, and to repay bonds and other borrowings. Note that indirect borrowing using accounts payable is not considered a financing activity—such borrowing would be classified as an operating activity.

EXAMPLE 1

Net Cash Flow from Investing Activities

A company recorded the following in Year 1:

Proceeds from issuance of long-term debt	$300,000
Purchase of equipment	$200,000
Loss on sale of equipment	$ 70,000
Proceeds from sale of equipment	$120,000
Equity in earnings of affiliate	$ 10,000

On the Year 1 cash flow statement, the company would report net cash flow from investing activities *closest* to:

A. −$150,000.
B. −$80,000.
C. $200,000.
D. $300,000.

Solution: The only two items that would affect the investing section are the purchase of equipment and the proceeds from sale of equipment. The loss on sale of equipment and the equity in earnings of affiliate affect net income but are not investing cash flows. The issuance of debt is a financing cash flow. B is correct: ($200,000) + $120,000 = ($80,000).

Under IFRS, there is some flexibility in reporting some items of cash flow, particularly interest and dividends. IAS No. 7 notes that while for a financial institution interest paid and received would normally be classified as operating activities, for other entities, alternative classifications may be appropriate. For this reason, under IFRS, interest received may be classified either as an operating activity or as an investing activity. Under IFRS, interest paid may be classified as either an operating activity or as a financing activity. Furthermore, under IFRS, dividends received may be classified as either an operating activity or an investing activity. On the other hand, dividends paid may be classified as either an operating activity or a financing activity. Companies must use a consistent classification from year to year and disclose where the amounts are reported.

Under U.S. GAAP, this discretion is not permitted: Interest received and paid is reported as operating activities for all companies.[2] Under U.S. GAAP, dividends received are always reported as operating activities and dividends paid are always reported as financing activities.

EXAMPLE 2

Operating versus Financing Cash Flows

On 31 December 2006, a company issued a $30,000, 90-day note at 8 percent to pay for inventory purchased that day and issued $110,000 long-term debt at 11 percent annually to pay for new equipment purchased that day. Which of the following *most* accurately reflects the combined effect of both transactions on the company's cash flows for the year ended 31 December 2006 under U.S. GAAP? Cash flow from:

A. operations increases $30,000.
B. financing increases $110,000.
C. operations decreases $30,000.
D. financing decreases $110,000.

Solution: C is correct. The increase in inventories would decrease cash flow from operations. The issuance of both short-term and long-term debt is part of financing activities. Equipment purchased is an investing activity. Note that because no interest was paid or received in this example, the answer would be the same under IFRS.

---

[2] See Financial Accounting Standard No. 95, *Statement of Cash Flows.* This was originally issued in 1987 and modified somewhat in recent years.

Companies may also engage in noncash investing and financing transactions. A noncash transaction is any transaction that does not involve an inflow or outflow of cash. For example, if a company exchanges one nonmonetary asset for another nonmonetary asset, no cash is involved. Similarly, no cash is involved when a company issues common stock either for dividends or in connection with conversion of a convertible bond or convertible preferred stock. Because no cash is involved in noncash transactions (by definition), these transactions are not incorporated in the cash flow statement. However, any significant noncash transaction is required to be disclosed, either in a separate note or a supplementary schedule to the cash flow statement.

2.2 A Summary of Differences between IFRS and U.S. GAAP

As highlighted in the previous section, there are some differences in cash flow statements prepared under IFRS and U.S. GAAP that the analyst should be aware of when comparing the cash flow statements of companies using U.S. GAAP or IFRS. The key differences are summarized in Exhibit 1. In short, the IASB allows more flexibility in the reporting of items such as interest paid or received and dividends paid or received, and in how income tax expense is classified.

U.S. GAAP classifies interest and dividends received from investments as operating activities, whereas IFRS allows companies to classify those items as either operating or investing cash flows. Likewise, U.S. GAAP classifies interest

EXHIBIT 1	Cash Flow Statements: Differences between IFRS and U.S. GAAP	
Topic	**IFRS**	**U.S. GAAP**
Classification of cash flows:		
Interest received	Operating or investing	Operating
Interest paid	Operating or financing	Operating
Dividends received	Operating or investing	Operating
Dividends paid	Operating or financing	Financing
Bank overdrafts	Considered part of cash equivalents	Not considered part of cash and cash equivalents and classified as financing
Taxes paid	Generally operating, but a portion can be allocated to investing or financing if it can be specifically identified with these categories	Operating
Format of statement	Direct or indirect; direct is encouraged	Direct or indirect; direct is encouraged. If direct is used, a reconciliation of net income and operating cash flow must also be provided

(Exhibit continued on next page . . .)

EXHIBIT 1	**(continued)**

Disclosures	Tax cash flows must be separately disclosed in the cash flow statement	Interest and taxes paid must be disclosed in footnotes if not presented on the cash flow statement

Sources: IAS No. 7, FAS No. 95, and "Similarities and Differences: A Comparison of IFRS and U.S. GAAP," PricewaterhouseCoopers, October 2004, available at www.pwc.com.

expense as an operating activity, even though the principal amount of the debt issued is classified as a financing activity. IFRS allows companies to classify interest expense as either an operating activity or a financing activity. U.S. GAAP classifies dividends paid to stockholders as a financing activity, whereas IFRS allows companies to classify dividends paid as either an operating activity or a financing activity.

U.S. GAAP classifies all income tax expenses as an operating activity. IFRS also classifies income tax expense as an operating activity, unless the tax expense can be specifically identified with an investing or financing activity (e.g., the tax effect of the sale of a discontinued operation could be classified under investing activities). Under either of the two sets of standards, companies currently have a choice of formats for presenting cash flow statements, as discussed in the next section.

2.3 Direct and Indirect Cash Flow Formats for Reporting Operating Cash Flow

There are two acceptable formats for reporting **cash flow from operations** (also known as **cash flow from operating activities** or **operating cash flow**), defined as the net amount of cash provided from operating activities: the direct and the indirect methods. The *amount* of operating cash flow is identical under both methods; only the *presentation format* of the operating cash flow section differs. The presentation format of the cash flows from investing and financing is exactly the same, regardless of which method is used to present operating cash flows.

The **direct method** shows the specific cash inflows and outflows that result in reported cash flow from operating activities. It shows each cash inflow and outflow related to a company's cash receipts and disbursements, adjusting income statement items to remove the effect of accruals. In other words, the direct method eliminates any impact of accruals and shows only cash receipts and cash payments. The primary argument in favor of the direct method is that it provides information on the specific sources of operating cash receipts and payments in contrast to the indirect method, which shows only the net result of these receipts and payments. Just as information on the specific sources of revenues and expenses is more useful than knowing only the net result—net income—the analyst gets additional information from a direct-format cash flow statement. The additional information is useful in understanding historical performance and in predicting future operating cash flows.

The **indirect method** shows how cash flow from operations can be obtained from reported net income as the result of a series of adjustments. The indirect format begins with net income. To reconcile net income with operating cash flow, adjustments are made for noncash items, for nonoperating items, and for the net changes in operating accruals. The main argument for the indirect approach is that it shows the reasons for differences between net income and operating cash flows. (It may be noted, however, that the differences between net income and operating cash flows are equally visible on an indirect-format cash flow statement and in the supplementary reconciliation required if the company uses the direct method.) Another argument for the indirect method is that it mirrors a forecasting approach that begins by forecasting future income and then derives cash flows by adjusting for changes in balance sheet accounts that occur due to the timing differences between accrual and cash accounting.

Under IFRS, IAS No. 7 encourages the use of the direct method but permits either. Similarly, under U.S. GAAP, the Financial Accounting Standards Board (FASB) in Financial Accounting Standard No. 95 encourages the use of the direct method but allows companies to use the indirect method. Under FAS No. 95, if the direct method is presented, footnote disclosure must also be provided of the indirect method. If the indirect method is chosen, no direct-format disclosures are required. As a result, few U.S. companies present the direct format for operating cash flows.

Many users of financial statements prefer the direct format, particularly analysts and commercial lenders, because of the importance of information about operating receipts and payments to assessing a company's financing needs and capacity to repay existing obligations. In 1987, at the time the FASB was adopting FAS No. 95, some companies argued that it is less costly to adjust net income to operating cash flow, as in the indirect format, than it is to report gross operating cash receipts and payments, as in the direct format. With subsequent progress in accounting systems and technology, it is not clear that this argument remains valid. CFA Institute has advocated that standard setters require the use of the direct format for the main presentation of the cash flow statement, with indirect cash flows as supplementary disclosure.[3]

2.3.1 An Indirect-Format Cash Flow Statement Prepared under IFRS

Exhibit 2 presents cash flow statements prepared under IFRS from Roche Group's annual report for the fiscal years ended 31 December 2005 and 2004, which show the use of the indirect method. Roche is a leading international healthcare company based in Switzerland.[4]

In the cash flows from operating activities section of Roche's cash flow statement, the company reconciles its net income to net cash provided by operating activities. Under IFRS, payments for interest and taxes are disclosed in the body of the cash flow statement. Note that Roche discloses the income taxes paid (CHF 1,997 million in 2005) as a separate item in the cash flows from operating activities section. Separate disclosure of this is not useful if an analyst is trying to assess the impact on cash flow of changes in tax rates (income tax expense provided on the income statement does not reflect the flow of cash due to prepaid and deferred items). Roche reports its interest paid in the cash flows from

---

[3] *A Comprehensive Business Reporting Model: Financial Reporting for Investors*, CFA Institute Centre for Financial Market Integrity, October 2005, p. 27.

[4] The cash flow statement presented here includes a reconciliation of net income to cash generated from operations, which Roche Group reported in the footnotes to the financial statement rather than on the statement itself.

EXHIBIT 2	Roche Group Consolidated Cash Flow Statements (Millions of CHF)	

Fiscal Years Ended 31 December	2005	2004
Cash flows from operating activities:		
Net income	6,730	7,063
Add back nonoperating (income) expense:		
Income from associated companies	(1)	43
Financial income	(678)	(369)
Financing costs	382	602
Exceptional income from bond conversion and redemption	–	(872)
Income taxes	2,224	1,865
Discontinued businesses	12	(2,337)
Operating profit	8,669	5,995
Depreciation of property, plant, and equipment	1,302	1,242
Amortization of goodwill	–	572
Amortization of intangible assets	1,011	1,000
Impairment of long-term assets	66	39
Changes in group organization	–	199
Major legal cases	356	–
Expenses for defined-benefit postemployment plans	313	532
Expenses for equity-settled equity compensation plans	364	169
Other adjustments	455	(335)
Cash generated from continuing operations	12,526	9,413
Operating cash flows generated from discontinued businesses	(5)	335
Cash generated from operations	12,521	9,748
(Increase) decrease in working capital	488	227
Vitamin case payments	(82)	(66)
Major legal cases	(98)	(65)
Payments made for defined-benefit postemployment plans	(303)	(653)
Utilization of restructuring provisions	(119)	(163)
Utilization of other provisions	(310)	(128)
Other operating cash flows	(125)	(75)
Income taxes paid	(1,997)	(1,490)
Total cash flows from operating activities	9,975	7,335
Cash flows from investing activities:		
Purchase of property, plant, and equipment	(3,319)	(2,344)
Purchase of intangible assets	(349)	(191)
Disposal of property, plant, and equipment	353	196
Disposal of intangible assets	2	12
Disposal of products	56	431

(Exhibit continued on next page . . .)

EXHIBIT 2	(continued)		
Fiscal Years Ended 31 December		**2005**	**2004**
Acquisitions of subsidiaries and associated companies		(233)	(1,822)
Divestments of discontinued businesses and associated companies		2,913	696
Interest and dividends received		383	255
Sales of marketable securities		9,859	4,965
Purchases of marketable securities		(15,190)	(4,281)
Other investing cash flows		(161)	64
Total cash flows from investing activities		(5,686)	(2,019)
Cash flows from financing activities:			
Proceeds from issue of long-term debt instruments		2,565	–
Repayment of long-term debt instruments		(1,178)	(3,039)
Increase (decrease) in other long-term debt		(1,083)	(1,156)
Transactions in own equity instruments		779	237
Increase (decrease) in short-term borrowings		(422)	(939)
Interest and dividends paid		(1,983)	(1,971)
Exercises of equity-settled equity compensation plans		1,090	643
Genentech and Chugai share repurchases		(2,511)	(1,699)
Other financing cash flows		(38)	61
Total cash flows from financing activities		(2,781)	(7,863)
Net effect of currency translation on cash and cash equivalents		115	(124)
Increase (decrease) in cash and cash equivalents		1,623	(2,671)
Cash and cash equivalents at 1 January		2,605	5,276
Cash and cash equivalents at 31 December		4,228	2,605

financing activities section, showing a total of CHF 1,983 million in interest and dividends paid in 2005. As noted earlier under U.S. GAAP, interest paid—or the reconciliation adjustment for the net change in interest payable—must be reported in the operating section of the cash flow statement. Furthermore, U.S. GAAP does not require that interest and taxes paid be disclosed as separate line items on the cash flow statement; however, it does require that these amounts be provided in a supplemental note.

Roche reports its dividends and interest received (CHF 383 million in 2005) in the cash flows from investing activities section. Under U.S. GAAP, investment income received (or the reconciliation adjustment for the net change in investment income receivable) must be reported in the operating section of the cash flow statement.

2.3.2 A Direct-Format Cash Flow Statement Prepared under IFRS

Exhibit 3 presents a direct-method format cash flow statement prepared under IFRS for Telefónica Group, a diversified telecommunications company based in Madrid.[5] Note that in this format of the cash flow statement, the cash received from customers, as well as other operating items, is clearly shown. The analyst can then contrast the change in revenues from the income statement with the change in cash received from customers. An increase in revenues coupled with a decrease in cash received from customers could signal collection problems. However, in the case of Telefónica Group, cash received from customers has increased.

EXHIBIT 3	Telefónica Group Consolidated Cash Flow Statements (Millions of Euros)		
Fiscal Years Ended 31 December		**2005**	**2004**
Cash flows from operating activities			
Cash received from customers		44,353.14	36,367.10
Cash paid to suppliers and employees		(30,531.54)	(24,674.10)
Dividends received		70.58	71.24
Net interest and other financial expenses paid		(1,520.00)	(1,307.11)
Taxes paid		(1,233.04)	(326.00)
Net cash from operating activities		11,139.14	10,131.13
Cash flows from investing activities			
Proceeds on disposals of property, plant, and equipment and intangible assets		113.20	241.27
Payments on investments in property, plant, and equipment and intangible assets		(4,423.22)	(3,488.15)
Proceeds on disposals of companies, net of cash, and cash equivalents disposed		501.59	531.98
Payments on investments in companies, net of cash, and cash equivalents acquired		(6,571.40)	(4,201.57)
Proceeds on financial investments not included under cash equivalents		147.61	31.64
Payments made on financial investments not included under cash equivalents		(17.65)	(76.35)
Interest received on short-term investments not included under cash equivalents		625.18	1,139.51
Capital grants received		32.67	13.51
Net cash used in investing activities		(9,592.02)	(5,808.16)

(Exhibit continued on next page . . .)

---

[5] Excludes supplemental cash flow reconciliation provided at the bottom of the original cash flow statement by the company.

EXHIBIT 3	(continued)		
Fiscal Years Ended 31 December		**2005**	**2004**
Cash flows from financing activities			
Dividends paid		(2,768.60)	(2,865.81)
Proceeds from issue of stock		(2,054.12)	(1,938.56)
Proceeds on issue of debentures and bonds		875.15	572.99
Proceeds on loans, credits, and promissory notes		16,533.96	10,135.11
Cancellation of debentures and bonds		(3,696.52)	(1,790.57)
Repayments of loans, credits, and promissory notes		(9,324.54)	(8,049.77)
Net cash from financing activities		(434.67)	(3,936.61)
Effect of foreign exchange rate changes on collections and payments		165.73	74.18
Effect of changes in consolidation methods and other nonmonetary effects		9.62	(36.76)
Net increase (decrease) in cash and cash equivalents during the year		1,287.80	423.78
Cash and cash equivalents at beginning of year		914.35	490.57
Cash and cash equivalents at end of year		2,202.15	914.35

2.3.3 Illustrations of Cash Flow Statements Prepared under U.S. GAAP

Previously, we presented a cash flow statement prepared under IFRS. In this section, we illustrate cash flow statements prepared under U.S. GAAP. This section presents the cash flow statements of two companies, Tech Data Corporation and Wal-Mart. Tech Data reports its operating activities using the direct method, whereas Wal-Mart reports its operating activities using the more common indirect method.

Tech Data Corporation is a leading distributor of information technology products. Exhibit 4 presents comparative cash flow statements from the company's annual report for the fiscal years ended 31 January 2005 and 2004.[6]

Tech Data Corporation prepares its cash flow statements under the direct method. In the cash flows from operating activities section of Tech Data's cash flow statements, the company identifies the amount of cash it received from customers, $19.7 billion for 2005, and the amount of cash that it paid to suppliers and employees, $19.6 billion for 2005. Net cash provided by operating activities of $106.9 million was adequate to cover the company's investing activities, primarily purchases of property and equipment ($25.9 million) and software development ($17.9 million). In 2005, the company issued $32.7 million of common stock, providing net cash from financing activities of $12.2 million after its debt repayments. Overall, the company's cash increased by $86.3 million, from $108.8 million at the beginning of the year to $195.1 million at the end of the year.

---

[6] Under U.S. GAAP, companies present three years of the cash flow statement. For purposes of presentation and comparison with the IFRS statements presented above, only two years are presented here.

EXHIBIT 4	Tech Data Corporation and Subsidiaries Consolidated Cash Flow Statements (in Thousands)		
Fiscal Years Ended 31 January		**2005**	**2004**
Cash flows from operating activities:			
Cash received from customers		$19,745,283	$17,390,674
Cash paid to suppliers and employees		(19,571,824)	(17,027,162)
Interest paid		(18,837)	(17,045)
Income taxes paid		(47,677)	(43,233)
Net cash provided by operating activities		106,945	303,234
Cash flows from investing activities:			
Acquisition of businesses, net of cash acquired		–	(203,010)
Proceeds from sale of property and equipment		5,130	4,484
Expenditures for property and equipment		(25,876)	(31,278)
Software development costs		(17,899)	(21,714)
Net cash used in investing activities		(38,645)	(251,518)
Cash flows from financing activities:			
Proceeds from the issuance of common stock		32,733	28,823
Net repayments on revolving credit loans		(11,319)	(138,039)
Principal payments on long-term debt		(9,214)	(1,492)
Net cash provided by (used in) financing activities		12,200	(110,708)
Effect of exchange rate changes on cash		5,755	10,602
Net increase (decrease) in cash and cash equivalents		86,255	(48,390)
Cash and cash equivalents at beginning of year		108,801	157,191
Cash and cash equivalents at end of year		$ 195,056	$ 108,801
Reconciliation of net income to net cash provided by operating activities:			
Net income		$ 162,460	$ 104,147
Adjustments to reconcile net income to net cash provided by operating activities:			
Depreciation and amortization		55,472	55,084
Provision for losses on accounts receivable		13,268	29,214
Deferred income taxes		(3,616)	7,369
Changes in operating assets and liabilities, net of acquisitions:			
Accounts receivable		(44,305)	(15,699)
Inventories		(119,999)	(140,203)
Prepaid and other assets		(32,193)	14,713
Accounts payable		55,849	300,350
Accrued expenses and other liabilities		20,009	(51,741)
Total adjustments		(55,515)	199,087
Net cash provided by operating activities		$ 106,945	$ 303,234

Whenever the direct method is used, FAS No. 95 mandates a disclosure note and schedule that reconciles net income with the net cash flow from operating activities. Tech Data shows this reconciliation at the bottom of its consolidated cash flow statements. The disclosure note and reconciliation schedule are exactly the information that would have been presented in the body of the cash flow statement if the company had elected instead to use the indirect method.

Wal-Mart is a global retailer that conducts business under the names of Wal-Mart and Sam's Club. Exhibit 5 presents the comparative cash flow statements from the company's annual report for the fiscal years ended 31 January 2005 and 2004.[7]

EXHIBIT 5	Wal-Mart Cash Flow Statements (in Millions)		
Fiscal Years Ended 31 January		**2005**	**2004**
Cash flows from operating activities:			
Income from continuing operations		$10,267	$ 8,861
Adjustments to reconcile net income to net cash provided by operating activities:			
Depreciation and amortization		4,405	3,852
Deferred income taxes		263	177
Other operating activities		378	173
Changes in certain assets and liabilities, net of effects of acquisitions:			
Decrease (increase) in accounts receivable		(304)	373
Increase in inventories		(2,635)	(1,973)
Increase in accounts payable		1,694	2,587
Increase in accrued liabilities		976	1,896
Net cash provided by operating activities of continuing operations		15,044	15,946
Net cash provided by operating activities of discontinued operations		–	50
Net cash provided by operating activities		15,044	15,996
Cash flows from investing activities:			
Payments for property and equipment		(12,893)	(10,308)
Investment in international operations		(315)	(38)
Proceeds from the disposal of fixed assets		953	481
Proceeds from the sale of McLane		–	1,500
Other investing activities		(96)	78
Net cash used in investing activities of continuing operations		(12,351)	(8,287)
Net cash used in investing activities of discontinued operations		–	(25)
Net cash used in investing activities		(12,351)	(8,312)

(Exhibit continued on next page . . .)

---

[7] Under U.S. GAAP, companies present three years of the cash flow statement. For purposes of presentation and comparison with the IFRS statements presented above, only two years are presented here.

EXHIBIT 5	(continued)		
Cash flows from financing activities:			
Increase in commercial paper		544	688
Proceeds from issuance of long-term debt		5,832	4,099
Purchase of company stock		(4,549)	(5,046)
Dividends paid		(2,214)	(1,569)
Payment of long-term debt		(2,131)	(3,541)
Payment of capital lease obligations		(204)	(305)
Other financing activities		113	111
Net cash used in financing activities		(2,609)	(5,563)
Effect of exchange rate changes on cash		205	320
Net increase in cash and cash equivalents		289	2,441
Cash and cash equivalents at beginning of year		5,119	2,758
Cash and cash equivalents at end of year		$ 5,488	$ 5,199
Income tax paid		$ 5,593	$ 4,358
Interest paid		1,163	1,024
Capital lease obligations incurred		377	252

Wal-Mart prepares its cash flow statements under the indirect method. In the cash flows from operating activities section of Wal-Mart's cash flow statement, the company reconciles its net income of $10.3 billion to net cash provided by operating activities of $15 billion. Whenever the indirect method is used, U.S. GAAP mandates a supplemental note that discloses how much cash was paid for interest and income taxes. Wal-Mart discloses the amount of cash paid for income tax ($5.6 billion), interest ($1.2 billion), and capital lease obligations (i.e., the interest expense component of the capital lease payments) at the bottom of its cash flow statements.

THE CASH FLOW STATEMENT: LINKAGES AND PREPARATION

3

The indirect format of the cash flow statement demonstrates that changes in balance sheet accounts are an important factor in determining cash flows. The next section addresses the linkages between the cash flow statement and other financial statements.

3.1 Linkages of the Cash Flow Statement with the Income Statement and Balance Sheet

Recall the accounting equation that summarizes the balance sheet:

Assets = Liabilities + Owners' equity

Cash is an asset. The cash flow statement ultimately shows the change in cash during an accounting period. The beginning and ending balances of cash are shown on the company's balance sheets for the previous and current years, and the bottom of the cash flow statement reconciles beginning cash with ending cash. For example, the Roche Group's cash flow statement for 2005, presented in Exhibit 2, shows that operating, investing, and financing activities during the year imply a CHF 1,623 increase in cash and cash equivalents, which is the amount by which end-of-year cash and cash equivalents (CHF 4,228) exceeds beginning-of-year cash and cash equivalents (CHF 2,605). The relationship, stated in general terms, is as shown below.

Beginning Balance Sheet at 31 December 20X6	Cash Flow Statement for Year Ended 31 December 20X7		Ending Balance Sheet at 31 December 20X7
Beginning cash	Plus: Cash receipts (from operating, investing, and financing activities)	Less: Cash payments (for operating, investing, and financing activities)	Ending cash

In the case of cash held in foreign currencies, there would also be an impact from changes in exchange rates. The body of the cash flow statement shows why the change in cash occurred; in other words, it shows the company's operating, investing, and financing activities (as well as the impact of foreign currency translation). The beginning and ending balance sheet values of cash and cash equivalents are linked through the cash flow statement. The linkage is similar to the one that relates net income and dividends as shown in the income statement to the beginning and ending values of retained earnings in the owners' equity section of the balance sheet, as shown below.

Beginning Balance Sheet at 31 December 20X6	Statement of Owners' Equity for Year Ended 31 December 20X7		Ending Balance Sheet at 31 December 20X7
Beginning retained earnings	Plus: Net income or minus net loss from the income statement for year ended 31 December 20X7	Minus: Dividends	Ending retained earnings

A company's operating activities are reported on an accrual basis in the income statement, and any differences between the accrual basis and the cash basis of accounting for an operating transaction result in an increase or decrease in some (usually) short-term asset or liability on the balance sheet. For example, if revenue reported using accrual accounting is higher than the cash actually collected, the result will be an increase in accounts receivable. If expenses reported using accrual accounting are lower than cash actually paid, the result will be a decrease in accounts payable.

A company's investing activities typically relate to the long-term asset section of the balance sheet, and its financing activities typically relate to the equity and long-term debt sections of the balance sheet. Each item on the balance sheet is also related to the income statement and/or cash flow statement through the change in the beginning and ending balance. Consider, for example, accounts receivable:

Beginning Balance Sheet at 31 December 20X6	Income Statement for Year Ended 31 December 20X7	Cash Flow Statement for Year Ended 31 December 20X7	Ending Balance Sheet at 31 December 20X7
Beginning accounts receivable	Plus: Revenues	Minus: Cash collected from customers	Ending accounts receivable

Knowing any three of these four items makes it easy to compute the fourth. For example, if you know beginning accounts receivable, revenues, and cash collected from customers, you can easily compute ending accounts receivable. Understanding these interrelationships between the balance sheet, income statement, and cash flow statement is useful in not only understanding the company's financial health but also in detecting accounting irregularities. The next section demonstrates the preparation of cash flow information based upon income statement and balance sheet information.

3.2 Steps in Preparing the Cash Flow Statement

The preparation of the cash flow statement uses data from both the income statement and the comparative balance sheets.

As noted earlier, companies often only disclose indirect operating cash flow information, whereas analysts prefer direct-format information. Understanding how cash flow information is put together will enable you to take an indirect statement apart and reconfigure it in a more useful manner. The following demonstration of how a cash flow statement is prepared uses the income statement and the comparative balance sheets for Acme Corporation (a fictitious retail company) shown in Exhibits 6 and 7.

EXHIBIT 6	Acme Corporation Income Statement Year Ended 31 December 2006 (in Thousands)

Revenue		$23,598
Cost of goods sold		11,456
Gross profit		12,142
Salary and wage expense	4,123	
Depreciation expense	1,052	
Other operating expenses	3,577	
Total operating expenses		8,752
Operating profit		3,390

(Exhibit continued on next page . . .)

EXHIBIT 6	(continued)

Other revenues (expenses):

Gain on sale of equipment	205	
Interest expense	(246)	(41)
Income before tax		3,349
Income tax expense		1,139
Net income		$ 2,210

EXHIBIT 7	Acme Corporation Comparative Balance Sheets 31 December 2006 and 2005 (in Thousands)

	2006	2005	Net Change
Cash	$ 1,011	$ 1,163	$ (152)
Accounts receivable	1,012	957	55
Inventory	3,984	3,277	707
Prepaid expenses	155	178	(23)
Total current assets	6,162	5,575	587
Land	510	510	–
Buildings	3,680	3,680	–
Equipment[a]	8,798	8,555	243
Less: accumulated depreciation	(3,443)	(2,891)	(552)
Total long-term assets	9,545	9,854	(309)
Total assets	$15,707	$15,429	278
Accounts payable	$ 3,588	$ 3,325	$ 263
Salary and wage payable	85	75	10
Interest payable	62	74	(12)
Income tax payable	55	50	5
Other accrued liabilities	1,126	1,104	22
Total current liabilities	4,916	4,628	288
Long-term debt	3,075	3,575	(500)
Common stock	3,750	4,350	(600)
Retained earnings	3,966	2,876	1,090
Total liabilities and equity	$15,707	$15,429	278

[a] During 2006, Acme purchased new equipment for a total cost of $1,300. No items impacted retained earnings other than net income and dividends.

The first step in preparing the cash flow statement is to determine the total cash flows from operating activities. The direct method of presenting cash from operating activities will be illustrated first, followed by the indirect method. Cash flows from investing activities and from financing activities are identical under either method.

3.2.1 Operating Activities: Direct Method

We first determine how much cash Acme received from its customers, followed by how much cash was paid to suppliers and to employees as well as how much cash was paid for other operating expenses, interest, and income taxes.

3.2.1.1 Cash Received from Customers The income statement for Acme reported revenue of $23,598 (in thousands) for the year ended 31 December 2006. To determine the cash receipts from its customers, it is necessary to adjust this revenue amount by the net change in accounts receivable for the year. If accounts receivable increase during the year, revenue on an accrual basis is higher than cash receipts from customers, and vice versa. For Acme Corporation, accounts receivable increased by $55, so cash received from customers was $23,543, as follows:

Revenue	$23,598
Less: Increase in accounts receivable	(55)
Cash received from customers	**$23,543**

Cash received from customers affects the accounts receivable account as follows:

Beginning accounts receivable	$ 957
Plus revenue	23,598
Minus cash collected from customers	**(23,543)**
Ending accounts receivable	$ 1,012

The accounts receivable account information can also be presented as follows:

Beginning accounts receivable	$ 957
Plus revenue	23,598
Minus ending accounts receivable	(1,012)
Cash collected from customers	**$23,543**

> ### EXAMPLE 3
>
> #### Computing Cash Received from Customers
>
> Blue Bayou, an advertising company, reported revenues of $50 million, total expenses of $35 million, and net income of $15 million in the most recent year. If accounts receivable decreased by $12 million, how much cash did the company receive from customers?
>
> A. $62 million.
> B. $50 million.
> C. $38 million.
> D. $15 million.
>
> **Solution:** A is correct. Revenues of $50 million plus the decrease in accounts receivable of $12 million equals $62 million in cash received from customers. The decrease in accounts receivable means that the company received more in cash than the amount of revenue it reported.

"Cash received from customers" is sometimes referred to as "cash collections from customers" or "cash collections."

3.2.1.2 Cash Paid to Suppliers   For Acme, the cash paid to suppliers was $11,900, determined as follows:

Cost of goods sold	$11,456
Plus: Increase in inventory	707
Equals purchases from suppliers	$12,163
Less: Increase in accounts payable	(263)
Cash paid to suppliers	**$11,900**

There are two pieces to this calculation: the amount of inventory purchased and the amount paid for it. To determine purchases from suppliers, cost of goods sold is adjusted for the change in inventory. If inventory increased during the year, then purchases during the year exceeded cost of goods sold, and vice versa. Acme reported cost of goods sold of $11,456 for the year ended 31 December 2006. For Acme Corporation, inventory increased by $707, so purchases from suppliers was $12,163. Purchases from suppliers affects the inventory account, as shown below:

Beginning inventory	3,277
Plus purchases	12,163
Minus cost of goods sold	(11,456)
Ending inventory	3,984

Acme purchased $12,163 of inventory from suppliers this year, but is this the amount of cash that Acme paid to its suppliers during the year? Not necessarily. Acme may not have yet paid for all of these purchases and may yet owe for some of the purchases made this year. In other words, Acme may have paid less cash to its suppliers than the amount of this year's purchases, in which case Acme's liability (accounts payable) will have increased by the difference. Alternatively, Acme may have paid even more to its suppliers than the amount of this year's purchases, in which case Acme's accounts payable will have decreased.

Therefore, once purchases have been determined, cash paid to suppliers can be calculated by adjusting purchases for the change in accounts payable. If the company made all purchases for cash, then accounts payable would not change and cash outflows would equal purchases. If accounts payable increased during the year, then purchases on an accrual basis are higher than they are on a cash basis, and vice versa. In this example, Acme made more purchases than it paid in cash, so the balance in accounts payable has increased. For Acme, the cash paid to suppliers was $11,900, determined as follows:

Purchases from suppliers	$12,163
Less: Increase in accounts payable	(263)
Cash paid to suppliers	**$11,900**

The amount of cash paid to suppliers is reflected in the accounts payable account, as shown below:

Beginning accounts payable	$ 3,325
Plus purchases	12,163
Minus cash paid to suppliers	**(11,900)**
Ending accounts payable	$ 3,588

EXAMPLE 4

Computing Cash Paid to Suppliers

Orange Beverages Plc., a manufacturer of tropical drinks, reported cost of goods sold for the year of $100 million. Total assets increased by $55 million, but inventory declined by $6 million. Total liabilities increased by $45 million, but accounts payable decreased by $2 million. How much cash did the company pay to its suppliers during the year?

A. $110 million.
B. $108 million.
C. $104 million.
D. $96 million.

Solution: D is correct. Cost of goods sold of $100 million less the decrease in inventory of $6 million equals purchases from suppliers of $94 million. The decrease in accounts payable of $2 million means that the company paid $96 million in cash ($94 million plus $2 million).

3.2.1.3 Cash Paid to Employees To determine the cash paid to employees, it is necessary to adjust salary and wage expense by the net change in salary and wage payable for the year. If salary and wage payable increased during the year, then salary and wage expense on an accrual basis is higher than the amount of cash paid for this expense, and vice versa. For Acme, salary and wage payable increased by $10, so cash paid for salary and wages was $4,113, as follows:

Salary and wage expense	$4,123
Less: Increase in salary and wage payable	(10)
Cash paid to employees	**$4,113**

The amount of cash paid to employees is reflected in the salary and wage payable account, as shown below:

Beginning salary and wages payable	$ 75
Plus salary and wage expense	4,123
Minus cash paid to employees	**(4,113)**
Ending salary and wages payable	$ 85

3.2.1.4 Cash Paid for Other Operating Expenses   To determine the cash paid for other operating expenses, it is necessary to adjust the other operating expenses amount on the income statement by the net changes in prepaid expenses and accrued expense liabilities for the year. If prepaid expenses increased during the year, other operating expenses on a cash basis were higher than on an accrual basis, and vice versa. Likewise, if accrued expense liabilities increased during the year, other operating expenses on a cash basis were lower than on an accrual basis, and vice versa. For Acme Corporation, the amount of cash paid for operating expenses in 2006 was $3,532, as follows:

Other operating expenses	$3,577
Less: Decrease in prepaid expenses	23
Less: Increase in other accrued liabilities	22
Cash paid for other operating expenses	**$3,532**

EXAMPLE 5

Computing Cash Paid for Other Operating Expenses

Black Ice, a sportswear manufacturer, reported other operating expenses of $30 million. Prepaid insurance expense increased by $4 million, and accrued utilities payable decreased by $7 million. Insurance and utilities are the only two components of other operating expenses. How much cash did the company pay in other operating expenses?

A. $41 million.
B. $33 million.
C. $27 million.
D. $19 million.

Solution: A is correct. Other operating expenses of $30 million plus the increase in prepaid insurance expense of $4 million plus the decrease in accrued utilities payable of $7 million equals $41 million.

3.2.1.5 Cash Paid for Interest The company is either subject to U.S. GAAP, which requires that interest expense be included in operating cash flows, or it is subject to IFRS, which gives companies the option to treat interest expense in this manner. To determine the cash paid for interest, it is necessary to adjust interest expense by the net change in interest payable for the year. If interest payable increases during the year, then interest expense on an accrual basis is higher than the amount of cash paid for interest, and vice versa. For Acme Corporation, interest payable decreased by $12 and cash paid for interest was $258, as follows:

Interest expense	$246
Plus: Decrease in interest payable	12
Cash paid for interest	**$258**

Alternatively, cash paid for interest may also be determined by an analysis of the interest payable account, as shown below:

Beginning interest payable	$ 74
Plus interest expense	246
Minus cash paid for interest	**(258)**
Ending interest payable	$ 62

3.2.1.6 Cash Paid for Income Taxes To determine the cash paid for income taxes, it is necessary to adjust the income tax expense amount on the income statement by the net changes in taxes receivable, taxes payable, and deferred income taxes for the year. If taxes receivable or deferred tax assets increase during the year, income taxes on a cash basis will be higher than on an accrual basis, and vice versa. Likewise, if taxes payable or deferred tax liabilities increase during the year, income tax expense on a cash basis will be lower than on an accrual basis, and vice versa. For Acme Corporation, the amount of cash paid for income taxes in 2006 was $1,134, as follows:

Income tax expense	$1,139
Less: Increase in income tax payable	(5)
Cash paid for income taxes	**$1,134**

3.2.2 Investing Activities: Direct Method

The second and third steps in preparing the cash flow statement are to determine the total cash flows from investing activities and from financing activities. The presentation of this information is identical, regardless of whether the direct or indirect method is used for operating cash flows. Investing cash flows are always presented using the direct method.

Purchases and sales of equipment were the only investing activities undertaken by Acme in 2006, as evidenced by the fact that the amounts reported for land and buildings were unchanged during the year. An informational note in Exhibit 7 tells us that Acme *purchased* new equipment in 2006 for a total cost of $1,300. However, the amount of equipment shown on Acme's balance sheet increased by only $243 (ending balance of $8,798 minus beginning balance of $8,555); therefore, Acme must have also *sold* some equipment during the year. To determine the cash inflow from the sale of equipment, we analyze the equipment and accumulated depreciation accounts as well as the gain on the sale of equipment from Exhibits 6 and 7.

The historical cost of the equipment sold was $1,057. This amount is determined as follows:

Beginning balance equipment (from balance sheet)	$8,555
Plus equipment purchased (from informational note)	1,300
Minus ending balance equipment (from balance sheet)	(8,798)
Equals historical cost of equipment sold	$1,057

The accumulated depreciation on the equipment sold was $500, determined as follows:

Beginning balance accumulated depreciation (from balance sheet)	$2,891
Plus depreciation expense (from income statement)	1,052
Minus ending balance accumulated depreciation (from balance sheet)	(3,443)
Equals accumulated depreciation on equipment sold	$500

The historical cost information, accumulated depreciation information, and information from the income statement about the gain on the sale of equipment can be used to determine the cash received from the sale.

Historical cost of equipment sold (calculated above)	$1,057
Less accumulated depreciation on equipment sold (calculated above)	(500)
Equals: Book value of equipment sold	557
Plus: Gain on sale of equipment (from the income statement)	205
Equals: Cash received from sale of equipment	$762

EXAMPLE 6

Computing Cash Received from the Sale of Equipment

Copper, Inc., a brewery and restaurant chain, reported a gain on the sale of equipment of $12 million. In addition, the company's income statement shows depreciation expense of $8 million, and the cash flow statement shows capital expenditure of $15 million, all of which was for the purchase of new equipment.

Balance sheet item	12/31/2005	12/31/2006	Change
Equipment	$100 million	$109 million	$9 million
Accumulated depreciation —equipment	$30 million	$36 million	$6 million

Using the information from the comparative balance sheets, how much cash did the company receive from the equipment sale?

A. $16 million.
B. $9 million.
C. $6 million.
D. $3 million.

Solution: A is correct. Selling price (cash inflow) minus book value equals gain or loss on sale; therefore, gain or loss on sale plus book value equals selling price (cash inflow). The amount of gain is given, $12 million. To calculate the book value of the equipment sold, find the historical cost of the equipment and the accumulated depreciation on the equipment.

► Beginning balance of equipment of $100 million plus equipment purchased of $15 million minus ending balance of equipment of $109 million equals historical cost of equipment sold, or $6 million.

► Beginning accumulated depreciation on equipment of $30 million plus depreciation expense for the year of $8 million minus ending balance of accumulated depreciation of $36 million equals accumulated depreciation on the equipment sold, or $2 million.

► Therefore, the book value of the equipment sold was $6 million minus $2 million, or $4 million.

► Because the gain on the sale of equipment was $12 million, the amount of cash received must have been $16 million.

3.2.3 Financing Activities: Direct Method

As with investing activities, financing activities are always presented using the direct method.

3.2.3.1 Long-Term Debt and Common Stock The change in long-term debt, based on the beginning and ending balance sheets in Exhibit 7, was a decrease of $500. Absent other information, this indicates that Acme retired $500 of long-term debt. Retiring long-term debt is a cash outflow relating to financing activities.

Similarly, the change in common stock during 2006 was a decrease of $600. Absent other information, this indicates that Acme repurchased $600 of its common stock. Repurchase of common stock is also a cash outflow related to financing activity.

3.2.3.2 Dividends Recall the following relationship:

Beginning retained earnings + Net income − Dividends
    = Ending retained earnings

Based on this relationship, the amount of cash dividends paid in 2006 can be determined from an analysis of retained earnings, as follows:

Beginning balance of retained earnings (from the balance sheet)	$2,876
Plus net income (from the income statement)	2,210
Minus ending balance of retained earnings (from the balance sheet)	(3,966)
Equals dividends paid	**$1,120**

3.2.4 Overall Cash Flow Statement: Direct Method

Exhibit 8 summarizes the information about Acme's operating, investing, and financing cash flows in the cash flow statement. At the bottom of the statement, the total net change in cash is shown to be a decrease of $152 (from $1,163 to $1,011). This can also be seen on the comparative balance sheet in Exhibit 7. The cash provided by operating activities of $2,606 was adequate to cover the net cash used in investing activities of $538; however, the company's debt repayments, cash payments for dividends, and repurchase of common stock (i.e., its financing activities) of $2,220 resulted in an overall decrease of $152.

EXHIBIT 8	Acme Corporation Cash Flow Statement (Direct Method) for Year Ended 31 December 2006 (in Thousands)

Cash flow from operating activities:	
Cash received from customers	$23,543
Cash paid to suppliers	(11,900)
Cash paid to employees	(4,113)
Cash paid for other operating expenses	(3,532)
Cash paid for interest	(258)
Cash paid for income tax	(1,134)
Net cash provided by operating activities	2,606
Cash flow from investing activities:	
Cash received from sale of equipment	762
Cash paid for purchase of equipment	(1,300)
Net cash used for investing activities	(538)
Cash flow from financing activities:	
Cash paid to retire long-term debt	(500)
Cash paid to retire common stock	(600)
Cash paid for dividends	(1,120)
Net cash used for financing activities	(2,220)
Net decrease in cash	(152)
Cash balance, 31 December 2005	1,163
Cash balance, 31 December 2006	$ 1,011

3.2.5 Overall Cash Flow Statement: Indirect Method

Using the alternative approach to reporting cash from operating activities, the indirect method, we will present the same amount of cash provided by operating activities. Under this approach, we reconcile Acme's net income of $2,210 to its operating cash flow of $2,606.

To perform this reconciliation, net income is adjusted for the following: a) any nonoperating activities; b) any noncash expenses; and c) changes in operating working capital items.

The only nonoperating activity in Acme's income statement, the sale of equipment, resulted in a gain of $205. This amount is removed from the operating cash flow section; the cash effects of the sale are shown in the investing section.

Acme's only noncash expense was depreciation expense of $1,052. Under the indirect method, depreciation expense must be added back to net income because it was a noncash deduction in the calculation of net income.

Changes in working capital accounts include increases and decreases in the current operating asset and liability accounts. The changes in these accounts arise from applying accrual accounting; that is, recognizing revenues when they are earned and expenses when they are incurred instead of when the cash is received or paid. To make the working capital adjustments under the indirect method, any increase in a current operating asset account is subtracted from net income while a net decrease is added to net income. As described above, the increase in accounts receivable, for example, resulted from Acme recording income statement revenue higher than the amount of cash received from customers; therefore, to reconcile back to operating cash flow, that increase in accounts receivable must be deducted from net income. For current operating liabilities, a net increase is added to net income while a net decrease is subtracted from net income. As described above, the increase in wages payable, for example, resulted from Acme recording income statement expenses higher than the amount of cash paid to employees.

Exhibit 9 presents a tabulation of the most common types of adjustments that are made to net income when using the indirect method to determine net cash flow from operating activities.

EXHIBIT 9	Adjustments to Net Income Using the Indirect Method

Additions   Noncash items

        Depreciation expense of tangible assets

        Amortization expense of intangible assets

        Depletion expense of natural resources

        Amortization of bond discount

    Nonoperating losses

        Loss on sale or write-down of assets

        Loss on retirement of debt

        Loss on investments accounted for under the equity method

    Increase in deferred income tax liability

    Changes in working capital resulting from accruing higher expenses than cash payments, or lower revenues than cash receipts

(Exhibit continued on next page . . .)

EXHIBIT 9	(continued)

	Increase in current operating liabilities (e.g., accounts payable and accrued expense liabilities)
	Decrease in current operating assets (e.g., accounts receivable, inventory, and prepaid expenses)
Subtractions	Noncash items (e.g., amortization of bond premium)
	Nonoperating items
	Gain on sale of assets
	Gain on retirement of debt
	Income on investments accounted for under the equity method
	Decrease in deferred income tax liability
	Changes in working capital resulting from accruing lower expenses than cash payments, or higher revenues than cash receipts
	Decrease in current operating liabilities (e.g., accounts payable and accrued expense liabilities)
	Increase in current operating assets (e.g., accounts receivable, inventory, and prepaid expenses)

Accordingly, for Acme Corporation, the $55 increase in accounts receivable and the $707 increase in inventory are subtracted from net income while the $23 decrease in prepaid expenses is added to net income. For Acme's current liabilities, the increases in accounts payable, salary and wage payable, income tax payable, and other accrued liabilities ($263, $10, $5, and $22, respectively) are added to net income while the $12 decrease in interest payable is subtracted from net income. Exhibit 10 presents the cash flow statement for Acme Corporation under the indirect method by using the information that we have determined from our analysis of the income statement and the comparative balance sheets. Note that the investing and financing sections are identical to the cash flow statement prepared using the direct method.

EXHIBIT 10	Acme Corporation Cash Flow Statement (Indirect Method) Year Ended 31 December 2006 (in Thousands)

Cash flow from operating activities:	
Net income	$2,210
Depreciation expense	1,052
Gain on sale of equipment	(205)
Increase in accounts receivable	(55)
Increase in inventory	(707)

(Exhibit continued on next page . . .)

EXHIBIT 10	(continued)	
Decrease in prepaid expenses		23
Increase in accounts payable		263
Increase in salary and wage payable		10
Decrease in interest payable		(12)
Increase in income tax payable		5
Increase in other accrued liabilities		22
Net cash provided by operating activities		2,606
Cash flow from investing activities:		
Cash received from sale of equipment		762
Cash paid for purchase of equipment		(1,300)
Net cash used for investing activities		(538)
Cash flow from financing activities:		
Cash paid to retire long-term debt		(500)
Cash paid to retire common stock		(600)
Cash paid for dividends		(1,120)
Net cash used for financing activities		(2,220)
Net decrease in cash		(152)
Cash balance, 31 December 2005		(1,163)
Cash balance, 31 December 2006		$ 1,011

EXAMPLE 7

Adjusting Net Income to Compute Operating Cash Flow

Based on the following information for Pinkerly Inc., what are the total adjustments that the company would make to net income in order to derive operating cash flow?

	Year Ended		
Income statement item	12/31/2006		
Net income	$30 million		
Depreciation	$7 million		
Balance sheet item	12/31/2005	12/31/2006	Change
Accounts receivable	$15 million	$30 million	$15 million
Inventory	$16 million	$13 million	($3 million)
Accounts payable	$10 million	$20 million	$10 million

A. Add $5 million.
B. Add $29 million.
C. Subtract $5 million.
D. Subtract $29 million.

Solution: A is correct. To derive operating cash flow, the company would make the following adjustments to net income: add depreciation (a noncash expense) of $7 million; add the decrease in inventory of $3 million; add the increase in accounts payable of $10 million; and subtract the increase in accounts receivable of $15 million. Total additions would be $20 million, and total subtractions would be $15 million for net additions of $5 million.

3.3 Conversion of Cash Flows from the Indirect to the Direct Method

An analyst may desire to review direct-format operating cash flow to review trends in cash receipts and payments (such as cash received from customers or cash paid to suppliers). If a direct-format statement is not available, cash flows from operating activities reported under the indirect method can be converted to the direct method. Accuracy of conversion depends on adjustments using data available in published financial reports. The method described here is sufficiently accurate for most analytical purposes.

The three-step conversion process is demonstrated for Acme Corporation in Exhibit 11. Referring again to Exhibits 6 and 7 for Acme Corporation's income statement and balance sheet information, begin by disaggregating net income of $2,210 into total revenues and total expenses (Step 1). Next, remove any nonoperating and noncash items (Step 2). For Acme, we therefore remove the nonoperating gain on the sale of equipment of $205 and the noncash depreciation expense of $1,052. Then, convert accrual amounts of revenues and expenses to cash flow amounts of receipts and payments by adjusting for changes in working capital accounts (Step 3). The results of these adjustments are the items of information for the direct format of operating cash flows. These line items are shown as the results of Step 3.

EXHIBIT 11	Conversion from the Indirect to the Direct Method	
Step 1	Total revenues	$23,803
Aggregate all revenue and all expenses	Total expenses	21,593
	Net income	$ 2,210

Step 2	Total revenue less noncash item revenues:	
Remove all noncash items from aggregated revenues and expenses and break out remaining items into relevant cash flow items	($23,803 − $205) =	$23,598
	Revenue	$23,598
	Total expenses less noncash item expenses:	
	($21,593 − $1,052) =	$20,541

(Exhibit continued on next page . . .)

EXHIBIT 11	(continued)	

	Cost of goods sold	$11,456
	Salary and wage expenses	4,123
	Other operating expenses	3,577
	Interest expense	246
	Income tax expense	1,139
	Total	$20,541

Step 3	Cash received from customers[a]	$23,543
Convert accrual amounts to cash flow amounts by adjusting for working capital changes	Cash paid to suppliers[b]	11,900
	Cash paid to employees[c]	4,113
	Cash paid for other operating expenses[d]	3,532
	Cash paid for interest[e]	258
	Cash paid for income tax[f]	1,134

Calculations for Step 3

[a] Revenue of $23,598 less increase in accounts receivable of $55.

[b] Cost of goods sold of $11,456 plus increase in inventory of $707 less increase in accounts payable of $263.

[c] Salary and wage expense of $4,123 less increase in salary and wage payable of $10.

[d] Other operating expenses of $3,577 less decrease in prepaid expenses of $23 less increase in other accrued liabilities of $22.

[e] Interest expense of $246 plus decrease in interest payable of $12.

[f] Income tax expense of $1,139 less increase in income tax payable of $5.

CASH FLOW STATEMENT ANALYSIS   4

The analysis of a company's cash flows can provide useful information for understanding a company's business and earnings and for predicting its future cash flows. This section describes tools and techniques for analyzing the cash flow statement, including the analysis of major sources and uses of cash, cash flow, common-size analysis, conversion of the cash flow statement from the indirect method to the direct method, and computation of free cash flow and cash flow ratios.

4.1 Evaluation of the Sources and Uses of Cash

Evaluation of the cash flow statement should involve an overall assessment of the sources and uses of cash between the three main categories as well as an assessment of the main drivers of cash flow within each category, as follows:

1. Evaluate where the major sources and uses of cash flow are between operating, investing, and financing activities.
2. Evaluate the primary determinants of operating cash flow.
3. Evaluate the primary determinants of investing cash flow.
4. Evaluate the primary determinants of financing cash flow.

Step 1 The major sources of cash for a company can vary with its stage of growth. For a mature company, it is desirable to have the primary source of cash be operating activities. Over the long term, a company must generate cash from its operating activities. If operating cash flow were consistently negative, a company would need to borrow money or issue stock (financing activities) to fund the shortfall. Eventually, these providers of capital need to be repaid from operations or they will no longer be willing to provide capital. Cash generated from operating activities can either be used in investing or financing activities. If the company has good opportunities to grow the business or other investment opportunities, it is desirable to use the cash in investing activities. If the company does not have profitable investment opportunities, the cash should be returned to capital providers, a financing activity. For a new or growth stage company, operating cash flow may be negative for some period of time as it invests in inventory and receivables (extending credit to new customers) in order to grow the business. This cannot sustain itself over the long term, so eventually the cash must start to come primarily from operating activities so that capital can be returned to the providers of capital. Lastly, it is desirable that operating cash flows are sufficient to cover capital expenditures (in other words, the company has free cash flow as discussed further below). In summary, major points to consider at this step are:

▶ What are the major sources and uses of cash flow?

▶ Is operating cash flow positive and sufficient to cover capital expenditures?

Step 2 Turning to the operating section, the analysts should examine the most significant determinates of operating cash flow. Some companies need to raise cash for use in operations (to hold receivables, inventory, etc.), while occasionally a company's business model generates cash flow (e.g., when cash is received from customers before it needs to be paid out to suppliers). Under the indirect method, the increases and decreases in receivables, inventory, payables, and so on can be examined to determine whether the company is using or generating cash in operations and why. It is also useful to compare operating cash flow with net income. For a mature company, because net income includes noncash expenses (depreciation and amortization), it is desirable that operating cash flow exceeds net income. The relationship between net income and operating cash flow is also an indicator of earnings quality. If a company has large net income but poor operating cash flow, it may be a sign of poor earnings quality. The company may be making aggressive accounting choices to increase net income but not be generating cash for its business. You should also examine the variability of both earnings and cash flow and consider the impact of this variability on the company's risk as well as the ability to forecast future cash flows for valuation purposes. In summary:

▶ What are the major determinants of operating cash flow?

▶ Is operating cash flow higher or lower than net income? Why?

▶ How consistent are operating cash flows?

Step 3 Within the investing section, you should evaluate each line item. Each line item represents either a source or use of cash. This enables you to understand where the cash is being spent (or received). This section will tell you how much cash is being invested for the future in property, plant, and equipment; how much is used to acquire entire companies; and how much is put aside in liquid investments, such as stocks and bonds. It will also tell you how much cash is being raised by selling these types of assets. If the company is making major capital investments, you should consider where the cash is coming from to cover these investments (e.g., is the cash coming from excess operating cash flow or from the financing activities described in Step 4?).

Step 4 Within the financing section, you should examine each line item to understand whether the company is raising capital or repaying capital and what the nature of its capital sources are. If the company is borrowing each year, you should consider when repayment may be required. This section will also present dividend payments and repurchases of stock that are alternative means of returning capital to owners.

Example 8 provides an example of a cash flow statement evaluation.

EXAMPLE 8

Analysis of the Cash Flow Statement

Derek Yee, CFA, is preparing to forecast cash flow for Groupe Danone as an input into his valuation model. He has asked you to evaluate the historical cash flow statement of Groupe Danone, which is presented in Exhibit 12. Groupe Danone prepares its financial statements in conformity with International Financial Reporting Standards as adopted by the European Union.

EXHIBIT 12	Groupe Danone Consolidated Financial Statements Consolidated Statements of Cash Flows (Millions of Euros)		
Fiscal Years Ended 31 December		**2004**	**2005**
Net income		449	1,464
Minority interests in net income of consolidated subsidiaries		189	207
Net income from discontinued operations		(47)	(504)
Net income (loss) of affiliates		550	(44)
Depreciation and amortization		481	478
Dividends received from affiliates		45	45
Other flows		(93)	70
Cash flows provided by operations		1,574	1,716
(Increase) decrease in inventories		(70)	(17)
(Increase) decrease in trade accounts receivable		(27)	(87)
Increase (decrease) in trade accounts payable		143	123
Changes in other working capital items		74	112
Net change in current working capital		120	131
Cash flows provided by operating activities		1,694	1,847
Capital expenditures		(520)	(607)
Purchase of businesses and other investments net of cash and cash equivalent acquired		(98)	(636)

(Exhibit continued on next page . . .)

EXHIBIT 12   (continued)

Proceeds from the sale of businesses and other investments net of cash and cash equivalent disposed of	650	1,659
(Increase) decrease in long-term loans and other long-term assets	130	(134)
Changes in cash and cash equivalents of discontinued operations	52	30
Cash flows provided by investing activities	214	312
Increase in capital and additional paid-in capital	38	61
Purchases of treasury stock (net of disposals)	(213)	(558)
Dividends	(456)	(489)
Increase (decrease) in noncurrent financial liabilities	(290)	(715)
Increase (decrease) in current financial liabilities	(536)	(191)
(Increase) decrease in marketable securities	(415)	(210)
Cash flows used in financing activities	(1,872)	(2,102)
Effect of exchange rate changes on cash and cash equivalents	(21)	53
Increase (decrease) in cash and cash equivalents	15	110
Cash and cash equivalents at beginning of period	451	466
Cash and cash equivalents at end of period	466	576
Supplemental disclosures:		
Cash paid during the year:		
Interest	152	172
Income tax	439	424

Yee would like answers to the following questions:

▶ What are the major sources of cash for Groupe Danone?

▶ What are the major uses of cash for Groupe Danone?

▶ What is the relationship between net income and cash flow from operating activities?

▶ Is cash flow from operating activities sufficient to cover capital expenditures?

▶ Other than capital expenditures, is cash being used or generated in investing activities?

▶ What types of financing cash flows does Groupe Danone have?

Solution: The major categories of cash flows can be summarized as follows (in millions of euros):

	2004	2005
Cash flows from operating activities	1,694	1,847
Cash flows from investing activities	214	312
Cash flows from financing activities	(1,872)	(2,102)
Exchange rate effects on cash	(21)	53
Increase in cash	15	110

The primary source of cash for Groupe Danone is operating activities. The secondary source of cash is investing activities. Most of this cash flow is being spent in financing activities. The fact that the primary source of cash is from operations is a good sign. Additionally, operating cash flow exceeds net income in both years—a good sign. Operating cash flows are much higher than capital expenditures, indicating that the company can easily fund capital expenditures from operations. The company has generated investing cash flows by selling business and investments in the two years presented. In the financing category, Groupe Danone is spending cash by repurchasing its own stock, paying dividends, and paying down debt. This could be an indicator that the company lacks investment opportunities and is, therefore, returning cash to the providers of capital.

4.2 Common-Size Analysis of the Cash Flow Statement

In common-size analysis of a company's income statement, each income and expense line item is expressed as a percentage of net revenues (net sales). For the common-size balance sheet, each asset, liability, and equity line item is expressed as a percentage of total assets. For the common-size cash flow statement, there are two alternative approaches. The first approach is to express each line item of cash inflow (outflow) as a percentage of total inflows (outflows) of cash, and the second approach is to express each line item as a percentage of net revenue.

Exhibit 13 demonstrates the total cash inflows/total outflows method for Acme Corporation. Under this approach, each of the cash inflows is expressed as a percentage of the total cash inflows, whereas each of the cash outflows is expressed as a percentage of the total cash outflows. In Panel A, Acme's common-size statement is based on a cash flow statement using the direct method of presenting operating cash flows. Operating cash inflows and outflows are separately presented on the cash flow statement and, therefore, the common-size cash flow statement shows each of these operating inflows (outflows) as a percentage of total inflows (outflows). In Panel B, Acme's common-size statement is based on a cash flow statement using the indirect method of presenting operating cash flows. When a cash flow statement has been presented using the indirect method, operating cash inflows and outflows are not separately presented; therefore, the common-size cash flow statement shows only the net operating cash flows as a percentage of total inflows or outflows, depending on whether the net amount was an in- or out-cash flow. Because Acme's net operating cash flow is positive, it is shown as a percentage of total inflows.

EXHIBIT 13	Acme Corporation Common-Size Cash Flow Statement: Year Ended 31 December 2006

Panel A. Direct Format for Operating Cash Flow

Inflows		Percentage of Total Inflows
Receipts from customers	$23,543	96.86%
Sale of equipment	762	3.14
Total	$24,305	100.00%

Outflows		Percentage of Total Outflows
Payments to suppliers	$11,900	48.66%
Payments to employees	4,113	16.82
Payments for other operating expenses	3,532	14.44
Payments for interest	258	1.05
Payments for income tax	1,134	4.64
Purchase of equipment	1,300	5.32
Retirement of long-term debt	500	2.04
Retirement of common stock	600	2.45
Dividend payments	1,120	4.58
Total	$24,457	100.00%

Panel B. Indirect Format for Operating Cash Flow

Inflows		Percentage of Total Inflows
Operations	$ 2,606	77.38%
Sale of equipment	762	22.62
Total	$ 3,368	100.00%

Outflows		Percentage of Total Outflows
Purchase of equipment	1,300	36.93%
Retirement of long-term debt	500	14.20
Retirement of common stock	600	17.05
Dividend payments	1,120	31.82
Total	$ 3,520	100.00%

Exhibit 14 demonstrates the net revenue common-size cash flow statement for Acme Corporation. Under the net revenue approach, each line item in the cash flow statement is shown as a percentage of net revenue. The common-size statement in this exhibit has been developed based on Acme's cash flow statement using the indirect method for operating cash flows. Each line item of the reconciliation between net income and net operating cash flows is expressed as a percentage of net revenue. The common-size format makes it easier to see trends in cash flow rather than just looking at the total amount. This method is also useful to the analyst in forecasting future cash flows because individual items in the common-size statement (e.g., depreciation, fixed capital expenditures, debt borrowing, and repayment) are expressed as a percentage of net revenue. Thus, once the analyst has forecast revenue, the common-size statement provides a basis for forecasting cash flows.

EXHIBIT 14	Acme Corporation Common-Size Cash Flow Statement: Indirect Format Year Ended 31 December 2006	
		Percentage of Net Revenue
Cash flow from operating activities:		
Net income	$2,210	9.37
Depreciation expense	1,052	4.46
Gain on sale of equipment	(205)	(0.87)
Increase in accounts receivable	(55)	(0.23)
Increase in inventory	(707)	(3.00)
Decrease in prepaid expenses	23	0.10
Increase in accounts payable	263	1.11
Increase in salary and wage payable	10	0.04
Decrease in interest payable	(12)	(0.05)
Increase in income tax payable	5	0.02
Increase in other accrued liabilities	22	0.09
Net cash provided by operating activities	2,606	11.04
Cash flow from investing activities:		
Cash received from sale of equipment	762	3.23
Cash paid for purchase of equipment	(1,300)	(5.51)
Net cash used for investing activities	(538)	(2.28)
Cash flow from financing activities:		
Cash paid to retire long-term debt	(500)	(2.12)
Cash paid to retire common stock	(600)	(2.54)
Cash paid for dividends	(1,120)	(4.75)
Net cash used for financing activities	(2,220)	(9.41)
Net decrease in cash	$ (152)	(0.64)

EXAMPLE 9

Analysis of a Common-Size Cash Flow Statement

Andrew Potter is examining an abbreviated common-size cash flow statement based on net revenues for Dell, which is reproduced below:

	Period Ending				
	3 Feb 2006	28 Jan 2005	30 Jan 2004	31 Jan 2003	1 Feb 2002
Net income	**6.39%**	**6.18%**	**6.38%**	**5.99%**	**4.00%**
Cash flows—operating activities					
Depreciation	0.70	0.68	0.63	0.60	0.77
Net income adjustments	0.93	−0.56	−0.92	−0.61	4.57
Changes in operating activities					
Accounts receivable	−1.84	0.00	−1.96	0.54	0.71
Inventory	−0.21	0.00	−0.13	−0.06	0.36
Other operating activities	−0.54	4.49	−0.34	−0.50	−0.20
Liabilities	3.22	0.00	5.19	4.04	1.98
Net cash flow—operating	**8.66%**	**10.79%**	**8.86%**	**9.99%**	**12.18%**
Cash flows—investing activities					
Capital expenditures	−1.30	−1.07	−0.79	−0.86	−0.97
Investments	8.24	−3.64	−4.88	−3.04	−6.28
Other investing activities	0.00	0.00	−1.12	0.00	0.00
Net cash flows—investing	**6.94%**	**−4.71%**	**−6.79%**	**−3.90%**	**−7.25%**
Cash flows—financing activities					
Sale and purchase of stock	−11.14	−6.36	−3.34	−5.72	−8.68
Other financing activities	0.00	0.00	0.00	0.00	0.01
Net cash flows—financing	**−11.14%**	**−6.36%**	**−3.34%**	**−5.72%**	**−8.67%**
Effect of exchange rate	−0.35	1.15	1.48	1.30	−0.33
Net cash flow	**4.10%**	**0.87%**	**0.21%**	**1.67%**	**−4.07%**

Based on the information in the above exhibit, address the following:

1. Characterize the importance of:
   A. depreciation.
   B. capital expenditures.
2. Contrast Dell's operating cash flow as a percentage of revenue with Dell's net profit margin (on a cash basis).
3. Identify Dell's major use of its positive operating cash flow.

Solution to 1:

A. Dell has very little depreciation expense (less than 1 percent), which is added back to determine operating cash flow.

B. Dell's level of capital expenditures is relatively small, less than 1 percent of revenues in most years, but this increased in the most recent year. This is consistent with Dell's low amount of depreciation.

Solution to 2: Dell's operating cash flow as a percentage of revenue is consistently much higher than net profit margin. Dell's business model appears to generate cash flow instead of requiring working capital, as many companies do. Dell collects cash flow from customers, on average, sooner than cash is paid out to suppliers.

Solution to 3: Most of Dell's operating cash flow has been used to repurchase large amounts of its own stock (financing activities).

4.3 Free Cash Flow to the Firm and Free Cash Flow to Equity

In the initial evaluation of the cash flow statement above, it was mentioned that it is desirable that operating cash flows are sufficient to cover capital expenditures. The excess of operating cash flow over capital expenditures is known generically as **free cash flow**. For purposes of valuing a company or its equity securities, an analyst may want to determine a more precise free cash flow measure, such as free cash flow to the firm (FCFF) or free cash flow to equity (FCFE).

FCFF is the cash flow available to the company's suppliers of debt and equity capital after all operating expenses (including income taxes) have been paid and necessary investments in working capital and fixed capital have been made. FCFF can be computed starting with net income as[8]

$$FCFF = NI + NCC + Int(1 - Tax\ rate) - FCInv - WCInv$$

where

NI	= Net income
NCC	= Noncash charges (such as depreciation and amortization)
Int	= Interest expense
FCInv	= Capital expenditures (fixed capital, such as equipment)
WCInv	= Working capital expenditures

The reason for adding back interest is that FCFF is the cash flow available to the suppliers of debt capital as well as equity capital. Conveniently, FCFF can also be computed from cash flow from operating activities as

$$FCFF = CFO + Int(1 - Tax\ rate) - FCInv$$

---

[8] See Stowe, Robinson, Pinto, and McLeavey (2002) for a detailed discussion of free cash flow computations.

CFO represents cash flow from operating activities under U.S. GAAP or under IFRS where the company has chosen to place interest expense in operating activities. Under IFRS, if the company has placed interest and dividends received in investing activities, these should be added back to CFO to determine FCFF. Additionally, if dividends paid were subtracted in the operating section, these should be added back in to compute FCFF.

The computation of FCFF for Acme Corporation (based on the data from Exhibits 6, 7, and 8) is as follows:

CFO	$2,606
Plus: Interest paid times (1 − income tax rate)	
{$258 [1 − ($1,139 ÷ $3,349)]}	170
Less: Net investments in fixed capital	
($1,300 − $762)	(538)
FCFF	$2,238

FCFE is the cash flow available to the company's common stockholders after all operating expenses and borrowing costs (principal and interest) have been paid and necessary investments in working capital and fixed capital have been made. FCFE can be computed as

$$FCFE = CFO - FCInv + Net\ borrowing - Net\ debt\ repayment$$

The computation of FCFE for Acme Corporation (based on the data from Exhibits 6, 7, and 8) is as follows:

CFO	$2,606
Less: Net investments in fixed capital [$1,300 − $762]	538
Less: Debt repayment	500
FCFE	$1,568

Positive FCFE means that the company has an excess of operating cash flow over amounts needed for investments for the future and repayment of debt. This cash would be available for distribution to owners.

4.4 Cash Flow Ratios

The cash flow statement provides information that can be analyzed over time to obtain a better understanding of the past performance of a company and its future prospects. This information can also be effectively used to compare the performance and prospects of different companies in an industry and of different industries. There are several ratios based on cash flow from operating activities that are useful in this analysis. These ratios generally fall into cash flow performance (profitability) ratios and cash flow coverage (solvency) ratios. Exhibit 15 summarizes the calculation and interpretation of some of these ratios.

EXHIBIT 15	Cash Flow Ratios	
Performance Ratios	**Calculation**	**What It Measures**
Cash flow to revenue	CFO ÷ Net revenue	Cash generated per dollar of revenue
Cash return on assets	CFO ÷ Average total assets	Cash generated from all resources
Cash return on equity	CFO ÷ Average shareholders' equity	Cash generated from owner resources
Cash to income	CFO ÷ Operating income	Cash-generating ability of operations
Cash flow per share	(CFO − Preferred dividends) ÷ Number of common shares outstanding	Operating cash flow on a per-share basis
Coverage Ratios	**Calculation**	**What It Measures**
Debt coverage	CFO ÷ Total debt	Financial risk and financial leverage
Interest coverage	(CFO + Interest paid + Taxes paid) ÷ Interest paid	Ability to meet interest obligations
Reinvestment	CFO ÷ Cash paid for long-term assets	Ability to acquire assets with operating cash flows
Debt payment	CFO ÷ Cash paid for long-term debt repayment	Ability to pay debts with operating cash flows
Dividend payment	CFO ÷ Dividends paid	Ability to pay dividends with operating cash flows
Investing and financing	CFO ÷ Cash outflows for investing and financing activities	Ability to acquire assets, pay debts, and make distributions to owners

EXAMPLE 10

A Cash Flow Analysis of Comparables

Andrew Potter is comparing the cash-flow-generating ability of Dell with that of several other computer manufacturers: Hewlett Packard, Gateway, and Apple. He collects the following information:

	Operating Cash Flow		
Revenue	**2005 (%)**	**2004 (%)**	**2003 (%)**
DELL	8.66	10.79	8.86
HPQ	9.26	6.37	8.29
GTW	−0.65	−11.89	2.15
AAPL	18.20	11.28	4.66

Average Total Assets	2005 (%)	2004 (%)	2003 (%)
DELL	20.89	24.97	21.10
HPQ	10.46	6.75	8.33
GTW	−1.35	−22.84	3.22
AAPL	25.87	12.57	4.41

AAPL = Apple, GTW = Gateway, HPQ = Hewlett Packard.

What is Potter likely to conclude about the relative cash-flow-generating ability of these companies?

Solution: Dell has consistently generated operating cash flow relative to both revenue and assets. Hewlett Packard also has a good level of operating cash flow relative to revenue, but its operating cash flow is not as strong as Dell relative to assets. This is likely due to Dell's lean business model and lack of a need for large amounts of property, plant, and equipment. Gateway has poor operating cash flow on both measures. Apple has dramatically improved its operating cash flow over the three years and in 2005 had the strongest operating cash flow of the group.

SUMMARY

The cash flow statement provides important information about a company's cash receipts and cash payments during an accounting period as well as information about a company's operating, investing, and financing activities. Although the income statement provides a measure of a company's success, cash and cash flow are also vital to a company's long-term success. Information on the sources and uses of cash helps creditors, investors, and other statement users evaluate the company's liquidity, solvency, and financial flexibility. Key concepts are as follows:

▶ Cash flow activities are classified into three categories: operating activities, investing activities, and financing activities. Significant noncash transaction activities (if present) are reported by using a supplemental disclosure note to the cash flow statement.

▶ The cash flow statement under IFRS is similar to U.S. GAAP; however, IFRS permits greater discretion in classifying some cash flow items as operating, investing, or financing activities.

▶ Companies can use either the direct or the indirect method for reporting their operating cash flow:

  ▶ The direct method discloses operating cash inflows by source (e.g., cash received from customers, cash received from investment income) and operating cash outflows by use (e.g., cash paid to suppliers, cash paid for interest) in the operating activities section of the cash flow statement.

  ▶ The indirect method reconciles net income to net cash flow from operating activities by adjusting net income for all noncash items and the net changes in the operating working capital accounts.

▶ The cash flow statement is linked to a company's income statement and comparative balance sheets and is constructed from the data on those statements.

▶ Although the indirect method is most commonly used by companies, the analyst can generally convert it to the direct format by following a simple three-step process.

▶ The analyst can use common-size statement analysis for the cash flow statement. Two prescribed approaches are the total cash inflows/total cash outflows method and the percentage of net revenues method.

▶ The cash flow statement can be used to determine FCFF and FCFE.

▶ The cash flow statement may also be used in financial ratios measuring a company's profitability, performance, and financial strength.

PRACTICE PROBLEMS FOR READING 34

1. The three major classifications of activities in a cash flow statement are:

    A. inflows, outflows, and balances.

    B. beginning balance, ending balance, and change.

    C. operating, investing, and financing.

2. The sale of a building for cash would be classified as what type of activity on the cash flow statement?

    A. Operating.

    B. Investing.

    C. Financing.

3. Which of the following is an example of a financing activity on the cash flow statement under U.S. GAAP?

    A. Payment of dividends.

    B. Receipt of dividends.

    C. Payment of interest.

4. A conversion of a face value $1,000,000 convertible bond for $1,000,000 of common stock would most likely be:

    A. reported as a $1,000,000 financing cash outflow and inflow.

    B. reported as supplementary information to the cash flow statement.

    C. reported as a $1,000,000 financing cash outflow and a $1,000,000 investing cash inflow.

5. Interest expense may be classified as an operating cash flow:

    A. under U.S. GAAP, but may be classified as either operating or investing cash flows under IFRS.

    B. under IFRS, but may be classified as either operating or investing cash flows under U.S. GAAP.

    C. under U.S. GAAP, but may be classified as either operating or financing cash flows under IFRS.

6. Tax cash flows:

    A. must be separately disclosed in the cash flow statement under IFRS only.

    B. must be separately disclosed in the cash flow statement under U.S. GAAP only.

    C. are not separately disclosed in the cash flow statement under IFRS or U.S. GAAP.

7. Which of the following components of the cash flow statement may be prepared under the indirect method under both IFRS and U.S. GAAP?

    A. Operating.

    B. Investing.

    C. Financing.

8. Which of the following is most likely to appear in the operating section of a cash flow statement under the indirect method under U.S. GAAP?

   A. Net income.

   B. Cash paid for interest.

   C. Cash paid to suppliers.

9. Red Road Company, a consulting company, reported total revenues of $100 million, total expenses of $80 million, and net income of $20 million in the most recent year. If accounts receivable increased by $10 million, how much cash did the company receive from customers?

   A. $110 million.

   B. $90 million.

   C. $30 million.

10. Green Glory Corp., a garden supply wholesaler, reported cost of goods sold for the year of $80 million. Total assets increased by $55 million, including an increase of $5 million in inventory. Total liabilities increased by $45 million, including an increase of $2 million in accounts payable. How much cash did the company pay to its suppliers during the year?

   A. $90 million.

   B. $83 million.

   C. $77 million.

11. Purple Fleur S.A., a retailer of floral products, reported cost of goods sold for the year of $75 million. Total assets increased by $55 million, but inventory declined by $6 million. Total liabilities increased by $45 million, and accounts payable increased by $2 million. How much cash did the company pay to its suppliers during the year?

   A. $85 million.

   B. $79 million.

   C. $67 million.

12. White Flag, a women's clothing manufacturer, reported wage expense of $20 million. The beginning balance of wages payable was $3 million, and the ending balance of wages payable was $1 million. How much cash did the company pay in wages?

   A. $24 million.

   B. $23 million.

   C. $22 million.

13. An analyst gathered the following information from a company's 2004 financial statements ($ millions):

Year Ended 31 December	2003	2004
Net sales	245.8	254.6
Cost of goods sold	168.3	175.9
Accounts receivable	73.2	68.3
Inventory	39.0	47.8
Accounts payable	20.3	22.9

Based only on the information above, the company's 2004 cash flow statement prepared using the direct method would include amounts ($ millions) for cash received from customers and cash paid to suppliers, respectively, that are *closest* to:

	Cash received from customers	Cash paid to suppliers
A.	249.7	182.1
B.	259.5	169.7
C.	259.5	182.1

14. Golden Cumulus Corp., a commodities trading company, reported interest expense of $19 million and taxes of $6 million. Interest payable increased by $3 million, and taxes payable decreased by $4 million. How much cash did the company pay for interest and taxes?

A. $22 million for interest and $2 million for taxes.

B. $16 million for interest and $2 million for taxes.

C. $16 million for interest and $10 million for taxes.

15. An analyst gathered the following information from a company's 2005 financial statements ($ millions):

Balances as of Year Ended 31 December	2004	2005
Retained earnings	120	145
Accounts receivable	38	43
Inventory	45	48
Accounts payable	36	29

The company declared and paid cash dividends of $10 million in 2005 and recorded depreciation expense in the amount of $25 million for 2005. The company's 2005 cash flow from operations ($ millions) was *closest* to:

A. 25.

B. 35.

C. 45.

16. Silverago Incorporated, an international metals company, reported a loss on the sale of equipment of $2 million. In addition, the company's income statement shows depreciation expense of $8 million and the cash flow statement shows capital expenditure of $10 million, all of which was for the purchase of new equipment. Using the following information from the comparative balance sheets, how much cash did the company receive from the equipment sale?

Balance Sheet Item	12/31/2005	12/31/2006	Change
Equipment	$100 million	$105 million	$5 million
Accumulated depreciation— equipment	$40 million	$46 million	$6 million

   A. $6 million.

   B. $5 million.

   C. $1 million.

17. Jaderong Plinkett Stores reported net income of $25 million, which equals the company's comprehensive income. The company has no outstanding debt. Using the following information from the comparative balance sheets (in millions), what should the company report in the financing section of the cash flow statement?

Balance Sheet Item	12/31/2005	12/31/2006	Change
Common stock	$100	$102	$2
Additional paid-in capital common stock	$100	$140	$40
Retained earnings	$100	$115	$15
Total stockholders' equity	$300	$357	$57

   A. Issuance of common stock $42 million; dividends paid of $10 million.

   B. Issuance of common stock $38 million; dividends paid of $10 million.

   C. Issuance of common stock $42 million; dividends paid of $40 million.

18. Based on the following information for Pinkerly Inc., what are the total net adjustments that the company would make to net income in order to derive operating cash flow?

	Year Ended	
Income Statement Item	**12/31/2006**	
Net income	$20 million	
Depreciation	$2 million	

Balance Sheet Item	**12/31/2005**	**12/31/2006**	**Change**
Accounts receivable	$25 million	$22 million	($3 million)
Inventory	$10 million	$14 million	$4 million
Accounts payable	$8 million	$13 million	$5 million

   A. Add $6 million.

   B. Add $8 million.

   C. Subtract $6 million.

19. The first step in evaluating the cash flow statement should be to examine:

   A. individual investing cash flow items.

   B. individual financing cash flow items.

   C. the major sources and uses of cash.

20. Which of the following would be valid conclusions from an analysis of the cash flow statement for Telefónica Group presented in Exhibit 3?

   A. The company does not pay dividends.

   B. The primary use of cash is financing activities.

   C. The primary source of cash is operating activities.

21. Which is an appropriate method of preparing a common-size cash flow statement?

   A. Begin with net income and show the items that reconcile net income and operating cash flows.

   B. Show each line item on the cash flow statement as a percentage of net revenue.

   C. Show each line item on the cash flow statement as a percentage of total cash outflows.

22. Which of the following is an appropriate method of computing free cash flow to the firm?

    A. Add operating cash flows plus capital expenditures and deduct after-tax interest payments.

    B. Add operating cash flows plus after-tax interest payments and deduct capital expenditures.

    C. Deduct both after-tax interest payments and capital expenditures from operating cash flows.

23. An analyst has calculated a ratio using as the numerator the sum of operating cash flow, interest, and taxes, and as the denominator the amount of interest. What is this ratio, what does it measure, and what does it indicate?

    A. This ratio is an interest coverage ratio, measuring a company's ability to meet its interest obligations and indicating a company's solvency.

    B. This ratio is an effective tax ratio, measuring the amount of a company's operating cash flow used for taxes, and indicating a company's efficiency in tax management.

    C. This ratio is an operating profitability ratio, measuring the operating cash flow generated accounting for taxes and interest and indicating a company's liquidity.

SOLUTIONS FOR READING 34

1. C is correct. Answers A and B are incorrect: These are items of information involved in making calculations for the statement of cash flows.

2. B is correct. Purchases and sales of long-term assets are considered investing activities. Note: Absent information to the contrary, it is assumed that the sale of a building involves cash. If, for example, the transaction had involved the exchange of a building for common stock or the exchange of a building for a long-term note payable, it would have been considered a significant noncash activity.

3. A is correct. Answers B and C are items that are included in operating cash flows. Note: International accounting standards allow companies to include receipt of interest and dividends as either operating or investing cash flows, and international accounting standards allow companies to include payment of interest and dividends as either operating or financing cash flows.

4. B is correct. Noncash transactions, if significant, are reported as supplementary information, not in the investing or financing sections of the cash flow statement.

5. C is correct. Interest expense is always classified as an operating cash flow under U.S. GAAP but may be classified as either an operating or financing cash flow under IFRS.

6. A is correct. Taxes are only required to be separately disclosed on the cash flow statement under IFRS.

7. A is correct. The operating section may be prepared under the indirect method. The other sections are always prepared under the direct method.

8. A is correct. Under the indirect method, the operating section would begin with net income and adjust it to arrive at operating cash flow. The other items would appear under the direct method as a cash flow statement prepared under U.S. GAAP. Note that cash paid for interest may appear on an indirect cash flow statement under IFRS if classified as a financing activity.

9. B is correct. Revenues of $100 million minus the increase in accounts receivable of $10 million equal $90 million cash received from customers. The increase in accounts receivable means that the company received less in cash than it reported as revenue.

10. B is correct. Cost of goods sold of $80 million plus the increase in inventory of $5 million equals purchases from suppliers of $85 million. The increase in accounts payable of $2 million means that the company paid $83 million in cash ($85 million minus $2 million) to its suppliers.

11. C is correct. Cost of goods sold of $75 million less the decrease in inventory of $6 million equals purchases from suppliers of $69 million. The increase in accounts payable of $2 million means that the company paid $67 million in cash ($69 million minus $2 million).

12. C is correct. Beginning wages payable of $3 million plus wage expense of $20 million, minus ending wages payable of $1 million equals $22 million. The expense of $20 million plus the $2 million decrease in wages payable equals $22 million.

13. C is correct. Cash received from customers = Sales + Decrease in accounts receivable = 254.6 + 4.9 = 259.5. Cash paid to suppliers = Cost of goods sold + Increase in inventory − Increase in accounts payable = 175.9 + 8.8 − 2.6 = 182.1

14. C is correct. Interest expense of $19 million less the increase in interest payable of $3 million equals $16 million. Tax expense of $6 million plus the decrease in taxes payable of $4 million equals $10 million.

15. C is correct. Net income (NI) for 2005 can be computed as the change in retained earnings, $25, plus the dividends paid in 2005, $10. NI can also be calculated from the formula: Beginning retained earnings + NI − Dividends paid = Ending retained earnings. Depreciation of $25 would be added back to net income while the increases in accounts receivable, $5, and in inventory, $3, would be subtracted from net income because they are uses of cash. The decrease in accounts payable is also a use of cash and, therefore, a subtraction from net income. Thus, cash flow from operations for 2005 is $25 + $10 + $25 − $5 − $3 − $7 = $45 ($ millions).

16. C is correct. Selling price (cash inflow) minus book value equals gain or loss on sale; therefore, gain or loss on sale plus book value equals selling price (cash inflow). The amount of loss is given, $2 million. To calculate the book value of the equipment sold, find the historical cost of the equipment and the accumulated depreciation on the equipment.

▶ Beginning balance of equipment of $100 million plus equipment purchased of $10 million minus ending balance of equipment of $105 million equals the historical cost of equipment sold, or $5 million.

▶ Beginning accumulated depreciation of $40 million plus depreciation expense for the year of $8 million minus ending balance of accumulated depreciation of $46 million equals accumulated depreciation on the equipment sold, or $2 million.

▶ Therefore, the book value of the equipment sold was $5 million minus $2 million, or $3 million.

▶ Because the loss on the sale of equipment was $2 million, the amount of cash received must have been $1 million.

17. A is correct. The increase of $42 million in common stock and additional paid-in capital indicates that the company issued stock during the year. The increase in retained earnings of $15 million indicates that the company paid $10 million in cash dividends during the year, determined as beginning retained earnings of $100 million plus net income of $25 million, minus ending retained earnings of $115, which equals $10 million in cash dividends.

18. A is correct. To derive operating cash flow, the company would make the following adjustments to net income: add depreciation (a noncash expense) of $2 million; add the decrease in accounts receivable of $3 million; add the increase in accounts payable of $5 million; and subtract the increase in inventory of $4 million. Total additions would be $10 million, and total subtractions would be $4 million for net additions of $6 million.

19. C is correct. Before examining individual cash flows, the major sources and uses of cash should be evaluated.

20. C is correct. The primary source of cash is operating activities. An examination of the financing section indicates that the company pays dividends. The primary use of cash is investing activities. Interest received for Telefónica is classified as an investing activity.

21. B is correct. Dividing each line item on the cash flow statement by net revenue is one of two acceptable approaches for preparing a common-size cash flow statement. The other acceptable approach involves expressing each line item of cash inflow (outflow) as a percentage of total inflows (outflows) of cash. Answer A is a description of the indirect method of determining cash flow from operations. Answer C is incorrect because in describing an alternative way to prepare a common-size cash flow statement it fails to distinguish between the divisor appropriate for cash outflows and cash inflows.

22. B is correct. Free cash flow to the firm can be computed as operating cash flows plus after-tax interest expense less capital expenditures.

23. A is correct. This is the interest coverage ratio using operating cash flow rather than earnings before interest, tax, depreciation, and amortization (EBITDA).

FINANCIAL ANALYSIS TECHNIQUES

by Thomas R. Robinson, CFA, Jan Hendrik van Greuning, CFA,
R. Elaine Henry, CFA, and Michael A. Broihahn, CFA

LEARNING OUTCOMES

The candidate should be able to:	Mastery
a. evaluate and compare companies using ratio analysis, common-size financial statements, and charts in financial analysis;	☐
b. describe the limitations of ratio analysis;	☐
c. describe the various techniques of common-size analysis and interpret the results of such analysis;	☐
d. calculate, classify, and interpret activity, liquidity, solvency, profitability, and valuation ratios;	☐
e. demonstrate how ratios are related and how to evaluate a company using a combination of different ratios;	☐
f. demonstrate the application of and interpret changes in the component parts of the DuPont analysis (the decomposition of return on equity);	☐
g. calculate and interpret the ratios used in equity analysis, credit analysis, and segment analysis;	☐
h. describe how ratio analysis and other techniques can be used to model and forecast earnings.	☐

THEME

Financial analysis techniques—such as ratio analysis and common-size financial statements—can provide valuable insight into a company's operations, risk characteristics, and valuation beyond what is readily apparent by examining raw data. When data are presented analytically, differences across time periods, interrelationships of financial statement accounts, and comparisons among companies are more easily understood. Furthermore, trends and relationships become more visible, thereby assisting in equity valuation and credit analysis.

International Financial Statement Analysis, by Thomas R. Robinson, CFA, Jan Hendrik van Greuning, CFA, R. Elaine Henry, CFA, and Michael A. Broihahn, CFA. Copyright © 2007 by CFA Institute. Reprinted with permission.

| 1 |

INTRODUCTION

Financial analysis applies analytical tools to financial data to assess a company's performance and trends in that performance. In essence, an analyst converts data into financial metrics that assist in decision making. Analysts seek to answer such questions as: How successfully has the company performed, relative to its own past performance and relative to its competitors? How is the company likely to perform in the future? Based on expectations about future performance, what is the value of this company or the securities it issues?

A primary source of data is a company's financial reports, including the financial statements, footnotes, and management's discussion and analysis. This reading focuses on data presented in financial reports prepared under international financial reporting standards (IFRS) and United States generally accepted accounting principles (U.S. GAAP). However, even financial reports prepared under these standards do not contain all the information needed to perform effective financial analysis. Although financial statements do contain data about the *past* performance of a company (its income and cash flows) as well as its *current* financial condition (assets, liabilities, and owners' equity), such statements may not provide some important nonfinancial information nor do they forecast *future* results. The financial analyst must be capable of using financial statements in conjunction with other information in order to reach valid conclusions and make projections. Accordingly, an analyst will most likely need to supplement the information found in a company's financial reports with industry and economic data.

The purpose of this reading is to describe various techniques used to analyze a company's financial statements. Financial analysis of a company may be performed for a variety of reasons, such as valuing equity securities, assessing credit risk, conducting due diligence related to an acquisition, or assessing a subsidiary's performance. This reading will describe the techniques common to any financial analysis and then discuss more specific aspects for the two most common categories: equity analysis and credit analysis.

Equity analysis incorporates an owner's perspective, either for valuation or performance evaluation. Credit analysis incorporates a creditor's (such as a banker or bondholder) perspective. In either case, there is a need to gather and analyze information to make a decision (ownership or credit); the focus of analysis varies due to the differing interest of owners and creditors. Both equity and credit analysis assess the entity's ability to generate and grow earnings and cash flow, as well as any associated risks. Equity analysis usually places a greater emphasis on growth, whereas credit analysis usually places a greater emphasis on risks. The difference in emphasis reflects the different fundamentals of these types of investments: The value of a company's equity generally increases as the company's earnings and cash flow increase, whereas the value of a company's debt has an upper limit.[1]

The balance of this reading is organized as follows: Section 2 recaps the framework for financial statements and the place of financial analysis techniques within it. Section 3 provides a description of analytical tools and techniques. Section 4 explains how to compute, analyze, and interpret common financial ratios. Sections 4 through 8 explain the use of ratios and other analytical data in equity analysis, debt analysis, segment analysis, and forecasting, respectively. A summary of the key points and practice problems in the CFA Institute multiple-choice format conclude the reading.

THE FINANCIAL ANALYSIS PROCESS   2

In financial analysis, as in any business task, a clear understanding of the end goal and the steps required to get there is essential. In addition, the analyst needs to know the typical questions to address when interpreting financial data and how to communicate the analysis and conclusions.

2.1 The Objectives of the Financial Analysis Process

Due to the variety of reasons for performing financial analysis, the numerous available techniques, and the often substantial amount of data, it is important that the analytical approach be tailored to the specific situation. Prior to embarking on any financial analysis, the analyst should clarify purpose and context, and clearly understand the following:

▶ What is the purpose of the analysis? What questions will this analysis answer?

▶ What level of detail will be needed to accomplish this purpose?

▶ What data are available for the analysis?

▶ What are the factors or relationships that will influence the analysis?

▶ What are the analytical limitations, and will these limitations potentially impair the analysis?

Having clarified the purpose and context of the analysis, the analyst can select the techniques (e.g., ratios) that will best assist in making a decision. Although there is no single approach to structuring the analysis process, a general framework is set forth in Exhibit 1.[2] The steps in this process were discussed in more detail in the reading that introduced financial statement analysis. The primary focus of this reading is on Phases 3 and 4, processing and analyzing data.

---

[1] The upper limit is equal to the undiscounted sum of the principal and remaining interest payments (i.e., the present value of these contractual payments at a zero percent discount rate).

[2] Components of this framework have been adapted from van Greuning and Bratanovic (2003, p. 300) and Benninga and Sarig (1997, pp. 134–156).

EXHIBIT 1	A Financial Statement Analysis Framework	
Phase	**Sources of Information**	**Output**
1. Articulate the purpose and context of the analysis	▶ The nature of the analyst's function, such as evaluating an equity or debt investment or issuing a credit rating. ▶ Communication with client or superior on needs and concerns. ▶ Institutional guidelines related to developing specific work product.	▶ Statement of the purpose or objective of analysis. ▶ A list (written or unwritten) of specific questions to be answered by the analysis. ▶ Nature and content of report to be provided. ▶ Timetable and budgeted resources for completion.
2. Collect input data	▶ Financial statements, other financial data, questionnaires, and industry/economic data. ▶ Discussions with management, suppliers, customers, and competitors. ▶ Company site visits (e.g., to production facilities or retail stores).	▶ Organized financial statements. ▶ Financial data tables. ▶ Completed questionnaires, if applicable.
3. Process data	▶ Data from the previous phase.	▶ Adjusted financial statements. ▶ Common-size statements. ▶ Ratios and graphs. ▶ Forecasts.
4. Analyze/interpret the processed data	▶ Input data as well as processed data.	▶ Analytical results.
5. Develop and communicate conclusions and recommendations (e.g., with an analysis report)	▶ Analytical results and previous reports. ▶ Institutional guidelines for published reports.	▶ Analytical report answering questions posed in Phase 1. ▶ Recommendation regarding the purpose of the analysis, such as whether to make an investment or grant credit.
6. Follow up	▶ Information gathered by periodically repeating above steps as necessary to determine whether changes to holdings or recommendations are necessary.	▶ Updated reports and recommendations.

2.2 Distinguishing between Computations and Analysis

An effective analysis encompasses both computations and interpretations. A well-reasoned analysis differs from a mere compilation of various pieces of information, computations, tables, and graphs by integrating the data collected into a cohesive whole. Analysis of past performance, for example, should address not only what happened but also why it happened and whether it advanced the company's strategy. Some of the key questions to address include:

▶ What aspects of performance are critical for this company to successfully compete in this industry?

► How well did the company's performance meet these critical aspects? (This is established through computation and comparison with appropriate benchmarks, such as the company's own historical performance or competitors' performance.)

► What were the key causes of this performance, and how does this performance reflect the company's strategy? (This is established through analysis.)

If the analysis is forward looking, additional questions include:

► What is the likely impact of an event or trend? (Established through interpretation of analysis.)

► What is the likely response of management to this trend? (Established through evaluation of quality of management and corporate governance.)

► What is the likely impact of trends in the company, industry, and economy on future cash flows? (Established through assessment of corporate strategy and through forecasts.)

► What are the recommendations of the analyst? (Established through interpretation and forecasting of results of analysis.)

► What risks should be highlighted? (Established by an evaluation of major uncertainties in the forecast.)

Example 1 demonstrates how a company's financial data can be analyzed in the context of its business strategy and changes in that strategy. An analyst must be able to understand the "why" behind the numbers and ratios, not just what the numbers and ratios are.

EXAMPLE 1

Change in Strategy Reflected in Financial Performance

Motorola (NYSE:MOT) and Nokia (NYSE:NOK) engage in the design, manufacture, and sale of mobility products worldwide. Selected financial data for 2003 through 2005 for these two competitors are given below.

Selected Financial Data for Motorola (in $Millions)

Years ended 31 December	2005	2004	2003
Net sales	36,843	31,323	23,155
Operating earnings	4,696	3,132	1,273

Selected Financial Data for Nokia Corporation (in €Millions)

Years ended 31 December	2005	2004	2003
Net sales	34,191	29,371	29,533
Operating profit	4,639	4,326	4,960

Source: Motorola 10-K and Nokia 20-F, both filed 2 March 2006.

Although the raw numbers for Motorola and Nokia are not directly comparable because Motorola reports in U.S. dollars and Nokia in euros, the relative changes can be compared. Motorola reported a 35 percent increase in net sales from 2003 to 2004 and a further increase in 2005 of approximately 18 percent. Also, the company's operating earnings more than doubled from 2003 to 2004 and grew another 50 percent in 2005. Over the 2003 to 2004 time period, industry leader Nokia reported a decrease in both sales and operating profits, although sales growth was about 16 percent in 2005.

What caused Motorola's dramatic growth in sales and operating profits? One of the most important factors was the introduction of new products, such as the stylish RAZR cell phone in 2004. Motorola's 2005 10-K indicates that more than 23 million RAZRs had been sold since the product was launched. The handset segment represents 54 percent of the company's 2004 sales and nearly 58 percent of 2005 sales, so the impact on sales and profitability of the successful product introduction was significant. The introduction of branded, differentiated products not only increased demand but also increased the potential for higher pricing. The introduction of the new products was one result of the company's strategic shift to develop a consumer marketing orientation as a complement to its historically strong technological position.

Analysts often need to communicate the findings of their analysis in a written report. Their reports should, therefore, communicate how conclusions were reached and why recommendations were made. For example, a report might present the following:[3]

- ▶ the purpose of the report, unless it is readily apparent;
- ▶ relevant aspects of the business context:
  - ▶ economic environment (country, macro economy, sector);
  - ▶ financial and other infrastructure (accounting, auditing, rating agencies);
  - ▶ legal and regulatory environment (and any other material limitations on the company being analyzed);
- ▶ evaluation of corporate governance;
- ▶ assessment of financial and operational data;
- ▶ conclusions and recommendations (including risks and limitations to the analysis).

An effective storyline and well-supported conclusions and recommendations are normally enhanced by using 3–10 years of data, as well as analytic techniques appropriate to the purpose of the report.

---

[3] The nature and content of reports will vary depending upon the purpose of the analysis and the ultimate recipient of the report. For an example of the contents of an equity research report, see Stowe, Robinson, Pinto, and McLeavey (2002, pages 22–28).

ANALYSIS TOOLS AND TECHNIQUES

3

The tools and techniques presented in this section facilitate evaluations of company data. Evaluations require comparisons. It is difficult to say that a company's financial performance was "good" without clarifying the basis for comparison.

In assessing a company's ability to generate and grow earnings and cash flow, and the risks related to those earnings and cash flows, the analyst draws comparisons to other companies (cross-sectional analysis) and over time (trend or time-series analysis).

For example, an analyst may wish to compare the profitability in 2004 of Dell and Gateway. These companies differ significantly in size, so comparing net income in raw dollars is not useful. Instead, ratios (which express one number in relation to another) and common-size financial statements can remove size as a factor and enable a more relevant comparison.

The analyst may also want to examine Dell's performance relative to its own historic performance. Again, the raw dollar amounts of sales or net income may not highlight significant changes. However, using ratios (see Example 2), horizontal financial statements, and graphs can make such changes more apparent.

EXAMPLE 2

Ratio Analysis

Dell computer reported the following data for three recent fiscal years:

Fiscal Year Ended (FY)	Net Income (Millions of USD)
1/31/2003	2,122
1/30/2004	2,645
1/28/2005	3,043

Overall net income has grown steadily over the three-year period. Net income for FY2005 is 43 percent higher than net income in 2003, which is a good sign. However, has profitability also steadily increased? We can obtain some insight by looking at the **net profit margin** (net income divided by revenue) for each year.

Fiscal Year Ended	Net Profit Margin (%)
1/31/2003	5.99
1/30/2004	6.38
1/28/2005	6.18

The net profit margin indicates that profitability improved from FY2003 to FY2004 but deteriorated slightly from FY2004 to FY2005. Further analysis is needed to determine the cause of the profitability decline and assess whether this decline is likely to persist in future years.

The following paragraphs describe the tools and techniques of ratio analysis in more detail.

3.1 Ratios

There are many relationships between financial accounts and between expected relationships from one point in time to another. Ratios are a useful way of expressing these relationships. Ratios express one quantity in relation to another (usually as a quotient).

Notable academic research has examined the importance of ratios in predicting stock returns (Ou and Penman, 1989; Abarbanell and Bushee, 1998) or credit failure (Altman, 1968; Ohlson, 1980; Hopwood et al., 1994). This research has found that financial statement ratios are effective in selecting investments and in predicting financial distress. Practitioners routinely use ratios to communicate the value of companies and securities.

Several aspects of ratio analysis are important to understand. First, the computed ratio is not "the answer." The ratio is an *indicator* of some aspect of a company's performance, telling what happened but not why it happened. For example, an analyst might want to answer the question: Which of two companies was more profitable? The net profit margin, which expresses profit relative to revenue, can provide insight into this question. Net profit margin is calculated by dividing net income by revenue:[4]

$$\frac{\text{Net income}}{\text{Revenue}}$$

Assume Company A has €100,000 of net income and €2,000,000 of revenue, and thus a net profit margin of 5 percent. Company B has €200,000 of net income and €6,000,000 of revenue, and thus a net profit margin of 3.33 percent. Expressing net income as a percentage of revenue clarifies the relationship: For each €100 of revenue, Company A earns €5 in net income, while Company B earns only €3.33 for each €100 of revenue. So, we can now answer the question of which company was more profitable in percentage terms: Company A was more profitable, as indicated by its higher net profit margin of 5 percent. We also note that Company A was more profitable despite the fact that Company B reported higher absolute amounts of net income and revenue. However, this ratio by itself does not tell us *why* Company A has a higher profit margin. Further analysis is required to determine the reason (perhaps higher relative sales prices or better cost control).

Company size sometimes confers economies of scale, so the absolute amounts of net income and revenue are useful in financial analysis. However, ratios reduce the effect of size, which enhances comparisons between companies and over time.

A second important aspect of ratio analysis is that differences in accounting policies (across companies and across time) can distort ratios, and a meaningful comparison may, therefore, involve adjustments to the financial data. Third, not all ratios are necessarily relevant to a particular analysis. The ability to select a

---

[4] The term "sales" is often used interchangeably with the term "revenues." Other times it is used to refer to revenues derived from sales of products versus services. Furthermore, the income statement usually reflects "revenues" or "sales" after returns and allowances (e.g., returns of products or discounts offered after a sale to induce the customer to not return a product). Additionally, in some countries including the United Kingdom, the term "turnover" is used in the sense of "revenue."

relevant ratio or ratios to answer the research question is an analytical skill. Finally, as with financial analysis in general, ratio analysis does not stop with computation; interpretation of the result is essential. In practice, differences in ratios across time and across companies can be subtle, and interpretation is situation specific.

3.1.1 The Universe of Ratios

There are no authoritative bodies specifying exact formulas for computing ratios or providing a standard, comprehensive list of ratios. Formulas and even names of ratios often differ from analyst to analyst or from database to database. The number of different ratios that can be created is practically limitless. There are, however, widely accepted ratios that have been found to be useful. Section 4 of this reading will focus primarily on these broad classes and commonly accepted definitions of key ratios. However, the analyst should be aware that different ratios may be used in practice and that certain industries have unique ratios tailored to the characteristics of that industry. When faced with an unfamiliar ratio, the analyst can examine the underlying formula to gain insight into what the ratio is measuring. For example, consider the following ratio formula:

$$\frac{\text{Operating income}}{\text{Average total assets}}$$

Never having seen this ratio, an analyst might question whether a result of 12 percent is better than 8 percent. The answer can be found in the ratio itself. The numerator is operating income and the denominator is average total assets, so the ratio can be interpreted as the amount of operating income generated per unit of assets. For every €100 of average total assets, generating €12 of operating income is better than generating €8 of operating income. Furthermore, it is apparent that this particular ratio is an indicator of profitability (and, to a lesser extent, efficiency in use of assets in generating operating profits). When facing a ratio for the first time, the analyst should evaluate the numerator and denominator to assess what the ratio is attempting to measure and how it should be interpreted. This is demonstrated in Example 3.

EXAMPLE 3

Interpreting a Financial Ratio

An insurance company reports that its "combined ratio" is determined by dividing losses and expenses incurred by net premiums earned. It reports the following combined ratios:

	2005	2004	2003	2002	2001
Combined ratio	90.1%	104.0%	98.5%	104.1%	101.1%

Explain what this ratio is measuring and compare and contrast the results reported for each of the years shown in the chart. What other information might an analyst want to review before concluding on this information?

Solution: The combined ratio is a profitability measure. The ratio is explaining how much the costs (losses and expenses) were for every dollar of revenue (net premiums earned). The underlying formula indicates that a lower ratio is better. The 2005 ratio of 90.1 percent means that for every dollar of net premiums earned, the costs were $.901, yielding a gross profit of $.099. Ratios greater than 100 percent indicate an overall loss. A review of the data indicates that there does not seem to be a consistent trend in this ratio. Profits were achieved in 2005 and 2003. The results for 2004 and 2002 show the most significant losses at 104 percent.

The analyst would want to discuss this data further with management and understand the characteristics of the underlying business. He or she would want to understand why the results are so volatile. The analyst would also want to determine what ratio should be used as a benchmark.

The Operating income/Average total assets ratio shown above is one of many versions of the **return on assets (ROA)** ratio. Note that there are other ways of specifying this formula based on how assets are defined. Some financial ratio databases compute ROA using the ending value of assets rather than average assets. In limited cases, one may also see beginning assets in the denominator. Which one is right? It depends upon what you are trying to measure and the underlying company trends. If the company has a stable level of assets, the answer will not differ greatly under the three measures of assets (beginning, average, and ending). If, however, the assets are growing (or shrinking), the results will differ. When assets are growing, operating income divided by ending assets may not make sense because some of the income would have been generated before some assets were purchased, and this would understate the company's performance. Similarly, if beginning assets are used, some of the operating income later in the year may have been generated only because of the addition of assets; therefore, the ratio would overstate the company's performance. Because operating income occurs throughout the period, it generally makes sense to use some average measure of assets. A good general rule is that when an income statement or statement of cash flows number is in the numerator of a ratio and a balance sheet number is in the denominator, then an average should be used for the denominator. It is generally not necessary to use averages when only balance sheet numbers are used in both the numerator and denominator because both are determined as of the same date. However, as we shall see later, there are occasions when even balance sheet data may be averages (e.g., in analyzing the components of **return on equity [ROE]**, which is defined as net income divided by average shareholders' equity).

If an average is used, there is also judgment required as to what average should be used. For simplicity, most ratio databases use a simple average of the beginning and end-of-year balance sheet amounts. If the company's business is seasonable so that levels of assets vary by interim period (semiannual or quarterly), then it may be beneficial to take an average over all interim periods, if available (if the analyst is working within a company and has access to monthly data, this can also be used).

3.1.2 Value, Purposes, and Limitations of Ratio Analysis

The value of ratio analysis is that it enables the equity or credit analyst to evaluate past performance, assess the current financial position of the company, and gain insights useful for projecting future results. As noted previously, the ratio itself is not "the answer" but an indicator of some aspect of a company's performance. Financial ratios provide insights into:

▶ microeconomic relationships within a company that help analysts project earnings and free cash flow;

▶ a company's financial flexibility, or ability to obtain the cash required to grow and meet its obligations, even if unexpected circumstances develop; and

▶ management's ability.

There are also limitations to ratio analysis:

▶ *The homogeneity of a company's operating activities.* Companies may have divisions operating in many different industries. This can make it difficult to find comparable industry ratios to use for comparison purposes.

▶ *The need to determine whether the results of the ratio analysis are consistent.* One set of ratios may indicate a problem, whereas another set may prove that the potential problem is only short term in nature.

▶ *The need to use judgment.* A key issue is whether a ratio for a company is within a reasonable range. Although financial ratios are used to help assess the growth potential and risk of a company, they cannot be used alone to directly value a company or its securities, or to determine its credit-worthiness. The entire operation of the company must be examined, and the external economic and industry setting in which it is operating must be considered when interpreting financial ratios.

▶ *The use of alternative accounting methods.* Companies frequently have latitude when choosing certain accounting methods. Ratios taken from financial statements that employ different accounting choices may not be comparable unless adjustments are made. Some important accounting considerations include the following:

▶ FIFO (first in, first out), LIFO (last in, first out), or average cost inventory valuation methods (IFRS no longer allow LIFO);

▶ Cost or equity methods of accounting for unconsolidated affiliates;

▶ Straight line or accelerated methods of depreciation; and

▶ Capital or operating lease treatment.

The expanding use of IFRS and the planned convergence between U.S. GAAP and IFRS seek to make the financial statements of different companies comparable and so overcome some of these difficulties. Nonetheless, there will remain accounting choices that the analyst must consider.

3.1.3 *Sources of Ratios*

Ratios may be computed using data directly from companies' financial statements or from a database such as Bloomberg, Baseline, FactSet, or Thomson Reuters. These databases are popular because they provide easy access to many years of historical data so that trends over time can be examined. They also allow for ratio calculations based on periods other than the company's fiscal year, such as for the trailing 12 months (TTM) or most recent quarter (MRQ).

Analysts should be aware that the underlying formulas may differ by vendor. The formula used should be obtained from the vendor, and the analyst should determine whether any adjustments are necessary. Furthermore, database providers often exercise judgment when classifying items. For example, operating income may not appear directly on a company's income statement, and the vendor may use judgment to classify income statement items as "operating" or "nonoperating." Variation in such judgments would affect any computation involving operating income. It is, therefore, a good practice to use the same source for data when comparing different companies or when evaluating the historical record of a single given company. Analysts should verify the consistency of formulas and data classifications of the data source. Analysts should also be mindful of the judgments made by a vendor in data classifications and refer back to the source financial statements until they are comfortable that the classifications are appropriate.

Systems are under development that collect financial data from regulatory filings and can automatically compute ratios. The eXtensible Business Reporting Language (XBRL) is a mechanism that attaches "smart tags" to financial information (e.g., total assets), so that software can automatically collect the data and perform desired computations. The organization developing XBRL (www.xbrl.org) is a worldwide nonprofit consortium of organizations, including the International Accounting Standards Board.

Analysts can compare a subject company to similar (peer) companies in these databases or use aggregate industry data. For nonpublic companies, aggregate industry data can be obtained from such sources as Annual Statement Studies by the Risk Management Association or Dun & Bradstreet. These publications provide industry data with companies sorted into quartiles. Twenty-five percent of companies' ratios fall within the lowest quartile, 25 percent have ratios between the lower quartile and median value, and so on. Analysts can then determine a company's relative standing in the industry.

3.2 Common-Size Analysis

Common-size analysis involves expressing financial data, including entire financial statements, in relation to a single financial statement item, or base. Items used most frequently as the bases are total assets or revenue. In essence, common-size analysis creates a ratio between every financial statement item and the base item.

Common-size analysis was demonstrated in readings for the income statement, balance sheet, and statement of cash flows. In this section, we present common-size analysis of financial statements in greater detail and include further discussion of their interpretation.

3.2.1 Common-Size Analysis of the Balance Sheet

A vertical[5] common-size balance sheet, prepared by dividing each item on the balance sheet by the same period's total assets and expressing the results as percentages, highlights the composition of the balance sheet. What is the mix of assets being used? How is the company financing itself? How does one company's balance sheet composition compare with that of peer companies, and what is behind any differences?

A horizontal common-size balance sheet, prepared by computing the increase or decrease in percentage terms of each balance sheet item from the

---

[5] The term vertical analysis is used to denote a common-size analysis using only one reporting period or one base financial statement, whereas horizontal analysis can refer either to an analysis comparing a specific financial statement with prior or future time periods or to a cross-sectional analysis of one company with another.

prior year, highlights items that have changed unexpectedly or have unexpectedly remained unchanged.

For example, Exhibit 2 presents a vertical common-size (partial) balance sheet for a hypothetical company in two different time periods. In this example, receivables have increased from 35 percent to 57 percent of total assets. What are possible reasons for such an increase? The increase might indicate that the company is making more of its sales on a credit basis rather than a cash basis, perhaps in response to some action taken by a competitor. Alternatively, the increase in receivables as a percentage of assets may have occurred because of a change in another current asset category—for example, a decrease in the level of inventory; the analyst would then need to investigate why that asset category had changed. Another possible reason for the increase in receivables as a percentage of assets is that the company has lowered its credit standards, relaxed its collection procedures, or adopted more aggressive revenue recognition policies. The analyst can turn to other comparisons and ratios (e.g., comparing the rate of growth in accounts receivable with the rate of growth in sales to help determine which explanation is most likely).

EXHIBIT 2	Vertical Common-Size (Partial) Balance Sheet for a Hypothetical Company	
	Period 1 **% of Total Assets**	**Period 2** **% of Total Assets**
Cash	25	15
Receivables	35	57
Inventory	35	20
Fixed assets, net of depreciation	5	8
Total assets	100	100

3.2.2 Common-Size Analysis of the Income Statement

A vertical common-size income statement divides each income statement item by revenue, or sometimes by total assets (especially in the case of financial institutions). If there are multiple revenue sources, a decomposition of revenue in percentage terms is useful. For example, Exhibit 3 presents a hypothetical company's vertical common-size income statement in two different time periods. Revenue is separated into the company's four services, each shown as a percentage of total revenue. In this example, revenues from Service A have become a far greater percentage of the company's total revenue (45 percent in Period 2). What are possible reasons for and implications of this change in business mix? Did the company make a strategic decision to sell more of Service A, perhaps because it is more profitable? Apparently not, because the company's earnings before interest, taxes, depreciation, and amortization (EBITDA) declined from 53 percent of sales to 45 percent, so other possible explanations should be examined. In addition, we note from the composition of operating expenses that the main reason for this decline in profitability is that salaries and employee benefits have increased from 15 percent to 25 percent of total revenue. Are more highly compensated employees required for Service A? Were higher training costs incurred in order to increase Service A revenues? If the analyst wants to predict future performance, the causes of these changes must be understood.

In addition, Exhibit 3 shows that the company's income tax as a percentage of sales has declined dramatically (from 15 percent to 8 percent). Furthermore, as a percentage of earnings before tax (EBT) (usually the more relevant comparison), taxes have decreased from 36 percent to 23 percent. Is Service A provided in a jurisdiction with lower tax rates? If not, what is the explanation?

The observations based on Exhibit 3 summarize the issues that can be raised through analysis of the vertical common-size income statement.

EXHIBIT 3	Vertical Common-Size Income Statement for Hypothetical Company	
	Period 1 % of Total Revenue	**Period 2 % of Total Revenue**
Revenue source: Service A	30	45
Revenue source: Service B	23	20
Revenue source: Service C	30	30
Revenue source: Service D	17	5
Total revenue	**100**	**100**
Operating expenses (excluding depreciation)		
Salaries and employee benefits	15	25
Administrative expenses	22	20
Rent expense	10	10
EBITDA	**53**	**45**
Depreciation and amortization	4	4
EBIT	**49**	**41**
Interest paid	7	7
EBT	**42**	**34**
Income tax provision	15	8
Net income	**27**	**26**

Note: EBIT = earnings before interest and tax.

3.2.3 Cross-Sectional Analysis

As noted previously, ratios and common-size statements derive part of their meaning through comparison to some benchmark. **Cross-sectional analysis** (sometimes called "relative analysis") compares a specific metric for one company with the same metric for another company or group of companies, allowing comparisons even though the companies might be of significantly different sizes and/or operate in different currencies.

Exhibit 4 presents a vertical common-size (partial) balance sheet for two hypothetical companies at the same point in time. Company 1 is clearly more liquid (liquidity is a function of how quickly assets can be converted into cash) than Company 2, which has only 12 percent of assets available as cash, compared with the highly liquid Company 1, where cash is 38 percent of assets. Given that cash

EXHIBIT 4	Vertical Common-Size (Partial) Balance Sheet for Two Hypothetical Companies	
	Company 1 % of Total Assets	Company 2 % of Total Assets
Cash	38	12
Receivables	33	55
Inventory	27	24
Fixed assets net of depreciation	1	2
Investments	1	7
Total assets	**100**	**100**

is generally a relatively low-yielding asset and thus not a particularly efficient use of the balance sheet, why does Company 1 hold such a large percentage of total assets in cash? Perhaps the company is preparing for an acquisition, or maintains a large cash position as insulation from a particularly volatile operating environment. Another issue highlighted by the comparison in this example is the relatively high percentage of receivables in Company 2's assets, which (as discussed in Section 3.2.1) may indicate a greater proportion of credit sales, overall changes in asset composition, lower credit or collection standards, or aggressive accounting policies.

3.2.4 Trend Analysis[6]

When looking at financial statements and ratios, trends in the data, whether they are improving or deteriorating, are as important as the current absolute or relative levels. Trend analysis provides important information regarding historical performance and growth and, given a sufficiently long history of accurate seasonal information, can be of great assistance as a planning and forecasting tool for management and analysts.

Exhibit 5A presents a partial balance sheet for a hypothetical company over five periods. The last two columns of the table show the changes for Period 5 compared with Period 4, expressed both in absolute currency (in this case, dollars) and in percentages. A small percentage change could hide a significant currency change and vice versa, prompting the analyst to investigate the reasons despite one of the changes being relatively small. In this example, the largest percentage change was in investments, which decreased by 33.3 percent.[7] However, an examination of the absolute currency amount of changes shows that investments changed by only $2 million and the more significant change was the $12 million increase in receivables.

Another way to present data covering a period of time is to show each item in relation to the same item in a base year (i.e., a horizontal common-size balance

---

[6] In financial statement analysis, the term "trend analysis" usually refers to comparisons across time periods of 3–10 years not involving statistical tools. This differs from the use of the term in the quantitative methods portion of the CFA curriculum, where "trend analysis" refers to statistical methods of measuring patterns in time-series data.

[7] Percentage change is calculated as: (Ending value − Beginning value)/Beginning value, or equivalently, (Ending value/Beginning value) − 1.

sheet). Exhibit 5B presents the same partial balance sheet as in Exhibit 5A but with each item indexed relative to the same item in Period 1. For example, in Period 2, the company had $29 million cash, which is 75 percent of the amount of cash it had in Period 1, or expressed as an index relative to Period 1, 75 ($29/$39 = 0.75 × 100 = 75). Presenting data this way highlights significant changes. In this example, we see easily that the company has less than half the amount of cash in Period 1, four times the amount of investments, and eight times the amount of property, plant, and equipment.

An analysis of horizontal common-size balance sheets highlights structural changes that have occurred in a business. Past trends are obviously not necessarily an accurate predictor of the future, especially when the economic or competitive environment changes. An examination of past trends is more valuable when the macroeconomic and competitive environments are relatively stable and when the analyst is reviewing a stable or mature business. However, even in less stable contexts, historical analysis can serve as a basis for developing expecta-

| EXHIBIT 5A | Partial Balance Sheet for a Hypothetical Company over Five Periods |

Assets ($ Millions)	Period 1	2	3	4	5	Change 4 to 5 ($ Million)	Change 4 to 5 (%)
Cash	39	29	27	19	16	−3	−15.8
Investments	1	7	7	6	4	−2	−33.3
Receivables	44	41	37	67	79	12	17.9
Inventory	15	25	36	25	27	2	8
Fixed assets net of depreciation	1	2	6	9	8	−1	−11.1
Total assets	100	105	112	126	133	8	5.6

| EXHIBIT 5B | Horizontal Common-Size (Partial) Balance Sheet for a Hypothetical Company over Five Periods, with Each Item Expressed Relative to the Same Item in Period One |

Assets	Period 1	2	3	4	5
Cash	1.00	0.75	0.69	0.48	0.41
Investments	1.00	7.35	6.74	6.29	4.00
Receivables	1.00	0.93	0.84	1.52	1.79
Inventory	1.00	1.68	2.40	1.68	1.78
Fixed assets net of depreciation	1.00	2.10	5.62	8.81	8.00
Total assets	1.00	1.05	1.12	1.26	1.33

tions. Understanding past trends is helpful in assessing whether these trends are likely to continue or if the trend is likely to change direction.

One measure of success is for a company to grow at a rate greater than the rate of the overall market in which it operates. Companies that grow slowly may find themselves unable to attract equity capital. Conversely, companies that grow too quickly may find that their administrative and management information systems cannot keep up with the rate of expansion.

3.2.5 Relationships among Financial Statements

Trend data generated by a horizontal common-size analysis can be compared across financial statements. For example, the growth rate of assets for the hypothetical company in Exhibit 5 can be compared with the company's growth in revenue over the same period of time. If revenue is growing more quickly than assets, the company may be increasing its efficiency (i.e., generating more revenue for every dollar invested in assets).

As another example, consider the following year-over-year percentage changes for a hypothetical company:

Revenue	+20%
Net income	+25%
Operating cash flow	−10%
Total assets	+30%

Net income is growing faster than revenue, which indicates increasing profitability. However, the analyst would need to determine whether the faster growth in net income resulted from continuing operations or from nonoperating, nonrecurring items. In addition, the 10 percent decline in operating cash flow despite increasing revenue and net income clearly warrants further investigation because it could indicate a problem with earnings quality (perhaps aggressive reporting of revenue). Lastly, the fact that assets have grown faster than revenue indicates the company's efficiency may be declining. The analyst should examine the composition of the increase in assets and the reasons for the changes. Example 4 provides a recent example of a company where comparisons of trend data from different financial statements can indicate aggressive accounting policies.

EXAMPLE 4

Use of Comparative Growth Information[8]

Sunbeam, a U.S. company, brought in new management to turn the company around during July 1996. For the following year, 1997, the following common-size trends were apparent:

Revenue	+19%
Inventory	+58%
Receivables	+38%

---

[8] Adapted from Robinson and Munter (2004, pp. 2–15).

It is generally more desirable to observe inventory and receivables growing at a slower (or similar) rate to revenue growth. Receivables growing faster than revenue can indicate operational issues, such as lower credit standards or aggressive accounting policies for revenue recognition. Similarly, inventory growing faster than revenue can indicate an operational problem with obsolescence or aggressive accounting policies, such as an improper overstatement of inventory to increase profits.

In this case, the explanation lay in aggressive accounting policies. Sunbeam was later charged by the U.S. SEC with improperly accelerating the recognition of revenue and engaging in other practices, such as billing customers for inventory prior to shipment.

3.3 The Use of Graphs as an Analytical Tool

Graphs facilitate comparison of performance and financial structure over time, highlighting changes in significant aspects of business operations. In addition, graphs provide the analyst (and management) with a visual overview of risk trends in a business. Graphs may also be used effectively to communicate the analyst's conclusions regarding financial condition and risk management aspects.

Exhibit 6 presents the information from Exhibit 5A in a stacked column format. The graph makes the significant decline in cash and growth in receivables (both in absolute terms and as a percentage of assets) readily apparent.

Choosing the appropriate graph to communicate the most significant conclusions of a financial analysis is a skill. In general, pie graphs are most useful to communicate the composition of a total value (e.g., assets over a limited amount of time, say one or two periods). Line graphs are useful when the focus is on the

EXHIBIT 6	Stacked Column Graph of Asset Composition of Hypothetical Company over Five Periods

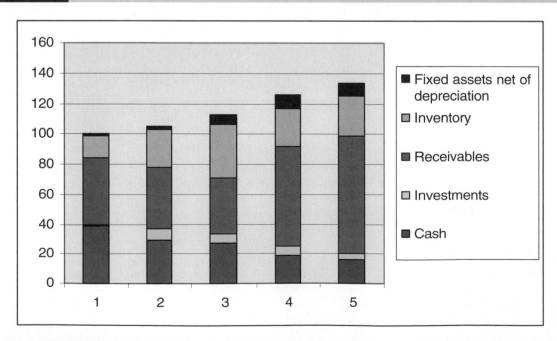

change in amount for a limited number of items over a relatively longer time period. When the composition and amounts, as well as their change over time, are all important, a stacked column graph can be useful.

When comparing Period 5 with Period 4, the growth in receivables appears to be within normal bounds, but when comparing Period 5 with earlier periods, the dramatic growth becomes apparent. In the same manner, a simple line graph will also illustrate the growth trends in key financial variables. Exhibit 7 presents the information from Exhibit 5 as a line graph, illustrating the growth of assets of a hypothetical company over five periods. The steady decline in cash, volatile movements of inventory, and dramatic growth of receivables is clearly illustrated.

EXHIBIT 7	**Line Graph of Growth of Assets of Hypothetical Company over Five Periods**

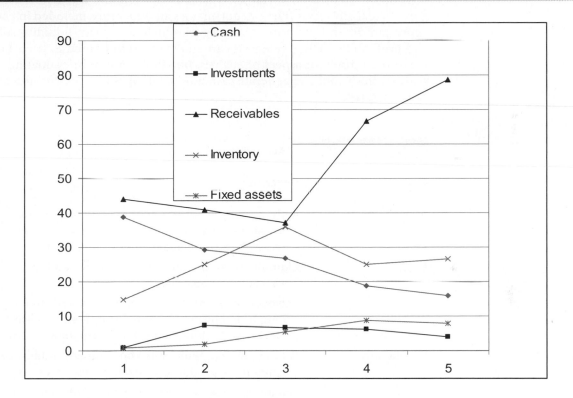

3.4 Regression Analysis

When analyzing the trend in a specific line item or ratio, frequently it is possible simply to visually evaluate the changes. For more complex situations, regression analysis can help identify relationships (or correlation) between variables. For example, a regression analysis could relate a company's sales to GDP over time, providing insight into whether the company is cyclical. In addition, the statistical relationship between sales and GDP could be used as a basis for forecasting sales.

Other examples of such relationships are the relation between a company's sales and inventory over time, or the relation between hotel occupancy and a company's hotel revenues. In addition to providing a basis for forecasting, regression analysis facilitates identification of items or ratios that are not behaving as expected, given historical statistical relationships.

4

COMMON RATIOS USED IN FINANCIAL ANALYSIS

In the previous section, we focused on ratios resulting from common-size analysis. In this section, we expand the discussion to include other commonly used financial ratios and the broad classes into which they are categorized. There is some overlap with common-size financial statement ratios. For example, a common indicator of profitability is the net profit margin, which is calculated as net income divided by sales. This ratio appears on a common-size vertical income statement. Other ratios involve information from multiple financial statements or even data from outside the financial statements.

Due to the large number of ratios, it is helpful to think about ratios in terms of broad categories based on what aspects of performance a ratio is intended to detect. Financial analysts and data vendors use a variety of categories to classify ratios. The category names and the ratios included in each category can differ. Common ratio categories include activity, liquidity, solvency, and profitability. These categories are summarized in Exhibit 8. Each category measures a different aspect of analysis, but all are useful in evaluating a company's overall ability to generate cash flows from operating its business and the associated risks.

EXHIBIT 8	Categories of Financial Ratios
Category	**Description**
Activity	**Activity ratios** measure how efficiently a company performs day-to-day tasks, such as the collection of receivables and management of inventory.
Liquidity	**Liquidity ratios** measure the company's ability to meet its short-term obligations.
Solvency	**Solvency ratios** measure a company's ability to meet long-term obligations. Subsets of these ratios are also known as "leverage" and "long-term debt" ratios.
Profitability	**Profitability ratios** measure the company's ability to generate profitable sales from its resources (assets).
Valuation	**Valuation ratios** measure the quantity of an asset or flow (e.g., earnings) associated with ownership of a specified claim (e.g., a share or ownership of the enterprise).

These categories are not mutually exclusive; some ratios are useful in measuring multiple aspects of the business. For example, an activity ratio measuring how quickly a company collects accounts receivable is also useful in assessing the company's liquidity because collection of revenues increases cash. Some profitability ratios also reflect the operating efficiency of the business. In summary, analysts appropriately use certain ratios to evaluate multiple aspects of the business. Analysts also need to be aware of variations in industry practice in the calculation of financial ratios. In the text that follows, alternative views on ratio calculations are often provided.

4.1 Interpretation and Context

Financial ratios can only be interpreted in the context of other information, including benchmarks. In general, the financial ratios of a company are compared with those of its major competitors (cross-sectional and trend analysis) and to the company's prior periods (trend analysis). The goal is to understand the underlying causes of divergence between a company's ratios and those of the industry. Even ratios that remain consistent require understanding because consistency can sometimes indicate accounting policies selected to smooth earnings. An analyst should evaluate financial ratios based on the following:

1. *Company goals and strategy.* Actual ratios can be compared with company objectives to determine whether objectives are being attained and whether the results are consistent with the company's strategy.

2. *Industry norms (cross-sectional analysis).* A company can be compared with others in its industry by relating its financial ratios to industry norms or to a subset of the companies in an industry. When industry norms are used to make judgments, care must be taken because:

   ▶ Many ratios are industry specific, and not all ratios are important to all industries.

   ▶ Companies may have several different lines of business. This will cause aggregate financial ratios to be distorted. It is better to examine industry-specific ratios by lines of business.

   ▶ Differences in accounting methods used by companies can distort financial ratios.

   ▶ Differences in corporate strategies can affect certain financial ratios.

3. *Economic conditions.* For cyclical companies, financial ratios tend to improve when the economy is strong and weaken during recessions. Therefore, financial ratios should be examined in light of the current phase of the business cycle.

The following sections discuss activity, liquidity, solvency, and profitability ratios in turn. Selected valuation ratios are presented later in the section on equity analysis.

4.2 Activity Ratios

Activity ratios are also known as **asset utilization ratios** or **operating efficiency ratios**. This category is intended to measure how well a company manages various activities, particularly how efficiently it manages its various assets. Activity ratios are analyzed as indicators of ongoing operational performance—how effectively assets are used by a company. These ratios reflect the efficient management of both working capital and longer-term assets. As noted, efficiency has a direct impact on liquidity (the ability of a company to meet its short-term obligations), so some activity ratios are also useful in assessing liquidity.

4.2.1 Calculation of Activity Ratios

Exhibit 9 presents the most commonly used activity ratios. The exhibit shows the numerator and denominator of each ratio.

EXHIBIT 9	Definitions of Commonly Used Activity Ratios	
Activity Ratios	**Numerator**	**Denominator**
Inventory turnover	Cost of goods sold	Average inventory
Days of inventory on hand (DOH)	Number of days in period	Inventory turnover
Receivables turnover	Revenue	Average receivables
Days of sales outstanding (DSO)	Number of days in period	Receivables turnover
Payables turnover	Purchases	Average trade payables
Number of days of payables	Number of days in period	Payables turnover
Working capital turnover	Revenue	Average working capital
Fixed asset turnover	Revenue	Average net fixed assets
Total asset turnover	Revenue	Average total assets

Activity ratios measure how efficiently the company utilizes assets. They generally combine information from the income statement in the numerator with balance sheet items in the denominator. Because the income statement measures what happened *during* a period whereas the balance sheet shows the condition only at the end of the period, average balance sheet data are normally used for consistency. For example, to measure inventory management efficiency, cost of goods sold (from the income statement) is divided by average inventory (from the balance sheet). Most databases, such as Bloomberg and Baseline, use this averaging convention when income statement and balance sheet data are combined. These databases typically average only two points: the beginning of the year and the end of the year. The examples that follow based on annual financial statements illustrate that practice. However, some analysts prefer to average more observations if they are available, especially if the business is seasonal. If a semiannual report is prepared, an average can be taken over three data points (beginning, middle, and end of year). If quarterly data are available, a five-point average can be computed (beginning of year and end of each quarterly period) or a four-point average using the end of each quarterly period. Note that if the company's year ends at a low or high point for inventory for the year, there can still be bias in using three or five data points, because the beginning and end of year occur at the same time of the year and are effectively double counted.

Because cost of goods sold measures the cost of inventory that has been sold, this ratio measures how many times per year the entire inventory was theoretically turned over, or sold. (We say that the entire inventory was "theoretically" sold because in practice companies do not generally sell out their entire inventory.) If, for example, a company's cost of goods sold for a recent year was €120,000 and its average inventory was €10,000, the inventory turnover ratio would be 12. The company theoretically turns over (i.e., sells) its entire inventory 12 times per year (i.e., once a month). (Again, we say "theoretically" because in practice the company likely carries some inventory from one month into another.) Turnover can then be converted to days of inventory on hand (DOH) by dividing inventory turnover into the number of days in the accounting period. In this example, the result is a DOH of 30.42 (365/12), meaning that, on average, the company's inventory was on hand for about 30 days, or, equivalently, the company kept on hand about 30 days' worth of inventory, on average, during the period.

Activity ratios can be computed for any annual or interim period, but care must be taken in the interpretation and comparison across periods. For example, if the same company had cost of goods sold for the first quarter (90 days) of the following year of €35,000 and average inventory of €11,000, the inventory turnover would be 3.18 times. However, this turnover rate is 3.18 times per quarter, which is not directly comparable to the 12 times per year in the preceding year. In this case, we can annualize the quarterly inventory turnover rate by multiplying the quarterly turnover by 4 (12 months/3 months; or by 4.06, using 365 days/90 days) for comparison to the annual turnover rate. So, the quarterly inventory turnover is equivalent to a 12.72 annual inventory turnover (or 12.91 if we annualize the ratio using a 90-day quarter and a 365-day year). To compute the DOH using quarterly data, we can use the quarterly turnover rate and the number of days in the quarter for the numerator—or, we can use the annualized turnover rate and 365 days; either results in DOH of around 28.3, with slight differences due to rounding (90/3.18 = 28.30 and 365/12.91 = 28.27). Another time-related computational detail is that for companies using a 52/53-week annual period and for leap years, the actual days in the year should be used rather than 365.

In some cases, an analyst may want to know how many days of inventory are on hand at the end of the year rather than the average for the year. In this case, it would be appropriate to use the year-end inventory balance in the computation rather than the average. If the company is growing rapidly or if costs are increasing rapidly, analysts should consider using cost of goods sold just for the fourth quarter in this computation because the cost of goods sold of earlier quarters may not be relevant. Example 5 further demonstrates computation of activity ratios using Hong Kong Exchange-listed Lenovo Group Limited.

EXAMPLE 5

Computation of Activity Ratios

Ya-Wen Yang would like to evaluate how efficient Lenovo Group Limited is at collecting its trade accounts receivable on average during the fiscal year ended 31 March 2005. Yang has gathered the following information from Lenovo's annual and interim reports:

	HK$ in Thousands
Trade receivables as of 31 March 2004	1,230,944
Trade receivables as of 31 March 2005	851,337
Revenue for year ended 31 March 2005	22,554,678

What is Lenovo's receivables turnover and number of days of sales outstanding (DSO) for the fiscal year ended 31 March 2005?

Solution:

$$Receivables\ turnover = Revenue/Average\ receivables$$
$$= 22,554,678/[(1,230,944 + 851,337)/2]$$
$$= 22,554,678/1,041,140.50$$
$$= 21.6634\ times$$

$$DSO = Number\ of\ days\ in\ period/Receivables\ turnover$$
$$= 365/21.6634$$
$$= 16.85\ days$$

On average, it took Lenovo 16.85 days to collect receivables during the fiscal year ended 31 March 2005.

4.2.2 Interpretation of Activity Ratios

In the following, we discuss the activity ratios that were defined in Exhibit 9.

Inventory Turnover and DOH   Inventory turnover lies at the heart of operations for many entities. It indicates the resources (money) tied up in inventory (i.e., the carrying costs) and can, therefore, be used to indicate inventory management effectiveness. The higher the inventory turnover ratio, the shorter the period that inventory is held and so the lower DOH. In general, inventory turnover (and DOH) should be benchmarked against industry norms.

A high inventory turnover ratio relative to industry norms might indicate highly effective inventory management. Alternatively, a high inventory turnover ratio (and commensurately low DOH) could possibly indicate the company does not carry adequate inventory, so shortages could potentially hurt revenue. To assess which explanation is more likely, the analyst can compare the company's revenue growth with that of the industry. Slower growth combined with higher inventory turnover could indicate inadequate inventory levels. Revenue growth at or above the industry's growth supports the interpretation that the higher turnover reflects greater inventory management efficiency.

A low inventory turnover ratio (and commensurately high DOH) relative to the rest of the industry could be an indicator of slow-moving inventory, perhaps due to technological obsolescence or a change in fashion. Again, comparing the company's sales growth with the industry can offer insight.

Receivables Turnover and DSO   The number of DSO represents the elapsed time between a sale and cash collection, reflecting how fast the company collects cash from customers it offers credit. Although limiting the numerator to sales made on credit would be more appropriate, credit sales information is not always available to analysts; therefore, revenue as reported in the income statement is generally used as an approximation.

A relatively high receivables turnover ratio (and commensurately low DSO) might indicate highly efficient credit and collection. Alternatively, a high receivables turnover ratio could indicate that the company's credit or collection policies are too stringent, suggesting the possibility of sales being lost to competitors offering more lenient terms. A relatively low receivables turnover ratio would typically raise questions about the efficiency of the company's credit and collections procedures. As with inventory management, comparison of the company's sales growth relative to the industry can help the analyst assess whether sales are being lost due to stringent credit policies. In addition, comparing the company's estimates of uncollectible accounts receivable and actual credit losses with past experience and with peer companies can help assess whether low turnover reflects credit management issues. Companies often provide details of receivables aging (how much receivables have been outstanding by age). This can be used along with DSO to understand trends in collection, as demonstrated in Example 6.

EXAMPLE 6

Evaluation of an Activity Ratio

Ya-Wen Yang has computed the average DSO for fiscal years ended 31 March 2004 and 2005:

	2005	2004
Days of sales outstanding	16.85	14.05

Yang would like to better understand why, on average, it took almost 17 days to collect receivables in 2005 versus 14 days in 2004. He collects accounts receivable aging information from Lenovo's annual reports and computes the percentage of accounts receivable by days outstanding. This information is presented below:

	31 March 2005		31 March 2004		31 March 2003	
	HK$000	Percent	HK$000	Percent	HK$000	Percent
0–30 days	588,389	69.11	944,212	76.71	490,851	88.68
31–60 days	56,966	6.69	84,481	6.86	27,213	4.92
61–90 days	40,702	4.78	20,862	1.69	10,680	1.93
Over 90 days	165,280	19.41	181,389	14.74	24,772	4.48
Total	851,337	100.00	1,230,944	100.00	553,516	100.00

From these data, it appears that over the past three years there has been a trend of fewer receivables due within 30 days and more due for periods of longer than 90 days. Lenovo's footnotes disclose that general trade customers are provided with 30-day credit terms but that systems integration customers (consulting jobs) are given 180 days. Furthermore, the footnotes reveal that consulting revenues increased dramatically over the 2003 to 2004 period. In the third quarter of fiscal year ending 31 March 2005, Lenovo spun off its systems integration business to another company, retaining a small percentage interest. Yang concludes that the higher DSO in fiscal year ending 31 March 2005 appears to be due to the higher revenue in systems integration, which has longer credit terms. Yang may further surmise that DSO should drop in the next fiscal year since this business has been spun off.

Payables Turnover and the Number of Days of Payables   The number of days of payables reflects the average number of days the company takes to pay its suppliers, and the payables turnover ratio measures how many times per year the company theoretically pays off all its creditors. For purposes of calculating these ratios, an implicit assumption is that the company makes all its purchases using credit. If the amount of purchases is not directly available, it can be computed as cost of goods sold plus ending inventory less beginning inventory. Alternatively, cost of goods sold is sometimes used as an approximation of purchases.

A payables turnover ratio that is high (low days payable) relative to the industry could indicate that the company is not making full use of available credit facilities; alternatively, it could result from a company taking advantage of early payment discounts. An excessively low turnover ratio (high days payable) could indicate trouble making payments on time, or alternatively, exploitation of lenient supplier terms. This is another example where it is useful to look simultaneously at other ratios. If liquidity ratios indicate that the company has sufficient cash and other short-term assets to pay obligations and yet the days payable ratio is relatively high, the analyst would favor the lenient supplier credit and collection policies as an explanation.

Working Capital Turnover   **Working capital** is defined as current (expected to be consumed or converted into cash within one year) assets minus current liabilities. Working capital turnover indicates how efficiently the company generates revenue with its working capital. For example, a working capital turnover ratio of 4.0 indicates that the company generates €4 of revenue for every €1 of working capital. A high working capital turnover ratio indicates greater efficiency (i.e., the company is generating a high level of revenues relative to working capital). For some companies, working capital can be near zero or negative, rendering this ratio incapable of being interpreted. The following two ratios are more useful in those circumstances.

Fixed Asset Turnover   This ratio measures how efficiently the company generates revenues from its investments in fixed assets. Generally, a higher fixed asset turnover ratio indicates more efficient use of fixed assets in generating revenue. A low ratio can indicate inefficiency, a capital-intensive business environment, or a new business not yet operating at full capacity—in which case the analyst will not be able to link the ratio directly to efficiency. In addition, asset turnover can be affected by factors other than a company's efficiency. The fixed asset turnover ratio would be lower for a company whose assets are newer (and, therefore, less depreciated and so reflected in the financial statements at a higher carrying value) than the ratio for a company with older assets (that are thus more depreciated and so reflected at a lower carrying value). The fixed asset ratio can be erratic because, although revenue may have a steady growth rate, increases in fixed assets may not follow a smooth pattern; so, every year-to-year change in the ratio does not necessarily indicate important changes in the company's efficiency.

Total Asset Turnover   The total asset turnover ratio measures the company's overall ability to generate revenues with a given level of assets. A ratio of 1.20 would indicate that the company is generating €1.20 of revenues for every €1 of average assets. A higher ratio indicates greater efficiency. Because this ratio includes both fixed and current assets, inefficient working capital management can distort overall interpretations. It is, therefore, helpful to analyze working capital and fixed asset turnover ratios separately.

A low asset turnover ratio can be an indicator of inefficiency or of relative capital intensity of the business. The ratio also reflects strategic decisions by management: for example, the decision whether to use a more labor-intensive (and less capital-intensive) approach to its business or a more capital-intensive (and less labor-intensive) approach.

When interpreting activity ratios, the analysts should examine not only the individual ratios but also the collection of relevant ratios to determine the overall efficiency of a company. Example 7 demonstrates the evaluation of activity ratios, both narrow (e.g., number of days inventory) and broad (total asset turnover) for a Taiwanese semiconductor manufacturer.

EXAMPLE 7

Evaluation of Activity Ratios

United Microelectronics Corp. (UMC) is a semiconductor foundry company based in Taiwan. As part of an analysis of management's operating efficiency, an analyst collects the following activity ratios from Bloomberg:

Ratio	2004	2003	2002	2001
DOH	35.68	40.70	40.47	48.51
DSO	45.07	58.28	51.27	76.98
Total asset turnover	0.35	0.28	0.23	0.22

These ratios indicate that the company has improved on all three measures of activity over the four-year period. The company has fewer DOH, is collecting receivables faster, and is generating a higher level of revenues relative to total assets. The overall trend is good, but thus far, the analyst has only determined *what* happened. A more important question is *why* the ratios improved, because understanding good changes as well as bad ones facilitates judgments about the company's future performance. To answer this question, the analyst examines company financial reports as well as external information about the industry and economy. In examining the annual report, the analyst notes that in the fourth quarter of 2004, the company experienced an "inventory correction" and that the company recorded an allowance for the decline in market value and obsolescence of inventory of TWD 1,786,493, or about 15 percent of year-end inventory value (compared with about a 5.9 percent allowance in the prior year). This reduction in the value of inventory accounts for a large portion of the decline in DOH from 40.7 in 2003 to 35.68 in 2004. Management claims that this inventory obsolescence is a short-term issue; analysts can watch DOH in future interim periods to confirm this assertion. In any event, all else being equal, the analyst would likely expect DOH to return to a level closer to 40 days going forward.

More positive interpretations can be drawn from the total asset turnover. The analyst finds that the company's revenues increased more than 35 percent while total assets only increased by about 6 percent. Based on external information about the industry and economy, the analyst attributes the increased revenues largely to the recovery of the semiconductor industry in 2004. However, management was able to achieve this growth in revenues with a comparatively modest increase in assets, leading to an improvement in total asset turnover. Note further that part of the reason for the modest increase in assets is lower DOH and DSO.

4.3 Liquidity Ratios

Liquidity analysis, which focuses on cash flows, measures a company's ability to meet its short-term obligations. Liquidity measures how quickly assets are converted into cash. Liquidity ratios also measure the ability to pay off short-term obligations. In day-to-day operations, liquidity management is typically achieved through efficient use of assets. In the medium term, liquidity in the nonfinancial sector is also addressed by managing the structure of liabilities. (See discussion on financial sector below.)

The level of liquidity needed differs from one industry to another. A particular company's liquidity position may also vary according to the anticipated need for funds at any given time. Judging whether a company has adequate liquidity requires analysis of its historical funding requirements, current liquidity position, anticipated future funding needs, and options for reducing funding needs or attracting additional funds (including actual and potential sources of such funding).

Larger companies are usually better able to control the level and composition of their liabilities than smaller companies. Therefore, they may have more potential funding sources, including public capital and money markets. Greater discretionary access to capital markets also reduces the size of the liquidity buffer needed relative to companies without such access.

Contingent liabilities, such as letters of credit or financial guarantees, can also be relevant when assessing liquidity. The importance of contingent liabilities varies for the nonbanking and banking sector. In the nonbanking sector, contingent liabilities (usually disclosed in the footnotes to the company's financial statements) represent potential cash outflows, and when appropriate, should be included in an assessment of a company's liquidity. In the banking sector, contingent liabilities represent potentially significant cash outflows that are not dependent on the bank's financial condition. Although outflows in normal market circumstances typically may be low, a general macroeconomic or market crisis can trigger a substantial increase in cash outflows related to contingent liabilities because of the increase in defaults and business bankruptcies that often accompany such events. In addition, such crises are usually characterized by diminished levels of overall liquidity, which can further exacerbate funding shortfalls. Therefore, for the banking sector, the effect of contingent liabilities on liquidity warrants particular attention.

4.3.1 Calculation of Liquidity Ratios

Common liquidity ratios are presented in Exhibit 10. These liquidity ratios reflect a company's position at a point in time and, therefore, typically use data from the ending balance sheet rather than averages. The current, quick, and cash ratios reflect three measures of a company's ability to pay current liabilities. Each uses a progressively stricter definition of liquid assets.

The defensive interval ratio measures how long a company can pay its daily cash expenditures using only its existing liquid assets, without additional cash flow coming in. This ratio is similar to the "burn rate" often computed for start-up internet companies in the late 1990s or for biotechnology companies. The numerator of this ratio includes the same liquid assets used in the quick ratio, and the denominator is an estimate of daily cash expenditures. To obtain daily cash expenditures, the total of cash expenditures for the period is divided by the number of days in the period. Total cash expenditures for a period can be approximated by summing all expenses on the income statement—such as cost

EXHIBIT 10	Definitions of Commonly Used Liquidity Ratios	
Liquidity Ratios	**Numerator**	**Denominator**
Current ratio	Current assets	Current liabilities
Quick ratio	Cash + Short-term marketable investments + Receivables	Current liabilities
Cash ratio	Cash + Short-term marketable investments	Current liabilities
Defensive interval ratio	Cash + Short-term marketable investments + Receivables	Daily cash expenditures

Additional Liquidity Measure

Cash conversion cycle (net operating cycle)	DOII + DSO − Number of days of payables	

of goods sold; selling, general, and administrative expenses; and research and development expenses—and then subtracting any noncash expenses, such as depreciation and amortization. (Typically, taxes are not included.)

The **cash conversion cycle**, a financial metric not in ratio form, measures the length of time required for a company to go from cash (invested in its operations) to cash received (as a result of its operations). During this period of time, the company needs to finance its investment in operations through other sources (i.e., through debt or equity).

4.3.2 Interpretation of Liquidity Ratios

In the following, we discuss the interpretation of the five basic liquidity ratios presented in Exhibit 10.

Current Ratio   This ratio expresses current assets (assets expected to be consumed or converted into cash within one year) in relation to current liabilities (liabilities falling due within one year). A higher ratio indicates a higher level of liquidity (i.e., a greater ability to meet short-term obligations). A current ratio of 1.0 would indicate that the book value of its current assets exactly equals the book value of its current liabilities.

A lower ratio indicates less liquidity, implying a greater reliance on operating cash flow and outside financing to meet short-term obligations. Liquidity affects the company's capacity to take on debt. The current ratio implicitly assumes that inventories and accounts receivable are indeed liquid (which is presumably not the case when related turnover ratios are low).

Quick Ratio   The quick ratio is more conservative than the current ratio because it includes only the more liquid current assets (sometimes referred to as "quick assets") in relation to current liabilities. Like the current ratio, a higher quick ratio indicates greater liquidity.

The quick ratio reflects the fact that certain current assets—such as prepaid expenses, some taxes, and employee-related prepayments—represent costs of the current period that have been paid in advance and cannot usually be converted back into cash. This ratio also reflects the fact that inventory might not be easily and quickly converted into cash, and furthermore, that a company would probably not be able to sell all of its inventory for an amount equal to its carrying value, especially if it were required to sell the inventory quickly. In situations where inventories are illiquid (as indicated, for example, by low inventory turnover ratios), the quick ratio may be a better indicator of liquidity than the current ratio.

Cash Ratio The cash ratio normally represents a reliable measure of an individual entity's liquidity in a crisis situation. Only highly marketable short-term investments and cash are included. In a general market crisis, the fair value of marketable securities could decrease significantly as a result of market factors, in which case even this ratio might not provide reliable information.

Defensive Interval Ratio This ratio measures how long the company can continue to pay its expenses from its existing liquid assets without receiving any additional cash inflow. A defensive interval ratio of 50 would indicate that the company can continue to pay its operating expenses for 50 days before running out of quick assets, assuming no additional cash inflows. A higher defensive interval ratio indicates greater liquidity. If a company's defensive interval ratio is very low relative to peer companies or to the company's own history, the analyst would want to ascertain whether there is sufficient cash inflow expected to mitigate the low defensive interval ratio.

Cash Conversion Cycle (Net Operating Cycle) This metric indicates the amount of time that elapses from the point when a company invests in working capital until the point at which the company collects cash. In the typical course of events, a merchandising company acquires inventory on credit, incurring accounts payable. The company then sells that inventory on credit, increasing accounts receivable. Afterwards, it pays out cash to settle its accounts payable, and it collects cash in settlement of its accounts receivable. The time between the outlay of cash and the collection of cash is called the "cash conversion cycle." A shorter cash conversion cycle indicates greater liquidity. The short cash conversion cycle implies that the company only needs to finance its inventory and accounts receivable for a short period of time. A longer cash conversion cycle indicates lower liquidity; it implies that the company must finance its inventory and accounts receivable for a longer period of time, possibly indicating a need for a higher level of capital to fund current assets. Example 8 demonstrates the advantages of a short cash conversion cycle as well as how a company's business strategies are reflected in financial ratios.

EXAMPLE 8

Evaluation of Liquidity Ratios

An analyst is evaluating the liquidity of Dell and finds that Dell provides a computation of the number of days of receivables, inventory, and accounts payable, as well as the overall cash conversion cycle, as follows:

Fiscal Year Ended	28 Jan 2005	30 Jan 2004	31 Jan 2003
DSO	32	31	28
DOH	4	3	3
Less: Number of days of payables	73	70	68
Equals: Cash conversion cycle	(37)	(36)	(37)

The minimal DOH indicates that Dell maintains lean inventories, which is attributable to key aspects of the company's business model—namely, the company does not build a computer until it is ordered. Furthermore, Dell has a sophisticated just-in-time manufacturing system. In isolation, the increase in number of days payable (from 68 days in 2003 to 73 days in 2005) might suggest an inability to pay suppliers; however, in Dell's case, the balance sheet indicates that the company has almost $10 billion of cash and short-term investments, which would be more than enough to pay suppliers sooner if Dell chose to do so. Instead, Dell takes advantage of the favorable credit terms granted by its suppliers. The overall effect is a negative cash cycle, a somewhat unusual result. Instead of requiring additional capital to fund working capital as is the case for most companies, Dell has excess cash to invest for about 37 days (reflected on the balance sheet as short-term investments) on which it is earning, rather than paying, interest.

For comparison, the analyst computes the cash conversion cycle for three of Dell's competitors:

Fiscal Year	2004	2003	2002
HP Compaq	27	37	61
Gateway	(7)	(9)	(3)
Apple	(40)	(41)	(40)

The analyst notes that of the group, only HP Compaq has to raise capital for working capital purposes. Dell is outperforming HP Compaq and Gateway on this metric, its negative cash conversion cycle of minus 37 days indicating stronger liquidity than either of those two competitors. Apple, however, is slightly more liquid than Dell, evidenced by its slightly more negative cash conversion cycle, and Apple also has a similarly stable negative cash conversion cycle.

4.4 Solvency Ratios

Solvency refers to a company's ability to fulfill its long-term debt obligations. Assessment of a company's ability to pay its long-term obligations (i.e., to make interest and principal payments) generally includes an in-depth analysis of the components of its financial structure. Solvency ratios provide information regarding the relative amount of debt in the company's capital structure and the adequacy of earnings and cash flow to cover interest expenses and other fixed charges (such as lease or rental payments) as they come due.

Analysts seek to understand a company's use of debt for several main reasons. One reason is that the amount of debt in a company's capital structure is important for assessing the company's risk and return characteristics, specifically its financial leverage. Leverage is a magnifying effect that results from the use of **fixed costs**—costs that stay the same within some range of activity—and can take two forms: **operating leverage** and **financial leverage**. Operating leverage results from the use of fixed costs in conducting the company's business. Operating leverage magnifies the effect of changes in sales on operating income. Profitable companies may use operating leverage because when revenues increase, with operating leverage, their operating income increases at a faster rate. The explanation is that, although **variable costs** will rise proportionally with revenue, fixed costs will not. When financing a firm (i.e., raising capital for it), the use of debt constitutes financial leverage because interest payments are essentially fixed financing costs. As a result of interest payments, a given percent change in EBIT results in a larger percent change in earnings before taxes (EBT). Thus, financial leverage tends to magnify the effect of changes in EBIT on returns flowing to equityholders. Assuming that a company can earn more on the funds than it pays in interest, the inclusion of some level of debt in a company's capital structure may lower a company's overall cost of capital and increase returns to equityholders. However, a higher level of debt in a company's capital structure increases the risk of default and results in higher borrowing costs for the company to compensate lenders for assuming greater credit risk. Starting with Modigliani and Miller (1958, 1963), a substantial amount of research has focused on a company's optimal capital structure, and the subject remains an important one in corporate finance. In analyzing financial statements, an analyst aims to understand levels and trends in a company's use of financial leverage in relation to past practices and the practices of peer companies. Analysts also need to be aware of the relationship between operating leverage and financial leverage. The greater a company's use of operating leverage, the greater the risk of the operating income stream available to cover debt payments; operating leverage can thus limit a company's capacity to use financial leverage.

A company's relative solvency is fundamental to valuation of its debt securities and its credit-worthiness. Finally, understanding a company's use of debt can provide analysts with insight into the company's future business prospects because management's decisions about financing often signal their beliefs about a company's future.

4.4.1 Calculation of Solvency Ratios

Solvency ratios are primarily of two types. Debt ratios, the first type, focus on the balance sheet and measure the amount of debt capital relative to equity capital. Coverage ratios, the second type, focus on the income statement and measure the ability of a company to cover its debt payments. All of these ratios are useful in assessing a company's solvency and, therefore, in evaluating the quality of a company's bonds and other debt obligations.

Exhibit 11 describes commonly used solvency ratios. The first three of the debt ratios presented use total debt in the numerator. The definition of total debt used in these ratios varies among informed analysts and financial data vendors, with some using the total of interest-bearing short-term and long-term debt, excluding liabilities such as accrued expenses and accounts payable. (For calculations in this reading, we use this definition.) Other analysts use defini-

EXHIBIT 11	Definitions of Commonly Used Solvency Ratios	
Solvency Ratios	**Numerator**	**Denominator**
Debt Ratios		
Debt-to-assets ratio[a]	Total debt[b]	Total assets
Debt-to-capital ratio	Total debt[b]	Total debt[b] + Total shareholders' equity
Debt-to-equity ratio	Total debt[b]	Total shareholders' equity
Financial leverage ratio	Average total assets	Average total equity
Coverage Ratios		
Interest coverage	EBIT	Interest payments
Fixed charge coverage	EBIT + Lease payments	Interest payments + Lease payments

[a] "Total debt ratio" is another name sometimes used for this ratio.

[b] In this reading, we take total debt in this context to be the sum of interest-bearing short-term and long-term debt.

tions that are more inclusive (e.g., all liabilities) or restrictive (e.g., long-term debt only, in which case the ratio is sometimes qualified as "long-term," as in "long-term debt-to-equity ratio"). If using different definitions of total debt materially changes conclusions about a company's solvency, the reasons for the discrepancies warrant further investigation.

4.4.2 Interpretation of Solvency Ratios

In the following, we discuss the interpretation of the basic solvency ratios presented in Exhibit 11.

Debt-to-Assets Ratio   This ratio measures the percentage of total assets financed with debt. For example, a debt-to-assets ratio of 0.40 or 40 percent indicates that 40 percent of the company's assets are financed with debt. Generally, higher debt means higher financial risk and thus weaker solvency.

Debt-to-Capital Ratio   The debt-to-capital ratio measures the percentage of a company's capital (debt plus equity) represented by debt. As with the previous ratio, a higher ratio generally means higher financial risk and thus indicates weaker solvency.

Debt-to-Equity Ratio   The debt-to-equity ratio measures the amount of debt capital relative to equity capital. Interpretation is similar to the preceding two ratios (i.e., a higher ratio indicates weaker solvency). A ratio of 1.0 would indicate equal amounts of debt and equity, which is equivalent to a debt-to-capital ratio of 50 percent. Alternative definitions of this ratio use the market value of stockholders' equity rather than its book value (or use the market values of both stockholders' equity and debt).

Financial Leverage Ratio   This ratio (often called simply the "leverage ratio") measures the amount of total assets supported for each one money unit of equity. For example, a value of 3 for this ratio means that each €1 of equity supports €3 of total assets. The higher the financial leverage ratio, the more leveraged the company is in the sense of using debt and other liabilities to finance assets. This ratio is often defined in terms of average total assets and average total equity and plays an important role in the DuPont decomposition of return on equity that will be presented in Section 4.6.2.

Interest Coverage   This ratio measures the number of times a company's EBIT could cover its interest payments. A higher interest coverage ratio indicates stronger solvency, offering greater assurance that the company can service its debt (i.e., bank debt, bonds, notes) from operating earnings.

Fixed Charge Coverage   This ratio relates fixed charges, or obligations, to the cash flow generated by the company. It measures the number of times a company's earnings (before interest, taxes, and lease payments) can cover the company's interest and lease payments.[9] Similar to the interest coverage ratio, a higher fixed charge coverage ratio implies stronger solvency, offering greater assurance that the company can service its debt (i.e., bank debt, bonds, notes, and leases) from normal earnings. The ratio is sometimes used as an indication of the quality of the preferred dividend, with a higher ratio indicating a more secure preferred dividend.

Example 9 demonstrates the use of solvency ratios in evaluating the creditworthiness of a company.

EXAMPLE 9

Evaluation of Solvency Ratios

A credit analyst is evaluating the solvency of Alcatel (now known as Alcatel-Lucent) as of the beginning of 2005. The following data are gathered from the company's 2005 annual report (in € millions):

	2004	2003
Total equity	4,389	4,038
Accrued pension	1,144	1,010
Other reserves	2,278	3,049
Total financial debt	4,359	5,293
Other liabilities	6,867	7,742
Total assets	19,037	21,132

---

[9] For computing this ratio, an assumption sometimes made is that one-third of the lease payment amount represents interest on the lease obligation and that the rest is a repayment of principal on the obligation. For this variant of the fixed charge coverage ratio, the numerator is EBIT plus one-third of lease payments and the denominator is interest payments plus one-third of lease payments.

The analyst concludes that, as used by Alcatel in its 2005 annual report, "total financial debt" consists of noncurrent debt and the interest-bearing, borrowed portion of current liabilities.

1. **A.** Calculate the company's financial leverage ratio for 2004.

   B. Interpret the financial leverage ratio calculated in Part A.

2. **A.** What are the company's debt-to-assets, debt-to-capital, and debt-to-equity ratios for the two years?

   B. Is there any discernable trend over the two years?

Solution to 1:

A. Average total assets was $(19,037 + 21,132)/2 = 20,084.50$ and average total equity was $(4,389 + 4,038)/2 = 4,213.5$. Thus, financial leverage was $20,084.50/4,213.5 = 4.77$.

B. For 2004, every €1 in total equity supported €4.77 in total assets, on average.

Solution to 2:

A. Debt-to-assets for 2003 $= 5,293/21,132 = 25.05\%$

Debt-to-assets for 2004 $= 4,359/19,037 = 22.90\%$

Debt-to-capital for 2003 $= 5,293/(5,293 + 4,038) = 56.72\%$

Debt-to-capital for 2004 $= 4,359/(4,359 + 4,389) = 49.83\%$

Debt-to-equity for 2003 $= 5,293/4,038 = 1.31$

Debt-to-equity for 2004 $= 4,359/4,389 = 0.99$

B. On all three metrics, the company's level of debt has declined. This decrease in debt as part of the company's capital structure indicates that the company's solvency has improved. From a creditor's perspective, higher solvency (lower debt) indicates lower risk of default on obligations.

4.5 Profitability Ratios

The ability to generate profit on capital invested is a key determinant of a company's overall value and the value of the securities it issues. Consequently, many equity analysts would consider profitability to be a key focus of their analytical efforts.

Profitability reflects a company's competitive position in the market, and by extension, the quality of its management. The income statement reveals the sources of earnings and the components of revenue and expenses. Earnings can be distributed to shareholders or reinvested in the company. Reinvested earnings enhance solvency and provide a cushion against short-term problems.

4.5.1 Calculation of Profitability Ratios

Profitability ratios measure the return earned by the company during a period. Exhibit 12 provides the definitions of a selection of commonly used profitability

EXHIBIT 12	Definitions of Commonly Used Profitability Ratios	
Profitability Ratios	**Numerator**	**Denominator**
Return on Sales[10]		
Gross profit margin	Gross profit	Revenue
Operating profit margin	Operating income[11]	Revenue
Pretax margin	EBT (earnings before tax but after interest)	Revenue
Net profit margin	Net income	Revenue
Return on Investment		
Operating ROA	Operating income	Average total assets
ROA	Net income	Average total assets
Return on total capital	EBIT	Short- and long-term debt and equity
ROE	Net income	Average total equity
Return on common equity	Net income − Preferred dividends	Average common equity

ratios. Return-on-sales profitability ratios express various subtotals on the income statement (e.g., gross profit, operating profit, net profit) as a percentage of revenue. Essentially, these ratios constitute part of a common-size income statement discussed earlier. Return on investment profitability ratios measure income relative to assets, equity, or total capital employed by the company. For operating ROA, returns are measured as operating income (i.e., prior to deducting interest on debt capital). For ROA and ROE, returns are measured as net income (i.e., after deducting interest paid on debt capital). For return on common equity, returns are measured as net income minus preferred dividends (because preferred dividends are a return to preferred equity).

4.5.2 Interpretation of Profitability Ratios

In the following, we discuss the interpretation of the profitability ratios presented in Exhibit 12. For each of the profitability ratios, a higher ratio indicates greater profitability.

Gross Profit Margin   Gross profit margin indicates the percentage of revenue available to cover operating and other expenditures. Higher gross profit margin indicates some combination of higher product pricing and lower product costs.

---

[10] "Sales" is being used as a synonym for "revenue."

[11] Some analysts use EBIT as a shortcut representation of operating income. Note that EBIT, strictly speaking, includes nonoperating items such as dividends received and gains and losses on investment securities. Of utmost importance is that the analyst compute ratios consistently whether comparing different companies or analyzing one company over time.

The ability to charge a higher price is constrained by competition, so gross profits are affected by (and usually inversely related to) competition. If a product has a competitive advantage (e.g., superior branding, better quality, or exclusive technology), the company is better able to charge more for it. On the cost side, higher gross profit margin can also indicate that a company has a competitive advantage in product costs.

Operating Profit Margin   Operating profit is calculated as gross margin minus operating costs. So, an operating margin increasing faster than the gross margin can indicate improvements in controlling operating costs, such as administrative overheads. In contrast, a declining operating profit margin could be an indicator of deteriorating control over operating costs.

Pretax Margin   Pretax income (also called "earnings before tax") is calculated as operating profit minus interest, so this ratio reflects the effects on profitability of leverage and other (nonoperating) income and expenses. If a company's pretax margin is rising primarily as a result of increasing nonoperating income, the analyst should evaluate whether this increase reflects a deliberate change in a company's business focus and, therefore, the likelihood that the increase will continue.

Net Profit Margin   Net profit, or net income, is calculated as revenue minus all expenses. Net income includes both recurring and nonrecurring components. Generally, the net profit margin adjusted for nonrecurring items offers a better view of a company's potential future profitability.

ROA   ROA measures the return earned by a company on its assets. The higher the ratio, the more income is generated by a given level of assets. Most databases compute this ratio as:

$$\frac{\text{Net income}}{\text{Average total assets}}$$

The problem with this computation is net income is the return to equityholders, whereas assets are financed by both equityholders and creditors. Interest expense (the return to creditors) has already been subtracted in the numerator. Some analysts, therefore, prefer to add back interest expense in the numerator. In such cases, interest must be adjusted for income taxes because net income is determined after taxes. With this adjustment, the ratio would be computed as:

$$\frac{\text{Net income } + \text{ Interest expense } (1 \ - \ \text{Tax rate})}{\text{Average total assets}}$$

Alternatively, some analysts elect to compute ROA on a pre-interest and pretax basis as:

$$\frac{\text{Operating income or EBIT}}{\text{Average total assets}}$$

As noted, returns are measured prior to deducting interest on debt capital (i.e., as operating income or EBIT). This measure reflects the return on all assets invested in the company, whether financed with liabilities, debt, or equity. Whichever form of ROA that is chosen, the analyst must use it consistently in comparisons to other companies or time periods.

Return on Total Capital Return on total capital measures the profits a company earns on all of the capital that it employs (short-term debt, long-term debt, and equity). As with ROA, returns are measured prior to deducting interest on debt capital (i.e., as operating income or EBIT).

ROE ROE measures the return earned by a company on its equity capital, including minority equity, preferred equity, and common equity. As noted, return is measured as net income (i.e., interest on debt capital is not included in the return on equity capital). A variation of ROE is return on common equity, which measures the return earned by a company only on its common equity.

Both ROA and ROE are important measures of profitability and will be explored in more detail below. As with other ratios, profitability ratios should be evaluated individually and as a group to gain an understanding of what is driving profitability (operating versus nonoperating activities). Example 10 demonstrates the evaluation of profitability ratios and the use of management's discussion that accompanies financial statements to explain the trend in ratios.

EXAMPLE 10

Evaluation of Profitability Ratios

An analyst is evaluating the profitability of DaimlerChrysler (NYSE: DCX) over a recent three-year period and collects the following profitability ratios:

	2004 (%)	2003 (%)	2002 (%)
Gross profit margin	19.35	19.49	18.99
Operating profit margin	3.19	2.83	3.35
Pretax margin	2.49	0.44	4.06
Net profit margin	1.74	0.33	3.15

DCX's 2003 Annual Report indicates that revenue declined in 2003. Furthermore, management's discussion of results in that report notes the following:

> General administrative expenses of €5.4 billion remained virtually flat on the prior-year level. General administrative expenses as a percentage of revenues were 3.9 percent in 2003 and 3.6 percent in 2002, reflecting the limited variability of these expenses. Slightly higher personnel expenses, primarily caused by higher net periodic pension and post-retirement benefit costs, resulted in a moderate increase of general administrative expenses.

1. Contrast gross profit margins and operating profit margins over 2002 to 2004.
2. Explain the decline in operating profit margin in 2003.
3. Explain why the pretax margin might decrease to a greater extent than the operating profit margin in 2003.

---

4. Compare and contrast net profit margins and pretax margins over 2002 to 2004.

Solution to 1: Gross margin improved from 2002 to 2003 as a result of some combination of price increases and/or cost control. However, gross margin declined slightly in 2004. Operating profit margin, on the other hand, declined from 2002 to 2003, and then improved in 2004.

Solution to 2: The decline in operating profit from 3.35 percent in 2002 to 2.83 percent in 2003 appears to be the result of DCX's operating leverage, discussed in management's discussion. Revenue declined in 2003 but, according to management, general administrative expenses were virtually flat compared with 2002. These expenses thus increased as a proportion of revenue in 2003, lowering the operating profit margin. This is an example of the effects of fixed cost on profitability. In general, as revenues rise, to the extent that costs remain fixed, operating margins should increase. However, if revenue declines, the opposite occurs.

Solution to 3: Pretax margin was down substantially in 2003, indicating that the company may have had some nonoperating losses or high interest expense in that year. A review of the company's financial statement footnotes confirms that the cause was nonoperating losses: Specifically, the company had a significant impairment loss on investments in 2003.

Solution to 4: Net profit margin followed the same pattern as pretax margin, declining substantially in 2003, then improving in 2004 but not reaching 2002 levels. In the absence of major variation in the applicable tax rates, this would be the expected as net income is $\text{EBT}(1 - \text{tax rate})$.

4.6 Integrated Financial Ratio Analysis

In prior sections, the text presented separately activity, liquidity, solvency, and profitability ratios. In the following, we illustrate the importance of examining a portfolio of ratios, not a single ratio or category of ratios in isolation, to ascertain the overall position and performance of a company. Experience shows that the information from one ratio category can be helpful in answering questions raised by another category and that the most accurate overall picture comes from integrating information from all sources. Section 4.6.1 provides some introductory examples of such analysis and Section 4.6.2 shows how return on equity can be analyzed into components related to profit margin, asset utilization (activity), and financial leverage.

4.6.1 The Overall Ratio Picture: Examples

This section presents two simple illustrations to introduce the use of a portfolio of ratios to address an analytical task. Example 11 shows how the analysis of a pair of activity ratios resolves an issue concerning a company's liquidity. Example 12 shows that examining the overall ratios of multiple companies can assist an analyst in drawing conclusions about their relative performances.

EXAMPLE 11

A Portfolio of Ratios

An analyst is evaluating the liquidity of a Canadian manufacturing company and obtains the following liquidity ratios:

	2005	2004	2003
Current ratio	2.1	1.9	1.6
Quick ratio	0.8	0.9	1.0

The ratios present a contradictory picture of the company's liquidity. Based on the increase in its current ratio from 1.6 to 2.1, the company appears to have strong and improving liquidity; however, based on the decline of the quick ratio from 1.0 to 0.8, its liquidity appears to be deteriorating. Because both ratios have exactly the same denominator, current liabilities, the difference must be the result of changes in some asset that is included in the current ratio but not in the quick ratio (e.g., inventories). The analyst collects the following activity ratios:

DOH	55	45	30
DSO	24	28	30

The company's DOH has deteriorated from 30 days to 55 days, meaning that the company is holding increasingly greater amounts of inventory relative to sales. The decrease in DSO implies that the company is collecting receivables faster. If the proceeds from these collections were held as cash, there would be no effect on either the current ratio or the quick ratio. However, if the proceeds from the collections were used to purchase inventory, there would be no effect on the current ratio and a decline in the quick ratio (i.e., the pattern shown in this example). Collectively, the ratios suggest that liquidity is declining and that the company may have an inventory problem that needs to be addressed.

EXAMPLE 12

A Comparison of Two Companies (1)

An analyst collects the following information for two companies:

Anson Industries	2005	2004	2003	2002
Inventory turnover	76.69	89.09	147.82	187.64
DOH	4.76	4.10	2.47	1.95

Anson Industries	2005	2004	2003	2002
Receivables turnover	10.75	9.33	11.14	7.56
DSO	33.95	39.13	32.77	48.29
Accounts payable turnover	4.62	4.36	4.84	4.22
Days payable	78.97	83.77	75.49	86.56
Cash from operations/ Total liabilities	31.41%	11.15%	4.04%	8.81%
ROE	5.92%	1.66%	1.62%	−0.62%
ROA	3.70%	1.05%	1.05%	−0.39%
Net profit margin (Net income/Revenue)	3.33%	1.11%	1.13%	−0.47%
Total asset turnover (Revenue/Average assets)	1.11	0.95	0.93	0.84
Leverage (Average assets/ Average equity)	1.60	1.58	1.54	1.60

Clarence Corporation	2005	2004	2003	2002
Inventory turnover	9.19	9.08	7.52	14.84
DOH	39.73	40.20	48.51	24.59
Receivables turnover	8.35	7.01	6.09	5.16
DSO	43.73	52.03	59.92	70.79
Accounts payable turnover	6.47	6.61	7.66	6.52
Days payable	56.44	55.22	47.64	56.00
Cash from operations/ Total liabilities	13.19%	16.39%	15.80%	11.79%
ROE	9.28%	6.82%	−3.63%	−6.75%
ROA	4.64%	3.48%	−1.76%	3.23%
Net profit margin (Net income/Revenue)	4.38%	3.48%	−1.60%	−2.34%
Total asset turnover (Revenue/Average assets)	1.06	1.00	1.10	1.38
Leverage (Average assets/ Average equity)	2.00	1.96	2.06	2.09

Which of the following choices best describes reasonable conclusions an analyst might make about the companies' efficiency?

A. Over the past four years, Anson has shown greater improvement in efficiency than Clarence, as indicated by its total asset turnover ratio increasing from 0.84 to 1.11.

B. In 2005, Anson's DOH of only 4.76 indicated that it was less efficient at inventory management than Clarence, which had DOH of 39.73.

C. In 2005, Clarence's receivables turnover of 8.35 times indicated that it was more efficient at receivables management than Anson, which had receivables turnover of 10.75.

D. Over the past four years, Clarence has shown greater improvement in efficiency than Anson, as indicated by its net profit margin of 4.38 percent.

Solution: A is correct. Over the past four years, Anson has shown greater improvement in efficiency than Clarence, as indicated by its total asset turnover ratio increasing from 0.84 to 1.11. Over the same period of time, Clarence's total asset turnover ratio has declined from 1.38 to 1.06. Choice B is incorrect because it misinterprets DOH. Choice C is incorrect because it misinterprets receivables turnover. Choice D is incorrect because net profit margin is not an indicator of efficiency.

4.6.2 DuPont Analysis: The Decomposition of ROE

As noted earlier, ROE measures the return a company generates on its equity capital. To understand what drives a company's ROE, a useful technique is to decompose ROE into its component parts. (Decomposition of ROE is sometimes referred to as **DuPont analysis** because it was developed originally at that company.) Decomposing ROE involves expressing the basic ratio (i.e., net income divided by average shareholders' equity) as the product of component ratios. Because each of these component ratios is an indicator of a distinct aspect of a company's performance that affects ROE, the decomposition allows us to evaluate how these different aspects of performance affected the company's profitability as measured by ROE.[12]

Decomposing ROE is useful in determining the reasons for changes in ROE over time for a given company and for differences in ROE for different companies in a given time period. The information gained can also be used by management to determine which areas they should focus on to improve ROE. This decomposition will also show why a company's overall profitability, measured by ROE, is a function of its efficiency, operating profitability, taxes, and use of financial leverage. DuPont analysis shows the relationship between the various categories of ratios discussed in this reading and how they all influence the return to the investment of the owners.

Analysts have developed several different methods of decomposing ROE. The decomposition presented here is one of the most commonly used and the one found in popular research databases, such as Bloomberg. Return on equity is calculated as:

ROE = Net income/Average shareholders' equity

---

[12] For purposes of analyzing ROE, this method usually uses average balance sheet factors; however, the math will work out if beginning or ending balances are used throughout. For certain purposes, these alternative methods may be appropriate. See Stowe et al. (2002, pp. 85–88).

The decomposition of ROE makes use of simple algebra and illustrates the relationship between ROE and ROA. Expressing ROE as a product of only two of its components, we can write:

$$\text{ROE} = \frac{\text{Net income}}{\text{Average shareholders' equity}}$$

$$= \frac{\text{Net income}}{\text{Average total assets}} \times \frac{\text{Average total assets}}{\text{Average shareholders' equity}} \qquad \textbf{(1a)}$$

which can be interpreted as:

$$\text{ROE} = \text{ROA} \times \text{Leverage}$$

In other words, ROE is a function of a company's ROA and its use of financial leverage ("leverage" for short, in this discussion). A company can improve its ROE by improving ROA or making more effective use of leverage. Consistent with the definition given earlier, leverage is measured as average total assets divided by average shareholders' equity. If a company had no leverage (no liabilities), its leverage ratio would equal 1.0 and ROE would exactly equal ROA. As a company takes on liabilities, its leverage increases. As long as a company is able to borrow at a rate lower than the marginal rate it can earn investing the borrowed money in its business, the company is making an effective use of leverage and ROE would increase as leverage increases. If a company's borrowing cost exceeds the marginal rate it can earn on investing, ROE would decline as leverage increased because the effect of borrowing would be to depress ROA.

Using the data from Example 12 for Anson Industries, an analyst can examine the trend in ROE and determine whether the increase from an ROE of -0.625 percent in 2002 to 5.925 percent in 2005 is a function of ROA or the use of leverage:

	ROE	=	ROA	×	Leverage
2005	5.92%		3.70%		1.60
2004	1.66%		1.05%		1.58
2003	1.62%		1.05%		1.54
2002	−0.62%		−0.39%		1.60

Over the four-year period, the company's leverage factor was relatively stable. The primary reason for the increase in ROE is the increase in profitability measured by ROA.

Just as ROE can be decomposed, the individual components such as ROA can be decomposed. Further decomposing ROA, we can express ROE as a product of three component ratios:

$$\frac{\text{Net income}}{\text{Average shareholders' equity}} = \frac{\text{Net income}}{\text{Revenue}} \times \frac{\text{Revenue}}{\text{Average total assets}}$$

$$\times \frac{\text{Average total assets}}{\text{Average shareholders' equity}} \qquad \textbf{(1b)}$$

which can be interpreted as:

$$\text{ROE} = \text{Net profit margin} \times \text{Asset turnover} \times \text{Leverage}$$

The first term on the right-hand side of this equation is the net profit margin, an indicator of profitability: how much income a company derives per one money unit (e.g., euro or dollar) of sales. The second term on the right is the asset turnover ratio, an indicator of efficiency: how much revenue a company generates per one money unit of assets. Note that ROA is decomposed into these two components: net profit margin and asset turnover. A company's ROA is a function of profitability (net profit margin) and efficiency (asset turnover). The third term on the right-hand side of Equation 1b is a measure of financial leverage, an indicator of solvency: the total amount of a company's assets relative to its equity capital. This decomposition illustrates that a company's ROE is a function of its net profit margin, its efficiency, and its leverage. Again, using the data from Example 12 for Anson Industries, the analyst can evaluate in more detail the reasons behind the trend in ROE:[13]

	ROE	=	Net profit margin	×	Asset turnover	×	Leverage
2005	5.92%		3.33%		1.11		1.60
2004	1.66%		1.11%		0.95		1.58
2003	1.62%		1.13%		0.93		1.54
2002	−0.62%		−0.47%		0.84		1.60

This further decomposition confirms that increases in profitability (measured here as net profit margin) are indeed an important contributor to the increase in ROE over the four-year period. However, Anson's asset turnover has also increased steadily. The increase in ROE is, therefore, a function of improving profitability and improving efficiency. As noted above, ROE decomposition can also be used to compare the ROEs of peer companies, as demonstrated in Example 13.

EXAMPLE 13

A Comparison of Two Companies (2)

Referring to the data for Anson Industries and Clarence Corporation in Example 12, which of the following choices best describes reasonable conclusions an analyst might make about the companies' ROE?

A. Anson's inventory turnover of 76.69 indicates it is more profitable than Clarence.

B. The main drivers of Clarence's superior ROE in 2005 are its greater use of debt financing and higher net profit margin.

C. The main driver of Clarence's superior ROE in 2005 is its more efficient use of assets.

D. Anson's days payable of 78.97 indicates it is more profitable than Clarence.

---

[13] Please note that ratios are expressed in terms of two decimal places and are rounded. Therefore, ROE may not be the exact product of the three ratios.

> **Solution:** B is correct. The main driver of Clarence's superior ROE (9.29 percent compared with only 5.94 percent for Anson) in 2005 is its greater use of debt financing (leverage of 2.00 compared with Anson's leverage of 1.60) and higher net profit margin (4.38 percent compared with only 3.33 percent for Anson). A and D are incorrect because neither inventory turnover nor days payable is an indicator of profitability. C is incorrect because Clarence has less-efficient use of assets than Anson, indicated by turnover of 1.06 for Clarence compared with Anson's turnover of 1.11.

To separate the effects of taxes and interest, we can further decompose the net profit margin and write:

$$\frac{\text{Net income}}{\text{Average shareholders' equity}} = \frac{\text{Net income}}{\text{EBT}} \times \frac{\text{EBT}}{\text{EBIT}} \times \frac{\text{EBIT}}{\text{Revenue}}$$

$$\times \frac{\text{Revenue}}{\text{Average total assets}} \times \frac{\text{Average total assets}}{\text{Average shareholders' equity}} \quad \textbf{(1c)}$$

which can be interpreted as:

$$\text{ROE} = \text{Tax burden} \times \text{Interest burden} \times \text{EBIT margin}$$
$$\times \text{Asset turnover} \times \text{Leverage}$$

This five-way decomposition is the one found in financial databases such as Bloomberg. The first term on the right-hand side of this equation measures the effect of taxes on ROE. Essentially, it reflects one minus the average tax rate, or how much of a company's pretax profits it gets to keep. This can be expressed in decimal or percentage form. So, a 30 percent tax rate would yield a factor of 0.70 or 70 percent. A higher value for the tax burden implies that the company can keep a higher percentage of its pretax profits, indicating a lower tax rate. A decrease in the tax burden ratio implies the opposite (i.e., a higher tax rate leaving the company with less of its pretax profits).

The second term on the right-hand side captures the effect of interest on ROE. Higher borrowing costs reduce ROE. Some analysts prefer to use operating income instead of EBIT for this factor and the following one (consistency is required!). In such a case, the second factor would measure both the effect of interest expense and nonoperating income.

The third term on the right-hand side captures the effect of operating margin (if operating income is used in the numerator) or EBIT margin (if EBIT is used) on ROE. In either case, this factor primarily measures the effect of operating profitability on ROE.

The fourth term on the right-hand side is again the asset turnover ratio, an indicator of the overall efficiency of the company (i.e., how much revenue it generates per unit of assets). The fifth term on the right-hand side is the financial leverage ratio described above—the total amount of a company's assets relative to its equity capital.

This decomposition expresses a company's ROE as a function of its tax rate, interest burden, operating profitability, efficiency, and leverage. An analyst can use this framework to determine what factors are driving a company's ROE. The decomposition of ROE can also be useful in forecasting ROE based upon expected efficiency, profitability, financing activities, and tax rates. The relationship of the individual factors, such as ROA to the overall ROE, can also be expressed in the form of an ROE tree to study the contribution of each of the five factors, as shown in Exhibit 13 for Anson Industries.[14]

Exhibit 13 shows that Anson's ROE of 5.92 percent in 2005 can be decomposed into ROA of 3.7 percent and leverage of 1.60. ROA can further be decomposed into a net profit margin of 3.33 percent and total asset turnover of 1.11. Net profit margin can be decomposed into a tax burden of 0.70 (an average tax rate of 30 percent), an interest burden of 0.90, and an EBIT margin of 5.29 percent. Overall ROE is decomposed into five components.

EXHIBIT 13	DuPont Analysis of Anson Industries' ROE: 2005

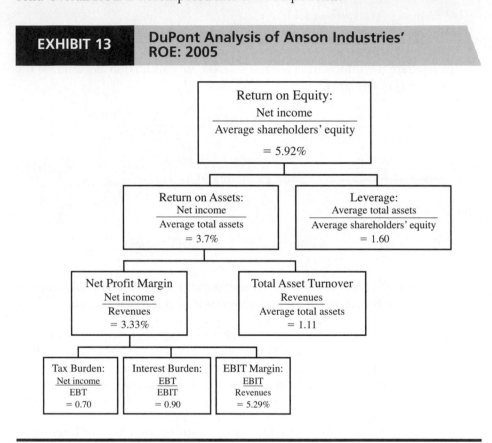

Example 14 demonstrates how the five-component decomposition can be used to determine reasons behind the trend in a company's ROE.

EXAMPLE 14

Five-Way Decomposition of ROE

An analyst examining BP PLC (BP) wishes to understand the factors driving the trend in ROE over a recent three-year period. The analyst obtains the following data from Bloomberg and ascertains that Bloomberg has included nonoperating income in the interest burden factor:

---

[14] Note that a breakdown of net profit margin was not provided in Example 12, but is added here.

	2004	2003	2002
ROE	20.62%	14.42%	10.17%
Tax burden	64.88%	62.52%	60.67%
Interest burden	130.54%	112.60%	130.50%
EBIT margin	6.51%	6.40%	4.84%
Asset turnover	1.55	1.38	1.19
Leverage	2.42	2.32	2.24

What might the analyst conclude?

Solution: Because the tax burden reflects the relation of after-tax profits to pretax profits, the increase from 60.67 percent to 64.88 percent indicates that taxes declined as a percentage of pretax profits. This decline in average tax rates could be due to lower tax rates from new legislation or revenue in a lower tax jurisdiction. An interest burden factor greater than 100 percent means that nonoperating income exceeded interest expense in all three years. Operating margin (EBIT margin) improved, particularly from 2002 to 2003, indicating the company's operations were more profitable. The company's efficiency (asset turnover) increased each year as did its leverage. Overall, the trend in ROE (doubling in three years) did not result from a single aspect of the company's performance, but instead was a function of lower average tax rates, increasing operating profits, greater efficiency, and increased use of leverage. Additional research on the causes of the various changes is required in order to develop expectations about the company's future performance.

The most detailed decomposition of ROE that we have presented is a five-way decomposition. Nevertheless, an analyst could further decompose individual components of a five-way analysis. For example, EBIT margin (EBIT/Revenue) could be further decomposed into a nonoperating component (EBIT/Operating income) and an operating component (Operating income/Revenues). The analyst can also examine which other factors contributed to these five components. For example, an improvement in efficiency (total asset turnover) may have resulted from better management of inventory (DOH) or better collection of receivables (DSO).

EQUITY ANALYSIS   5

One application of financial analysis is to select securities as part of the equity portfolio management process. Analysts are interested in valuing a security to assess its merits for inclusion or retention in a portfolio. The valuation process has several steps, including:[15]

---

[15] Stowe et al. (2002, p. 6).

1. understanding the business and the existing financial profile
2. forecasting company performance
3. selecting the appropriate valuation model
4. converting forecasts to a valuation
5. making the investment decision

Financial analysis assists in providing the core information to complete the first two steps of this valuation process: understanding the business and forecasting performance.

Fundamental equity analysis involves evaluating a company's performance and valuing its equity in order to assess its relative attractiveness as an investment. Analysts use a variety of methods to value a company's equity, including valuation ratios (e.g., the price-to-earnings or P/E ratio), discounted cash flow approaches, and residual income approaches (ROE compared with the cost of capital), among others. The following section addresses the first of these approaches—the use of valuation ratios.

5.1 Valuation Ratios

Valuation ratios have long been used in investment decision making. A well-known example is the P/E ratio—probably the most widely used indicator in discussing the value of equity securities—which relates share price to the earnings per share (EPS). Additionally, some analysts use other market multiples, such as price to book value (P/B) and price to cash flow (P/CF). The following sections explore valuation ratios and other quantities related to valuing equities.

5.1.1 Calculation of Valuation Ratios and Related Quantities

Exhibit 14 describes the calculation of some common valuation ratios and related quantities.

The P/E ratio expresses the relationship between the price per share and the amount of earnings attributable to a single share. In other words, the P/E ratio tells us how much an investor in common stock pays per dollar of current earnings.

Because P/E ratios are calculated using net income, the ratios can be sensitive to nonrecurring earnings or one-off earnings events. In addition, because net income is generally considered to be more susceptible to manipulation than are cash flows, analysts may use **price to cash flow** as an alternative measure— particularly in situations where earnings quality may be an issue. EBITDA per share, because it is calculated using income before interest, taxes, and depreciation, can be used to eliminate the effect of different levels of fixed asset investment across companies. It facilitates comparison between companies in the same sector but at different stages of infrastructure maturity. **Price to sales** is calculated in a similar manner and is sometimes used as a comparative price metric when a company does not have positive net income.

Another price-based ratio that facilitates useful comparisons of companies' stock prices is **price to book value**, or P/B, which is the ratio of price to book value per share. This ratio is often interpreted as an indicator of market judgment about the relationship between a company's required rate of return and its actual rate of return. Assuming that book values reflect the fair values of the assets, a price to book ratio of one can be interpreted as an indicator that the company's future returns are expected to be exactly equal to the returns required by the market. A

EXHIBIT 14	Definitions of Selected Valuation Ratios and Related Quantities	
	Numerator	**Denominator**
Valuation Ratios		
P/E	Price per share	Earnings per share
P/CF	Price per share	Cash flow per share
P/S	Price per share	Sales per share
P/BV	Price per share	Book value per share
Per-Share Quantities		
Basic EPS	Net income minus preferred dividends	Weighted average number of ordinary shares outstanding
Diluted EPS	Adjusted income available for ordinary shares, reflecting conversion of dilutive securities	Weighted average number of ordinary and potential ordinary shares outstanding
Cash flow per share	Cash flow from operations	Average number of shares outstanding
EBITDA per share	EBITDA	Average number of shares outstanding
Dividends per share	Common dividends declared	Weighted average number of ordinary shares outstanding
Dividend-Related Quantities		
Dividend payout ratio	Common share dividends	Net income attributable to common shares
Retention rate (b)	Net income attributable to common shares − Common share dividends	Net income attributable to common shares
Sustainable growth rate	$b \times \text{ROE}$	

ratio greater than one would indicate that the future profitability of the company is expected to exceed the required rate of return, and values of this ratio less than one indicate that the company is not expected to earn excess returns.[16]

5.1.2 Interpretation of Earnings per Share

Exhibit 14 presented a number of per-share quantities that can be used in valuation ratios. In the following, we discuss the interpretation of one such critical quantity, EPS.

---

[16] For more detail on valuation ratios as used in equity analysis, see Stowe et al. (2002).

EPS is simply the amount of earnings attributable to each share of common stock. In isolation, EPS does not provide adequate information for comparison of one company with another. For example, assume that two companies have only common stock outstanding and no dilutive securities outstanding. In addition, assume the two companies have identical net income of $10 million, identical book equity of $100 million and, therefore, identical profitability (10 percent, using ending equity in this case for simplicity). Furthermore, assume that Company A has 100 million weighted average common shares outstanding, whereas Company B has 10 million weighted average common shares outstanding. So, Company A will report EPS of $0.10 per share, and Company B will report EPS of $1 per share. The difference in EPS does not reflect a difference in profitability—the companies have identical profits and profitability. The difference reflects only a different number of common shares outstanding.

Analysts should understand in detail the types of EPS information that companies report:

Basic EPS provides information regarding the earnings attributable to each share of common stock. International Accounting Standards (IAS) No. 33 contains the international principles for the determination and presentation of EPS. This standard applies to entities whose shares are publicly traded or in the process of being issued in public securities markets, and other entities that choose to disclose EPS. U.S. Financial Accounting Standards Board Statement No. 128 contains the standards for computing and presenting EPS.

To calculate basic EPS, the weighted average number of shares outstanding during the period is first calculated. The weighted average number of shares consists of the number of ordinary shares outstanding at the beginning of the period, adjusted by those bought back or issued during the period, multiplied by a time-weighting factor.

Accounting standards generally require the disclosure of basic as well as diluted EPS (**diluted EPS** includes the effect of all the company's securities whose conversion or exercise would result in a reduction of basic EPS; dilutive securities include convertible debt, convertible preferred, warrants, and options). Basic EPS and diluted EPS must be shown with equal prominence on the face of the income statement for each class of ordinary share. Disclosure includes the amounts used as the numerators in calculating basic and diluted EPS, and a reconciliation of those amounts to the company's profit or loss for the period. Because both basic and diluted EPS are presented in a company's financial statements, an analyst does not need to calculate these measures for reported financial statements. Understanding the calculations is, however, helpful for situations requiring an analyst to calculate expected future EPS.

To calculate diluted EPS, earnings are adjusted for the after-tax effects assuming conversion, and the following adjustments are made to the weighted number of shares:

► The weighted average number of shares for basic EPS, *plus* those that would be issued on conversion of all dilutive potential ordinary shares. Potential ordinary shares are treated as dilutive when their conversion would decrease net profit per share from continuing ordinary operations.

► These shares are deemed to have been converted into ordinary shares at the beginning of the period or, if later, at the date of the issue of the shares.

► Options, warrants (and their equivalents), convertible instruments, contingently issuable shares, contracts that can be settled in ordinary shares or cash, purchased options, and written put options should be considered.

5.1.3 Dividend-Related Quantities

In the following, we discuss the interpretation of the dividend-related quantities presented in Exhibit 14. These quantities play a role in some present value models for valuing equities.

Dividend Payout Ratio   The dividend payout ratio measures the percentage of earnings that the company pays out as dividends to shareholders. The amount of dividends per share tends to be relatively fixed because any reduction in dividends has been shown to result in a disproportionately large reduction in share price. Because dividend amounts are relatively fixed, the dividend payout ratio tends to fluctuate with earnings. Therefore, conclusions about a company's dividend payout policies should be based on examination of payout over a number of periods. Optimal dividend policy, similar to optimal capital structure, has been examined in academic research and continues to be a topic of significant interest in corporate finance.

Retention Rate   The retention rate is the complement of the payout ratio (i.e., 1 − payout ratio). Whereas the payout ratio measures the percentage of earnings that a company pays out as dividends, the retention rate is the percentage of earnings that a company retains. It is simply one minus the payout ratio. (Note that both the dividend payout ratio and retention rate are both percentages of earnings. The difference in terminology—"ratio" versus "rate" versus "percentage"—reflects common usage rather than any substantive differences.)

Sustainable Growth Rate   A company's sustainable growth rate is viewed as a function of its profitability (measured as ROE) and its ability to finance itself from internally generated funds (measured as the retention rate). A higher ROE and a higher retention rate result in a higher sustainable growth rate. This calculation can be used to estimate a company's growth rate, a factor commonly used in equity valuation.

5.2 Industry-Specific Ratios

As stated earlier in this reading, a universally accepted definition and classification of ratios do not exist. The purpose of ratios is to serve as indicators of important aspects of a company's performance and value. Aspects of performance that are considered important in one industry may be irrelevant in another, and industry-specific ratios reflect these differences. For example, companies in the retail industry may report same-store sales changes because, in the retail industry, it is important to distinguish between growth that results from opening new stores and growth that results from generating more sales at existing stores. Industry-specific metrics can be especially important to the value of equity in early stage industries, where companies are not yet profitable.

In addition, regulated industries—especially in the financial sector—often are required to comply with specific regulatory ratios. For example, the banking sector's liquidity and cash reserve ratios provide an indication of banking liquidity and reflect monetary and political requirements. Banking capital adequacy requirements, although not perfect, do relate banks' solvency requirements directly to their specific levels of risk exposure.

Exhibit 15 presents some industry-specific and task-specific ratios.[17]

---

[17] These are provided for illustrative purposes only. There are many other industry-specific ratios that are outside the scope of this reading. Resources such as Standard and Poor's Industry Surveys present useful ratios for each industry.

EXHIBIT 15	Definitions of Some Common Industry and Task-Specific Ratios	

Ratios	Numerator	Denominator
Business Risk		
Coefficient of variation of operating income	Standard deviation of operating income	Average operating income
Coefficient of variation of net income	Standard deviation of net income	Average net income
Coefficient of variation of revenues	Standard deviation of revenue	Average revenue
Financial Sector Ratios		
Capital adequacy—banks	Various components of capital	Risk-weighted assets, market risk exposure, and level of operational risk assumed
Monetary reserve requirement	Reserves held at central bank	Specified deposit liabilities
Liquid asset requirement	Approved "readily marketable" securities	Specified deposit liabilities
Net interest margin	Net interest income	Total interest-earning assets
Retail Ratios		
Same (or comparable) store sales	Average revenue growth year over year for stores open in both periods	Not applicable
Sales per square foot (meter)	Revenue	Total retail space in feet or meters
Service Companies		
Revenue per employee	Revenue	Total number of employees
Net income per employee	Net income	Total number of employees
Hotel		
Average daily rate	Room revenue	Number of rooms sold
Occupancy rate	Number of rooms sold	Number of rooms available

5.3 Research on Ratios in Equity Analysis

Some ratios should be expected to be particularly useful in equity analysis. The end product of equity analysis is often a valuation and investment recommendation. Theoretical valuation models are useful in selecting ratios that would be useful in this process. For example, a company's P/B is theoretically linked to ROE, growth, and the required return. ROE is also a primary determinate of residual income in a residual income valuation model. In both cases, higher ROE relative to the required return denotes a higher valuation. Similarly, profit margin is related to justified price-to-sales (P/S) ratios. Another common valuation method involves forecasts of future cash flows that are discounted back to the present. Trends in ratios can be useful in forecasting future earnings and cash flows (e.g., trends in operating profit margin and collection of customer receivables). Future growth expectations are a key component of all of these valuation models. Trends may be useful in assessing growth prospects (when used in conjunction with overall economic and industry trends). The variability in ratios and common-size data can be useful in assessing risk, an important component of the required rate of return in valuation models. A great deal of academic research has focused on the use of these fundamental ratios in evaluating equity investments.

A classic study, Ou and Penman (1989a and 1989b), found that ratios and common-size metrics generated from accounting data were useful in forecasting earnings and stock returns. Ou and Penman examined a variety of 68 such metrics and found that these variables could be reduced to a more parsimonious list and combined in a statistical model that was particularly useful for selecting investments. These variables included:

- percentage change in current ratio;
- percentage change in quick ratio;
- percentage change in inventory turnover;
- inventory/Total assets (a common-size measure) and the percentage change in this metric;
- percentage change in inventory;
- percentage change in sales;
- percentage change in depreciation;
- change in dividend per share;
- percentage change in depreciation to plant assets ratio;
- ROE;
- change in ROE;
- percentage change in capital expenditures to total assets ratio (contemporaneously and lagged);
- debt-to-equity ratio and the percentage change in this ratio;
- percentage change in total asset turnover;
- ROA;
- gross margin;
- pretax margin;
- sales to total cash;
- percentage change in total assets;
- cash flow to debt;
- working capital to total assets;

► operating ROA;

► repayment of long-term debt to total long-term debt;

► cash dividend to cash flows.

Subsequent studies have also demonstrated the use of ratios in evaluation of equity investments and valuation. Lev and Thiagarajan (1993) examined fundamental financial variables used by analysts to assess whether they are useful in security valuation. They found that fundamental variables add about 70 percent to the explanatory power of earnings alone in predicting excess returns (stock returns in excess of those expected). The fundamental variables they found useful included percentage changes in inventory and receivables relative to sales, gross margin, sales per employee, and the change in bad debts relative to the change in accounts receivable, among others. Abarbanell and Bushee (1997) found some of the same variables useful in predicting future accounting earnings. Abarbanell and Bushee (1998) devised an investment strategy using these same variables and found that they can generate excess returns under this strategy.

Piotroski (2000) used financial ratios to supplement a value investing strategy and found that he can generate significant excess returns. Variables used by Piotroski include ROA, cash flow ROA, change in ROA, change in leverage, change in liquidity, change in gross margin, and change in inventory turnover.

This research shows that in addition to being useful in evaluating the past performance of a company, ratios can be useful in predicting future earnings and equity returns.

6   CREDIT ANALYSIS

Credit risk is the risk of loss caused by a counterparty's or debtor's failure to make a promised payment. For example, credit risk with respect to a bond is the risk that the obligor (the issuer of the bond) is not able to pay interest and principal according to the terms of the bond indenture (contract). **Credit analysis** is the evaluation of credit risk.

Approaches to credit analysis vary and, as with all financial analysis, depend on the purpose of the analysis and the context in which it is done. Credit analysis for specific types of debt (e.g., acquisition financing and other highly leveraged financing) often involves projections of period-by-period cash flows similar to projections made by equity analysts. Whereas the equity analyst may discount projected cash flows to determine the value of the company's equity, a credit analyst would use the projected cash flows to assess the likelihood of a company complying with its financial covenants in each period and paying interest and principal as due.[18] The analysis would also include expectations about asset sales and refinancing options open to the company.

Credit analysis may relate to the borrower's credit risk in a particular transaction or to its overall credit-worthiness. In assessing overall credit-worthiness, one general approach is credit scoring, a statistical analysis of the determinants of credit default.

Another general approach to credit analysis is the credit rating process that is used, for example, by credit rating agencies to assess and communicate the proba-

---

[18] Financial covenants are clauses in bond indentures relating to the financial condition of the bond issuer.

bility of default by an issuer on its debt obligations (e.g., commercial paper, notes, and bonds). A credit rating can be either long term or short term and is an indication of the rating agency's opinion of the credit-worthiness of a debt issuer with respect to a specific debt security or other obligation. Where a company has no debt outstanding, a rating agency can also provide an issuer credit rating that expresses an opinion of the issuer's overall capacity and willingness to meet its financial obligations. The following sections review research on the use of ratios in credit analysis and the ratios commonly used in credit analysis.

6.1 The Credit Rating Process

The rating process involves both the analysis of a company's financial reports as well as a broad assessment of a company's operations. The credit rating process includes many of the following procedures:[19]

- ▶ Meeting with management, typically including the chief financial officer, to discuss, for example, industry outlook, overview of major business segments, financial policies and goals, distinctive accounting practices, capital spending plans, and financial contingency plans.

- ▶ Tours of major facilities, time permitting.

- ▶ Meeting of a ratings committee where the analyst's recommendations are voted on, after considering factors that include:

  - ▶ Business risk, including the evaluation of:

    - ▶ operating environment;

    - ▶ industry characteristics (e.g., cyclicality and capital intensity);

    - ▶ success factors and areas of vulnerability;

    - ▶ company's competitive position, including size and diversification;

  - ▶ Financial risk, including:

    - ▶ the evaluation of capital structure, interest coverage, and profitability using ratio analysis;

    - ▶ the examination of debt covenants;

  - ▶ Evaluation of management.

- ▶ Monitoring of publicly distributed ratings—including reconsideration of ratings due to changing conditions.

In assigning credit ratings, rating agencies emphasize the importance of the relationship between a company's business risk profile and its financial risk. "The company's business risk profile determines the level of financial risk appropriate for any rating category."[20]

When analyzing financial ratios, rating agencies normally investigate deviations of ratios from the median ratios of the universe of companies for which such ratios have been calculated and also use the median ratings as an indicator for the ratings grade given to a specific debt issuer. This so-called universe of rated companies changes constantly, and any calculations are obviously affected by economic factors as well as by mergers and acquisitions. International ratings include the influence of country and economic risk factors. Exhibit 16 presents

---

[19] Based on Standard & Poor's Corporate Ratings Criteria (2006).
[20] Standard & Poor's Corporate Ratings Criteria (2006), p. 23.

EXHIBIT 16	Selected Credit Ratios Used by Standard & Poor's

Credit Ratio	Numerator[a]	Denominator[b]
EBIT interest coverage	EBIT	Gross interest (prior to deductions for capitalized interest or interest income)
EBITDA interest coverage	EBITDA	Gross interest (prior to deductions for capitalized interest or interest income)
Funds from operations to total debt	FFO (net income adjusted for non-cash items)[c]	Total debt
Free operating cash flow to total debt	CFO (adjusted) less capital expenditures[d]	Total debt
Total debt to EBITDA	Total debt	EBITDA
Return on capital	EBIT	Capital = Average equity (common and preferred stock) and short-term portions of debt, noncurrent deferred taxes, minority interest
Total debt to total debt plus equity	Total debt	Total debt plus equity

[a] Emphasis is on earnings from *continuing* operations.

[b] Note that both the numerator and denominator definitions are adjusted from ratio to ratio and may not correspond to the definitions used in this reading.

[c] FFO = funds from operations.

[d] CFO = cash flow from operations.

Source: Based on data from Standard & Poor's Corporate Ratings Criteria 2006, p. 43.

key financial ratios used by Standard & Poor's in evaluating industrial companies. Note that before calculating ratios, rating agencies make certain adjustments to reported financials such as adjusting debt to include off-balance sheet debt in a company's total debt.

6.2 Research on Ratios in Credit Analysis

A great deal of academic and practitioner research has focused on determining which ratios are useful in assessing the credit risk of a company, including the risk of bankruptcy.

One of the earliest studies examined individual ratios to assess their ability to predict failure of a company up to five years in advance. Beaver (1967) found that six ratios could correctly predict company failure one year in advance 90 percent of the time and five years in advance at least 65 percent of the time. The ratios found effective by Beaver were cash flow to total debt, ROA, total debt to total assets, working capital to total assets, the current ratio, and the no-credit interval ratio (the length of time a company could go without borrowing).

Altman (1968) and Altman, Haldeman, and Narayanan (1977) found that financial ratios could be combined in an effective model for predicting bankruptcy. Altman's initial work involved creation of a Z-score that was able to correctly predict financial distress. The Z-score was computed as

$$
\begin{aligned}
Z = {} & 1.2 \times (\text{Current assets} - \text{Current liabilities})/\text{Total assets} \\
& + 1.4 \times (\text{Retained earnings}/\text{Total assets}) \\
& + 3.3 \times (\text{EBIT}/\text{Total assets}) \\
& + 0.6 \times (\text{Market value of stock}/\text{Book value of liabilities}) \\
& + 1.0 \times (\text{Sales}/\text{Total assets})
\end{aligned}
$$

In his initial study, a Z-score of lower than 1.81 predicted failure, and the model was able to accurately classify 95 percent of companies studied into a failure group and a nonfailure group. The original model was designed for manufacturing companies. Subsequent refinements to the models allow for other company types and time periods. Generally, the variables found to be useful in prediction include profitability ratios, coverage ratios, liquidity ratios, capitalization ratios, and earnings variability (Altman 2000).

Similar research has been performed on the ability of ratios to predict bond ratings and bond yields. For example, Ederington, Yawtiz, and Roberts (1987) found that a small number of variables (total assets, interest coverage, leverage, variability of coverage, and subordination status) were effective in explaining bond yields. Similarly, Ederington (1986) found that nine variables in combination could correctly classify more than 70 percent of bond ratings. These variables included ROA, long-term debt to assets, interest coverage, cash flow to debt, variability of coverage and cash flow, total assets, and subordination status. These studies have shown that ratios are effective in evaluating credit risk, bond yields, and bond ratings.

BUSINESS AND GEOGRAPHIC SEGMENTS   7

Analysts often need to evaluate the performance underlying business segments (subsidiary companies, operating units, or simply operations in different geographic areas) to understand in detail the company as a whole. Unfortunately, companies are not required to provide full financial statements for segments for which all of the traditional ratios can be computed. Publicly traded companies are required to provide limited segment information under both IFRS and U.S. GAAP.

7.1 IAS 14 Requirements

Under IAS 14 (Segment Reporting), disclosures are required for reportable segments. U.S. GAAP requirements are similar to IFRS but less detailed. One noticeable omission under U.S. GAAP is the disclosure of segment liabilities.

A reportable segment is defined as a business or geographical segment where both of the following apply:

► the majority (greater than 50 percent) of its revenue is earned externally, and

► its income from sales, segment result, or assets is greater than or equal to 10 percent of the appropriate total amount of all segments.

A business segment is a distinguishable component of a company that is engaged in providing an individual product or service or a group of related products or services and that is subject to risks and returns that are different from those of other business segments. A geographical segment is a distinguishable component of a company that is engaged in providing products or services within a particular economic environment.

Different business and geographical segments should be identified. A company's business and geographical segments for external reporting purposes should be those organizational units for which information is reported to the board of directors and to the chief executive officer. If a company's internal organizational and management structure and its system of internal financial reporting to the board of directors and the chief executive officer are not based on individual products, services, groups of related products or services, or on geography, the directors and management of the company should choose either business segments or geographical segments as the company's primary segment reporting format, based on their assessment of which type of segment reflects the primary source of the company's risks and returns. Under this standard, most entities would identify their business and geographical segments as the organizational units for which information is reported to the nonexecutive board of directors and senior management.

If the total revenue from external customers for all reportable segments combined is less than 75 percent of the total company revenue, additional reportable segments should be identified until the 75 percent level is reached. Small segments might be combined as one if they share a substantial number of factors that define a business or geographical segment, or they might be combined with a similar significant reportable segment. If they are not separately reported or combined, they are included as an unallocated reconciling item.

The company must identify a primary segment reporting format (either business or geographical) with the other segment used for the secondary reporting format. The dominant source and nature of risks and returns govern whether a company's primary segment reporting format will be its business segments or its geographical segments. The company's internal organization and management structure, and its system of internal financial reporting to the board of directors and the chief executive officer, are normally the basis for identifying the predominant source and nature of risks and differing rates of return facing the company.

For each primary segment, the following should be disclosed:

▶ segment revenue, distinguishing between revenue to external customers and revenue from other segments;

▶ segment result (segment revenue minus segment expenses);

▶ carrying amount of segment assets;

▶ segment liabilities;

▶ cost of property, plant, and equipment, and intangible assets acquired;

▶ depreciation and amortization expense;

▶ other noncash expenses;

▶ share of the net profit or loss of an investment accounted for under the equity method;

▶ reconciliation between the information of reportable segments and the consolidated financial statements in terms of segment revenue, result, assets, and liabilities.

For each secondary segment, the following should be disclosed:

► revenue from external customers;
► carrying amount of segment assets;
► cost of property, plant, and equipment, and intangible assets acquired.

Other required disclosures are as follows:

► revenue of any segment whereby the external revenue of the segment is greater than or equal to 10 percent of company revenue but that is not a reportable segment (because a majority of its revenue is from internal transfers);
► basis of pricing intersegment transfers;
► changes in segment accounting policies;
► types of products and services in each business segment;
► composition of each geographical segment.

7.2 Segment Ratios

Based on the limited segment information that companies are required to present, a variety of useful ratios can be computed, as shown in Exhibit 17.

EXHIBIT 17	Definitions of Segment Ratios	
Segment Ratios	**Numerator**	**Denominator**
Segment margin	Segment profit (loss)	Segment revenue
Segment turnover	Segment revenue	Segment assets
Segment ROA	Segment profit (loss)	Segment assets
Segment debt ratio	Segment liabilities	Segment assets

The segment margin measures the operating profitability of the segment relative to revenues, whereas the segment ROA measures the operating profitability relative to assets. Segment turnover measures the overall efficiency of the segment: how much revenue is generated per unit of assets. The segment debt ratio examines the level of liabilities (hence solvency) of the segment. Example 15 demonstrates the evaluation of segment ratios.

EXAMPLE 15

The Evaluation of Segment Ratios

The following information relates to the business segments of Nokia for 2004 in millions of euros. Evaluate the performance of the segments using the segment margin, segment ROA, and segment turnover.

	Revenue	Operating Profit	Segment Assets
Mobile phones	18,429	3,768	3,758
Multimedia	3,636	179	787
Enterprise solutions	806	−199	210
Networks	6,367	878	3,055

	Segment Margin (%)	Segment ROA (%)	Segment Turnover
Mobile phones	20.45	100.27	4.90
Multimedia	4.92	22.74	4.62
Enterprise solutions	−24.69	−94.76	3.84
Networks	13.79	28.74	2.08

Solution: Mobile Phones is the best performing segment with the highest segment margin, segment ROA, and efficiency. Networks is the second highest in terms of profitability but lowest in efficiency (the ability to generate revenue from assets). Enterprise Solutions is not profitable; however, it is the smallest segment and may still be in the development stage.

8   MODEL BUILDING AND FORECASTING

Analysts often need to forecast future financial performance. For example, EPS forecasts of analysts are widely followed by Wall Street. Analysts use data about the economy, industry, and company in arriving at a company's forecast. The results of an analyst's financial analysis, including common-size and ratio analysis, are integral to this process, along with the judgment of the analysts.

Based upon forecasts of growth and expected relationships among the financial statement data, the analyst can build a model (sometimes referred to as an "earnings model") to forecast future performance. In addition to budgets, pro forma financial statements are widely used in financial forecasting within companies, especially for use by senior executives and boards of directors. Last but not least, these budgets and forecasts are also used in presentations to credit analysts and others in obtaining external financing.

For example, based on a revenue forecast, an analyst may budget expenses based on expected common-size data. Forecasts of balance sheet and statement of cash flows can be derived from expected ratio data, such as DSO. Forecasts are not limited to a single point estimate but should involve a range of possibilities. This can involve several techniques:

▶ **Sensitivity analysis**: Also known as "what if" analysis, sensitivity analysis shows the range of possible outcomes as specific assumptions are changed; this could, in turn, influence financing needs or investment in fixed assets.

▶ **Scenario analysis**: Scenario analysis shows the changes in key financial quantities that result from given (economic) events, such as the loss of customers, the loss of a supply source, or a catastrophic event. If the list of events is mutually exclusive and exhaustive and the events can be assigned probabilities, the analyst can evaluate not only the range of outcomes but also standard statistical measures such as the mean and median value for various quantities of interest.

▶ **Simulation**: This is computer-generated sensitivity or scenario analysis based on probability models for the factors that drive outcomes. Each event or possible outcome is assigned a probability. Multiple scenarios are then run using the probability factors assigned to the possible values of a variable.

SUMMARY

Financial analysis techniques, including common-size and ratio analysis, are useful in summarizing financial reporting data and evaluating the performance and financial position of a company. The results of financial analysis techniques provide important inputs into security valuation. Key facets of financial analysis include the following:

▶ Common-size financial statements and financial ratios remove the effect of size, allowing comparisons of a company with peer companies (cross-sectional analysis) and comparison of a company's results over time (trend or time-series analysis).

▶ Activity ratios measure the efficiency of a company's operations, such as collection of receivables or management of inventory. Major activity ratios include inventory turnover, days of inventory on hand, receivables turnover, days of sales outstanding, payables turnover, number of days of payables, working capital turnover, fixed asset turnover, and total asset turnover.

▶ Liquidity ratios measure the ability of a company to meet short-term obligations. Major liquidity ratios include the current ratio, quick ratio, cash ratio, and defensive interval ratio.

▶ Solvency ratios measure the ability of a company to meet long-term obligations. Major solvency ratios include debt ratios (including the debt-to-assets ratio, debt-to-capital ratio, debt-to-equity ratio, and financial leverage ratio) and coverage ratios (including interest coverage and fixed charge coverage).

▶ Profitability ratios measure the ability of a company to generate profits from revenue and assets. Major profitability ratios include return on sales ratios (including gross profit margin, operating profit margin, pretax margin, and net profit margin) and return on investment ratios (including operating ROA, ROA, ROE, and return on common equity).

▶ Ratios can also be combined and evaluated as a group to better understand how they fit together and how efficiency and leverage are tied to profitability.

▶ ROE can be analyzed as the product of the net profit margin, asset turnover, and financial leverage.

▶ Ratio analysis is useful in the selection and valuation of debt and equity securities and is a part of the credit rating process.

▶ Ratios can also be computed for business segments to evaluate how units within a business are doing.

▶ The results of financial analysis provide valuable inputs into forecasts of future earnings and cash flow.

PRACTICE PROBLEMS FOR READING 35

1. Comparison of a company's financial results to other peer companies for the same time period is called:

   A. horizontal analysis.

   B. time-series analysis.

   C. cross-sectional analysis.

2. In order to assess a company's ability to fulfill its long-term obligations, an analyst would *most likely* examine:

   A. activity ratios.

   B. liquidity ratios.

   C. solvency ratios.

3. Which ratio would a company *most likely* use to measure its ability to meet short-term obligations?

   A. Current ratio.

   B. Payables turnover.

   C. Gross profit margin.

4. Which of the following ratios would be *most useful* in determining a company's ability to cover its debt payments?

   A. ROA.

   B. Total asset turnover.

   C. Fixed charge coverage.

5. John Chan is interested in assessing both the efficiency and liquidity of Spherion PLC. Chan has collected the following data for Spherion:

	2005	2004	2003
Days of inventory on hand	32	34	40
Days' sales outstanding	28	25	23
Number of days of payables	40	35	35

   Based on this data, what is Chan *least likely* to conclude?

   A. Inventory management has contributed to improved liquidity.

   B. Management of payables has contributed to improved liquidity.

   C. Management of receivables has contributed to improved liquidity.

6. Marcus Lee is examining the solvency of Apex Manufacturing and has collected the following data (in millions of euros):

	2005	2004	2003
Total debt	€2,000	€1,900	€1,750
Total equity	€4,000	€4,500	€5,000

Which of the following would be the *most appropriate* conclusion for Lee?

   A. The company is becoming increasingly less solvent, as evidenced by the increase in its debt-to-equity ratio from 0.35 to 0.50 from 2003 to 2005.

   B. The company is becoming less liquid, as evidenced by the increase in its debt-to-equity ratio from 0.35 to 0.50 from 2003 to 2005.

   C. The company is becoming increasingly more liquid, as evidenced by the increase in its debt-to-equity ratio from 0.35 to 0.50 from 2003 to 2005.

7. With regard to the data in Problem 6, what would be a reasonable explanation of these financial results?

   A. The decline in the company's equity results from a decline in the market value of this company's common shares.

   B. The increase in the company's debt of €250 from 2003 to 2005 indicates that lenders are viewing the company as increasingly creditworthy.

   C. The decline in the company's equity indicates that the company may be incurring losses on its operations, paying dividends greater than income, and/or repurchasing shares.

8. Linda Roper observes a decrease in a company's inventory turnover. Which of the following would explain this trend?

   A. The company installed a new inventory management system, allowing more efficient inventory management.

   B. Due to problems with obsolescent inventory last year, the company wrote off a large amount of its inventory at the beginning of the period.

   C. The company installed a new inventory management system but experienced some operational difficulties resulting in duplicate orders being placed with suppliers.

9. Which of the following would best explain an increase in receivables turnover?

   A. The company adopted new credit policies last year and began offering credit to customers with weak credit histories.

   B. Due to problems with an error in its old credit scoring system, the company had accumulated a substantial amount of uncollectible accounts and wrote off a large amount of its receivables.

   C. To match the terms offered by its closest competitor, the company adopted new payment terms now requiring net payment within 30 days rather than 15 days, which had been its previous requirement.

10. Brown Corporation had an average days sales outstanding of 19 days in 2005. Brown wants to decrease its collection period in 2006 to match the industry average of 15 days. Credit sales in 2005 were $300 million, and Brown expects credit sales to increase to $390 million in 2006. To achieve Brown's goal of decreasing the collection period, the change in the average accounts receivable balance from 2005 to 2006 that must occur is *closest* to:

  A. –$1.22 million.

  B. –$0.42 million.

  C. $0.42 million.

11. An analyst gathered the following data for a company:

	2003	2004	2005
ROE	19.8%	20.0%	22.0%
Return on total assets	8.1%	8.0%	7.9%
Total asset turnover	2.0	2.0	2.1

Based only on the information above, the *most* appropriate conclusion is that, over the period 2003 to 2005, the company's:

  A. net profit margin and financial leverage have decreased.

  B. net profit margin and financial leverage have increased.

  C. net profit margin has decreased but its financial leverage has increased.

12. A decomposition of ROE for Integra SA is as follows:

	2005	2004
ROE	18.90%	18.90%
Tax burden	0.70	0.75
Interest burden	0.90	0.90
EBIT margin	10.00%	10.00%
Asset turnover	1.50	1.40
Leverage	2.00	2.00

Which of the following choices *best* describes reasonable conclusions an analyst might make based on this ROE decomposition?

  A. Profitability and the liquidity position both improved in 2005.

  B. The higher average tax rate in 2005 offset the improvement in profitability, leaving ROE unchanged.

  C. The higher average tax rate in 2005 offset the improvement in efficiency, leaving ROE unchanged.

13. A decomposition of ROE for Company A and Company B is as follows:

	Company A		Company B	
	2005	**2004**	**2005**	**2004**
ROE	26.46%	18.90%	26.33%	18.90%
Tax burden	0.7	0.75	0.75	0.75
Interest burden	0.9	0.9	0.9	0.9
EBIT margin	7.00%	10.00%	13.00%	10.00%
Asset turnover	1.5	1.4	1.5	1.4
Leverage	4	2	2	2

Which of the following choices *best* describes reasonable conclusions an analyst might make based on this ROE decomposition?

A. Company A's ROE is higher than Company B's in 2005, but the difference between the two companies' ROE is very small and was mainly the result of Company A's increase in its financial leverage.

B. Company A's ROE is higher than Company B's in 2005, apparently reflecting a strategic shift by Company A to a product mix with higher profit margins.

C. Company A's ROE is higher than Company B's in 2005, which suggests that Company A may have purchased new, more efficient equipment.

14. Rent-A-Center reported the following information related to total debt and shareholders' equity in its 2003 annual report.

	As of 31 December				
($ in Thousands)	**2003**	**2002**	**2001**	**2000**	**1999**
Total debt	698,000	521,330	702,506	741,051	847,160
Stockholders' equity	794,830	842,400	405,378	309,371	206,690

What would an analyst's most appropriate conclusion be based on this data?

A. The company's solvency has improved from 1999 to 2002.

B. The company's solvency has improved from 2002 to 2003.

C. The data suggest the company increased debt in 2002.

15. Frank Collins observes the following data for two companies:

	Company A ($)	Company B ($)
Revenue	4,500	6,000
Net income	50	1,000
Current assets	40,000	60,000
Total assets	100,000	700,000
Current liabilities	10,000	50,000
Total debt	60,000	150,000
Shareholders' equity	30,000	500,000

Which of the following choices best describes reasonable conclusions that Collins might make about the two companies' ability to pay their current and long-term obligations?

A. Company A's current ratio of 4.0x indicates it is more liquid than Company B, whose current ratio is only 1.2x, but Company B is more solvent, as indicated by its lower debt-to-equity ratio.

B. Company A's current ratio of 25 percent indicates it is less liquid than Company B, whose current ratio is 83 percent, and Company A is also less solvent, as indicated by a debt-to-equity ratio of 200 percent compared with Company B's debt-to-equity ratio of only 30 percent.

C. Company A's current ratio of 4.0x indicates it is more liquid than Company B, whose current ratio is only 1.2x, and Company A is also more solvent, as indicated by a debt-to-equity ratio of 200 percent compared with Company B's debt-to-equity ratio of only 30 percent.

Use the following information to answer Questions 16–19

The data below appear in the five-year summary of a major international company. A business combination with another major manufacturer took place in 2003. The term "turnover" in this financial data is a synonym for revenue.

	2000	2001	2002	2003	2004
Financial statements	GBP m	GBP m	GBP m	GBP m	GBP m
Income statements					
Turnover (i.e., revenue)	4,390	3,624	3,717	8,167	11,366
Profit before interest and taxation (EBIT)	844	700	704	933	1,579
Net interest payable	–80	–54	–98	–163	–188
Taxation	–186	–195	–208	–349	–579
Minorities	–94	–99	–105	–125	–167
Profit for the year	484	352	293	296	645
Balance sheets					
Fixed assets	3,510	3,667	4,758	10,431	11,483
Current asset investments, cash at bank and in hand	316	218	290	561	682
Other current assets	558	514	643	1,258	1,634
Total assets	4,384	4,399	5,691	12,250	13,799
Interest bearing debt (long term)	–602	–1,053	–1,535	–3,523	–3,707
Other creditors and provisions (current)	–1,223	–1,054	–1,102	–2,377	–3,108
Total liabilities	–1,825	–2,107	–2,637	–5,900	–6,815
Net assets	2,559	2,292	3,054	6,350	6,984
Shareholders' funds	2,161	2,006	2,309	5,572	6,165
Equity minority interests	398	286	745	778	819
Capital employed	2,559	2,292	3,054	6,350	6,984
Cash flow					
Working capital movements	–53	5	71	85	107
Net cash inflow from operating activities	864	859	975	1,568	2,292

16. The company's total assets at year-end 1999 were GBP 3,500 million. Which of the following choices *best* describes reasonable conclusions an analyst might make about the company's efficiency?

    A. Comparing 2004 with 2000, the company's efficiency improved, as indicated by a total asset turnover ratio of 0.86 compared with 0.64.

    B. Comparing 2004 with 2000, the company's efficiency deteriorated, as indicated by its current ratio.

    C. Comparing 2004 with 2000, the company's efficiency deteriorated due to asset growth faster than turnover (i.e., revenue) growth.

17. Which of the following choices *best* describes reasonable conclusions an analyst might make about the company's solvency?

    A. Comparing 2004 with 2000, the company's solvency improved, as indicated by an increase in its debt-to-assets ratio from 0.14 to 0.27.

    B. Comparing 2004 with 2000, the company's solvency deteriorated, as indicated by a decrease in interest coverage from 10.6 to 8.4.

    C. Comparing 2004 with 2000, the company's solvency improved, as indicated by the growth in its profits to GBP 645 million.

18. Which of the following choices *best* describes reasonable conclusions an analyst might make about the company's liquidity?

    A. Comparing 2004 with 2000, the company's liquidity improved, as indicated by an increase in its debt-to-assets ratio from 0.14 to 0.27.

    B. Comparing 2004 with 2000, the company's liquidity deteriorated, as indicated by a decrease in interest coverage from 10.6 to 8.4.

    C. Comparing 2004 with 2000, the company's liquidity improved, as indicated by an increase in its current ratio from 0.71 to 0.75.

19. Which of the following choices *best* describes reasonable conclusions an analyst might make about the company's profitability?

    A. Comparing 2004 with 2000, the company's profitability improved, as indicated by an increase in its debt-to-assets ratio from 0.14 to 0.27.

    B. Comparing 2004 with 2000, the company's profitability deteriorated, as indicated by a decrease in its net profit margin from 11.0 percent to 5.7 percent.

    C. Comparing 2004 with 2000, the company's profitability improved, as indicated by the growth in its shareholders' equity to GBP 6,165 million.

20. In general, a creditor would consider a decrease in which of the following ratios to be positive news?

    A. Interest coverage (times interest earned).

    B. Debt to total assets.

    C. Return on assets.

21. Assuming no changes in other variables, which of the following would decrease ROA?

    A. A decrease in the effective tax rate.

    B. A decrease in interest expense.

    C. An increase in average assets.

22. What does the P/E ratio measure?

    A. The "multiple" that the stock market places on a company's EPS.

    B. The relationship between dividends and market prices.

    C. The earnings for one common share of stock.

SOLUTIONS FOR READING 35

1. **C is correct.** Cross-sectional analysis involved the comparison of companies with each other for the same time period. Time-series analysis is the comparison of financial data across different time periods.

2. **C is correct.** Solvency ratios are used to evaluate the ability of a company to meet its long-term obligations.

3. **A is correct.** The current ratio is a liquidity ratio. It compares the net amount of current assets expected to be converted into cash within the year, compared with liabilities falling due in the same period. A current ratio of 1.0 would indicate that the company would have just enough current assets to pay current liabilities.

4. **C is correct.** Solvency ratios measure the ability to cover debt payments. There are two main types of solvency ratios. Debt ratios focus on the balance sheet and measure the amount of capital raised by debt relative to equity. Coverage ratios focus on the income statement and measure the ability of a company to cover its debt payments. The fixed charge coverage ratio is a coverage ratio that relates known fixed obligations to the cash flow generated by the entity.

5. **C is correct.** Chan is very *unlikely* to reach the conclusion given in Statement C because days' sales outstanding increased from 23 days in 2003 to 25 days in 2004 to 28 days in 2005, indicating that the time required to collect receivables has increased over the period, which is a negative factor for Spherion's liquidity. By contrast, days of inventory on hand dropped over the period 2003 to 2005, a positive for liquidity. Thus Statement A is an appropriate conclusion. The company's increase in days' payable from 35 days' to 40 days shorted its cash collection cycle, thus contributing to improved liquidity; therefore, Statement B is also an appropriate conclusion.

6. **A is correct.** The company is becoming increasingly less solvent, as evidenced by its debt-to-equity ratio increasing from 0.35 to 0.50 from 2003 to 2005. B is incorrect because it incorrectly interprets the debt-to-equity ratio as a measure of liquidity. C is incorrect because it incorrectly interprets the direction of the trend and misinterprets the ratio as an indicator of liquidity.

    Debt to equity:
2005:	$2,000/4,000 = 0.5000$	
2004:	$1,900/4,500 = 0.4222$	
2003:	$1,750/5,000 = 0.3500$	

7. **C is correct.** The decline in the company's equity indicates that the company may be incurring losses on its operations, paying dividends greater than income, or repurchasing shares. Recall that Beginning equity + New shares issuance − Shares repurchased + Net income − Dividends = Ending equity. A is incorrect because the book value of a company's equity is not affected by changes in the market value of its common stock. B is incorrect because an increased amount of lending does not necessarily indicate that lenders view a company as increasingly creditworthy. Credit-worthiness is not evaluated based on how much a company has increased its debt but rather on its willingness to pay its

obligations and its ability to pay. (Its financial strength is indicated by its solvency, liquidity, profitability, efficiency, and other aspects of credit analysis.)

8. C is correct. The company's problems with its inventory management system causing duplicate orders would result in a higher amount of inventory than needed and would, therefore, likely result in a decrease in inventory turnover. A is incorrect because a more efficient inventory management system would likely be reflected in the inventory turnover ratio, an indicator of more efficient inventory management. B is incorrect because a write-off of inventory at the beginning of the period would decrease the average inventory for the period (the denominator of the inventory turnover ratio), thus increasing the ratio rather than decreasing it.

9. B is correct. A write-off of receivables would decrease the average amount of accounts receivable (the denominator of the receivables turnover ratio), thus increasing this ratio. A is incorrect because weaker credit customers are more likely to make payments more slowly or to pose collection difficulties, which would likely increase the average amount of accounts receivable and thus decrease receivables turnover. C is incorrect because a longer payment period would likely increase the average amount of accounts receivable and thus decrease receivables turnover.

10. C is correct because accounts receivable turnover can be calculated to determine the average DSO. Turnovers are equal to 365/19 (DSO) = 19.2 for 2005 and 365/15 = 24.3 in 2004. Sales/turnovers are equal to accounts receivable balances. For 2005, \$300,000,000/19.2 = \$15,625,000, and for 2006, \$390,000,000/24.3 = \$16,049,383. The difference is an increase in receivables of \$424,383.

   A is incorrect because the accounts receivable balance must increase.

   B is incorrect because the accounts receivable balance must increase.

11. C is correct. ROE = Return on assets × Financial leverage. ROA can be decomposed into the product of net profit margin (net income divided by revenue) and total asset turnover (revenue divided by average total assets). Because ROA has been decreasing over 2003 to 2005 while total asset turnover has been increasing, it must be the case that the net profit margin has been declining. Furthermore, because ROE has increased despite the drop in ROA, financial leverage must have increased. Statement C is the only statement that correctly identifies the trends in net profit margin and financial leverage.

12. C is correct. The increase in the average tax rate in 2005, as indicated by the decrease in the value of the tax burden (the tax burden equals one minus the average tax rate), offset the improvement in efficiency indicated by higher asset turnover; as a result, ROE remained unchanged at 18.90 percent. Statement A is not correct because the EBIT margin, measuring profitability, was unchanged in 2005; furthermore, no information is given on liquidity. Statement B is not correct because profitability was unchanged in 2005.

13. A is correct. The difference between the two companies' ROE in 2005 is very small and is mainly the result of Company A's increase in its financial leverage, indicated by the increase in its assets/equity ratio from 2 to 4. B is incorrect because Company A has experienced a significant decline in its operating margin, from 10 percent to 7 percent which, all else equal, would not suggest that it is selling more of products with higher profit margin.

C is incorrect because the impact of efficiency on ROE is identical for the two companies, as indicated by both companies' asset turnover ratios of 1.5. Furthermore, if Company A had purchased newer equipment to replace older, depreciated equipment, then the company's asset turnover ratio (computed as sales/assets) would have declined, assuming constant sales.

14. A is correct. The debt-to-equity ratio has improved from 1999 to 2002 from 410 percent to 88 percent (calculations below). The decrease in total debt implies that debt has been repaid, not borrowed. B is incorrect because the company's solvency has deteriorated from 2002 to 2003, as indicated by the higher debt-to-equity ratio. C is incorrect because lower total debt in 2002 suggests repayment of debt.

	2003	2002	2001	2000	1999
Total debt	698,000	521,330	702,506	741,051	847,160
Stockholders' equity	794,830	842,400	405,378	309,371	206,690
Total debt-to-equity ratio	88%	62%	173%	240%	410%

15. A is correct. Company A's current ratio of 4.0× ($40,000/$10,000 = 4.0) indicates it is more liquid than Company B, whose current ratio is only 1.2× ($60,000/$50,000 = 1.2). Company B is more solvent, as indicated by its lower debt-to-equity ratio of 30 percent ($150,000/$500,000 = 0.30) compared with Company A's debt-to-equity ratio of 200 percent ($60,000/$30,000 = 2.0). The other choices are incorrect either because the current ratio is incorrectly calculated or because the debt-to-equity ratio was incorrectly interpreted.

16. C is correct. The company's efficiency deteriorated, as indicated by the decline in its total asset turnover ratio from 1.11 (GBP 4,390/ [(GBP 4,384 + 3,500)/2 = 1.11]) for the year 2000 to 0.87 (GBP 11,366/[(GBP 12,250 + GBP 13,799)/2] = 0.87) for the year 2004. The decline in the total asset turnover ratio resulted from an increase in average assets from GBP 3,942 (GBP 4,384 + 3,500)/2 = GBP 3,942 in 2000 to GBP 13,024.5 in 2004, an increase of 330 percent, compared with an increase in turnover (i.e., revenues) from GBP 4,390 in 2000 to GBP 11,366 in 2004, an increase of only 259 percent. A is incorrect because the asset turnover ratio is calculated incorrectly. B is incorrect because the current ratio is not an indicator of efficiency.

17. B is correct. Comparing 2004 with 2000, the company's solvency deteriorated, as indicated by a decrease in interest coverage from 10.6 (GBP 844/GBP 80=10.6) in 2000 to 8.4 (GBP 1,579/GBP 188 = 8.4). A is incorrect because it misinterprets the debt-to-asset ratio. C is incorrect because, in isolation, the amount of profits does not provide enough information to assess solvency.

18. C is correct. Comparing 2004 with 2000, the company's liquidity improved, as indicated by an increase in its current ratio from 0.71 ([GBP 316 + GBP 558]/GBP 1,223 = 0.71) in 2000 to 0.75 ([GBP 682 + GBP 1,634]/GBP 3,108 = 0.75) in 2004. Note, however, comparing only current investments with the level of current liabilities shows a decline in liquidity from 0.25 (316/1223 = 0.25) in 2000 to 0.22 (GBP 682/GBP 3,108 = 0.22) in 2004. A is incorrect because the debt-to-assets ratio is not an indicator of liquidity. B is incorrect because interest coverage is not an indicator of liquidity.

19. B is correct. Comparing 2004 with 2000, the company's profitability deteriorated, as indicated by a decrease in its net profit margin from 11 percent (484/4,390 = 0.11) to 5.7 percent (645/11,366 = 0.057). A is incorrect because the debt-to-assets ratio is not an indicator of profitability. C is incorrect because growth in shareholders' equity, in isolation, does not provide enough information to assess profitability.

20. B is correct. In general, a creditor would consider a decrease in debt to total assets as positive news. A higher level of debt in a company's capital structure increases the risk of default and will result in higher borrowing costs for the company to compensate lenders for assuming greater credit risk.

21. C is correct. Assuming no changes in other variables, an increase in average assets would decrease ROA.

22. A is correct. The P/E ratio measures the "multiple" that the stock market places on a company's EPS.

23⅜ 24

4⅝ 4¹¹⁄₁₆ ...

5½ 5½ — ⅜

5½ 5½ — ⅛

20⅝ 21³⁄₁₆ — ⅛

17⅜ 18⅛ + ⅞

18½ 6½ 6½ — ½

7¼ 6½ 3¹⅛₃₂ — ⅛

15⁄₁₆ 15⁄₁₆

9⁄₁₆ 9⁄₁₆

1⅛₃₂

7⅕₁₆ 7¹³⁄₁₆ 7¹⁵⁄₁₆

2⅝ 2¹¹⁄₃₂ 2½ +

23¾ 2¼ 2¼

6⅒ 12¹⁄₁₆ 11⅜ 11¾ +

87 33¾ 33 33⅛ —

832 25⅝ 24⁹⁄₁₆ 25⅜ +

833 12 11⅝ 11⅛ +

16 10½ 10½ 10½ —

78 15⅞ 15¹³⁄₁₆ 15⅞ —

908 9¹⁄₁₆ 8¼ 8⅛ +

11¼ 10½

STUDY SESSION 9
FINANCIAL REPORTING AND ANALYSIS:
Inventories, Long-Term Assets, Deferred Taxes, and On- and Off-Balance Sheet Debt

The readings in this study session examine specific categories of assets and liabilities that are particularly susceptible to the impact of alternative accounting policies and estimates. Analysts must understand the effects of alternative policies on financial statements and ratios and be able to execute appropriate adjustments to enhance comparability between companies. In addition, analysts must be alert to differences between a company's reported financial statements and economic reality.

The description and measurement of inventories require careful attention because the investment in inventories is frequently the largest current asset for merchandizing and manufacturing companies. For these companies, the measurement of inventory cost (i.e., cost of goods sold) is a critical factor in determining gross profit and other measures of company profitability. Long-term operating assets are often the largest category of assets on a company's balance sheet. The analyst needs to scrutinize management's choices with respect to recognizing expenses associated with the operating assets because of the potentially large impact such choices can have on reported earnings and the opportunities for financial statement manipulation during longer time periods.

A company's accounting policies (such as depreciation choices) can cause differences in taxes reported in financial statements and taxes reported on tax returns. The reading "Income Taxes" discusses several issues that arise relating to deferred taxes.

Both on- and off-balance sheet debt affect a company's liquidity and solvency and have consequences for its long-term growth and viability. The notes of the financial statements must be carefully reviewed to ensure that all potential liabilities (e.g., leasing arrangements and other contractual commitments) are

375

appropriately evaluated for their conformity to economic reality. Adjustments to the financial statements may be required to achieve comparability when evaluating several companies and may also be required to improve credit and investment decision-making.

READING ASSIGNMENTS

Reading 36   Inventories
International Financial Statement Analysis, by Thomas R. Robinson, CFA, Jan Hendrik van Greuning, CFA, R. Elaine Henry, CFA, and Michael A. Broihahn, CFA

Reading 37   Long-Lived Assets
International Financial Statement Analysis, by Thomas R. Robinson, CFA, Jan Hendrik van Greuning, CFA, R. Elaine Henry, CFA, and Michael A. Broihahn, CFA

Reading 38   Income Taxes
International Financial Statement Analysis, by Thomas R. Robinson, CFA, Jan Hendrik van Greuning, CFA, R. Elaine Henry, CFA, and Michael A. Broihahn, CFA

Reading 39   Long-Term Liabilities and Leases
International Financial Statement Analysis, by Thomas R. Robinson, CFA, Jan Hendrik van Greuning, CFA, R. Elaine Henry, CFA, and Michael A. Broihahn, CFA

INVENTORIES

by Elbie Antonites, CFA and Michael A. Broihahn, CFA

LEARNING OUTCOMES

The candidate should be able to:	Mastery
a. explain IFRS and U.S. GAAP rules for determining inventory cost, including which costs are capitalized and methods of allocating costs between cost of goods sold and inventory;	☐
b. discuss how inventories are reported on the financial statements and how the lower of cost or net realizable value is used and applied;	☐
c. compute ending inventory balances and cost of goods sold using the FIFO, weighted average cost, and LIFO methods to account for product inventory and explain the relationship among and the usefulness of inventory and cost of goods sold data provided by the FIFO, weighted average cost, and LIFO methods when prices are 1) stable, 2) decreasing, or 3) increasing;	☐
d. discuss and calculate ratios useful for evaluating inventory management;	☐
e. analyze the financial statements of companies using different inventory accounting methods by comparing and describing the effect of the different methods on cost of goods sold, inventory balances, and other financial statement items;	☐
f. compute and describe the effects of the choice of inventory method on profitability, liquidity, activity, and solvency ratios;	☐
g. calculate adjustments to reported financial statements related to inventory assumptions to aid in comparing and evaluating companies;	☐
h. discuss the reasons that a LIFO reserve might rise or decline during a given period and discuss the implications for financial analysis.	☐

International Financial Statement Analysis, by Thomas R. Robinson, CFA, Jan Hendrik van Greuning, CFA, R. Elaine Henry, CFA, and Michael A. Broihahn, CFA. Copyright © 2008 by CFA Institute. Reprinted with permission.

THEME

Inventory cost flow is a major determinant of net income for merchandising and manufacturing companies. In addition, inventories are often a significant asset on the balance sheets of these companies. Companies can choose among several methods that comply with accounting standards to account for inventory. The choice of method can result in significantly different values being assigned to cost of goods sold and to inventory. The company's financial statements and related notes provide important information that the analyst can use to assess financial performance and to compare financial performance with other companies.

1   INTRODUCTION

Merchandising and manufacturing companies generate their sales and profits through inventory transactions on a regular basis. Merchandisers (wholesalers and retailers) purchase their inventory from manufacturers and thus account for only one type of inventory—finished goods inventory. Manufacturers, however, must account for three different types of inventory: raw materials, work-in-process, and finished goods. A manufacturer purchases raw materials from supplier companies and then adds value by transforming the raw materials into work-in-process and, ultimately, finished goods through the application of direct labor and factory overhead costs. Work-in-process inventories are those inventories that have started the conversion process from raw materials but have not yet been completed or "finished." Manufacturers may report the separate carrying values of their raw materials, work-in-process, and finished goods inventories on the balance sheet or choose instead to report just the total inventory value. If the latter approach is used, the company must disclose the carrying values of its raw materials, work-in-process, and finished goods inventories in a footnote to the financial statements.

An important consideration in calculating profits for these types of companies is measuring the cost of goods sold when inventory is sold to business customers. The measurement process would be simple if inventory costs remained constant over time; however, that is simply not economic reality. Also, financial analysis would be much easier if all companies used the same inventory cost flow assumption; however, that is not an accounting reality in today's complex business environment. International Financial Reporting Standards (IFRS) as promulgated by the International Accounting Standards Board allow companies complying with IFRS to opt from three sanctioned methods: specific identification, weighted average cost, and first-in, first-out (FIFO). U.S. GAAP allows the same three methods, but also includes a fourth method called last-in, first-out (LIFO).

Given the complexity introduced by having several allowable inventory accounting methods, the analyst must clearly understand the various approaches to inventory costing that companies use and be able to understand the related impact on financial statements and financial ratios. A beneficial outcome of this knowledge will be an improved evaluation of a company's performance and better comparisons of a company with industry peers.

INVENTORY COST AND INVENTORY ACCOUNTING METHODS

2

Because inventory purchase costs and manufacturing conversion costs generally change over time, the allocation of these total inventory costs (cost of goods available for sale) between cost of goods sold on the income statement and inventory on the balance sheet will vary depending on the cost flow assumption used by the company. If more cost is allocated to cost of goods sold under one inventory method than another (with a corresponding lower cost allocated to inventory), that inventory method will cause reported gross profit (and thus net income) to be lower and reported inventory carrying value to be lower than if the other inventory method had been used. Accounting for inventory, and consequently the allocation of costs, thus has a direct impact on the financial statements.

2.1 Determination of Inventory Cost

According to IAS 2, the IFRS rule governing inventory accounting, the cost of inventories, **capitalized inventory costs**, shall comprise all costs of purchase, costs of conversion, and other costs incurred in bringing the inventories to their present location and condition. Companies must also allocate to inventory a portion of fixed production overhead based on normal capacity levels, though any unallocated portion of the overhead is expensed when incurred. IAS 2 excludes from inventory cost all abnormal costs incurred due to waste of materials and abnormal waste incurred for labor and overhead conversion costs from the production process, any storage costs (unless required as part of the production process), and all administrative overhead and selling costs. These excludable costs are expensed and treated as period costs instead of being capitalized as inventory product costs. Under U.S. GAAP, ARB 43 and SFAS No. 151 provide similar treatment for the determination of inventory cost.

Capitalizing inventory related costs defers their recognition as an expense in the income statement until the inventory is sold. Any capitalization of costs that should otherwise be expensed will overstate profitability on the income statement (due to the inappropriate deferral of cost recognition) and create an overstated inventory value on the balance sheet. WorldCom used a variation of this ploy (i.e., capitalization of expenses to long-term fixed assets) to construct the fictitious financial statements that resulted in very costly accounting fraud for the deceived creditors and investors.

EXAMPLE 1

Capitalization of Inventory Related Costs

Acme Enterprises, a hypothetical company, produces folding tables at a factory that has a normal capacity of 1 million folding tables per year. Acme prepares its financial statements in accordance with IFRS. In 2008, the factory produced 900,000 finished folding tables and incurred €2 million of fixed production overhead costs. Raw material costs for the finished folding tables were €9 million and labor conversion costs were €18 million. In addition, Acme scrapped 1,000 folding tables (attributable to abnormal waste) at a total production cost of €30,000 (€10,000 raw material cost and €20,000 labor conversion costs). During the year, Acme spent €1 million for freight-in charges and also incurred €500,000 for storage related costs prior to selling the manufactured folding tables. Acme does not have any work-in-process inventory at the end of the year.

1. What are the total capitalized inventory costs for Acme in 2008?
2. What is the finished goods inventory cost of an Acme folding table in 2008?
3. What costs did Acme treat as period costs and, therefore, expense in 2008?

Solution to 1: Capitalized inventory costs will include 90 percent (900,000 units produced ÷ 1,000,000 units normal capacity) of the fixed production overhead costs or €1.8 million (.90 × €2 million total fixed production overhead costs), the €9 million cost of raw materials and the €18 million labor conversion costs for the 900,000 finished good folding tables, and also €1 million for the raw material freight-in costs. The total capitalized inventory costs are thus €29.8 million.

Solution to 2: The finished good inventory cost of one folding table is €33.11 (€29.8 million capitalized inventory costs ÷ 900,000 finished good folding tables).

Solution to 3: The period costs include the remaining unallocated fixed production overhead of €200,000, the €30,000 incurred cost for abnormal waste, and the €500,000 spent for storage related costs prior to selling the manufactured folding tables. The total period costs that Acme expensed in 2008 are thus €730,000.

2.2 Declines in Inventory Value

IAS 2 states that inventories shall be measured at the lower of cost and "net realizable value." **Net realizable value** is the estimated selling price in the ordinary course of business less the estimated costs necessary to make the sale. In the event that the value of inventory declines below the cost carried on the balance sheet (historical cost), a write-down (loss) must be recorded. Reversal (limited to the amount of the original write-down) is required for a subsequent increase in value of inventory previously written down. The amount of any write-down of inventories to net realizable value and all losses of inventories are recognized as an expense in the period the write-down or loss occurs. Likewise, the amount of any reversal of any write-down of inventories, arising from an increase in net realizable value, is recognized as a reduction in the amount of inventories recognized as an expense (cost of sales) in the period in which the reversal occurs.

In certain industries, inventories may be valued and recorded at amounts greater than their historical cost. IAS 41 allows the inventories of producers and dealers of agricultural and forest products, agricultural produce at the point of harvest, and minerals and mineral products to be carried at net realizable value even if above historical cost. If an active market exists for these products, the quoted market price in that market is the appropriate basis for determining the fair value of that asset. If an active market does not exist, a company may use market-determined prices or values (such as the most recent market transaction price) when available. A gain or loss from the change in fair value is included in net profit or loss for the period in which it arises.

U.S. GAAP (ARB 43) is broadly consistent with IFRS, in that the lower of cost and market is used to value inventories. Market value (frequently referred to as fair value following the receipt of SFAS No. 157) is defined as being current replacement cost subject to an upper limit of net realizable value and a lower limit of net realizable value less a normal profit margin. Reversal of a write-down is prohibited, as a write-down creates a new cost basis. The treatment is similar to IFRS for inventories of agricultural and forest products and mineral ores. Mark-to-market inventory accounting is allowed for refined bullion of precious metals.

EXAMPLE 2

Accounting for Declines and Recoveries of Inventory Value

Acme Enterprises, a hypothetical company, manufactures folding tables and prepares its financial statements in accordance with IFRS. In 2007, the carrying (book) value of its inventory was €5.2 million before a €0.3 million write-down was recorded. In 2008, the fair value of Acme's inventory was €0.5 million greater than the carrying value.

1. What was the effect of the write-down on Acme's 2007 financial statements? What was the effect of the recovery on Acme's 2008 financial statements?

2. What would be the effect of the recovery on Acme's 2008 financial statements if Acme's inventory were agricultural assets instead of folding tables?

Solution to 1: For 2007, Acme would record the €0.3 million write-down as a loss, thereby decreasing inventory and increasing cost of goods sold. For 2008, Acme would record a €0.3 million recovery as a gain, thereby increasing inventory and decreasing cost of goods sold. Acme is limited to a €0.3 million recovery because its inventories are not agricultural, forest, or mineral products.

Solution to 2: If Acme's inventory were agricultural assets instead of folding tables, IAS 41 would be applicable. Acme would, therefore, record a €0.5 million gain for 2008.

2.3 Inventory Accounting Methods

According to IAS 2, the cost of inventories is generally assigned by using either the first-in, first-out (FIFO) or weighted average cost method. The specific identification method is used for inventories of items that are not ordinarily interchangeable and for goods or services produced and segregated for specific projects (i.e., for products that are not typically purchased, manufactured, or sold to customers in the ordinary course of business). Specific identification is also commonly used for costly goods that are uniquely identifiable, such as precious gemstones. The FIFO and weighted average methods (as well as the LIFO method that is permissible under U.S. GAAP) are cost flow *assumptions,* whereas the specific identification method is not. A business entity must use the same cost formula for all inventories having a similar nature and use to the entity. For inventories with a different nature or use, different cost formulas may be justified (e.g., using the weighted average method for one type of product and FIFO or specific identification methods for another). When inventories are sold, the carrying amount of the inventory is recognized as an expense according to the inventory cost flow formula. U.S. GAAP is similar in all respects to IFRS with the exception that the last-in, first-out (LIFO) method is also permissible. The LIFO inventory method will be discussed and illustrated in Section 4 of this reading.

The choice of inventory method would not be much of an issue if inventory unit costs remained relatively constant from period to period. That is because the allocation of cost flow between cost of goods sold and inventory carrying value would be very similar under the specific identification, weighted average cost, and FIFO inventory methods. But because inventory unit costs typically change from period to period, the choice of inventory method does in fact matter to a company.

The specific identification method matches the physical flow of the specific inventory items sold to their actual historic cost. Under the weighted average cost method, inventory value and inventory cost recognition are determined by using a weighted average mix of the actual costs incurred for all inventory items available for sale. The FIFO method assumes that companies sell their oldest purchased inventory units first before selling the next oldest purchased inventory units, and so on. Under the FIFO method, ending inventory will always consist of those units that have been most recently purchased and are valued at their historic purchase costs (subject to subsequent potential net realizable value inventory declines and recoveries as discussed in Section 2.2).

EXAMPLE 3

Inventory Cost Flow Illustration for the Specific Identification, Weighted Average Cost, and FIFO Methods

Global Sales, Inc. (GSI), a hypothetical company, sells electric razors at retail. GSI began operations in 2006, during which it purchased 50,000 razors and sold 46,000 razors. The razors were purchased at a cost of €20.00 per unit. In 2007, GSI purchased another 53,000 razors at a cost of €23.00 per unit. GSI sold 55,000 razors during 2007 (3,000 of

---

the razors sold were purchased in 2006 and 52,000 sold were purchased in 2007). GSI's sales price for razors was €30.00 per unit in 2006 and €33.00 per unit in 2007.

1. What is the reported cost of goods sold on GSI's income statement for 2007 under the specific identification method? What is the carrying value of inventory on GSI's balance sheet at year-end 2007 under the specific identification method?

2. What is the reported cost of goods sold on GSI's income statement for 2007 under the weighted average cost method? What is the carrying value of inventory on GSI's balance sheet at year-end 2007 under the weighted average cost method?

3. What is the reported cost of goods sold on GSI's income statement for 2007 under the FIFO cost method? What is the carrying value of inventory on GSI's balance sheet at year-end 2007 under the FIFO method?

Solution to 1: Under the specific identification method, the physical flow of the specific inventory items sold is matched to their actual historic cost. GSI's cost of goods sold for 2007 is €1,256,000 (52,000 razors sold at €23.00 cost per razor and 3,000 razors sold at €20.00 cost per razor). The inventory carrying value at year-end 2007 is €43,000 (1,000 razors remaining from those purchased in 2006 at €20.00 cost per razor and 1,000 razors remaining from those purchased in 2007 at €23.00 cost per razor).

Solution to 2: Under the weighted average cost method, inventory value and inventory cost recognition are determined by using a weighted average mix of the actual costs incurred for all inventory items. The weighted average cost of the razor inventory available for sale in 2007 is €1,299,000 (4,000 razors in beginning inventory purchased at €20.00 cost per razor and the 53,000 razors purchased in 2007 at €23.00 cost per razor). Accordingly, the weighted average cost of a razor inventory unit that was available for sale in 2007 is €22.7895 (€1,299,000 total purchase cost of the razor inventory available for sale divided by 57,000 razors available). The cost of goods sold is thus €1,253,421 (55,000 razors sold at €22.7895 weighted average cost per razor) and the inventory carrying value at year-end 2007 is €45,579 (2,000 razors remaining in inventory at a weighted average cost of €22.7895 cost per razor).

Solution to 3: Under the FIFO method, the cost flow assumption is that the oldest inventory units acquired are the first units to be sold. Ending inventory, therefore, consists of those inventory units most recently acquired. GSI's cost of goods sold for 2007 is €1,253,000 (4,000 razors sold at €20.00 cost per razor and 51,000 razors sold at €23.00 cost per razor). The inventory carrying value at year-end 2007 is €46,000 (2,000 razors remaining in inventory from those purchased in 2007 at €23.00 cost per razor).

The following table summarizes the ending inventory and the cost of goods sold that was calculated for each of the three inventory methods. Note that, as would be expected, the sum (the total cost of goods available for sale) is the same under all three methods.

Inventory Method	Specific ID	Weighted Average Cost	FIFO
Cost of goods sold	€1,256,000	€1,253,421	€1,253,000
Ending inventory	43,000	45,579	46,000
Total cost of goods available for sale	€1,299,000	€1,299,000	€1,299,000

2.4 Comparison of Inventory Accounting Methods

As shown in Example 3, the allocated cost of inventories available for sale to cost of goods sold on the income statement and to ending inventory on the balance sheet are each different under the specific identification, weighted average, and FIFO methods. The allocation of cost will be different again if the LIFO method were applied under U.S. GAAP.

In an environment of rising inventory unit costs and constant or increasing inventory quantities, FIFO (in comparison with weighted average cost) will allocate a lower amount of cost flow to cost of goods sold on the income statement and a greater amount of cost flow to the carrying value of inventory on the balance sheet. Accordingly, because cost of goods sold will be lower under FIFO, a company's gross profit, operating profit, and income before taxes will be higher. The book value of inventories under FIFO will more closely reflect current replacement values because inventories consist of the most recently purchased items that are carried at their higher purchase costs.

Conversely, in an environment of declining inventory unit costs and constant or increasing inventory quantities, FIFO (in comparison with weighted average cost) will allocate a greater amount of cost flow to cost of goods sold on the income statement and a lower amount of cost flow to the carrying value of inventory on the balance sheet. Accordingly, because cost of goods sold will be greater under FIFO, a company's gross profit, operating profit, and income before taxes will be lower. Once again, the book value of inventories under FIFO will more closely reflect current replacement values because inventories consist of the most recently purchased items that are carried at their lower purchase costs.

3   FINANCIAL ANALYSIS OF INVENTORIES

The choice of inventory method impacts the financial statements and any financial ratios that are derived from them. As a consequence, the analyst must carefully consider inventory method differences when evaluating a company's performance or when comparing a company with industry data or industry competitors.

3.1 Inventory Ratios

The **inventory turnover** ratio, **number of days of inventory** ratio, and **gross profit margin** ratio are directly and fully impacted by a company's choice of inventory method.[1] Analysts should be aware, however, that many other ratios are also affected by the choice of inventory method, although less directly. Some examples include the current ratio because inventory is a component of current assets, return on assets ratio because cost of goods sold is a component in deriving net income and inventory is a component of total assets, and even the debt-to-equity ratio because the cumulative measured net income from the inception of a business is an aggregate component of retained earnings.

The inventory turnover ratio indicates the resources tied up in inventory (the carrying costs) and can be used to evaluate inventory management effectiveness. The higher the inventory turnover ratio, the shorter the period that inventory is held, and so the lower the number of days of inventory ratio. In general, inventory turnover and the number of days of inventory should be benchmarked against industry norms.

A high inventory turnover ratio to industry norms might indicate highly effective inventory management. Alternatively, a high inventory ratio (and commensurately low number of days of inventory) could possibly indicate the company does not carry adequate inventory, so shortages could potentially result in lost sales and reduced revenue. To assess which explanation is more likely, the analyst can compare the company's revenue growth with that of the industry. Slower growth combined with higher inventory turnover could indicate inadequate inventory levels. Revenue growth at or above the industry's growth supports the interpretation that the higher turnover reflects greater inventory management efficiency.

A low inventory turnover ratio (and commensurately high number of days of inventory) relative to the rest of the industry could be an indicator of slow-moving or obsolete inventory. Again, comparing the company's sales growth with the industry can provide insight.

3.2 Financial Analysis Illustration

Selected consolidated financial statements and financial notes for Alcatel-Lucent (NYSE: ALU) are presented in Exhibits 1, 2, and 3. Note 1 (i) from Exhibit 3 discloses that ALU's finished goods inventories and work-in-process are valued at the lower of cost or net realizable value and that cost is primarily determined by the weighted average cost method.[2] Note 2 (a) in Exhibit 3 discloses that the impact of inventory and work-in-process write-down on Alcatel-Lucent income before tax was a net charge of €77 million in 2006, a net charge of €18 million in 2005, and a net gain of €20 million in 2004. These amounts are included as a component (additions/reversals) of ALU's change in valuation allowance as disclosed in Note 19 (b) from Exhibit 3. Observe also that ALU breaks out the valuation allowance at 31 December 2006, 2005, and 2004 (€378 million for 2006) in Note 19 (b) for inventories (€355 million for 2006) and for construction contracts (€23 million for 2006). Finally, observe that the €2,259 net value for inventories at 31 December 2006 (excluding construction contracts) in

---

[1] The number of days of inventory ratio is also commonly referred to as the average inventory processing period.

[2] Alcatel-Lucent's financial statements and notes refer to "work-in-progress" rather than "work-in-process." Both terms are commonly used and mean the same thing.

Note 19 (a) reconciles to the balance sheet amount for inventories and work-in-process, net on 31 December 2006 as presented in Exhibit 2.

Some companies use and disclose an inventory valuation allowance in their financial footnotes. The inventory valuation allowance represents the total amount of inventory write-down that was taken for the inventory reported on the balance sheet (which is measured at the lower of cost or net realizable value). The analyst can, therefore, determine the historical cost of the company's inventory by adding the inventory valuation allowance to the reported inventory carrying value on the balance sheet.

EXHIBIT 1	Alcatel-Lucent Consolidated Income Statements (Euros in Millions except per Share Data)		
For Years Ended 31 December	**2006**	**2005**	**2004**
Revenues	€12,282	€11,219	€10,263
Cost of sales	(8,212)	(7,085)	(6,169)
Gross profit	4,070	4,134	4,094
Administrative and selling expenses	(1,910)	(1,815)	(1,771)
Research and development costs	(1,466)	(1,298)	(1,320)
Income from operating activities before restructuring costs, impairment of intangible assets and gain on disposal of consolidated assets	694	1,021	1,003
Restructuring costs	(707)	(79)	(313)
Impairment of intangible assets	(141)	—	(88)
Gain on disposal of consolidated entities	15	129	—
Income (loss) from operating activities	(139)	1,071	602
Financial interest on gross financial debt	(241)	(215)	(211)
Financial interest on cash and cash equivalents	143	122	103
Finance costs	(98)	(93)	(108)
Other financial income (loss)	(112)	43	32
Share in net income (losses) of equity affiliates	22	(14)	(61)
Income (loss) before tax, related reduction of goodwill and discontinued operations	(327)	1,007	465
Reduction of goodwill related to realized unrecognized loss carryforwards	(5)	—	—
Income tax expense (benefit)	42	(146)	(34)
Income (loss) from continuing operations	(290)	861	431
Income from discontinued operations	159	110	214
Net income (loss)	€(131)	€971	€645
Attributable to:			
▶ **Equity holders of parent**	(176)	930	576
▶ Minority interests	45	41	69

(Exhibit continued on next page . . .)

EXHIBIT 1	(continued)			

Net income (loss) attributable to the equity holders of the parent per share

▶ Basic earnings per share		€(0.12)	€0.68	€0.43
▶ Diluted earnings per share		(0.12)	0.68	0.42

Net income (loss) before discontinued operations attributable to the equity holders of the parent per share

▶ Basic earnings per share		(0.23)	0.60	0.27
▶ Diluted earnings per share		(0.23)	0.60	0.26

Net income (loss) of discontinued operations per share

▶ Basic earnings per share		0.11	0.08	0.16
▶ Diluted earnings per share		0.11	0.08	0.16

EXHIBIT 2	Alcatel-Lucent Consolidated Balance Sheets (Euros in Millions)

31 December	2006	2005	2004
Goodwill, net	€10,977	€3,772	€3,774
Intangible assets, net	5,347	819	705
Goodwill and intangible assets, net	16,324	4,591	4,479
Property, plant and equipment, net	2,026	1,111	1,095
Share in net assets of equity affiliates	682	606	604
Other non-current financial assets, net	803	306	554
Deferred tax assets	1,692	1,768	1,638
Prepaid pension costs	2,734	294	287
Marketable securities, net	697	—	—
Other non-current assets	203	468	332
Total non-current assets	25,161	9,144	8,989
Inventories and work in progress, net	2,259	1,438	1,273
Amounts due from customers on construction contracts	615	917	729
Trade receivables and related accounts, net	3,877	3,420	2,693
Advances and progress payments	87	124	90
Other current assets	1,006	827	1,418
Assets held for sale	2,117	50	196
Current income taxes	256	45	78
Marketable securities, net	1,245	640	552
Cash and cash equivalents	4,749	4,510	4,611
Total current assets	16,211	11,971	11,640
Total assets	€41,372	€21,115	€20,629

(Exhibit continued on next page . . .)

EXHIBIT 2   (continued)

Capital stock (€2 nominal value: 2,309,679,141 shares issued at 31 December 2006; 1,428,541,640 ordinary shares issued at 31 December 2005; and 1,305,455,461 ordinary shares issued and 120,780,519 shares to be issued related to Orane at 31 December 2004)	€4,619	€2,857	€2,852
Additional paid-in capital	16,443	8,308	8,226
Less treasury stock at cost	(1,572)	(1,575)	(1,607)
Retained earnings, fair value and other reserves	(3,706)	(4,467)	(4,951)
Cumulative translation adjustments	(115)	174	(183)
Net income (loss)—attributable to the equity holders of the parent	(176)	930	576
Shareholders' equity—attributable to the equity holders of the parent	15,493	6,227	4,913
Minority interests	498	477	373
Total shareholders' equity	15,991	6,704	5,286
Pensions, retirement indemnities and other post-retirement benefits	5,331	1,468	1,466
Bonds and notes issued, long-term	4,901	2,393	3,089
Other long-term debt	147	359	402
Deferred tax liabilities	2,524	162	132
Other non-current liabilities	303	295	201
Total non-current liabilities	13,206	4,677	5,290
Provisions	2,331	1,621	2,049
Current portion of long-term debt	1,161	1,046	1,115
Customers' deposits and advances	778	1,144	973
Amounts due to customers on construction contracts	273	138	133
Trade payables and related accounts	4,022	3,755	3,350
Liabilities related to disposal groups held for sale	1,606	—	97
Current income tax liabilities	66	99	179
Other current liabilities	1,938	1,931	2,157
Total current liabilities	12,175	9,734	10,053
Total liabilities and shareholders' equity	€41,372	€21,115	€20,629

| EXHIBIT 3 | Alcatel-Lucent Selected Notes to Consolidated Financial Statements |

Note 1—Summary of Significant Accounting Policies

(i) Inventories and work in progress

Inventories and work in progress are valued at the lower of cost (including indirect production costs where applicable) or net realizable value. Cost is primarily calculated on a weighted average basis. Net realizable value is the estimated sales revenue for a normal period of activity less expected completion and selling costs.

Note 2—Principal Uncertainties Regarding the Use of Estimates

(a) Valuation allowance for inventories and work in progress

Inventories and work in progress are measured at the lower of cost or net realizable value. Valuation allowances for inventories and work in progress are calculated based on an analysis of foreseeable changes in demand, technology or the market, in order to determine obsolete or excess inventories and work in progress.

The valuation allowances are accounted for in cost of sales or in restructuring costs depending on the nature of the amounts concerned.

The impact of inventory and work in progress write-down on Alcatel-Lucent income before tax was a net charge of €77 million in 2006 (a net charge of €18 million in 2005 and a net gain of €20 million in 2004), representing new write-down taken in 2006 which more than offset the reversal of existing provisions of €98 million due to asset sales that occurred in 2006.[1]

Note 19—Inventories and Work in Progress

(a) Analysis of Net Value

(in Millions of Euros)	2006	2005	2004
Raw materials and goods	542	467	501
Work in progress excluding construction contracts	752	712	592
Finished goods	1,320	653	645
Gross value (excluding construction contracts)	2,614	1,832	1,738
Valuation allowance	(355)	(394)	(465)
Net value (excluding construction contracts)	2,259	1,438	1,273
Work in progress on construction contracts, gross (*)	137	281	291
Valuation allowance	(23)	(29)	(30)
Work in progress on construction contracts, net	114	252	261
Total, net	2,373	1,690	1,534

(*) Included in the amounts due from/to construction contracts

[1] For 2006, €175 million was added to the allowance for inventory write-downs; however, €98 million was reversed because inventory that had been written down in earlier years was sold in 2006. Because the company uses a valuation allowance, the inventory that is sold would have the valuation allowance associated with the sold inventory removed from the total valuation.

(Exhibit continued on next page . . .)

EXHIBIT 3	(continued)		

**(b) Change in Valuation Allowance
(in Millions of Euros)** | **2006** | **2005** | **2004** |

	2006	2005	2004
At January 1	(423)	(495)	(978)
(Additions)/reversals	(77)	(18)	20
Utilization	54	131	427
Changes in consolidation group	54	11	40
Net effect of exchange rate changes and other changes	14	(52)	(4)
At December 31	(378)	(423)	(495)

EXAMPLE 4

Financial Analysis Illustration

The consolidated income statements and consolidated balance sheets for Alcatel-Lucent (NYSE: ALU) are provided in Exhibits 1 and 2, respectively. Exhibit 3 includes selected financial note disclosures concerning ALU's inventory accounting policies.

1. What are ALU's inventory turnover ratios, number of days of inventory ratios, gross margin ratios, current ratios, return on total assets ratios, and debt-to-equity ratios for 2006, 2005, and 2004, respectively, under the weighted average cost method?

2. What trends are apparent for ALU's inventory turnover ratio, number of days of inventory, and gross profit margin ratios?

3. If ALU had used the FIFO inventory method instead of the weighted average cost method during 2004, 2005, and 2006, what would be the effect on ALU's reported cost of goods sold and inventory values? What would be the directional impact on the financial ratios that were calculated in part 1 above for ALU?

Solution to 1: The financial ratios are as follows:

	2006	2005	2004
Inventory turnover ratio	3.64	4.93	4.85
Number of days of inventory	100.4 days	74.1 days	75.3 days
Gross profit margin	33.14%	36.85%	39.89%
Current ratio	1.33	1.23	1.16
Return on assets	−0.32%	4.60%	3.13%
Debt-to-equity ratio	1.59	2.15	2.90

▶ The inventory turnover ratio (cost of goods sold ÷ ending inventory) is 3.64 (€8,212 ÷ €2,259) for 2006, 4.93 (€7,085 ÷ €1,438) for 2005, and 4.85 (€6,169 ÷ €1,273) for 2004.[3]

▶ The number of days of inventory (365 days ÷ inventory turnover ratio) is 100.4 days (365 days ÷ 3.64) for 2006, 74.1 days (365 days ÷ 4.93) for 2005, and 75.3 days (365 days ÷ 4.85) for 2004.

▶ The gross profit margin (gross profit ÷ total revenue) is 33.14% (€4,070 ÷ €12,282) for 2006, 36.85% (€4,134 ÷ €11,219) for 2005, and 39.89% (€4,094 ÷ €10,263) for 2004.

▶ The current ratio (current assets ÷ current liabilities) for ALU is 1.33 (€16,211 ÷ €12,175) for 2006, 1.23 (€11,971 ÷ €9,734) for 2005, and 1.16 (€11,640 ÷ €10,053) for 2004.

▶ The return on assets (net income ÷ ending total assets) is −0.32% (−€131 ÷ €41,372) for 2006, 4.60% (€971 ÷ €21,115) for 2005, and 3.13% (€645 ÷ €20,629) for 2004.[3]

▶ The debt-to-equity ratio (total debt ÷ total shareholders' equity) for ALU is 1.59 (€25,381 ÷ €15,991) for 2006, 2.15 (€14,411 ÷ €6,704) for 2005, and 2.90 (€15,343 ÷ €5,286) for 2004.

Solution to 2: The inventory turnover ratio declined sharply in 2006, and the number of days of inventory increased in 2006 from the relatively constant levels that existed in 2005 and 2004. ALU's gross profit margin declined sharply in 2005 and declined sharply again in 2006 (more than a 3 percent margin erosion in each successive year from 2004). The analyst should investigate the reasons for the sharp decline in ALU's gross profit margin.

Solution to 3: If inventory replacement costs were increasing during 2004, 2005, and 2006 (and inventory quantity levels were stable or increasing), ALU's cost of goods sold would have been lower under the FIFO inventory method than what it reported under the weighted average cost method (assuming no inventory write-downs that would otherwise neutralize the differences between the inventory methods). Consequently, ALU's reported gross profit, net income, and retained

---

[3] For simplicity of example, the ending values of balance sheet accounts were used in calculating the financial ratios in this example (e.g., ending inventory, ending total assets). In practice, it is generally preferable to use average values (e.g., average inventory, average total assets).

earnings would also be higher for those years. Because FIFO always allocates the oldest inventory costs to cost of goods sold, the reported cost of goods sold would be lower under the FIFO method. Under the FIFO method, inventory carrying values would be higher than under weighted average cost because the more recently purchased inventory items would be included in inventory at their higher costs (again assuming no inventory write-downs that would otherwise neutralize the differences between the inventory methods).

▶ The inventory turnover ratios would all be lower under the FIFO inventory method because the numerator (cost of goods sold) would be lower and the denominator (inventory) would be higher than what was reported by ALU under the weighted average cost method.

▶ The number of days of inventory ratios would all be longer under the FIFO inventory method because the inventory turnover ratios would be lower under FIFO.

▶ The gross profit margin ratios would all be higher under the FIFO inventory method because cost of goods sold would be lower under FIFO than under the weighted average method.

▶ The current ratios would all be higher under the FIFO inventory method because inventory carrying values would be higher under FIFO (current liabilities would be the same under both methods).

▶ The return on assets ratios would all be higher under the FIFO inventory method because the incremental profit added to the numerator (net income) has a greater impact than the incremental increase to the denominator (total assets). By way of example, assume that a company has €3 million in net income and €100 million in total assets using the weighted average cost method. If the company earns another €1 million in net income by using FIFO instead of weighted average cost, it would then also have another €1 million in total assets (after tax). Based on this example, the return on assets under the weighted average cost method is 3.00 percent (€3/€100), and 3.96 percent (€4/€101) under the FIFO method.

▶ The debt-to-equity ratios would all be lower under the FIFO inventory method because retained earnings would be higher under FIFO (again assuming no inventory write-downs that would otherwise neutralize the differences between the inventory methods).

If inventory replacement costs were decreasing during 2004, 2005, and 2006 (and inventory quantity levels were stable or increasing), ALU's cost of goods sold would have been higher under the FIFO inventory method than what it reported under the weighted average cost method (assuming no inventory write-downs that would otherwise neutralize the differences between the inventory methods). As a consequence, the ratio assessment that was performed above would result in directly opposite conclusions.

LIFO ACCOUNTING METHOD UNDER U.S. GAAP   4

In the United States, there are four basic methods that companies may choose from to report inventory value and to allocate inventory cost. They are the specific identification, weighted average cost, first-in, first-out (FIFO), and last-in, first-out (LIFO) methods. The specific identification, weighted average cost, and FIFO methods are also permissible under IFRS; however, the LIFO method is not. In the United States, the LIFO method is widely used (approximately 30 percent of U.S. companies use the LIFO method) because of potential income tax savings.[4] Under the "LIFO conformity rule," the U.S. tax code requires that companies using LIFO for tax purposes must also use LIFO for financial reporting.

4.1 The LIFO Method

The LIFO method assumes that companies sell their most recently purchased inventory units first before selling the next most recently purchased inventory units, and so on. Under this method, ending inventory will consist of those units that have been held the longest and valued at their historic purchase costs.

EXAMPLE 5

LIFO Inventory Method Illustration

American Sales, Inc. (ASI), a hypothetical company, sells portable hair dryers on a retail basis. ASI began operations in 2006, during which it purchased 50,000 hair dryers and sold 46,000 hair dryers. The hair dryers were purchased at a cost of $20.00 per unit. In 2007, ASI purchased another 60,000 hair dryers at a cost of $23.00 per unit. ASI sold 55,000 hair dryers during 2007. ASI's sales price for hair dryers was $30.00 per unit in 2006 and $33.00 per unit in 2007. ASI uses the LIFO inventory method.

1. What is the reported cost of goods sold on ASI's income statement for 2007 under LIFO?

2. What is the reported gross profit on ASI's income statement for 2007 on a LIFO basis?

3. What is the carrying value of inventory on ASI's balance sheet at year-end 2007 under LIFO?

4. What would be the reported cost of goods sold, gross profit, and inventory carrying value if ASI used the weighted average cost inventory method instead of LIFO?

5. What would be the reported cost of goods sold, gross profit, and inventory carrying value if ASI used the FIFO inventory method instead of LIFO?

---

[4] The tax consequences and their effect on cash flows are a unique consequence of the U.S. tax system. Many countries specify the tax treatment independent of whether a particular treatment is adopted in the accounts.

Solution to 1: ASI's cost of goods sold for 2007 is $1,265,000 (55,000 hair dryers sold at $23.00 cost per hair dryer). Under the LIFO method, the cost flow assumption is that the most recently purchased inventory units are the first units to be sold. Because ASI purchased more hair dryers than it sold in 2007, the units allocated to cost of goods sold are those that were purchased in 2007 at a unit cost of $23.00 per hair dryer.

Solution to 2: ASI's gross profit for 2007 is $550,000. The reported sales are $1,815,000 (55,000 hair dryers sold at $33.00 sales price per hair dryer) and the reported cost of goods sold is $1,265,000.

Solution to 3: ASI's inventory carrying value at year-end 2007 is $195,000 (4,000 hair dryers purchased in 2006 at $20.00 per hair dryer plus 5,000 hair dryers purchased in 2007 at $23.00 per hair dryer). Under the LIFO method, the ending inventory consists of those units that have been held the longest at their historical purchase cost. Because there were 4,000 unsold hair dryers at the end of 2006 (ASI's first year of operations), ASI's beginning inventory for 2007 carries those 4,000 hair dryers at a historical cost of $80,000. Furthermore, because 5,000 more hair dryers were purchased than sold by ASI in 2007, the ending inventory at year-end 2007 will increase by an additional $115,000 over year-end 2006.

Solution to 4: Under the weighted average cost method, inventory value and inventory cost recognition are determined by using a weighted average mix of the actual costs incurred for all inventory items. The weighted average cost of the hair dryer inventory available for sale in 2007 is $1,460,000 (4,000 hair dryers in beginning inventory purchased at $20.00 cost per hair dryer and the 60,000 hair dryers purchased in 2007 at $23.00 cost per hair dryer). Accordingly, the weighted average cost of a hair dryer inventory unit that was available for sale in 2007 is $22.8125 ($1,460,000 total purchase cost of the hair dryer inventory available for sale divided by 64,000 hair dryers available). The cost of goods sold is thus $1,254,688 (55,000 hair dryers sold at $22.8125 weighted average cost per hair dryer). ASI's gross profit for 2007 is $560,312. The reported sales are $1,815,000 (55,000 hair dryers sold at $33.00 sales price per hair dryer). Ending inventory carrying value at year-end 2007 under the weighted average cost method is $205,313 (9,000 hair dryers remaining in inventory at a weighted average cost of $22.8125 cost per hair dryer).

Solution to 5: Under the FIFO method, the cost flow assumption is that the oldest inventory units acquired are the first units to be sold. ASI's cost of goods sold for 2007 is $1,253,000 (4,000 hair dryers sold at $20.00 cost per hair dryer and 51,000 hair dryers sold at $23.00 cost per hair dryer). ASI's gross profit for 2007 is $562,000. The reported sales are $1,815,000 (55,000 hair dryers sold at $33.00 sales price per hair dryer). Ending inventory thus consists of those inventory units most recently acquired. The inventory carrying value at year-end 2007 under

FIFO is $207,000 (9,000 hair dryers remaining in inventory from those purchased in 2007 at $23.00 cost per hair dryer).

The following table summarizes the cost of goods sold, ending inventory, and gross profit that were calculated for each of the three inventory methods. Note that any difference in gross profit among the three methods is attributable by the same amount of difference in their respective ending inventory balances. Finally, it should be noted that because inventory unit purchase costs increased in 2007 relative to the inventory unit purchase costs that were incurred in 2006 (the initial year of business), the LIFO method will report the lowest gross profit and the lowest ending inventory balance, and the FIFO method will report the highest gross profit and the highest ending inventory balance. Whether inventory unit purchase costs are increasing or decreasing over time, the weighted average cost method will always result in a gross profit and ending inventory balance that falls somewhere between the LIFO and FIFO methods.

Inventory Method	LIFO	Weighted Average Cost	FIFO
Cost of goods sold	$1,265,000	$1,254,688	$1,253,000
Ending inventory	195,000	205,312	207,000
Total cost of goods available for sale	$1,460,000	$1,460,000	$1,460,000
Gross profit	$550,000	$560,312	$562,000

In general, the weighted average cost method valuations assigned to cost of goods sold and ending inventory are typically near or approximately the valuations that would otherwise be allocated under the FIFO method. This is primarily due to the fact that the cost flow allocation using the weighted average method closely trails the cost flows that are allocated under the FIFO method. Because the differences between the two inventory methods are often immaterial, an analyst will not typically make adjustments when comparing a company using the weighted average cost method with a company using FIFO. This is not the case, however, when the analyst is comparing a company using the LIFO method with a company using FIFO. Over a period of time, a continuous cycle of increasing inventory unit purchase costs and stable or rising inventory unit levels will often lead to significant and material differences between the LIFO and FIFO inventory methods. For this reason, the analyst must carefully evaluate valuations allocated to cost of goods sold and ending inventory for LIFO reporting companies when comparing them to FIFO reporting companies.

4.2 LIFO Reserve

Under the LIFO method, inventory write-downs are less likely to occur than under other inventory methods (assuming a long-term environment of rising inventory costs). This is mostly attributable to LIFO inventories being valued at older and lower costs (and thus less likely to be carried at values that are greater than their net realizable values) than are inventories valued under the FIFO and weighted average cost methods.

Under U.S. GAAP, companies that use the LIFO inventory method must disclose in their financial notes the amount of the **LIFO reserve** or the amount that would have been reported in inventory if the FIFO method had been used. The LIFO reserve is the difference between inventory reported at FIFO and inventory reported at LIFO (FIFO inventory value less LIFO inventory value). When inventory unit costs are rising over time, the FIFO inventory value will always exceed the LIFO inventory value. Accordingly, when inventory unit costs are rising over time and new LIFO unit layers are added to inventory, the LIFO reserve will increase. Likewise, to the extent that older LIFO unit layers are depleted, the LIFO reserve will decrease. The analyst may, therefore, determine whether LIFO liquidations are occurring by closely examining the change in the LIFO reserve from year to year (or by deriving the LIFO reserve for each year by taking the difference between inventory reported at FIFO and inventory reported at LIFO).

The LIFO reserve disclosure may also be used by the analyst to compare a U.S. company that uses LIFO accounting with another company in its industry that uses FIFO accounting. This comparison is especially critical when comparing a U.S. company that uses the LIFO accounting method with international companies for which this method is not allowable.

EXHIBIT 4	Caterpillar Inc. Consolidated Results of Operation (Dollars in Millions except per Share Data)		
For the Years Ended 31 December	**2006**	**2005**	**2004**
Sales and revenues:			
Sales of Machinery and Engines	$38,869	$34,006	$28,336
Revenue of Financial Products	2,648	2,333	1,970
Total sales and revenues	41,517	36,339	30,306
Operating costs:			
Cost of goods sold	29,549	26,558	22,497
Selling, general and administrative expenses	3,706	3,190	2,926
Research and development expenses	1,347	1,084	928
Interest expense of Financial Products	1,023	768	524
Other operating expenses	971	955	747
Total operating costs	36,596	32,555	27,622

(Exhibit continued on next page . . .)

EXHIBIT 4	**(continued)**		

Operating profit	4,921	3,784	2,684
Interest expense excluding Financial Products	274	260	230
Other income (expense)	214	377	253
Consolidated profit before taxes	4,861	3,901	2,707
Provision for income taxes	1,405	1,120	731
Profit of consolidated companies	3,456	2,781	1,976
Equity in profit of unconsolidated affiliated companies	81	73	59
Profit	$3,537	$2,854	$2,035
Profit per common share	$5.37	$4.21	$2.97
Profit per common share—diluted	$5.17	$4.04	$2.88
Weighted-average common shares outstanding (millions):			
▶ Basic	658.7	678.4	684.5
▶ Diluted	683.8	705.8	707.4
Cash dividends declared per common share	$1.15	$0.96	$0.80

EXHIBIT 5	**Caterpillar Inc. Consolidated Financial Position (Dollars in Millions)**		

31 December	**2006**	**2005**	**2004**
Assets			
Current assets:			
Cash and short-term investments	$ 530	$ 1,108	$ 445
Receivables—trade and other	8,168	7,526	7,463
Receivables—finance	6,804	6,442	5,182
Deferred and refundable income taxes	733	255	330
Prepaid expenses and other current assets	507	2,146	1,369
Inventories	6,351	5,224	4,675
Total current assets	$23,093	$22,701	$19,464
Property and equipment—net	8,851	7,988	7,682
Long-term receivables—trade and other	860	1,037	764
Long-term receivables—finance	11,531	10,301	9,903
Investments in unconsolidated companies	562	565	517
Deferred income taxes	1,949	857	742
Intangible assets	387	424	315
Goodwill	1,904	1,451	1,450
Other assets	1,742	1,745	2,258
Total assets	$50,879	$47,069	$43,095

(Exhibit continued on next page . . .)

EXHIBIT 5	(continued)

Liabilities

Current liabilities:

Short-term borrowings:

Machinery and Engines	$ 165	$ 871	$ 93
Financial Products	4,990	4,698	4,064
Accounts payable	4,085	3,412	3,524
Accrued expenses	2,923	2,617	2,261
Accrued wages, salaries and employee benefits	938	1,601	1,543
Customer advances	921	454	503
Dividends payable	194	168	141
Deferred and current income taxes payable	575	528	259

Long-term debt due within one year:

Machinery and Engines	418	340	6
Financial Products	4,043	4,159	3,525
Total current liabilities	19,252	18,848	15,919

Long-term debt due after one year:

Machinery and Engines	3,694	2,717	3,663
Financial Products	13,986	12,960	12,174
Liability for postemployment benefits	5,879	3,161	3,126
Deferred income taxes and other liabilities	1,209	951	746
Total liabilities	44,020	38,637	35,628

Commitments and contingencies (Notes 22 and 23)

Stockholders' equity

Common stock of $1.00 par value:

Authorized shares: 900,000,000

Issued shares (2006, 2005 and 2004—814,894,624) at paid-in amount	2,465	1,859	1,231
Treasury stock (2006—169,086,448 shares; 2005—144,027,405 shares and 2004—129,020,726 shares) at cost	(7,352)	(4,637)	(3,277)
Profit employed in the business	14,593	11,808	9,937
Accumulated other comprehensive income	(2,847)	(598)	(424)
Total stockholders' equity	6,859	8,432	7,467
Total liabilities and stockholders' equity	$50,879	$47,069	$43,095

| EXHIBIT 6 | Caterpillar Inc. Selected Notes to Consolidated Financial Statements |

Note 1. Operations and Summary of Significant Accounting Policies

D. Inventories

Inventories are stated at the lower of cost or market. Cost is principally determined using the last-in, first-out (LIFO) method. The value of inventories on the LIFO basis represented about 75% of total inventories at December 31, 2006 and about 80% of total inventories at December 31, 2005 and 2004.

If the FIFO (first-in, first-out) method had been in use, inventories would have been $2,403 million, $2,345 million and $2,124 million higher than reported at December 31, 2006, 2005 and 2004, respectively.

L. New accounting standards

SFAS 151—In November 2004, the Financial Accounting Standards Board (FASB) issued Statement of Financial Accounting Standards No. 151 (SFAS 151), "Inventory Costs—an amendment of ARB No. 43, Chapter 4." SFAS 151 discusses the general principles applicable to the pricing of inventory. Paragraph 5 of ARB 43, Chapter 4 provides guidance on allocating certain costs to inventory. This Statement amends ARB 43, Chapter 4, to clarify that abnormal amounts of idle facility expense, freight, handling costs, and wasted materials (spoilage) should be recognized as current-period charges. In addition, this Statement requires that allocation of fixed production overheads to the costs of conversion be based on the normal capacity of production facilities. As required by SFAS 151, we adopted this new accounting standard on January 1, 2006. The adoption of SFAS 151 did not have a material impact on our financial statements.

EXAMPLE 6

LIFO Reserve Illustration

The Consolidated Results of Operations (Income Statements) and Consolidated Financial Position (Balance Sheets) for Caterpillar Inc. (NYSE: CAT) are provided in Exhibits 4 and 5, respectively. Exhibit 6 includes selected financial note disclosures concerning CAT's inventory accounting policies.

1. What inventory value would CAT report on its 2006 balance sheet if it used the FIFO inventory method instead of LIFO?

2. What amount would cost of goods sold be on CAT's 2006 income statement if it used the FIFO inventory method instead of LIFO?

3. What amount would net income (profit) be on CAT's 2006 income statement if it used the FIFO inventory method instead of LIFO?

4. What is the cumulative amount of income tax savings that CAT has generated through 2006 by using the LIFO inventory method instead of FIFO?

5. What amounts would be added to CAT's deferred income tax liabilities and retained earnings (profit employed in the business) respectively, at 31 December 2006 if CAT used the FIFO inventory method instead of LIFO?

6. What is CAT's inventory turnover ratio, number of days of inventory ratio, gross margin ratio, current ratio, return on total assets ratio, and debt-to-equity ratio for 2006 under the LIFO method? What would CAT's inventory turnover ratio, number of days of inventory ratio, gross margin ratio, current ratio, return on total assets ratio, and debt-to-equity ratio be for 2006 if the company used the FIFO inventory method instead of LIFO?

Solution to 1: CAT's 2006 inventory value would be $8,754 (in millions) if the FIFO inventory method was used instead of LIFO. Exhibit 5 reports that CAT's inventories (valued on a LIFO basis) at 31 December 2006 were $6,351. Financial note D in Exhibit 6 discloses that CAT's inventories would have been $2,403 higher than reported at 31 December 2006 if the FIFO method had been used instead.

Solution to 2: CAT's cost of goods sold for 2006 would be $29,491 (in millions) if the FIFO inventory method was used instead of LIFO. Exhibit 4 reports that CAT's cost of goods sold (valued on a LIFO basis) for 2006 was $29,549. Financial note D in Exhibit 6 discloses that CAT's inventories would have been $2,403 higher and $2,345 higher than reported at 31 December 2006 and 2005, respectively, if the FIFO method had been used instead. Because the LIFO reserve increased by $58 during 2006 ($2,403 LIFO Reserve at 31 December 2006 less $2,345 LIFO reserve at 31 December 2005), the reported cost of goods sold would accordingly be lower by that amount if the FIFO method had been used instead of LIFO.

Solution to 3: CAT's net income (profit) for 2006 would be $3,578 (in millions) if the FIFO inventory method was used instead of LIFO. Exhibit 4 reports that CAT's profit (based on the LIFO method) for 2006 was $3,537. Under the FIFO method, CAT's cost of goods sold would have been $58 lower than what CAT reported under the LIFO method (determined in the solution to 2 above). The resulting $58 increase to CAT's gross profit would, however, be reduced by income taxes of $17 because CAT's 2006 income tax rate was approximately 29% ($1,405 provision for income taxes ÷ $4,861 consolidated profit before taxes). CAT's profit for 2006 would thus be $41 ($58 incremental gross profit less $17 incremental income tax expense) higher if the FIFO inventory method had been used instead of LIFO.

Solution to 4: The cumulative amount of income tax savings that CAT has generated by using the LIFO method instead of FIFO is approximately $697 (in millions). Financial note D in Exhibit 6 discloses that the LIFO reserve at 31 December 2006 is $2,403. Accordingly, under the FIFO inventory method, cumulative gross profits would have been $2,403 higher. Because CAT's income tax rate is approximately 29% (determined in the solution to 3 above), the cumulative additional income tax expense would be approximately $697 ($2,403 LIFO reserve × 29% income tax rate). The estimated savings would be higher (lower) if income tax rates in prior years were higher (lower) than the 29% average tax rate incurred by CAT in 2006.

Solution to 5: The amount that would be added to CAT's deferred income tax liabilities at 31 December 2006 is $697 (in millions). The $2,403 LIFO reserve would be taxed at an income tax rate of approximately 29%. Likewise, the amount that would be added to CAT's retained earnings (profit employed in the business) is $1,706 because CAT would keep approximately 71 percent (after income taxes) of the $2,403 LIFO reserve.

Solution to 6: The LIFO and FIFO ratios are as follows:

	LIFO	FIFO
Inventory turnover ratio	4.65	3.37
Number of days of inventory	78.5 days	108.3 days
Gross profit margin	28.83%	28.97%
Current ratio	1.20	1.28
Return on assets	6.95%	6.72%
Debt-to-equity ratio	6.42	5.22

The inventory turnover ratio (cost of goods sold ÷ ending inventory) under LIFO is 4.65 ($29,549 ÷ $6,351) and under FIFO is 3.37 ($29,491 ÷ $8,754). The ratio is higher under LIFO than under FIFO because, in a long-term environment of rising inventory costs, cost of goods sold will be higher and inventory carrying value will be lower under LIFO than what it would otherwise be under FIFO.[5]

The number of days of inventory (365 days ÷ inventory turnover ratio) under LIFO is 78.5 days (365 days ÷ 4.65) and under FIFO is 108.3 days (365 days ÷ 3.37). The number of days of inventory is lower under LIFO than under FIFO because the inventory turnover ratio is higher under LIFO in a long-term environment of rising inventory costs.

The gross profit margin (gross profit ÷ total revenue) under LIFO is 28.83 percent [($41,517 − $29,549) ÷ $41,517] and under FIFO is 28.97 percent [($41,517 − $29,491) ÷ $41,517]. The gross profit margin is lower under LIFO than under FIFO because cost of goods sold is higher under LIFO in an environment of rising inventory costs.

The current ratio (current assets ÷ current liabilities) for CAT under LIFO is 1.20 ($23,093 ÷ $19,252) and under FIFO is 1.28 [($23,093 + $2,403 LIFO reserve) ÷ ($19,252 + $697 deferred income tax liability)]. The current ratio is lower under LIFO primarily because

---

[5] As before, the ending values of balance sheet accounts were used in calculating the financial ratios in this example. In practice, it is generally preferable to use average values.

inventories are carried at a lower value (in an environment of rising inventory costs) than what it would otherwise be carried at under FIFO.

The return on assets (net income ÷ ending total assets) under LIFO is 6.95 percent ($3,537 ÷ $50,879) and under FIFO is 6.72 percent [$3,578 ÷ ($50,879 + $2,403 LIFO reserve)]. In this instance, the return on assets is higher under LIFO than under FIFO. This is due to the current year's increase in the LIFO reserve having less of an impact on FIFO net income than the impact of the total LIFO reserve on FIFO total assets.

Lastly, the debt-to-equity ratio (total debt ÷ total shareholders' equity) for CAT under LIFO is 6.42 ($44,020 ÷ $6,859) and under FIFO is 5.22 [($44,020 + $697 additional deferred income tax liability from the LIFO reserve) ÷ ($6,859 + $1,706 after-tax addition to retained earnings from the LIFO reserve)]. In this instance, the ratio is higher under LIFO than under FIFO. This is due to the current year's increase in the deferred income tax liability having less of an impact on FIFO total debt than the total after-tax addition to retained earnings from the LIFO reserve on FIFO total equity.

4.3 LIFO Liquidations

LIFO liquidation occurs when the number of units in ending inventory declines from the number of units that were present at the beginning of the year. This occurs whenever the sale of units from inventory exceeds the purchase or production of new inventory units within any given year. If inventory unit costs have generally risen from year to year, the phenomenon of inventory-related "phantom" gross profits occurs. Inventory phantom gross profits occur because the lower inventory costs of the liquidated units are matched with unit sales to generate a higher gross profit than what would otherwise occur if those sold units were matched with units purchased at current replacement costs. Phantom inventory profits are one-time accounting events that are not sustainable in the future. Accordingly, the analyst must be attuned to the fact that some companies may potentially manipulate and inflate their reported gross profits at critical times by intentionally liquidating older layers of LIFO inventory.

Companies may also incur LIFO liquidations because of recession, labor strikes, or declining product demand. The ensuing liquidation may result in outsized phantom profits that boost reported gross profit during economic downturns (a somewhat paradoxical phenomenon).

LIFO liquidations are most likely to occur if a company uses a specific-goods LIFO approach. If LIFO layers of individual inventory items are temporarily depleted and not replaced by fiscal year-end, LIFO liquidation will occur, resulting in phantom profits. In order to mitigate this liquidation problem, companies can opt to combine individual inventory items into inventory pools or groups of items that are similar in nature. Under the pooled approach, a decrease of some individual inventory items may be offset by an increase in other individual items within the pool.

EXAMPLE 7

LIFO Liquidation Illustration

Industrial Fan Sales, Inc. (IFS), a hypothetical company, sells an industrial grade fan at retail and has been in business since 2004. Exhibit 7 provides relevant data and financial statement information about IFS's inventory purchases and sales of fan inventory for the years 2004 through 2007. IFS uses the LIFO inventory method. What is IFS's inventory phantom gross profit for 2007?

EXHIBIT 7	IFS Financial Statement Information under LIFO			
	2004	**2005**	**2006**	**2007**
Fans units purchased	12,000	12,000	12,000	12,000
Purchase cost per fan	$100	$105	$110	$115
Fans units sold	10,000	10,000	10,000	16,000
Sales price per fan	$200	$205	$210	$215
LIFO Method				
Beginning inventory	$0	$200,000	$410,000	$630,000
Purchases	1,200,000	1,260,000	1,320,000	1,380,000
Goods available for sale	1,200,000	1,460,000	1,730,000	2,010,000
Ending inventory	(200,000)	(410,000)	(630,000)	(200,000)
Cost of goods sold	$1,000,000	1,050,000	$1,100,000	$1,810,000
Income Statement				
Sales	$2,000,000	$2,050,000	$2,100,000	$3,440,000
Cost of goods sold	1,000,000	1,050,000	1,100,000	1,810,000
Gross profit	$1,000,000	$1,000,000	$1,000,000	$1,630,000
Balance Sheet				
Inventory	$200,000	$410,000	$630,000	$200,000

Solution: IFS's phantom gross profit for 2007 is $30,000. The reported gross profit is $1,630,000. If IFS had purchased 16,000 fans in 2007 rather than 12,000 fans, the cost of goods sold under the LIFO method would have been $1,840,000 (16,000 fans sold at $115.00 purchase cost per fan), and the reported gross profit would have been $1,600,000 ($3,440,000 reported sales less $1,840,000 cost of goods sold). The phantom gross profit is thus $30,000 ($1,630,000 reported gross profit less the $1,600,000 gross profit that would have been reported without the LIFO liquidation). The phantom gross profit may alternatively be determined by multiplying the number of units liquidated times the difference between the replacement cost of the units liquidated and their historical purchase cost. For IFS, the $30,000 phantom gross profit would be the 2,000 fans that are liquidated from its LIFO inventory from 2006 multiplied by $5.00 per fan ($115.00 replacement cost per fan less the $110.00 historical cost per fan) plus the 2,000 fans that are liquidated from its LIFO inventory from 2005 multiplied by $10.00 per fan ($115.00 replacement cost per fan less the $105.00 historical cost per fan).

4.4 Inventory Financial Note Disclosures

As stated in Section 4.2 above, U.S. GAAP requires companies that use the LIFO inventory method to disclose in their financial notes the amount of the LIFO reserve or the amount that would have been reported in inventory if the FIFO method had been used (see note D in Exhibit 6 for an example of this disclosure). In addition to this disclosure, U.S. GAAP requires all companies, regardless of the inventory method used, to disclose any changes in accounting for their inventories. Financial note L in Exhibit 6 describes Caterpillar's changes in accounting for its inventories because of the adoption of SFAS No. 151 (which was mandatory for all manufacturing companies under U.S. GAAP) in 2006. Another required financial note disclosure for manufacturing companies is the breakout of the inventory values for raw materials, work-in-process, and finished goods inventories if these values are not already separately reported on the balance sheet. Exhibit 8 below provides an example of this required disclosure from Note 9 of Caterpillar's 2006 annual report. See that the total inventories in the note disclosure ($6,351 for CAT at 31 December 2006) must reconcile to the inventories amount stated on the balance sheet (the $6,351 for inventories in Exhibit 5).

EXHIBIT 8	Caterpillar Inc. Selected Notes to Consolidated Financial Statements

Note 9. Inventories

31 December (Millions of Dollars)	2006	2005	2004
Raw materials	$2,182	$1,689	$1,592
Work-in-process	977	814	664
Finished goods	2,915	2,493	2,209
Supplies	277	228	210
Total inventories	$6,351	$5,224	$4,675

We had long-term material purchase obligations of approximately $231 million at December 31, 2006.

5   EFFECTS OF INVENTORY METHOD CHOICE

As was discussed earlier, the choice of inventory method would not be much of an issue if inventory unit costs remained relatively constant from period to period because the allocation of cost flow between cost of goods sold and inventory carrying value would be very similar under the weighted average cost, FIFO, and LIFO inventory methods. But because inventory unit costs typically change from period to period, the choice of inventory method does in fact matter to a company. In an environment of rising inventory unit costs and generally constant or increasing inventory quantities, U.S. companies have an economic incentive to use the LIFO method because of the related income tax savings.

5.1 Financial Statement Effects of Using LIFO

In an environment of rising inventory unit costs and constant or increasing inventory quantities, LIFO (in comparison with FIFO) will allocate a greater amount of cost flow to cost of goods sold on the income statement and a lesser amount of cost flow to the carrying value of inventory on the balance sheet. Accordingly, because cost of goods sold will be greater under LIFO, a company's gross profit, operating profit, and income before taxes will be lower. Income tax expense will thus be lower under LIFO, causing the company's net operating cash flow to increase. On the balance sheet, a lower inventory carrying value will also cause reported working capital and total assets to be lower.

When the financial statement impact from using LIFO is significantly different from the impact of using FIFO, the company's profitability, liquidity, activity, and solvency ratios will be materially affected as well. When confronted with these conditions, a restatement to the FIFO method (see Example 5) is critical for the analyst to make a valid comparison with other companies using FIFO (or other companies reporting under IFRS).

Although an environment of rising inventory unit costs is far more prevalent than an environment of falling unit prices, there are some industries (such as the computer hardware and peripheral equipment industry) where declining unit prices are the norm. Companies do not usually select the LIFO method when they conduct business in a normal environment of falling inventory unit costs. In such an environment, these companies would more likely opt for the FIFO method because using this method would generate the lowest amount of income tax expense. In fact, the effect on financial statements and ratios from using FIFO (in comparison with LIFO) in an environment of declining inventory unit costs is the same as when using LIFO (in comparison with FIFO) in an environment of rising inventory unit costs.

5.2 Inventory Method Changes

Companies sometimes decide to change inventory methods. Under IFRS, changes in accounting policy are accounted for retrospectively. According to IAS 8, a change in policy is acceptable only if the change results in the financial statements providing reliable and more relevant information about the effects of transactions, other events, or conditions on the business entity's financial position, financial performance, or cash flows. If the change is justifiable, historical information is restated for all accounting periods (typically the previous one or two years that are presented for comparability purposes with the current year in annual financial reports). Adjustment amounts relating to accounting periods that are prior to those financial statements presented and restated are adjusted against the opening balance of retained earnings of the earliest year presented for comparison purposes. An exemption to the restatement applies when it is impracticable to determine either the period-specific effects or the cumulative effect of the change.

Under U.S. GAAP, accounting for a change in inventory policy is now similar to IFRS due to the adoption of SFAS No. 154 for fiscal years beginning after 15 December 2005. Because of U.S. GAAP consistency requirements, a company must thoroughly explain why the newly adopted inventory accounting method is superior and preferable to the old method. In addition, U.S. tax regulations may also restrict changes and require permission from the Internal Revenue Service

(IRS). If a company decides to change from LIFO to another inventory method, U.S. GAAP requires a retrospective restatement of inventory and retained earnings. Historical financial statements are also restated for the effects of the change. If a company decides to change to the LIFO method, it must do so on a prospective basis. Retrospective adjustments are not made to the financial statements. Instead, the carrying value of inventory under the old method will become the initial LIFO layer in the year of LIFO adoption.

SUMMARY

Inventory cost flow is a major determinant in measuring income for merchandising and manufacturing companies. In addition, inventories are usually a significant asset on the balance sheets of these companies. The financial statements and financial notes of a company provide important information that the analyst needs to correctly assess and compare financial performance with other companies. Key concepts in this reading are as follows:

▶ Inventories are a major factor in the analysis of merchandising and manufacturing companies. Such companies generate their sales and profits through inventory transactions on a regular basis. An important consideration in determining profits for these companies is measuring the cost of goods sold when inventories are sold to business customers.

▶ The cost of inventories comprises all costs of purchase, costs of conversion, and other costs incurred in bringing the inventories to their present location and condition. Also, any allocation of fixed production overhead is based on normal capacity levels, with unallocated production overhead expensed as incurred.

▶ Under IFRS, the cost of inventories is assigned by using either the first-in, first-out (FIFO) or weighted average cost formula. The specific identification method is required for inventories of items that are not ordinarily interchangeable and for goods or services produced and segregated for specific projects. A business entity must use the same cost formula for all inventories having a similar nature and use to the entity.

▶ Inventories are measured at the lower of cost or "net realizable value." Net realizable value is the estimated selling price in the ordinary course of business less the estimated costs necessary to make the sale. Reversals of write-downs are permissible under IFRS but not U.S. GAAP.

▶ The choice of inventory method impacts the financial statements and any financial ratios that are derived from them. As a consequence, the analyst must carefully consider inventory method differences when evaluating a company's performance or when comparing a company with industry data or industry competitors.

▶ The inventory turnover ratio, number of days of inventory ratio, and gross profit margin ratio are directly and fully affected by a company's choice of inventory method.

▶ Under U.S. GAAP, the LIFO method is widely used for both tax and financial reporting purposes because of potential income tax savings.

▶ LIFO reserve liquidation occurs when the number of units in ending inventory declines from the number of units that were present at the beginning of the year. If inventory unit costs have generally risen from year to year, the phenomenon of inventory "phantom" gross profits occurs on liquidation.

▶ Under U.S. GAAP, companies that use the LIFO inventory method must disclose in their financial notes the amount of the LIFO reserve or the amount that would have been reported in inventory if the FIFO method had been used.

▶ Consistency of inventory costing is required under both U.S. GAAP and IFRS. If a company changes an accounting policy, the change must be justifiable and all financial statements are accounted for retrospectively.

PRACTICE PROBLEMS FOR READING 36

1. Inventory cost is *least likely* to include:

   A. production-related storage costs.

   B. costs incurred due to normal waste of materials.

   C. transportation costs of shipping inventory to customers.

2. Ajax Factories produces pencils at a factory designed to produce 10 million pencils per year. In 2007 the fixed production overhead related to the factory was $1 million and the factory produced 9 million pencils. The inventory cost for each pencil related to the fixed production overhead is *closest* to:

   A. $0.00.

   B. $0.10.

   C. $0.11.

3. Mustard Seed PLC adheres to IFRS. It recently purchased inventory for €100 million and spent €5 million for storage prior to selling the goods. The amount it charged to inventory expense (in € millions) was *closest* to:

   A. €95.

   B. €100.

   C. €105.

4. Carrying inventory at a value above its historical cost would *most likely* be permitted if:

   A. the inventory was held by a produce dealer.

   B. financial statements were prepared using U.S. GAAP.

   C. the change resulted from a reversal of a previous write-down.

5. Eric's Used Bookstore prepares its financial statements in accordance with U.S. GAAP. Inventory was purchased for $1 million and later marked down to $550,000. However, one of the books was later discovered to be a rare collectible item, and the inventory is now worth an estimated $3 million. The inventory is *most likely* reported on the balance sheet at:

   A. $550,000.

   B. $1,000,000.

   C. $3,000,000.

6. Fernando's Pasta purchased inventory and later wrote it down, though the current realizable value is higher than the value when written down. Fernando's inventory balance will *most likely* be:

   A. higher if it complies with IFRS.

   B. higher if it complies with U.S. GAAP.

   C. the same under U.S. GAAP and IFRS.

7. Cinnamon Corp. started business in 2007 and uses the weighted average cost inventory method. During 2007 it purchased 45,000 units of inventory at €10 each and sold 40,000 units for €20 each. In 2008 it purchased another 50,000 units at €11 each and sold 45,000 units for €22 each. Its 2008 cost of goods sold (in € thousands) was *closest* to:

    A. €490.

    B. €491.

    C. €495.

8. Zimt AG started business in 2007 and uses the FIFO inventory method. During 2007 it purchased 45,000 units of inventory at €10 each and sold 40,000 units for €20 each. In 2008 it purchased another 50,000 units at €11 each and sold 45,000 units for €22 each. Its 2008 ending inventory balance (in € thousands) was *closest* to:

    A. €105.

    B. €109.

    C. €110.

9. Zimt AG uses the FIFO inventory accounting method, and Nutmeg Inc. uses the LIFO method. Compared to the cost of replacing the inventory, during periods of rising prices the cost of goods sold reported by:

    A. Zimt is too low.

    B. Nutmeg is too low.

    C. Nutmeg is too high.

10. Zimt AG uses the FIFO inventory accounting method, and Nutmeg Inc. uses the LIFO method. Compared to the cost of replacing the inventory, during periods of rising prices the ending inventory balance reported by:

    A. Zimt is too high.

    B. Nutmeg is too low.

    C. Nutmeg is too high.

11. Like many technology companies, TechnoTools operates in an environment of declining prices. Its reported profits will tend to be *highest* if it accounts for inventory using the:

    A. FIFO method.

    B. LIFO method.

    C. weighted average cost method.

12. Compared to using the weighted average cost method to account for inventory, during a period in which prices are generally rising, the current ratio of a company using the FIFO method would *most likely* be:

    A. lower.

    B. higher.

    C. dependent upon the interaction with accounts payable.

13. Zimt AG wrote down the value of inventory in 2007 and reversed the write-down in 2008. Compared to ratios calculated if the write-down had never occurred, Zimt's reported 2007:

   A. current ratio was too high.

   B. gross margin was too high.

   C. inventory turnover was too high.

14. Zimt AG wrote down the value of inventory in 2007 and reversed the write-down in 2008. Compared to results reported if the write-down had never occurred, Zimt's reported 2008:

   A. profit was overstated.

   B. cash flow from operations was overstated.

   C. year-end inventory balance was overstated.

15. Compared to a company that uses the FIFO inventory accounting method, during periods of rising prices a company that uses the LIFO method will *most likely* appear more:

   A. liquid.

   B. efficient.

   C. profitable.

16. Nutmeg, Inc. uses the LIFO method to account for inventory. During years in which inventory unit costs are generally rising and in which the company purchases more inventory than it sells to customers its reported gross profit margin will *most likely* be:

   A. lower than it would have been if the company used the FIFO method.

   B. higher than it would have been if the company used the FIFO method.

   C. about the same as it would have been if the company used the FIFO method.

17. Sauerbraten Corp. reported 2007 sales ($ in millions) of $2,157 and cost of goods sold of $1,827. The company uses the LIFO method for inventory valuation and discloses that if the FIFO inventory valuation method had been used, inventories would have been $63.3 million and $56.8 million higher in 2007 and 2006, respectively. If Sauerbraten used the FIFO method exclusively, it would have reported 2007 gross profit *closest* to:

   A. $324.

   B. $330.

   C. $337.

18. Sauerbraten Corp. reported 2007 sales ($ in millions) of $2,157 and cost of goods sold of $1,827. Inventories at year-end 2007 and 2006, respectively, were $553 and $562. The company uses the LIFO method for inventory valuation and discloses that if the FIFO inventory valuation method had been used, inventories would have been $63.3 million and $56.8 million higher in 2007 and 2006, respectively. Compared to the inventory turnover ratio reported, if Sauerbraten had exclusively used the FIFO method its inventory turnover ratio would have been *closest* to:

   A. 2.96.

   B. 3.28.

   C. 3.49.

19. Compared to using the FIFO method to account for inventory, during periods of rising prices a company that uses the LIFO method is *most likely* to report higher:

   A. net income.

   B. cost of sales.

   C. income taxes.

20. In order to compare the results of a company that uses the LIFO method to one using FIFO, the required adjustments to the financial statements of the LIFO user include adding the:

   A. LIFO reserve to inventory.

   B. change in the LIFO reserve to inventory.

   C. change in the LIFO reserve to cost of goods sold.

21. Carey Company adheres to U.S. GAAP, while Jonathan Company adheres to IFRS. It is *least likely* that:

   A. Carey has reversed an inventory write-down.

   B. Jonathan has reversed an inventory write-down.

   C. Jonathan and Carey both use the FIFO inventory accounting method.

SOLUTIONS FOR READING 36

1. C is correct. Transportation costs incurred to ship inventory to customers is an expense and may not be capitalized in inventory. (Transportation costs incurred to bring inventory to the business location can be capitalized in inventory.) Storage costs required as part of production, as well as costs incurred due to normal waste of materials can be capitalized in inventory. (Costs incurred due to abnormal waste must be expensed.)

2. B is correct. Ajax can allocate to inventory cost a portion of fixed production overhead based on normal capacity levels. Normal capacity is 10 million pencils, and fixed production costs are $1 million, so capitalized inventory costs will include 90% (9 million pencils produced ÷ 10 million capacity) of the fixed production overhead costs of $1 million. The inventory cost for each pencil related to the fixed production overhead allocated to each pencil is thus $0.10 (90% × $1 million ÷ 9 million pencils). The remaining $100,000 of fixed production overhead costs would be expensed as incurred.

3. B is correct. Inventory expense includes costs of purchase, costs of conversion, and other costs incurred in bringing the inventories to their present location and condition. It does not include storage costs not required as part of production.

4. A is correct. IAS 41 allows (and U.S. GAAP treatment is similar) the inventories of producers and dealers of agricultural and forest products, agricultural produce after harvest, and minerals and mineral products to be carried at net realizable value even if above historical cost.

5. A is correct. Under U.S. GAAP, inventory is carried at the lower of cost or market value. After being written down, a new cost basis is determined and further revisions may only reduce the value further.

6. A is correct. IFRS permit the reversal of inventory write-downs; U.S. GAAP does not.

7. B is correct. Cinnamon uses the weighted average cost method, so in 2008 5,000 units of inventory were 2007 units at €10 each and the 50,000 were 2008 purchases at €11. The weighted average cost of inventory during 2008 was thus (5,000 × 10) + (50,000 × 11) = 50,000 + 550,000 = €600,000 and the weighted average cost was €600,000/55,000 = €10.91. Cost of goods sold were €10.9091 × 45,000, which is approximately €490,909.

8. C is correct. Zimt uses the FIFO method, and thus the first 5,000 units sold in 2008 depleted the 2007 inventory. Of the inventory purchased in 2008, 40,000 units were sold and 10,000 remain, valued at €11 each for a total of €110,000.

9. A is correct. Zimt uses the FIFO method, so its cost of goods sold represents units purchased at a (no longer available) lower price. Nutmeg uses the LIFO method, so its cost of goods sold is approximately equal to the current replacement cost of inventory.

10. B is correct. Nutmeg uses the LIFO method and thus some of the inventory on the balance sheet was purchased at a (no longer available) lower price. Zimt uses the FIFO method, so the carrying value on the balance sheet represents the most recently purchased units and thus approximates the current replacement cost.

International Financial Statement Analysis, by Thomas R. Robinson, CFA, Jan Hendrik van Greuning, CFA, R. Elaine Henry, CFA, and Michael A. Broihahn, CFA. Copyright © 2008 by CFA Institute. Reprinted with permission.

11. B is correct. In a declining price environment, the newest inventory is the lowest cost inventory. In such circumstances, using the LIFO method (selling the newer, cheaper inventory first) will result in lower cost of goods sold and higher profit.

12. B is correct. In a rising price environment, inventory balances will be higher for the company using the FIFO method. Accounts payable are based on amounts due to suppliers, not the amounts accrued based on inventory accounting.

13. C is correct. The write-down reduced the value of inventory and increased cost of goods sold in 2007. The higher numerator and lower denominator mean that the inventory turnover ratio as reported was too high. Gross margin and the current ratio were both too low.

14. A is correct. The reversal shifted cost of sales from 2008 to 2007. As a result, the reported 2008 profits were overstated. Inventory balance would have been the same because the write-down and reversal cancel each other out. Cash flow from operations is not affected by the non-cash write-down, but the higher profits in 2008 likely resulted in higher taxes and thus lower cash flow from operations.

15. B is correct. LIFO will result in lower inventory and higher cost of sales. Gross margin (a profitability ratio) will be lower, the current ratio (a liquidity ratio) will be lower, and inventory turnover (an efficiency ratio) will be higher.

16. A is correct. Because inventory purchases exceed product sales there is no LIFO liquidation and thus no abnormal "phantom" profits. Consequently, LIFO results in lower gross margin than FIFO.

17. C is correct. Under FIFO, cost of goods sold would be lower than LIFO by an amount equal to the increase in the LIFO reserve (in this case, $63.3 − $56.8 = $6.5). So, $1,827 − $6.5 = $1,820.5 meaning gross profit is $2,157 − $1,820.5 = $336.5.

18. A is correct. Inventory turnover is cost of goods sold divided by average inventory. As reported, this was $1,827/$557.5 = 3.28. Under FIFO, cost of goods sold would have been $1,820.5 and inventory would have been $616.3 and $618.8 (average $617.6). Adjusted inventory turnover would thus be 2.96.

19. B is correct. The LIFO method increases cost of sales, thus reducing profits and the taxes thereon.

20. A is correct. The adjustments are to add the LIFO reserve to inventory and subtract the change in LIFO reserve from cost of goods sold.

21. A is correct. U.S. GAAP does not permit inventory write-downs to be reversed.

4⅝ 4¹¹⁄₁₆
5½ 5½ − ⅜
5½ 21³⁄₁₆ − ¹⁄₁₆
20⅝ 21³⁄₁₆ − ¹⁄₁₆
17⅜ 18⅛ + ⅞
6½ 6½ − ½
7¼ 3³¹⁄₃₂ − ⅛
15⁄₁₆ ⁹⁄₁₆
9⁄₁₆
7¹⁵⁄₁₆ 7¹³⁄₁₆ 7¹⁵⁄₁₆
2⅝ 2¹¹⁄₃₂ 2½ +
2¾ 2¼ 2¼
12¹⁄₁₆ 11⅜ 11¾ +
33¾ 33 33¼ −
25⅝ 24⁹⁄₁₆ 25⅜ +
12 11⅝ 11⅝ +
16 10½ 10½ 10½ −
78 15⅞ 15¹³⁄₁₆ 15⅞ −
9¹⁄₁₆ 8¼ 8⅛ +
430 11¼ 10⅛

LONG-LIVED ASSETS

by R. Elaine Henry, CFA and Elizabeth A. Gordon

LEARNING OUTCOMES

The candidate should be able to:	Mastery
a. explain the accounting standards related to the capitalization of expenditures as part of long-lived assets, including interest costs;	☐
b. compute and describe the effects of capitalizing versus expensing on net income, shareholders' equity, cash flow from operations, and financial ratios, including the effect on the interest coverage ratio of capitalizing interest costs;	☐
c. explain the circumstances in which software development costs and research and development costs are capitalized;	☐
d. identify the different depreciation methods for long-lived tangible assets, and discuss how the choice of method, useful lives, and salvage values affect a company's financial statements, ratios, and taxes;	☐
e. discuss the use of fixed asset disclosures to compare companies' average age of depreciable assets and calculate, using such disclosures, the average age and average depreciable life of fixed assets;	☐
f. describe amortization of intangible assets with finite useful lives and the estimates that affect the amortization calculations;	☐
g. discuss the liability for closure, removal, and environmental effects of long-lived operating assets, and discuss the financial statement impact and ratio effects of that liability;	☐
h. discuss the impact of sales or exchanges of long-lived assets on financial statements;	☐
i. define impairment of long-lived tangible and intangible assets and explain what effect such impairment has on a company's financial statements and ratios;	☐
j. calculate and describe both the initial and long-lived effects of asset revaluations on financial ratios.	☐

International Financial Statement Analysis, by Thomas R. Robinson, CFA, Jan Hendrik van Greuning, CFA, R. Elaine Henry, CFA, and Michael A. Broihahn, CFA. Copyright © 2008 by CFA Institute. Reprinted with permission.

THEME

Accounting for long-lived assets involves several stages: initially recording the asset, recognizing associated expenses as the asset is used up, valuing the asset during the course of its economic life, and reporting the disposal of the asset. For both tangible and intangible assets, companies' decisions about accounting methods and estimates can affect the financial statements and various ratios commonly used in analysis.

1

INTRODUCTION

Long-lived assets, also commonly referred to as long-term assets, are assets that are expected to provide economic benefits over a future period of time, typically greater than one year.[1] Long-lived assets may be tangible, intangible, or financial assets. Examples of **tangible assets** include land (property), plant, and equipment; examples of **intangible assets** (assets lacking physical substance) include patents and trademarks; and examples of financial assets include investments in equity or debt securities issued by other companies. In this reading, we cover long-lived tangible and intangible assets. A subsequent reading will discuss financial assets.

The costs of most long-lived assets are allocated as expenses over the period of time during which they are expected to provide economic benefits. The two main types of long-lived assets whose costs are *not* allocated over time are land, which is not depreciated, and those intangible assets with indefinite useful lives. Intangible assets with indefinite lives are tested periodically for any reduction in their fair value as compared to their recorded value, known as an impairment, which is reflected as an impairment loss on the income statement.

This reading is organized as follows. Sections 2 and 3 describe and illustrate accounting for the acquisition of long-lived tangible assets and long-lived intangible assets. Sections 4 and 5 describe the allocation of the costs of long-lived assets over their useful lives. Section 6 discusses the treatment of obligations arising in connection with the ultimate retirement of an asset. Section 7 describes accounting for the disposal of long-lived operating assets. Sections 8 and 9 cover the concepts of impairment (reduction in the value of an asset) and revaluation (change in the value of an asset). A summary of the key points and practice problems in the CFA Institute multiple-choice format conclude the reading.

---

[1] In some instances, it is industry practice (such as with tobacco and alcohol distillers) to include as current assets rather than long-lived assets those assets with lives that are longer than one year, e.g. leaf tobacco, which is cured and aged over a period longer than one year, and whiskey which is barrel-aged for a period longer than one year.

ACCOUNTING FOR THE ACQUISITION OF LONG-LIVED TANGIBLE ASSETS

2

Upon acquisition, a long-lived asset is recorded on the balance sheet at its cost, which is typically the same as its fair value.[2] In addition to the purchase price, the buyer also records, as part of the cost of an asset, all the expenditures necessary to prepare the asset for its intended use. The following paragraphs discuss accounting for the acquisition of long-lived tangible assets and selected relevant analytical issues.

2.1 Accounting Standards Related to Capitalization of Expenditures

Expenditures related to long-lived assets are included as part of the recorded value of assets on the balance sheet, i.e., capitalized, if they are expected to provide benefits in the future, typically beyond one year; alternatively, expenditures are treated as an expense if they are not expected to provide benefits in future periods. Before turning to specific instances, we will consider the general financial statement impact of capitalizing versus expensing and two analytical issues related to the decision—namely the effect on an individual company's trend analysis and on comparability across companies.

In the period of the expenditure, an expenditure that is capitalized increases the amount of assets on the balance sheet and appears as an investing cash outflow on the statement of cash flows. In subsequent periods, a company allocates the capitalized amount over the asset's useful life (except land and intangible assets with indefinite lives) as depreciation or amortization expense. This expense reduces net income on the income statement and reduces the value of the asset on the balance sheet. Depreciation is a non-cash expense and therefore, apart from its effect on taxable income, has no impact on the statement of cash flows. In the section of the statement of cash flows that reconciles net income to operating cash flow, depreciation expense is added back to net income.

Alternatively, an expenditure that is expensed reduces net income by the entire amount of the expenditure in the period it is made. No asset is recorded on the balance sheet and thus no depreciation or amortization can occur in subsequent periods. The lower amount of net income is reflected in lower retained earnings on the balance sheet. An expenditure that is expensed appears as operating cash outflow in the period it is made. There is no effect on the financial statements of subsequent periods.

Example 1 illustrates the impact on the financial statements of capitalizing versus expensing an expenditure.

---

[2] Fair value is defined formally in the Statement of Financial Accounting Standards (SFAS) No. 157, Paragraph 5 as "the price that would be received to sell an asset or paid to transfer a liability in an orderly transaction between market participants at the measurement date."

EXAMPLE 1

Financial Statement Impact of Capitalizing versus Expensing

Assume two identical (hypothetical) companies, CAP Inc. and NOW Inc., start up with €1,000 cash and €1,000 common stock. Each year the companies receive total revenues of €1,500 cash and pay cash expenses, excluding an equipment purchase, of €500. At the beginning of operations, each company spends €900 to purchase equipment. CAP estimates the equipment will have a useful life of three years and an estimated salvage value of €0 at the end of the three years. NOW estimates a much shorter useful life and expenses the equipment immediately. The companies have no other assets and make no other asset purchases during the three-year period. Assume the companies pay no dividends, earn zero interest on cash balances, have a tax rate of 30 percent, and use the same accounting method for financial and tax purposes.

The first table below shows CAP's financial statements, with the expenditure capitalized and depreciated at €300 per year based on the straight-line method of depreciation (€900 cost minus €0 salvage value equals €900, divided by a three-year life equals €300 per year). The second table below shows NOW's financial statements, with the entire €900 expenditure treated as an expense in the first year.

| | CAP Inc. Capitalize €900 as Asset and Depreciate | | |
For Year	1	2	3
Revenue	€1,500	€1,500	€1,500
Cash expenses	500	500	500
Depreciation	300	300	300
Income before tax	€700	€700	€700
Tax at 30%	210	210	210
Net income	€490	€490	€490
Cash from operations	€790	€790	€790
Cash used in investing	(900)	0	0
Total change in cash	(€110)	€790	€790

For Year	NOW Inc. Expense €900 Immediately		
	1	**2**	**3**
Revenue	€1,500	€1,500	€1,500
Cash expenses	1,400	500	500
Depreciation	0	0	0
Income before tax	€100	€1,000	€1,000
Tax at 30%	30	300	300
Net income	€70	€700	€700
Cash from operations	€70	€700	€700
Cash used in investing	0	0	0
Total change in cash	€70	€700	€700

1. Which company reports higher net income over the three years? Total cash flow? Cash from operations?

2. Based on ROE and net profit margin, how do the two companies' profitability compare?

3. Why does NOW Inc. report change in cash of €70 in year 1, while CAP Inc. reports total change in cash of (€110)?

Solution to 1: Neither company reports higher net income nor total cash flow over the three years. The sum of net income over the three years is identical (€1,470 total) whether the €900 is capitalized or expensed. Also, the sum of the change in cash (€1,470 total) is identical under either scenario. CAP Inc. reports higher cash from operations by an amount of €900 because, under the capitalization scenario, the €900 purchase is treated as an investing cash flow.

Note: Because the companies use the same accounting method for both financial and taxable income, absent the assumption of zero interest on cash balances, expensing the €900 would have resulted in higher income and cash flow for NOW Inc. because the lower taxes paid in the first year (€30 versus €210) would have allowed NOW Inc. to earn interest income on the tax savings.

Solution to 2: Computing ROE requires forecasting shareholders' equity. In general, Ending shareholders' equity = Beginning shareholders' equity + Net income + Other comprehensive income − Dividends + Net capital contributions from shareholders. Because the companies in this example do not have other comprehensive income, did not pay dividends, and reported no capital contributions from shareholders, Ending retained earnings = Beginning retained earnings + Net income, and Ending shareholders' equity = Beginning shareholders' equity + Net income. The forecasts are presented below.

CAP Inc. Capitalize €900 as Asset and Depreciate				
Time	**0**	**1**	**2**	**3**
Retained earnings	€0	€490	€980	€1,470
Common stock	1,000	1,000	1,000	1,000
Total shareholders' equity	1,000	1,490	1,980	2,470

NOW Inc. Expense €900 Immediately				
Time	**0**	**1**	**2**	**3**
Retained earnings	€0	€70	€770	€1,470
Common stock	1,000	1,000	1,000	1,000
Total shareholders' equity	1,000	1,070	1,770	2,470

ROE is calculated as net income divided by average shareholders' equity, and net profit margin is calculated as net income divided by total revenue. For example, CAP Inc. had year 1 ROE of 39 percent (€490/[(€1,000 + €1,490)/2]), and year 1 net profit margin of 33 percent (€490/€1,500).

CAP Inc. Capitalize €900 as Asset and Depreciate			
For Year	**1**	**2**	**3**
ROE	39%	28%	22%
Net profit margin	33%	33%	33%

NOW Inc. Expense €900 Immediately			
For Year	**1**	**2**	**3**
ROE	7%	49%	33%
Net profit margin	5%	47%	47%

As shown, capitalizing results in higher profitability ratios (ROE and net profit margin) in the first year, and lower profitability ratios in the subsequent years. For example, CAP Inc.'s year 1 ROE of 39 percent was higher than NOW Inc.'s year 1 ROE of 7 percent, but in years 2 and 3, NOW Inc. reports superior profitability.

Note also that NOW's superior growth in net income between year 1 and year 2 is not attributable to superior performance but rather to a different accounting decision, namely to recognize the expense sooner than CAP. In general, all else equal, accounting decisions that result in recognizing expenses sooner will give the appearance of greater subsequent growth. Comparison of the growth of the two companies' net income without an awareness of the difference in accounting methods would be misleading. As a corollary, NOW's income and profitability exhibit greater volatility across the three years, not because of more volatile performance but rather because of the different accounting decision.

Solution to 3: NOW Inc. reports change in cash of €70 in year 1, while CAP Inc. reports total change in cash of €110 because NOW's taxes were €180 lower than CAP Inc.'s (€30 versus €210).

Note that this example assumes the two companies use identical accounting methods for financial reporting and taxes. Recall that in the United States, companies are allowed to use different depreciation methods for financial reporting and taxes, which, in practice, often gives rise to deferred taxes.

As shown, discretion regarding whether to expense or capitalize expenditures can impede comparability across companies. Example 1 assumes the companies purchase a single asset in one year. Because the sum of net income over the three-year period is identical whether the asset is capitalized or expensed, it illustrates that although capitalizing results in higher profitability compared to expensing in the first year, it results in lower profitability ratios in the subsequent years. Conversely, expensing results in lower profitability in the first year, but higher profitability in later years, indicating a favorable trend.

Similarly, shareholders' equity for a firm that capitalizes the expenditure will be higher in the early years because the initially higher profits result in initially higher retained earnings. Example 1 assumes the companies purchase a single asset in one year and report identical amounts of total net income over the three-year period, so shareholders' equity (and retained earnings) for the firm that expenses will be identical to shareholders' equity (and retained earnings) for the capitalizing firm at the end of the three-year period.

Although the example above shows companies purchasing an asset only in the first year, if a company continues to purchase similar or increasing amounts of assets each year, the profitability-enhancing effect of capitalizing continues so long as the amount of the expenditure in a period is more than the depreciation expense for a single year. Example 2 illustrates this point.

EXAMPLE 2

Impact of Capitalizing versus Expensing for Ongoing Purchases

A company buys a £300 computer in year 1 and capitalizes the expenditure. The computer has a useful life of 3 years and an expected salvage value of £0, so the annual depreciation expense using the straight-line method is £100 per year. Compared to expensing the entire £300 immediately, the company's pre-tax profit in year 1 is £200 greater.

1. Assume that the company continues to buy an identical computer each year at the same price. Assuming the company uses an identical accounting treatment for each of the computers, when does the profit-enhancing effect of capitalizing versus expensing end?

2. If the company buys another identical computer in year 4, using identical accounting treatment as the prior years, what is the effect on year 4 profits of capitalizing versus expensing these expenditures?

Solution to 1: The profit-enhancing effect of capitalizing versus expensing would end in year 3. In year 3, the depreciation expense on each of the three computers bought in years 1, 2, and 3 would total £300 (£100 + £100 + £100). Therefore, the total depreciation expense for year 3 will be exactly equal to the capital expenditure in year 3. The expense in year 3 would be £300, regardless of whether the company capitalized or expensed the annual computer purchases.

Solution to 2: There is no impact on year 4 profits. As in the previous year, the depreciation expense on each of the three computers bought in years 2, 3, and 4 would total £300 (£100 + £100 + £100). Therefore, the total depreciation expense for year 4 will be exactly equal to the capital expenditure in year 4. Pre-tax profits would be reduced by £300, regardless of whether the company capitalized or expensed the annual computer purchases.

Capitalizing an expenditure rather than expensing it also results in greater amounts reported as cash from operations. Cash from operations is an important consideration in valuation, so companies may aim to maximize reported cash from operations. WorldCom is an infamous example of a company violating U.S. GAAP to maximize reported cash from operations: in 2001, the company wrongly capitalized over $3 billion in line costs (charges paid for access to telecommunication lines) that should have been expensed. It is, of course, important to distinguish between WorldCom's fraudulent financial reporting and allowable accounting discretion. Nonetheless, the general concept is that a capitalized expenditure would typically be shown as an investment cash outflow whereas an expense would reduce operating cash.

The discussion now turns to specific instances of the capitalization of expenditures.

2.2 Costs Incurred at Acquisition

The most obvious cost incurred to acquire a tangible asset (such as property, plant, and equipment) is its purchase price. In addition to the purchase price, the buyer also records, as part of the cost of an asset, all the expenditures necessary to get the asset ready for its intended use. For example, freight costs borne by the purchaser and special installation costs are included in the total cost of the asset.

In a monetary exchange, the purchase price is easily determined. If an asset is acquired in a nonmonetary exchange, its cost is based on the fair value of the asset given up, or the fair value of the asset acquired if it is more readily determinable.[3] Examples of nonmonetary exchanges of operating assets include exchanges of mineral leases or real estate. For an example, refer to the disclosure of a nonmonetary exchange shown in Exhibit 1.

| EXHIBIT 1 | Example of a Nonmonetary Exchange |

Massey Energy Company (NYSE: MEE) disclosed a nonmonetary exchange in its 2006 financial statements:

> "During the third quarter of 2005, we exchanged coal reserves with a third party, recognizing a gain of $38.2 million (pre-tax) in accordance with SFAS 153. The fair value of the assets surrendered by both parties was determined by use of a future cashflows valuation model. The difference in the fair value of the assets surrendered and their book basis resulted in the gain recognized. The gain from this transaction is recorded in Other revenue. The acquired coal reserves were recorded in Property, plant and equipment at the fair value of the reserves surrendered."

Source: Massey Energy Company's Form 10-K filed with the SEC on 1 March 2007, page 60.

An analyst would want to understand the nature of a nonmonetary exchange that gave rise to a significant gain or loss. Presumably, neither counterparty to an exchange would be willing to sacrifice an asset of higher value to obtain an asset of lower value. Therefore, one reason for an exchange giving rise to a significant gain or loss would be differences between the values placed on the assets exchanged by the different counterparties. Another explanation for an exchange is to achieve a fair value measurement of assets. As we will discuss below, IFRS, unlike U.S. GAAP, allows companies the option to value long-lived assets based on historical costs or based on fair value. The net result of the exchange described in Exhibit 1 was that the company now reports the exchanged coal reserves at fair value, which is $38.2 million higher than the book value of the assets exchanged.

2.3 Capitalization of Interest Costs

Companies generally must capitalize interest costs associated with acquiring or constructing an asset that requires a long period of time to get ready for its intended use.[4] For example, constructing a building to sell or for a company's own

---

[3] APB 29 and SFAS No. 153 specify U.S. GAAP accounting for assets acquired in non-monetary exchanges, and the latter standard uses language similar to that in IAS 16, *Property, Plant and Equipment*, and IAS 38, *Intangible Assets*.

[4] SFAS No. 34 specifies U.S. GAAP accounting for capitalization of interest costs. Under the recently revised IAS 23 (March, 2007), international standards now require capitalization of interest costs. Although the standards are not completely converged, the new international standard eliminates the previously allowed alternative of immediately expensing interest costs.

use typically requires a substantial amount of time; any interest cost incurred in order to finance construction is capitalized as part of the cost of the asset. The company determines the interest rate to use based on its existing borrowings or, if applicable, on a borrowing specifically incurred for constructing the asset. If a company takes out a loan specifically to construct a building, the interest cost on that loan during the time of construction would be capitalized as part of the building's cost.

As a consequence of this accounting treatment, a company's interest costs for a period can appear either on the balance sheet (to the extent they are capitalized) or on the income statement (to the extent they are expensed).

If the interest expenditure is incurred in connection with constructing an asset for the company's own use, the capitalized interest appears on the balance sheet as a part of the relevant long-lived asset, i.e., property, plant, and equipment. The capitalized interest is expensed over time as the property is depreciated—and is thus part of depreciation expense rather than interest expense. If the interest expenditure is incurred in connection with constructing an asset to sell, for example by a home builder, the capitalized interest appears on the company's balance sheet as part of inventory. The capitalized interest is expensed as part of the cost of goods sold when the asset is sold.

The treatment of capitalized interest poses certain issues that analysts may want to consider. First, capitalized interest appears as part of investing cash outflows, whereas expensed interest reduces operating cash flow. Although the treatment is consistent with accounting standards, an analyst may want to examine the impact on reported cash flows. Second, recall that interest coverage ratios are solvency indicators measuring the extent to which a company's earnings (or cash flow) in a period covered its interest costs. To provide a true picture of a company's interest coverage, the entire amount of interest expenditure, both the capitalized portion and the expensed portion, should be used in calculating interest coverage ratios. Additionally, if a company is depreciating interest that it capitalized in a previous period, income should be adjusted to eliminate the effect of that depreciation. Example 3 illustrates the calculation.

EXAMPLE 3

Effect of Capitalized Interest Costs on Coverage Ratios and Cash Flow

MTR Gaming Group, Inc. (NasdaqGS: MNTG) disclosed the following information in one of the footnotes to its financial statements: "Interest is capitalized to construction in progress based on the product resulting from applying the company's cost of borrowing rate to qualifying assets. Interest capitalized in 2005 was $1,301,000. There was no interest capitalized during 2004 and 2003 (Form 10-K filed 29 March 2006, F-6)."

EXHIBIT 2   MTR Gaming Group Selected Data, as Reported

(Dollars in Thousands)	2005	2004	2003
EBIT (from income statement)	$25,736	$36,321	$35,869
Interest expense (from income statement)	12,179	13,599	11,896
Interest capitalized (from footnote)	1,301	0	0
Net cash provided by operating activities	$39,484	$46,569	$37,806
Net cash used in investing activities	(45,778)	(45,922)	(46,541)

1. Calculate and interpret MTR's interest coverage ratio, with and without capitalized interest.

2. Calculate MTR's percentage change in operating cash flow from 2004 to 2005. What were the effects of capitalized interest on operating and investing cash flows?

Solution to 1: MTR did not capitalize any interest during 2003 or 2004, so the interest coverage ratio for each of those two years is not affected by capitalized interest. The interest coverage ratio, measured as earnings before interest and taxes (EBIT) divided by interest expense, was as follows:

3.02 ($35,869 divided by $11,896) for 2003; and
2.67 ($36,321 divided by $13,599) for 2004.

For the year 2005, interest coverage ratios with and without capitalized interest were as follows:

2.11 ($25,736 divided by $12,179) excluding capitalized interest; and
1.91 ($25,736 divided by the sum of $12,179 and $1,301) including capitalized interest.

Because MTR did not capitalize interest in previous years, no adjustment for depreciation of capitalized interest costs is required.

The above calculations indicate that MTR's interest coverage deteriorated over the three-year period from 2003 to 2005. In addition, the 2005 interest coverage ratio of 1.91 that includes capitalized interest is substantially lower than the ratio with capitalized interest excluded.

Solution to 2: If the interest had been expensed rather than capitalized, operating cash flows would have shown an even greater decline and investing cash outflows would have declined rather than remaining stable over the 2004 to 2005 period.

For 2005 compared with 2004, MTR's operating cash flow declined by 15.2 percent ($39,484 /$46,569 − 1). If the $1,301 of interest had been expensed rather than capitalized, the decline in cash flow would have been even greater, 18.0 percent [($39,484 − $1,301)/$46,569 − 1].

Further, including capitalized interest in investing activities, as reported, the company's investing cash flows appear approximately flat between 2004 and 2005. However, excluding capitalized interest from investing activities, the company's investing cash flows declined over the period by 3.1 percent [($45,778 − $1,301)/$45,922 − 1].

Generally, including capitalized interest in the calculation of interest coverage ratios provides a better assessment of a company's solvency. In assigning credit ratings, rating agencies include capitalized interest in coverage ratios. For example, Standard & Poor's calculates the EBIT interest coverage ratio as EBIT divided by gross interest (defined as interest prior to deductions for capitalized interest or interest income).

Maintaining a minimum interest coverage ratio is a financial covenant often included in bank loans. The definition of the coverage ratio can be found in the company's credit agreement. The definition is relevant because treatment of capitalized interest in calculating coverage ratios would affect an assessment of how close a company's actual ratios are to the levels specified by its financial covenants and thus the probability of breaching those covenants.

3 ACCOUNTING FOR THE ACQUISITION OF LONG-LIVED INTANGIBLE ASSETS

Intangible assets are assets lacking physical substance. Intangible assets include items that involve exclusive rights such as patents, copyrights, trademarks, and franchises. Intangible assets also include goodwill, which arises when one company purchases another and the acquisition price exceeds the fair value of the identifiable assets acquired. Accounting for an intangible asset depends on how it is acquired. The following sections describe accounting for intangible assets obtained in three ways: purchased in situations other than business combinations, developed internally, and acquired in business combinations.

3.1 Intangible Assets Purchased in Situations Other than Business Combinations

Intangible assets purchased in situations other than business combinations are treated the same as long-lived tangible assets, namely they are recorded at their fair value when acquired, which is assumed to be equivalent to the purchase price.[5] If several intangible assets are acquired as part of a group, the purchase price is allocated to each asset based on its fair value.

In deciding how to treat individual intangible assets for analytical purposes, analysts are particularly aware that companies must use a substantial amount of judgment and numerous assumptions to determine the fair value of individual intangible assets. For analysis, therefore, understanding the types of intangible assets acquired can often be more useful than focusing on the values assigned to the individual assets.

3.2 Intangible Assets Developed Internally

Costs to internally develop intangible assets are generally expensed when incurred, although there are some exceptions, described in the following sections. The general analytical issues related to the capitalizing-versus-expensing decision apply here, namely comparability across companies and the effect on an individual company's trend analysis.

3.2.1 Effect of Differences in Strategy (Developing Internally versus Acquiring)

The general requirement that costs of internally developing intangible assets be expensed should be compared with capitalizing the cost of acquiring intangible assets, described in the previous section. Because costs associated with internally developing intangible assets are usually expensed, a company that has obtained its intangible assets such as patents, copyrights, or brands internally through

---

[5] SFAS No. 142 specifies U.S. GAAP accounting for intangible assets, and IAS 38 specifies requirements under international standards.

expenditures on R&D or advertising will reflect a lower amount of assets than a company that has obtained its intangible assets by acquisition. In addition, on the statement of cash flows, costs of internally developing intangible assets are treated as operating cash outflows, while costs of acquiring intangible assets are investing cash outflows. Differences in strategy (developing versus acquiring intangible assets) can thus impact financial ratios.

3.2.2 Research and Development (R&D)

IFRS (IAS 38) requires that expenditures on research (or during the research phase of an internal project) be expensed rather than capitalized as an intangible asset. Research is defined in IAS 38, paragraph 8, as "original and planned investigation undertaken with the prospect of gaining new scientific or technical knowledge and understanding." The "research phase of an internal project" refers to the period during which a company cannot demonstrate that an intangible asset is being created— for example, the search for alternative materials or systems to use in a production process. IFRS allows companies to recognize an internal asset arising from development (or the development phase of an internal project) if certain criteria are met, including a demonstration of the technical feasibility of completing the intangible asset and the intent to use or sell the asset. Development is defined in IAS 38 as "the application of research findings or other knowledge to a plan or design for the production of new or substantially improved materials, devices, products, processes, systems or services before the start of commercial production or use."

Generally, U.S. accounting standards require that research and development costs be expensed. But the standards do require that certain costs related to software development be capitalized.[6] Costs incurred to develop a software product for sale are expensed until the product's feasibility is established, and capitalized after the product's feasibility has been established. In addition, companies capitalize costs related directly to developing software for internal use, such as the costs of employees who help build and test the software.

Even though standards require companies to capitalize software development costs after a product's feasibility is established, judgment in determining feasibility means that companies' capitalization practices differ. For example, as illustrated in Exhibit 3, Microsoft judges product feasibility to be established very shortly before manufacturing begins and therefore effectively expenses—rather than capitalizing—research and development costs.

| EXHIBIT 3 | Disclosure on Software Development Costs |

Excerpt from Management Discussion and Analysis (MD&A) of Microsoft Corporation (NasdaqGS: MSFT):

> "Judgment is required in determining when technological feasibility of a product is established. We have determined that technological feasibility for our software products is reached shortly before the products are released to manufacturing. Costs incurred after technological feasibility is established have not been material, and accordingly, we have expensed all research and development costs when incurred."

Source: Microsoft 2005 10-K filed 26 August 2006, page 39.

---

[6] SFAS No. 86 and SOP 98-1 specify U.S. GAAP accounting for software development costs.

Expensing rather than capitalizing development costs results in lower net income in the current period. The cumulative effect will also reduce net income so long as the amount of the current period development costs is higher than the expense that would have resulted from amortizing prior periods' capitalized development costs—the typical situation when a company's development costs are increasing. On the statement of cash flows, expensing rather than capitalizing development costs lowers net operating cash flows and lowers investing cash outflows.

In comparing the financial performance of one company that expenses all software development costs, such as Microsoft, with another company that capitalizes software development costs, adjustments can be made to make the two comparable. For the company that capitalizes software development costs, an analyst can adjust a) the income statement to include software development costs as an expense and to exclude amortization of prior years' software development costs; b) the balance sheet to exclude capitalized software; and c) the statement of cash flows to decrease operating cash flows and decrease cash used in investing by the amount of the current period development costs. Any ratios that

EXAMPLE 4

Software Development Costs

You are working on a project involving the analysis of JHH Software, a (hypothetical) software development company that established technical feasibility for its first product in 2004. Part of your analysis involves computing certain market-based ratios, which you will use to compare JHH to another company that expenses all of its software development expenditures. Relevant data and extracts from the company's annual report are included in the following exhibit.

EXHIBIT 4   JHH Software

(Dollars in Thousands, except per-Share Amounts)

CONSOLIDATED STATEMENT OF EARNINGS—abbreviated

For year ended 31 December	2006	2005	2004
Total revenue	$91,424	$91,134	$96,293
Total operating expenses	78,107	78,908	85,624
Operating income	$13,317	$12,226	$10,669
Provision for income taxes	3,825	4,232	3,172
Net income	$9,492	$7,934	$7,479
Earnings per share (EPS)	$1.40	$0.81	$0.68

STATEMENT OF CASH FLOWS—abbreviated

For year ended 31 December	2006	2005	2004
Net cash provided by operating activities	$15,007	$14,874	$15,266
Net cash used in investing activities*	(11,549)	(4,423)	(5,346)
Net cash used in financing activities	(8,003)	(7,936)	(7,157)
Net change in cash and cash equivalents	($4,545)	$2,515	$2,763
*Includes software development expenses of	($6,000)	($4,000)	($2,000)
and includes capital expenditures of	($2,000)	($1,600)	($1,200)

(Exhibit continued on next page . . .)

EXHIBIT 4	**(continued)**

Additional information:

For year ended 31 December	2006	2005	2004
Market value of outstanding debt	0	0	0
Amortization of capitalized software development expenses	($2,000)	($667)	0
Depreciation expense	($2,200)	($1,440)	($1,320)
Market price per share of common stock	$42	$26	$17
Shares of common stock outstanding (thousands)	6,780	9,765	10,999

---

1. Compute the following ratios for JHH based on the reported financial statements for fiscal year ended 31 December 2006, with no adjustments, and determine the approximate impact on these ratios if the company had expensed rather than capitalized its investments in software. (Assume the financial reporting does not affect reporting for income taxes, so there would be no change in the effective tax rate.)

   A. P/E: Price/Earnings per share

   B. P/CFO: Price/Operating cash flow per share

   C. EV/EBITDA: Enterprise value/EBITDA, where enterprise value is defined as the total market value of all sources of a company's financing, including equity and debt, and EBITDA is earnings before interest tax, depreciation, and amortization

2. Interpret the changes in the ratios.

Solution to 1: (Dollars are in thousands, except per-share amounts.) JHH's 2006 ratios are presented in the following table:

	Ratios	Solution to 1 (as Reported)	Solution to 2 (as Adjusted)
A.	P/E ratio	30.0	42.9
B.	P/CFO	19.0	31.6
C.	EV/EBITDA	16.3	24.7

A. Based on information as reported, the P/E ratio was 30.0 ($42/$1.40). Based on EPS adjusted to expense software development costs, the P/E ratio was 42.9 ($42/$0.98).

▶ Price: Assuming that the market value of the company's equity is based on its fundamentals, the price per share is $42, regardless of a difference in accounting.

▶ EPS: As reported, EPS was $1.40. Adjusted EPS was $0.98. Expensing software development costs would have reduced JHH's 2006 operating income by $6,000, but the company would have reported no amortization of prior years' software costs, which would have increased operating income by $2,000. The net change of $4,000 would have reduced operating income from the reported $13,317 to $9,317. The effective tax rate for 2006 ($3,825/$13,317) is 28.72%, and using this effective tax rate would give an adjusted net income of $6,641 [$9,317 × (1 – 0.2872)], compared to $9,492 before the adjustment. The EPS would therefore be reduced from the reported $1.40 to $0.98 (adjusted net income of $6,641 divided by 6,780 shares).

B. Based on information as reported, the P/CFO was 19.0 ($42/$2.21). Based on CFO adjusted to expense software development costs, the P/CFO was 31.6 ($42/$1.33).

▶ Price: Assuming that the market value of the company's equity is based on its fundamentals, the price per share is $42, regardless of a difference in accounting.

▶ CFO per share, as reported, was $2.21 (total operating cash flows $15,007 divided by 6,780 shares).

▶ CFO per share, as adjusted, was $1.33. The company's $6,000 expenditure on software development costs was reported as a cash outflow from investing activities, so expensing those costs would reduce cash from operating activities by $6,000, from the reported $15,007 to $9,007. Dividing adjusted total operating cash flow of $9,007 by 6,780 shares results in cash flow per share of $1.33.

C. Based on information as reported, the EV/EBITDA was 16.3 ($284,760/$17,517). Based on EBITDA adjusted to expense software development costs, the EV/EBITDA was 24.7 ($284,760/$11,517).

▶ Enterprise Value: Enterprise value is the sum of the market value of the company's equity and debt. JHH has no debt, and therefore the enterprise value is equal to the market value of its equity. The market value of its equity is $284,760 ($42 per share times 6,780 shares).

▶ EBITDA, as reported, was $17,517 (earnings before interest and taxes of $13,317 plus $2,200 depreciation plus $2,000 amortization).

▶ EBITDA, adjusted for expensing software development costs by the inclusion of $6,000 development expense and the exclusion of $2,000 amortization of prior expense, would be $11,517 (earnings before interest and taxes of $9,317 plus $2,200 depreciation plus $0 amortization).

Solution to 2: Expensing software development costs would decrease historical profits, operating cash flow, and EBITDA, and would thus increase all market multiples. So JHH's stock would appear more expensive if it expensed rather than capitalized the software development costs.

If the unadjusted market-based ratios were used in the comparison of JHH to its competitor that expenses all software development expenditures, then JHH might appear to be under-priced when the difference is solely related to accounting factors. JHH's adjusted market-based ratios provide a better basis for comparison.

Footnote disclosure of accounting policy for software development:
Expenses that are related to the conceptual formulation and design of software products are expensed to research and development as incurred. The company capitalizes expenses that are incurred to produce the finished product after technological feasibility has been established.

include income, long-lived assets, or cash flow from operations—such as return on equity—will also be affected.

For the company in Example 4, current period software development expenditures exceed the amortization of prior periods' capitalized software development expenditures. As a result, expensing rather than capitalizing software development costs would have the effect of lowering income. If, however, software development expenditures slowed such that current expenditures were lower than the amortization of prior periods' capitalized software development expenditures, then expensing software development costs would have the effect of increasing income relative to capitalizing it.

3.3 Intangible Assets Acquired in a Business Combination

When one company acquires another company, the transaction is accounted for using the **purchase method** of accounting.[7] Under the purchase method, the company identified as the acquirer allocates the purchase price to each asset acquired (and each liability assumed) on the basis of its fair value. If the purchase price exceeds the sum of the amounts that can be allocated to individual assets and liabilities, the excess is recorded as goodwill. Goodwill is an intangible asset that cannot be identified separately from the business as a whole.

U.S. accounting standards present two criteria to judge whether an intangible asset should be treated separately from goodwill, namely it must be either an item arising from contractual or legal rights, or an item that can be separated from the acquired company. Examples of intangible assets that are treated separately from goodwill include the intangible assets mentioned above that involve exclusive rights (patents, copyrights, franchises, licenses), as well as items such as internet domain names, video and audiovisual materials, and numerous others. International accounting standards specify that an intangible asset meet the definition of an intangible asset and be capable of being measured reliably.

Exhibit 5, for example, describes how one company allocated a portion of the $19 million purchase price of an acquisition to intangible assets—licenses, customer lists, and goodwill.

EXHIBIT 5	Acquisition of Intangible Assets Through a Business Combination

Excerpt from annual report of United States Cellular Corporation (AMEX: USM):

> "On April 21, 2006, U.S. Cellular purchased the remaining ownership interest in the Tennessee RSA No. 3 Limited Partnership, a wireless market operator in which it had previously owned a 16.7% interest, for approximately $19.0 million in cash, subject to a working capital adjustment. This acquisition increased investments in licenses, goodwill and customer lists by $5.5 million, $4.1 million and $2.0 million, respectively."

Source: Company's 10-K filed 23 April 2007, page 61.

---

[7] SFAS No. 141 specifies U.S. GAAP accounting for business combinations, and IFRS 3 specifies requirements under international standards. Both sets of standards require use of the purchase method.

One item with somewhat different accounting treatment under U.S. GAAP is in-process research and development (R&D). Amounts considered in-process R&D are amounts related to a particular project that is incomplete at the time of an acquisition. Any part of the purchase price that is allocated to in-process R&D must be expensed at the time of acquisition.

In analyzing a company reporting a write-off of in-process R&D, items to consider are the effect on a company's future earnings trend and relevance to forecasting earnings. Appearance of a favorable earnings trend would result from a company's decision to allocate a greater amount of the acquisition price to in-process R&D, which would reduce earnings in the current year but contribute to a more favorable earnings trend in future years. With respect to forecasting, if the current period earnings are used as a baseline for forecasting future earnings, they should usually be adjusted to eliminate the effect of an in-process R&D write-off because such an item would not typically be viewed as a recurring part of operations.

Exhibit 6 illustrates how one company provided information, adjusted for the effects of in-process R&D, and the rationale for doing so. The example disclosures in Exhibit 6 should facilitate an analyst's evaluation of the trend in the company's R&D expenditures, both including and excluding R&D expenditures related to acquisitions.

EXHIBIT 6	Disclosure of In-Process R&D

Excerpt from Earnings Announcement by Becton, Dickinson and Company (NYSE: BDX):

> "We present research and development expense, both alone and as a percentage of revenues, for the first six months of fiscal year 2007 after excluding the impact of the in-process research and development ("R&D") charge relating to the acquisition of TriPath Imaging, Inc. . . . We also present these measures for the second quarter and first six months of fiscal year 2006 after excluding the impact of the in-process R&D charge relating to the acquisition of GeneOhm Sciences Inc. . . . These noncash charges are not considered by management to be part of ordinary operations and served to increase reported R&D expense for the period in which they were incurred. Management believes that these adjusted measures are more indicative of BD's R&D activities for the period presented. Management also presents these adjusted measures in order to assist investors in comparing BD's R&D expense for the period to other periods."

Source: Company's Form 8-K filed 25 April 2007 announcing results for the second fiscal quarter ending 31 March 2007.

Unlike U.S. GAAP, IFRS does not require the immediate write-off of in-process R&D acquired in a business combination. A company may either identify the amount of in-process R&D as a separate asset with a finite life, or include the asset as part of goodwill. Exhibit 7 provides an example of the disclosures by one Dutch company that reports under IFRS, but reconciles their results to U.S. GAAP.

To summarize accounting treatment for R&D, Exhibit 8 shows the types of R&D expenditures discussed in this section and their treatment under IFRS and U.S. GAAP.

EXHIBIT 7	Differences in Accounting for In-Process R&D between U.S. GAAP and IFRS

Excerpt from earnings announcement by CRUCELL NV (Euronext, NASDAQ: CRXL; Swiss Exchange: CRX):

> "RECONCILIATION IFRS TO U.S. GAAP
>
> Shareholders equity under U.S. GAAP is €413.4 million, €50.9 million lower than under IFRS. This is primarily due to the different method to determine the Berna acquisition price and write-off of in-process R&D of €61.8 million required under U.S. GAAP . . . Net loss under U.S. GAAP for the six months ended June 30, 2006, is €102.4 million versus a loss of €40.9 million under IFRS. The difference is mainly due to the write-off of in-process R&D under U.S. GAAP as well as some other minor differences."

Source: Company's Form 6-K filed 29 August 2006 announcing results for the second quarter of 2006.

EXHIBIT 8		
Type of Expenditure	**IFRS**	**U.S. GAAP**
Research	Expense as incurred	Expense as incurred
Development	Capitalize if certain criteria are met	Expense as incurred, except for: ▶ Costs to develop a software product to sell after feasibility established ▶ Certain costs to develop software for internal use
In-process R&D (IPRD) acquired in a business combination	Either identify IPRD as a separate asset with a finite life, or include as part of goodwill	Expense immediately upon acquisition

Having described the accounting for acquisition of long-lived assets, we turn to the topic of allocating their costs to subsequent periods.

DEPRECIATING LONG-LIVED TANGIBLE ASSETS   4

As described in an earlier reading, the capitalized cost of a long-lived tangible asset (other than land, which is not depreciated) is allocated to subsequent periods as a depreciation expense. The sum of historical depreciation expenses, i.e. accumulated depreciation, is netted against the asset's historical cost on the balance sheet. Detail on depreciation expense and the amount of accumulated depreciation typically appears in a footnote to the financial statements. Companies also describe the depreciation method used along with information on the assumptions used. The following paragraphs review depreciation methods, discuss estimates required for depreciation calculations, and present an analytical tool for using fixed asset disclosure to estimate the average age of companies' depreciable assets.

4.1 Depreciation Methods

As described in the reading "Understanding the Income Statement," depreciation methods include: the straight-line method, in which the cost of an asset is evenly distributed over its useful life; accelerated methods, in which the allocation of cost is greater in earlier years; and units-of-production methods, in which the allocation of cost corresponds to the actual use of an asset in a particular period.

The straight-line method is calculated as depreciable cost divided by estimated useful life, where depreciable cost is the historical cost minus the estimated salvage (i.e., residual) value. A common accelerated method is the declining balance method, in which the amount of depreciation expense is calculated as some percentage of the remaining balance of cost, net of accumulated depreciation, i.e. carrying value. In a units-of-production method, the amount of depreciation expense is based on the proportion of the asset's production during a period compared to the total estimated productive capacity of the asset over its useful life. Example 5 provides a review of these depreciation methods.

EXAMPLE 5

Review of Depreciation Methods

You are analyzing three (hypothetical) companies: EVEN-LI Co., SOONER Inc., and AZUSED Co. Each of the companies buys an identical piece of box-manufacturing equipment, but each uses a different method of depreciation. Each company's depreciation method, as disclosed in the footnotes to their financial statements, and assumptions are as follows:

Depreciation method
- ► EVEN-LI Co.: straight-line method.
- ► SOONER Inc.: double-declining balance method for the first year, switching to straight-line for the remaining years.
- ► AZUSED Co.: units-of-production method.

Assumptions
- ► Cost of equipment: $2,300.
- ► Estimated salvage value: $100.
- ► Useful life: 4 years.
- ► Total productive capacity: 800 boxes.
- ► Production in each of the four years: 200 boxes in the first year, 300 in the second year, 200 in the third year, and 100 in the fourth year.
- ► For each company, revenues in each year were $3,000 and expenses, other than depreciation, were $1,000. The tax rate is 32 percent.

1. Using the following sample template, record each company's beginning and ending net book value, end-of-year accumulated depreciation, and annual depreciation expense for the box-manufacturing equipment.
2. Explain the significant differences in the timing of the recognition of the depreciation expense.

3. Calculate each company's net profit margin (net income divided by sales) for each of the four years, and assess the impact of the depreciation methods on that ratio.

Sample template:

	Beginning Net Book Value	Depreciation Expense	Accumulated Depreciation	Ending Net Book Value
Year 1				
Year 2				
Year 3				
Year 4				

Solution to 1: For *every* company, the following apply: Accumulated year-end depreciation equals the balance from the previous year plus the current year's depreciation expense; ending net book value equals original cost minus accumulated year-end depreciation (which is the same as beginning net book value minus depreciation expense); beginning net book value in year one equals the purchase price; and beginning net book value in years two and three equals the ending net book value of the prior year. The following notes describe how depreciation *expense* is calculated for each company.

EVEN-LI Co. uses the straight-line method, so depreciation expense in each year equals $550, which is calculated as ($2,300 original cost − $100 salvage value)/4 years.

	Beginning Net Book Value	Depreciation Expense	Accumulated Year-End Depreciation	Ending Net Book Value
Year 1	$2,300	$550	$550	$1,750
Year 2	1,750	550	1,100	1,200
Year 3	1,200	550	1,650	650
Year 4	650	550	2,200	100

SOONER Inc. uses the double-declining balance method for the first year, switching to straight-line for the remaining years. The depreciation rate for the double-declining balance method is double the depreciation rate for the straight-line method. The straight-line method is depreciating at a rate of one-fourth (1/4) per year, thus the depreciation rate for the double-declining balance method is one-half (1/2). So the depreciation expense for the first year is one-half of the beginning balance $1,150 (1/2 of initial balance of $2,300). Note that under this method, the depreciation rate of 1/2 is applied to the total cost of the asset, without adjustment for expected salvage value. After the first year, the ending net book value is $1,150 (original cost of

$2,300 minus accumulated depreciation of $1,150.) Switching to the straight-line method for the remaining years gives a depreciation expense of $350, calculated as ($1,150 remaining book value – $100 salvage value)/3 years.

	Beginning Net Book Value	Depreciation Expense	Accumulated Year-End Depreciation	Ending Net Book Value
Year 1	$2,300	$1,150	$1,150	$1,150
Year 2	1,150	350	1,500	800
Year 3	800	350	1,850	450
Year 4	450	350	2,200	100

AZUSED Co. uses the units-of-production method. Dividing the equipment's total depreciable cost by its total productive capacity gives a cost per unit of $2.75, calculated as ($2,300 original cost – $100 salvage value)/800. So the depreciation expense each year is the number of units produced times $2.75. For year 1, the amount of depreciation expense is $550 (200 units times $2.75). For year 2, the amount is $825 (300 units times $2.75). For year 3, the amount is $550. For year 4, the amount is $275.

	Beginning Net Book Value	Depreciation Expense	Accumulated Year-End Depreciation	Ending Net Book Value
Year 1	$2,300	$550	$550	$1,750
Year 2	1,750	825	1,375	925
Year 3	925	550	1,925	375
Year 4	375	275	2,200	100

Solution to 2: All three methods result in the same total depreciation expense over the life of the equipment. The significant differences are simply in the timing of the recognition of the expense with the straight-line method recognizing the expense evenly, the accelerated method recognizing most of the expense in the first year, and the units-of-production method recognizing the expense based on usage.

Under all three methods, the ending net book value is $100; however, because the accelerated method recognizes depreciation expense earlier, the net book value declines more quickly under the accelerated method.

Solution to 3: Because revenues and expenses other than depreciation are assumed equal in each year, EVEN-LI, which uses straight-line depreciation, reports the same income before tax, net income, and net profit margin for each of the four years. SOONER, which uses an accelerated depreciation method in the first year, reports lower income before tax, net income, and net profit margin in the initial year because its depreciation expense is higher in that year. AZUSED, which employs a usage-based depreciation method, reports income before tax, net income, and a net profit margin that varies with the variations in usage of the asset.

Calculations in the table below are as follows:
- ▶ Income before tax equals revenues of $3,000 minus expenses (other than depreciation) of $1,000 minus depreciation expense for each company.
- ▶ Net income equals income before tax times (1 minus tax rate).
- ▶ Net profit margin equals net income divided by sales.

EVEN-LI Co.	Income before Tax	Net Income	Net Profit Margin
Year 1	$1,450	$986	32.9%
Year 2	1,450	986	32.9
Year 3	1,450	986	32.9
Year 4	1,450	986	32.9
SOONER Inc.			
Year 1	$850	$578	19.3%
Year 2	1,650	1,122	37.4
Year 3	1,650	1,122	37.4
Year 4	1,650	1,122	37.4
AZUSED Co.			
Year 1	$1,450	$986	32.9%
Year 2	1,175	799	26.6
Year 3	1,450	986	32.9
Year 4	1,725	1,173	39.1

Recall that in the United States, a company need not use the same depreciation method for financial reporting and taxes. (In many countries, a company must follow the same accounting methods for financial and tax reporting.) Typically companies use the straight-line method for financial reporting and an accelerated depreciation method prescribed by the Internal Revenue Service, known as MACRS (Modified Accelerated Cost Recovery System), for tax purposes. Differences in depreciation methods create differences in the amount of taxes computed, based on financial reporting and the amount of taxes actually owed. Although these differences eventually reverse because the total depreciation is the same regardless of the timing of its recognition in the financial statements versus the tax return, during the period of the difference the balance sheet will show deferred taxes.

Specifically, if a company uses straight-line depreciation for financial reporting and an accelerated depreciation method for tax purposes, the company's financial statements will report lower depreciation expenses and thus higher pre-tax income in the first year, compared with the amount of depreciation expense and taxable income included in its tax reporting. (Compare the depreciation expense in year one for EVEN-LI and SOONER, Inc. in the above example.) Tax expense calculated based on pre-tax income shown in the financial statements will be higher than taxes payable based on taxable income; the difference between the two amounts is deferred tax.

4.2 Estimates Required for Depreciation Calculations

As mentioned in an earlier reading, significant estimates required for depreciation calculations include the useful life of the equipment (or its total lifetime productive capacity) and its expected residual value at the end of that useful life. A longer useful life and higher expected residual value decrease the amount of annual depreciation relative to a shorter useful life and lower expected residual value.

Additional estimates are required to allocate depreciation expense between the cost of goods sold and sales, general, and administrative expenses (SG&A). Footnotes to the financial statements often disclose some information regarding which income statement line item includes depreciation, although the exact amount of detail disclosed by individual companies varies. Including a higher proportion of depreciation expense in cost of goods sold lowers the gross margin, and lowers the operating expenses, but does not affect the operating margin. When comparing two companies, apportionment of depreciation to cost of goods versus SG&A can contribute to explaining differences in gross margins and operating expenses.

4.3 Using Fixed Asset Disclosures to Compare Companies' Average Age of Depreciable Assets

Under U.S. GAAP, companies value long-lived assets at historical cost net of accumulated depreciation. International accounting standards (IAS 16) permit companies to measure property, plant, and equipment (PPE) either under a cost model, i.e. historical cost minus accumulated depreciation, or under a revaluation model, i.e. fair value.[8] Under the revaluation model, the relationship between carrying value, accumulated depreciation, and depreciation expense will differ when the carrying value differs significantly from the historical cost. The following discussion applies primarily to PPE reported under a historical cost model.

The balance sheet reports PPE at historical cost net of accumulated depreciation. The statement of cash flows typically shows depreciation expense (or depreciation plus amortization) as a line item in the adjustments of net income

---

[8] Research indicates that revaluations of property, plant, and equipment permitted under IFRS but prohibited under U.S. GAAP are an important cause of the lack of comparability of financial statements prepared under the two sets of standards. For example see, J. L. Haverty, "Are IFRS and U.S. GAAP converging? Some evidence from People's Republic of China companies listed on the New York Stock Exchange," *Journal of International Accounting, Auditing and Taxes,* Volume 15, Issue 1 (2006): 48–71.

to cash from operations. The notes to the financial statements describe the company's accounting method(s), the range of estimated useful lives, historical cost by main category of fixed asset, and annual depreciation expense.

The reading on applications of financial statement analysis provides an example of using the amount of depreciation expense and the balance of net property, plant, and equipment (PPE) to estimate the average remaining useful life of a company's asset base. Specifically, the average remaining useful life of a company's assets can be estimated as net PPE divided by depreciation expense. In this section, we review that analysis as well as the estimation of the average age of a company's depreciable assets. To estimate the average age of the asset base, divide accumulated depreciation by depreciation expense.

These estimates simply reflect the following relationships for assets accounted for on a historical cost basis: total historical cost minus accumulated depreciation equals net PPE; and, under straight-line depreciation, total historical cost less salvage value divided by estimated useful life equals annual depreciation expense. Equivalently, total historical cost less salvage value divided by annual depreciation expense equals estimated useful life.

Assuming, for simplicity, straight-line depreciation and no salvage value, we have the following:

Estimated total useful life	=	Time elapsed since purchase (age)	+	Estimated remaining life
Historical cost ÷ Annual depreciation expense	=	Estimated total useful life		
Historical cost	=	Accumulated depreciation	+	Net PPE

Equivalently,

Estimated total useful life	=	Estimated age of equipment	+	Estimated remaining life
Historical cost ÷ Annual depreciation expense	=	Accumulated depreciation ÷ Annual depreciation expense	+	Net PPE ÷ Annual depreciation expense

The application of these estimates can be illustrated by a hypothetical example of a company with a single depreciable asset. Assume the asset initially cost $100, had an estimated useful life of 10 years, and an estimated salvage value of $0. Each year, the company records a depreciation expense of $10, so accumulated depreciation will equal $10 times the number of years since the asset was acquired (when the asset is 7 years old, accumulated depreciation will be $70) and, equivalently, the age of the asset will equal accumulated depreciation divided by the annual depreciation expense.

In practice, such estimates are difficult to make with great precision. Companies use depreciation methods other than the straight-line method and have numerous assets with varying useful lives and salvage values, including some assets that are fully depreciated, so this approach produces an estimate only. Moreover, fixed asset disclosures are often quite general. Consequently, these estimates may be primarily useful to identify areas for further investigation.

One further general metric compares annual capital expenditures to annual depreciation expense. The metric provides a very general indicator of the rate at which a company is replacing its PPE relative to the rate at which the PPE is being depreciated.

EXAMPLE 6

Using Fixed Asset Disclosure to Compare Companies' Average Age of Depreciable Assets

You are analyzing the property, plant, and equipment of three international paper and paper products companies:

▶ Abitibi-Consolidated Inc. (NYSE: ABY; TSX: A) is a Canadian company that manufactures newsprint, commercial printing papers, and other wood products.

▶ International Paper Company (NYSE: IP) is a U.S. paper and packaging company.

▶ UPM-Kymmene Corporation (UPM) is a Finnish company that manufactures fine and specialty papers, newsprint, magazine papers, and other related products. The company's common stock is listed on the Helsinki and New York stock exchanges.

The following table presents selected information from the companies' financial statements.

	ABY	IP	UPM
Currency, millions of:	Canadian $	U.S. $	Euro €
Historical cost total PPE	$7,768	$23,043	€16,997
Accumulated depreciation	3,784	14,050	10,497
Net PPE	3,984	8,993	6,500
Land included in PPE	Not separated	Not separated	632
Annual depreciation expense (annual impairment)	424	1,158	804 (239)
Capital expenditure	165	1,009	635
Accounting standards	Canadian GAAP	U.S. GAAP	IFRS
PPE measurement	Historical cost	Historical cost	Historical cost
Depreciation method	Straight-line	Units-of-production for pulp and paper mills;* straight-line for other	Straight-line
Useful life of assets, in years, except as noted	20–25 (buildings, pulp and paper mills); 10–12 (sawmill equip.); 10–20 (roads, camps, woodlands); 40 (power plants)	Straight-line depreciation rates are 2.5% to 8.5% (buildings), and 5% to 33% (machinery and equipment)	25–40 (buildings); 15–20 (heavy equip.); 5–15 (light equip.)

*Pulp and paper mills' historical costs as disclosed in a footnote total $16,665 million. Depreciation expense and accumulated depreciation is not separately reported for mills.

1. Based on the above data for each company, use the standard formulas to estimate the total useful life, age, and remaining useful life of PPE.

2. Interpret the estimates. What items might affect comparisons across these companies?

3. How does each company's 2006 depreciation expense compare to its capital expenditures for the year?

Solution to 1: The following table presents the estimated total useful life, estimated age, and estimated remaining useful life of PPE using the standard formulas.

Estimates	ABY	IP	UPM
Estimated total useful life (years)	18.3	19.9	21.1
Estimated age (years)	8.9	12.1	13.1
Estimated remaining life (years)	9.4	7.8	8.1

The computations are explained using UPM's data. The estimated total useful life of PPE is total historical cost of PPE of €16,997 divided by annual depreciation expense of €804, giving 21.1 years. Estimated age and estimated remaining life are obtained by dividing accumulated depreciation of €10,497 and net PPE of €6,500 by the annual depreciation expense of €804, giving 13.1 years and 8.1 years respectively.

Ideally, the estimates of asset lives illustrated in this example should exclude land, which is not depreciable, when the information is available; however, UPM is the only one of the three companies for which land appeared to be disclosed separately and the above table thus presents the estimates without adjusting UPM for land costs in order to compare it with the other two companies. As an illustration of the calculations to exclude land, excluding UPM's land would give an estimated total useful life of 20.4 years ([total cost €16,997 minus land cost of €632] divided by annual depreciation expense of €804 million).

Solution to 2: The estimated total useful life suggests that UPM depreciates its PPE over the longest period—21.1 years versus 19.9 and 18.3 for IP and ABY, respectively—although the differences are not dramatic across the companies. This result can be compared, to an extent, to the useful life of assets noted by the companies. UPM depreciates its buildings over 25 to 40 years, while ABY depreciates its buildings over 20 to 25 years. IP depreciates its buildings (other than pulp and paper mills) over 12 years (1 divided by a depreciation rate of 8.5 percent) to 40 years (1 divided by a depreciation rate of 2.5 percent).

The estimated age of the equipment suggests that ABY has the newest PPE with an estimated age of 8.9 years. Additionally, the estimates suggest that only 49 percent of ABY's assets' useful lives have passed (8.9 years divided by 18.3 years, or equivalently, C$3,784 million divided by C$7,768 million). In comparison, over 60 percent of the useful lives of the PPE of both IP and UPM have passed.

Items that can affect comparisons across the companies include business differences, such as differences in composition of the companies' operations and differences in acquisition and divestiture activity. In addition, the companies all use different sets of accounting standards, and IP discloses that it uses the units-of-production method for the largest component of its PPE. Differences in disclosures, e.g. in the categories of assets disclosed, also can affect comparisons.

Solution to 3: Capital expenditure as a percentage of depreciation is 39 percent for ABY, 87 percent for IP, and 79 percent for UPM. Based on this metric, IP is replacing its PPE at a rate almost comparable to the rate its PPE is being depreciated. Because IP uses the units-of-production method of depreciation, this implies that IP is replacing its PPE at nearly the same rate of usage. ABY's metric suggests the company is replacing its PPE at a slower rate than the PPE is being depreciated, suggesting that further examination of the company's capital expenditure policies may be needed.

Sources:

For ABY, Form 40-F for the year ended 31 December 2006, filed 15 March 2007.

For IP, Form 10-K for the year ended 31 December 2006, filed 28 February 2007.

For UPM, Form 20-F for the year ended 31 December 2006, filed 15 March 2007.

5   AMORTIZING INTANGIBLE ASSETS WITH FINITE USEFUL LIVES

This section discusses cost allocation for intangible assets with finite useful lives, i.e. amortization. As noted, amortization is effectively the same concept as depreciation. The term amortization applies to intangible assets, and the term depreciation applies to tangible assets.[9]

5.1 Amortizing Intangible Assets with Finite Useful Lives

Intangible assets with finite useful lives are amortized over their useful lives, following the pattern in which the benefits are used up. Assets without a finite useful life, i.e., with an indefinite useful life, are not amortized. In both cases, the assets are periodically reviewed for impairment (discussed in Section 8).

Examples of intangible assets with finite useful lives include: an acquired customer list expected to provide benefits to a direct-mail marketing company for two to three years; an acquired patent or copyright with a specific expiration date; an acquired license with a specific expiration date and no right to renew the license; or an acquired trademark for a product that a company plans to phase out over a specific number of years. Examples of intangible assets with

---

[9] Depletion is the term applied to a similar concept for natural resources; costs associated with those resources are allocated to a period based on the usage or extraction of those resources.

indefinite useful lives include: an acquired license which, although it has a specific expiration date, can be renewed at little or no cost; or an acquired trademark which, although it has a specific expiration, can be renewed at a minimal cost and relates to a product that a company plans to continue selling for the foreseeable future.

5.2 Estimates Required for Amortization Calculations

As with tangible assets, the estimates required for amortization calculations include the original amount at which the intangible asset is valued, its residual value at the end of its useful life, and the length of its useful life. Useful lives are estimated based on the expected use of the asset, considering any factors that may limit the life of the asset such as legal, regulatory, contractual, competitive, or economic.

ASSET RETIREMENT OBLIGATIONS

6

For many types of long-lived tangible assets, ownership involves not only a right to use the asset but also an obligation that must be fulfilled at the end of the asset's service life. For example, a company that owns and operates a landfill will have legal obligations, such as covering the land with topsoil and planting vegetation when sections of the landfill become full, and legal obligations after the end of the asset's service life, such as monitoring the ground water and air quality. These obligations are referred to as **asset retirement obligations (AROs)**.

As soon as a company is able to make a reasonable estimate of the costs it will incur as a result of those asset retirement obligations, the company reports the fair value of these estimated costs, with the fair value determined using a discounted cash flow approach. The fair value of the asset retirement obligations is reported as a liability, with the balancing offset being an increase in the carrying value of the asset. Afterward, the amount added to the asset's carrying value is expensed systematically (a concept similar to depreciation). The amount reported as a liability increases each year with the passage of time because it is based on the discounted present value of future cash flows. The increase in the amount of the liability is recognized as an operating expense, referred to as accretion expense.

EXAMPLE 7

Reporting an Asset Retirement Obligation

A (hypothetical) company, Wastaway Inc., disposes of waste at a landfill site. The landfill site is recorded as an asset, which the company is depreciating on a straight-line basis over its useful life of 10 years.[10] In the future, after the company finishes using the landfill site, state and federal laws require that the company undertake procedures to cap and close the landfill. Landfill caps range from a single layer of soil to a multi-layer system of soils and synthetic materials. Regulations also require that the location be monitored after closure to prevent future

---

[10] While land in and of itself is not depreciated, Wastaway Inc. can depreciate the landfill site (including site improvements and capital expenditures necessary to prepare the site) over its useful life.

damage to the air and water around the site. Wastaway Inc. estimates that the costs for capping, closing, and post-closure monitoring its landfill at the end of its 10-year useful life will total $450,000 (adjusted for inflation), equal to a present value of $200,872 when discounted at a rate of 8.4%, which is based on the company's credit standing. So the company will record the asset retirement costs of $200,872 as part of the cost of the long-lived asset (landfill site) and an ARO liability equal to $200,872.

The company will write off the asset at the same rate that it depreciates the landfill site asset and show this as a depreciation expense. The company will show changes in the ARO liability that occur because of the passage of time as an accretion expense. In this example, each year the company will recognize a depreciation expense equal to one-tenth (1/10) of the asset retirement costs ($20,087), and an accretion expense equal to 8.4 percent of the ARO liability balance. In year 1, the accretion expense will be $16,873 (8.4 percent times $200,872). For year 1, the total expense associated with the asset retirement obligation will be $36,960 ($20,087 + $16,873). At the end of year 1, i.e., the beginning of year 2, the ARO liability balance will have grown to $217,745 ($200,872 + $16,873), so the accretion expense for year 2 will be $18,291 (8.4 percent times $217,745). The total expense associated with the asset retirement obligation in year 2 will be $38,378 ($20,087 + $18,291).

1. What will be the accretion expense for year 3?

2. What will be the total expense associated with the asset retirement obligation in year 3?

3. At the end of the useful life of the landfill, what will be the balance of the ARO? What will be the balance of the asset?

Solution to 1: The accretion expense for year 3 will be $19,827. At the beginning of year 3, the ARO liability balance will have grown to $236,036 (the $217,745 balance at the beginning of year 2 plus the accretion expense of $18,291 for year 2). This ARO liability balance can also be computed as the present value of $450,000 discounted at a rate of 8.4 percent for the remaining period of 8 years. The accretion expense for year 3 equals $19,827 (8.4% × $236,036).

Solution to 2: The total expense associated with the asset retirement obligation in year 3 will be $39,914, which is determined by adding the accretion expense of $19,827 for year 3 to the annual depreciation expense of $20,087.

Solution to 3: At the end of the useful life of the landfill, the balance of the ARO liability will be $450,000. The beginning balance of the ARO liability was determined as the present value of $450,000 for 10 years at 8.4 percent, and each year's accretion reflects the increase in the ARO liability for 1 year at 8.4 percent; so after 10 years, the ARO liability equals $450,000. At the end of the useful life of the landfill, the balance of the asset will be $0. Each year's depreciation expense reduces the balance of the asset by 1/10; therefore, after 10 years, the balance of the asset will be zero.

For financial analysis, and particularly credit analysis, adjustments can reflect the debt-like nature of AROs. These adjustments, described in Standard & Poor's Corporate Ratings Criteria (2006), consider the AROs as debt and treat the related financial statement items in a manner consistent with debt. For example, to treat the AROs as debt, increase the amount of debt by the amount of the AROs, adjusted for such offsetting items as dedicated retirement fund assets and any tax savings that the company is likely to utilize. Anticipated tax savings reduce any deferred tax asset. To reclassify items consistent with treating the AROs as debt, reclassify the accretion amount, which is similar to an interest accrual, as an interest expense.

Some companies, such as utilities, have trust funds in excess of their asset retirement obligations. For example, Exhibit 9 shows that Constellation Energy Group Inc. (CEG) had an asset retirement obligation, primarily nuclear decommissioning costs, totaling $974.8 million at the end of 2006. However, the company's nuclear decommissioning trust fund totaled $1,240.1 million (i.e., $265.3 million more than the amount of the ARO). In addition, the company's net investments in the trust fund were $8.8 million for the year, compared to $3.1 million of new ARO liabilities, indicating that in 2006, the fund increased by more than the amount of the AROs. The U.S. Nuclear Regulatory Commission (NRC) requires nuclear power plant owners to decommission nuclear plants. Owners are required to pre-fund the decommissioning over the plants' 40-year life. For CEG, changes in the trust fund relative to the ARO liability reflect in part actions by utility regulators that control the rates customers can be charged and amounts allocated to decommissioning funds. Although the size of the asset retirement obligation and the trust fund are each large enough to merit separate disclosure on the face of the company's

EXHIBIT 9	Asset Retirement Obligations Constellation Energy Group Inc (NYSE: CEG) Selected Information for 2006		
Line Item ($ in Millions)		**As Reported**	**Where Reported**
Nuclear decommissioning trust funds (asset)		$1,240.1	B/S
Asset retirement obligations (liability)		$974.8	B/S
Investment in nuclear decommissioning trust fund securities		$394.6	CF
Proceeds from nuclear decommissioning trust fund securities		$385.8	CF
Net investments in nuclear decommissioning trust fund securities		$8.8	calculated
ARO liabilities incurred, net of liabilities settled		$3.1	FT 1

B/S—balance sheet; CF—statement of cash flows; FT—footnote

Explanation in the MD&A (page 37)

"Our nuclear decommissioning costs represent our largest asset retirement obligation. This obligation primarily results from the requirement to decommission and decontaminate our nuclear generating facilities in connection with their future retirement. We utilize site-specific decommissioning cost estimates to determine our nuclear asset retirement obligations. However, given the magnitude of the amounts involved, complicated and ever-changing technical and regulatory requirements, and the very long time horizons involved, the actual obligation could vary from the assumptions used in our estimates, and the impact of such variations could be material."

Source: Constellation Energy Group Inc. and Subsidiaries Form 10-K for the year ending 31 December 2006, filed 27 February 2007.

balance sheet, the significant size of the trust fund relative to the ARO indicates that the ARO would not have a negative credit impact.

In contrast with the company in Exhibit 9, the following example illustrates a company in which the amounts of the asset retirement obligation were not significant enough to warrant separate line item disclosure on the face of the company's balance sheet; however, there is a noticeable, if not dramatic, impact on the company's solvency ratios.

EXAMPLE 8

Asset Retirement Obligation

The following exhibit provides selected information on Waste Management, Inc. (WMI), a company involved in the collection, treatment, disposal, and recycling of waste.

1. Adjust the company's reported financial information to reflect the ARO liability as part of long-term debt. Assume that the company will be able to use all tax deductions when the ARO liability is paid. Then calculate and compare the company's interest coverage ratio and debt-to-equity ratio based on the information as reported and as adjusted.

2. Interpret the ratios.

EXHIBIT 10	Waste Management, Inc. Selected Information for 2006	
Line Item ($ Millions)	**As Reported**	**Where Reported**
Income from continuing operations before taxes	$1,474	I/S
Interest expense (including capitalized interest)	563	FT 3
EBIT	2,037	I/S
Total long-term debt	$8,317	B/S
Common shareholders' equity	6,222	B/S
Other information		
Trust funds and escrow accounts for environmental remediation obligations (asset)	$219	FT 3
Landfill and environment remediation liabilities (liability)	1,389	FT 4
Accretion on liability	79	FT 4
Effective tax rate	22.1%	FT 8

I/S—income statement; B/S—balance sheet; FT—footnote.

Source: Waste Management Inc. Form 10-K for the year ended 31 December 2006, filed 15 February 2007.

Solution to 1: To calculate the company's interest coverage ratio and debt-to-equity ratio reflecting the ARO liability as part of long-term debt, first adjust the ARO for the following offsetting items:

▶ $219 million trust funds and escrow accounts for environmental remediation obligations,

▶ $307 million tax savings when the ARO is paid (22.1 percent tax rate times $1,389 million ARO). The adjustment is made on a tax-adjusted basis because it is considered likely that the company will be able to make use of the tax deduction.

The ARO, after deducting these offsetting adjustments is $863 million.

Interest expense for the period is adjusted by the amount of the accretion, which is $79 million.

The following table summarizes these adjustments and presents the ratios before and after these adjustments.

Line Item	As Reported	Adjustment	As Adjusted
Income from continuing operations before taxes	$1,474		$1,474
Interest expense (including capitalized interest)	$ 563	$79	$ 642
EBIT	$2,037	$79	$2,116
Total long term debt	$8,317	$863	$9,180
Common shareholders' equity	$6,222		$6,222
Ratios			
Interest coverage	3.6x		3.3x
Debt-to-equity	1.34		1.48

The interest coverage ratio is 3.6 ($2,037 million/$563 million) before any adjustment and 3.3 ($2,116 million/$642 million) after the adjustment. The debt-to-equity ratio before adjustment is 1.34 ($8,317 million/$6,222 million) and 1.48 ($9,180 million/$6,222 million) after the adjustment.

Solution to 2: The interest coverage ratio, after adjusting to treat the current period accretion as interest expense, declines from 3.6x to 3.3x. This solvency indicator shows that the company's coverage is lower, i.e. the company has a somewhat lower safety cushion against a decline in income on an adjusted basis.

The company's debt-to-equity ratio increases from 1.34 to 1.48. Prior to adjustment, the company had $1.34 in debt for every $1 of equity, but after adjusting to treat the asset retirement obligation as debt, the company has $1.48 in debt for every $1 of equity. This ratio indicates that the company's solvency position is weaker after adjusting to treat the asset retirement obligation as debt.

DISPOSAL OF LONG-LIVED OPERATING ASSETS 7

A company may dispose of a long-lived operating asset by selling it, exchanging it, or abandoning it. Assets that are to be sold are classified as assets held for sale, in contrast to assets held for use.

7.1 Sale of Long-Lived Assets

The gain or loss on the sale of long-lived assets is computed as the sales proceeds minus the carrying value of the asset at the time of sale. An asset's carrying value is typically the net book value, i.e. the historical cost minus accumulated depreciation (unless the asset's carrying value has been changed to reflect impairment and/or revaluation, as discussed in Sections 8 and 9).

EXAMPLE 9

Calculation of Gain or Loss on the Sale of Long-Lived Assets

Moussilauke Diners Inc. (hypothetical company), as a result of revamping its menus to focus on healthier food items, sells 450 used pizza ovens and reports a gain on the sale of $1.2 million. The ovens had a carrying value of $1.9 million (original cost $5.1 million less $3.2 million of accumulated depreciation). At what price did Moussilauke sell the ovens?

A. $0.7 million.

B. $0.9 million.

C. $3.1 million.

D. $3.3 million.

Solution: C is correct. Moussilauke sold the ovens at a price of $3.1 million, and recognized a gain of $1.2 million ($3.1 million minus $1.9 million) on the sale.

A gain or loss on the sale of an asset is disclosed on the income statement, either as a component of other gains and losses or in a separate line item when the amount is material. A company typically discloses further detail about the sale in the management discussion and analysis (MD&A) and/or financial statement footnotes. In addition, a statement of cash flows prepared using the indirect method adjusts net income to remove any gain or loss on the sale from operating cash flow, and to include the amount of proceeds from the sale in cash from investing activities. Recall that the indirect method of the statement of cash flows begins with net income and makes all adjustments to arrive at cash from operations, including removal of gains or losses from nonoperating activities.

During an accounting period in which a company makes the decision to dispose of a long-lived operating asset by selling it and commences the sale process, the company classifies the asset (or group of assets) as held for sale. The asset or group of assets, referred to as a "component of an entity," can be a subsidiary, a business segment, or an asset group (defined in SFAS No. 144 as the "lowest level for which identifiable cash flows are largely independent of the cash flows of other groups of assets and liabilities"). So a component could be a subsidiary or a division that produces some product or a manufacturing plant within that division, so long as the plant's cash flows could be clearly distinguished. In IFRS 5, a "component of an entity" is defined as "Operations and cash flows that can be clearly distinguished, operationally and for financial reporting purposes, from the rest of the entity."

The company measures the value of the held-for-sale asset at the lower of its carrying value or fair value less cost to sell.[11] Costs to sell include items such as legal fees and title transfer fees. The company no longer records depreciation on

---

[11] SFAS No. 144 specifies U.S. GAAP accounting for long-lived assets to be disposed of by sale, and IFRS 5 specifies requirements under international standards. Accounting for long-lived assets held for sale and the classification and presentation of discontinued items is considered to be substantially the same under the two standards (IFRS 5, IN5).

the asset. If the fair value of the asset, net of the cost to sell it, is less than its carrying value, the company records an impairment loss. Assets that comprise a component of a company (defined above) are reported in "discontinued operations" if they have been sold or classified as held for sale in an accounting period.

To illustrate the financial statement impact of an asset sale, consider the sale by Pfizer Inc. (Pfizer) of its Consumer Healthcare business in 2006. Pfizer's MD&A in its 2006 annual report (page 8) discloses that, "In the fourth quarter of 2006, we sold our Consumer Healthcare business for $16.6 billion, and recorded a gain of approximately $10.2 billion ($7.9 billion, net of tax)." Exhibit 11 illustrates the impact on the company's balance sheet, income statement, and statement of cash flows. At year-end 2005, Pfizer's balance sheet shows $6.7 billion in assets of discontinued operations and other assets held for sale, a significant portion of which related to the consumer healthcare business. Pfizer's income statement for 2006 shows the $7.9 billion gain on the sale, net of tax. The statement of cash flows shows a reconciliation item to remove the $10.2 billion gain (pre-tax) from net income. Because most of the sale proceeds were apparently received in the form of short-term investments rather than cash, Pfizer discloses a non-cash transaction of $16.4 billion as supplemental information on its statement of cash flows. The $200 million difference between the total sales proceeds disclosed in the MD&A and the amount received as short term investments ($16.6 billion minus $16.4 billion) would be included among the company's investing cash inflows.

EXHIBIT 11	Disclosures on Pfizer's Financial Statements Related to the Consumer Healthcare Business

On Balance Sheet as of 31 December 2005

Assets of discontinued operations and other assets held for sale	$6,659 million

On Income Statement for the year ended 31 December 2006

Gains on sales of discontinued items – net of tax	$7,880 million

On Statement of Cash Flows for the year ended 31 December 2006

Operating activities	
Adjustments to reconcile net income to net cash provided by operating activities:	
Gains on sales of discontinued operations	($10,243 million)
Supplemental Cash Flow Information	
Non-cash transactions:	
Sale of the Consumer Healthcare business (portion of proceeds received in the form of short-term investments)	$16,429 million

Differences in asset sales transactions result in different presentations. Example 10 shows an instance where a portion of a sale was considered to be the sale of assets that were part of the company's continuing operations, and the other portion of the sale was considered to be the sale of assets that constituted discontinued operations by the company. The gain on the portion of the sale transaction considered part of the company's continuing operations is shown in operating income. The gain on the portion considered discontinued operations of the company is shown as a gain on the sale of discontinued operations. The amount of Jupitermedia's 2005 asset sale was relatively large and had a significant impact on reported financial performance. Evaluating the company, excluding the asset sales, can provide a better picture of the company's past operating performance and the outlook for its future performance.

EXAMPLE 10

Financial Statement Reporting of the Sale of Long-Lived Assets

Jupitermedia (NasdaqGS: JUPM) sells photos, clip art, music, and online information to customers in information technology and media design. For the year ended 2005, the company's income statement and statement of cash flow (abbreviated versions below) provide information about an asset sale, which is further described in the management discussion and analysis (MD&A). From the company's MD&A:

► "On August 5, 2005, Jupitermedia sold its Search Engine Strategies and its ClickZ.com Network of Web sites (collectively known as "SES") to Incisive Media plc, a London Stock Exchange listed media company, for $43.0 million in cash, subject to certain post-closing adjustments." (Company's 2006 10-K, page 26)

► "As part of the sale of SES on August 5, 2005, we sold our ClickZ.com Network of Web sites to Incisive Media plc, which resulted in a gain of $13.3 million." (Company's 2006 10-K, page 30)

EXHIBIT 12	**Excerpts from Jupitermedia Corporation Financial Statements [Abbreviated] Consolidated Statements of Operations**

	Year Ended 31 December		
Line Items ($ Thousands)	2004	2005	2006
Revenues	$52,636	$113,754	$137,530
Cost of revenues (exclusive of items shown separately below)	15,917	36,841	50,683
Advertising, selling, general	19,929	40,170	57,112
Depreciation and amortization	2,970	6,579	13,386
Gain on sale of assets, net	0	13,259	0
Total operating expenses	$38,816	$70,331	$121,181
Operating income	$13,820	$43,423	$16,349
Interest and investment income (loss), net	353	392	138
Interest expense	(130)	(3,508)	(5,544)
Income before income taxes, minority interests and equity income (loss) from investments, net	$14,043	$40,307	$10,943
Provision (benefit) for income taxes	288	(19,692)	3,625
Minority interests	(89)	(46)	(34)
Equity income (loss) from investments, net	(31)	270	256
Income from continuing operations	$13,635	$60,223	$7,540
Income from discontinued operations, net of taxes	2,102	2,332	11
Gain on sale of discontinued operations, net of taxes	0	15,844	5,573
Net income	$15,737	$78,399	$13,124

A footnote discloses that the benefit for income taxes of $19.7 million in 2005 was the result of reversing a valuation allowance related to a deferred tax asset.

(Exhibit continued on next page . . . .)

EXHIBIT 12 (continued)			
	Year Ended 31 December		
Line Items ($ Thousands)	**2004**	**2005**	**2006**
Cash flows from operating activities:			
Income from continuing operations	$13,635	$60,223	$7,540
Adjustments to reconcile income from continuing operations to net cash provided by operating activities:			
Depreciation and amortization	2,970	6,579	13,386
Gain on sale of assets, net	0	(13,259)	0
Deferred income taxes	0	(24,549)	1,665
All other non-operating or non-cash items	(204)	(228)	3,065
Changes in current assets and liabilities:			
Accounts receivable, net	(1,155)	(606)	(3,653)
Prepaid expenses and other	134	1,230	72
Accounts payable and accrued expenses	(470)	(4,451)	(11,325)
Deferred revenues	2,208	101	1,644
Discontinued operations	2,693	1,287	1,054
Net cash provided by operating activities	$19,811	$26,327	$13,448
Cash flows from investing activities:			
Purchases of property, equipment, images, businesses	(37,088)	(149,024)	(41,013)
Proceeds from sale of assets and other	211	14,911	368
Proceeds from sale of discontinued operations	0	28,135	9,600
Distribution from internet.com venture funds	148	105	0
Net cash used in investing activities	($36,729)	($105,873)	($31,045)
Net cash provided by financing activities	$37,537	$68,136	$7,692

Source: Jupitermedia Corporation 10-K filed 27 March 2007.

1. Where do Jupitermedia's income statement and statement of cash flows reflect the disposal of SES?

2. What was the company's operating profit margin in 2005? What is the operating profit margin excluding the gain on the sale of assets?

3. What was the company's net profit margin in 2005? What is the effect on this profitability measure of considering only continuing operations and excluding the gain on the sale of assets?

4. By what percentage did the company's operating income and cash from operations change from 2005 to 2006? Excluding the gain on the sale of assets, what were the changes in these metrics?

Solution to 1: Jupitermedia's disclosures indicate that they sold SES for $43 million. On the income statement, a gain of $13.3 million on a portion of the disposal (sale of assets) appears in operating income and a gain of $15.8 million on a portion classified as discontinued operations appears separately at the bottom of the statement. From the MD&A excerpt above indicating a gain of $13.3 million from the sale of ClickZ.com's network of websites, we infer that the gain of $15.8 million is from the sale of the other part of SES, namely Search Engine Strategies.

On the statement of cash flows, the $43 million cash proceeds from the sale appear in the investing section, approximately $14.9 million from asset sales and $28.1 million from the sale of discontinued operations. (The $14.9 million is an approximation because it may not be entirely from the asset sale based on the label "proceeds from sale of assets and other.") From the statement of cash flows, we infer that the $13.3 million gain on asset sales was realized from the $14.9 million proceeds from asset sales, and the gain of $15.8 million occurred on the $28.1 million proceeds from the sale of discontinued operations.

Solution to 2: The company's operating profit margin in 2005 was 38.2 percent (operating income of $43,423 divided by revenues of $113,754), as reported. Excluding the gain on the sale of assets, the operating profit margin would be 26.5 percent [(operating income of $43,423 minus $13,259) divided by revenues of $113,754].

Solution to 3: The company's net profit margin in 2005 was 68.9 percent (net income $78,399 divided by revenues of $113,754). Using income from continuing operations, however, rather than net income better reflects the ongoing profitability of the company, and on this basis, the net margin is 52.9 percent (income from continuing operations $60,223 divided by revenues of $113,754). Excluding the asset sale, the net margin would be 41.3 percent [(income from continuing operations $60,223 minus $13,259) divided by revenues of $113,754].

Solution to 4: The company's operating income declined by 62.3 percent ($16,349/$43,423 − 1). Excluding the 2005 sale of assets, the company's operating income declined by 45.8 percent ($16,349/($43,423 − $13,259) − 1). The company's cash from operations declined by 48.9 percent ($13,448/$26,327 − 1). Because the sale of assets was excluded from operating cash and shown in investing cash, the 2005 sale of assets had no impact on reported operating cash flow.

7.2 Long-Lived Assets Disposed of Other than by a Sale

Long-lived assets to be disposed of other than by a sale, e.g. abandoned, exchanged for another asset, or distributed to owners in a spin-off, are classified as held for use until disposal.[12] Thus, the long-lived assets continue to be depreciated and tested for impairment as required for other long-lived assets owned by the company.

---

[12] In a spin-off, shareholders of the parent company receive a proportional number of shares in a new, separate entity.

When an asset is retired or abandoned, the accounting is similar to a sale, except that the company does not record cash proceeds. Assets are reduced by the carrying value of the asset at the time of retirement or abandonment, and a loss is recorded.

When an asset is exchanged for another asset, the asset acquired is recorded at the fair value of the asset given up or the fair value of the asset acquired, whichever is more readily available. Accounting for the exchange involves reducing assets by the carrying value of the asset given up, increasing assets by the value of the asset acquired, and reporting any difference as a gain or loss. A gain would be reported when the newly acquired asset's value exceeds the carrying value of the asset given up.

As an illustration of a spin-off, Altria Group, Inc. ("Altria") effected a spin-off of Kraft Foods ("Kraft") on 30 March 2007 by distributing about 89 percent of Kraft's shares to Altria's shareholders. The company prepared unaudited pro forma income statements and balance sheets (for illustrative purposes only) as if the spin-off had occurred at the beginning of the year. Exhibit 13 summarizes information from the asset portion of the company's pro forma balance sheets. The items in Column (b) reflect Kraft's assets being removed from Altria's balance sheet at the time of the spin-off. For example, Kraft's property, plant, and equipment (net of depreciation) total $9.7 billion.

EXHIBIT 13	Altria Group, Inc. and Subsidiaries Pro Forma Condensed Consolidated Balance Sheet [Partial] as of 31 December 2006 (Unaudited)			
Assets ($ Millions)	Historical Altria[a]	Spin-off of Kraft[b]	Adjustments[c]	Pro Forma Altria
Cash and cash equivalents	$5,020	($239)	$369	$5,150
Receivables, net	6,070	(3,869)		2,201
Inventories	12,186	(3,506)		8,680
Other current assets	2,876	(640)		2,236
Total current assets	$26,152	($8,254)	$369	$18,267
Property, plant and equipment, net	17,274	(9,693)		7,581
Goodwill	33,235	(25,553)	($1,485)	6,197
Other intangible assets, net	12,085	(10,177)		1,908
Other assets	8,734	(1,897)	$305	7,142
Total consumer products assets	$97,480	($55,574)	($811)	$41,095
Financial services assets	6,790	0		6,790
Total assets	$104,270	($55,574)	($811)	$47,885

[a] Historical consolidated balance sheet of Altria.

[b] Reflects the removal of Kraft's consolidated balance sheet from the Altria historical consolidated balance sheet.

[c] Represents adjustments, such as for pro forma cash payments by Kraft to Altria, arising from modifications to existing stock awards and tax contingencies, adjustments to goodwill, and other.

Source: Altria's Form 8-K filed with the SEC on 5 April 2007.

8

IMPAIRMENT OF LONG-LIVED ASSETS

In contrast with depreciation and amortization charges, which serve to allocate the cost of a long-lived asset over its useful life, impairment charges reflect an unanticipated decline in the fair value of an asset. Accounting for impairment charges differs with assets held for use versus assets held for sale. Further, within the category of assets held for use, accounting for impairment may differ depending on the type of asset. The differences primarily involve when to test for impairment and what test is applied. The following paragraphs describe the accounting treatments and discuss implications for financial statement analysis.

8.1 Impairment of Long-Lived Tangible Assets Held for Use

For long-lived tangible assets held for use, impairment losses are recognized when the asset's carrying amount is not recoverable and its carrying value exceeds its fair value. Both of these concepts are based on the asset's carrying amount relative to its expected future cash flows. Recoverability, under U.S. standards, relates to undiscounted future cash flows, and fair value relates to discounted cash flows. The asset is considered not recoverable when the asset's carrying amount exceeds the undiscounted expected future cash flows. Then, if the asset is considered not recoverable, the impairment loss is measured as the difference between its fair value and carrying amount.

The impairment loss will reduce the carrying value of the asset on the balance sheet and will reduce net income on the income statement. The impairment loss is a non-cash item and will not affect cash from operations. As with any accounting estimate, management's estimate of an impairment loss may be affected by motivations to manage earnings.

EXAMPLE 11

Implications of Impairment Charges in Financial Statement Analysis

Assume a (hypothetical) company, OmeTech, owns one asset with a carrying value of $2,000, manufacturing equipment that produces two products: the Ome-Gizmo and the Tech-Gizmo. An adverse event occurs that requires evaluation for impairment, namely one of OmeTech's competitors wins a lawsuit confirming their right to a patent on the technology underlying the Tech-Gizmo, leaving OmeTech with a single product. Because the equipment is highly specialized and can now only be used to manufacture a single product for which there is finite demand, OmeTech believes that this adverse event reduces the recoverable value of their manufacturing equipment to an amount below its carrying cost. Based on new estimates that the future cash flows from the equipment will total $300 per year for the next five years, and an assumed discount rate of 10 percent, the company estimates the fair value of the equipment is now $1,137 (calculated as the present value of a $300 per year cash flow for five years.) The company thus determines it has an impairment loss of $863.

---

1. Where will the impairment loss appear in the company's financial statements?
2. How should the impairment loss be viewed in the context of evaluating past earnings and cash flow?
3. How should the impairment loss be viewed in the context of projecting future earnings and cash flow?

Solution to 1: On the balance sheet, the impairment loss will reduce the carrying amount of the relevant long-lived asset, with detail on the impairment loss itself in the footnotes to the financial statements and the MD&A. On the income statement (and thus ultimately in the retained earnings account on the balance sheet), the impairment loss will reduce income. In the operating section of the statement of cash flows, the reconciliation of net income to cash flows from operating activities will add back the impairment charge because it represents a non-cash item.

Solution to 2: Because the historical depreciation charge was insufficient to represent the full decline in the equipment's value, historical earnings may have been overstated. In evaluating past earnings, it should be understood that recognition and measurement of impairment charges are highly judgmental and thus can offer the potential for a company to manage its earnings. The direction of earnings management, to the extent that it exists, is driven by the motivational context. For example, a new management team might be motivated to show improvements in future performance, so recognizing a substantial impairment charge in the current period will contribute to presenting a favorable trend. Alternatively, a management team that is close to missing a targeted earnings benchmark might be motivated to underestimate the impairment loss. In the context of evaluating past cash flow, an impairment charge does not affect cash flow. However, if the impairment loss relates to an asset that was relatively recently acquired, comparing the impairment loss to the amount invested to acquire the asset may offer some insight into management's ability to make successful acquisitions.

Solution to 3: In projecting future earnings, impairment losses would typically be considered non-recurring and thus would not be included in future projections. In projecting future cash flows, the impairment loss can provide some guidance. In this hypothetical example with only a single machine, the disclosures would provide a fairly transparent picture of management's expectations about its future cash flows. If an analyst or other user of the financial statements made identical assumptions of a five year remaining life of the equipment and a 10 percent discount rate, the user could derive the expected future annual cash flows by calculating what annuity a present value of $1,137 would yield over five years at an interest rate of 10 percent, namely $300 per annum. The information from the impairment loss could be used as input to an analyst's own future cash flow projections, based on his own expectations about the company's sales and profit margins, given information and assumptions about future demand for the product and competitive pressures.

In practice, neither companies' businesses nor their disclosures are as simplistic as the above example. Nonetheless, impairment disclosures can provide similarly useful information. The exhibit below provides a footnote from the financial statements of Abitibi-Consolidated. The footnotes provide information about three properties assessed for potential impairment. Based on the information, we can estimate that the company forecasts undiscounted future cash flows on the three properties of around C\$1,014 million (32 percent more than the book value of the three properties: C\$250 million plus C\$174 million plus C\$344 million). An assumption that the average remaining life of these assets is approximately the same as the estimated remaining life of the company's overall PP&E asset base of 9.4 years (calculated in Example 6), would indicate projected annual future cash flows from these three properties of C\$108 million (C\$1,014 million divided by 9.4 years). While this cash flow projection is clearly a broad estimate, it could provide a useful basis of comparison for an analyst's own projections based on his own assumptions about the future cash flows of the company.

EXHIBIT 14   Disclosure of Impairment of Long-Lived Assets

Excerpt from Financial Statement Footnotes of Abitibi-Consolidated Inc. (NYSE: ABY; TSX: A):

"IMPAIRMENT OF LONG-LIVED ASSETS

During the fourth quarter of 2006, the Company conducted the initial step of the impairment tests on the Bridgewater, United Kingdom, paper mill and on the "Wood products" segment as a result of operating losses. The Company also conducted the initial step on the indefinitely idled Lufkin, Texas, paper mill. Estimates of future cash flows used to test the recoverability of a long-lived asset are mainly derived in the same manner as the projections of cash flows used in the initial step of the goodwill impairment test. In addition, the impairment test for the Lufkin paper mill was performed in light of a scenario of the mill's restart producing lightweight coated paper under a partnership structure.

"The Company concluded that the recognition of an impairment charge for the business units analyzed was not required, as the estimated undiscounted cash flows exceeded the book values by at least 32%. Certain paper mills and sawmills are particularly sensitive to the key assumptions. Given the inherent imprecision and corresponding importance of the key assumptions used in the impairment test, it is reasonably possible that changes in future conditions may lead management to use different key assumptions, which could require a material change in the book value of these assets. The total book value of these assets was \$250 million, \$174 million and \$344 million for the "Newsprint", "Commercial printing papers" and "Wood products" segments, respectively, as at December 31, 2006."

Source: Form 40-F for the year ended 31 December 2006, page 5, filed 15 March 2007.

Continuously testing the value of all these assets would obviously be impractical, so accounting standards set guidelines for when the tests must be done. SFAS No. 144 provides examples of events that give rise to the need to test for impairment, including a significant adverse change in an asset's physical condition, a significant adverse change in legal or economic factors, or a significant decrease in the market price.

International standards differ somewhat in both the guidelines for determining that impairment has occurred and in the measurement of an impairment loss. For example, under IAS 36, measurement of an impairment loss is based on the recoverable amount of the asset (defined as "the higher of its fair value less costs to sell and its value in use") rather than its fair value (generally based on discounted cash flows) as in the United States.

8.2 Impairment of Intangible Assets with a Finite Life

Impairment accounting for intangible assets with a finite life is essentially the same as for tangible assets.

Intangible assets with a finite life are amortized. They may become impaired, but are not tested annually for impairment. Instead, they are tested only when significant events suggest the need to test. Examples of such events include a significant decrease in the market price or a significant adverse change in legal or economic factors.

8.3 Impairment of Goodwill and Other Intangibles with Indefinite Lives

Goodwill and other intangible assets with indefinite lives are not amortized. Instead they are carried on the balance sheet at historical cost but tested at least annually for impairment. Impairment exists when the carrying value exceeds its fair value.[13] Measuring the value of goodwill differs somewhat from measurement of other assets because the nature of goodwill is that it cannot be separated from an overall business. Because of this inseparability, goodwill is valued for an overall reporting unit, defined as an operating segment or some component of an operating segment.

Testing for an impairment loss to goodwill in accordance with SFAS No. 142 involves two steps. First, if the carrying value of the reporting unit (including associated goodwill) exceeds its fair value, the second step is required; otherwise, there is no impairment and the second step is not required. The second step compares the carrying value of the goodwill to the fair value of the goodwill based on the valuation in the first step. If the carrying value exceeds the fair value, an impairment loss is reported. Example 12 provides an illustration.

EXAMPLE 12

Calculating Goodwill Impairment

Destroblow Inc., a (hypothetical) manufacturing company reporting under U.S. GAAP, acquired Subblow Company in 2006 for $1.2 billion. The fair value of the net assets of Subblow were $900 million, so Destroblow recorded $300 million in goodwill and will perform a goodwill impairment test at the end of each year. Subblow continues to

---

[13] According to U.S. GAAP (SFAS No. 141, paragraphs 23–25), the fair value of an asset (or liability) is the amount at which that asset (or liability) could be bought (or incurred) or sold (or settled) in a current transaction between willing parties, that is, other than in a forced or liquidation sale. Perhaps the best source of fair values is the quoted market prices in active markets, if available. If not available, other methods such as the present value of future cash flows or multiples of earnings or revenues can be used.

operate as a separate company. At the end of 2007, the carrying value of Subblow is $1,010 million, including the $300 million in goodwill. The fair value of Subblow at that date is now only $950 million, and the fair value of the net assets is $875 million.

The goodwill impairment test involves two steps: 1) determining whether the fair value of Subblow is less than its carrying amount including goodwill, in which case an impairment loss exists; and 2) if an impairment loss exists, measuring the goodwill impairment loss as the difference between the carrying value of goodwill and the implied value of goodwill.

The first step of the test determines that an impairment loss exists because the $950 million fair value of Subblow is less than the $1,010 million carrying value. The second step of the test determines that the impairment loss equals $225 million, which is the excess of the $300 million book value of goodwill over the $75 million implied value of goodwill ($950 million fair value of Subblow minus $875 million fair value of Subblow's net assets equals $75 million implied value of goodwill.)

1. If at the end of 2007, the fair value of Subblow was determined to be $950 million and the fair value of its net assets were $900 million, what would be the amount of the goodwill impairment loss?

2. If, at the end of 2007, the fair value of Subblow was determined to be $1.1 billion and the fair value of its net assets were $1 billion, what would be the amount of the goodwill impairment loss?

Solution to 1: The first step of the goodwill impairment test indicates that an impairment loss exists because Subblow's fair value of $950 million is less than its carrying value of $1,010 million. The second step determines that the amount of the goodwill impairment loss equals $250 million, which is the excess of the $300 million book value of goodwill over the $50 million implied value of goodwill ($950 million fair value of Subblow minus $900 million fair value of Subblow's net assets).

Solution to 2: The first step of the goodwill impairment tests indicates that an impairment loss would not exist because Subblow's fair value of $1.1 billion exceeds its carrying value of $1,010 million. The amount of goodwill impairment loss would be $0.

Goodwill accounting under U.S. GAAP and IFRS are fairly similar conceptually, although there are several differences. Under IFRS, annual tests of goodwill (under IAS 36) relate to a "cash-generating unit" rather than a reporting unit, as under U.S. GAAP. Under IFRS, calculation of impairment of goodwill involves only one step rather than two steps, namely a comparison of the carrying value of the cash-generating unit with its "recoverable amount." The recoverable amount of an asset, as defined in IAS 36, paragraph 6, is "the higher of its fair value less costs to sell and its value in use." The fair value less costs to sell is based on the amount that would be obtained from selling the asset, and value in use is based on the present value of future cash flows that would be obtained from using the asset. If the carrying value is higher than the recoverable amount, an impairment loss is reported.

8.4 Impairment of Long-Lived Assets Held for Sale

Long-lived assets held for sale are tested for impairment at the time they are categorized as held for sale. If the carrying value exceeds the fair value less costs to sell, an impairment loss is recognized.

8.5 Reversals of Impairments of Long-Lived Assets

After an asset has been deemed impaired and an impairment loss reported, the asset's value could potentially increase. For instance, a lawsuit appeal may successfully challenge a patent infringement. The accounting for reversals of impairments depends on whether the asset is classified as held for use or held for sale. Under U.S. GAAP, once an impairment loss has been recognized for assets held for use it cannot be reversed. In other words, once the value of an asset held for use has been decreased by an impairment charge, it cannot be increased.[14] For assets held for sale, if the fair value of an asset increases after an impairment loss, the loss can be reversed.[15]

In contrast, international accounting standards permit impairment losses to be reversed if the value of an asset increases regardless of whether the asset was held for use or held for sale. The reversal is reported in profit.

8.6 Implications for Financial Statement Analysis

Significant judgment is involved in projecting the future cash flows that an asset will generate and in assessing fair values. Companies, therefore, have considerable discretion about the timing of loss recognition. One important consideration in financial statement analysis is how these charges should be included in analyzing past performance and in projecting future performance.

REVALUATION OF LONG-LIVED ASSETS   9

As previously discussed, under U.S. accounting standards, the value of long-lived assets is reported at depreciated historical cost and adjusted for impairments (decreases in value). In contrast, international accounting standards (IAS 16) allow companies to value long-lived assets either under a cost model, i.e., historical cost minus accumulated depreciation, or under a revaluation model, i.e., fair value. A key difference between the two is that where U.S. GAAP allows only decreases in the value of long-lived assets held for use (due to impairments), IFRS also permits increases in value to an amount above historical cost.

Under IFRS, whether an asset **revaluation** affects earnings depends on whether the revaluation initially increases or decreases an asset's carrying value. If an asset revaluation initially decreases the carrying value, the decrease is recognized in profit or loss (similar to an asset impairment). Later, if the asset's carrying value increases, the increase is recognized in profit or loss to the extent that it reverses a revaluation decrease of the same asset previously recognized in profit or loss. Contrast this treatment with an upward revaluation where the increase in the asset's carrying value bypasses the income statement and goes

---

[14] See SFAS No. 144, paragraph 14.
[15] See SFAS No. 144, paragraph 37.

directly to equity under the heading of revaluation surplus. Any subsequent decrease in the asset's value first decreases the revaluation surplus then goes to income.

Exhibit 15 provides an example of a company's disclosures concerning revaluation. The exhibit shows an excerpt from the annual report of KPN, the Dutch telecommunications and multimedia company. The excerpt is from the section in which the company explains differences between its reporting under IFRS and its reporting under U.S. GAAP. One of these differences, as noted above, is that U.S. GAAP does not allow revaluation of fixed assets held for use. KPN explains that they elected to report fixed assets at fair value, so under U.S. GAAP (historical cost), the value of the assets at the end of 2006 would have been EUR 350 million lower.

EXHIBIT 15	Selected Excerpts from Annual Report of Koninklijke KPN N.V. (NYSE: KPN)

Excerpt from the explanation of certain differences between IFRS and U.S. GAAP regarding "Deemed cost fixed assets:"

> "KPN elected the exemption to revalue certain of its fixed assets upon the transition to IFRS to fair value and to use this fair value as their deemed cost. KPN applied the depreciated replacement cost method to determine this fair value. The revalued assets pertain to certain cables, which form part of property, plant & equipment. Under U.S. GAAP, this revaluation is not allowed and therefore results in a reconciling item. As a result, the value of these assets as of December 31, 2006 under U.S. GAAP is EUR 350 million lower (2005: EUR 415 million; 2004: EUR 487 million) than under IFRS."

Source: Company's Form 20-F, page 168, filed 1 March 2007.

Asset revaluations offer several considerations for financial statement analyses. First, an increase in the carrying value of depreciable long-lived assets increases total assets and shareholders' equity; so, asset revaluations that increase the carrying value of an asset can be used to reduce reported leverage (recall leverage is defined as average total assets divided by average shareholders' equity).[16] Therefore, the leverage motivation for the revaluation should be considered in analysis. For example, a company may revalue assets up if it is seeking new capital or approaching leverage limitations set by financial covenants. Second, assets revaluations that decrease the carrying value of the assets reduce net income. In the year of the revaluation, profitability measures such as return on assets and return on equity decline. However, because total assets and shareholders' equity are also lower, the company may appear more profitable in future years. Additionally, reversals of downward revaluations also go through income, thus increasing earnings. Managers can then opportunistically time the reversals to manage earnings and increase income. Third, assets revaluations that increase the carrying value of an asset initially increase depreciation expense, total assets, and shareholders' equity. Therefore, profitability measures, such as

---

[16] Though both the numerator (assets) and denominator (equity) increase, we know that leverage decreases because mathematically, when a ratio is greater than one, as in this case, an increase in both the numerator and the denominator by the same amount leads to a decline in the ratio.

return on assets and return on equity, would decline. Although upward asset revaluations also generally decrease income (through higher depreciation expense), the increase in the value of the long-lived asset is presumably based on increases in the operating capacity of the asset, which will be likely evidenced in increased future revenues. Finally, an analyst would also want to understand who does the appraisal, i.e., an independent external appraiser or management, and how often revaluations are made. Appraisals of the fair value of long-lived assets involve considerable judgment and discretion. Presumably, appraisals of assets from independent external sources are more reliable. How often assets are revalued can provide an indicator of whether their reported value continues to be representative of their fair values.

EXAMPLE 13

Asset Revaluation

You are analyzing a company (hypothetical), RevUp PLC, that is planning to raise new debt in the coming year. Part of your analysis involves understanding the company's solvency to help determine its capacity to handle additional debt. You observe that in 2006 RevUp made an asset revaluation that increased the reported value of its assets by €150 million and increased depreciation expense by €25 million. Other relevant data and extracts from the company's annual report are included in the following exhibit.

EXHIBIT 16	RevUp PLC Excerpts from Financial Statements	
Line Items (€ in Millions)	**2005**	**2006**
At 31 December		
Property, plant, and equipment, net	€700	€750
Total assets	3,000	3,650
Total liabilities	1,400	1,900
Revaluation surplus (part of shareholders' equity)	—	150
Total shareholders' equity	1,600	1,750
For the year ended 31 December		
Depreciation expense	€100	€125
Income before taxes	1,000	975
Tax expense	400	400
Net income	600	575

1. Compute the company's financial leverage (defined as average total assets divided by average shareholders' equity) based on reported financial statements fiscal year 2006, with no adjustments, and with adjustment for the impact of the asset revaluation on leverage. (Assume the asset revaluation is not taxable and any increases in

depreciation expense related to the revaluation are not tax-deductible, so there would be no change in taxes.)

2. Interpret the change in leverage.

Solution to 1: RevUp's 2006 ratios are as follows:

	With Asset Revaluation (as Reported)	Without Asset Revaluation (as Adjusted)
Leverage	1.99	2.03

Based on information as reported, leverage with the asset revaluation was 1.99 (average total assets divided by average shareholders' equity).

► Average total assets: €3,325. Beginning assets of €3,000 plus ending total assets of €3,650 divided by 2.

► Average shareholders' equity: €1,675. Beginning shareholders' equity of €1,600 plus ending shareholders' equity of €1,750 divided by 2.

Based on information as reported, leverage without the asset revaluation was 2.03 (average total assets divided by average shareholders' equity).

► Average total assets: €3,250. Beginning assets of €3,000 plus ending total assets of €3,500 (€3,650 minus the €150 increase in the value of the asset surplus) divided by 2.

► Average shareholders' equity: €1,600. Beginning shareholders' equity of €1,600 plus ending shareholders' equity of €1,600 (€1,750 minus the €150 asset surplus) divided by 2.

Solution to 2: Increasing the value of the assets through revaluation would decrease leverage. So, RevUp would appear to have more capacity for any new debt issues.

SUMMARY

Key points include the following:

▶ Expenditures related to long-lived assets are included as part of the value of assets on the balance sheet, i.e. capitalized, if they are expected to provide future benefits, typically beyond one year.

▶ Although capitalizing expenditures, rather than expensing, results in higher reported profitability in the initial year, it results in lower profitability in subsequent years; however, if a company continues to purchase similar or increasing amounts of assets each year, the profitability-enhancing effect of capitalizing continues.

▶ Capitalizing an expenditure rather than expensing it results in greater amounts reported as cash from operations.

▶ If an asset is acquired in a nonmonetary exchange, its cost is based on the fair value of the asset given up, or the fair value of the asset acquired if it is more reliably determinable.

▶ Companies must capitalize interest costs associated with acquiring or constructing an asset that requires a long period of time to prepare for its intended use.

▶ Including capitalized interest in the calculation of interest coverage ratios provides a better assessment of a company's solvency.

▶ Generally, U.S. accounting standards require that research and development costs be expensed; however, certain costs related to software development are required to be capitalized. IFRS also requires research costs be expensed but allows development costs to be capitalized under certain conditions.

▶ If companies apply different approaches to capitalizing software development costs, adjustments can be made to make the two comparable.

▶ When one company acquires another company, the transaction is accounted for using the purchase method of accounting in which the company identified as the acquirer allocates the purchase price to each asset acquired (and each liability assumed) on the basis of its fair value.

▶ Under purchase accounting, if the purchase price of an acquisition exceeds the sum of the amounts that can be allocated to individual assets and liabilities, the excess is recorded as goodwill.

▶ U.S. GAAP requires the immediate write-off of in-process R&D acquired in a business combination, but IFRS does not.

▶ Depreciation methods include the straight-line method, in which the cost of an asset is allocated in equal amounts over its useful life; accelerated methods, in which the allocation of cost is greater in earlier years; and units-of-production methods, in which the allocation of cost corresponds to the actual use of an asset in a particular period.

▶ Significant estimates required for depreciation calculations include the useful life of the equipment (or its total lifetime productive capacity) and its expected residual value at the end of that useful life. A longer useful life and higher expected residual value decrease the amount of annual depreciation relative to a shorter useful life and lower expected residual value.

▶ Estimates of average age and remaining useful life of a company's assets reflect the relationship between assets accounted for on a historical cost basis and depreciation amounts.

▶ The average remaining useful life of a company's assets can be estimated as net PP&E divided by depreciation expense.

▶ To estimate the average age of the asset base, divide accumulated depreciation by depreciation expense.

▶ Intangible assets with finite useful lives are amortized over their useful lives.

▶ Intangible assets without a finite useful life, i.e. with an indefinite useful life, are not amortized, but are reviewed for impairment whenever changes in events or circumstances indicate that the carrying amount of an asset may not be recoverable.

▶ For many types of long-lived tangible assets, ownership involves obligations that must be fulfilled at the end of the asset's service life, referred to as asset retirement obligations (AROs). Financial analysts often adjust financial statements to treat AROs in a manner consistent with debt.

▶ The gain or loss on the sale of long-lived assets is computed as the sales proceeds minus the carrying value of the asset at the time of sale.

▶ Long-lived assets to be disposed of other than by a sale—e.g., abandoned, exchanged for another asset, or distributed to owners in a spin-off—are classified as held for use until disposal. Thus, they continue to be depreciated and tested for impairment.

▶ In contrast with depreciation and amortization charges, which serve to allocate the cost of a long-lived asset over its useful life, impairment charges reflect a decline in the fair value of an asset to an amount lower than its carrying value.

▶ Impairment disclosures can provide useful information about a company's expected cash flows.

▶ Under U.S. accounting standards, the value of long-lived assets is reported at depreciated historical cost. This value may be decreased by impairment charges, but cannot be increased. International accounting standards, however, permit impairment losses to be reversed, with the reversal reported in profit.

PRACTICE PROBLEMS FOR READING 37

1. The Schneider Candy Company has decided to capitalize the interest costs it incurs during and related to construction of its new storage and shipping facility. This practice is:

    A. permitted only if the company complies with U.S. GAAP.

    B. permitted only if the company complies with International Financial Reporting Standards (IFRS).

    C. permissible under either U.S. GAAP or IFRS.

2. The Juniper Juice Company reports that it has capitalized the interest costs it incurred during and related to construction of its new bottling plant. A creditor assessing Juniper Juice's solvency ratios would *most likely*:

    A. add capitalized interest to reported interest expense.

    B. subtract capitalized interest from reported interest expense.

    C. add any depreciation from previously capitalized interest to interest expense.

3. Anna Lyssette is evaluating the performance of two biotechnology companies: Biotech Holdings and Advanced Biotech. Both companies released their first new drugs early in the year, but Lyssette is worried about a possible lack of comparability due to differing strategies. Biotech Holdings acquired the research and development for its drug from another company while Advanced Biotech developed its drug internally. In the current accounting period, all else equal, Biotech Holdings would *most likely* report:

    A. lower total assets.

    B. higher net income.

    C. similar cash flow from operations.

4. Amerisoft complies with U.S. GAAP, while EuroWare complies with International Financial Reporting Standards (IFRS). When comparing the two companies, it would *most likely* be necessary to adjust the financial statements of:

    A. Amerisoft to remove charges related to acquired in-process R&D.

    B. EuroWare to remove charges related to acquired in-process R&D.

    C. Both companies to remove charges related to acquired in-process R&D.

5. When comparing a company that complies with International Financial Reporting Standards (IFRS) to a company that complies with U.S. GAAP, it is *most* important to remember that under IFRS:

    A. research-phase R&D expenditures are capitalized.

    B. acquired in-process R&D is expensed immediately.

    C. development-phase R&D expenditures may be capitalized.

The following information relates to Questions 6–9

The Asset Intensive Company (AIC) has purchased equipment for $1 million. The equipment is expected to have a three-year useful life and a salvage value of $100,000. AIC reports under U.S. GAAP.

6. Over the full life of the machine, all else equal, the volatility of AIC's net income will be:

   A. the same regardless of whether AIC expenses or capitalizes the cost of the machine.

   B. highest if the company expenses the entire cost of the machine in the year of its purchase.

   C. highest if the company capitalizes the cost of the machine and depreciates it over its useful life.

7. Assuming AIC capitalizes the cost of the equipment, depreciation expense over the life of the machine will be:

   A. the same regardless of the chosen depreciation method.

   B. lowest if the company uses the double-declining balance method.

   C. highest if the company uses the double-declining balance method.

8. In year 3, the return on equity will *most likely* be:

   A. highest if the company expenses the cost of the equipment.

   B. highest if the company capitalizes the cost of the equipment.

   C. the same regardless of whether the cost of the equipment is expensed or capitalized.

9. Regardless of the depreciation method used for reporting purposes, the company will use MACRS for tax purposes. In year 1, the reported income tax expense will be:

   A. the same regardless of depreciation method.

   B. highest if the company uses the straight-line method.

   C. highest if the company uses the double-declining balance method.

---

10. Bobcat Company's balance sheet shows property, plant, and equipment valued at a historical cost of $22,983 million and accumulated depreciation of $7,879. Depreciation expense in the most recent year was $2,459. What is the average remaining useful life of Bobcat's assets?

   A. 3.2 years.

   B. 6.1 years.

   C. 9.3 years.

11. Francis Acana is comparing the property and equipment disclosures for three airline companies, as summarized in the following table:

	Airline A	Airline B	Airline C
Historical cost, aircraft	$17,239	£23,584	€45,266
Accumulated depreciation, aircraft	6,584	13,654	21,745
Net cost, aircraft	10,655	9,930	23,521
Annual depreciation expense	575	786	1,509

Acana finds that the average fleet age is:
  A. lowest for Airline A.
  B. lowest for Airline B.
  C. lowest for Airline C.

12. Relative to assets with finite lives, an intangible asset determined to have an indefinite life will result in lower reported:
  A. assets.
  B. net income.
  C. amortization expense.

13. With regard to intangible assets, a company's reported profit margin the year the asset is acquired will be highest if it estimates a:
  A. six-year useful life and no salvage value.
  B. six-year useful life and a positive salvage value.
  C. five-year useful life and a positive salvage value.

14. With regard to intangible assets, the company's cash flow from operating activities the year the asset is acquired will *most likely* be highest if it estimates a:
  A. five-year useful life and no salvage value.
  B. six-year useful life and a positive salvage value.
  C. five-year useful life and a positive salvage value.

15. When a company is able to estimate the future costs it will incur when an asset is retired, it is *least likely* to:
  A. increase the carrying value of the asset.
  B. decrease the carrying value of the liability through an accretion charge.
  C. decrease the carrying value of the asset over time through an accretion charge.

16. Compared to an asset that will not require a retirement obligation, an asset that will require a retirement obligation is *most likely* to result in a:
  A. one-time charge at the time of retirement.
  B. rising debt/equity ratio as the retirement date approaches.
  C. declining debt/equity ratio as the retirement date approaches.

17. A credit analyst reviewing a company with asset retirement obligations (ARO) would *least likely* adjust:

 A. interest expense by the amount of accretion.

 B. shareholders' equity by the amount of the ARO.

 C. the reported ARO by the amount of any related trust funds or escrow.

18. Fisherman Enterprises purchased $1 million of equipment with an estimated 10-year useful life and a $100,000 expected salvage value. The company uses the straight-line method of depreciation. At the end of five years it sells the equipment for $500,000. Fisherman's income statement will include a $50,000:

 A. loss recorded as a separate line-item.

 B. gain recorded as a separate line-item.

 C. offset to depreciation and amortization.

19. A company that has decided to sell an asset is *least likely* to record a:

 A. gain at the time the asset is sold.

 B. loss at the time the decision is made.

 C. gain at the time the decision is made.

20. An asset is considered impaired when:

 A. its fair value exceeds its carrying value.

 B. its carrying value exceeds its fair value.

 C. it ceases to provide an economic benefit.

21. An asset impairment is *most likely* to impact reported:

 A. depreciation expense in future periods.

 B. depreciation expense in the year impaired.

 C. cash flow from operating activities in the year impaired.

22. When comparing the reported results of a company that complies with U.S. GAAP to a company that complies with International Financial Reporting Standards (IFRS), return on assets is *least likely* to require an adjustment for:

 A. goodwill amortization.

 B. upwardly revalued assets.

 C. acquired in-process research and development charges.

23. In the year of the revaluation, an asset revaluation that increases the carrying value of an asset is *most likely* to:

 A. increase return on equity.

 B. decrease reported leverage.

 C. decrease shareholders' equity.

SOLUTIONS FOR READING 37

1. C is correct. Capitalization of interest costs incurred during construction is permitted under both U.S. GAAP and IFRS.

2. A is correct. To adjust solvency ratios, interest capitalized during the period should be *added* to interest expense. Any related depreciation expense would be added to *income*.

3. B is correct. By acquiring its drug, Biotech Holdings will have higher total assets (because it would capitalize the intangible asset) and higher cash flow from operations (because the drug purchase would appear as an investing cash flow). All else equal, Biotech Holdings would initially report higher net income because only a portion of the cost would reduce revenues in the current accounting period (through depreciation). In future periods, Advanced Biotech would report higher net income so that total net income over time would be unaffected by whether R&D was expensed or amortized.

4. A is correct. Under U.S. GAAP, acquired in-process research and development costs are expensed upon acquisition. In contrast, companies reporting under IFRS may either identify in-process R&D as a separate asset with a finite life, or include it as part of goodwill.

5. C is correct. Under IFRS, development-phase R&D may be capitalized, whereas it must be expensed under U.S. GAAP (except for software under certain circumstances). Both standards require *expensing* of research-phase expenditures, and IFRS requires acquired in-process R&D to be capitalized.

6. B is correct. All else equal, net income would be more volatile if AIC expensed the cost of the machine because the entire cost would detract from net income in the year of its purchase.

7. A is correct. Over the life of the asset, depreciation expense will be $900,000 regardless of the depreciation method chosen.

8. A is correct. Expensing results in the lower ROE in the first year, but a higher ROE in subsequent years.

9. B is correct. Depreciation expense will be lower if the straight-line method is used. That will increase reported income and therefore reported income taxes. Although the company will use MACRS for tax purposes, the difference will be in deferred taxes on the balance sheet until reversed.

10. B is correct. The average remaining life is calculated as net PPE divided by annual depreciation expense. Net PPE is $15,104 ($22,983 − $7,879). Annual depreciation expense is $2,459, giving an average remaining life of 6.14 years ($15,104/$2,459).

11. A is correct. Average age is calculated as accumulated depreciation divided by annual depreciation expense. It is 11.5, 17.4, and 14.4 for airlines A, B and C, respectively.

12. C is correct. Assets with indefinite lives are not amortized. Therefore, no deduction is taken from the asset over time or charged to the income statement. Assets and net income are both higher.

13. B is correct. Amortization expense is determined by dividing the difference between the acquisition and salvage values over the useful life. Higher salvage values and longer lives equate to lower amortization expense and thus higher profit margins.

International Financial Statement Analysis, by Thomas R. Robinson, CFA, Jan Hendrik van Greuning, CFA, R. Elaine Henry, CFA, and Michael A. Broihahn, CFA. Copyright © 2008 by CFA Institute. Reprinted with permission.

14. A is correct. Higher amortization expense reduces reported income and the taxes paid on the income. On the statement of cash flows, the amortization is added back as a non-cash expense. Therefore, the cash flow will be highest when amortization is highest because the amortization is added back, but the tax outflow is reduced. Amortization is highest for shorter useful lives and lower salvage value estimates.

15. B is correct. At the time the expense is estimable, the company must create a new liability equal to the discounted value of the future cash outlay. The liability will increase in size over time as the maturity approaches (the discount is reduced). Only at the time of disposal will the liability be reduced (removed). When first established, the liability is offset by increasing the carrying value of the asset. Over time, the asset value is reduced by charging it to expense.

16. B is correct. AROs do not result in one-time charges but in a liability that increases over time and offset by charges to income. The result is rising liability and lower equity (relative to assets that will not require a retirement obligation) as the retirement date approaches.

17. B is correct. A credit analyst would want to treat the ARO as an interest-bearing liability. The necessary adjustments would be to reduce the ARO by the value of any offsetting assets and future tax benefits, to reclassify accretion expense as interest expense, and to increase total debt by the amount of the ARO. No adjustments to shareholders' equity are needed.

18. A is correct. Fisherman is depreciating $90,000 annually [($1,000,000 − $100,000)/10]. After five years the depreciation totals $450,000 and the book value of the asset is $550,000 ($1,000,000 − $450,000). It must record a $50,000 loss on the sale. Material losses are recorded as a separate line item.

19. C is correct. At the time an asset is sold, the company records a gain or loss equal to the difference between the sale price and the carrying price. At the time the decision is made, the carrying value is adjusted to the lower of book value or estimated fair value. Either a gain or loss can occur at the time of sale, but only a loss can result at the time the decision is made.

20. B is correct. An asset is impaired when its carrying value exceeds its fair value.

21. A is correct. Asset impairments do not affect cash flow or current period depreciation. However, by reducing the value of the asset (and thus the difference between book and salvage value) the impairment will affect future depreciation expense.

22. A is correct. Neither U.S. GAAP nor IFRS permits goodwill amortization. By contrast, each of the other choices is treated differently depending on which standards are applied.

23. B is correct. Upward revaluations increase total assets, shareholders' equity, and depreciation expense. Therefore, profitability ratios (e.g. ROE) would decrease. Reported leverage (average total assets divided by average shareholders' equity) would also decrease.

INCOME TAXES

by Elbie Antonites, CFA and Michael A. Broihahn, CFA

LEARNING OUTCOMES

The candidate should be able to:	Mastery
a. explain the differences between accounting profit and taxable income, and define key terms, including deferred tax assets, deferred tax liabilities, valuation allowance, taxes payable, and income tax expense;	☐
b. explain how deferred tax liabilities and assets are created and the factors that determine how a company's deferred tax liabilities and assets should be treated for the purposes of financial analysis;	☐
c. determine the tax base of a company's assets and liabilities;	☐
d. calculate income tax expense, income taxes payable, deferred tax assets, and deferred tax liabilities, and calculate and interpret the adjustment to the financial statements related to a change in the income tax rate;	☐
e. evaluate the impact of tax rate changes on a company's financial statements and ratios;	☐
f. distinguish between temporary and permanent items in pre-tax financial income and taxable income;	☐
g. discuss the valuation allowance for deferred tax assets—when it is required and what impact it has on financial statements;	☐
h. compare and contrast a company's deferred tax items;	☐
i. analyze disclosures relating to deferred tax items and the effective tax rate reconciliation, and discuss how information included in these disclosures affects a company's financial statements and financial ratios;	☐
j. identify the key provisions of and differences between income tax accounting under IFRS and U.S. GAAP.	☐

1   INTRODUCTION

For those companies reporting under International Financial Reporting Standards (IFRS), IAS 12 covers accounting for a company's income taxes and the reporting of deferred taxes. For those companies reporting under United States generally accepted accounting principles (U.S. GAAP), SFAS No. 109 is the primary source for information on accounting for income taxes. Although IFRS and U.S. GAAP follow similar conventions on many income tax issues, there are some key differences that will be discussed in the reading.

Differences between how and when transactions are recognized for financial reporting purposes relative to tax reporting can give rise to differences in tax expense and related tax assets and liabilities. To reconcile these differences, companies that report under either IFRS or U.S. GAAP create a provision on the balance sheet called deferred tax assets or deferred tax liabilities, depending on the nature of the situation.

Deferred tax assets or liabilities usually arise when accounting standards and tax authorities recognize the timing of revenues and expenses at different times. Because timing differences such as these will eventually reverse over time, they are called "temporary differences." Deferred tax assets represent taxes that have been recognized for tax reporting purposes (or often the carrying forward of losses from previous periods) but have not yet been recognized on the income statement prepared for financial reporting purposes. Deferred tax liabilities represent tax expense that has appeared on the income statement for financial reporting purposes, but has not yet become payable under tax regulations.

This reading provides a primer on the basics of income tax accounting and reporting. The reading is organized as follows. Section 2 describes the differences between taxable income and accounting profit. Section 3 explains the determination of tax base, which relates to the valuation of assets and liabilities for tax purposes. Section 4 discusses several types of timing differences between the recognition of taxable and accounting profit. Section 5 examines unused tax losses and tax credits. Section 6 describes the recognition and measurement of current and deferred tax. Section 7 discusses the disclosure and presentation of income tax information on companies' financial statements and illustrates its practical implications for financial analysis. Section 8 provides an overview of the similarities and differences for income-tax reporting between IFRS and U.S. GAAP. A summary of the key points and practice problems in the CFA Institute multiple-choice format conclude the reading.

DIFFERENCES BETWEEN ACCOUNTING PROFIT AND TAXABLE INCOME

2

A company's **accounting profit** is reported on its income statement in accordance with prevailing accounting standards. Accounting profit (also referred to as income before taxes or pretax income) does not include a provision for income tax expense.[1] A company's **taxable income** is the portion of its income that is subject to income taxes under the tax laws of its jurisdiction. Because of different guidelines for how income is reported on a company's financial statements and how it is measured for income tax purposes, accounting profit and taxable income may differ.

A company's taxable income is the basis for its **income tax payable** (a liability) or recoverable (an asset), which is calculated on the basis of the company's tax rate and appears on its balance sheet. A company's **tax expense**, or tax benefit in the case of a recovery, appears on its income statement and is an aggregate of its income tax payable (or recoverable in the case of a tax benefit) and any changes in deferred tax assets and liabilities.

When a company's taxable income is greater than its accounting profit, then its income taxes payable will be higher than what would have otherwise been the case had the income taxes been determined based on accounting profit. **Deferred tax assets**, which appear on the balance sheet, arise when an excess amount is paid for income taxes (taxable income higher than accounting profit) and the company expects to recover the difference during the course of future operations. Actual income taxes payable will thus exceed the financial accounting income tax expense (which is reported on the income statement and is determined based on accounting profit). Related to deferred tax assets is a **valuation allowance**, which is a reserve created against deferred tax assets. The valuation allowance is based on the likelihood of realizing the deferred tax assets in future accounting periods. **Deferred tax liabilities**, which also appear on the balance sheet, arise when a deficit amount is paid for income taxes and the company expects to eliminate the deficit over the course of future operations. In this case, financial accounting income tax expense exceeds income taxes payable.

Income tax paid in a period is the actual amount paid for income taxes (not a provision, but the actual cash outflow). The income tax paid may be less than the income tax expense because of payments in prior periods or refunds received in the current period. Income tax paid reduces the income tax payable, which is carried on the balance sheet as a liability.

---

[1] As defined under IAS 12, paragraph 5.

The **tax base** of an asset or liability is the amount at which the asset or liability is valued for tax purposes, whereas the **carrying amount** is the amount at which the asset or liability is valued according to accounting principles.[2] Differences between the tax base and the carrying amount also result in differences between accounting profit and taxable income. These differences can carry through to future periods. For example, a **tax loss carry forward** occurs when a company experiences a loss in the current period that may be used to reduce future taxable income. The company's tax expense on its income statement must not only reflect the taxes payable based on taxable income, but also the effect of these differences.

2.1 Current Tax Assets and Liabilities

A company's current tax liability is the amount payable in taxes and is based on current taxable income. If the company expects to receive a refund for some portion previously paid in taxes, the amount recoverable is referred to as a current tax asset. The current tax liability or asset may, however, differ from what the liability would have been if it was based on accounting profit rather than taxable income for the period. Differences in accounting profit and taxable income are the result of the application of different rules. Such differences between accounting profit and taxable income can occur in several ways, including:

▶ Revenues and expenses may be recognized in one period for accounting purposes and a different period for tax purposes;

▶ Specific revenues and expenses may be either recognized for accounting purposes and not for tax purposes; or not recognized for accounting purposes but recognized for tax purposes;

▶ The carrying amount and tax base of assets and/or liabilities may differ;

▶ The deductibility of gains and losses of assets and liabilities may vary for accounting and income tax purposes;

▶ Subject to tax rules, tax losses of prior years might be used to reduce taxable income in later years, resulting in differences in accounting and taxable income (tax loss carryforward); and

▶ Adjustments of reported financial data from prior years might not be recognized equally for accounting and tax purposes or might be recognized in different periods.

2.2 Deferred Tax Assets and Liabilities

Deferred tax assets represent taxes that have been paid (or often the carrying forward of losses from previous periods) but have not yet been recognized on the income statement. Deferred tax liabilities occur when financial accounting income tax expense is greater than regulatory income tax expense. Deferred tax assets and liabilities usually arise when accounting standards and tax author-

---

[2] The terms "tax base" and "tax basis" are interchangeable. "Tax basis" is more commonly used in the United States. Similarly, "carrying amount" and "book value" refer to the same concept.

ities recognize the timing of taxes due at different times; for example, when a company uses accelerated depreciation when reporting to the tax authority (to increase expense and lower tax payments in the early years) but uses the straight-line method on the financial statements. Although not similar in treatment on a year-to-year basis (e.g., depreciation of 5 percent on a straight-line basis may be permitted for accounting purposes whereas 10 percent is allowed for tax purposes) over the life of the asset, both approaches allow for the total cost of the asset to be depreciated (or amortized). Because these timing differences will eventually reverse or self-correct over the course of the asset's depreciable life, they are called "temporary differences."

Under IFRS, deferred tax assets and liabilities are always classified as noncurrent. Under U.S. GAAP, however, deferred tax assets and liabilities are classified on the balance sheet as current and noncurrent based on the classification of the underlying asset or liability.

Any deferred tax asset or liability is based on temporary differences that result in an excess or a deficit amount paid for taxes, which the company expects to recover from future operations. Because taxes will be recoverable or payable at a future date, it is only a temporary difference and a deferred tax asset or liability is created. Changes in the deferred tax asset or liability on the balance sheet reflect the difference between the amounts recognized in the previous period and the current period. The changes in deferred tax assets and liabilities are added to income tax payable to determine the company's income tax expense (or credit) as it is reported on the income statement.

At the end of each fiscal year, deferred tax assets and liabilities are recalculated by comparing the tax bases and carrying amounts of the balance sheet items. Identified temporary differences should be assessed on whether the difference will result in future economic benefits. For example, Pinto Construction (a hypothetical company) depreciates equipment on a straight-line basis of 10 percent per year. The tax authorities allow depreciation of 15 percent per year. At the end of the fiscal year, the carrying amount of the equipment for accounting purposes would be greater than the tax base of the equipment thus resulting in a temporary difference. A deferred tax item may only be created if it is not doubtful that the company will realize economic benefits in future. In our example, the equipment is used in the core business of Pinto Construction. If the company is a going concern and stable, there should be no doubt that future economic benefits will result from the equipment and it would be appropriate to create the deferred tax item.

Should it be doubtful that future economic benefits will be realized from a temporary difference (such as Pinto Construction being under liquidation), the temporary difference will not lead to the creation of a deferred tax asset or liability. If a deferred tax asset or liability resulted in the past, but the criteria of economic benefits is not met on the current balance sheet date, then, under IFRS, an existing deferred tax asset or liability related to the item will be reversed. Under U.S. GAAP, a valuation allowance is established. In assessing future economic benefits, much is left to the discretion of the auditor in assessing the temporary differences and the issue of future economic benefits.

EXAMPLE 1

The following information pertains to a fictitious company, Reston Partners:

Reston Partners
Consolidated Income Statement

Period Ending 31 March (£ Millions)	2006	2005	2004
Revenue	£40,000	£30,000	£25,000
Other net gains	2,000	0	0
Changes in inventories of finished goods and work in progress	400	180	200
Raw materials and consumables used	(5,700)	(4,000)	(8,000)
Depreciation expense	(2,000)	(2,000)	(2,000)
Other expenses	(6,000)	(5,900)	(4,500)
Interest expense	(2,000)	(3,000)	(6,000)
Profit before tax	£26,700	£15,280	£4,700

The financial performance and accounting profit of Reston Partners on this income statement is based on accounting principles appropriate for the jurisdiction in which Reston Partners operates. The principles used to calculate accounting profit (profit before tax in the example above) may differ from the principles applied for tax purposes (the calculation of taxable income). For illustrative purposes, however, assume that all income and expenses on the income statement are treated identically for tax and accounting purposes *except* depreciation.

The depreciation is related to equipment owned by Reston Partners. For simplicity, assume that the equipment was purchased at the beginning of the 2004 fiscal year. Depreciation should thus be calculated and expensed for the full year. Assume that accounting standards permit equipment to be depreciated on a straight-line basis over a 10-year period, whereas the tax standards in the jurisdiction specify that equipment should be depreciated on a straight-line basis over a 7-year period. For simplicity, assume a salvage value of £0 at the end of the equipment's useful life. Both methods will result in the full depreciation of the asset over the respective tax or accounting life.

The equipment was originally purchased for £20,000. In accordance with accounting standards, over the next 10 years the company will recognize annual depreciation of £2,000 (£20,000 ÷ 10) as an expense on its income statement and for the determination of accounting profit. For tax purposes, however, the company will recognize £2,857 (£20,000 ÷ 7) in depreciation each year. Each fiscal year the depreciation expense related to the use of the equipment will, therefore, differ for tax and accounting purposes (tax base vs. carrying amount), resulting in a difference between accounting profit and taxable income.

The income statement above reflects accounting profit (depreciation at £2,000 per year). The following table shows the taxable income for each fiscal year.

Taxable Income (£ Millions)	2006	2005	2004
Revenue	£40,000	£30,000	£25,000
Other net gains	2,000	0	0
Changes in inventories of finished goods and work in progress	400	180	200
Raw materials and consumables used	(5,700)	(4,000)	(8,000)
Depreciation expense	(2,857)	(2,857)	(2,857)
Other expenses	(6,000)	(5,900)	(4,500)
Interest expense	(2,000)	(3,000)	(6,000)
Taxable income	£25,843	£14,423	£3,843

The carrying amount and tax base for the equipment is as follows:

(£ Millions)	2006	2005	2004
Equipment value for accounting purposes (*carrying amount*) (depreciation of £2,000/year)	£14,000	£16,000	£18,000
Equipment value for tax purposes (*tax base*) (depreciation of £2,857/year)	£11,429	£14,286	£17,143
Difference	£2,571	£1,714	£857

At each balance sheet date, the tax base and carrying amount of all assets and liabilities must be determined. The income tax payable by Reston Partners will be based on the taxable income of each fiscal year. If a tax rate of 30 percent is assumed, then the income taxes payable for 2004, 2005, and 2006 are £1,153 (30% × 3,843), £4,327 (30% × 14,423), and £7,753 (30% × 25,843).

Remember, though, that if the tax obligation is calculated based on accounting profits, it will differ because of the differences between the tax base and the carrying amount of equipment. The difference in each fiscal year is reflected in the table above. In each fiscal year the carrying amount of the equipment exceeds its tax base. For tax purposes, therefore, the asset tax base is less than its carrying value under financial accounting principles. The difference results in a deferred tax liability.

(£ Millions)	2006	2005	2004
Deferred tax liability	£771	£514	£257

(Difference between tax base
and carrying amount)

2004: £(18,000 − 17,143) × 30% = 257

2005: £(16,000 − 14,286) × 30% = 514

2006: £(14,000 − 11,429) × 30% = 771

The comparison of the tax base and carrying amount of equipment shows what the deferred tax liability should be on a particular balance sheet date. In each fiscal year, only the change in the deferred tax liability should be included in the calculation of the income tax expense reported on the income statement prepared for accounting purposes.

On the income statement, the company's income tax expense will be the sum of the deferred tax liability and income tax payable.

(£ Millions)	2006	2005	2004
Income tax payable (based on tax accounting)	£7,753	£4,327	£1,153
Deferred tax liability	257	257	257
Income tax (based on financial accounting)	£8,010	£4,584	£1,410

(Difference between tax base
and carrying amount)

2004: £(18,000 − 17,143) × 30% = 257

2005: £(16,000 − 14,286) × 30% − 257 = 257

2006: £(14,000 − 11,429) × 30% − 514 = 257

Note that because the different treatment of depreciation is a temporary difference, the income tax on the income statement is 30 percent of the accounting profit, although only a part is income tax payable and the rest is a deferred tax liability.

The consolidated income statement of Reston Partners including income tax is presented as follows:

Reston Partners Consolidated Income Statement			
Period Ending 31 March (£ Millions)	**2006**	**2005**	**2004**
Revenue	£40,000	£30,000	£25,000
Other net gains	2,000	0	0
Changes in inventories of finished goods and work in progress	400	180	200
Raw materials and consumables used	(5,700)	(4,000)	(8,000)
Depreciation expense	(2,000)	(2,000)	(2,000)
Other expenses	(6,000)	(5,900)	(4,500)
Interest expense	(2,000)	(3,000)	(6,000)
Profit before tax	£26,700	£15,280	£4,700
Income tax	(8,010)	(4,584)	(1,410)
Profit after tax	£18,690	£10,696	£3,290

Any amount paid to the tax authorities will reduce the liability for income tax payable and be reflected on the statement of cash flows of the company.

DETERMINING THE TAX BASE OF ASSETS AND LIABILITIES

3

As mentioned in Section 2, temporary differences arise from a difference in the tax base and carrying amount of assets and liabilities. The tax base of an asset or liability is the amount attributed to the asset or liability for tax purposes, whereas the carrying amount is based on accounting principles. Such a difference is considered temporary if it is expected that the taxes will be recovered or payable at a future date.

3.1 Determining the Tax Base of an Asset

The tax base of an asset is the amount that will be deductible for tax purposes in future periods as the economic benefits become realized and the company recovers the carrying amount of the asset.

For example, our previously mentioned Reston Partners (from Example 1) depreciates equipment on a straight-line basis at a rate of 10 percent per year.

The tax authorities allow depreciation of approximately 15 percent per year. At the end of the fiscal year, the carrying amount of equipment for accounting purposes is greater than the asset tax base thus resulting in a temporary difference.

EXAMPLE 2

Determining the Tax Base of an Asset

The following information pertains to Entiguan Sports, a hypothetical developer of products used to treat sports-related injuries. (The treatment of items for accounting and tax purposes is based on fictitious accounting and tax standards and is not specific to a particular jurisdiction.) Calculate the tax base and carrying amount for each item.

1. *Dividends receivable*: On its balance sheet, Entiguan Sports reports dividends of €1 million receivable from a subsidiary. Assume that dividends are not taxable.

2. *Development costs*: Entiguan Sports capitalized development costs of €3 million during the year. Entiguan amortized €500,000 of this amount during the year. For tax purposes amortization of 25 percent per year is allowed.

3. *Research costs*: Entiguan incurred €500,000 in research costs, which were all expensed in the current fiscal year for financial reporting purposes. Assume that applicable tax legislation requires research costs to be expensed over a four-year period rather than all in one year.

4. *Accounts receivable*: Included on the income statement of Entiguan Sports is a provision for doubtful debt of €125,000. The accounts receivable amount reflected on the balance sheet, after taking the provision into account, amounts to €1,500,000. The tax authorities allow a deduction of 25 percent of the gross amount for doubtful debt.

Solutions:

	Carrying Amount (€)	Tax Base (€)	Temporary Difference (€)
1. Dividends receivable	1,000,000	1,000,000	0
2. Development costs	2,500,000	2,250,000	250,000
3. Research costs	0	375,000	(375,000)
4. Accounts receivable	1,500,000	1,218,750	281,250

Comments:

1. *Dividends receivable*: Although the dividends received are economic benefits from the subsidiary, we are assuming that dividends are not taxable. Therefore, the carrying amount equals the tax base for dividends receivable.

2. *Development costs*: First, we assume that development costs will generate economic benefits for Entiguan Sports. Therefore, it may

be included as an asset on the balance sheet for the purposes of this example. Second, the amortization allowed by the tax authorities exceeds the amortization accounted for based on accounting rules. Therefore, the carrying amount of the asset exceeds its tax base. The carrying amount is (€3,000,000 − €500,000) = €2,500,000 whereas the tax base is [€3,000,000 − (25% × €3,000,000)] = €2,250,000.

3. *Research costs*: We assume that research costs will result in future economic benefits for the company. If this were not the case, creation of a deferred tax asset or liability would not be allowed. The tax base of research costs exceeds their carrying amount. The carrying amount is €0 because the full amount has been expensed for financial reporting purposes in the year in which it was incurred. Therefore, there would not have been a balance sheet item "Research costs" for tax purposes, and only a proportion may be deducted in the current fiscal year. The tax base of the asset is (€500,000 − €500,000/4) = €375,000.

4. *Accounts receivable*: The economic benefits that should have been received from accounts receivable have already been included in revenues included in the calculation of the taxable income when the sales occurred. Because the receipt of a portion of the accounts receivable is doubtful, the provision is allowed. The provision, based on tax legislation, results in a greater amount allowed in the current fiscal year than would be the case under accounting principles. This results in the tax base of accounts receivable being lower than its carrying amount. Note that the example specifically states that the balance sheet amount for accounts receivable after the provision for accounting purposes amounts to €1,500,000. Therefore, accounts receivable before any provision was €1,500,000 + €125,000 = €1,625,000. The tax base is calculated as (€1,500,000 + €125,000) − [25% × (€1,500,000 + €125,000)] = €1,218,750.

3.2 Determining the Tax Base of a Liability

The tax base of a liability is the carrying amount of the liability less any amounts that will be deductible for tax purposes in the future. With respect to payments from customers received in advance of providing the goods and services, the tax base of such a liability is the carrying amount less any amount of the revenue that will not be taxable in future. Keep in mind the following fundamental principle: In general, a company will recognize a deferred tax asset or liability when recovery/settlement of the carrying amount will affect future tax payments by either increasing or reducing the taxable profit. Remember, an analyst is not only evaluating the difference between the carrying amount and the tax base, but the relevance of that difference on future profits and losses and thus by implication future taxes.

IFRS offers specific guidelines with regard to revenue received in advance: IAS 12 states that the tax base is the carrying amount less any amount of the revenue that will not be taxed at a future date. Under U.S. GAAP, an analysis of the tax base would result in a similar outcome. The tax legislation within the jurisdiction will determine the amount recognized on the income statement and whether the liability (revenue received in advance) will have a tax base greater than zero. This will depend on how tax legislation recognizes revenue received in advance.

EXAMPLE 3

Determining the Tax Base of a Liability

The following information pertains to Entiguan Sports for the 2006 year-end. The treatment of items for accounting and tax purposes is based on fictitious accounting and tax standards and is not specific to a particular jurisdiction. Calculate the tax base and carrying amount for each item.

1. *Donations*: Entiguan Sports made donations of €100,000 in the current fiscal year. The donations were expensed for financial reporting purposes, but are not tax deductible based on applicable tax legislation.

2. *Interest received in advance*: Entiguan Sports received in advance interest of €300,000. The interest is taxed because tax authorities recognize the interest to accrue to the company (part of taxable income) on the date of receipt.

3. *Rent received in advance*: Entiguan recognized €10 million for rent received in advance from a lessee for an unused warehouse building. Rent received in advance is deferred for accounting purposes but taxed on a cash basis.

4. *Loan*: Entiguan Sports secured a long-term loan for €550,000 in the current fiscal year. Interest is charged at 13.5 percent per annum and is payable at the end of each fiscal year.

Solutions:

	Carrying Amount (€)	Tax Base (€)	Temporary Difference (€)
1. Donations	0	0	0
2. Interest received in advance	300,000	0	(300,000)
3. Rent received in advance	10,000,000	0	(10,000,000)
4. Loan (capital)	550,000	550,000	0
Interest paid	0	0	0

Comments:

1. *Donations*: The amount of €100,000 was immediately expensed on Entiguan's income statement; therefore, the carrying amount is €0. Tax legislation does not allow donations to be deducted for tax

purposes, so the tax base of the donations equals the carrying amount. Note that while the carrying amount and tax base are the same, the difference in the treatment of donations for accounting and tax purposes (expensed for accounting purposes, but not deductible for tax purposes) represents a permanent difference (a difference that will not be reversed in future). Permanent and temporary differences are elaborated on in Section 4 and it will refer to this particular case with an expanded explanation.

2. *Interest received in advance*: Based on the information provided, for tax purposes, interest is deemed to accrue to the company on the date of receipt. For tax purposes, it is thus irrelevant whether it is for the current or a future accounting period; it must be included in taxable income in the financial year received. Interest received in advance is, for accounting purposes though, included in the financial period in which it is deemed to have been earned. For this reason, the interest income received in advance is a balance sheet liability. It was not included on the income statement because the income relates to a future financial year. Because the full €300,000 is included in taxable income in the current fiscal year, the tax base is €300,000 − 300,000 = €0. Note that although interest received in advance and rent received in advance are both taxed, the timing depends on how the particular item is treated in tax legislation.

3. *Rent received in advance*: The result is similar to interest received in advance. The carrying amount of rent received in advance would be €10,000,000 while the tax base is €0.

4. *Loan*: Repayment of the loan has no tax implications. The repayment of the capital amount does not constitute an income or expense. The interest paid is included as an expense in the calculation of taxable income as well as accounting income. Therefore, the tax base and carrying amount is €0. For clarity, the interest paid that would be included on the income statement for the year amounts to 13.5% × €550,000 = €74,250 if the loan was acquired at the beginning of the current fiscal year.

3.3 Changes in Income Tax Rates

The measurement of deferred tax assets and liabilities is based on current tax law. But if there are subsequent changes in tax laws or new income tax rates, existing deferred tax assets and liabilities must be adjusted for the effects of these changes. The resulting effects of the changes are also included in determining accounting profit in the period of change.

When income tax rates change, the deferred tax assets and liabilities are adjusted to the new tax rate. If income tax rates increase, deferred taxes (that is, the deferred tax assets and liabilities) will also increase. Likewise, if income tax rates decrease, deferred taxes will decrease. A decrease in tax rates decreases deferred tax liabilities, which reduces future tax payments to the taxing authorities. A decrease in tax rates will also decrease deferred tax assets, which reduces their value toward the offset of future tax payments to the taxing authorities.

To illustrate the effect of a change in tax rate, consider Example 1 again. In that illustration, the timing difference that led to the recognition of a deferred tax liability for Reston Partners was attributable to differences in the method of depreciation and the related effects on the accounting carrying value and the asset tax base. The relevant information is restated below.

The carrying amount and tax base for the equipment is:

(£ Millions)	2006	2005	2004
Equipment value for accounting purposes (*carrying amount*) (depreciation of £2,000/year)	£14,000	£16,000	£18,000
Equipment value for tax purposes (*tax base*) (depreciation of £2,857/year)	£11,429	£14,286	£17,143
Difference	£2,571	£1,714	£857

At a 30 percent income tax rate, the deferred tax liability was then determined as follows:

(£ Millions)	2006	2005	2004
Deferred tax liability	£771	£514	£257
(Difference between tax base and carrying amount)			
2004: £(18,000 − 17,143) × 30% = £257			
2005: £(16,000 − 14,286) × 30% = £514			
2006: £(14,000 − 11,429) × 30% = £771			

For this illustration, assume that the taxing authority has changed the income tax rate to 25 percent for 2006. Although the difference between the carrying amount and the tax base of the depreciable asset are the same, the deferred tax liability for 2006 will be £643 (instead of £771 or a reduction of £128 in the liability). 2006: £(14,000 − 11,429) × 25% = £643.

Reston Partners' provision for income tax expense is also affected by the change in tax rates. Taxable income for 2006 will now be taxed at a rate of 25 percent. The benefit of the 2006 accelerated depreciation tax shield is now only £214 (£857 × 25%) instead of the previous £257 (a reduction of £43). In addition, the reduction in the beginning carrying value of the deferred tax liability for 2006 (the year of change) further reduces the income tax expense for 2006. The reduction in income tax expense attributable to the change in tax rate is £85. 2006: (30% − 25%) × £1,714 = £85. Note that these two components together account for the reduction in the deferred tax liability (£43 + £85 = £128).

As may be seen from this discussion, changes in the income tax rate have an effect on a company's deferred tax asset and liability carrying values as well as an effect on the measurement of income tax expense in the year of change. The analyst must thus note that proposed changes in tax law can have a quantifiable effect on these accounts (and any related financial ratios that are derived from them) if the proposed changes are subsequently enacted into law.

TEMPORARY AND PERMANENT DIFFERENCES BETWEEN TAXABLE AND ACCOUNTING PROFIT

Temporary differences arise from a difference between the tax base and the carrying amount of assets and liabilities. The creation of a deferred tax asset or liability from a temporary difference is only possible if the difference reverses itself at some future date and to such an extent that the balance sheet item is expected to create future economic benefits for the company. IFRS and U.S. GAAP both prescribe the balance sheet liability method for recognition of deferred tax. This balance sheet method focuses on the recognition of a deferred tax asset or liability should there be a temporary difference between the carrying amount and tax base of balance sheet items.[3]

Permanent differences are differences between tax and financial reporting of revenue (expenses) that *will not* be reversed at some future date. Because they will not be reversed at a future date, these differences do not give rise to deferred tax. These items typically include

▶ Income or expense items not allowed by tax legislation, and

▶ Tax credits for some expenditures that directly reduce taxes.

Because no deferred tax item is created for permanent differences, all permanent differences result in a difference between the company's effective tax rate and statutory tax rate. The effective tax rate is also influenced by different statutory taxes should an entity conduct business in more than one tax jurisdiction. The formula for the reported effective tax rate is thus equal to:

$$\text{Reported effective tax rate} = \text{Income tax expense} \div \text{Pretax income (accounting profit)}$$

The net change in deferred tax during a reporting period is the difference between the balance of the deferred tax asset or liability for the current period and the balance of the previous period.

4.1 Taxable Temporary Differences

Temporary differences are further divided into two categories, namely taxable temporary differences and deductible temporary differences. **Taxable temporary differences** are temporary differences that result in a taxable amount in a future period when determining the taxable profit as the balance sheet item is recovered or settled. Taxable temporary differences result in a deferred tax liability when the carrying amount of an asset exceeds its tax base and, in the case of a liability, when the tax base of the liability exceeds its carrying amount.

Under U.S. GAAP, a deferred tax asset or liability is not recognized for unamortizable goodwill. Under IFRS, a deferred tax account is not recognized

---

[3] Previously, IAS 12 required recognition of deferred tax based on the deferred method (also known as the income statement method), which focused on timing differences. Timing differences are differences in the recognition of income and expenses for accounting and tax purposes that originate in one period and will reverse in a future period. Given the definition of timing differences, all timing differences are temporary differences, such as the different treatment of depreciation for tax and accounting purposes (although the timing is different with regard to the allowed depreciation for tax and accounting purposes, the asset will eventually be fully depreciated).

for goodwill arising in a business combination. Since goodwill is a residual, the recognition of a deferred tax liability would increase the carrying amount of goodwill. Discounting deferred tax assets or liabilities is generally not allowed for temporary differences related to business combinations as it is for other temporary differences.

IFRS provides an exemption (that is, deferred tax is not provided on the temporary difference) for the initial recognition of an asset or liability in a transaction that: a) is not a business combination (e.g., joint ventures, branches and unconsolidated investments); and b) affects neither accounting profit nor taxable profit at the time of the transaction. U.S. GAAP does not provide an exemption for these circumstances.

As a simple example of a temporary difference with no recognition of deferred tax liability, assume that a fictitious company, Corporate International, a holding company of various leisure related businesses and holiday resorts, buys an interest in a hotel in the current financial year. The goodwill related to the transaction will be recognized on the financial statements, but the related tax liability will not, as it relates to the initial recognition of goodwill.

4.2 Deductible Temporary Differences

Deductible temporary differences are temporary differences that result in a reduction or deduction of taxable income in a future period when the balance sheet item is recovered or settled. Deductible temporary differences result in a deferred tax asset when the tax base of an asset exceeds its carrying amount and, in the case of a liability, when the carrying amount of the liability exceeds its tax base. The recognition of a deferred tax asset is only allowed to the extent there is a reasonable expectation of future profits against which the asset or liability (that gave rise to the deferred tax asset) can be recovered or settled.

To determine the probability of sufficient future profits for utilization, one must consider the following: 1) Sufficient taxable temporary differences must exist that are related to the same tax authority and the same taxable entity; and 2) The taxable temporary differences that are expected to reverse in the same periods as expected for the reversal of the deductible temporary differences.

As with deferred tax liabilities, IFRS states that deferred tax assets should not be recognized in cases that would arise from the initial recognition of an asset or liability in transactions that are not a business combination and when, at the time of the transaction, there is no impact on either accounting or taxable profit. Subsequent to initial recognition under IFRS and U.S. GAAP, any deferred tax assets that arise from investments in subsidiaries, branches, associates, and interests in joint ventures are recognized as a deferred tax asset.

IFRS and U.S. GAAP allow the creation of a deferred tax asset in the case of tax losses and tax credits. These two unique situations will be further elaborated on in Section 6. IAS 12 *does not* allow the creation of a deferred tax asset arising from negative goodwill. Negative goodwill arises when the amount that an entity pays for an interest in a business is less than the net fair market value of the portion of assets and liabilities of the acquired company, based on the interest of the entity.

4.3 Examples of Taxable and Deductible Temporary Differences

Exhibit 1 summarizes how differences between the tax bases and carrying amounts of assets and liabilities give rise to deferred tax assets or deferred tax liabilities.

EXHIBIT 1	Treatment of Temporary Differences

Balance sheet item	Carrying amount vs. tax base	Results in deferred tax asset/liability
Asset	Carrying amount > tax base	Deferred tax liability
Asset	Carrying amount < tax base	Deferred tax asset
Liability	Carrying amount > tax base	Deferred tax asset
Liability	Carrying amount < tax base	Deferred tax liability

EXAMPLE 4

Taxable and Deductible Temporary Differences

Examples 2 and 3 illustrated how to calculate the tax base of assets and liabilities, respectively. Based on the information provided in Examples 2 and 3, indicate whether the difference in the tax base and carrying amount of the assets and liabilities are temporary or permanent differences and whether a deferred tax asset or liability will be recognized based on the difference identified.

Solution to Example 2:

	Carrying Amount(€)	Tax Base(€)	Temporary Difference(€)	*Will Result in Deferred Tax Asset/Liability*
1. Dividends receivable	1,000,000	1,000,000	0	*N/A*
2. Development costs	2,500,000	2,250,000	250,000	*Deferred tax liability*
3. Research costs	0	375,000	(375,000)	*Deferred tax asset*
4. Accounts receivable	1,500,000	1,218,750	281,250	*Deferred tax liability*

Example 2 included comments on the calculation of the carrying amount and tax base of the assets.

1. *Dividends receivable*: As a result of non-taxability, the carrying amount equals the tax base of dividends receivable. This constitutes a permanent difference and will not result in the recognition of any deferred tax asset or liability. A temporary difference constitutes a difference that will, at some future date, be reversed. Although the timing of recognition is different for tax and accounting purposes, in the end the full carrying amount will be expensed/recognized as income. A permanent difference will never be reversed. Based on tax legislation, dividends from a subsidiary are not recognized as income. Therefore, no amount will be reflected as dividend income when calculating the taxable income, and the tax base of dividends receivable must be the total amount received, namely €1,000,000. The taxable income and accounting profit will permanently differ with the amount of dividends receivable, even on future financial statements as an effect on the retained earnings reflected on the balance sheet.

2. *Development costs*: The difference between the carrying amount and tax base is a temporary difference that, in the future, will reverse. In this fiscal year, it will result in a deferred tax liability.

3. *Research costs*: The difference between the carrying amount and tax base is a temporary difference that results in a deferred tax asset. Remember the explanation in Section 2 for deferred tax assets—a deferred tax asset arises because of an excess amount paid for taxes (when taxable

income is greater than accounting profit), which is expected to be recovered from future operations. Based on accounting principles, the full amount was deducted resulting in a lower accounting profit, while the taxable income by implication, should be greater because of the lower amount expensed.

4. *Accounts receivable*: The difference between the carrying amount and tax base of the asset is a temporary difference that will result in a deferred tax liability.

Solution to Example 3:

	Carrying Amount(€)	Tax Base(€)	Temporary Difference(€)	*Will Result in Deferred Tax Asset/Liability*
1. Donations	0	0	0	*N/A*
2. Interest received in advance	300,000	0	(300,000)	*Deferred tax asset*
3. Rent received in advance	10,000,000	0	(10,000,000)	*Deferred tax asset*
4. Loan (capital)	550,000	550,000	0	*N/A*
Interest paid	0	0	0	*N/A*

Example 3 included extensive comments on the calculation of the carrying amount and tax base of the liabilities.

1. *Donations*: It was assumed that tax legislation does not allow donations to be deducted for tax purposes. No temporary difference results from donations, and thus a deferred tax asset or liability will not be recognized. This constitutes a permanent difference.

2. *Interest received in advance*: Interest received in advance results in a temporary difference that gives rise to a deferred tax asset. A deferred tax asset arises because of an excess amount paid for taxes (when taxable income is greater than accounting profit), which is expected to be recovered from future operations.

3. *Rent received in advance*: The difference between the carrying amount and tax base is a temporary difference that leads to the recognition of a deferred tax asset.

4. *Loan*: There are no temporary differences as a result of the loan or interest paid, and thus no deferred tax item is recognized.

4.4 Temporary Differences at Initial Recognition of Assets and Liabilities

In some situations the carrying amount and tax base of a balance sheet item may vary at initial recognition. For example, a company may deduct a government grant from the initial carrying amount of an asset or liability that appears on the balance sheet. For tax purposes, such grants may not be deducted when determining the tax base of the balance sheet item. In such circumstances, the carrying amount of the asset or liability will be lower than its tax base. Differences in the tax base of an asset or liability as a result of the circumstances described above may not be recognized as deferred tax assets or liabilities.

For example, a government may offer grants to Small, Medium, and Micro Enterprises (SMME) in an attempt to assist these entrepreneurs in their endeavors that contribute to the country's GDP and job creation. Assume that a particular grant is offered for infrastructure needs (office furniture, property, plant, and equipment, etc). In these circumstances, although the carrying amount will be lower than the tax base of the asset, the related deferred tax may not be recognized. As mentioned earlier, deferred tax assets and liabilities should not be recognized in cases that would arise from the initial recognition of an asset or liability in transactions that are not a business combination and when, at the time of the transaction, there is no impact on either accounting or taxable profit.

A deferred tax liability will also not be recognized at the initial recognition of goodwill. Although goodwill may be treated differently across tax jurisdictions, which may lead to differences in the carrying amount and tax base of goodwill, IAS 12 does not allow the recognition of such a deferred tax liability. Any impairment that an entity should, for accounting purposes, impose on goodwill will again result in a temporary difference between its carrying amount and tax base. Any impairment that an entity should, for accounting purposes, impose on goodwill and if part of the goodwill is related to the initial recognition, that part of the difference in tax base and carrying amount should not result in any deferred taxation because the initial deferred tax liability was not recognized. Any future differences between the carrying amount and tax base as a result of amortization and the deductibility of a portion of goodwill constitute a temporary difference for which provision should be made.

4.5 Business Combinations and Deferred Taxes

The fair value of assets and liabilities acquired in a business combination is determined on the acquisition date and may differ from the previous carrying amount. It is highly probable that the values of acquired intangible assets, including goodwill, would differ from their carrying amounts. This temporary difference will affect deferred taxes as well as the amount of goodwill recognized as a result of the acquisition.

4.6 Investments in Subsidiaries, Branches, Associates and Interests in Joint Ventures

Investments in subsidiaries, branches, associates and interests in joint ventures may lead to temporary differences on the consolidated versus the parent's financial statements. The related deferred tax liabilities as a result of temporary differences will be recognized unless both of the following criterion are satisfied:

▶ The parent is in a position to control the timing of the future reversal of the temporary difference, and

▶ It is probable that the temporary difference will not reverse in the future.

With respect to deferred tax assets related to subsidiaries, branches, and associates and interests, deferred tax assets will only be recognized if the following criteria are satisfied:

▶ The temporary difference will reverse in the future, and

▶ Sufficient taxable profits exist against which the temporary difference can be used.

5   UNUSED TAX LOSSES AND TAX CREDITS

IAS 12 allows the recognition of unused tax losses and tax credits only to the extent that it is probable that in the future there will be taxable income against which the unused tax losses and credits can be applied. Under U.S. GAAP, a deferred tax asset is recognized in full but is then reduced by a valuation allowance if it is more likely than not that some or all of the deferred tax asset will not be realized. The same requirements for creation of a deferred tax asset as a result of deductible temporary differences also apply to unused tax losses and tax credits. The existence of tax losses may indicate that the entity cannot reasonably be expected to generate sufficient future taxable income. All other things held constant, the greater the history of tax losses, the greater the concern regarding the company's ability to generate future taxable profits.

Should there be concerns about the company's future profitability, then the deferred tax asset may not be recognized until it is realized. When assessing the probability that sufficient taxable profit will be generated in the future, the following criteria can serve as a guide:

▶ If there is uncertainty as to the probability of future taxable profits, a deferred tax asset as a result of unused tax losses or tax credits is only recognized to the extent of the available taxable temporary differences;

▶ Assess the probability that the entity will in fact generate future taxable profits before the unused tax losses and/or credits expire pursuant to tax rules regarding the carry forward of the unused tax losses;

▶ Verify that the above is with the same tax authority and based on the same taxable entity;

▶ Determine whether the past tax losses were a result of specific circumstances that are unlikely to be repeated; and

▶ Discover if tax planning opportunities are available to the entity that will result in future profits. These may include changes in tax legislation that is phased in over more than one financial period to the benefit of the entity.

It is imperative that the timing of taxable and deductible temporary differences also be considered before creating a deferred tax asset based on unused tax credits.

6   RECOGNITION AND MEASUREMENT OF CURRENT AND DEFERRED TAX

Current taxes payable or recoverable from tax authorities are based on the applicable tax rates at the balance sheet date. Deferred taxes should be measured at the tax rate that is expected to apply when the asset is realized or the liability settled. With respect to the income tax for a current or prior period not yet paid, it is recognized as a tax liability until paid. Any amount paid in excess of any tax obligation is recognized as an asset. The income tax paid in excess or owed to tax authorities is separate from deferred taxes on the company's balance sheet.

When measuring deferred taxes in a jurisdiction, there are different forms of taxation such as income tax, capital gains tax (any capital gains made), or secondary tax on companies (tax payable on the dividends that a company declares) and possibly different tax bases for a balance sheet item (as in the case of government grants influencing the tax base of an asset such as property). In assessing which tax laws should apply, it is dependent on how the related asset or liability will be settled. It would be prudent to use the tax rate and tax base that is consistent with how it is expected the tax base will be recovered or settled.

Although deferred tax assets and liabilities are related to temporary differences expected to be recovered or settled at some future date, neither are discounted to present value in determining the amounts to be booked. Both must be adjusted for changes in tax rates.

Deferred taxes as well as income taxes should always be recognized on the income statement of an entity unless it pertains to:

▶ Taxes or deferred taxes charged directly to equity, or

▶ A possible provision for deferred taxes relates to a business combination.

The carrying amount of the deferred tax assets and liabilities should also be assessed. The carrying amounts may change even though there may have been no change in temporary differences during the period evaluated. This can result from:

▶ Changes in tax rates;

▶ Reassessments of the recoverability of deferred tax assets; or

▶ Changes in the expectations for how an asset will be recovered and what influences the deferred tax asset or liability.

All unrecognized deferred tax assets and liabilities must be reassessed at the balance sheet date and measured against the criteria of probable future economic benefits. If such a deferred asset is likely to be recovered, it may be appropriate to recognize the related deferred tax asset.

Different jurisdictions have different requirements for determining tax obligations that can range from different forms of taxation to different tax rates based on taxable income. When comparing financial statements of entities that conduct business in different jurisdictions subject to different tax legislation, the analyst should be cautious in reaching conclusions because of the potentially complex tax rules that may apply.

6.1 Recognition of a Valuation Allowance

Deferred tax assets must be assessed at each balance sheet date. If there is any doubt whether the deferral will be recovered, then the carrying amount should be reduced to the expected recoverable amount. Should circumstances subsequently change and suggest the future will lead to recovery of the deferral, the reduction may be reversed.

Under U.S. GAAP, deferred tax assets are reduced by creating a valuation allowance. Establishing a valuation allowance reduces the deferred tax asset and income in the period in which the allowance is established. Should circumstances change to such an extent that a deferred tax asset valuation allowance may be reduced, the reversal will increase the deferred tax asset and operating income. Because of the subjective judgment involved, an analyst should carefully scrutinize any such changes.

6.2 Recognition of Current and Deferred Tax Charged Directly to Equity

In general, IFRS and U.S. GAAP require that the recognition of deferred tax liabilities and current income tax should be treated similarly to the asset or liability that gave rise to the deferred tax liability or income tax based on accounting treatment. Should an item that gives rise to a deferred tax liability be taken directly to equity, the same should hold true for the resulting deferred tax.

The following are examples of such items:

▶ Revaluation of property, plant, and equipment (revaluations are not permissible under U.S. GAAP);

▶ Long-term investments at fair value;

▶ Changes in accounting policies;

▶ Errors corrected against the opening balance of retained earnings;

▶ Initial recognition of an equity component related to complex financial instruments; and

▶ Exchange rate differences arising from the currency translation procedures for foreign operations.

Whenever it is determined that a deferred tax liability will not be reversed, an adjustment should be made to the liability. The deferred tax liability will be reduced and the amount by which it is reduced should be taken directly to equity. Any deferred taxes related to a business combination must also be recognized in equity.

Depending on the items that gave rise to the deferred tax liabilities, an analyst should exercise judgment regarding whether the taxes should be included with deferred tax liabilities or whether it should be taken directly to equity. It may be more appropriate simply to ignore deferred taxes.

EXAMPLE 5

Taxes Charged Directly to Equity

The following information pertains to Anderson Company (a hypothetical company). A building owned by Anderson Company was originally purchased for €1,000,000 on 1 January 2004. For accounting purposes, buildings are depreciated at 5 percent a year on a straight-line basis, and depreciation for tax purposes is 10 percent a year on a straight-line basis. On the first day of the 2006, the building is revalued at €1,200,000. It is estimated that the remaining useful life of the building from the date of revaluation is 20 years. *Important*: For tax purposes the revaluation of the building is not recognized.

Based on the information provided, the following illustrates the difference in treatment of the building for accounting and tax purposes.

	Carrying Amount of Building	Tax Base of Building
Balance on 1 January 2004	€1,000,000	€1,000,000
Depreciation 2004	50,000	100,000
Balance on 31 December 2004	€950,000	€900,000
Depreciation 2005	50,000	100,000
Balance on 31 December 2005	€900,000	€800,000
Revaluation on 1 January 2006	300,000	n/a
Balance on 1 January 2006	€1,200,000	€800,000
Depreciation 2006	60,000	100,000
Balance on 31 December 2006	€1,140,000	€700,000
Accumulated depreciation		
Balance on 1 January 2004	€0	€0
Depreciation 2004	50,000	100,000
Balance on 31 December 2004	€50,000	€100,000
Depreciation 2005	50,000	100,000
Balance on 31 December 2005	€100,000	€200,000
Revaluation at 1 January 2006	(100,000)	n/a
Balance on 1 January 2006	€0	€200,000
Depreciation 2006	60,000	100,000
Balance on 30 November 2006	€60,000	€300,000

	Carrying Amount	Tax Base
On 31 December 2004	€950,000	€900,000
On 31 December 2005	€900,000	€800,000
On 31 December 2006	€1,140,000	€700,000

31 December 2004: On 31 December 2004, different treatments for depreciation expense result in a temporary difference that gives rise to a deferred tax liability. The difference in the tax base and carrying amount of the building was a result of different depreciation amounts for tax and accounting purposes. Depreciation appears on the income statement. For this reason the deferred tax liability will also be reflected on the income statement. If we assume that the applicable tax rate in 2004 was 40 percent, then the resulting deferred tax liability will be $40\% \times (€950,000 - €900,000) = €20,000$.

31 December 2005: As of 31 December 2005, the carrying amount of the building remains greater than the tax base. The temporary difference again gives rise to a deferred tax liability. Again, assuming the applicable tax rate to be 40 percent, the deferred tax liability from the building is $40\% \times (€900,000 - €800,000) = €40,000$.

31 December 2006: On 31 December 2006, the carrying amount of the building again exceeds the tax base. This is not the result of disposals or additions, but is a result of the revaluation at the beginning of the 2006 fiscal year and the different rates of depreciation. The deferred tax liability would seem to be 40% × (€1,140,000 − €700,000) = €176,000, *but* the treatment is different than it was for the 2004 and 2005. In 2006, revaluation of the building gave rise to a balance sheet liability, namely "Revaluation Surplus" in the amount of €300,000, which is not recognized for tax purposes.

The deferred tax liability would usually have been calculated as follows:

	2006	2005	2004
Deferred tax liability (closing balance at end of fiscal year)	€176,000	€40,000	€20,000

(Difference between tax base and carrying amount)

2004: €(950,000 − 900,000) × 40% = 20,000

2005: €(900,000 − 800,000) × 40% = 40,000

2006: €(1,140,000 − 700,000) × 40% = 176,000

The change in the deferred tax liability in 2004 is €20,000, in 2005: €20,000 (€40,000 − €20,000) and, it would seem, in 2006: €136,000 (€176,000 − €40,000). In 2006, although it would seem that the balance for deferred tax liability should be €176,000, the revaluation is not recognized for tax purposes. Only the portion of the difference between the tax base and carrying amount that is not a result of the revaluation is recognized as giving rise to a deferred tax liability.

The effect of the revaluation surplus and the associated tax effects are accounted for in a direct adjustment to equity. The revaluation surplus is reduced by the tax provision associated with the excess of the fair value over the carry value and it affects retained earnings (€300,000 × 40% = €120,000).

The deferred tax liability that should be reflected on the balance sheet is thus not €176,000 but only €56,000 (€176,000 − €120,000). Given the balance of deferred tax liability at the beginning of the 2006 fiscal year in the amount of €40,000, the change in the deferred tax liability is only €56,000 − €40,000 = €16,000.

In the future, at the end of each year, an amount equal to the depreciation as a result of the revaluation minus the deferred tax effect will be transferred from the revaluation reserve to retained earnings. In 2006 this will amount to a portion of depreciation resulting from the revaluation, €15,000 (€300,000 ÷ 20), minus the deferred tax effect of €6,000 (€15,000 × 40%), thus €9,000.

PRESENTATION AND DISCLOSURE   7

We will discuss the presentation and disclosure of income tax related information by way of example. The Consolidated Statements of Operations (Income Statements) and Consolidated Balance Sheets for Micron Technology (MU) are provided in Exhibits 2 and 3, respectively. Exhibit 4 provides the income tax note disclosures for MU for the 2004, 2005, and 2006 fiscal years.

MU's income tax provision (i.e., income tax expense) for fiscal year 2006 is $18 million (see Exhibit 2). The income tax note disclosure in Exhibit 4 reconciles how the income tax provision was determined beginning with MU's reported income before taxes (shown in Exhibit 2 as $433 million for fiscal year 2006). The note disclosure then denotes the income tax provision for 2006 that is current ($42 million), which is then offset by the deferred tax benefit for foreign taxes ($24 million), for a net income tax provision of $18 million. Exhibit 4 further shows a reconciliation of how the income tax provision was derived from the U.S. federal statutory rate. Many public companies comply with this required disclosure by displaying the information in percentage terms, but MU has elected to provide the disclosure in absolute dollar amounts. From this knowledge, we can see that the dollar amount shown for U.S. federal income tax provision at the statutory rate ($152 million) was determined by multiplying MU's income before taxes by the 35 percent U.S. federal statutory rate ($433 \times 0.35 = $152). Furthermore, after considering tax credits and changes in the valuation allowance for deferred tax assets, MU's $18 million tax provision for 2006 is only 4.16 percent of its income before taxes ($18 \div $433 = 4.16%).

In addition, the note disclosure in Exhibit 4 provides detailed information about the derivation of the deferred tax assets ($26 million current and $49 million noncurrent) and deferred tax liabilities ($28 million noncurrent) that are shown on MU's consolidated balance sheet for fiscal year 2006 in Exhibit 3.

EXHIBIT 2	Micron Technology, Inc. Consolidated Statements of Operations (Amounts in Millions except per Share)		
For the Year Ended	**31 Aug. 2006**	**1 Sept. 2005**	**2 Sept. 2004**
Net sales	$5,272	$4,880	$4,404
Cost of goods sold	4,072	3,734	3,090
Gross margin	1,200	1,146	1,314
Selling, general and administrative	460	348	332
Research and development	656	604	755
Restructure	—	(1)	(23)
Other operating (income) expense, net	(266)	(22)	—
Operating income	350	217	250
Interest income	101	32	15
Interest expense	(25)	(47)	(36)
Other non-operating income (expense), net	7	(3)	3
Income before taxes	433	199	232

(Exhibit continued on next page . . .)

EXHIBIT 2　(continued)

For the Year Ended	31 Aug. 2006	1 Sept. 2005	2 Sept. 2004
Income tax (provision)	(18)	(11)	(75)
Noncontrolling interests in net income	(7)	—	—
Net income	$408	$188	$157
Earnings per share:			
Basic	$0.59	$0.29	$0.24
Diluted	$0.56	$0.27	$0.24
Number of shares used in per share calculations:			
Basic	692	648	641
Diluted	725	702	646

EXHIBIT 3　Micron Technology, Inc. Consolidated Balance Sheets (Dollars in Millions)

As of	31 Aug. 2006	1 Sept. 2005
Assets		
Cash and equivalents	$1,431	$524
Short-term investments	1,648	766
Receivables	956	794
Inventories	963	771
Prepaid expenses	77	39
Deferred income taxes	26	32
Total current assets	5,101	2,926
Intangible assets, net	388	260
Property, plant and equipment, net	5,888	4,684
Deferred income taxes	49	30
Goodwill	502	16
Other assets	293	90
Total assets	$12,221	$8,006
Liabilities and shareholders' equity		
Accounts payable and accrued expenses	$1,319	$753
Deferred income	53	30
Equipment purchase contracts	123	49
Current portion of long-term debt	166	147
Total current liabilities	1,661	979

(Exhibit continued on next page . . .)

EXHIBIT 3	(continued)		
As of		**31 Aug. 2006**	**1 Sept. 2005**
Long-term debt		405	1,020
Deferred income taxes		28	35
Other liabilities		445	125
Total liabilities		2,539	2,159
Commitments and contingencies		—	—
Noncontrolling interests in subsidiaries		1,568	—
Common stock of $0.10 par value, authorized 3 billion shares, issued and outstanding 749.4 million and 616.2 million shares		75	62
Additional capital		6,555	4,707
Retained earnings		1,486	1,078
Accumulated other comprehensive loss		(2)	—
Total shareholders' equity		8,114	5,847
Total liabilities and shareholders' equity		$12,221	$8,006

EXHIBIT 4	Micron Technology, Inc. Income Taxes Note to the Consolidated Financial Statements

Income (loss) before taxes and the income tax (provision) benefit consisted of the following:

(Millions)	2006	2005	2004
Income (loss) before taxes:			
U.S.	$351	$108	($19)
Foreign	82	91	251
	$433	$199	$232
Income tax (provision) benefit:			
Current:			
U.S. federal	($12)	$—	$—
State	(1)	(3)	—
Foreign	(29)	(18)	(12)
	(42)	(21)	(12)
Deferred:			
U.S. federal	—	—	—
State	—	—	—
Foreign	24	10	(63)
	24	10	(63)
Income tax (provision)	($18)	($11)	($75)

(Exhibit continued on next page . . .)

EXHIBIT 4   (continued)

The company's income tax (provision) computed using the U.S. federal statutory rate and the company's income tax (provision) benefit is reconciled as follows:

(Millions)	2006	2005	2004
U.S. federal income tax (provision) benefit at statutory rate	$(152)	$(70)	$(81)
State taxes, net of federal benefit	5	6	(9)
Foreign operations	3	9	(44)
Change in valuation allowance	103	(7)	(11)
Tax credits	7	28	7
Export sales benefit	13	16	16
Resolution of tax matters	—	—	37
Other	3	7	10
	$(18)	$(11)	$(75)

State taxes reflect investment tax credits of $23 million, $14 million, and $9 million for 2006, 2005, and 2004, respectively. Deferred income taxes reflect the net tax effects of temporary differences between the bases of assets and liabilities for financial reporting and income tax purposes. The company's deferred tax assets and liabilities consist of the following as of the end of the periods shown below:

($ Millions)	2006	2005
Deferred tax assets:		
Net operating loss and credit carryforwards	$929	$1,202
Basis differences in investments in joint ventures	301	—
Deferred revenue	160	76
Accrued compensation	51	40
Accounts payable	43	25
Inventories	16	33
Accrued product and process technology	11	12
Other	36	87
Gross deferred assets	1,547	1,475
Less valuation allowance	(915)	(1,029)
Deferred tax assets, net of valuation allowance	632	446

(Exhibit continued on next page . . . .)

EXHIBIT 4	(continued)		
($ Millions)		**2006**	**2005**
Deferred tax liabilities:			
Excess tax over book depreciation		(308)	(315)
Receivables		(91)	—
Intangibles		(68)	—
Unremitted earnings on certain subsidiaries		(58)	(49)
Product and process technology		(45)	(39)
Other		(15)	(16)
Deferred tax liabilities		(585)	(419)
Net deferred tax assets		$47	$27
Reported as:			
Current deferred tax assets		$26	$32
Noncurrent deferred tax assets		49	30
Noncurrent deferred tax liabilities		(28)	(35)
Net deferred tax assets		$47	$27

The company has a valuation allowance against substantially all of its U.S. net deferred tax assets. As of 31 August 2006, the company had aggregate U.S. tax net operating loss carryforwards of $1.7 billion and unused U.S. tax credit carryforwards of $164 million. The company also has unused state tax net operating loss carryforwards of $1.4 billion and unused state tax credits of $163 million. During 2006, the company utilized approximately $1.1 billion of its U.S. tax net operating loss carryforwards as a result of IMFT, MP Mask, and related transactions.[4] Substantially all of the net operating loss carryforwards expire in 2022 to 2025 and substantially all of the tax credit carryforwards expire in 2013 to 2026.

The changes in valuation allowance of ($114) million and $25 million in 2006 and 2005, respectively, are primarily a result of uncertainties of realizing certain U.S. net operating losses and certain tax credit carryforwards. The change in the valuation allowance in 2006 and 2005 includes $12 million and $2 million, respectively, for stock plan deductions, which will be credited to additional capital if realized.

Provision has been made for deferred taxes on undistributed earnings of non-U.S. subsidiaries to the extent that dividend payments from such companies are expected to result in additional tax liability. Remaining undistributed earnings of $686 million as of 31 August 2006 have been indefinitely reinvested; therefore, no provision has been made for taxes due upon remittance of these earnings. Determination of the amount of unrecognized deferred tax liability on these unremitted earnings is not practicable.

---

[4] Micron Technology entered into profitable joint ventures and acquired profitable companies in 2006. The company was able to apply its net operating tax loss carryforwards (NOLs) toward these profits thereby reducing the income tax payments that would otherwise have been made without the NOLs.

EXAMPLE 6

Financial Analysis Example

Use the financial statement information and disclosures provided by MU in Exhibits 2, 3, and 4 to answer the following questions:

1. MU discloses a valuation allowance of $915 million (see Exhibit 4) against total deferred assets of $1,547 million in 2006. Does the existence of this valuation allowance have any implications concerning MU's future earning prospects?

2. How would MU's deferred tax assets and deferred tax liabilities be affected if the federal statutory tax rate was changed to 32 percent? Would a change in the rate to 32 percent be beneficial to MU?

3. How would reported earnings have been affected if MU were not using a valuation allowance?

4. How would MU's $929 million in net operating loss carryforwards in 2006 (see Exhibit 4) affect the valuation that an acquiring company would be willing to offer?

5. Under what circumstances should the analyst consider MU's deferred tax liability as debt or as equity? Under what circumstances should the analyst exclude MU's deferred tax liability from both debt and equity when calculating the debt-to-equity ratio?

Solution to 1: According to Exhibit 4, MU's deferred tax assets expire gradually until 2026 (2022 to 2025 for the net operating loss carryforwards and 2013 to 2026 for the tax credit carryforwards). Because the company is relatively young, it is likely that most of these expirations occur toward the end of that period. Because cumulative federal net operating loss carryforwards total $1.7 billion, the valuation allowance could imply that MU is not reasonably expected to earn $1.7 billion over the next 20 years. However, as we can see in Exhibit 2, MU has earned profits for 2006, 2005, and 2004, thereby showing that the allowance could be adjusted downward if the company continues to generate profits in the future, making it more likely than not that the deferred tax asset would be recognized.

Solution to 2: MU's total deferred tax assets exceed total deferred tax liabilities by $47 million. A change in the federal statutory tax rate to 32 percent from the current rate of 35 percent would make these net deferred assets less valuable. Also, because it is possible that the deferred tax asset valuation allowance could be adjusted downward in the future (see discussion to solution 1 above), the impact could be far greater in magnitude.

Solution to 3: The disclosure in Exhibit 4 shows that the reduction in the valuation allowance reduced the income tax provision as reported on the income statement by $103 million in 2006. Additional potential reductions in the valuation allowance could similarly reduce reported income taxes (actual tax income taxes would not be affected by a valuation allowance established for financial reporting) in future years (see discussion to solution 1 above).

Solution to 4: If an acquiring company is profitable, it may be able to use MU's tax loss carryforwards to offset its own tax liabilities. The value to an acquirer would be the present value of the carryforwards, based on the acquirer's tax rate and expected timing of realization. The higher the acquiring company's tax rate, and the more profitable the acquirer, the sooner it would be able to benefit. Therefore, an acquirer with a high current tax rate would theoretically be willing to pay more than an acquirer with a lower tax rate.

Solution to 5: The analyst should classify the deferred tax liability as debt if the liability is expected to reverse with subsequent tax payment. If the liability is not expected to reverse, there is no expectation of a cash outflow and the liability should be treated as equity. By way of example, future company losses may preclude the payment of any income taxes, or changes in tax laws could result in taxes that are never paid. The deferred tax liability should be excluded from both debt and equity when both the amounts and timing of tax payments resulting from the reversals of temporary differences are uncertain.

COMPARISON OF IFRS AND U.S. GAAP   8

As mentioned earlier, though IFRS and U.S. GAAP follow similar conventions on many tax issues, there are some notable differences (such as revaluation). Exhibit 5 summarizes many of the key similarities and differences between IFRS and U.S. GAAP. Though both frameworks require a provision for deferred taxes, there are differences in the methodologies.

EXHIBIT 5	Deferred Income Tax Issues IFRS and U.S. GAAP Methodology Similarities and Differences	
Issue	**IFRS**	**U.S. GAAP**
General considerations:		
General approach	Full provision.	Similar to IFRS.
Basis for deferred tax assets and liabilities	Temporary differences—i.e., the difference between carrying amount and tax base of assets and liabilities (see exceptions below).	Similar to IFRS.
Exceptions (i.e., deferred tax is not provided on the temporary difference)	Nondeductible goodwill (that which is not deductible for tax purposes) does not give rise to taxable temporary differences.	Similar to IFRS, except no initial recognition exemption and special requirements apply in computing deferred tax on leveraged leases.

(Exhibit continued on next page . . .)

| EXHIBIT 5 | (continued) | |

Issue	IFRS	U.S. GAAP
General considerations:		
	Initial recognition of an asset or liability in a transaction that: a) is not a business combination; and b) affects neither accounting profit nor taxable profit at the time of the transaction. Other amounts that do not have a tax consequence (commonly referred to as permanent differences) exist and depend on the tax rules and jurisdiction of the entity.	
Specific applications:		
Revaluation of plant, property, and equipment and intangible assets	Deferred tax recognized in equity.	Not applicable, as revaluation is prohibited.
Foreign nonmonetary assets/liabilities when the tax reporting currency is not the functional currency	Deferred tax is recognized on the difference between the carrying amount, determined using the historical rate of exchange, and the tax base, determined using the balance sheet date exchange rate.	No deferred tax is recognized for differences related to assets and liabilities that are remeasured from local currency into the functional currency resulting from changes in exchange rates or indexing for tax purposes.
Investments in subsidiaries—treatment of undistributed profit	Deferred tax is recognized except when the parent is able to control the distribution of profit and it is probable that the temporary difference will not reverse in the foreseeable future.	Deferred tax is required on temporary differences arising after 1992 that relate to investments in domestic subsidiaries, unless such amounts can be recovered tax-free and the entity expects to use that method. No deferred taxes are recognized on undistributed profits of foreign subsidiaries that meet the indefinite reversal criterion.
Investments in joint ventures—treatment of undistributed profit	Deferred tax is recognized except when the venturer can control the sharing of profits and if it is probable that the temporary difference will not reverse in the foreseeable future.	Deferred tax is required on temporary differences arising after 1992 that relate to investment in domestic corporate joint ventures. No deferred taxes are recognized on undistributed profits of foreign corporate joint ventures that meet the indefinite reversal criterion.

(Exhibit continued on next page . . .)

EXHIBIT 5   (continued)

Issue	IFRS	U.S. GAAP
Investment in associates—treatment of undistributed profit	Deferred tax is recognized except when the investor can control the sharing of profits and it is probable that the temporary difference will not reverse in the foreseeable future.	Deferred tax is recognized on temporary differences relating to investments in investees.
Uncertain tax positions	Reflects the tax consequences that follow from the manner in which the entity expects, at the balance sheet date, to be paid to (recovered from) the taxation authorities.	A tax benefit from an uncertain tax position may be recognized only if it is "more likely than not" that the tax position is sustainable based on its technical merits. The tax position is measured as the largest amount of tax benefit that is greater than 50 percent likely of being realized upon ultimate settlement.
Measurement of deferred tax:		
Tax rates	Tax rates and tax laws that have been enacted or substantively enacted.	Use of substantively enacted rates is not permitted. Tax rate and tax laws used must have been enacted.
Recognition of deferred tax assets	A deferred tax asset is recognized if it is probable (more likely than not) that sufficient taxable profit will be available against which the temporary difference can be utilized.	A deferred tax asset is recognized in full but is then reduced by a valuation allowance if it is more likely than not that some or all of the deferred tax asset will not be realized.
Business combinations—Acquisitions:		
Step-up of acquired assets/liabilities to fair value	Deferred tax is recorded unless the tax base of the asset is also stepped up.	Similar to IFRS.
Previously unrecognized tax losses of the acquirer	A deferred tax asset is recognized if the recognition criteria for the deferred tax asset are met as a result of the acquisition. Offsetting credit is recorded in income.	Similar to IFRS, except the offsetting credit is recorded against goodwill.
Tax losses of the acquiree (initial recognition)	Similar requirements as for the acquirer except the offsetting credit is recorded against goodwill.	Similar to IFRS.
Subsequent resolution of income tax uncertainties in a business combination	If the resolution is more than one year after the year in which the business combination occurred, the result is recognized on the income statement.	The subsequent resolution of any tax uncertainty relating to a business combination is recorded against goodwill.

(Exhibit continued on next page . . .)

EXHIBIT 5	(continued)	
Issue	**IFRS**	**U.S. GAAP**
Subsequent recognition of deferred tax assets that were not "probable" at the time of the business combination	A deferred tax asset that was not considered probable at the time of the business combination but later becomes probable is recognized. The adjustment is to income tax expense with a corresponding adjustment to goodwill. The income statement shows a debit to goodwill expense and a credit to income tax expense. There is no time limit for recognition of this deferred tax asset.	The subsequent resolution of any tax uncertainty relating to a business combination is recorded first against goodwill, then noncurrent intangibles, and then income tax expense. There is no time limit for recognition of this deferred tax asset.
Presentation of deferred tax:		
Offset of deferred tax assets and liabilities	Permitted only when the entity has a legally enforceable right to offset and the balance relates to tax levied by the same authority.	Similar to IFRS.
Current/noncurrent	Deferred tax assets and liabilities are classified net as noncurrent on the balance sheet, with supplemental note disclosure for 1) the components of the temporary differences, and 2) amounts expected to be recovered within 12 months and more than 12 months from the balance sheet date.	Deferred tax assets and liabilities are either classified as current or noncurrent, based on the classification of the related non-tax asset or liability for financial reporting. Tax assets not associated with an underlying asset or liability are classified based on the expected reversal period.
Reconciliation of actual and expected tax expense	Required. Computed by applying the applicable tax rates to accounting profit, disclosing also the basis on which the applicable tax rates are calculated.	Required for public companies only. Calculated by applying the domestic federal statutory tax rates to pre-tax income from continuing operations.

Sources: IFRS: IAS 1, IAS 12, and IFRS 3.
U.S. GAAP: FAS 109 and FIN 48.
"Similarities and Differences–A Comparison of IFRS and U.S. GAAP," PricewaterhouseCoopers, October 2006.

SUMMARY

Income taxes are a significant category of expense for profitable companies. Analyzing income tax expenses is often difficult for the analyst because there are many permanent and temporary timing differences between the accounting that is used for income tax reporting and the accounting that is used for financial reporting on company financial statements. The financial statements and notes to the financial statements of a company provide important information that the analyst needs to assess financial performance and to compare a company's financial performance with other companies. Key concepts in this reading are as follows:

▶ Differences between the recognition of revenue and expenses for tax and accounting purposes may result in taxable income differing from accounting profit. The discrepancy is a result of different treatments of certain income and expenditure items.

▶ The tax base of an asset is the amount that will be deductible for tax purposes as an expense in the calculation of taxable income as the company expenses the tax basis of the asset. If the economic benefit will not be taxable, the tax base of the asset will be equal to the carrying amount of the asset.

▶ The tax base of a liability is the carrying amount of the liability less any amounts that will be deductible for tax purposes in the future. With respect to revenue received in advance, the tax base of such a liability is the carrying amount less any amount of the revenue that will not be taxable in future.

▶ Temporary differences arise from recognition of differences in the tax base and carrying amount of assets and liabilities. The creation of a deferred tax asset or liability as a result of a temporary difference will only be allowed if the difference reverses itself at some future date and to the extent that it is expected that the balance sheet item will create future economic benefits for the company.

▶ Permanent differences result in a difference in tax and financial reporting of revenue (expenses) that will not be reversed at some future date. Because it will not be reversed at a future date, these differences do not constitute temporary differences and do not give rise to a deferred tax asset or liability.

▶ Current taxes payable or recoverable are based on the applicable tax rates on the balance sheet date of an entity; in contrast, deferred taxes should be measured at the tax rate that is expected to apply when the asset is realized or the liability settled.

▶ All unrecognized deferred tax assets and liabilities must be reassessed on the appropriate balance sheet date and measured against their probable future economic benefit.

▶ Deferred tax assets must be assessed for their prospective recoverability. If it is probable that they will not be recovered at all or partly, the carrying amount should be reduced. Under U.S. GAAP, this is done through the use of a valuation allowance.

PRACTICE PROBLEMS FOR READING 38

1. Using the straight-line method of depreciation for reporting purposes and accelerated depreciation for tax purposes would *most likely* result in a:
   A. valuation allowance.
   B. deferred tax asset.
   C. temporary difference.

2. In early 2009 Sanborn Company must pay the tax authority €37,000 on the income it earned in 2008. This amount was recorded on the company's 31 December 2008 financial statements as:
   A. taxes payable.
   B. income tax expense.
   C. a deferred tax liability.

3. Income tax expense reported on a company's income statement equals taxes payable, plus the net increase in:
   A. deferred tax assets and deferred tax liabilities.
   B. deferred tax assets, less the net increase in deferred tax liabilities.
   C. deferred tax liabilities, less the net increase in deferred tax assets.

4. Analysts should treat deferred tax liabilities that are expected to reverse as:
   A. equity.
   B. liabilities.
   C. neither liabilities nor equity.

5. Deferred tax liabilities should be treated as equity when:
   A. they are not expected to reverse.
   B. the timing of tax payments is uncertain.
   C. the amount of tax payments is uncertain.

6. When both the timing and amount of tax payments are uncertain, analysts should treat deferred tax liabilities as:
   A. equity.
   B. liabilities.
   C. neither liabilities nor equity.

7. When accounting standards require recognition of an expense that is not permitted under tax laws, the result is a:
   A. deferred tax liability.
   B. temporary difference.
   C. permanent difference.

8. When certain expenditures result in tax credits that directly reduce taxes, the company will *most likely* record:
   A. a deferred tax asset.
   B. a deferred tax liability.
   C. no deferred tax asset or liability.

9. When accounting standards require an asset to be expensed immediately but tax rules require the item to be capitalized and amortized, the company will *most likely* record:

   A. a deferred tax asset.

   B. a deferred tax liability.

   C. no deferred tax asset or liability.

10. A company incurs a capital expenditure that may be amortized over five years for accounting purposes, but over four years for tax purposes. The company will *most likely* record:

   A. a deferred tax asset.

   B. a deferred tax liability.

   C. no deferred tax asset or liability.

11. A company receives advance payments from customers that are immediately taxable but will not be recognized for accounting purposes until the company fulfills its obligation. The company will *most likely* record:

   A. a deferred tax asset.

   B. a deferred tax liability.

   C. no deferred tax asset or liability.

Use the following disclosure related to income taxes to answer Questions 12–14

Note I
Income Taxes

The components of earnings before income taxes are as follows ($ thousands):

	2007	2006	2005
Earnings before income taxes:			
United States	$ 88,157	$ 75,658	$ 59,973
Foreign	116,704	113,509	94,760
Total	$204,861	$189,167	$154,733

The components of the provision for income taxes are as follows ($ thousands):

	2007	2006	2005
Income taxes			
Current:			
Federal	$30,632	$22,031	$18,959
Foreign	28,140	27,961	22,263
	$58,772	$49,992	$41,222
Deferred:			
Federal	($4,752)	$5,138	$2,336
Foreign	124	1,730	621
	(4,628)	6,868	2,957
Total	$54,144	$56,860	$44,179

12. In 2007, the company's U.S. GAAP income statement recorded a provision for income taxes *closest* to:

A. $30,632.

B. $54,144.

C. $58,772.

13. The company's effective tax rate was *highest* in:

A. 2005.

B. 2006.

C. 2007.

14. Compared to the company's effective tax rate on U.S. income, its effective tax rate on foreign income was:

A. lower in each year presented.

B. higher in each year presented.

C. higher in some periods and lower in others.

15. Zimt AG presents its financial statements in accordance with U.S. GAAP. In 2007, Zimt discloses a valuation allowance of $1,101 against total deferred tax assets of $19,201. In 2006, Zimt disclosed a valuation allowance of $1,325 against total deferred tax assets of $17,325. The change in the valuation allowance *most likely* indicates that Zimt's:

A. deferred tax liabilities were reduced in 2007.

B. expectations of future earning power has increased.

C. expectations of future earning power has decreased.

16. Cinnamon, Inc. recorded a total deferred tax asset in 2007 of $12,301, offset by a $12,301 valuation allowance. Cinnamon *most likely*:

A. fully utilized the deferred tax asset in 2007.

B. has an equal amount of deferred tax assets and deferred tax liabilities.

C. expects not to earn any taxable income before the deferred tax asset expires.

Use the following income tax disclosure to answer Questions 17–19

The tax effects of temporary differences that give rise to deferred tax assets and liabilities are as follows ($ thousands):

	2007	2006
Deferred tax assets:		
Accrued expenses	$8,613	$7,927
Tax credit and net operating loss carryforwards	2,288	2,554
LIFO and inventory reserves	5,286	4,327
Other	2,664	2,109
Deferred tax assets	18,851	16,917
Valuation allowance	(1,245)	(1,360)
Net deferred tax assets	$17,606	$15,557
Deferred tax liabilities:		
Depreciation and amortization	$(27,338)	$(29,313)
Compensation and retirement plans	(3,831)	(8,963)
Other	(1,470)	(764)
Deferred tax liabilities	(32,639)	(39,040)
Net deferred tax liability	($15,033)	($23,483)

17. A reduction in the statutory tax rate would *most likely* benefit the company's:

    A. income statement and balance sheet.

    B. income statement but not the balance sheet.

    C. balance sheet but not the income statement.

18. If the valuation allowance had been the same in 2007 as it was in 2006, the company would have reported $115 *higher*:

    A. net income.

    B. deferred tax asset.

    C. income tax expense.

19. Compared to the provision for income taxes in 2007, the company's cash tax payments were:

    A. lower.

    B. higher.

    C. the same.

Use the following income tax disclosure to answer Questions 20–22

A company's provision for income taxes resulted in effective tax rates attributable to loss from continuing operations before cumulative effect of change in accounting principles that varied from the statutory federal income tax rate of 34 percent, as summarized in the table below.

Year Ended 30 June	2007	2006	2005
Expected federal income tax expense (benefit) from continuing operations at 34 percent	($112,000)	$768,000	$685,000
Expenses not deductible for income tax purposes	357,000	32,000	51,000
State income taxes, net of federal benefit	132,000	22,000	100,000
Change in valuation allowance for deferred tax assets	(150,000)	(766,000)	(754,000)
Income tax expense	$227,000	$56,000	$82,000

20. In 2007, the company's net income (loss) was *closest* to:

  A. ($217,000).

  B. ($329,000).

  C. ($556,000).

21. The $357,000 adjustment in 2007 *most likely* resulted in:

  A. an increase in deferred tax assets.

  B. an increase in deferred tax liabilities.

  C. no change to deferred tax assets and liabilities.

22. Over the three years presented, changes in the valuation allowance for deferred tax assets were *most likely* indicative of:

  A. decreased prospect for future profitability.

  B. increased prospects for future profitability.

  C. assets being carried at a higher value than their tax base.

SOLUTIONS FOR READING 38

1. C is correct. Because the differences between tax and financial accounting will correct over time, the resulting deferred tax liability, for which the expense was charged to the income statement but the tax authority has not yet been paid, will be a temporary difference. A valuation allowance would only arise if there was doubt over the company's ability to earn sufficient income in the future to require paying the tax.

2. A is correct. The taxes a company must pay in the immediate future are taxes payable.

3. C is correct. Higher reported tax expense relative to taxes paid will increase the deferred tax liability, whereas lower reported tax expense relative to taxes paid increases the deferred tax asset.

4. B is correct. If the liability is expected to reverse (and thus require a cash tax payment) the deferred tax represents a future liability.

5. A is correct. If the liability will not reverse, there will be no required tax payment in the future and the "liability" should be treated as equity.

6. C is correct. The deferred tax liability should be excluded from both debt and equity when both the amounts and timing of tax payments resulting from the reversals of temporary differences are uncertain.

7. C is correct. Accounting items that are not deductible for tax purposes will not be reversed and thus result in permanent differences.

8. C is correct. Tax credits that directly reduce taxes are a permanent difference, and permanent differences do not give rise to deferred tax.

9. A is correct. The capitalization will result in an asset with a positive tax base and zero carrying value. The amortization means the difference is temporary. Because there is a temporary difference on an asset resulting in a higher tax base than carrying value, a deferred tax asset is created.

10. B is correct. The difference is temporary, and the tax base will be lower (because of more rapid amortization) than the carrying value of the asset. The result will be a deferred tax liability.

11. A is correct. The advances represent a liability for the company. The carrying value of the liability exceeds the tax base (which is now zero). A deferred tax asset arises when the carrying value of a liability exceeds its tax base.

12. B is correct. The income tax provision in 2007 was $54,144, consisting of $58,772 in current income taxes, of which $4,628 were deferred.

13. B is correct. The effective tax rate of 30.1 percent ($56,860/$189,167) was higher than the effective rates in 2005 and 2007.

14. A is correct. In 2007 the effective tax rate on foreign operations was 24.2 percent [($28,140 + $124)/$116,704] and the effective U.S. tax rate was [($30,632 − $4,752)/$88,157] = 29.4 percent. In 2006 the effective tax rate on foreign operations was 26.2 percent and the U.S. rate was 35.9 percent. In 2005 the foreign rate was 24.1 percent and the U.S. rate was 35.5 percent.

International Financial Statement Analysis, by Thomas R. Robinson, CFA, Jan Hendrik van Greuning, CFA, R. Elaine Henry, CFA, and Michael A. Broihahn, CFA. Copyright © 2008 by CFA Institute. Reprinted with permission.

15. B is correct. The valuation allowance is taken against deferred tax assets to represent uncertainty that future taxable income will be sufficient to fully utilize the assets. By decreasing the allowance, Zimt is signaling greater likelihood that future earnings will be offset by the deferred tax asset.

16. C is correct. The valuation allowance is taken when the company will "more likely than not" fail to earn sufficient income to offset the deferred tax asset. Because the valuation allowance equals the asset, by extension the company expects *no* taxable income prior to the expiration of the deferred tax assets.

17. A is correct. A lower tax rate would increase net income on the income statement, and because the company has a net deferred tax liability, the net liability position on the balance sheet would also improve (be smaller).

18. C is correct. The reduction in the valuation allowance resulted in a corresponding reduction in the income tax provision.

19. B is correct. The net deferred tax liability was smaller in 2007 than it was in 2006, indicating that in addition to meeting the tax payments provided for in 2007 the company also paid taxes that had been deferred in prior periods.

20. C is correct. The income tax provision at the statutory rate of 34 percent is a benefit of $112,000, suggesting that the pre-tax income was a loss of $112,000/0.34 = ($329,412). The income tax provision was $227,000. ($329,412) − $227,000 = ($556,412).

21. C is correct. Accounting expenses that are not deductible for tax purposes result in a permanent difference, and thus do not give rise to deferred taxes.

22. B is correct. Over the three-year period, changes in the valuation allowance reduced cumulative income taxes by $1,670,000. The reductions to the valuation allowance were a result of the company being "more likely than not" to earn sufficient taxable income to offset the deferred tax assets.

LONG-TERM LIABILITIES AND LEASES
by Elizabeth A. Gordon and R. Elaine Henry, CFA

LEARNING OUTCOMES

The candidate should be able to:	Mastery
a. compute the effects of debt issuance and amortization of bond discounts and premiums on financial statements and ratios;	☐
b. explain the role of debt covenants in protecting creditors by restricting a company's ability to invest, pay dividends, or make other operating and strategic decisions;	☐
c. describe the presentation of, and disclosures relating to, financing liabilities;	☐
d. determine the effects of changing interest rates on the market value of debt and on financial statements and ratios;	☐
e. describe two types of debt with equity features (convertible debt and debt with warrants) and calculate the effect of issuance of such instruments on a company's debt ratios;	☐
f. discuss the motivations for leasing assets instead of purchasing them and the incentives for reporting the leases as operating leases rather than finance leases;	☐
g. determine the effects of finance and operating leases on the financial statements and ratios of the lessees and lessors;	☐
h. distinguish between a sales-type lease and a direct financing lease, and determine the effects on the financial statements and ratios of the lessors;	☐
i. describe the types and economic consequences of off-balance sheet financing and determine how take-or-pay contracts, throughput arrangements, and the sale of receivables affect financial statements and selected financial ratios.	☐

International Financial Statement Analysis, by Thomas R. Robinson, CFA, Jan Hendrik van Greuning, CFA, R. Elaine Henry, CFA, and Michael A. Broihahn, CFA. Copyright © 2008 by CFA Institute. Reprinted with permission.

513

> **THEME**
>
> Companies' long-term obligations include bonds payable, long-term notes, finance leases, and similar instruments. Accounting for long-term debt involves several stages: initially recording the debt, recording periodic interest expense and interest payment (if required), amortizing any discount or premium on the debt, and extinguishing debt. Various types of "off-balance sheet financing," though not reported as debt, are nonetheless obligations of the company that an analyst considers in assessing a company's solvency.

1 INTRODUCTION

A **long-term liability** broadly represents a probable sacrifice of economic benefits over a future period generally greater than one year. Common types of long-term liabilities reported in a company's financial statements include long-term debt (i.e. bonds payable, long-term notes payable), finance leases, and pension liabilities. Other contractual obligations, referred to as "off-balance sheet financing," are not reported as debt in the financial statements, yet represent probable future cash outflows that are similar in nature to debt and must be disclosed. This reading focuses on bonds payable, leases, and off-balance sheet financing. A subsequent reading will cover pension liabilities.

This reading is organized as follows. Section 2 describes and illustrates the accounting for long-term bonds, including issuing bonds, recording interest expense and interest payments, amortizing any discount or premium, extinguishing debt, and disclosing information about debt financings. Section 3 describes the treatment of debt with equity features. Section 4 describes accounting for leases, including benefits of leasing, finance versus operating leases, and direct financing versus sales-type leases. Section 5 discusses other types of off-balance sheet financing, their economic consequences, and their effect on selected financial ratios. A summary of the key points and practice problems in the CFA Institute multiple-choice format conclude the reading.

2 BONDS PAYABLE

This section discusses accounting for bonds payable, the most common form of long-term debt. In some contexts, e.g. some government debt obligations, the word "bond" is used only for a debt security with a maturity of 10 years or longer, with "note" referring to a debt security with a maturity between 2 and 10 years and "bill" referring to a debt security with a maturity of less than 2 years. In this reading, we will use the terms bond and note interchangeably. In the following sections, we discuss bond issuance, bond interest expense and payment, repayment of bonds, including retirements and redemptions, and other issues concerning disclosures related to debt. We will also present debt covenants and an issue related to market rates and fair values.

2.1 Accounting for Bond Issuance

Bonds are contractual promises of cash payments in the future in exchange for cash received today, issued by a company (or other borrowing entity) to its lenders (i.e., bondholders). The cash a company receives when it issues bonds (sales proceeds) is based on the value of the bonds when issued, determined as the present value of future cash payments the company promises in the bond agreement.

Ordinarily, bonds consist of two types of future cash payments that are discounted to present value: 1) the face value of the bonds and 2) periodic interest payments. The **face value** of the bonds is the amount of cash payable by the company to the bondholders when the bonds mature. The face value is also referred to as the principal, par value, stated value, or maturity value. The maturity of the bonds (the date on which the face value is paid to bondholders) is also stated in the bond contract and is generally a number of years in the future. Periodic interest payments are made based on the interest rate promised in the bond contract applied to the bonds' face value. The rate at which the periodic interest payments are calculated is also referred to as the **stated rate**, nominal rate, or coupon rate. For fixed-rate bonds (the primary focus of our discussion here), the stated rate remains unchanged throughout the life of the bonds. How often interest payments are made (i.e., frequency) is also stated in the bond agreement. For instance, bonds paying interest semi-annually will make two interest payments a year.

The **market rate** of interest is the rate demanded by purchasers of the bonds, given the risks associated with future cash payment obligations of the particular bond issue. The market rate of interest often differs from the stated rate because of interest rate fluctuations that occur between the time the issuer establishes the stated rate and the day the bonds are actually available to investors. If the market rate of interest when the bonds are issued equals the stated rate, the market value of the bonds, and thus the amount of cash the company receives (the selling price produces the sales proceeds), will equal the face value of the bonds. When a bond is issued at a price equal to its face value, the bond is said to have been issued at par. Alternatively, if the stated rate of interest when the bonds are issued is higher than the market rate, the market value of the bonds, and thus the amount of cash the company receives, will be higher than the face value of the bonds. In other words, the bonds will sell at a premium to face value. If the stated rate of interest is lower than the market rate, the market value and thus the sale proceeds from the bonds will be less than the face value of the bonds (i.e., will sell at a discount to face value). The market rate at the time of issuance is the effective interest rate or borrowing rate that the company incurs on the debt. For the issuing company, interest expense reported for the bonds in the financial statements is based on the effective interest rate.

On the issuing company's statement of cash flows, the cash received (sales proceeds) from issuing bonds is reported as a financing cash inflow. On the issuing company's balance sheet, bonds payable are normally reported at **net book value**, i.e., the face value of the bonds minus any unamortized discount, or plus any unamortized premium. In a later section, we will briefly discuss instances where bonds payable are not reported at net book value.

The following two examples illustrate accounting for bonds issued at face value and then accounting for bonds issued at a discount to face value. Accounting for bonds issued at a premium involves steps similar to the steps followed in the examples below. For simplicity, these examples assume a flat interest rate yield curve, i.e., that the market rate of interest is the same for each period. More precise bond valuations use the interest rate applicable to each time period in which a payment of interest or principal occurs.

EXAMPLE 1

Bonds Issued at Face Value

Debond Corp. (a hypothetical company) issues £1,000,000 worth of five-year bonds, dated 1 January 2008, when the market interest rate is 5 percent per annum. The bonds pay 5 percent interest annually on 31 December. What are the sales proceeds of the bonds when issued, and how is the issuance reflected in the financial statements?

Solution: The sales proceeds of the bonds when issued are £1,000,000. The issuance is reflected on the balance sheet as a long-term liability, bonds payable, of £1,000,000. The issuance is reflected in the statement of cash flows as a financing cash inflow of £1,000,000.

Calculating the value of the bonds at issuance and thus the sales proceeds involves three steps: identifying key features of the bonds, determining future cash flows, and discounting the future cash flows to the present.

First, identify key features of the bonds to determine sales proceeds:

Face value (principal):	£1,000,000
Time to maturity:	5 years
Stated interest rate:	5%
Market rate at issuance:	5%
Frequency of interest payments:	1 per year
Interest payment:	£50,000

Each annual interest payment is the face value times the stated interest rate. Here, £1,000,000 × 5 percent. If interest is paid other than annually, adjust the interest rate to match the interest payment period (e.g., divide the annual stated rate by two for semi-annual interest payments).

Second, determine future cash outflows. Debond will pay bondholders £1,000,000 when the bonds mature in five years. On 31 December of each year until the bonds mature, Debond will make an interest payment of £50,000 (£1,000,000 face value times 5 percent stated interest rate).

Date	Interest Payment	Present Value at Market Rate (5%)	Face Value Payment	Present Value at Market Rate (5%)	Total
31 December 2008	£50,000	£47,619			
31 December 2009	50,000	45,351			
31 December 2010	50,000	43,192			
31 December 2011	50,000	41,135			
31 December 2012	50,000	39,176	£1,000,000	£783,526	
Total		£216,474		£783,526	£1,000,000
					Sales Proceeds: Cash inflow when bonds are issued

Third, sum the present value of the future payments of interest and principal to obtain the value of the bonds and thus the sales proceeds from issuing the bonds. In this example, the sum is £1,000,000 (£216,474 + £783,526).

The present value of each cash outflow shown in the table above is calculated as:

$$PV = \frac{\text{Cash outflow}}{(1 + r)^t}$$

where:

r = market rate
t = number of periods

For example, the present value of the £50,000 interest payment to be made at the end of 2011 is calculated as £50,000 ÷ $(1.05)^4$ = £41,135.

Because it is assumed that the market rate is the same for each year, an alternative way to calculate the present value of interest payments is to treat the five annual interest payments as an annuity and use the formula for finding the present value of an annuity:

$$PV = PMT \left[\frac{1 - \dfrac{1}{(1 + r)^t}}{r} \right]$$

where:

PMT = annual payment
r = market rate
t = number of periods

In this example, the present value of the five annual interest payments is:

£50,000 × [(1 − (1 ÷ $(1.05)^5$) ÷ 0.05]
= £50,000 × [(1 − 0.7835) ÷ 0.05]
= £50,000 × 4.3295
= £216,474.

The amount of sales proceeds is reported as a financing cash inflow in the issuing company's statement of cash flows. Because these bonds are issued at par, there is no discount or premium to face value. Therefore, the amount of debt reported as a long-term liability on the issuing company's balance sheet (i.e., the net book value) is equal to the face value of the bonds.

The price of bonds is also expressed in terms of face value. For instance, the price of bonds issued at par, as in the above example, is 100 (i.e., 100 percent of face value). In the following example, in which bonds are issued at a discount, the price is 95.79 (i.e., 95.79 percent of face value).

EXAMPLE 2

Bonds Issued at a Discount

Debond Corp. (a hypothetical company) issues £1,000,000 worth of five-year bonds, dated 1 January 2008, when the market interest rate is 6 percent. The bonds pay 5 percent interest annually on 31 December. What are the sales proceeds of the bonds when issued, and how is the issuance reflected in the financial statements?

Solution: The sales proceeds from the bond issuance is £957,876. The issuance is reflected on the balance sheet as a long-term liability, bonds payable, of £957,876, which is composed of the face value of £1,000,000 minus a discount of £42,124. The issuance is reflected in the statement of cash flows as a financing cash inflow of £957,876.

Calculating the value of the bonds at issuance and thus the sales proceeds involves three steps: identifying key features of the bonds, determining future cash flows, and discounting the future cash flows to the present.

First, identify key features of the bonds to determine sales proceeds:

Face value (principal):	£1,000,000	
Time to maturity:	5 years	
Stated interest rate:	5%	
Market rate at issuance:	6%	
Frequency of interest payments:	1 per year	
Interest payment:	£50,000	Each annual interest payment is the face value times the stated interest rate. Here, £1,000,000 × 5%. If interest is paid other than annually, adjust the interest rate to match the interest payment period (e.g., divide the annual stated rate by two for semi-annual interest payments).

Second, determine future cash outflows. Debond will pay bondholders £1,000,000 when the bonds mature in five years. On 31 December each year until the bonds mature, Debond makes an interest payment of £50,000 (£1,000,000 face value times 5 percent stated interest rate).

Date	Interest Payment	Present Value at Market Rate (6%)	Face Value Payment	Present Value at Market Rate (6%)	Total
31 December 2008	£50,000	£47,170			
31 December 2009	50,000	44,500			
31 December 2010	50,000	41,981			
31 December 2011	50,000	39,605			
31 December 2012	50,000	37,363	£1,000,000	£747,258	
Total		£210,618		£747,258	£957,876
					Sales Proceeds: Cash inflow when bonds are issued

Third, sum the present value of the principal payment and the present value of the interest payments to obtain the value of the bonds at issuance of £957,876 (£210,618 + £747,258). This is the amount of sales proceeds at issuance. Because the market rate when the bonds are issued (6 percent) is greater than the bonds' stated rate (5 percent), the bonds sell at a discount of £42,124 (£1,000,000 − £957,876). Present values are calculated as in the previous example.

Cash of £957,876 from the bonds issuance is reported as a financing cash inflow in the issuing company's statement of cash flows. The amount of debt reported as a long-term liability on the issuing company's balance sheet is also £957,876, which is composed of the face value of the bonds of £1,000,000 minus a discount of £42,124.

In Example 2, the bonds were issued at a discount to face value because the bonds' stated rate of 5 percent was less than the market rate. Bonds may also be issued with a stated rate of zero, i.e., zero-coupon bonds. The value of zero-coupon bonds is based on the present value of the principal payment only (because there are no periodic interest payments), so zero-coupon bonds are always issued at a discount to face value.

Most corporate bonds, other than zero-coupon bonds, are currently issued at face value. Exhibit 1 lists four new issues of corporate bonds, including two that were priced at other than par. The list provides information about each issue's credit rating, coupon rate, coupon frequency, maturity date, issue price,

| EXHIBIT 1 | **List of Corporate Bond New Issues (Prices as of 7 June 2007, Total Cost for 25 Bonds)** | | | | | | | | |

Credit Ratings			Coupon						Est.
S&P	Moody's	Description	Rate	Frequency	Maturity	Price	YTM	Callable	Total Cost
AAA	Aaa	GENL ELEC CAP CP INTERNOTES 36966RS80 New Issue	5.45	Semi-Annual	6/15/2018	100	5.45	No	$25,000.00
A	A2	GENWORTH FINL SR NOTES 37247DAJ5 New Issue	5.65	Semi-Annual	6/15/2012	100.098	5.627	Yes	$25,024.50
A+	A1	LEHMAN BROS HLDG* 6.2%2752517P2S9 New Issue	6.2	Semi-Annual	6/15/2027	97.2	6.451	Yes	$24,300.00
AAA	Aaa	TOYOTA MTR CRDT CORENOTE 89240AGP9 New Issue	5.25	Semi-Annual	6/20/2012	100	5.25	Yes	$25,000.00

*Barclays has acquired Lehman Brothers and will maintain the family of Lehman Brothers indices and the associated index calculation, publication, and analytical infrastructure and tools.

yield to maturity (YTM) or market rate, and call provisions (provisions allowing the issuer to redeem the bonds prior to maturity). The final column in the list shows the estimated total cost to buy 25 bonds with a face value of $1,000 each, simply because these examples were obtained in response to a requested price quote for purchasing $25,000 face value of bonds. (Note that a bond purchaser pays the quoted price plus any interest accrued since the last interest payment. Because these bonds are all new issues, there is no accrued interest in the estimated total cost of the bonds.)

The first issue in the exhibit is an offering of 11-year, non-callable notes by General Electric Capital, with a credit rating of AAA/Aaa. The coupon rate of 5.45 percent is equal to the market rate of 5.45 percent, so the price per bond is 100.[1] The total price of 25 bonds with a face value of $1,000 each would be $25,000. The second issue in the exhibit is an offering of 5-year, callable notes by Genworth Financial with a rating of A/A2. Because the coupon rate of 5.65 percent is higher than the market rate of 5.627 percent, the price per note is 100.098. Similarly, the 97.2 price of the 20-year bonds issued by Lehman Brothers reflects the fact that the coupon rate of 6.2 percent is less than the market rate of 6.451 percent. One reason for the difference in rates is that the coupon may be set several days prior to the bonds' issuance date, and market rates may change in the interim.

Costs such as printing, legal fees, commissions, and other types of charges are incurred when bonds are issued. Under International Financial Reporting Standards (IFRS), all debt issue costs are included in the measurement of the liability. Under U.S. GAAP, companies generally show these debt issue costs as an asset (a prepaid expense), which is amortized over the life of the bonds.

2.2 Accounting for Bond Amortization, Interest Expense, and Interest Payments

As discussed above, companies initially report bonds as a liability on their balance sheet at the amount of the sales proceeds. The amount at which bonds are reported on the company's balance sheet is referred to as the book value, net book value, or carrying value. If the bonds are issued at par, the book value will be identical to the face value, and usually the book value will not change over the life of the bonds. For bonds issued at face value, the amount of periodic interest *expense* will be the same as the amount of the periodic interest *payment* to bondholders.

If, however, the market rate differs from the bonds' stated rate at issuance such that the bonds are issued at a premium or discount, the premium or discount is amortized systematically over the life of the bonds as a component of interest expense. For bonds issued at a premium to face value, the book value of the bonds is initially greater than the face value. As the premium is amortized, the book value of the bonds will decrease to the face value, reducing reported debt. For bonds issued at a discount to face value, the book value of the bonds is initially less than the face value. As the discount is amortized, the book value of the bonds will increase, increasing reported debt.

This accounting treatment for bonds issued at a discount, for example, reflects the fact that the company essentially paid some of its borrowing costs at issuance by selling its bonds at a discount. Rather than a cash transfer, this "payment" was made in the form of accepting less than face value for the bonds. The

---

[1] We are using market rate in this discussion to refer to the specific rate investors demand for the particular bonds in question based on risks unique to the particular bond issue as well as on risks relating to all bonds.

remaining borrowing cost occurs as a cash interest payment to investors each period. The total interest expense reflects both components of the borrowing cost. When the bonds mature, the book value will be equal to the face value.

Two methods for amortizing the book value of bonds that were issued at a price other than par are the effective interest rate method and the straight-line method. The effective interest rate method applies the market rate in effect when the bonds were issued (historical market rate) to the current amortized cost (book value) of the bonds to obtain interest expense for the period. The difference between the interest expense and the interest payment made is the **amortization** of the discount or premium. The straight-line method of amortization evenly amortizes the premium or discount over the life of the bond, similar to straight-line depreciation on long-lived assets. The effective interest rate method is required under IFRS and preferred under U.S. GAAP because it better reflects the economic substance of the transaction.

Interest payments on bonds are based on the bonds' stated rate applied to its face value. Example 3 illustrates both methods of amortization for bonds issued at a discount.

EXAMPLE 3

Amortizing a Bond Discount

Debond Corp. (a hypothetical company) issues £1,000,000 worth of five-year bonds, dated 1 January 2008, when the market interest rate is 6 percent. The bonds pay 5 percent interest annually on 31 December.

1. What is the interest *payment* on the bonds each year?
2. What amount of interest *expense* on the bonds would be reported in 2008 and 2009, using the effective interest rate method?
3. Determine the reported value of the bonds (i.e., the book value) at 31 December 2008 and 2009, assuming the effective interest rate method is used to amortize the discount.
4. What amount of interest expense on the bonds would be reported under the straight-line method of amortizing the discount?

Solution to 1: The interest payment, as shown in the previous example, equals £50,000 annually (£1,000,000 × 5%).

Solution to 2: As shown in the previous example, the bonds are issued at £957,876. The sales proceeds are less than the face value, i.e., the bonds were issued at a discount of £42,124 (£1,000,000 − £957,876). Over time, the discount is amortized.

Under the effective interest rate method, interest expense on the bonds is determined based on the bonds' book value times the market rate in effect when the bonds are issued (historical market rate). For 2008, interest expense is £57,473 (£957,876 × 6 percent). The amount of the discount that will be amortized in 2008 is the difference between the interest expense of £57,473 and the interest payment of £50,000, i.e., £7,473. The bonds' book value increases by the discount amortization, so at 31 December 2008 the bonds' book value is £965,349 (beginning balance of £957,876 plus £7,473 discount amortization). At this point, the book value reflects the remaining unamortized discount of £34,651 (£42,124 discount at issuance minus £7,473 amortized).

For 2009, interest expense is £57,921 (£965,349 × 6 percent). The amount of the discount that will be amortized in 2009 is the difference between the interest expense of £57,921 and the interest payment of £50,000, i.e., £7,921. The bonds' book value increases by the discount amortization, so at 31 December 2009 the bonds' book value is £973,270 (beginning balance of £965,349 plus £7,921 discount amortization).

The following table illustrates interest expense, discount amortization, and book value over the life of the bonds.

Year	Book Value (Beginning of Year)	Interest Expense (at Market Interest Rate of 6%)	Interest Payment (at Stated Interest Rate of 5%)	Amortization of Discount	Book Value (End of Year)
	(a)	(b)	(c)	(d)	(e)
2008	£957,876	£57,473	£50,000	£7,473	£965,349
2009	965,349	57,921	50,000	7,921	973,270
2010	973,270	58,396	50,000	8,396	981,666
2011	981,666	58,900	50,000	8,900	990,566
2012	990,566	59,434	50,000	9,434	1,000,000
Total				£42,124	

Column (a) shows the book value at the beginning of the year. The beginning amount in 2008 reflects the proceeds from the bonds' issuance of £957,876. The amounts in each subsequent year equal the ending book value from the prior year.

Column (b) shows interest expense for the year calculated as the book value at the beginning of the year multiplied by the historical market rate of interest when the bonds were issued.

Column (c) shows the annual interest payment on the bonds calculated as the bonds' face value multiplied by the bonds' stated interest rate.

Column (d) shows the amortization of the discount, calculated as the difference between the interest expense and interest payment. It is the amount of the original issuance discount allocated to this period and the amount by which the book value increases during the year.

Column (e) shows the book value at the end of the year, calculated as the book value at the beginning of the year (Column a) plus the amortization of the discount (Column d).

Solution to 3: From Column (e) in the table above, the book values of the bonds at 31 December 2008 and 2009 are £965,349 and £973,270, respectively. Observe that the book value of the bonds issued at a discount is increasing over the life of the bonds. At maturity, 31 December 2012, the book value of the bonds will equal face value.

Solution to 4: Under the straight-line method, the discount (or premium) is evenly reduced over the life of the bonds. In this example, the £42,124 discount would be amortized by £8,424.80 (£42,124 divided by 5 years) each year under the straight-line method. So, the annual interest expense under the straight-line method would be £58,424.80 (£50,000 plus £8,424.80).

The section in which interest payments are reported on the statement of cash flows can differ under IFRS and U.S. GAAP. U.S. GAAP requires interest payments on bonds to be shown as a reduction of operating cash flows. (Some financial statement users consider the placement of interest payments in the operating section to be inconsistent with the placement of bond issue proceeds in the financing section of the statement of cash flows.) Typically, cash interest paid is not shown directly on the statement of cash flows, but companies are required to disclose interest paid separately. Under IFRS interest payments on bonds can be shown as an outflow in the operating section, consistent with U.S. GAAP, or may be shown as an outflow in the financing section.

Amortization of a discount (premium) is a non-cash expense (reduction in expense) and thus, apart from its effect on taxable income, has no effect on cash flow. In the section of the statement of cash flows that reconciles net income to operating cash flow, amortization of a discount (premium) is added back to (subtracted from) net income.

The bonds in the examples above pay a periodic interest payment. The accounting and reporting for zero-coupon bonds is similar to the examples above except that no interest payments are made, so the amount of interest expense each year is the same as the amount of the discount amortization for the year.

2.3 Debt Extinguishment

Once bonds are issued, a company can leave the bonds outstanding until they mature, or can redeem bonds before maturity either by calling the bonds (if the bond issue includes a call provision) or by purchasing the bonds in the open market. If the bonds remain outstanding until the maturity date, the company pays bondholders the face value of the bonds at maturity. Repayment appears in the statement of cash flows as a financing cash outflow. On the balance sheet, repayment reduces bonds payable by the net book value. Recall that any discount or premium on the bonds would be fully amortized by the time the bonds mature such that net book value equals face value. So, at maturity, the repayment reduces the balance in bonds payable by the face value of the bonds.

If a company decides to redeem bonds before maturity and thus extinguish the liability, a gain or loss on the extinguishment is computed by subtracting the cash required to pay off the bonds from the book value of the bonds at the time of redemption. For example, assume a $10 million bond issuance with a current book value equal to its face value is called at a call price of 103; the company's loss on redemption would be $300 thousand ($10 million book value minus $10.3 million cash paid to call the bonds). Recall that under U.S. GAAP debt issue costs are accounted for separately, so any remaining debt issue costs must be written off and are also included in the gain or loss on debt extinguishment. Under IFRS, debt issue costs are included in the measurement of the liability and are thus part of its book value.

A gain or loss on the extinguishment of debt is disclosed on the income statement, in a separate line item, when the amount is material. A company typically discloses further detail about the extinguishment in the management discussion and analysis (MD&A) and/or financial statement footnotes.[2] In

---

[2] We use the term MD&A generally to refer to any management commentary that may be provided on a company's financial condition, changes in financial condition, and results of operations. In the United States, the SEC requires a management discussion and analysis for companies listed on U.S. public markets. For IFRS reporters, reporting requirements for a commentary such as the SEC-required MD&A vary across exchanges, but some are similar to the SEC requirements. Currently, the IASB is developing a standard for a management commentary, which would be consistent for all IFRS reporters.

addition, a statement of cash flows prepared using the indirect method adjusts net income to remove any gain or loss on the extinguishment of debt from operating cash flow, and to include the amount of payment in cash used for financing activities. (Recall that the indirect method of the statement of cash flows begins with net income and makes necessary adjustments to arrive at cash from operations, including removal of gains or losses from non-operating activities.)

As illustration of the financial statement impact of the extinguishment of debt, consider the notes payable repurchase by Ciena Corporation below.

EXAMPLE 4

Debt Extinguishment Disclosure

Ciena Corporation (NASDAQ: CIEN) reported a gain on the extinguishment of debt of $6.7 million in the "Management's Discussion and Analysis of Financial Condition and Results of Operations" section of its first quarter 2006, 10-Q filing as follows:

> **Gain on extinguishment of debt** for the first quarter of fiscal 2006 resulted from our repurchase of $106.5 million in aggregate principal on our outstanding 3.75 percent convertible notes in open market transactions for $98.8 million. We recorded a gain on the extinguishment of debt in the amount of $6.7 million, which consists of the $7.7 million gain from the repurchase of the notes, less $1.0 million of associated debt issuance costs.

The company's income statement includes a line entitled "Gain on extinguishment of debt" showing the $6.7 million. On the statement of cash flows, the gain is subtracted from net income as a non-cash adjustment to arrive at operating cash flows. Under financing cash flows, the $98.8 million repurchase costs appear as a cash outflow.

Using the information provided in the financial statements and 10-Q filing, the gain can be summarized as follows (dollars in millions):

Aggregate principal on notes	$106.5
Less: Cash required to repurchase notes	98.8
Gain before deducting unamortized debt issue costs	7.7
Less: Debt issue costs	1.0
Gain on repurchase of notes	$6.7

2.4 Debt Covenants

Borrowing agreements often include restrictions called covenants that protect creditors by restricting a company's ability to invest, pay dividends, or make other operating and strategic decisions that might adversely affect the company's ability to pay interest and principal. Debt covenants also benefit borrowers to the extent that they lower default risk and thus reduce the cost of borrowing.

Common covenants include limitations on how borrowed monies can be used, maintenance of collateral pledged as security (if any), restrictions on future borrowings, requirements that limit dividends, and requirements to meet specific working capital requirements. Covenants may also include minimum acceptable liquidity and solvency, expressed by particular levels of financial ratios such as debt-to-equity, current ratio, or interest coverage. The example below illustrates common disclosures on debt covenants included in financial statement footnotes.

EXAMPLE 5

Illustration of Debt Covenant Disclosures

The following excerpt from American Greeting Corporation's (NYSE:AM) 2006 financial statements illustrates common debt covenants and their disclosure:

> **NOTE 11—LONG AND SHORT-TERM DEBT** *Excerpt*
> The credit agreement contains certain restrictive covenants that are customary for similar credit arrangements, including covenants relating to limitations on liens, dispositions, issuance of debt, investments, payment of dividends, repurchases of capital stock, acquisitions and transactions with affiliates. There are also financial performance covenants that require the corporation to maintain a maximum leverage ratio and a minimum interest coverage ratio. The credit agreement also requires the corporation to make certain mandatory prepayments of outstanding indebtedness using the net cash proceeds received from certain dispositions, events of loss and additional indebtedness that the corporation may incur from time to time.

When a company violates a debt covenant, it is said to be in default. Lenders can choose to waive the covenant, renegotiate, or call for payment of the debt. Bond issues typically require that the decision about whether to call for immediate repayment be made on behalf of all the bondholders by holders of some minimum percentage of the principal amount of the bond issue.

2.5 Presentation and Disclosure of Long-Term Debt

The long-term liabilities section of the balance sheet usually includes a single line item of the total amount of a company's long-term debt due after one year, with the portion of long-term debt due in the next twelve months shown as a short-term liability. Financial statement footnotes provide more information on the types and nature of a company's debt. These footnote disclosures can be used to determine the amount and timing for future cash outflows. The footnotes generally include stated and effective interest rates, maturity dates, restrictions imposed by creditors, and collateral pledged (if any). The amount of scheduled debt repayments for the next five years is also shown in the footnotes. The following is an excerpt from Johnson & Johnson's 2006 10-K filing that illustrates common disclosures.

EXAMPLE 6

Illustration of Long-Term Debt Disclosures

The excerpt from footnote 6 of Johnson & Johnson's (NYSE:JNJ) 2006 financial statements illustrates financial statement disclosure for long-term debt, including type and nature of long-term debt, effective interest rates, and required payments over the next five years.

6. Borrowings *(Excerpt)*
The components of long-term debt are as follows:

(Dollars in Millions)	2006	Effective Rate%	2005	Effective Rate%
3% Zero Coupon Convertible Subordinated Debentures due 2020	$182	3.00	$202	3.00
4.95% Debentures due 2033	500	4.95	500	4.95
3.80% Debentures due 2013	500	3.82	500	3.82
6.95% Notes due 2029	293	7.14	293	7.14
6.73% Debentures due 2023	250	6.73	250	6.73
6.625% Notes due 2009	199	6.80	199	6.80
Industrial Revenue Bonds	29	5.21	31	3.90
Other	70	—	55	—
	2,023	5.23(1)	2,030	5.18(1)
Less current portion	9		13	
	$2,014		$2,017	

(1) Weighted average effective rate.

The Company has access to substantial sources of funds at numerous banks worldwide. Total unused credit available to the Company approximates $10.8 billion, including $9 billion of credit commitments, of which $3.75 billion expire September 27, 2007, $4 billion expire October 30, 2007 and $1.25 billion expire September 28, 2011. Also included are $0.75 billion of uncommitted lines with various banks worldwide that expire during 2007. Interest charged on borrowings under the credit line agreements is based on either bids provided by banks, the prime rate or London Interbank Offered Rates (LIBOR), plus applicable margins. Commitment fees under the agreement are not material.

Aggregate maturities of long-term obligations commencing in 2007 are (dollars in millions):

2007	2008	2009	2010	2011	After 2011
$9	9	240	9	6	1,750

In addition to disclosures in the financial statement footnotes, an MD&A commonly provides other information on a company's capital resources, including debt financing and off-balance sheet financing. In the MD&A, management often provides a qualitative discussion on any material trends, favorable or unfavorable, in capital resources and indicates any expected material changes in their mix and relative cost. Additional quantitative information is typically provided, including schedules summarizing a company's contractual obligations (such as bond payables) and other commitments (such as lines of credit and guarantees) in total and over the next five years.

2.6 Current Market Rates and Fair Values

Recall in the discussion of reporting bonds on the balance sheet, the reported value (net book value) of bonds is based on the market rate at the time the bonds were issued (i.e., historical rate). Over time, as market rates change, the bonds' book value diverges from the bonds' fair market value. For instance, when interest rates decline, the market value of debt increases, so a company's reported debt—based on historical market rates—will be lower than the value of its economic liabilities. Using financial statement amounts will then underestimate a company's debt-to-total capital employed and similar leverage ratios.

The availability of fair value information of financial liabilities has been limited. For example, under U.S. financial accounting standards for derivatives (SFAS No. 133), if a company hedged its obligations under fixed rate bonds by entering into an interest rate swap (i.e., a swap to receive fixed and pay floating that converts the fixed rate obligation into a floating rate), the company would be allowed to mark the hedged bonds to market value. Any loss in the bonds' value would be offset by a gain on the swap, and any gain in the bonds' value would be offset by a loss on the swap. A hedge qualifying for such treatment is known as a "fair value hedge." Implementing SFAS No. 133 created difficulties for a number of companies resulting in a significant number of restatements. A recently issued U.S. accounting standard (SFAS No. 159) is expected to reduce some of the difficulty in accounting for financial liabilities (and thus reduce the number of restatements associated with hedge accounting) because it provides companies with more flexibility in reporting both financial assets and liabilities at fair value. Overall, recently issued U.S. accounting standards (SFAS No. 159 and SFAS No. 157) and international standards (IAS 32, IAS 39, and IFRS 7) expand disclosures of fair value of financial assets and liabilities and allow companies to report fair values on the balance sheet.[3]

DEBT WITH EQUITY FEATURES ◣ 3

This section discusses two types of debt with equity features—**convertible debt** and **debt with warrants**—and briefly describes reporting for certain financial instruments with characteristics of both liabilities and equity.

---

[3] Statement of Financial Accounting Standard No. 159, "The Fair Value Option for Financial Assets and Financial Liabilities—Including an amendment of SFAS No. 115," and SFAS No. 157, "Fair Value Measurements."

3.1 Convertible Debt

Some bonds include provisions allowing the bondholders to convert the bonds to equity in the future. The economic effect of issuing such instruments is substantially the same as issuing a debt instrument with an early settlement provision and options to purchase shares. The convertibility feature of the debt usually provides financing at a lower interest rate than straight debt (debt without a conversion feature) because the option to convert is valuable to the bond purchaser. The conversion feature typically gives bondholders the right to convert the bonds into a pre-specified number of common equity shares, equivalently expressed as the right to convert at a specific price.

Accounting for convertible debt differs under U.S. GAAP and IFRS. Under U.S. GAAP, accounting for convertible bond issues is essentially the same as accounting for regular bond issues. The issue proceeds (composed of face value adjusted for any discount or premium) are classified as a liability on the balance sheet and as a cash inflow from financing activities. If the bonds are converted, liabilities decrease by the book value of the bonds and equity increases by the same amount. This method for recording the amount of equity at conversion is referred to as the book value method and does not reflect the market value of the equity issued at conversion. When bonds are converted, there is no effect on cash flows. However, the conversion is a significant non-cash financing activity and is reported as supplemental information on the statement of cash flows.

Accounting under IFRS recognizes the economic effect of issuing convertible debt. Accordingly, a company presents the liability and equity (option) components separately on its balance sheet. The debt is initially valued at fair value. Any difference between the debt's fair value and issue proceeds is allocated to the conversion feature and reported as equity.

When evaluating a company's capital structure, convertible debt may merit special consideration. As debt, convertible bonds are classified as a liability on the balance sheet, yet at conversion the amount of the bonds would appear as equity. If the conversion features are such that a conversion is imminent, for example if the current market price is well above the conversion price and the company may force conversion by calling the bonds, an analyst can estimate the effect of treating the convertibles as equity rather than debt. In calculating ratios, for example debt-to-total capital, convertible bonds would change both the numerator and denominator. Because accounting at the conversion is based on the bonds carrying value (or book value), the numerator decreases and the denominator increases by the carrying value of the convertible bonds. It is, however, difficult to predict when and if the company's stock price will rise above the conversion price, and thus when the debt is more likely to be converted. Even when market prices are well above conversion prices, the timing of conversions is not necessarily easy to predict. Finally, convertible bonds are potentially dilutive securities that decrease the claims of current shareholders. As discussed in another reading, the dilutive effect of these securities is considered when reporting diluted earnings per share. The example below illustrates how common disclosures provided on convertible bonds may be used to assess the effect on equity and debt-to-total capital ratio if the debt were to be converted.

EXAMPLE 7

Convertible Debt

Below is an excerpt from Sirius Satellite Radio, Inc.'s (NasdaqGS: SIRI) long-term debt footnote. The company's shareholders' equity at 31 December 2006 was ($389,071), and the number of shares outstanding was 1,434,635,501. All dollar amounts are in thousands. For 2006, use the disclosures and additional information provided to estimate the following:

1. The number of additional shares that would be issued and the percentage increase in shares that would result if all convertible bonds were converted to common stock.

2. The effect on the debt-to-capital ratio if all convertible bonds were converted.

Long-Term Debt and Accrued Interest (*excerpt from footnote*)
Our long-term debt consists of the following:

	Conversion Price (per Share)	Book Value as of 31 December 2006	2005
9⅝% Senior Notes due 2013	N/A	$500,000	$500,000
3¼% Convertible Notes due 2011	$5.3	230,000	230,000
2½% Convertible Notes due 2009	4.41	300,000	300,000
3½% Convertible Notes due 2008	1.38	36,505	52,693
8¾% Convertible Subordinated Notes due 2009	28.4625	1,744	1,744
Total long-term debt		$1,068,249	$1,084,437

3½% Convertible Notes due 2008

In May 2003, we issued $201,250 in aggregate principal amount of our 3½% convertible notes due 2008 resulting in net proceeds of $194,224. These notes are convertible, at the option of the holder, into shares of our common stock at any time at a conversion rate of 724.6377 shares of common stock for each $1,000.00 principal amount, or $1.38 per share of common stock, subject to certain adjustments. Our 3½% convertible notes due 2008 mature on June 1, 2008 and interest is payable semi-annually on June 1 and December 1 of each year. The obligations under our 3½% convertible notes due 2008 are not secured by any of our assets.

During the year ended December 31, 2006, holders of $16,188 in aggregate principal amount of our 3½% convertible notes due 2008 presented such notes for conversion in accordance with the terms of the indenture. We issued 11,730,431 shares of our common stock upon conversion of these notes. During the year ended December 31, 2005, we issued 10,548,545 shares of our common stock in exchange for $14,557 in aggregate principal amount of our 3½% Convertible Notes due 2008, including accrued interest.

Solution to 1: The disclosures indicate the conversion price of the convertible bonds. Dividing the amount of bonds by the conversion price gives the additional shares if the bonds are converted. As shown in the table below, the number of additional shares that would be issued if all convertible debt were converted to common stock is 137,938,000, representing a 9.6 percent increase in the number of shares outstanding (137,938,000 divided by 1,434,635,501).

	Conversion Price (per Share)	Convertible Debt 31 Dec. 2006	Additional Shares (in Thousands), if Converted
3¼% Convertible notes due 2011	$5.3	$230,000	43,396
2½% Convertible notes due 2009	4.41	300,000	68,027
3½% Convertible notes due 2008	1.38	36,505	26,453
8¾% Convertible subordinated notes due 2009	28.4625	1,744	61
Total long-term convertible debt		$568,249	137,938

Solution to 2: The company's debt-to-capital ratio at 31 December 2006 is 1.57. If all convertible debt were converted, the ratio would decrease to 0.74, reflecting a strengthening in the company's capital structure.

	Current	Adjustment to Convert Debt to Equity at Book Value	If Converted
Shareholder's equity	(389,071)	568,249	179,178
Long-term debt	1,068,249	(568,249)	500,000
Debt-to-capital ratio	1.57		0.74

In the Sirius example above, conversion prices range from $1.38 to over $28 per common share. Given the company's recent share price range from $2.66 to $4.84, only the 3.5 percent notes due 2008 are "in the money" (i.e., the conversion price is below the share price). As indicated in the footnote excerpt, some holders of those bonds exercised the conversion option in 2005 and 2006.

3.2 Debt with Warrants

Some bonds are issued with warrants giving holders the right to purchase additional shares of the issuer's common stock at a specific price, similar to stock options. Warrants, issued directly by a company, share many characteristics of stock options, such as requiring a specific payment to acquire the stock (strike price), a certain time when they can be exercised (like an American or European option), and an expiration date. A company will also specify a conversion ratio defining the number of warrants required to acquire a share of stock. Like the conversion feature of convertible bonds, warrants provide a purchaser of debt with additional value and thus lower the required interest rate on the bonds. Warrants are also included in debt offerings to attract buyers, who may value the opportunity to participate in any future appreciation of the company's equity.

One difference between warrants and the conversion feature of convertible bonds is that the conversion feature is an integral part of convertible bonds, but warrants are usually detachable from bonds. Under both IFRS and U.S. GAAP, accounting for bonds issued with warrants essentially accounts for the bonds and the warrants as two separate securities. The issuer records the issuance by allocating the issue price between the bonds and the warrants, based on their respective fair values that are determined as follows. Initially, debt is valued at fair value, as if there is no warrant. Any difference between the debt's fair value and issue proceeds is allocated to the warrants, which are reported in equity. Warrants, too, are potentially dilutive securities that are considered when reporting diluted earnings per share.

Issuance of bonds with warrants is more common by non-U.S. companies. Example 8 provides an illustrative announcement of an issuance of bonds with warrants by a small German company, and Example 9 provides an example of a financial statement disclosure of bonds with warrants by a major Japanese company.

EXAMPLE 8

Press Release Announcing an Issuance of Bonds with Warrants

The following excerpts are from a press release issued by a German company with market capitalization of around €500 million, listed on the Frankfurt Stock Exchange:

"ORCO Germany S.A.: Bond with warrants issued by Orco Germany for €100 million

"Orco Germany issues €100 million of bonds with warrants attached. This marks the first significant fund raising realized by Orco Germany.

"The characteristics of the offer are the following: the maturity of the bond is 5 years (2012) and the bond coupon is 4 percent. 9,328,851 warrants were issued with a maturity of seven years (2014) and an exercise price of €16.90. Each warrant gives the holder the right to subscribe to one share.

"'The deal was placed to institutional investors and the bond will be used to finance our further growth and to further develop our property portfolio' says Rainer Bormann, CEO of Orco Germany."

Source: Release of a Corporate News (1 June 2007), transmitted by DGAP; a company of EquityStory AG. Retrieved from Lexis-Nexis.

EXAMPLE 9

Financial Statement Disclosure of Bonds with Warrants

The following excerpt is from the Form 20-F of Sony Corporation, filed 1 September 2006. (Form 20-F is the form filed annually with the SEC by non-U.S. companies that list their shares on a major U.S. stock exchange. It is the equivalent of Form 10-K for U.S. companies.)

11. Short-term borrowings and long-term debt (Excerpt)
**SONY CORPORATION AND CONSOLIDATED SUBSIDIARIES NOTES
TO CONSOLIDATED FINANCIAL STATEMENTS—(Continued)**
A summary of the exercise rights of the detachable warrants as of March 31, 2006 is as follows:

Issued on	Exercisable during	Exercise Price		Number of Shares per Warrant	Status of Exercise
		Yen	**Dollars**		
October 19, 2000	November 1, 2001 through October 18, 2006	12,457	106	100 shares of common stock of Sony Corporation	9,224 warrants outstanding
December 21, 2001	January 6, 2003 through December 20, 2007	6,039	52	100 shares of common stock of Sony Corporation	11,459 warrants outstanding

3.3 Financial Instruments with Characteristics of Both Debt and Equity

This section provides a brief description of accounting standards regarding how an issuer characterizes and measures financial instruments with characteristics of both debt and equity (SFAS No. 150). Broadly, the standards now require that issuers report as liabilities any financial instruments that will require repayment of principal in the future. A few representative examples of financial instruments that must be reported as debt are the following: 1) a financial instrument that includes an unconditional obligation for the issuing company to redeem it in the future (mandatorily redeemable financial securities); 2) a financial instrument that includes an obligation for the issuing company to repurchase its own equity in the future (forward purchase contract); and 3) an obligation that the company must settle by issuing a variable number of its own shares, when the amount of the obligation is a fixed monetary amount, known at inception.

These accounting standards are particularly applicable to structured finance transactions that aim to achieve favorable accounting, i.e., treatment as equity rather than debt. When a company issues a financial instrument that is reported as equity rather than debt, solvency ratios based on the financial statements appear stronger. Accounting standards now limit this favorable treatment for many financial instruments with characteristics of both debt and equity. For instance, mandatorily redeemable preferred stock has many of the same characteristics as bonds with required payments (dividends in the case of preferred stock) at a stated rate. Importantly, the feature that the preferred stock must be redeemed, rather than have an unlimited life, is similar to the final payment of principal on bonds. Previously, mandatorily redeemable preferred stock appeared as equity, or in the mezzanine section of the balance sheet, between debt and equity; but it must now be reported as debt. Dividends on mandatorily preferred stock are reported as interest expense, consistent with the view that mandatorily redeemable preferred stock is debt. The example below illustrates the implications of and financial statement effects of the change in classification of mandatorily preferred stock from equity to a liability.

EXAMPLE 10

The Effect of SFAS No. 150

The following excerpts illustrate how SFAS No. 150 affected several companies with mandatorily redeemable securities outstanding.

► CMS Energy Corp.
"At July 1, 2003, mandatorily redeemable preferred securities totaling $883 million, were reclassified from the mezzanine equity section to the liability section of CMS Energy's consolidated balance sheet.

"Consumers is subject to covenants in its financing agreements . . .[including] agreements to maintain specified levels of cash coverage of its interest requirements and to not allow its indebtedness to exceed specified levels of its consolidated capitalization . . . Consumers is in compliance with these requirements as of the most recent measurement date, June 30, 2003 . . . After giving effect to the adoption of SFAS No. 150 regarding the balance sheet classification of its Trust Preferred Securities and to expected future use of its revolving credit facilities, Consumers currently estimates that its ratio of indebtedness to total capitalization at the end of the third and fourth quarters of 2003 will still comply with the Debt Percentage Tests but will approach the limits specified in some of the Debt Percentage Tests. Consumers plans to seek amendments to the relevant financing agreements to modify the terms of the Debt Percentage Tests in order to, among other things, remove the effect of the adoption of SFAS No. 150 regarding Trust Preferred Securities on the calculations. Consumers believes that it will receive the necessary consents of its lenders to these amendments."

Source: CMS Energy Corp. 10-Q for the period ended 30 June 2003, filed 14 August 2003.

▶ AOL Time Warner Inc.

**Abbreviated Balance Sheet as of 30 June 2003
(Amounts in Millions)**

Long-term debt	$25,898
All other liabilities	36,759
Shareholders' equity	
Convertible preferred stock	1,500
Common stock	45
Paid-in capital	155,388
Accumulated other comprehensive loss	(460)
Retained earnings (loss)	(100,474)
Total shareholders' equity	55,999
Total liabilities and shareholders' equity	118,656

Source: AOL Time Warner Inc. 10-Q for the period ended 30 June 2003, filed 13 August 2003.

1. What were the concerns faced by CMS Energy Inc. when the accounting standards began requiring mandatorily redeemable preferred stock to be shown as debt rather than equity?

2. How did the reclassification required by SFAS No. 150 affect AOL's reported leverage (as measured by its debt-to-equity and debt-to-total-capital ratios)?

Solution to 1: CMS expressed concern that reclassifying its mandatorily redeemable preferred securities from mezzanine equity to debt would approach the limits specified in one of the financial covenants contained in its financing arrangements, namely the ratio of indebtedness to total capitalization. Accordingly, the company planned to seek consent from its lenders to amend the calculation of the ratio.

Solution to 2: The reclassification of its mandatorily redeemable preferred stock from equity to debt would significantly increase AOL's reported leverage. AOL's long-term debt-to-equity ratio would increase from 46.2 percent ($25,898/$55,999) to 50.3 percent ($27,398/$54,499), and the company's debt-to-capital ratio would increase from 31.6 percent [$25,898/($25,898 + $55,999)] to 33.5 percent [$27,398/($27,398 + $54,499)].

	As Reported	Adjusted
Long-term debt	$25,898	$27,398
All other liabilities	36,759	36,759
Shareholders' equity		
Convertible preferred stock	1,500	0
Common stock	45	45
Paid-in capital	155,388	155,388
Accumulated other comprehensive loss	−460	−460
Retained earnings (loss)	−100,474	−100,474
Total shareholders' equity	55,999	54,499
Total liabilities and shareholders' equity	$118,656	$118,656
Long-term debt-to-equity	46.2%	50.3%
Debt-to-capital	31.6%	33.5%

While the recent standards solved many of the accounting problems created by financial instruments with characteristics of both debt and equity, structured finance is an active field, and new products and financial instruments are continuously created, some of which may serve to enhance an issuer's reported financial position. Therefore, where new transactions similar to those covered by these accounting standards are treated as equity, an analyst should evaluate whether the classification as equity significantly enhances the appearance of strong solvency ratios; if so, further analysis of the specifics of the transactions may be warranted.

LEASES   4

A company wishing to obtain the use of an asset can borrow money and purchase the asset. Alternatively, a company can lease the asset for some finite period of time or lease the asset as a means of buying the asset over time. The following paragraphs first describe some advantages to leasing from the viewpoint of the **lessee** (the party obtaining the use of an asset through a lease) and then describe the accounting treatment of different types of leases. The final portion of this section evaluates leases from the perspective of the owner of the asset.

4.1 Advantages of Leasing

A lease is a contract between the owner of an asset—the **lessor**—and another party seeking use of the assets—the lessee. Through the lease, the lessor grants the right to use the asset to the lessee. The right to use the asset could be a long period, such as 20 years, or a much shorter period such as a month. In exchange for the right to use the asset, the lessee makes periodic lease payments to the lessor. A lease, then, is a form of financing to the lessee provided directly from the lessor in order to enable the lessee to purchase the *use* of the leased asset.

There are several advantages to leasing an asset compared to purchasing it. Leases can provide less costly financing, usually require little, if any, down payment, and are often at fixed interest rates. Because the lease contract is negotiated between the lessor and lessee, the lease may contain less restrictive provisions than other forms of borrowing. A lease can also reduce the risk of obsolescence to the lessee because the lessee does not own the asset.

Importantly, leases also have potential financial and tax reporting advantages. While providing a form of financing, certain types of leases are not shown as debt on the balance sheet. The items leased under these types of leases also do not appear as assets on the balance sheet. Therefore, no interest expense or depreciation expense is included in the income statement. In addition, in the United States, because financial reporting rules differ from tax regulations, in some cases a company may own an asset for tax purposes (and thus obtain deductions for depreciation expense for tax purposes) while not reflecting the ownership in its financial statements. A lease that is structured to provide a company with the tax benefits of ownership while not requiring the asset to be reflected on the company's financial statements is known as a synthetic lease. Next, we will discuss the two main types of leases—finance and operating—and the lessee's and lessor's accounting for them.

4.2 Finance (or Capital) Leases versus Operating Leases

The economic substance of a finance (or capital) lease is very different from an operating lease, as are the implications of each for the financial statements for the lessee and lessor.[4] In substance, a **finance lease** is the purchase of some asset (lease to own) by the buyer (lessee) that is directly financed by the seller (lessor). An **operating lease** is an agreement allowing the lessee to use some asset for a period of time, essentially a rental.

U.S. accounting standards have four specific requirements that define when a lease is a finance lease:

1. Ownership of the leased asset transfers to lessee at end of lease.
2. The lease contains an option for the lessee to purchase the leased asset cheaply (bargain purchase option).
3. The lease term is 75 percent or more of the useful life of the leased asset.
4. The present value of lease payments is 90 percent or more of the fair value of the leased asset.

Only one of these requirements has to be met for the lease to be considered a finance lease by the lessee. On the lessor side, satisfying only one of these four specific requirements determines a finance lease plus the lessor must also meet revenue recognition requirements (that is, be reasonably assured of cash collection and have performed substantially under the lease). If none of the four specific requirements are met or if at least one is met but the revenue recognition requirement is not, the lessor reports the lease as an operating lease. International standards are less prescriptive in their criteria for categorizing finance and operating leases, relying on broad definitions of economic substance and managerial judgment to determine whether a lease is a finance or operating lease.

---

[4] Finance leases are also commonly referred to as capital leases, particularly in the United States.

4.2.1 *Accounting and Reporting by the Lessee*

Because a finance lease is economically similar to borrowing money and buying an asset, a company that enters into a finance lease as the lessee reports an asset (leased asset) and related debt (lease payable) on the balance sheet. The initial value of both the leased asset and lease payable is the present value of future lease payments. On the income statement, the company reports interest expense on the debt, and if the asset acquired is depreciable, the company reports depreciation expense. (The lessor, as we will illustrate in the next section, reports the sale of an asset and a lease as receivable.)

Because an operating lease is economically similar to renting an asset, a company that enters into an operating lease as the lessee records a lease expense on its income statement during the period it uses the asset. No asset or liability is recorded on its balance sheet. The main accounting differences between a finance lease and an operating lease, then, are that reported debt is higher and expenses are generally higher in the early years under a finance lease. Because of the higher debt and expenses, lessees often prefer operating leases to finance leases. As we will illustrate in the next section, lessors' preferences generally differ. Lessors would prefer a finance lease because under an operating lease, lessors continue to show the asset and its associated financing on their balance sheets.

On the lessee's statement of cash flows, for an operating lease, the full lease payment is shown as an operating cash outflow. For a finance lease, only the portion of the lease payment relating to interest expense reduces operating cash flow; the portion of the lease payment that reduces the lease liability appears as a cash outflow in the financing section.

The example below illustrates the effect on a lessee's income, debt, and cash flows when reporting a lease as a finance versus operating lease.

EXAMPLE 11

Financial Statement Impact of a Finance versus Operating Lease for the Lessee

Assume two similar (hypothetical) companies CAPBS Inc. and OPIS Inc. enter into similar lease agreements for a piece of machinery on 1 January 2008. The leases require four annual payments of €28,679 starting on 1 January 2008. The useful life of the machine is four years and its salvage value is zero. CAPBS accounts for the lease as a finance lease while OPIS has determined the lease is an operating lease. For simplicity, this example assumes that the accounting rules governing these hypothetical companies do not mandate either type of lease. The present value of lease payments and fair value of the equipment is €100,000. (A reminder relevant for present value calculations: Lease payments are made at the beginning of each period.)

At the beginning of 2008, before entering into the lease agreements, both companies reported liabilities of €100,000 and equity of €200,000. Each year the companies receive total revenues of €50,000 cash. Assume the companies have a tax rate of 30 percent, and use the same accounting for financial and tax purposes. Both companies' discount rate is 10 percent. In order to focus only on the differences in the type of lease, assume neither company incurs expenses other than those associated with the lease and neither invests excess cash.

1. Which company reports higher expenses/net income in 2008? Over the four years?

2. Which company reports higher total cash flow over the four years? Cash flow from operations?

3. Based on return on equity (ROE), how do the two companies' profitability measures compare?

4. Based on the ratio of debt-to-equity, how do the two companies' solvency positions compare?

Solution to 1: In 2008 and 2009, CAPBS reports higher expenses because the depreciation expense and interest expense of its finance lease exceeds the lease expense of OPIS's operating lease. Therefore, OPIS reports higher net income in 2008 and 2009. The companies' total expense over the entire four year period, however, is equal as is the companies' total net income.

Each year, OPIS reports lease expense of €28,679 associated with its operating lease. For CAPBS, its finance lease is treated as being economically similar to borrowing money and purchasing an asset. So, on its income statement, CAPBS reports depreciation expense on the leased asset acquired and interest expense on the lease liability.

The table below shows by year CAPBS's depreciation expense and book values on the leased asset.

Year	Acquisition Cost	Depreciation Expense	Accumulated Depreciation	Book Value (Year End)
	(a)	(b)	(c)	(d)
2008	€100,000	€25,000	€25,000	€75,000
2009	100,000	25,000	50,000	50,000
2010	100,000	25,000	75,000	25,000
2011	100,000	25,000	100,000	0
		€100,000		

▶ Column (a) is acquisition cost of €100,000 of the leased equipment.

▶ Column (b) is depreciation expense of €25,000 per year, calculated using the straight line convention, as the acquisition costs less salvage value divided by useful life [(€100,000 − €0)/4 years].

▶ Column (c) is the accumulated depreciation on the leased asset calculated as the prior year's accumulated depreciation plus the current year's depreciation expense.

▶ Column (d) is the book value of the leased equipment, which is the difference between the acquisition cost and accumulated depreciation.

The table below shows CAPBS's lease payment, interest expense, and carrying values for its lease liability by year.[5]

	Lease Liability 1 January	Annual Lease Payment, 1 January	Interest (at 10%; Accrued in Previous Year)	Reduction of Lease Liability, 1 January	Lease Liability on 31 December after Lease Payment on 1 January Same Year
	(a)	(b)	(c)	(d)	(e)
2008	€100,000	€28,679	€0	€28,679	€71,321
2009	71,321	28,679	7,132	21,547	49,774
2010	49,774	28,679	4,977	23,702	26,072
2011	26,072	28,679	2,607	26,072	0
		€114,717	€14,717	€100,000	

► Column (a) is the lease liability at the beginning of the year.

  ► 2008: €100,000

  ► Years thereafter: lease liability at end of previous year

► Column (b) is the annual lease payment made at the beginning of the year. A portion of the lease payment reduces any interest accrued in the previous year, and the remainder of the lease payment reduces the lease liability.

  ► For example, in 2009, the €28,679 paid on 1 January reduces the interest payable of €7,132 that accrued in 2008 (0.10 × 71,321) and then reduces the lease liability by €21,547.

► Column (c) is the interest portion of the 1 January lease payment made on that date. This amount of interest was accrued as interest payable during the *prior* year and is reported as the interest expense of the *prior* year.

► Column (d) is the reduction of the lease liability, which is the difference between the annual lease payment and the interest portion.

► Column (e) is the lease liability on 31 December of a given year just before the lease payment is made on the first day of the next year. It is equal to the lease liability on 1 January of the same year (column a) less the reduction of the lease liability (column d).

---

[5] The computations included throughout the example were made using an Excel worksheet; small apparent discrepancies in the calculations are due to the rounding.

The table below summarizes and compares the income statement effects of the lease for CAPBS and OPIS. Notice that over the four year lease, both companies report the same total amount of expense but CAPBS shows higher expenses earlier in the life of the lease.

	CAPBS			OPIS	
Year	Depreciation Expense	Interest Expense	Total	Lease Expense	Difference
2008	€25,000	€7,132	€32,132	€28,679	€3,453
2009	25,000	4,977	29,977	28,679	1,298
2010	25,000	2,607	27,607	28,679	(1,072)
2011	25,000	—	25,000	28,679	(3,679)
Total	€100,000	€14,717	€114,717	€114,717	€(0)

The complete income statements for CAPBS and OPIS are presented below. Notice under the assumptions that the same accounting is used for financial and tax purposes, CAPBS's taxes are lower in 2008 and 2009. The lower taxes in the earlier years reflect the higher expenses in those years.

	CAPBS				
Income Statements	2008	2009	2010	2011	Total
Sales	€50,000	€50,000	€50,000	€50,000	€200,000
Depreciation expense	25,000	25,000	25,000	25,000	€100,000
Interest expense	7,132	4,977	2,607		14,717
Lease expense					
Income before taxes	17,868	20,023	22,393	25,000	85,283
Tax expense	5,360	6,007	6,718	7,500	25,585
Net income	€12,508	€14,016	€15,675	€17,500	€59,698

	OPIS				
Income Statements	2008	2009	2010	2011	Total
Sales	€50,000	€50,000	€50,000	€50,000	€200,000
Depreciation expense					
Interest expense					
Lease expense	28,679	28,679	28,679	28,679	114,717
Income before taxes	21,321	21,321	21,321	21,321	85,283
Tax expense	6,396	6,396	6,396	6,396	25,585
Net income	€14,925	€14,925	€14,925	€14,925	€59,698

Solution to 2: On the statement of cash flows, observe that over the four years, both CAPBS and OPIS report the same total change in cash of €59,698. Operating cash flows reported by CAPBS are higher because a portion of the lease payment each year is categorized as a financing cash flow rather than an operating cash flow. In the first two years, CAPBS's change in cash is higher due to its lower taxes in those years.

Statements of Cash Flows	CAPBS				
	2008	2009	2010	2011	Total
Sales	€50,000	€50,000	€50,000	€50,000	€200,000
Interest paid	—	7,132	4,977	2,607	€14,717
Taxes paid	5,360	6,007	6,718	7,500	25,585
Lease expense	—	—	—	—	—
Operating cash flows	44,640	36,861	38,305	39,893	159,698
Payment to reduce lease liability	(28,679)	(21,547)	(23,702)	(26,072)	(100,000)
Financing cash flows	(28,679)	(21,547)	(23,702)	(26,072)	(100,000)
Total change in cash	€15,960	€15,314	€14,603	€13,821	€59,698

Statements of Cash Flows	OPIS				
	2008	2009	2010	2011	Total
Sales	€50,000	€50,000	€50,000	€50,000	€200,000
Interest paid					
Taxes paid	6,396	6,396	6,396	6,396	€25,585
Lease expense	28,679	28,679	28,679	28,679	114,717
Operating cash flows	14,925	14,925	14,925	14,925	59,698
Payment to reduce lease liability					
Financing cash flows	—	—	—		—
Total change in cash	€14,925	€14,925	€14,925	€14,925	€59,698

Solution to 3: Based on ROE, CAPBS looks less profitable than OPIS in the earlier years. Computing ROE requires forecasting shareholders' equity. In general, Ending shareholders' equity = Beginning shareholders' equity + Net income + Other comprehensive income − Dividends + Net capital contributions by shareholders. Because the companies in this example do not have other comprehensive income, did not pay dividends, and experienced no capital contributions from shareholders, Ending shareholders' equity = Beginning shareholders' equity + Net income. The forecasts are presented below.

CAPBS	2007	2008	2009	2010	2011
Retained earnings	€0	€12,508	€26,523	€42,198	€59,698
Common stock	200,000	200,000	200,000	200,000	200,000
Total shareholders' equity	€200,000	€212,508	€226,523	€242,198	€259,698

OPIS	2007	2008	2009	2010	2011
Retained earnings	€0	€14,925	€29,849	€44,774	€59,698
Common stock	200,000	200,000	200,000	200,000	200,000
Total shareholders' equity	€200,000	€214,925	€229,849	€244,774	€259,698

ROE is calculated as net income divided by average shareholders' equity. For example, CAPBS Inc. had 2008 ROE of 6.1 percent: €12,508/[(€200,000 + €212,508)/2].

	CAPBS				OPIS			
	2008	2009	2010	2011	2008	2009	2010	2011
ROE	6.1%	6.4%	6.7%	7.0%	7.2%	6.7%	6.3%	5.9%

Solution to 4: Based on the ratio of debt-to-equity, the solvency position of CAPBS is weaker than that of OPIS.

For the debt-to-equity ratio, take the total shareholders' equity from part 3 above. Initially, both companies had reported liabilities of €100,000. For OPIS, the amount of total liabilities remains constant at €100,000. For CAPBS, add the lease liability at the end of the year and the amount of accrued interest payable at the end of each year from part 1 above. So for year end 2008, CAPBS's total liabilities are €178,453 (€100,000 + €71,321 lease liability + €7,132 accrued interest payable at the end of the year), and its debt-to-equity ratio is 0.84 (€178,453 / €212,508). For year end 2009, CAPBS total liabilities equal €154,751 (€100,000 + €49,774 lease liability + €4,977 accrued interest payable at the end of the year). The table below presents the ratios for each year.

CAPBS				
	2008	**2009**	**2010**	**2011**
Total debt	178,453	154,751	128,679	100,000
Shareholders' equity	212,508	226,523	242,198	259,698
Debt-to-equity ratio	0.84	0.68	0.53	0.39

OPIS				
	2008	**2009**	**2010**	**2011**
Total debt	100,000	100,000	100,000	100,000
Shareholders' equity	214,925	229,849	244,774	259,698
Debt-to-equity ratio	0.47	0.44	0.41	0.39

In summary, a company reporting a lease as an operating lease will typically show higher profits in early years, higher return measures in early years, and a stronger solvency position than an identical company reporting an identical lease as a finance lease.[6] However, the company reporting the lease as a finance lease will show higher operating cash flows because a portion of the lease payment will be reflected as a financing cash outflow rather than an operating cash outflow.

Because of the well-defined accounting standards in the United States that determine when a company should report an operating versus finance lease, a company can structure a lease to avoid the four finance lease criteria and so record an operating lease. Similar to debt disclosures, lease disclosures show payments under both capital and operating leases for the next five years and afterwards. These disclosures can help to estimate the extent of a company's off-balance sheet lease financing through operating leases. The example below illustrates the disclosures and how these disclosures can be used to determine the effect on the financial statements if all operating leases were capitalized.

---

[6] Example 11 assumes the company uses the straight-line depreciation method, which is common under IFRS and U.S. GAAP. But if the company estimated depreciation expense based on the "economic" depreciation of the leased asset, there would be no difference in reported income under a finance lease and operating lease.

EXAMPLE 12

Financial Statement Impact of Treating Operating Leases as Finance Leases for the Lessee

CEC Entertainment, Inc. (NYSE: CEC) has significant commitments under finance (capital) and operating leases. Presented below is selected financial statement information and footnote disclosure to the financial statements for the company.

Commitments and Contingencies Footnote from CEC's Financial Statements:

6. Commitments and contingencies:

The company leases certain restaurants and related property and equipment under operating and capital leases. All leases require the company to pay property taxes, insurance, and maintenance of the leased assets. The leases generally have initial terms of 10 to 20 years with various renewal options.

Scheduled annual maturities of the obligations for capital and operating leases as of December 31, 2006, are as follows:

Years	Capital	Operating
	(Thousands)	
2007	$1,679	$62,521
2008	1,679	61,199
2009	1,679	59,892
2010	1,679	61,858
2011	1,679	59,777
2012–2028 (aggregate payments)	13,080	486,831
Minimum future lease payments	21,475	$792,078
Less amounts representing interest	(7,894)	
Present value of future minimum lease payments	13,581	
Less current portion	(693)	
Long-term finance lease obligation	$12,888	

Selected Financial Statement Information for CEC:

	31 December 2006	1 January 2006
Total liabilities	$344,979	$308,737
Shareholders' equity	$359,206	$343,183

1. **A.** Calculate the implicit interest rate used to discount the "scheduled annual maturities" under finance leases to obtain the "present value of future minimum lease payments" of $13,851 disclosed in the Commitments and Contingencies footnote. To simplify the calculation, assume that future minimum lease payments on the company's finance leases are $1,679 on 31 December of each year from 2012 to 2018 and $1,327 in 2019. This is approximately the average annual minimum lease payment for the period 2007 to 2011.

   B. Why is the implicit interest rate estimate in Part A important in assessing a company's leases?

2. If the operating agreements had been treated as finance leases, what additional amount would be reported as a lease obligation on the balance sheet at 31 December 2006? To simplify the calculation, assume that future minimum lease payments on the company's operating leases are $59,777 on 31 December each year from 2012 to 2019 and $8,615 in 2020 ($59,777 is the latest annual minimum lease payment disclosed). Use the implicit interest rate obtained in Part 1A to discount future cash flows on the operating leases.

3. What would be the effect on the debt-to-equity ratio of treating all operating leases as finance leases (i.e., the ratio of total liabilities to equity) at 31 December 2006?

Solution to 1:

A. The implicit interest rate on finance leases is 7.4 percent. The implicit interest rate used to discount the finance lease payments is the internal rate of return on the stream of cash flows, i.e., the interest rate that will make the present value of the lease payments equal to $13,581. You can use an Excel spreadsheet or a financial calculator for the computations. Set the cash flow at time zero equal to $13,581 (note on Excel and on most financial calculators, you will input this amount as a negative number), input each of the annual payments on the finance leases, and solve for the internal rate of return.

   To demonstrate how the internal rate of return corresponds to the individual present values, refer to the following schedule of the undiscounted minimum lease payments based on information from footnote 6 and the assumptions given. The following table presents the present value computations.

Implicit Interest Rate (the Internal Rate of Return)				7.4%
Fiscal Year	Years to Discount	Minimum Lease Payment	Times Present Value Factor	Equals Present Value
2007	1	$1,679	$1/(1+\text{interest rate})^1$	$1,563
2008	2	1,679	$1/(1+\text{interest rate})^2$	1,456
2009	3	1,679	$1/(1+\text{interest rate})^3$	1,355
2010	4	1,679	$1/(1+\text{interest rate})^4$	1,262
2011	5	1,679	$1/(1+\text{interest rate})^5$	1,175
2012	6	1,679	$1/(1+\text{interest rate})^6$	1,094
2013	7	1,679	$1/(1+\text{interest rate})^7$	1,019
2014	8	1,679	$1/(1+\text{interest rate})^8$	948
2015	9	1,679	$1/(1+\text{interest rate})^9$	883
2016	10	1,679	$1/(1+\text{interest rate})^{10}$	822
2017	11	1,679	$1/(1+\text{interest rate})^{11}$	766
2018	12	1,679	$1/(1+\text{interest rate})^{12}$	713
2019	13	1,327	$1/(1+\text{interest rate})^{13}$	525
Undiscounted sum of minimum future lease payments		$21,475		
Present value of future minimum lease payments			$13,581	$13,581

The interest rate of 7.4 percent equates the future minimum lease payments with the present value of future minimum lease payments of $13,581 that CEC reports.

B. The implicit interest rate is important because it will be used to estimate the present value of the lease obligations reported as a liability, the value of the leased assets on the balance sheet, the interest expense, and the lease amortization on the income statement. For instance, by selecting a higher rate a company can opportunistically reduce reported debt, if desired. The reasonableness of the implicit interest rate can be gauged by comparing it to the interest rates of the company's other debt outstanding, which are disclosed in financial statement footnotes, and considering recent market conditions.

Solution to 2: If the operating leases had been treated as finance leases, the additional amount that would be reported as a lease obligation on the balance sheet at 31 December 2006 using a discount rate of 7.4 percent determined in part 1 above is $497,078. The table that follows presents the present value computations. An alternative shortcut approach is to divide the discounted finance lease cash flows of $13,581 by the undiscounted finance lease cash flows of $21,475, and then apply the resulting percentage of 63.24 percent to the undiscounted operating lease cash flows of $792,078. The shortcut approach estimates the present value of the operating lease payments as $500,918, which is close to the estimate obtained using the longer method. It is likely to be most accurate when the temporal pattern of the two sets of cash flows is similar.

Implicit Interest Rate				7.4%
Fiscal Year	Years to Discount	Operating Lease Payments	Times Present Value Factor	Equal Present Value
2007	1	$62,521	$1/(1+0.074)^1$	$58,213
2008	2	61,199	$1/(1+0.074)^2$	53,056
2009	3	59,892	$1/(1+0.074)^3$	48,345
2010	4	61,858	$1/(1+0.074)^4$	46,492
2011	5	59,777	$1/(1+0.074)^5$	41,832
2012	6	59,777	$1/(1+0.074)^6$	38,950
2013	7	59,777	$1/(1+0.074)^7$	36,266
2014	8	59,777	$1/(1+0.074)^8$	33,768
2015	9	59,777	$1/(1+0.074)^9$	31,441
2016	10	59,777	$1/(1+0.074)^{10}$	29,275
2017	11	59,777	$1/(1+0.074)^{11}$	27,258
2018	12	59,777	$1/(1+0.074)^{12}$	25,379
2019	13	59,777	$1/(1+0.074)^{13}$	23,631
2020	14	8,615	$1/(1+0.074)^{14}$	3,171
Undiscounted sum of future operating lease payment		$792,078		
Present value of future operating lease payments				$497,078

Solution to 3: The debt-to-equity ratio increases to 234.4 percent from 96.0 percent when capitalizing the operating leases. The adjusted debt-to-equity ratio is computed as follows:

	Unadjusted for Operating Leases	Adjustment to Capitalize Operating Leases	Adjusted to Capitalize Operating Leases
Total liabilities	$344,979	$497,078	$842,057
Common shareholders' equity	$359,206		$359,206
Debt-to-equity ratio	96.0%		234.4%

4.2.2 Accounting and Reporting by the Lessor

As previously mentioned, lessors that report under U.S. GAAP determine whether a lease is a finance (also called "capital lease") or operating lease using the same four criteria as a lessee, plus additional revenue recognition criteria. If a lessor enters into an operating lease, the lessor records any lease revenue when earned. The lessor also continues to report the leased asset on the balance sheet and the asset's associated depreciation expense on the income statement.

From the lessor's perspective, there are two types of finance leases: 1) direct financing leases, and 2) sales-type leases.[7] A direct financing lease results when the present value of lease payments (and thus the amount recorded as a lease receivable) equals the carrying value of the leased asset. Because there is no "profit" on the asset itself, the lessor is essentially providing financing to the lessee, and the revenues earned by the lessor are financing in nature (i.e., interest revenue). If, however, the present value of lease payments (and thus the amount recorded as a lease receivable) exceeds the carrying value of the leased asset, the lease is treated as a sale.

Both types of finance lease have two similar effects on the balance sheet: the lessor reports a lease receivable based on the present value of future lease payments, and the lessor also reduces its assets by the carrying value of the asset leased. The carrying value of the asset leased relative to the present value of lease payments distinguishes a direct financing lease from a sales-type lease. The income statement effect will thus differ based on the type of lease.

In a sales-type lease, the lessor "sells" the asset to the lessee and also provides financing on the sale. Therefore, in a sales-type lease, a lessor reports revenue from the sale, cost of goods sold (i.e., the carrying value of the asset leased), profit on the sale, and interest revenue earned from financing the sale.

EXAMPLE 13

Financial Statement Impact of a Direct Financing Lease versus Operating Lease for the Lessor

Assume two similar (hypothetical) companies, DIRFIN Inc. and LOPER Inc., own a similar piece of machinery and make similar agreements to lease the machinery on 1 January 2008. In the lease contract, each company requires four annual payments of €28,679 starting on 1 January 2008. The useful life of the machine is four years and its salvage value is zero. DIRFIN Inc. accounts for the lease as a direct financing lease while LOPER has determined the lease is an operating lease. (For simplicity, this example assumes that the accounting rules governing these hypothetical companies do not mandate either type of lease.) The present value of lease payments and fair value of the equipment is €100,000.

At the beginning of 2008, before entering into the lease agreement, both companies reported liabilities of €100,000 and equity of €200,000. Assets on hand include the asset about to be leased. Each year the companies receive total revenues of €50,000 cash, apart from any revenue earned on the lease. Assume the companies have a tax rate of 30 percent, and use the same accounting for financial and tax purposes. Both

---

[7] IFRS do not make the distinction between a sales-type lease and a direct financing lease. However, a similar treatment to "sales-type" is allowed for finance leases originated by "manufacturer or dealer lessors," within the general provisions for finance leases.

companies' discount rate is 10 percent. In order to focus only on the differences in the type of lease, assume neither company incurs expenses other than those associated with the lease and neither invests excess cash.

1. Which company reports higher expenses/net income in 2008? Over the four years?
2. Which company reports higher total cash flow over the four years? Cash flow from operations?
3. Based on ROE, how do the two companies' profitability measures compare?

Solution to 1: LOPER reports higher expenses in 2008 because under an operating lease, the lessor retains ownership of the asset and continues to report associated depreciation expense. DIRFIN, treating the lease as a finance lease, does not reflect ownership of the asset or associated depreciation expense. DIRFIN has higher net income in 2008 because the interest revenue component of the lease payment in that year exceeds the lease revenue net of depreciation reported by LOPER.

On its income statement, LOPER reports depreciation expense for the asset it has leased and lease revenue based on the lease payment received. The table below shows LOPER's depreciation and book values on leased equipment by year.[8]

Year	Cost	Depreciation Expense	Accumulated Depreciation	Book Value (Year End)
	(a)	(b)	(c)	(d)
2008	€100,000	€25,000	€25,000	€75,000
2009	100,000	25,000	50,000	50,000
2010	100,000	25,000	75,000	25,000
2011	100,000	25,000	100,000	0
		€100,000		

▶ Column (a) is the cost of €100,000 of the leased equipment.
▶ Column (b) is depreciation expense of €25,000 per year, calculated using the straight-line method as the cost less the salvage value divided by the useful life [(€100,000 − €0)/4 years].
▶ Column (c) is the accumulated depreciation on the leased asset calculated as the prior year's accumulated depreciation plus the current year's depreciation expense.
▶ Column (d) is the ending book value of the leased equipment, which is the difference between the cost and accumulated depreciation.

---

[8] The computations included throughout the example were made using an Excel worksheet: small apparent discrepancies in the calculations are due to the rounding.

On the other hand, DIRFIN records the lease as a direct financing lease. It removes the leased asset from its records and records a lease receivable. On its income statement, DIRFIN reports interest revenues earned from financing the lease. The table below shows DIRFIN's interest revenue and carrying values on the lease receivable.

Year	Lease Receivable, 1 January	Annual Lease Payment Received, 1 January	Interest (at 10%; Accrued in Previous Year)	Reduction of Lease Receivable, 1 January	Lease Receivable on 31 December after Lease Payment on 1 January of Same Year
	(a)	(b)	(c)	(d)	(e)
2008	€100,000	€28,679	€0	€28,679	€71,321
2009	71,321	28,679	7,132	21,547	49,774
2010	49,774	28,679	4,977	23,702	26,072
2011	26,072	28,679	2,607	26,072	0
		€114,717	€14,717	€100,000	

- ▶ Column (a) is the lease receivable at the beginning of the year.
- ▶ Column (b) is annual lease payment received at the beginning of the year, which is allocated to interest and reduction of the lease receivable.
- ▶ Column (c) is interest for the year calculated as the lease receivable outstanding for the year multiplied by the interest rate.
- ▶ Column (d) is the reduction of the lease receivable, which is the difference between the annual lease payments received and interest. Because the lease payment is due on 1 January, this amount of interest is a receivable at the end of the *prior* year and the interest revenue of the *prior* year.
- ▶ Column (e) is the lease receivable after the lease payment is received and at the end of the year. It is the lease receivable at 1 January (Column a) less the reduction of the lease receivable (Column d).

The table below summarizes and compares the income statement effects of the lease for DIRFIN and LOPER. Notice that over the four year lease, both companies report the same total amount of revenue, but DIRFIN's revenues in the earlier years of the lease are higher than the net of lease revenues less depreciation reported by LOPER in those years.

Year	DIRFIN Lease Revenue	LOPER Lease Revenue	Depreciation Expense	Total	Difference
2008	€7,132	€28,679	€25,000	€3,679	€3,453
2009	4,977	28,679	25,000	3,679	1,298
2010	2,607	28,679	25,000	3,679	(1,072)
2011	—	28,679	25,000	3,679	(–3,679)
Total	€14,717	€114,717	€100,000	€14,717	€0

The complete income statements for DIRFIN and LOPER are presented below. Notice that, under the assumption that the same accounting is used for financial and tax purposes, DIRFIN's taxes are higher than those of LOPER in 2008 and 2009.

	DIRFIN				
Income Statements	2008	2009	2010	2011	Total
Sales	€50,000	€50,000	€50,000	€50,000	€200,000
Depreciation expense					
Interest revenue	7,132	4,977	2,607		14,717
Lease revenue					
Income before taxes	€57,132	€54,977	€52,607	€50,000	€214,717
Tax expense	17,140	16,493	15,782	15,000	64,415
Net income	€39,992	€38,484	€36,825	€35,000	€150,302

	LOPER				
Income Statements	2008	2009	2010	2011	Total
Sales	€50,000	€50,000	€50,000	€50,000	€200,000
Depreciation expense	(25,000)	(25,000)	(25,000)	(25,000)	(100,000)
Interest revenue					
Lease revenue	28,679	28,679	28,679	28,679	114,717
Income before taxes	€53,679	€53,679	€53,679	€53,679	€214,717
Tax expense	16,104	16,104	16,104	16,104	64,415
Net income	€37,575	€37,575	€37,575	€37,575	€150,302

Solution to 2: Looking at the statement of cash flows, observe that operating cash flows reported by DIRFIN are lower, but investing cash flows are higher than LOPER. Over the four years, both DIRFIN and LOPER report the same total change in cash.

Statements of Cash Flows	DIRFIN				
	2008	2009	2010	2011	Total
Net income	€39,992	€38,484	€36,825	€35,000	€150,302
Increase(decrease) in interest receivable	7,132	(2,155)	(2,370)	(2,607)	0
Add back depreciation expense					
Operating cash flows	€32,860	€40,639	€39,195	€37,607	€150,302
Payments received on finance leases	28,679	21,547	23,702	26,072	100,000
Investing cash flows	28,679	21,547	23,702	26,072	100,000
Change in cash	€61,540	€62,186	€62,897	€63,679	€250,302

Statements of Cash Flows	LOPER				
	2008	2009	2010	2011	Total
Net income	€37,575	€37,575	€37,575	€37,575	€150,302
Increase(decrease) in interest receivable					
Add back depreciation expense	25,000	25,000	25,000	25,000	100,000
Operating cash flows	€62,575	€62,575	€62,575	€62,575	€250,302
Payments received on finance leases					
Investing cash flows					
Change in cash	€62,575	€62,575	€62,575	€62,575	€250,302

Solution to 3: Based on ROE, DIRFIN appears more profitable than LOPER in the early years of the lease.

Computing ROE requires forecasting shareholders' equity. In general, ending Shareholders' equity = Beginning shareholders' equity + Net income + Other comprehensive income − Dividends + Net capital contributions by shareholders. Because the companies in this example do not have other comprehensive income, do not pay dividends, and have no capital contributions, Ending shareholders' equity = Beginning shareholders' equity + Net income. The forecasts are presented below.

DIRFIN	2007	2008	2009	2010	2011
Retained earnings	€0	€39,992	€78,477	€115,302	€150,302
Common stock	200,000	200,000	200,000	200,000	200,000
Total shareholders' equity	€200,000	€239,992	€278,477	€315,302	€350,302

LOPER	2007	2008	2009	2010	2011
Retained earnings	€0	€37,575	€75,151	€112,726	€150,302
Common stock	200,000	200,000	200,000	200,000	200,000
Total shareholders' equity	€200,000	€237,575	€275,151	€312,726	€350,302

ROE is calculated as net income divided by average shareholders' equity. For example, DIRFIN Inc. had 2008 ROE of 18.2 percent: €39,992/[(€200,000 + €239,992)/2].

	DIRFIN				LOPER			
	2008	2009	2010	2011	2008	2009	2010	2011
ROE	18.2%	14.8%	12.4%	10.5%	17.2%	14.7%	12.8%	11.3%

From the comparisons above, DIRFIN looks more profitable in the early years of the lease, but less profitable in the later years.

When a company enters into a sales-type lease, a lease agreement where the present value of lease payment is greater than the value of the leased asset to the lessor, it will show a profit on the transaction in the year of inception and interest revenue over the life of the lease.

EXAMPLE 14

Financial Statement Impact of a Sales-type Lease for the Lessor

Assume a (hypothetical) company, Selnow Inc., owns a piece of machinery and enters into an agreement to lease the machinery on 1 January 2008. In the lease contract, the company requires four annual payments of €28,679 starting on 1 January 2008. The present value of the lease payments (using a 10 percent discount rate) is €100,000, and the fair value of the equipment is €90,000. The useful life of the machinery is four years and its salvage value is zero.

1. Is the lease above a direct financing or sales-type lease?
2. What is Selnow's income related to the lease in 2008? In 2009? Ignore taxes.

Solution to 1: The above lease is a sales-type lease. The present value of lease payments is more than the lessor's carrying value of the leased asset, the difference being the lessors' profit from selling the machinery. The lessor will record a profit of €10,000 on the sale of the leased equipment in 2008 (€100,000 present value of lease payments receivable less €90,000 value of leased equipment).

Solution to 2: In 2008, Selnow shows income of €17,132 related to the lease. One part of this is the €10,000 gain on the sale of the lease equipment (sales revenues of €100,000 less costs of goods sold of €90,000). Selnow also shows interest revenue of €7,132 on its financing of the lease (lease receivable of €71,321 after the initial lease payment is received times the 10 percent discount rate). In 2009, Selnow reports only the interest revenue of €4,977 (lease receivable of €49,774 after the 1 January lease payment is received times the 10 percent discount rate). The table below shows lease payments received, interest revenue, and reduction of the lease receivable for Selnow's sales-type lease. Note that this table is the same as DIRFIN's table in the previous example with the direct financing lease. They are the same because the present value of the lease payments in both cases is the same. It is the fair value of the equipment that differs between the two examples.

	Lease Receivable, 1 January	Annual Lease Payment Received, 1 January	Interest (at 10%; Accrued in Previous Year)	Reduction of Lease Receivable, 1 January	Lease Receivable on 31 December after Lease Payment on 1 January Same Year
	(a)	(b)	(c)	(d)	(e)
2008	€100,000	€28,679	€0	€28,679	€71,321
2009	71,321	28,679	7,132	21,547	49,774
2010	49,774	28,679	4,977	23,702	26,072
2011	26,072	28,679	2,607	26,072	0
		€114,717	€14,717	€100,000	

OTHER TYPES OF OFF-BALANCE SHEET FINANCING

## 5

An operating lease is only one type of contractual obligation that is not recognized as a liability on the balance sheet. Companies can engage in other types of off-balance sheet arrangements that do not result in additional liabilities reported on the balance sheet but nonetheless create economic obligations. Examples include (but are not limited to) take-or-pay contracts, throughput arrangements, and the sale of receivables. Each of these is described below. An analyst should consider the effect on financial statements and financial ratios of adjustments to reflect the economic reality of **off-balance sheet financing** activities.

5.1 Take-or-Pay and Throughput

With a take-or-pay contract, a company commits to buying a minimum quantity of an item (such as raw materials and other inputs) over a certain time period. Even if the company does not take delivery, it must still pay for the item. Similarly, with a throughput arrangement, a company commits to pay a minimum amount for transporting its production through a delivery channel. For example, a gas company or group of gas companies may commit to pay a minimum amount periodically to use a pipeline for delivering gas. Prices in the arrangements can be fixed or related to market prices. One reason for making such arrangements is to secure access to raw materials or to transport capacity. Another reason for making such arrangements is to facilitate the financing of a large project, such as a pipeline, on a standalone basis by providing a committed stream of cash inflows to the project.

Even though the company has committed to make minimum payments under take-or-pay and throughput arrangements, accounting standards do not require the liability to be recognized on the balance sheet. As a corollary, the standards also do not require the item being purchased to be recognized as an asset on the balance sheet. However, the purchaser commonly discloses the nature and minimum required payments in the footnotes to the financial statements and in the MD&A. The U.S. SEC (in a 2003 rule adopted at the direction of the Sarbanes–Oxley Act of 2002) specifically requires companies to explain off-balance sheet arrangements in a separately captioned disclosure in the MD&A and also to provide a tabular summary of known contractual obligations, including both on- and off-balance sheet obligations. Footnote disclosures about obligations not reflected on a company's balance sheet generally appear under the caption "Commitments and Contingencies."

For analytical purposes, disclosures about financial commitments are useful in assessing how a company's solvency position, as reflected in leverage ratios, is affected by off-balance sheet items. Example 15 illustrates the effect of adjusting a company's debt-to-capital ratio by adding the commitments under a take-or-pay arrangement to the company's total debt. For ratios involving assets, the adjustment would include adding both the assets to be purchased and the associated debt commitments to the relevant balance sheet amounts. Disclosures about financial commitments in forthcoming years are also useful when assessing a company's liquidity position.

EXAMPLE 15

Financial Statement Impact of Off-Balance Sheet Take-or-Pay Arrangements

Wheeling-Pittsburgh Corporation (NASDAQGM:WPSC) provides information about contractual obligations in its "Management's Discussion and Analysis (MD&A) of Financial Condition and Results of Operations" section of its 2006 10-K filing and in the footnotes to its 2006 financial statements.

The first excerpt is from the contractual obligations disclosures in the company's MD&A, and the second excerpt is from the "Commitments and Contingencies" footnote to the company's financial statements.

Excerpt from the Contractual Obligations table included in the company's MD&A showing the company's purchase commitments

		Contractual Obligations as of December 31, 2006			
		Contractual Payments Due (Dollars in Millions)			
	Total	Less than 1 Year	1–3 Years	3–5 Years	More than 5 Years
Purchase commitments:					
Oxygen supply	93.3	10.0	20.0	23.2	40.1
Electricity	83.7	7.5	15.0	14.0	47.2
Coal	8.4	8.4	—	—	—
Coal	11.3	11.3	—	—	—

We entered into a 15-year take-or-pay contract in 1999 that was amended in 2003. The contract requires us to purchase oxygen, nitrogen and argon each month with a minimum monthly charge of approximately $0.7 million, subject to escalation clauses.

We entered into a 20-year take-or-pay contract in 1999, which was amended in 2003. The contract requires us to purchase steam and electricity each month or pay a minimum monthly charge of approximately $0.5 million, subject to increases for inflation, and a variable charge calculated at a minimum of $3.75 times the number of tons of iron produced each month with an agreed-to minimum of 3,250 tons per day, regardless of whether any tons are produced. At December 31, 2006, a maximum termination payment of $27.7 million would have been required to terminate the contract.

In 2004, we amended our contract to purchase coal each month to a minimum monthly charge of approximately $0.7 million. The term of the contract expires on December 31, 2007.

In 2005, we entered into contracts to purchase 20,000 tons of coal each month from August 2006 through May 2007 at a price approximating $94.50 per ton.

Excerpt from the Commitments and Contingencies footnote to 2006 financial statements:

Commitments

The Company entered into a 15-year take-or-pay contract in 1999, which was amended in 2003 and requires the Company to purchase oxygen, nitrogen and argon each month with a minimum monthly charge of approximately $600, subject to escalation clauses. Payments for deliveries under this contract totaled $12,150, $10,621 and $14,200 during 2006, 2005 and 2004, respectively.

The Company entered into a 20-year contract in 1999, which was amended in 2003 and requires the Company to purchase steam and electricity each month or pay a minimum monthly charge of approximately $500, subject to increases for inflation, and a variable charge calculated at a minimum of $3.75 times the number of tons of iron produced each month, with an agreed-to minimum of 3,250 tons per day, regardless of whether any tons are produced. Payments for delivery of steam and electricity under this contract totaled $12,867, $9,652 and $9,150 during 2006, 2005 and 2004, respectively. At December 31, 2006, a maximum termination payment of approximately $27,750 would have been required to terminate the contract.

Additional information:

The company's shareholders' equity at 31 December 2006 was $286.2 million, and total debt was $287.1 million. All dollar amounts are in millions.

Required: Use the disclosures and additional information provided to estimate the effect on WPSC's debt-to-capital ratio for 2006 if the purchase commitments were included as debt.

Solution: The company's debt-to-capital ratio increases to 0.63 from 0.50 when its purchase commitments are included on the balance sheet. The company has two take-or-pay contracts disclosed in its MD&A and the footnotes to its financial statements totaling commitments of $196.7 million (93.3 + 83.7 + 8.4 + 11.3) at 31 December 2006. Including these off-balance sheet arrangements in the financial statement would reflect a deterioration in the company's ratio.

	As Reported	Adjustment for Purchase Commitments	Adjusted
Total debt	$287.1	$196.7	$483.8
Total capital (debt plus equity)	573.3	196.7	770.0
Debt-to-capital ratio	0.50		0.63

In this example, the purchase commitments do not dramatically increase the debt-to-total capital ratio. If the debt-to-capital ratio increased enough to be of concern, the analyst might discount the purchase commitments to their present value, which would provide a better estimate. Such an estimate would produce a debt-to-capital ratio between 0.50 and 0.63.

5.2 Sale of Receivables

To accelerate cash flows, a company can sell its accounts receivable to a third party. A securitization of receivables typically involves the company first selling the receivables to a trust (set up as a special purpose entity, or SPE), and then the SPE selling debt securities backed by the receivables. The receivables may be trade receivables, mortgages, or various other types of financial assets.

The company selling the receivables, however, often retains some of the risk that the receivable is not collected. Roughly, this means if the borrower owing under the receivable sold to the SPE defaults, the company that sold the receivables would be obligated to reimburse the SPE for some of the amount of the default. Depending on the amount of default risk that the company retains, the sale of receivables can be viewed as the economic equivalent of collateralized borrowing. Accounting standards (SFAS No. 140 and IAS 39) discuss the circumstances in which a company recognizes the transaction as a collateralized borrowing (in which the company's financial statements would reflect a liability) versus a sale (in which the company would not reflect a liability). Additionally, companies disclose information about securitized assets in the footnotes to their financial statements, including the principal amounts and losses arising from defaults (SFAS No. 140 and IFRS 7).

Disclosures about accounts receivable facilitate assessment of a company's financial position. When receivables are transferred, and the transfer is accounted for as a sale, accounts receivable decrease and operating cash flows increase. To the extent that an analyst considers the transfer of receivables as borrowings, the cash received should be reclassified to financing cash flows from operating cash flows. Additionally, accounts receivable and current liabilities should be increased by the amount of receivables that were sold before computing ratios.

EXAMPLE 16

Financial Statement Impact of Sale of Receivables

Stanley Works (NYSE: SWK) discloses the following information on the sale of accounts receivable in its 2006 financial statement footnotes:

> **Excerpt from footnotes to 2006 financial statements:**
>
> **B. ACCOUNTS AND NOTES RECEIVABLE**
> The Company has agreements to sell, on a revolving basis, undivided interests in defined pools of notes receivable to a Qualified Special Purpose Entity ("QSPE"). The entity is designed to facilitate the securitization of certain trade accounts receivable and is used as an additional source of liquidity. . . . The proceeds from sales of such eligible receivables to the QSPE in revolving-period securitizations were $43.9 million in 2006 and $4.7 million in 2005. There were no gains or losses on these sales. The amounts deducted from receivables in the December 30, 2006 and December 31, 2005 Consolidated Balance Sheets under this arrangement were $60.3 million and $16.4 million, respectively. The Company is responsible for servicing and collecting the receivables sold and held in the QSPE. . . .

The company's statement of cash flows shows that operating cash flows for fiscal 2006 were $439.1 million. Its balance sheet at 30 December 2006 shows total current assets and total current liabilities of $1,638.5 million and $1,251.1 million, respectively. All dollar amounts are in millions.

Use the disclosures and additional information provided to estimate the following for 2006:

▶ the effect on the operating cash flows if the proceeds from the sale of accounts receivable had been classified as financing cash flows, and

▶ the effect on the current ratio of treating the asset transfer as a collateralized borrowing, i.e., continuing to include the receivables in both current assets and current liabilities.

Solution: The company's operating cash flows decrease by approximately 10 percent to $395.2 million from $439.1 million when proceeds from the sale of accounts receivable are reclassified to financing cash flows. Its current ratio decreases only slightly from 1.31 to 1.30.

	As Reported	Adjustment for Sale of Trade A/R	Adjusted
Operating cash flows	$439.1	$43.9	$395.2
Total current assets	1,638.5	60.3	1,698.8
Total current liabilities	1,251.1	60.3	1,311.4
Current ratio	1.31		1.30

SUMMARY

Key points include the following:

- ▶ The sales proceeds of a bond issue are determined by discounting future cash payments using the market rate of interest. The reported interest expense on bonds is based on the market interest rate.

- ▶ Future cash payments on bonds usually include periodic interest payments (made at the stated rate) and the principal amount at maturity.

- ▶ When the market rate of interest is the stated rate for the bonds, the bonds will sell at par, i.e., at a price equal to the face value. When the market rate of interest is higher than the bonds' stated rate, the bonds will sell at a discount. When the market rate of interest is lower than the bonds' stated rate, the bonds will sell at a premium.

- ▶ An issuer amortizes any issuance discount or premium on bonds over the life of the bonds.

- ▶ If a company redeems bonds before maturity, it may show a gain or loss on debt extinguishment computed as the net book value of the bonds (including bond issuance costs under IFRS) less the amount required to redeem the bonds.

- ▶ Debt covenants impose restrictions on borrowers such as limitations on future borrowing or requirements to maintain a minimum debt-to-equity ratio.

- ▶ The book value of bonds is based on the face value adjusted for any unamortized discount or premium, which can differ from its fair value. Such a difference will be due to the implicit discount rate, established at the time of issue, being different from the current market rate.

- ▶ Under U.S. GAAP, convertible bonds, which allow bondholders to convert the bonds to equity, are reported at issuance with no separate value attributed to the conversion feature. IFRS separates the debt from the conversion feature, which is reported as equity.

- ▶ Bonds with warrants giving the holder the right to purchase additional shares of the issuer's common stock are reported at issuance with the issue proceeds allocated between the bonds and the warrants.

- ▶ Some financial instruments have characteristics of both debt and equity. If the financial instruments are treated as equity, solvency ratios based on the financial statements appear stronger.

- ▶ Accounting standards generally define two types of leases: operating leases and finance (or capital) leases. U.S. accounting standards have four specific requirements that define when a lease is a finance lease. International standards are less prescriptive.

- ▶ When a lessee reports a lease as an operating lease rather than a finance lease, it usually appears more profitable in early years of the lease and less so later, and it appears more solvent over the whole period.

- ▶ When a company has a substantial amount of operating leases, adjusting reported financials to include the impact of capitalizing these leases better reflects the company's solvency position.

- ▶ When a lessor reports a lease as a finance lease rather than an operating lease, it usually appears more profitable in early years of the lease.

▶ In direct financing leases, a lessor earns only interest revenue. In a sales-types lease, a lessor earns both interest revenue and a profit (or loss) on the sale of the leased asset.

▶ Companies can engage in other types of off-balance sheet arrangements to avoid reporting additional liabilities on the balance sheet such as take-or-pay contracts, throughput arrangements, and the sale of receivables. Analysis should assess the impact on financial statements and financial ratios of adjustments reflecting the economic reality of off-balance sheet financing activities.

PRACTICE PROBLEMS FOR READING 39

1. A company issues $1,000,000 of bonds at face value. When the bonds are issued, the company will record a:

   A. cash inflow from investing activities.

   B. cash inflow from financing activities.

   C. cash inflow from operating activities.

2. Alpha Aircraft receives $1 million for bonds issued at face value, and Beta Bizjets receives $1 million for bonds issued at a discount. As a result of the bond issue, compared to Alpha Aircraft, Beta Bizjets will *most likely* record higher:

   A. periodic interest expense on the income statement.

   B. liabilities on the balance sheet at the time of issue.

   C. periodic interest payments on the statement of cash flows.

3. Oil Exploration LLC paid $45,000 related to printing, legal fees, commissions, and other costs associated with its recent bond issue. Under U.S. GAAP it is most likely to record these costs on its financial statements as:

   A. an asset.

   B. a liability.

   C. a cash outflow from investing activities.

4. On 1 January 2008, Elegant Fragrances Company issues $1 million worth of five-year bonds with annual interest payments of $55,000 paid each 31 December. The market interest rate is 6.0 percent. Using the effective interest rate method of amortizing, Elegant Fragrances is *most likely* to record:

   A. interest expense of $55,000 on its 2008 income statement.

   B. a liability of $982,674 on the 31 December 2008 balance sheet.

   C. a $58,736 cash outflow from operating activity on the 2008 statement of cash flows.

5. Consolidated Enterprises issues $10 million worth of five-year bonds with a stated rate of 6.5 percent at a time when the market interest rate is 6.0 percent. Using the effective interest rate method of amortizing, the carrying value after one year will be *closest to*:

   A. $10.17 million.

   B. $10.21 million.

   C. $10.28 million.

6. Innovative Inventions, Inc. needs to raise $10 million and typically would issue coupon-bearing bonds at par value. If the company chooses to issue zero-coupon bonds instead, its debt-to-equity ratio will:

   A. rise as the maturity date approaches.

   B. decline as the maturity date approaches.

   C. remain constant throughout the life of the bond.

7. Fairmont Golf issued fixed rate debt when interest rates were 6 percent. Rates have since risen to 7 percent. Using the values reported on the financial statements would *most likely* cause an analyst to:

    A. overestimate Fairmont's economic liabilities.

    B. underestimate Fairmont's economic liabilities.

    C. underestimate Fairmont's interest coverage ratio.

8. Debt covenants are *least likely* to place restrictions on the issuer's ability to:

    A. pay dividends.

    B. issue additional debt.

    C. issue additional equity.

9. Sheila Cummins is analyzing the financial statements of a company that has issued convertible bonds that are currently reported as debt. Cummins is considering potential adjustments to the debt-to-equity ratio as part of her analysis. The *least appropriate* action would be to:

    A. make no adjustment.

    B. adjust debt but not equity.

    C. adjust equity but not debt.

10. Why-Fi Incorporated reports total equity of $10 million. It has also issued convertible bonds with a book value of $10 million that are convertible into equity with a current market value of $15 million. Under U.S. GAAP, if the bonds are converted, Why-Fi will report total equity *closest to*:

    A. $10 million.

    B. $20 million.

    C. $25 million.

11. When analyzing the financial statements of Energy Resources, Inc., Frederico Montalban, CFA is treating its convertible bonds issue as equity rather than debt. Montalban's analysis is *most likely* appropriate:

    A. if the conversion price is near the current market price of the stock.

    B. if the conversion price is significantly above the current market price of the stock.

    C. if the conversion price is significantly below the current market price of the stock.

12. Capitol Services Corp. has $300 million in shareholders' equity and $400 million in long-term debt, of which $200 million are convertible bonds. What would Capitol's long-term debt-to-equity ratio be if the bonds were converted?

    A. 0.40.

    B. 0.80.

    C. 0.67.

13. Assets that are being used under a synthetic lease are reported as though the lessee owns them:

    A. for tax purposes and on the financial statements.

    B. on the financial statements but not for tax purposes.

    C. for tax purposes but not on the financial statements.

14. Compared to using a finance lease, a lessee that makes use of an operating lease will report higher:

    A. debt.

    B. rent expense.

    C. cash flow from operating activity.

15. The notes to the financial statements of Bargain Apparel Corp. disclose that the company has finance lease commitments with minimum future payments of $20 million, of which $6 million represents interest payments. It also has operating leases with minimum future payments of $25 million. If Robert Xu, CFA wishes to adjust the financial statements to treat all leases as debt, he should increase reported total liabilities by an amount *closest to*:

    A. $17.5 million.

    B. $25.0 million.

    C. $45.0 million.

16. Compared to an identical company that uses an operating lease, a company that uses a finance lease will *most likely* produce a reported return on equity (ROE) that:

    A. starts lower but rises during the life of the lease.

    B. starts higher but declines during the life of the lease.

    C. starts lower and remains so during the life of the lease.

17. For a lessor, the leased asset appears on the balance sheet and continues to be depreciated when the lease is classified as:

    A. a sales-type lease.

    B. an operating lease.

    C. a direct financing lease.

18. A lessor's reported revenues at lease inception will be *highest* if the lease is classified as:

    A. a sales-type lease.

    B. an operating lease.

    C. a direct financing lease.

19. The lessor will record interest income if the lease is classified as:

    A. sales-type only.

    B. direct financing only.

    C. either sales-type or direct financing.

20. Cavalier Copper Mines has $840 million in total liabilities and $520 million in shareholders' equity. It has disclosed $100 million in purchase commitments over the next five years. An analyst wishing to treat the purchase commitments as debt would calculate a debt to total capital ratio *closest to*:

    A. 0.58.

    B. 0.59.

    C. 0.64.

21. Charles McKimmon, CFA, is analyzing the financial statements of Computers On Credit, Inc. (COC). COC has sold $60 million of accounts receivable for proceeds of $50 million, and McKimmon wishes to treat the transaction as collateralized borrowing. McKimmon's financial statement adjustments will *most likely* include adding:

   A. $50 million to accounts receivable.

   B. $50 million to cash flows from financing activity.

   C. $50 million to cash flows from operating activity.

SOLUTIONS FOR READING 39

1. B is correct. The company receives $1 million in cash from investors at the time the bonds are issued. This is recorded as a financing activity.

2. A is correct. At the time of issue, both companies will record a $1,000,000 liability and cash from financing inflow. The income statement will reflect interest expense equal to the cash interest payments *plus* amortization of the initial discount. Because both companies received the same amount, the bonds issued at a discount will have a higher face value and higher periodic interest expense on the income statement. However, the amortization is a non-cash expense and will not appear on the statement of cash flows.

3. A is correct. In the United States, expenses incurred when issuing bonds are generally recorded as an asset and amortized to the related expense (legal, etc.) over the life of the bonds. The related cash flows are financing and operating activities, not investing activities.

4. B is correct. The bonds will be issued at a discount because the market interest rate is higher than the stated rate. Discounting the future payments to their present value indicates that at the time of issue the company will record $978,938 as both a liability and a cash inflow from financing activities. During the year, the company will pay a cash outflow from operating activities of $55,000 related to the interest payment, but interest expense on the income statement will also reflect $3,736 related to amortization of the initial discount, for a total interest expense of $58,736. The value of the liability at 31 December 2008 will reflect the initial value plus the amortized discount, for a total of $982,674.

5. A is correct. The stated rate on the bonds is higher than the market rate, which indicates the bonds will be issued at a premium. Taking the present value of each payment indicates an issue date value of $10,210,618. The interest expense is determined by multiplying the book value at the beginning of the period ($10,210,618) by the market interest rate at the time of issue (6.0 percent) for an interest expense of $612,637. The value after one year will equal the beginning value less the amortized premium, which is the difference between the amount paid ($650,000) and the expense accrued ($612,637) or $37,363. $10,210,618 − $37,363 = $10,173,255 or $10.17 million.

6. A is correct. Both bonds will add $10 million to debt and nothing to equity, and thus have the same effect on the debt/equity ratio at the time they are issued. However, the value of the liability for zero-coupon bonds increases as the discount is amortized over time while the liability will not change for the par bonds. Furthermore, the amortized interest will reduce earnings at an increasing rate over time as the value of the liability increases. Higher relative debt and lower relative equity (through retained earnings) will cause the debt/equity ratio to increase as the zero-coupon bonds approach maturity, compared to the bonds issued at par.

7. A is correct. When interest rates rise, bonds decline in value. Thus, the book value of the bonds being carried on the balance sheet is higher than the market value. The company could repurchase the bonds for less than book value, so the economic liabilities are overestimated. Because the bonds are fixed rates, there is no effect on interest coverage.

International Financial Statement Analysis, by Thomas R. Robinson, CFA, Jan Hendrik van Greuning, CFA, R. Elaine Henry, CFA, and Michael A. Broihahn, CFA. Copyright © 2008 by CFA Institute. Reprinted with permission.

8. C is correct. Covenants protect debtholders from excessive risk-taking, typically by limiting the issuer's ability to use cash or by limiting the overall levels of debt relative to income and equity. Issuing additional equity would increase the company's ability to meet its obligations, so debtholders would not restrict that ability.

9. B is correct. Because convertible bonds have characteristics of both debt and equity, at times it can be appropriate to treat it as debt, equity, or both. Because it is already classified as debt, adjusting debt but not adjusting equity would have the effect of ignoring it altogether. Such treatment would be inappropriate.

10. B is correct. If the bonds are converted, liabilities decrease by the book value of the bonds and equity increases by the same amount.

11. C is correct. If the current market price is significantly above the conversion price, the bonds are more likely to be converted into equity than redeemed at face value. Therefore, it would be appropriate to treat the bonds as equity.

12. A is correct. If converted, debt would decrease by $200 million and equity would increase by the same amount. The resulting debt-to-equity ratio would be $200/$500 = 0.40.

13. C is correct. Assets held under a synthetic lease enjoy the tax benefits of ownership (depreciation expense) but are not held as assets or liabilities on the financial statements.

14. B is correct. An operating lease is not recorded on the balance sheet (debt is lower), and lease payments are entirely categorized as rent (interest expense is lower.) Because the rent expense is an operating outflow but principal repayments are financing cash flows, the operating lease will result in lower cash flow from operating activity.

15. A is correct. The finance leases are carried as liabilities in the amount of the present value of future minimum lease payments (equals the sum of future minimum lease payments *minus* the sum of amounts representing interest). Using the alternative shortcut approach shown in Example 12 (solution to 2), Xu could estimate the present value of the operating lease payments by multiplying the aggregate minimum future operating lease payments ($25 million) by the ratio of the present value of minimum finance lease payments ($20 million − $6 million = $14 million) to the undiscounted minimum finance lease payments ($20 million). The result is: ($14 million ÷ $20 million) × $25 million = $17.5 million.

16. A is correct. In the early years, a finance lease generally results in higher reported expenses, lower profitability, and a lower ROE. This difference reverses over the life of the lease such that finance leases will result in an ROE that rises over time and ends higher than would result if an operating lease were used.

17. B is correct. When a lease is classified as an operating lease, the underlying asset remains on the lessor's balance sheet. The lessor will record a depreciation expense that reduces the assets value over time.

18. A is correct. A sales-type lease treats the lease as a sale of the asset, and revenue is recorded at the time of sale equal to the present value of future lease payments. Under a direct financing lease, only interest income is reported as earned. Under an operating lease, revenue from rent is reported when collected.

19. C is correct. With an operating lease, all revenue is recorded as rental revenue. A portion of the payments for either direct financing or sales-type leases is reported as interest income.

20. C is correct. The current debt to total capital ratio is 840/(840 + 520) = 0.62. To adjust for the purchase commitments, an analyst should add 100 to both the numerator and denominator: 940/(940 + 520) = 0.64.

21. B is correct. McKinnon should add $60 million to accounts receivable, reduce cash from operating activities by $50 million, and increase cash from financing activities by $50 million.

STUDY SESSION 10
FINANCIAL REPORTING AND ANALYSIS:
Applications and International Standards Convergence

The readings in this study session discuss financial statement analysis applications and the international convergence of accounting standards.

The most frequently used tools and techniques to evaluate companies include common size analysis, cross-sectional analysis, trend analysis, and ratio analysis. Beyond mere knowledge of these tools, however, the analyst must recognize the implications of accounting choices on the quality of a company's reported financial results. Then the analyst can apply these financial analysis techniques to major analyst tasks including the evaluation of past and future financial performance, credit risk, and the screening of potential equity investments. The readings also discuss analyst adjustments to reported financials. Such adjustments are often needed to put companies' reported results on a comparable basis.

This study session concludes with a reading on convergence of international and U.S. accounting standards. Although there has been much progress in harmonizing accounting standards globally, as this reading discusses, significant variations still exist among generally accepted accounting principles from one country to another.

READING ASSIGNMENTS

FINANCIAL REPORTING QUALITY: RED FLAGS AND ACCOUNTING WARNING SIGNS

by Thomas R. Robinson, CFA and Paul Munter

LEARNING OUTCOMES

The candidate should be able to:	Mastery
a. describe incentives that might induce a company's management to overreport or underreport earnings;	☐
b. describe activities that will result in a low quality of earnings;	☐
c. describe the "fraud triangle";	☐
d. describe the risk factors that may lead to fraudulent accounting related to 1) incentives and pressures, 2) opportunities, and 3) attitudes and rationalizations;	☐
e. describe common accounting warning signs and methods for detecting each;	☐
f. describe the accounting warning signs related to the Enron accounting scandal;	☐
g. describe the accounting warning signs related to the Sunbeam accounting scandal.	☐

INTRODUCTION   1

Recent years have seen numerous accounting scandals, some resulting in bankruptcies and even the demise of a major CPA firm. Unfortunately, these scandals are not a new phenomenon. Looking back, we see that scandals such as these have occurred from time to time, in particular when there is a downturn in the economy and managers have felt pressure to meet market earnings expectations or debt covenants or to maintain or increase their personal wealth. By examining recent scandals, we can learn more about warning signs of danger and the techniques used to manipulate reported financial results.

This reading takes a look at red flags and aggressive accounting techniques that have resulted in a reduction of the financial reporting quality of corporate financial statements. Financial reporting quality goes beyond the traditional view of conservatism and earnings quality. Financial reporting quality relates the overall quality of the financial statements and related disclosures to ask how well the reported results fairly present the operations and financial position of a company. In the United States, audits are intended to ensure this fair presentation in accordance with U.S. generally accepted accounting principles (GAAP). Similarly, in the United Kingdom and in the international accounting standards (IAS), there is a desire to achieve a true and fair view of the company. Additionally, CEOs and CFOs of public companies are now required by Section 302 of the Sarbanes-Oxley Act (SOA) to provide quarterly certifications that the information included in Securities and Exchange Commission (SEC) filings represents a fair presentation of operations and financial position.[1]

This reading discusses financial reporting quality and activities that result in low financial reporting quality. We describe some prominent accounting scandals over the years, SEC studies, and related auditing literature to identify nonaccounting red flags that can be used to identify potential problem areas. We also discuss a variety of accounting warning signs, such as aggressive reporting of revenues or off-balance sheet activities. Finally, we show how the red flags can be applied to accounting scandals, using Enron and Sunbeam as examples.

2   FINANCIAL REPORTING QUALITY

The concept of financial reporting quality is not new. The Association for Investment Management and Research (AIMR) has periodically published surveys and other documents on the subject. In a recent survey, AIMR found that a vast majority of portfolio managers and securities analysts surveyed found corporate disclosures and the quality of financial reporting to be very important (43 percent), extremely important (30 percent), or somewhat important (22 percent). Unfortunately, on a 5.0-point scale, these same analysts rated public companies they follow on average 3.4 (C+).[2]

A principal concern of many users of financial statements has been whether or not earnings are overstated. There is a preference by some for the use of conservative accounting practices; those that result in lower earnings in early periods relative to later periods. This is certainly an important consideration, but it is not the only factor that should be used in evaluating financial reporting quality. Companies may be motivated to increase earnings in a particular period

---

[1] *See also* SEC Release No. 33-8124, *Certification of Disclosure in Companies' Quarterly and Annual Reports*, August 29, 2002.

[2] 2003 AIMR Member Survey of Global Corporate Financial Reporting Quality and Corporate Communications and Disclosure Practices, October 2003, www.aimr.org.

to meet analysts' earnings expectations, to meet debt covenants, or to improve incentive compensation. Importantly, management also may have incentives to lower reported earnings in a particular period. For example, management may be motivated to report lower earnings to obtain trade relief, negotiate lower payments to other counterparties from a prior business transaction, or negotiate concessions from unions or others.

In addition to making sure earnings are presented fairly, it also is important that the financial position of the company is presented fairly, particularly from the standpoint of creditors. Just as management might be motivated to overstate earnings, it may have an incentive to overstate assets or understate liabilities to make the company's financial position appear to be more solvent. Conversely, management may want to understate assets to improve certain ratios, such as return on assets. Likewise, it may want to appear less solvent in a quest to negotiate concessions from creditors, vendors, and employees.

The quality of reported cash flow is another factor that needs to be examined. In some recent scandals, companies have been creative in generating operating cash flow from borrowing activities.[3] Financial disclosures or lack thereof also are important.[4] For example, when a company enters into a guarantee to others, this is an obligation that is important to creditors. Some guarantees are required to be measured and reported on the balance sheet as a liability. Other guarantees are not required to be measured and reported, but must be disclosed.[5] Clearly, the adequacy of these disclosures affects financial reporting quality.

Further, a simultaneous examination of all of the financial statements is a useful tool in detecting financial irregularities. For example, a combination of increasing earnings and decreasing operating cash flow may indicate aggressive reporting of earnings. Similarly, fraudulent activities to inflate sales and understate expenses generally lead to a buildup in assets on the balance sheet (often assets, such as receivables and inventory, but, as in the case of WorldCom, it can involve long-lived assets, as well).

We define high financial reporting quality as overall financial reporting, including disclosures, which results in a fair presentation of a company's operations (including both earnings and cash flow) and financial position. Low financial reporting quality, on the other hand, can result from a variety of activities, including the following:

▶ Following GAAP but selecting alternatives within GAAP that bias or distort reported results to achieve a desired outcome (e.g., selecting a depreciation method that results in higher earnings than the economic depreciation of the assets warrant).

▶ Using loopholes or bright-lines in accounting principles (e.g., the lessee has a capital lease if the present value of the lease payments is 90 percent or more of the fair value of the property) to structure transactions to achieve a desired outcome that differs from the economic structure of the transaction (e.g., that allows a lessor to structure a lease solely to qualify for immediate sales treatment while still allowing the lessee to treat it as an off-balance sheet arrangement).

---

[3] See, e.g., SEC Accounting and Auditing Enforcement Release No. 1631, *In the Matter of Dynegy, Inc.*, September 24, 2002.

[4] See, e.g., SEC Accounting and Auditing Enforcement Release No. 1555, *In the Matter of Edison Schools, Inc.*, May 14, 2002, in which the SEC determined that, even though the company's accounting was appropriate, its disclosures were lacking.

[5] See SEC Release No. 33-8182, *Disclosure in Management's Discussion and Analysis about Off-Balance Sheet Arrangements and Aggregate Contractual Obligations*, January 27, 2003.

► Using unrealistic or inappropriate estimates and assumptions to achieve a desired outcome (e.g., using extraordinarily long depreciable lives for assets or unrealistically optimistic assumptions about collectibility of receivables and loans).

► Stretching accounting principles to achieve a desired outcome (e.g., using a narrowly defined rule on consolidation of special-purpose entities (SPEs) for a leasing transaction to justify nonconsolidation of SPEs in other types of transactions).

► Engaging in fraudulent financial reporting. Rather than low financial reporting quality, this category actually has no financial reporting quality.

3 RED FLAGS AND ACCOUNTING WARNING SIGNS

The auditing literature can help an analyst, creditor, or investor to begin to identify red flags. In October 2002, the American Institute of Certified Public Accountants (AICPA) published the Statement on Auditing Standards (SAS) No. 99, *Consideration of Fraud in a Financial Statement Audit* (SAS-99). SAS-99 warns practitioners to be alert for the "fraud triangle," or three conditions that are generally present when fraud occurs:

1. *Incentives or pressures* exist that can lead to fraudulent financial reporting, such as pressure to meet debt covenants or analysts' earnings expectations.

2. *Opportunities* to commit fraud exist, such as poor internal control.

3. The individuals themselves are able to *rationalize* their behavior, such as a desire to get the company through a difficult time, after which they plan to undo their accounting games.

Management has a unique ability to perpetrate fraud because it frequently is in a position to directly or indirectly manipulate accounting records and present fraudulent financial information. Fraudulent financial reporting often involves management override of controls that otherwise may appear to be operating effectively. Management can either direct employees to perpetrate fraud or solicit help in carrying it out. In addition, management personnel at a component of the entity may be in a position to manipulate the accounting records of the component in a manner that causes a material misstatement in the consolidated financial statements of the entity. Management override of controls can occur in unpredictable ways.

SAS-99 provides examples of fraud risk factors for each of the conditions of the fraud triangle, as set forth in Exhibits 1, 2, and 3. While these were written with auditors in mind, analysts and others can easily use them as red flags. For example, as shown in Exhibit 3, one risk factor is disputes with auditors. Significant disputes must be reported to the company's audit committee and in SEC filings so that the audit committee and analysts can have access to information for this red flag.

It is important that we learn from previous scandals. In fact, there is much to be learned from reviewing prior accounting scandals. Such postmortem reviews can be very useful in identifying common accounting warning signs that can serve as contemporaneous red flags that help auditors, analysts, and others identify future fraud schemes. In response to the mandate of Section 704 of the SOA, the SEC conducted a study to examine the root causes of recent enforcement actions.[6] In addition, the AICPA and others have examined the frequency of

---

[6] SEC, *Report Pursuant to Section 704 of the Sarbanes-Oxley Act of 2002*, January 2003.

EXHIBIT 1	Risk Factors Related to Incentives/Pressures

▶ Financial stability or profitability is threatened by economic, industry, or entity operating conditions, such as (or as indicated by):

  ▶ high degree of competition or market saturation, accompanied by declining margins

  ▶ high vulnerability to rapid changes, such as changes in technology, product obsolescence, or interest rates

  ▶ significant declines in customer demand and increasing business failures in either the industry or overall economy

  ▶ operating losses making the threat of bankruptcy, foreclosure, or hostile takeover imminent

  ▶ recurring negative cash flows from operations or an inability to generate cash flows from operations while reporting earnings and earnings growth

  ▶ rapid growth or unusual profitability, especially compared to that of other companies in the same industry

  ▶ new accounting, statutory, or regulatory requirements

▶ Excessive pressure exists for management to meet the requirements or expectations of third parties due to the following:

  ▶ profitability or trend-level expectations of investment analysts, institutional investors, significant creditors, or other external parties (particularly expectations that are unduly aggressive or unrealistic), including expectations created by management in, for example, overly optimistic press releases or annual report messages

  ▶ need to obtain additional debt or equity financing to stay competitive—including financing of major research and development or capital expenditures

  ▶ marginal ability to meet exchange listing requirements or debt repayment or other debt covenant requirements

  ▶ perceived or real adverse effects of reporting poor financial results on significant pending transactions, such as business combinations or contract awards

▶ Information available indicates that management or the board of directors' personal financial situation is threatened by the entity's financial performance arising from the following:

  ▶ significant financial interests in the entity

  ▶ significant portions of their compensation (e.g., bonuses, stock options, and earn-out arrangements) being contingent upon achieving aggressive targets for stock price, operating results, financial position, or cash flow

  ▶ personal guarantees of debts of the entity

▶ There is excessive pressure on management or operating personnel to meet financial targets set up by the board of directors or management, including sales or profitability incentive goals.

Source: AICPA, SAS No. 99, Consideration of Fraud in a Financial Statement Audit, October 2002.

EXHIBIT 2	Risk Factors Related to Opportunities

▶ The nature of the industry or the entity's operations provides opportunities to engage in fraudulent financial reporting that can arise from the following:

   ▶ significant related-party transactions not in the ordinary course of business or with related entities not audited or audited by another firm

   ▶ a strong financial presence or ability to dominate a certain industry sector that allows the entity to dictate terms or conditions to suppliers or customers that may result in inappropriate or non-arm's-length transactions

   ▶ assets, liabilities, revenues, or expenses based on significant estimates that involve subjective judgments or uncertainties that are difficult to corroborate

   ▶ significant, unusual, or highly complex transactions, especially those close to period end that pose difficult "substance over form" questions

   ▶ significant operations located or conducted across international borders in jurisdictions where differing business environments and cultures exist

   ▶ significant bank accounts or subsidiary or branch operations in tax-haven jurisdictions for which there appear to be no clear business justification

▶ There is ineffective monitoring of management as a result of the following:

   ▶ domination of management by a single person or small group (in a non-owner-managed business) without compensating controls

   ▶ ineffective board of directors or audit committee oversight over the financial reporting process and internal control

▶ There is a complex or unstable organizational structure, as evidenced by the following:

   ▶ difficulty in determining the organization or individuals that have controlling interest in the entity

   ▶ overly complex organizational structure involving unusual legal entities or managerial lines of authority

   ▶ high turnover of senior management, counsel, or board members

▶ Internal control components are deficient as a result of the following:

   ▶ inadequate monitoring of controls, including automated controls and controls over interim financial reporting (when external reporting is required)

   ▶ high turnover rates or employment of ineffective accounting, internal audit, or information technology staff

   ▶ ineffective accounting and information systems, including situations involving reportable conditions

---

Source: AICPA, SAS No. 99, Consideration of Fraud in a Financial Statement Audit, October 2002.

---

financial statement restatements by SEC registrants in recent years. Those studies show a disturbing trend of steadily increasing restatements:

▶ 157 in 2000;

▶ 270 in 2001;

▶ 330 in 2002;

▶ more than 350 in 2003 (as of September 30).

EXHIBIT 3	Risk Factors Related to Attitudes/ Rationalizations

Risk factors reflective of attitudes/rationalizations by board members, management, or employees that allow them to engage in and/or justify fraudulent financial reporting may not be susceptible to observation by the auditor. Nevertheless, the auditor who becomes aware of the existence of such information should consider it in identifying the risks of material misstatement arising from fraudulent financial reporting. For example, auditors may become aware of the following information that may indicate a risk factor:

- ineffective communication, implementation, support, or enforcement of the entity's values or ethical standards by management or the communication of inappropriate values or ethical standards

- nonfinancial management's excessive participation in or preoccupation with the selection of accounting principles or the determination of significant estimates

- known history of violations of securities laws or other laws and regulations or claims against the entity, its senior management, or board members alleging fraud or violations of laws and regulations

- excessive interest by management in maintaining or increasing the entity's stock price or earnings trend

- a practice by management of committing to analysts, creditors, and other third parties to achieve aggressive or unrealistic forecasts

- management failing to correct known reportable conditions on a timely basis

- an interest by management in employing inappropriate means to minimize reported earnings for tax-motivated reasons

- recurring attempts by management to justify marginal or inappropriate accounting on the basis of materiality

- the relationship between management and the current or predecessor auditor is strained, as exhibited by the following:

  - frequent disputes with the current or predecessor auditor on accounting, auditing, or reporting matters

  - unreasonable demands on the auditor, such as unreasonable time constraints regarding the completion of the audit or the issuance of the auditor's report

  - formal or informal restrictions on the auditor that inappropriately limit access to people or information or the ability to communicate effectively with the board of directors or audit committee

  - domineering management behavior in dealing with the auditor, especially involving attempts to influence the scope of the auditor's work or the selection or continuance of personnel assigned to or consulted on the audit engagement

Source: AICPA, SAS No. 99, Consideration of Fraud in a Financial Statement Audit, October 2002.

The SEC study, *Report Pursuant to Section 704 of the Sarbanes-Oxley Act of 2002*, reviews 515 enforcement actions between July 31, 1997, and July 30, 2002. The study classified improper accounting practices into four categories:

1. Improper revenue recognition (126 cases), including reporting revenue in advance through techniques, such as holding the accounting period open, billing without shipping (bill and hold), fictitious revenue, and improper valuation of revenue.

2. Improper expense recognition (101 cases), including improper capitalization, overstating inventory, understating bad debts/loan losses, improper use of restructuring reserves, and failure to record asset impairments.

3. Improper accounting in connection with business combinations (23 cases).

4. Other accounting and reporting issues (130 cases), including inadequate disclosures, failure to disclose related party transactions, inappropriate accounting for nonmonetary and round-trip transactions, improper accounting for foreign payments in violation of the Foreign Corrupt Practices Act, improper use of off-balance sheet arrangements, and improper use of non-GAAP financial measures.

Based on these studies and a review of accounting scandals, several common accounting warning signs are apparent:

▶ **Aggressive revenue recognition**. More than half of the restatements and SEC enforcement cases involve inappropriate revenue recognition practices. Companies are required to disclose in the financial statement footnotes their revenue recognition practices. These disclosures and any other information available about a company's revenue recognition policies should be scrutinized. Aggressive techniques are those that result in the reporting of revenue earlier than may be appropriate (even though they may not technically violate GAAP). These include:

  ▶ Bill-and-hold sales arrangements (invoicing a sale without shipping merchandise);

  ▶ Sales-type leases (lessor reporting leases as a sale, particularly when the lessee is treating the transaction as an operating lease);

  ▶ Recording revenue at the time a contract is signed but before delivery of goods or services;

  ▶ Recording revenue prior to fulfilling all of the terms of contracts (e.g., installation or verification that computer equipment/software is functioning according to contract terms); and

  ▶ Using swaps or barter arrangements to generate sales.

▶ **Operating cash flow out of line with reported earnings**. If a company is reporting positive and perhaps growing earnings but operating cash flow is negative or declining, this could indicate accounting irregularities. A cash flow earnings index (operating cash flow divided by net income) is useful in identifying potential problems (a ratio consistently below 1.0 or a ratio that is declining from one period to the next).

▶ **Growth in revenues out of sync with economy, industry, or peer companies and with growth in receivables**. If a company is reporting high revenue growth that is inconsistent with other companies in its industry or peer group, this could be the result of superior management or products, but also could indicate that the analyst should pay close attention to the quality of these revenues. Particular attention should be paid when receivables are growing faster than revenues or days' receivables are increasing over time. This could indicate nonexistent sales.

▶ **Growth in inventory out of line with sales growth or days inventory increasing over time**. This could indicate problems with:

　　▶ inventory management;

　　▶ potentially obsolete inventory; or, in some cases

　　▶ inappropriate overstatement of inventory to increase gross and net profits.

▶ **Classification of nonoperating or nonrecurring income as revenue**. Some companies may attempt to move income items up the income statement to mask deteriorating revenues or show higher revenue growth.

▶ **Deferral of expenses**. The accounting policies of a company may indicate that current expenditures are being capitalized and deferred to future years through amortization or some other means (e.g., WorldCom). It is important to identify if this is a common industry practice or if the company is boosting current period profits. This often results in an increase in assets with terms, such as "deferred customer acquisition costs," so any assets that appear unusual also can be scrutinized to identify this activity.

▶ **Excessive use of operating leases by lessees**. While there are legitimate reasons for leasing assets and use of leasing does not violate GAAP, some companies structure equipment acquisitions in the form of operating leases to achieve desirable financial ratios (low debt ratios, higher return on assets). If a company is using these to a greater extent than its peers, this is a potential red flag. It is usually best to adjust the financial statements to see what the ratios would look like if the equipment had been purchased.

▶ **Classification of expenses or losses as extraordinary or nonrecurring**. While some companies try to move income up the income statement to report certain gains as revenues, the opposite occurs for expenses. If a company has "special" charges year after year, it is usually best to classify them as ordinary operating expenses for evaluation purposes.

▶ **LIFO liquidations**. For companies using the last-in, first-out (LIFO) method of inventory, they can get an artificial boost to earnings by running the inventory balance low at year-end. Unfortunately, this results in a higher tax bill. This red flag can be identified by reviewing the inventory footnotes for a decline in the LIFO reserve.

▶ **Gross margins or operating margins out of line with peer companies**. While indicative of good management and cost control, this also can indicate that accounting methods are being selected to improve financial results relative to peers. It is useful to compare the accounting methods in the footnotes to see if they are more or less conservative than peer companies. This also could indicate use of other techniques described previously, such as overstatement of inventory or capitalization of costs.

▶ **Use of long useful lives for depreciation and amortization**. These should be compared with other peer companies to see if they are reasonable.

▶ **Use of aggressive pension plan assumptions**. This can result in a misstatement of both earnings and financial leverage. Particularly watch for high discount rates (lowers pension expense and liability) and high expected return on plan assets (lowers pension expense).

EXHIBIT 5	Enron 10K, 2000 (Summary of Footnote 19)	
Quarter	1999 (Millions)	2000 (Millions)
First	$7,632	$13,145
Second	9,672	16,886
Third	11,835	30,007
Fourth	10,973	40,751
Total	$40,112	$100,789

movements are recognized as "Other Revenues." Changes in the assets and liabilities from price risk management activities result primarily from changes in the valuation of the portfolio of contracts, newly originated transactions and the timing of settlement relative to the receipt of cash for certain contracts. The market prices used to value these transactions reflect management's best estimate considering various factors including closing exchange and over-the-counter quotations, time value and volatility factors underlying the commitments.

The use of the mark-to-market method for other types of contracts is somewhat unusual and presents ample opportunities to report revenues and income in any amount that management desires. The bankruptcy examiner's report notes that at least one analyst raised this issue as early as 1999. The analyst pointed out that Enron could recognize revenue from projects before they became operational, and this front-end loading of revenue and profits was limited only by Enron's "financial engineering skills."[11] The market-to-market gains were reported as other revenue on Enron's income statement as follows:

► 1998: $4,045 million
► 1999: $5,338 million
► 2000: $7,232 million

These amounts exceeded 10 percent of total revenues in 1998 and 1999. Further, without these "other revenues," operating income would have been negative. Enron's risk-management activities were reported as part of its wholesale services business segment, which comprised $94,906 million of revenue out of Enron's total revenue of $100,789 million. Adding to the red flags concerning revenue is the quarterly revenue reported in footnote 19 of Form 10K, as shown in Exhibit 5. In 2000, a disproportionate amount of revenues were reported in the third and fourth quarters, which is out of line with the seasonal trend.

Enron also engaged in securitizations of assets in its so-called price-risk-management business. In some cases, these resulted in sales to SPEs of assets with inflated values, which were really financing-type activities. In one case, Enron reported a gain on the sale of a portion of a joint venture with a major video rental company, when the technology for the venture did not exist.[12]

---

[11] Second Interim Report of Neal Batson, Court Appointed Examiner, US Bankruptcy Court, Southern District of New York, January 21, 2003, p. 26, discussing June 1999 report of JPMorgan.
[12] Id at pp. 29–31.

Enron's footnotes indicate that in some cases Enron effectively protected investors in these SPEs from risk:[13]

> Securitizations. From time to time, Enron sells interests in certain of its financial assets. Some of these sales are completed in securitizations, in which Enron concurrently enters into swaps associated with the underlying assets which limits the risks assumed by the purchaser. Such swaps are adjusted to fair value using quoted market prices, if available, or estimated fair value based on management's best estimate of the present value of future cash flow. These swaps are included in Price Risk Management activities above as equity investments. During 2000, gains from sales representing securitizations were $381 million and proceeds were $2,379 million ($545 million of the proceeds related to sales to Whitewing Associates, L.P.).

Assets related to price-risk-management activities when mark-to-market accounting was used increased drastically on the balance sheet during 2000 by $15,872 million. The scope and unusual accounting for these transactions should have been cause for concern.

Enron extended its mark-to-market accounting to equity-method investments. As noted previously, the equity method enables companies to keep assets and liabilities off of the balance sheet. Under the equity method of accounting, Enron should report its percentage share of GAAP income on its income statements. Enron, however, used the market-value method for some equity investees.[14]

> Investments in Unconsolidated Affiliates. Investments in unconsolidated affiliates are accounted for by the equity method, except for certain investments resulting from Enron's merchant investment activities which are included at market value in "Other Investments" in the Consolidated Balance Sheet.

Overall, Enron's disclosures of significant equity-method investment are another red flag, particularly since the income-sharing ratios differ from the voting interests and some entities were valued at fair value, as shown in Exhibit 6.[15]

Enron's net trade receivables on the balance sheet grew from $3,030 million in 1999 to $10,396 million in 2000. The allowance for doubtful accounts grew from $40 million to only $130 million, which calls into question the quality of the receivables and underlying revenues. Other transactions, such as barter of cable capacity, are also recorded, but probably the most disturbing disclosure is that about related-party transactions:

Related Party Transactions

In 2000 and 1999, Enron entered into transactions with limited partnerships (the Related Party) whose general partner's managing member is a senior officer of Enron. The limited partners of the Related Party are unrelated to Enron. Management believes that the terms of the transactions with the Related Party were reasonable compared to those which could have been negotiated with unrelated third parties.

---

[13] Enron, Form 10K, December 31, 2000, n.3.

[14] *Id.* at n.1.

[15] *Id.* at n.9.

EXHIBIT 6	Enron Annual Report, 2000 (Unconsolidated Equity Affiliates)

Enron's investment in and advances to unconsolidated affiliates that are accounted for by the equity method is as follows (in millions):

	Net Voting Interest[a]	December 31, 2000	December 31, 1999
Azurix Corp.	34%	$ 325	$ 762
Bridgeline Holdings	40%	229	—
Citrus Corp.	50%	530	480
Dabhol Power Company	50%	693	466
Joint Energy Development Investments L.P. (JEDI)[b]	50%	399	211
Joint Energy Development Investments II L.P. (JEDI II)[b]	50%	220	162
SK—Enron Co. Ltd.	50%	258	269
Transportadora de Gas del Sur S.A.	35%	479	452
Whitewing Associates, L.P.[b]	50%	558	662
Other		1,603	1,572
		$5,294	$5,036

[a] Certain investments have income sharing ratios that differ from Enron's voting interests.
[b] JEDI and JEDI II account for their investments at fair value. Whitewing accounts for certain of its investments at fair value. These affiliates held fair value investments totaling $1,823 million and $1,128 million, respectively, at December 31, 2000, and 1999.

In 2000, Enron entered into transactions with the Related Party to hedge certain merchant investments and other assets. As part of the transactions, Enron i) contributed to newly-formed entities (the Entities) assets valued at approximately $1.2 billion, including $150 million in Enron notes payable, 3.7 million restricted shares of outstanding Enron common stock and the right to receive up to 18.0 million shares of outstanding Enron common stock in March 2003 (subject to certain conditions) and ii) transferred to the Entities assets valued at approximately $309 million, including a $50 million note payable and an investment in an entity that indirectly holds warrants convertible into common stock of an Enron equity method investee. In return, Enron received economic interests in the Entities, $309 million in notes receivable, of which $259 million is recorded at Enron's carryover basis of zero, and a special distribution from the Entities in the form of $1.2 billion in notes receivable, subject to changes in the principal for amounts payable by Enron in connection with the execution of additional derivative instruments. Cash in these Entities of $172.6 million is invested in Enron demand notes. In addition, Enron paid $123 million to purchase share-settled options from the Entities on 21.7 million shares of Enron common stock. The Entities paid Enron $10.7 million to terminate the share-settled options on 14.6 million shares of Enron common stock outstanding. In late 2000,

Enron entered into share-settled collar arrangements with the Entities on 15.4 million shares of Enron common stock. Such arrangements will be accounted for as equity transactions when settled.

In 2000, Enron entered into derivative transactions with the Entities with a combined notional amount of approximately $2.1 billion to hedge certain merchant investments and other assets. Enron's notes receivable balance was reduced by $36 million as a result of premiums owed on derivative transactions. Enron recognized revenues of approximately $500 million related to the subsequent change in the market value of these derivatives, which offset market value changes of certain merchant investments and price risk management activities. In addition, Enron recognized $44.5 million and $14.1 million of interest income and interest expense, respectively, on the notes receivable from and payable to the Entities.

It appears that the assets of this related party consisted primarily of receivables from Enron and other Enron securities. Further, Enron engaged in billions of dollars of "derivatives" transactions with the related party. We have only included a portion of the related-party disclosure here. The footnotes go on to describe sales of assets to the related parties on which revenues and income were recognized. This type of self-dealing amounting to billions of dollars is what ultimately led to the collapse of Enron when potential write-downs related to these activities were announced in October 2001.

There were ample red flags outside of SEC filings. In May 2001, Enron's vice chairman resigned; in August 2001, the president resigned. The proxy statement shows that top management pay was largely from bonus and stock awards. The chairman of the board, for example, received more than 90 percent of his compensation from bonus and stock awards and only a small portion from salary.

ACCOUNTING SCANDALS: SUNBEAM   5

As noted previously, the most common improper accounting techniques have involved the recognition of revenue. Sunbeam provides a good case study in accelerating revenue and the accounting warning signs that indicate its presence. In July 1996, Sunbeam's board of directors hired Albert J. Dunlap to turn the company around. According to the SEC, Dunlap and his colleagues engaged in a variety of improper activities to achieve promised sales and earnings targets, as well as to increase the stock price for a sale of the company.[16] The SEC charged that Sunbeam in 1996, 1997, and the first quarter of 1998:

► created "cookie jar" reserves in 1996 to draw on in future years to improve earnings;

► recorded revenue from contingent sales;

► accelerated sales from later periods into the present quarter;

► used improper bill-and-hold transactions.

---

[16] SEC Release No. 2001-49, *SEC Sues Former CEO, CFO, Other Top Former Officers of Sunbeam Corporation in Massive Financial Fraud,* May 15, 2001.

EXHIBIT 7	Sunbeam (Relative Growth in Sales, Receivables, and Inventory)	
	1996	**1997**
Sales	−3.21%	18.69%
Inventory	−22.41%	57.89%
Receivables	−1.28%	38.47%

To uncover accounting warning signs, we examined financial data reported in Sunbeam's Form 10K for 1996 and 1997. As noted previously, increases in sales, receivables, and inventory should generally be in line. Exhibit 7 shows the relative growth in these amounts for Sunbeam for 1996 and 1997.

Note that for 1996, when the new management came in, sales declined slightly, as did receivables. This relationship would be expected. The larger decline in inventory is not usual. It is potentially the result of restructuring charges taken by new management in 1996, as shown in Exhibit 8.[17]

These are the cookie jar reserves referred to by the SEC. By expensing these in 1996, Sunbeam recorded a loss in the current year but set the stage for increasing income in future years. For example, if the cost of sales write-off included some write-offs of inventory, the company would have a higher profit when that inventory was sold in future years. The increase in revenues in 1997 is about 19 percent, but receivables increased by 38 percent, calling into question the quality of both the receivables and sales. Further, the increase in inventory is out of line at 58 percent, which could result from the prior year write-off and subsequent return to more normal levels. It could also indicate an overstatement of inventory to boost profits. The company reported an increase in gross margin in 1997 in spite of the need for a turnaround of the business.

Another indicator of problems with sales and cookie jar reserves is an examination of Sunbeam's cash flow compiled from Form 10K filings, as shown in Exhibit 9. The relationship of net income and operating cash flow in 1994 and 1995 is not unusual. In 1996, net income is a large negative number, yet operating cash flow is positive. The primary reason for this is the large noncash restructuring charges, which reduced 1996 income but not cash flow. In 1997, net income reached record levels for recent years, yet operating cash flow was

EXHIBIT 8	Sunbeam (Restructuring Charges, 1996)
	Pretax Dollar Amount
Restructuring, Impairment, and Other Costs	$154.9
Cost of Sales	92.3
Selling, General, and Administrative	42.5
Estimated Loss from Discontinued Operations	47.9
Total	**$337.6**

---

[17] Sunbeam, Form 10K, 1996, p. 14.

EXHIBIT 9	Sunbeam (Cash Flow Compiled from Form 10K Filings)			
Thousands of Dollars	**1994**	**1995**	**1996**	**1997**
Net Income	107,011	50,511	(228,262)	109,415
Operating Cash Flow	80,835	81,516	14,163	(8,249)

negative. This was primarily due to the increase in receivables and inventory. The difference would have been greater if not for a sale of receivables that increased operating cash flow by $59 million in 1997.[18]

An additional warning sign comes in a change in the company's revenue recognition policy footnote from 1996 to 1997:

▶ 1996: "The Company recognizes revenue from product sales at the time of shipment. Net sales is comprised of gross sales less provisions for expected customer returns, discounts, promotional allowances and cooperative advertising."

▶ 1997: "The Company recognizes revenues from product sales principally at the time of shipment to customers. In limited circumstances, at the customers' request, the Company may sell seasonal product on a bill and hold basis provided that the goods are completed, packaged and ready for shipment, such goods are segregated and the risks of ownership and legal title have passed to the customer. The amount of such bill and hold sales at December 29, 1997, was approximately 3 percent of consolidated revenues. Net sales is comprised of gross sales less provisions for expected customer returns, discounts, promotional allowances and cooperative advertising."

Further, it appears that the company reduced its bad-debt reserves relative to the increase in receivables. The allowance for doubtful accounts only increased about $1 million from 1996 to 1997, in spite of the large increase in receivables ($82 million). The company's bad-debt expense was about $23.4 million in 1996, but only 8.4 million in 1997.[19]

The company reports in its footnotes that its business is not seasonal, stating:[20]

On a consolidated basis, Sunbeam sales do not exhibit substantial seasonality. However, sales of outdoor cooking products are strongest in the first half of the year, while sales of appliances and personal care and comfort products are strongest in the second half of the year. In addition, sales of a number of the Company's products, including warming blankets, vaporizers, humidifiers and grills may be impacted by unseasonable weather conditions. During 1997, the Company initiated early buy programs for highly seasonal products such as grills and warming blankets in order to more levelize production and distribution activities.

---

[18] Sunbeam, Form 10K, 1997, p. 18.

[19] *Id.* at p. F-29.

[20] *Id.* at p. 6.

EXHIBIT 10	Sunbeam (Fourth-Quarter Sales Boost Suggests Aggressive Revenue Recognition)	
Percentage of Revenue in Each Quarter	**1996**	**1997**
First Quarter	23.34%	21.70%
Second Quarter	25.80%	24.62%
Third Quarter	23.55%	24.74%
Fourth Quarter	27.31%	28.94%

This provides a hint about the use of aggressive techniques to accelerate revenue into the fourth quarter. Exhibit 10 was compiled from quarterly disclosures in Sunbeam's 1996 and 1997 Form 10K filings. The increase in fourth-quarter revenues in a nonseasonal business is a warning sign.

6   BE ALERT FOR WARNING SIGNS

Studies of prior accounting scandals give us clues to evaluating other companies. While companies may look for more sophisticated methods to manage earnings, many of the recent scandals have involved the same techniques employed in the early years of U.S. capital markets. For example, in the 1930s, McKesson & Robbins created fictitious revenues, overstating receivables and inventory. In the 1980s, Crazy Eddie, Inc., engaged in much the same activities as did Sunbeam in the 1990s. Being alert for red flags that have occurred in past accounting scandals can help to identify potential problems early.

PRACTICE PROBLEM FOR READING 40

1. The accounting warning signs of early revenue recognition for Sunbeam included:

    A.   significant sales to related parties.

    B.   the use of bill-and-hold transactions.

    C.   the use of marked-to-market method for contracts.

SOLUTION FOR READING 40

1. B is correct. Sunbeam used bill-and-hold transactions. Enron used the other two methods.

ACCOUNTING SHENANIGANS ON THE CASH FLOW STATEMENT

by Marc A. Siegel

LEARNING OUTCOMES

The candidate should be able to analyze and discuss the following ways to manipulate the cash flow statement:

Mastery
☐

► stretching out payables,

► financing of payables,

► securitization of receivables, and

► using stock buybacks to offset dilution of earnings.

INTRODUCTION   1

CPAs typically focus on uncovering items that would impact the reported earnings or the balance sheet of a company. Knowing that investors use the balance sheet and the income statement to make investment decisions, companies sometimes engage in unusual or aggressive accounting practices in order to flatter their reported figures, especially earnings.

In the wake of recent high-profile scandals, the landscape is beginning to change. The majority of investors are now keenly aware of the concept of quality of earnings. It is now fairly common knowledge in the investment community that corporate management can in various ways manipulate earnings as reflected on the income statement. As a result, certain investors shun reported earnings and instead focus more attention on other metrics to evaluate the operational health of a business. Some metrics are non-GAAP, such as backlog, same-store

Marc A. Siegel, CPA, is director of research of the Center for Financial Research & Analysis (www.cfraonline.com).

sales, and bookings. Many analysts have also embraced cash flow measurements. These analysts believe that, notwithstanding the fraud at Parmalat Finanziaria SpA, cash cannot be manipulated. But this, too, is a misconception. While quality of earnings is now a buzzword, it may be another 10 years before it is as widely understood that the quality of cash flows is just as valid a concern.

Most conceptual definitions of materiality include the concept of factors that affect an investment decision. As Wall Street analysts have lost faith in earnings-based metrics in the wake of Enron, WorldCom, and others, many have gravitated toward the cash flow statement. Companies are regularly evaluated on the basis of free cash flow yield and other measures of cash generation. The focus of audits must change in order to devote more attention to the cash flow statement; the users of financial statements demand it.

2   DISPELLING THE MYTH ABOUT CASH FLOWS

Investors' increased focus on the cash flow statement is beneficial. Analyzing the cash flow statement is integral to understanding a company's financial performance and position because it often provides a check to the quality of the earnings shown in the income statement. Certain accounting shenanigans can, however, either artificially boost reported operating cash flow or present unsustainable cash flows. The increased scrutiny has alerted people to how some companies mask declines in operating cash flow. For example, after WorldCom's reverse-engineering subterfuge, many have learned to look for excessive capitalization of cash expenditures. Others now scrutinize the cash flow statement for nonrecurring sources of cash, such as the receipt of an income tax refund. Certain complex situations can arise that cause reported cash flow from operations to appear higher than it would have otherwise.

As the investment community begins to focus on this metric, auditors should adapt as well. Auditors have little to work with, however; only SFAS 95, Statement of Cash Flows, specifically addresses the cash flow statement, and only 15 paragraphs within SFAS 95 discuss the appropriate categorization of cash expenditures within the cash flow statement. On the other hand, a plethora of authoritative guidance surrounds the calculation and presentation of earnings. The following examples show how companies can employ certain techniques (many of which are within GAAP) to show improved reported cash flows.

3   STRETCHING OUT PAYABLES

The simplest thing that companies can do to improve reported operating cash flow is to slow down the rate of payments to their vendors. Extending out vendors used to be interpreted as a sign that a company was beginning to struggle with its cash generation. Companies now "spin" this as a prudent cash-management strategy. Another consequence of this policy is to boost the reported growth in cash flows from operations. In other words, reported operating cash flows can be improved due solely to a change in policy to slow the payment rate to vendors. If analysts or investors expect the current period improvement to continue, they may be mistaken; vendors will eventually put increasing pressure on the company to pay more timely. Therefore, any benefit may be unsustainable or, at minimum, any year-over-year improvement in operating cash flow may be unsustainable.

EXHIBIT 1	General Electric: Days Sales Payable, Annual Trend			
Year Ending December 31,	2003	2002	2001	2000
Days Sales Payable (DSP)	53.1	51.5	47.7	40.2

The extension of payables can be identified by monitoring days sales in payables (DSP). This metric is calculated as the end-of-period accounts-payable balance divided by the cost of goods sold and multiplied by the number of days in the period. As DSP grow, operating cash flows are boosted. As Exhibit 1 shows, General Electric Corporation began stretching out its payables in 2001 and therefore received boosts to operating cash flow. The figures show, however, that while the company received a significant benefit to cash flows from operations in 2001, that benefit began to slow in subsequent periods, indicating that GE will probably be unable to continue to fuel growth in operating cash flow using this method. Interestingly, GE modified some executive compensation agreements to include cash flow from operations as a metric on which management is evaluated.

FINANCING OF PAYABLES   4

A more complicated version of stretching out payables is the financing of payables. This occurs when a company uses a third-party financial institution to pay the vendor in the current period, with the company then paying back the bank in a subsequent period. An arrangement between Delphi Corporation and General Electric Capital Corporation shows how seemingly innocuous ventures can affect operating cash flows. The arrangement allowed Delphi to finance its accounts payable through GE Capital. Specifically, GE Capital would pay Delphi's accounts payable each quarter. In return, Delphi would reimburse GE Capital the following quarter and pay a fee for the service.

This agreement provided Delphi with a means to change the timing of its operating cash flows. In the first quarter of the venture, Delphi did not have to expend any cash with respect to accounts payable to vendors. The impact to operating cash flows can be seen in Delphi's accounting for the agreement with GE Capital. After GE Capital paid the amounts due from Delphi to its vendors, Delphi reclassified these items from accounts payable to short-term loans due to GE Capital. Delphi did this in a quarter in which cash flows were seasonally strong and it had access to the accounts-receivable securitization facilities. The reclassification resulted in a decrease to operating cash flow in that quarter, and an increase in financing cash flows. In the subsequent quarter, when Delphi paid GE Capital, the cash outflow was accounted for as a financing activity because it was a repayment of a loan. Normally, cash expenditures for accounts payable are included in operating activities. Therefore, because of the arrangement, Delphi was able to manage the timing of reported operating cash flows each period because the timing and extent of the vendor financing (and offsetting receivables securitizations) was at the discretion of company management.

Another example shows that the accounting profession has been slow to adapt to these types of transactions. During 2004, three companies in the same industry—AutoZone, Pep Boys, and Advance Auto Parts—all financed payments to vendors through a third-party financial institution. In other words, similar to Delphi above, the financial institution paid the vendors on behalf of the respective automotive company. Subsequently, the company paid back the bank, thereby slowing down its rate of payment to the vendors and boosting its operating cash flow. While each of these auto parts companies used a similar process for financing payables, each reflected it differently on its cash flow statement. Interestingly, two of these companies had the same auditor. This disparity in accounting treatment made analysts' comparisons of free cash flow yields for each of these companies irrelevant.

The lesson here is that auditors should ask questions whenever financial intermediaries are inserted in between parties that usually have no financial intermediary.

5   SECURITIZATIONS OF RECEIVABLES

A particularly significant item that could obfuscate both true cash flows and earnings is the securitization of receivables. Securitizations of receivables occur when companies package their receivables, most often those that have a longer term and higher credit quality, and transfer them to a financial institution or a variable interest entity (VIE). If the VIE is bankruptcy-remote (i.e., creditors cannot attach the assets of the VIE if the VIE sponsor files for bankruptcy), then GAAP indicates that the receivables have effectively been sold and the proceeds received should be reflected in the operating section of the cash flow statement.

The issue relates to nonfinancial companies, which are in effect able to boost reported operating cash flow by deciding how much and when to securitize accounts receivable. To the extent that proceeds received from the securitizations increase, any reported improvement in cash flow from operations should be considered unsustainable, because there is a limit to how much a company can securitize.

An interesting corollary to the impact on operating cash flow from securitizations is the impact on earnings. Specifically, in many cases companies can report gains when long-term accounts receivable are securitized. This occurs because the book value of the receivables at the time they are securitized does not include all the future interest income that is to be earned, yet the entity purchasing the receivables will have to pay for that interest. As a result, in this simplified example, because the amount received for the receivables is greater than the book value, a gain is generated. The amount of the gain can be affected as well by a variety of management assumptions, such as the expected default rate of the receivables securitized, the expected prepayment rate, and the discount rate used.

GAAP does not prescribe where on the income statement this gain is to be recorded. While one company may report the gain on sale of the receivables within revenues (the most aggressive approach), another might record it as an offset to selling, general, or administrative expenses. Another company might report the gain "below the line" in other nonoperating income. Marriott Corporation used to record the gain on securitizations of timeshare notes receivable within revenue. Specifically, in 2000, Marriott reported a gain on sale of $20 million within revenue from the securitization of these receivables. In 2001, the company reflected a $40 million gain on sale within revenues, helping to boost both reported revenues growth and pretax earnings growth. In 2002, Marriott's gain on sale was $60 million, again included in revenues, which further fueled reported revenues and earnings growth. In 2003, however, the gain on sale was flat at $60 million. Perhaps coincidentally, Marriott changed its accounting for these gains in 2003 and reported the gains on sale for all years presented as a component of "other" (nonoperating) income.

TAX BENEFITS FROM STOCK OPTIONS

6

Most companies currently follow Accounting Principles Board (APB) Opinion 25, which generally allows companies to avoid recording stock options as an expense when granted. Current IRS rules do not allow a company to take a deduction on its tax return when options are granted. At the time the stock option is exercised, however, the company is permitted to take a deduction on its tax return for that year reflecting the difference between the strike price and the market price of the option. On the external financial statements reported to investors, that deduction reduces (debits) taxes payable on the balance sheet, with the corresponding credit going to increase the equity section (additional paid-in-capital). Exhibit 2 shows the growing benefit that Cisco Corporation's operating cash flow received from this tax benefit.

EXHIBIT 2	Cisco Corporation's Statement of Cash Flows for Three Years Ended July 30, 2004

Cisco Corporation Consolidated Statements of Cash Flows

Years Ended	July 31, 2004	July 28, 2003	July 27, 2002
Cash flows from operating activities:			
Net income	$ 4,401	$ 3,578	$ 1,893
Adjustments to reconcile net income to net cash provided by operating activities:			
Cumulative effect of accounting change, net of tax	567	—	—
Depreciation and amortization	1,443	1,591	1,957
Provision for doubtful accounts	19	(59)	91
Provision for inventory	205	70	131
Deferred income taxes	552	(14)	(573)
Tax benefits from employee stock option plans	537	132	61
In-process research and development	3	4	53
Net (gains) losses and impairment charges on investments	(155)	520	1,127
Change in operating assets and liabilities:			
Accounts receivable	(488)	(125)	270
Inventories	(538)	(17)	673

(Exhibit continued on next page . . .)

EXHIBIT 2	(continued)			

Prepaid expenses and other current assets	**(42)**	(61)	(28)
Accounts payable	**54**	35	(174)
Income taxes payable	**260**	(125)	389
Accrued compensation	**(7)**	104	307
Deferred revenue	**688**	(84)	678
Other accrued liabilities	**(378)**	(309)	(268)
Net cash provided by operating activities	**7,121**	5,240	6,587

Cash flows from investing activities:

Purchases of short-term investments	**(12,206)**	(9,396)	(5,473)
Proceeds from sales and maturities of short-term investments	**13,570**	10,319	5,868
Purchases of investments	**(20,848)**	(18,063)	(15,760)
Proceeds from sales and maturities of investments	**20,757**	12,497	15,317
Purchases of restricted investments	—	—	(291)
Proceeds from sales and maturities of restricted investments	—	—	1,471
Acquisition of property and equipment	**(613)**	(717)	(2,641)
Acquisition of businesses, net of cash and cash equivalents	**(104)**	33	16
Change in lease receivables, net	**(159)**	79	380
Change in investments in privately held companies	**(13)**	(223)	(58)
Lease deposits	—	—	320
Purchase of minority interest of Cisco Systems, K.K. (Japan)	**(71)**	(59)	(115)
Other	**153**	94	159
Net cash provided by (used in) investing activities	**466**	(5,436)	(807)

Cash flows from financing activities:

Issuance of common stock	**1,257**	578	655
Repurchase of common stock	**(9,080)**	(5,984)	(1,854)
Other	**33**	43	30
Net cash used in financing activities	**(7,790)**	(5,363)	(1,169)
Net (decrease) increase in cash and cash equivalents	**(203)**	(5,559)	4,611
Cash and cash equivalents, beginning of fiscal year	**3,925**	9,484	4,873
Cash and cash equivalents, end of fiscal year	**$ 3,722**	$ 3,925	$ 9,484

A question developed over how to classify this tax benefit (reduction of the taxes payable) on the cash flow statement. Some companies had been including it as an addback to net income in the operating section of the cash flow statement; others included it as a financing activity. FASB's Emerging Issues Task Force (EITF) Issue 00-15, released in July 2000, specifically indicated that a reduction in taxes payable should, if significant, be shown as a separate line item on the cash flow statement in the operating section (i.e., as a source of cash). [SFAS 123(R), Share-Based Payment, which requires options to be expensed, also relegates the excess tax benefit to the financing section of the cash flow statement. SFAS 123(R) takes effect for fiscal years beginning after June 15, 2005.] If the company does not disclose the tax benefit in the operating section or in the statement of changes in stockholders equity, then EITF 00-15 provided that the company should disclose any material amounts in the notes to the financial statements. The tax benefit is sometimes disclosed only in the annual statement of stockholders equity, rather than as a separate line item in the operating section of the cash flow statement for investors to analyze.

To the extent that operating cash flow is affected by a growing impact from the tax benefit on stock options, an investor should question whether the reported operating cash flow growth is in fact sustainable and is indicative of improved operations. In fact, the boost to operating cash flow is often greatest in a period when the stock price has increased. In other words, when the stock is performing well, more stock options are exercised, resulting in a higher tax benefit, which is included as a source of operating cash flow, implying improving growth of operating cash flow. Because companies in the technology sector use stock options to a higher degree, these entities may require more-careful scrutiny. (This is an issue, however, only when a company has taxable income and the taxes that it would have paid are avoided by this tax benefit. If a company has a loss, there is no boost to operating cash flow.) Analysts and investors should thoroughly review the cash flow statement, the stockholders equity statement, and the notes to the financial statements to glean the volume of options exercised during the period, and the related tax benefit included as a source of operating cash flow.

STOCK BUYBACKS TO OFFSET DILUTION

7

A second issue related to stock options that affects reported cash flows is the buyback of company stock. A large number of companies have, in recent periods, been buying back their own stock on the open market. In a majority of cases, this activity is due to stock-option activity. Specifically, as stock prices generally increased in 2003, many of those who held stock options exercised those relatively cheap options. If companies did nothing to offset the larger number of outstanding shares that existed as a result of the growing number of in-the-money options, earnings per share would be negatively affected. Management of such companies therefore face a choice: They can allow earnings per share to be diluted by the growing share count or they can buy back company stock to offset that dilution.

From an accounting standpoint, the impact of options on the income statement is usually minimal, as discussed above. On the cash flow statement, the tax benefit of option exercises is a source of operating cash flow, benefiting those companies whose option exercises grow. Cash expended by a company for the buyback of corporate stock, however, is considered a financing activity on the cash flow statement. Consequently, as option exercises grow, so does the boost to operating cash flows for the tax benefit, but the outflows for stock buybacks to offset dilution of earnings are recorded in the financing section of the cash flow statement.

Interestingly, as a company's stock price rises, more options are generally exercised and the company must buy back more stock at the ever-higher market prices. In some cases, the entire amount of cash flow generated by operations in recent periods could be expended to buy back company stock to offset the dilution from in-the-money options. (See Cisco's cash flow statements in Exhibit 2.) Therefore, when analyzing the true earnings power of a company as measured by cash flows, it is important to consider the cash expended to buy back stock to offset dilution. This cash outflow should be subtracted from the operating cash flow in order to calculate the true free cash flow the company generated in the period in question.

8   OTHER MEANS

Many other means exist by which companies can influence the timing or the magnitude of reported free cash flows. Increasing the use of capital lease transactions as a way to acquire fixed assets obfuscates free cash flow because capital expenditures may be understated on a year-over-year basis. The accounting for outstanding checks and financing receivables are additional examples. In fact, General Motors and others have restated prior years' reported cash flow results in order to reflect the SEC's increased scrutiny of finance receivables. The restatement amounted to a downward revision of almost half of the reported operating cash flow.

Some companies have pointed analysts toward different metrics, such as operating cash flows, which are believed to be a more transparent indicator of a company's performance. The quality of a company's cash flows must be assessed, as highly motivated and intelligent management teams have created new ways to obfuscate the true picture of a company's operations. Auditors must be aware of the new focus by users of financial statements on operating cash flows, and adjust their work accordingly in order to provide the most value to the public.

PRACTICE PROBLEM FOR READING 41

1. Which of the following is *least likely* to be a reason a company would securitize its accounts receivable? To increase:

A. net income.

B. operating cash flows.

C. financing cash flows.

SOLUTION FOR READING 41

1. C is correct. The securitization of accounts receivable results in an increase in operating cash flows (as receivables decrease), and they are frequently sold at a gain, which increases net income. Financing cash flows are not affected.

FINANCIAL STATEMENT ANALYSIS: APPLICATIONS

by Thomas R. Robinson, CFA, Jan Hendrik van Greuning, CFA, R. Elaine Henry, CFA, and Michael A. Broihahn, CFA

LEARNING OUTCOMES

The candidate should be able to:	Mastery
a. evaluate a company's past financial performance and explain how a company's strategy is reflected in past financial performance;	☐
b. prepare a basic projection of a company's future net income and cash flow;	☐
c. describe the role of financial statement analysis in assessing the credit quality of a potential debt investment;	☐
d. discuss the use of financial statement analysis in screening for potential equity investments;	☐
e. determine and justify appropriate analyst adjustments to a company's financial statements to facilitate comparison with another company.	☐

THEME

Although certain steps are common to almost all analyses of financial statements, given the variety of purposes and contexts, no single approach is uniformly applicable. This reading examines several basic applications of financial statement analysis.

INTRODUCTION   1

This reading presents several important applications of financial statement analysis. Among the issues we will address are the following:

► What are the key questions to address in evaluating a company's past financial performance?

International Financial Statement Analysis, by Thomas R. Robinson, CFA, Jan Hendrik van Greuning, CFA, R. Elaine Henry, CFA, and Michael A. Broihahn, CFA. Copyright © 2007 by CFA Institute. Reprinted with permission.

▶ How can an analyst approach forecasting a company's future net income and cash flow?

▶ How can financial statement analysis be used to evaluate the credit quality of a potential fixed-income investment?

▶ How can financial statement analysis be used to screen for potential equity investments?

▶ How can differences in accounting methods affect financial ratio comparisons between companies, and what are some adjustments analysts make to reported financials in the interests of comparability?

Prior to undertaking any analysis, an analyst should explore the purpose and context of the analysis because purpose and context guide further decisions about the approach, the tools, the data sources, and the format in which to report results of the analysis, and also suggest which aspects of the analysis are most important. The analyst should then be able to formulate the key questions that the analysis must address. The questions will suggest the data the analyst needs to collect to objectively address the questions. The analyst then processes and analyzes the data to answer these questions. Conclusions and decisions based on the analysis are communicated in a format appropriate to the context, and follow-up is undertaken as required. Although this reading will not formally present applications as a series of steps, the process just described is generally applicable.

Section 2 describes the use of financial statement analysis to evaluate a company's past financial performance, and Section 3 describes basic approaches to projecting a company's future financial performance. Section 4 presents the use of financial statement analysis in assessing the credit quality of a potential debt investment. Section 5 concludes the survey of applications by describing the use of financial statement analysis in screening for potential equity investments. Analysts often encounter situations in which they must make adjustments to a company's reported financial results to increase their accuracy or comparability with the financials of other companies. Section 6 illustrates several typical types of analyst adjustments. A summary of the key points and practice problems in the CFA Institute multiple-choice format conclude the reading.

2   APPLICATION: EVALUATING PAST FINANCIAL PERFORMANCE

Analysts often analyze a company's past financial performance to determine the comparability of companies for a market-based valuation,[1] to provide a basis for a forward-looking analysis of the company, or to obtain information for evaluating the company's management.

---

[1] Stowe, Robinson, Pinto, and McLeavey (2002) describe market-based valuation as using price multiples ratios of a stock's market price to some measure of value per share (e.g., price-to-earnings ratios). Although the valuation method may be used independently of an analysis of a company's past financial performance, such an analysis may explain reasons for differences in companies' price multiples.

An evaluation of a company's past performance addresses not only *what* happened (i.e., how the company performed) but also *why* it happened—the causes behind the performance and how the performance reflects the company's strategy. Evaluative judgments assess whether the performance is better or worse, compared with a relevant benchmark such as the company's own historical performance, a competitor's performance, or market expectations. Some of the key analytical questions include:

► How have corporate measures of profitability, efficiency, liquidity, and solvency changed over the period being analyzed? Why?

► How do the level and trend in a company's profitability, efficiency, liquidity, and solvency compare with the corresponding results of other companies in the same industry? What explains any differences?

► What aspects of performance are critical for a company to successfully compete in its industry, and how did the company perform relative to those critical performance aspects?

► What are the company's business model and strategy, and how did they influence the company's performance as reflected, for example, in its sales growth, efficiency, and profitability?

Data available to answer these questions include the company's (and its competitors') financial statements, materials from the company's investor relations department, corporate press releases, and nonfinancial statement regulatory filings, such as proxies. Useful data also include industry information (e.g., from industry surveys, trade publications, and government sources), consumer information (e.g., from consumer satisfaction surveys), and information that is gathered by the analyst firsthand (e.g., through on-site visits). Processing the data will typically involve creating common-size financial statements, calculating financial ratios, and reviewing or calculating industry-specific metrics. Example 1 illustrates the effects of strategy on performance and the use of basic economic reasoning in interpreting results.

EXAMPLE 1

A Change in Strategy Reflected in a Change in Financial Performance

In analyzing the historical performance of Motorola (NYSE: MOT) as of the beginning of 2006, an analyst might refer to the information presented in Exhibit 1. Panel A presents selected data for Motorola from 2003 to 2005. Panel B presents an excerpt from the segment footnote, giving data for Motorola's mobile device business segment (the segment that manufactures and sells cellular phones). Panel C presents excerpts from the Management Discussion and Analysis (MD&A) describing the results of the segment.

Looking back to 1996, Motorola was the market leader with its Star-TAC cellular phone, but since 1998, Nokia had become the largest player in the global mobile phone market. "The mood inside Motorola was grim in early 2003. Nokia, whose 'candy bar' phone designs were all the rage had snatched Motorola's No. 1 worldwide market share" (*Fortune*, 12 June 2006, p. 126).

Following the arrival of new CEO Edward Zander at the end of 2003, Motorola radically revamped its strategy for new products: "Design leads, and engineering follows" (*Business Week*, 8 August 2005, p. 68). Motorola's strategy thereafter evolved to include a strong consumer marketing orientation to complement its historically strong technological position. The company launched 60 new products in 2004, an important one of which was the RAZR cellular phone with an ultra-thin profile that served to differentiate it from competitors' offerings. The successful introduction of new products in 2004 enabled the company to gain market share and increase profitability.

The changes at Motorola extended beyond the product strategy. An article in *Barron's* noted that in addition to the shift in product strategy, "Motorola has undergone a financial overhaul . . . The company has reduced the percentage of working capital to sales to less than 12 percent from about 22 percent, a sign of increased efficiency" (*Barron's* 25 July 2005, p. 23).

EXHIBIT 1	Selected Data for Motorola (Years Ended 31 December)

Panel A: Data for Motorola

(Dollars in Millions)	2005	2004	2003
Net sales	36,843	31,323	23,155
Gross margin	11,777	10,354	7,503
Operating earnings	4,696	3,132	1,273
Total assets	35,649	30,922	26,809

Panel B: Data for Motorola's Mobile Device Segment from Segment Footnote

(Dollars in Millions)	2005	2004	2003
Net sales	21,455	17,108	11,238
Operating earnings	2,198	1,728	511
Assets	7,548	5,442	3,900

Panel C: Excerpt from MD&A

2004	"Our wireless handset business had a very strong year in 2004, reflected by a 53% increase in net sales, a 257% increase in operating earnings and increased market share. The increase in net sales was driven by an increase in unit shipments, which increased 39% in 2004 compared to 2003, and improved ASP [average selling price], which increased 15% in 2004 compared to 2003 . . . This increase in net sales, accompanied by process improvements in the supply chain and benefits from ongoing

(Exhibit continued on next page . . .)

EXHIBIT 1   **(continued)**

cost reduction activities resulted in increased gross margin, which drove the increase in overall operating earnings for the business. . . ."

2005   "Net sales increased by $4.3 billion, or 25%, to $21.5 billion and operating earnings increased by 27% to $2.2 billion. We shipped 146 million handsets in 2005, up 40% from 2004 . . . The increase in unit shipments was attributed to an increase in the size of the total market and a gain in the segment's market share. The gain in market share reflected strong demand for GSM handsets and consumers' desire for the segment's compelling products that combine innovative style and leading technology. The segment had increased net sales in all regions of the world as a result of an improved product portfolio, strong market growth in emerging markets, and high replacement sales in more mature markets. Average selling price ("ASP") decreased approximately 10% compared to 2004, driven primarily by a higher percentage of lower-tier, lower-priced handsets in the overall sales mix."

Source: Motorola's 2005 10-K filed 2 March 2006 and 2004 10-K filed 4 March 2005.

Using the information provided, address the following:

1. Typically, products that are differentiated either through recognizable brand names, proprietary technology, or both can be sold at a higher price than commodity products.

   A. In general, would the selling prices of differentiated products be more directly reflected in a company's operating profit margin or gross profit margin?

   B. Does Motorola's segment footnote (Panel B) reflect a successful differentiation strategy in its mobile devices business?

   C. Based on the excerpts from Motorola's MD&A (Panel C), compare and contrast the drivers of the growth in sales in Motorola's mobile device business in 2005 with the drivers in 2004.

2. The *Barron's* article refers to working capital as a percentage of sales, an indicator of efficiency.

   A. In general, what other ratios indicate a company's efficiency?

   B. Does the financial data for Motorola shown in this example reflect increased efficiency?

Solution to 1:

A. Sales of differentiated products at premium prices would generally be reflected more directly in the gross profit margin, increasing it, all else equal. The effect of premium pricing generally would also be reflected in a higher operating margin. However, expenditures on advertising and/or research in support of differentiating features mean that the effect on operating profit margins is often weaker than the effect on gross profit margins.

B. Although Motorola's segment footnote does not include information on gross margins by segment, it does include sufficient information for calculating operating profit margins, which should also be positively correlated with premium pricing. Dividing operating earnings by net sales, we find that operating margins in the mobile devices business increased from 4.5 percent ($511/11,238) in 2003 to 10.1 percent ($1,728/17,108) in 2004 and 10.2 percent ($2,198/21,455) in 2005. The data indicate successful results from the differentiation strategy in 2004, but no further meaningful improvement in 2005.

C. In both years, the MD&A attributes sales growth to an increase in Motorola's share of the handset market. The 2005 MD&A explicitly mentions growth of the total wireless handset market as another factor in sales growth for that year. The 2004 results benefited from both a 39 percent increase in units sales (compared with 2003) and a 15 percent increase in ASP. The sources of growth shifted somewhat from 2004 to 2005. Lower-tier, lower-price handsets became a larger part of Motorola's product mix in 2005, and ASP declined by 10 percent. Because sales grew by 25.4 percent [= (21,455 − 17,108)/17,108] in 2005, it is clear, however, that the growth in handset unit sales more than overcame the decline in ASP.

Solution to 2:

A. Other ratios that indicate a company's efficiency include asset turnover, fixed asset turnover, working capital turnover, receivables turnover, and inventory turnover. In addition, efficiency is indicated by days of inventory on hand, days of sales outstanding, and days of payables.

B. Yes, they do indicate increased efficiency. The data given permit the calculation of one efficiency ratio, total asset turnover. Motorola's total asset turnover improved from 0.864 (23,155/26,809) for 2003 to 1.013 (31,323/30,922) for 2004 to 1.033 (36,843/35,649) for 2005.

In calculating financial statement ratios, an analyst needs to be aware of the potential impact of companies reporting under different accounting standards, such as U.S. generally accepted accounting principles (U.S. GAAP) and international financial reporting standards (IFRS). Furthermore, even within a given set of accounting standards, companies still have discretion to choose among acceptable methods and also must make certain estimates even when applying the same method. Therefore, it may be useful to make selected adjustments to a company's financial statement data in order to facilitate comparisons with other companies or with the industry overall. Examples of such analyst adjustments will be discussed in Section 6. Example 2 illustrates how differences in accounting standards can affect financial ratio comparisons.

EXAMPLE 2

The Effect of U.S. GAAP versus IFRS on ROE Comparisons

Despite convergence between U.S. GAAP and IFRS, differences remain. Non-U.S. companies that use IFRS (or any other acceptable body of accounting standards) and file with the U.S. Securities and Exchange Commission (because their shares or depositary receipts based on their shares trade in the United States) are required to reconcile their net income and shareholders' equity accounts to U.S. GAAP. In comparing the historical performance of Motorola and Nokia, you have prepared Exhibit 2 to evaluate whether the difference in accounting standards affects the comparison of the two companies' return on equity (ROE). Panel A presents selected data for Motorola for 2004 and 2005, and Panel B presents data for Nokia under IFRS and under U.S. GAAP.

EXHIBIT 2	Data for Motorola and Nokia for a ROE Calculation (Years Ended 31 December)

Panel A: Selected Data for Motorola (Dollars in Millions)	2005	2004
U.S. GAAP		
Net income	4,599	2,191
Shareholders' equity	16,676	13,331

Panel B: Selected Data for Nokia Corporation (Euros in Millions)	2005	2004
IFRS		
Net income	3,616	3,192
Shareholders' equity	12,155	14,231
U.S. GAAP		
Net income	3,582	3,343
Shareholders' equity	12,558	14,576

Sources: Motorola's 10-K and Nokia's 20-F, both filed 2 March 2006.

Does the difference in accounting standards affect the ROE comparison?

Solution: Motorola's return on average shareholders' equity for 2005 at 30.7 percent [net income of $4,599 divided by average shareholders' equity, calculated as ($16,676 + $13,331)/2] was higher than Nokia's, whether calculated under IFRS or U.S. GAAP. The difference in accounting standards does *not* affect the conclusion, though it does affect the magnitude of the difference in profitability. Under IFRS, Nokia's ROE was 27.4 percent [net income of €3,616 divided by average shareholders' equity, calculated as (€12,155+ €14,231)/2]. Under U.S. GAAP, Nokia's ROE was slightly lower at 26.4 percent [net income of €3,582 divided by average shareholders' equity, calculated as (€12,558 + €14,576)/2]. Results of the calculations are summarized in the following table:

Panel A: Motorola

U.S. GAAP

Return on average shareholders' equity	30.7%

Panel B: Nokia Corporation

IFRS

Return on average shareholders' equity	27.4%

U.S. GAAP

Return on average shareholders' equity	26.4%

In Example 2, Nokia's ROE for 2005 under IFRS and U.S. GAAP differed only slightly. In some cases, the effect of applying IFRS and U.S. GAAP on ROE and other profitability ratios can be substantial. For example, the Swiss drug company Novartis, which has undertaken historically numerous business combinations, shows a return on average shareholders' equity of 19.0 percent in 2005 under IFRS compared with 13.7 percent under U.S. GAAP; the differences are largely due to differences in accounting for business combinations.[2] Research indicates that for most non-U.S. companies filing with the U.S. Securities and Exchange Commission (SEC), differences between U.S. GAAP and home-country GAAP net income average around 1 to 2 percent of market value of equity, but with large variation.[3]

Comparison of the levels and trends in the company's performance provide information for statements about *how* the company performed. The company's management presents its view about causes underlying its performance in the MD&A section of its annual report and during periodic conference calls. To gain additional understanding on the causes underlying a company's performance, an analyst can review industry information or seek additional sources of information.

The results of an analysis of past performance provide a basis for reaching conclusions and making recommendations. For example, an analysis undertaken as the basis for a forward-looking study might result in conclusions about whether a company's future performance is likely to reflect continuation of recent historical trends or not. As another example, an analysis to support a market-based valuation of a company might focus on whether the company's better (worse) profitability and growth outlook compared with the peer group median justify its relatively high (low) valuation, as judged by market multiples such as price-to-earnings ratio (P/E), market-to-book ratio (MV/BV), and total invested capital to

---

[2] Henry and Yang (2006).

[3] Pownall and Schipper (1999). "Home country GAAP" can refer to IFRS in addition to non-IFRS GAAP other than U.S. GAAP.

earnings before interest, taxes, depreciation, and amortization (TIC/EBITDA).[4] As another example, an analysis undertaken as a component of an evaluation of the company's management might result in conclusions about whether the company has grown as fast as another company, or as the industry overall, and whether the company has maintained profitability while growing.

APPLICATION: PROJECTING FUTURE FINANCIAL PERFORMANCE

3

In some cases, evaluating a company's past performance provides a basis for forward-looking analyses. An evaluation of a company's environment and history may persuade the analyst that historical data constitute a valid basis for such analyses and that the analyst's projections may be based on the continuance of past trends, perhaps with some adjustments. Alternatively, in the case of a major acquisition or divestiture, or for a start-up company, or for a company operating in a volatile industry, past performance may be less relevant to future performance.

Projections of future financial performance are used in determining the value of a company or of its equity component. Projections of future financial performance are also used in credit analysis—particularly in project finance or acquisition finance—to determine whether a company's cash flows will be adequate to pay the interest and principal on its debt and to evaluate whether a company will likely be in compliance with its financial covenants.

Sources of data for analysts' projections include some or all of the following: the company's projections; the company's previous financial statements; industry structure and outlook; and macroeconomic forecasts.

Projections of a company's near-term performance may be used as an input to market-based valuation (valuation based on price multiples). Such projections may involve projecting next years' sales and using the common-size income statement to project major expense items or particular margins on sales (e.g., gross profit margin or operating profit margin). More complex projections of a company's future performance involve developing a more detailed analysis of components across multiple periods—for example, projections of sales and gross margin by product line, projection of operating expenses based on historical patterns, and projection of interest expense based on requisite debt funding, interest rates, and applicable taxes. Furthermore, a projection should include sensitivity analyses related to the major assumptions.

3.1 Projecting Performance: An Input to Market-Based Valuation

One application of financial statement analysis involves projecting a company's near-term performance as an input to market-based valuation. For example, one might project a company's sales and profit margin to estimate earnings per share (EPS) and then apply a projected P/E to establish a target price for a company's stock.

Analysts often take a top-down approach to projecting a company's sales.[5] First, industry sales are projected based on their historical relation with some

---

[4] **Total invested capital** is the sum of market value of common equity, book value of preferred equity, and face value of debt.

[5] The discussion in this paragraph is indebted to Benninga and Sarig (1997).

macroeconomic indicator or indicators such as real gross domestic product. In researching the automobile industry, for example, the analyst may find that the industry's annual domestic unit automobile sales (numbers of cars sold in domestic markets) bears a relation to annual changes in real GDP. Regression analysis is often used in establishing the parameters of such relations. Other factors in projecting sales may include consumer income or tastes, technological developments, and the availability of substitute products or services. After industry sales are projected, a company's market share is projected. Company-level market share projections may be based on historical market share and a forward-looking assessment of the company's competitive position. The company's sales are then estimated as its projected market share multiplied by projected total industry sales.

After developing a sales forecast for a company, an analyst can choose among various methods for forecasting income and cash flow. One decision is the level of detail in forecasts. For example, separate forecasts may be made for individual expense items or for more aggregated expense items, such as total operating expenses. Rather than stating a forecast in terms of expenses, the forecast might be stated in terms of a forecasted profit margin (gross, operating, or net). The net profit margin, in contrast to the gross or operating profit margins, is affected by financial leverage and tax rates, which are subject to managerial and legal/regulatory revisions; therefore, historical data may sometimes be more relevant for projecting gross or operating margins. Whatever the margin used, the forecasted amount of profit for a given period is the product of the forecasted amount of sales and the forecast of the selected profit margin.

As Example 3 illustrates, for relatively mature companies operating in nonvolatile product markets, historical information on operating profit margins can provide a useful starting point for forecasting future operating profits (at least over short forecasting horizons). For a new or relatively volatile business, or one with significant fixed costs (which can magnify the volatility of operating margins), historical operating profit margins are typically less reliable for projecting future margins.

EXAMPLE 3

Using Historical Operating Profit Margins to Forecast Operating Profit

One approach to projecting operating profit is to determine a company's average operating profit margin over the previous three years and apply that margin to a forecast of the company's sales. Consider the following three companies:

► Johnson & Johnson (JNJ). This U.S. health care conglomerate founded in 1887 had 2005 sales of around $50.5 billion from its three main businesses: pharmaceuticals, medical devices and diagnostics, and consumer products.

► BHP Billiton (BHP). This company, with group headquarters in Australia and secondary headquarters in London, is the world's largest natural resources company, reporting revenue of approximately US$32 billion for the fiscal year ended June 2006. The company mines, processes, and markets coal, copper, nickel, iron, bauxite, and silver and also has substantial petroleum operations.

▶ TomTom. This Dutch company, which went public on the Amsterdam Stock Exchange in 2005, provides personal navigation products and services in Europe, North America, and Australia. The company's revenues for 2005 were €720 million, an increase of 275 percent from 2004 and more than 18 times greater than revenues in 2003.

Address the following problems:

1. For each of the three companies given, state and justify whether the suggested forecasting method would be a reasonable starting point for projecting future operating profit.

2. Assume the suggested approach was applied to each of the three companies based on the realized level of sales provided. Consider the following additional information:

▶ JNJ: For the three years prior to 2005, JNJ's average operating profit margin was approximately 26.6 percent. The company's actual operating profit for 2005 was $13.4 billion.

▶ BHP: For the three years prior to the year ending June 2006, BHP's average operating profit margin was approximately 22.5 percent, based on data from Thompson Financial. The company's actual operating profit for the year ended June 2006, excluding profits from a jointly controlled entity, was $9.7 billion.

▶ TomTom: Over the three years prior to 2005, TomTom's average operating profit margin was approximately 23.5 percent. The company's actual operating profit for 2005 was €195 million.

Using the additional information given, state and justify whether actual results supported the usefulness of the stable operating margin assumption.

Solution to 1:

JNJ. Because JNJ is an established company with diversified operations across relatively stable businesses, the suggested approach to projecting the company's operating profit might provide a reasonable starting point.

BHP. Because commodity prices tend to be volatile and the mining industry is relatively capital intensive, the suggested approach to projecting BHP's operating profit would probably not have provided a useful starting point.

TomTom. A new company such as TomTom has little operating history on which to judge stability of margins. Two aspects about the company suggest that the broad approach to projecting operating profit would not be a useful starting point for TomTom. First, the company operates in an area of rapid technological change, and second, the company appears to be in a period of rapid growth.

Solution to 2:

JNJ. JNJ's actual operating profit margin for 2005 was 26.5 percent ($13.4 billion divided by sales of $50.5 billion), which is very close to the company's three-year average operating profit margin of approximately 26.6 percent. If the average operating profit margin had been applied to perfectly forecasted 2005 sales to obtain forecasted operating profit, the forecasting error would have been minimal.

BHP. BHP's actual operating profit margin for the year ended June 2006 was 30.3 percent ($9.7 billion divided by sales of $32 billion). If the company's average profit margin of 22.5 percent had been applied to perfectly forecasted sales, the forecasted operating profit would have been approximately $7.2 billion, 26 percent less than actual operating profit.

TomTom. TomTom's actual operating profit margin for 2005 was 27.1 percent (€195 million divided by sales of €720 million). If the average profit margin of 23.5 percent had been applied to perfectly forecasted sales, the forecasted operating profit would have been approximately €169 million, or 13 percent below TomTom's actual operating profit.

Although prior years' profit margins can provide a useful starting point in projections for companies with relatively stable business, the underlying data should, nonetheless, be examined to identify items that are not likely to reoccur. Such nonrecurring (i.e., transitory) items should be removed from computations of any profit amount or profit margin that will be used in projections. Example 4 illustrates this principle.

EXAMPLE 4

Issues in Forecasting

In reviewing Motorola's 2005 performance, an analyst notes the following items. What is the relevance of each item in forecasting the item given in italics?

1. Of Motorola's $4,696 million of operating earnings, $458 million was from other income, primarily payment received from a former customer that had defaulted several years ago on obligations to Motorola. *Operating earnings.*

2. Motorola's income included $1.9 billion from gains on sales of investments. Investments at the end of 2005 were $1.6 billion compared with $3.2 billion at the end of 2004. *Net income.*

3. Motorola's effective tax rate for 2005 was 29.5 percent compared with 32.6 percent for each of the previous two years. A main reason

for the lower effective tax rate was a one-time tax incentive for U.S. multinational companies to repatriate accumulated earnings from their foreign subsidiaries. *Net income.*

4. Motorola had losses from discontinued operations of $21 million and $659 million for the years 2005 and 2004, respectively. *Net income.*

Solution to 1: This item related to a specific former customer and is not an ongoing source of operating earnings. Therefore, it is not relevant in forecasting operating earnings.

Solution to 2: Gains on sales of investments are not a core part of Motorola's business, and the sale in 2005 halved the amount of Motorola's investments. Thus, this item should not be viewed as an ongoing source of earnings, and it is, therefore, not relevant to forecasting net income.

Solution to 3: The lower tax rate does not appear to reflect an ongoing change and, therefore, a projection would probably consider the previous years' higher rate as more representative and more useful in forecasting net income.

Solution to 4: Results of discontinued items should not be included either when assessing past performance or when forecasting future net income.

In general, when earnings projections are used as a basis for market-based valuations, an analyst will make appropriate allowance for transitory components of past earnings.

3.2 Projecting Multiple-Period Performance

Projections of future financial performance over multiple periods are needed in valuation models that estimate the value of a company or its equity by discounting future cash flows. The value of a company or its equity developed in this way can then be compared with the market price as a basis for investment decisions.

Projections of future performance are also used for credit analysis, in which case conclusions include an assessment of a borrower's ability to repay interest and principal of debt obligations. Investment recommendations depend on the needs and objectives of the client and on an evaluation of the risk of the investment relative to its expected return—both of which are a function of the terms of the debt obligation itself as well as financial market conditions. Terms of the debt obligation include amount, interest rate, maturity, financial covenants, and collateral.

Example 5 presents an elementary illustration of net income and cash flow forecasting to illustrate a format for analysis and some basic principles. In Example 5, assumptions are shown first and the period-by-period abbreviated financial statement that results from the assumption is shown below.

Depending on the use of the forecast, an analyst may choose to compute further, specific cash flow metrics. For example, free cash flow to equity, used in discounted cash flow approaches to equity valuation, can be found as net income adjusted for noncash items, minus investment in net working capital and in net fixed assets, plus net borrowing.[6]

EXAMPLE 5

Basic Example of Financial Forecasting

Assume a company is formed with $100 of equity capital, all of which is immediately invested in working capital. Assumptions are as follows:

Dividends	Nondividend paying
First-year sales	$100
Sales growth	10% per annum
Cost of goods sold/sales	20%
Operating expense/sales	70%
Interest income rate	5%
Tax rate	30%
Working capital as percent of sales	90%

Based on the above information, forecast the company's net income and cash flow for five years.

Solution: Exhibit 3 below shows the net income forecasts in Line 7 and cash flow forecasts ("change in cash") in Line 18.

EXHIBIT 3   Basic Financial Forecasting

				Time		
	0	**1**	**2**	**3**	**4**	**5**
1) Sales		100.0	110.0	121.0	133.1	146.4
2) Cost of goods sold		(20.0)	(22.0)	(24.2)	(26.6)	(29.3)
3) Operating expenses		(70.0)	(77.0)	(84.7)	(93.2)	(102.5)
4) Interest income		0.0	0.9	0.8	0.8	0.7
5) Income before tax		10.0	11.9	12.9	14.1	15.3
6) Taxes		(3.0)	(3.6)	(3.9)	(4.2)	(4.6)
7) Net income		7.0	8.3	9.0	9.9	10.7
8) Cash/Borrowing	0.0	17.0	16.3	15.4	14.4	13.1
9) Working capital (non cash)	100.0	90.0	99.0	108.9	119.8	131.8
10) Total assets	100.0	107.0	115.3	124.3	134.2	144.9
11) Liabilities	0.0	0.0	0.0	0.0	0.0	0.0
12) Equity	100.0	107.0	115.3	124.3	134.2	144.9
13) Total liabilities + Equity	100.0	107.0	115.3	124.3	134.2	144.9
14) Net income		7.0	8.3	9.0	9.9	10.7

(Exhibit continued on next page . . .)

---

[6] See Stowe et al. (2002) for further information.

	EXHIBIT 3	(continued)				

	Time					
	0	**1**	**2**	**3**	**4**	**5**
15) Plus noncash items		0.0	0.0	0.0	0.0	0.0
16) Less: investment in working capital		−10.0	9.0	9.9	10.9	12.0
17) Less: investment in fixed capital		0.0	0.0	0.0	0.0	0.0
18) Change in cash		17.0	−0.7	−0.9	−1.0	−1.3
19) Beginning cash		0.0	17.0	16.3	15.4	14.4
20) Ending cash		17.0	16.3	15.4	14.4	13.1

To explain the exhibit, at time zero, the company is formed with $100 of equity capital (Line 12). All of the company's capital is assumed to be immediately invested in working capital (Line 9). In future periods, because it is assumed that no dividends are paid, equity increases each year by the amount of net income. Future periods' working capital is assumed to be 90 percent of annual sales.

Sales are assumed to be $100 in the first period and to grow at a constant rate of 10 percent per annum (Line 1). The cost of goods sold is assumed constant at 20 percent of sales (Line 2), so the gross profit margin is 80 percent. Operating expenses are assumed to be 70 percent of sales each year (Line 3). Interest income (Line 4) is calculated as 5 percent of the beginning cash/borrowing balance (Line 8) and is an income item when there is a cash balance, as it is in this example. (If available cash is inadequate to cover required cash outflows, the shortfall is presumed to be covered by borrowing. This borrowing would be shown as a negative balance on Line 8 and an associated interest expense on Line 4. Alternatively, a forecast can be presented with separate lines for cash and borrowing.) Taxes of 30 percent are deducted to obtain net income (Line 7).

To calculate each period's cash flow, we begin with net income (Line 7 = Line 14), add back any noncash items such as depreciation (Line 15), deduct investment in working capital (Line 16), and deduct investment in fixed capital (Line 17).[7] In this simple example, we are assuming that the company does not invest in any fixed capital (long-term assets) but, rather, rents furnished office space. Therefore, there is no depreciation, and thus noncash items are zero. Each period's change in cash (Line 18) is added to the beginning cash balance (Line 19) to obtain the ending cash balance (Line 20 = Line 8).

Example 5 is simplified to demonstrate some principles of forecasting. In practice, each aspect of a forecast presents substantial challenges. Sales forecasts may be very detailed, with separate forecasts for each year of each product line, and/or each geographical or business segment. Sales forecasts may be based on past results (for relative stable businesses), management forecasts, industry studies,

---

[7] Working capital represents funds that must be invested in the daily operations of a business such as to carry inventory and accounts receivable. The term "investment" in this context means "the addition to" or "increase." The "investment in fixed capital" is also referred to as "capital expenditure" or "capex." See Stowe et al. (2002), Chapter 3, for further information.

and/or macroeconomic forecasts. Similarly, gross margins may be detailed and may be based on past results or forecast relationships. Expenses other than cost of goods sold may be broken down into more detailed line items, each of which may be forecasted based on its relationship with sales (if variable) or on its historical levels. Working capital requirements may be estimated as a proportion of the amount of sales (as in the example) or the change in sales, or as a compilation of specific forecasts for inventory, receivables, and payables. Most forecasts will involve some investment in fixed assets, in which case depreciation amounts affect taxable income and net income but not cash flow. Example 5 makes the simplifying assumption that interest is paid on the beginning-of-year cash balance.

Example 5 developed a series of point estimates for future net income and cash flow. In practice, forecasting generally includes an analysis of the risk in forecasts—in this case, an assessment of the impact on income and cash flow if the realized values of variables differ significantly from the assumptions used in the base case or if actual sales are much different from forecasts. Quantifying the risk in forecasts requires an analysis of the economics of the company's businesses and expense structures, and the potential impact of events affecting the company, the industry, and the economy in general. That investigation done, the analyst can assess risk using scenario analysis or Monte Carlo simulation. Scenario analysis involves specifying assumptions that differ from those included as the base case assumptions. In the above example, the projections of net income and cash flow could be recast using a more pessimistic scenario, with assumptions changed to reflect slower sales growth and higher costs. A Monte Carlo simulation involves specifying probability distributions of values for variables and random sampling from those distributions. In the above analysis, the projections would be repeatedly recast using randomly selected values for the drivers of net income and cash flow, thus permitting the analyst to evaluate the range of results possible and the probability of simulating the possible actual outcomes.

An understanding of financial statements and ratios can enable an analyst to make more detailed projections of income statement, balance sheet, and statement of cash flows items. For example, an analyst may collect information on normal inventory and receivables turnover ratios and use this information to forecast accounts receivable, inventory, and cash flows based on sales projections rather than use a composite working capital investment assumption, as in the above example.

As the analyst makes detailed forecasts, he or she must ensure that they are mutually consistent. For instance, in Example 6, the analyst's forecast concerning days of sales outstanding (which is an estimate of the average time to collect payment from sales made on credit) should flow from a model of the company that yields a forecast of the change in the average accounts receivable balance given as the solution to the problem. Otherwise, predicted days of sales outstanding and accounts receivable would not be mutually consistent.

EXAMPLE 6

Consistency of Forecasts[8]

Brown Corporation had an average days-of-sales-outstanding (DSO) period of 19 days in 2005. An analyst thinks that Brown's DSO will decline to match the industry average of 15 days in 2006. Total sales (all on credit) in 2005 were $300 million, and Brown expects total sales (all

---

[8] Adapted from a past CFA Institute examination question.

on credit) to increase to $320 million in 2006. To achieve the lower DSO, the change in the average accounts receivable balance from 2005 to 2006 that must occur is *closest* to:

A. −$3.51 million.

B. −$2.46 million.

C. $2.46 million.

D. $3.51 million.

Solution: B is correct. The first step is to calculate **accounts receivable turnover** from the DSO collection period. Receivable turnover equals 365/19 (DSO) = 19.2 for 2005, and 365/15 = 24.3 in 2006. Next, we use the fact that the average accounts receivable balance equals sales/receivable turnover to conclude that for 2005, average accounts receivable was $300,000,000/19.2 = $15,625,000, and for 2006, it must equal $320,000,000/24.3 = $13,168,724. The difference is a reduction in receivables of $2,456,276.

The next section illustrates the application of financial statement analysis to credit risk analysis.

APPLICATION: ASSESSING CREDIT RISK

4

Credit risk is the risk of loss caused by a counterparty's or debtor's failure to make a promised payment. For example, credit risk with respect to a bond is the risk that the obligor (the issuer of the bond) is not able to pay interest and principal according to the terms of the bond indenture (contract). **Credit analysis** is the evaluation of credit risk. Credit analysis may relate to the credit risk of an obligor in a particular transaction or to an obligor's overall credit-worthiness.

In assessing an obligor's overall credit-worthiness, one general approach is credit scoring, a statistical analysis of the determinants of credit default. As noted above, credit analysis for specific types of debt (e.g., acquisition financing and other highly leveraged financing) typically involves projections of period-by-period cash flows.

Whatever the techniques adopted, the analytical focus of credit analysis is on debt-paying ability. Unlike payments to equity investors, payments to debt investors are limited by the agreed contractual interest. If a company experiences financial success, its debt becomes less risky, but its success does not increase the amount of payments to its debtholders. In contrast, if a company experiences financial distress, it may be unable to pay interest and principal on its debt obligations. Thus, credit analysis has a special concern with the sensitivity of debt-paying ability to adverse events and economic conditions—cases in which the creditor's promised returns may be most at risk. Because those returns are generally paid in cash, credit analysis usually focuses on cash flow rather than accrual-income returns. Typically, credit analysts use return measures related to operating cash flow because it represents cash generated internally, which is available to pay creditors.

These themes are reflected in Example 7, which illustrates the application of four groups of quantitative factors in credit analysis to an industry group: scale and diversification, tolerance for leverage, operational efficiency, and margin stability. Scale and diversification relate to a company's sensitivity to adverse events and economic conditions as well as to other factors—such as market leadership, purchasing power with suppliers, and access to capital markets—that can affect debt-paying ability. Financial policies or tolerance for leverage relates to the obligor's ability to service its indebtedness (i.e., make the promised payments on debt). In the example, various solvency ratios are used to measure tolerance for leverage. One set of tolerance-for-leverage measures is based on retained cash flow (RCF). RCF is defined by Moody's as operating cash flow before working capital changes less dividends. A ratio of RCF/total debt of 0.5, for example, indicates that the company may be able to pay off debt in approximately $1/0.5 = 2$ years from cash flow retained in the business (at current levels of RCF and debt), assuming no capital expenditures; a ratio adjusting for capital expenditures is also used. Other factors include interest coverage ratios based on EBITDA, which is also chosen by Moody's in specifying factors for operational efficiency and margin stability. "Operational efficiency" as defined by Moody's relates to cost structure: Companies with lower costs are better positioned to deal with financial stress. "Margin stability" relates to the past volatility of profit margins: Higher stability should be associated with lower credit risk.

EXAMPLE 7

Moody's Evaluation of Quantifiable Rating Factors[9]

Moody's Investors Service indicates that when assigning credit ratings for the global paper and forest products industry, they look at a number of factors, including quantitative measures of four broad factors. These factors are weighted and aggregated in determining the overall credit rating assigned. The four broad factors, the subfactors, and weightings are as follows:

Broad Factor	Subfactors	Subfactor Weighting (%)	Broad Factor Weighting (%)
Scale and diversification	Average annual revenues	6.00	15
	Segment diversification	4.50	
	Geographic diversification	4.50	
Financial policies (tolerance for leverage)	Retained cash flow (RCF)/Total debt	11.00	55
	(RCF − Capital expenditures)/Total debt	11.00	
	Total debt/EBITDA	11.00	
	(EBITDA − Capital expenditures)/Interest	11.00	
	EBITDA/Interest	11.00	
Operational efficiency	Vertical integration	5.25	15
	EBITDA margin	5.25	
	EBITDA/Average assets	4.50	
Margin stability	Average percentage change in EBITDA margin	15.00	15
Total		100.00	100

---

[9] Moody's Investors Service, "Rating Methodology: Global Paper & Forest Products Industry," June 2006, pp. 8–19.

1. What are some reasons why Moody's may have selected these four broad factors as being important in assigning a credit rating?

2. Why might financial policies be weighted so heavily?

Solution to 1:

Scale and Diversification:

► Large scale can result in purchasing power over suppliers, leading to cost savings.

► Product and geographic diversification should lower risk.

Financial Policies:

► Strong financial policies should be associated with the ability of cash flow to service debt.

Operational Efficiency:

► Companies with high operational efficiency should have lower costs and higher margins than less efficient companies and so be able to withstand a downturn easier.

Margin Stability:

► Lower volatility in margins would imply lower risk relative to economic conditions.

Solution to 2: The level of debt relative to earnings and cash flow is a critical factor in assessing credit-worthiness. The higher the current level of debt, the higher the risk of default.

A point to note regarding Example 7 is that the rating factors and the metrics used to represent each can vary by industry group. For example, for heavy manufacturing (manufacturing of the capital assets used in manufacturing and production processes), Moody's distinguishes order trends and quality as distinctive credit factors affecting future revenues, factory load, and profitability patterns.

Analyses of a company's historical and projected financial statements are an integral part of the credit evaluation process. As noted by Moody's, the rating process makes:

> . . . extensive use of historic financial statements. Historic results help with understanding the pattern of a company's results and how the company compares to others. They also provide perspective, helping to ensure that estimated future results are grounded in reality.[10]

As noted in the above example, Moody's computes a variety of ratios in assessing credit-worthiness. A comparison of a company's ratios to its peers is informative in evaluating relative credit-worthiness, as demonstrated in Example 8.

---

[10] Ibid., p. 6.

EXAMPLE 8

Peer Comparison of Ratios

A credit analyst is assessing the tolerance for leverage for two paper companies based on the following subfactors identified by Moody's:[11]

	International Paper	Louisiana-Pacific
RCF/Debt	8.2 %	59.1%
(RCF − Capital expenditures)/Debt	0.2%	39.8%
Debt/EBITDA	5.6x	1.0x
(EBITDA − Capital expenditures)/Interest	1.7x	8.1x
EBITDA/Interest	3.1x	10.0x

Based solely on the data given, which company is more likely to be assigned a higher credit rating?

Solution: The ratio comparisons are all in favor of Louisiana-Pacific. Louisiana-Pacific has a much higher level of retained cash flow relative to debt whether capital expenditures are netted from RCF or not. Louisiana-Pacific has a lower level of debt relative to EBITDA and a higher level of EBITDA relative to interest expense. Louisiana-Pacific is likely to be assigned a higher credit rating.

Before calculating ratios such as those presented in Example 8, rating agencies make certain adjustments to reported financial statements, such as adjusting debt to include off-balance sheet debt in a company's total debt.[12] A later section will describe some common adjustments. Financial statement analysis, especially financial ratio analysis, can also be an important tool used in selecting equity investments, as discussed in the next section.

5 APPLICATION: SCREENING FOR POTENTIAL EQUITY INVESTMENTS

Ratios using financial statement data and market data are used to screen for potential equity investments. **Screening** is the application of a set of criteria to reduce a set of potential investments to a smaller set having certain desired characteristics. Criteria involving financial ratios generally involve comparing one or more ratios with some prespecified cutoff values.

---

[11] Ibid., p. 12; the values reported are based on average historical data.

[12] Ibid., p. 6.

A security selection approach incorporating financial ratios may be used whether the investor uses top-down analysis or bottom-up analysis. **Top-down analysis** involves identifying attractive geographic segments and/or industry segments and then the most attractive investments within those segments. **Bottom-up analysis** involves selection from all companies within a specified investment universe. Regardless of the direction, screening for potential equity investments aims to identify companies that meet specific criteria. An analysis of this type may be used as the basis for directly forming a portfolio, or it may be undertaken as a preliminary part of a more thorough analysis of potential investment targets.

Fundamental to this type of analysis are decisions about which metrics to use as screens, how many metrics to include, what values of those metrics to use as cutoff points, and what weighting to give each metric. Metrics can include not only financial ratios but also characteristics such as market capitalization or membership as a component security in a specified index. Exhibit 4 is an example of a hypothetical simple stock screen based on the following criteria: a valuation ratio (price-to-sales) less than a specified value; a solvency ratio measuring financial leverage (total assets/equity) not exceeding a specified value; dividend payments; and positive one-year-ahead forecast EPS. The exhibit shows the results of applying the screen to a set of 4,203 U.S. securities that comprise a hypothetical equity manager's investment universe.

EXHIBIT 4	Example of a Stock Screen	
	Stocks Meeting Criterion	
Criterion	**Number**	**Percent of Total**
Price per share/Sales per share < 1.5	1,560	37.1
Total assets/Equity ≤ 2.0	2,123	50.5
Dividends > 0	2,497	59.4
Consensus forecast EPS > 0	2,956	70.3
Meeting all four criteria simultaneously	473	11.3

Source: http://finance.yahoo.com.

Several points about the screen in Exhibit 4 are observed in many screens seen in practice:

▶ Some criteria serve as checks on the interpretation of other criteria. In this hypothetical example, the first criterion selects stocks that are relatively cheaply valued. However, the stocks might be cheap for a good reason, such as poor profitability or excessive financial leverage. So, the criteria requiring forecast EPS and dividends to be positive serve as checks on profitability, and the criterion limiting financial leverage serves as a check on financial risk. Of course, financial ratios or other statistics cannot generally control for exposure to certain types of risk (e.g., related to regulatory developments or technological innovation).

▶ If all the criteria were completely independent of each other, the set of stocks meeting all four criteria would be 329, equal to 4,203 times 7.8 percent—the product of the fraction of stocks satisfying the four criteria individually (i.e., $0.371 \times 0.505 \times 0.594 \times 0.703 = 0.078$, or 7.8 percent). As the screen illustrates, criteria are often not independent, and the result is more securities passing the screen. In this example, 473 (or 11.3 percent) of the securities passed all four screens. As an example of the lack of independence, dividend-paying status is probably positively correlated with the ability to generate positive earnings and the value of the fourth criterion. If stocks that pass one test tend to also pass the other, fewer would be eliminated after the application of the second test.

▶ The results of screens can sometimes be relatively concentrated in a subset of the sectors represented in the benchmark. The financial leverage criterion in Exhibit 4 would exclude all banking stocks, for example. What constitutes a high or low value of a measure of a financial characteristic can be sensitive to the industry in which a company operates.

Screens can be used by both **growth investors** (focused on investing in high-earnings-growth companies), **value investors** (focused on paying a relatively low share price in relation to earnings or assets per share), and **market-oriented investors** (an intermediate grouping for investors whose investment disciplines cannot be clearly categorized as value or growth). The criteria of growth screens would typically feature criteria related to earnings growth and/or momentum. Value screens, as a rule, feature criteria setting upper limits for the value of one or more valuation ratios. Market-oriented screens would not strongly emphasize valuation or growth criteria. The use of screens involving financial ratios may be most common among value investors.

There have been many studies researching the most effective items of accounting information for screening equity investments. Some research suggests that certain items of accounting information can help explain (and potentially predict) market returns (e.g., Chan et al. 1991; Lev and Thiagarajan 1993; Lakonishok et al. 1994; Davis 1994; Arbanell and Bushee 1998). Representative of such investigations is Piotroski (2000), whose screen uses nine accounting-based fundamentals that aim to identify financially strong and profitable companies among those with high book value/market value ratios. For example, the profitability measures relate to whether the company reported positive net income, positive cash flow, and an increase in return on assets (ROA).

An analyst may want to evaluate how a portfolio based on a particular screen would have performed historically, using a process known as "backtesting." **Backtesting** applies the portfolio selection rules to historical data and calculates what returns would have been earned if a particular strategy had been used. The relevance of backtesting to investment success in practice can, however, be limited. Haugen and Baker (1996) describe some of these limitations:

▶ Survivorship bias: If the database used in backtesting eliminates companies that cease to exist because of a merger or bankruptcy, then the remaining companies collectively will appear to have performed better.

▶ Look-ahead bias: If a database includes financial data updated for restatements (where companies have restated previously issued financial statements to correct errors or reflect changes in accounting principles),[13]

---

[13] In the United States, restatements of previously issued financial statements have increased in recent years. The U.S. Government Accounting Office (2002) reports 919 restatements by 834 public companies in the period from January 1997 to June 2002. The number of restatements increased from 613 in 2004 to 1,195 in 2005 (*Wall Street Journal*, 2006).

then there is a mismatch between what investors would have actually known at the time of the investment decision and the information used in backtesting.

▶ Data-snooping bias: If researchers build models based on previous researchers' findings, then using the same database to test the model is not actually a test. Under this scenario, the same rules may or may not produce similar results in the future. One academic study argues that the apparent ability of value strategies to generate excess returns is largely explainable as the result of collective data snooping (Conrad, Cooper, and Kaul, 2003).

EXAMPLE 9

Ratio-Based Screening for Potential Equity Investments

Below are two alternative strategies under consideration by an investment firm:

Strategy A invests in stocks that are components of a global equity index, have a ROE above the median ROE of all stocks in the index, and a P/E ratio less than the median P/E.

Strategy B invests in stocks that are components of a broad-based U.S. equity index, have price to operating cash flow in the lowest quartile of companies in the index, and have shown increases in sales for at least the past three years.

Both strategies were developed with the use of backtesting.

1. How would you characterize the two strategies?
2. What concerns might you have about using such strategies?

Solution to 1: Strategy A appears to aim for global diversification and combines a requirement for profitability with a traditional measure of value (low P/E). Strategy B focuses on both large and small companies in a single market and apparently aims to identify companies that are growing and yet managing to generate positive cash flow from operations.

Solution to 2: The use of *any* approach to investment decisions depends on the objectives and risk profile of the investor. With that crucial consideration in mind, ratio-based benchmarks can offer an efficient way to screen for potential equity investments. However, in doing so, many types of questions arise.

First, unintentional selections can be made if criteria are not specified carefully. For example, Strategy A might unintentionally select a loss-making company with negative shareholders' equity because negative net income divided by negative shareholders' equity would arithmetically result in a positive ROE. Strategy B might unintentionally select a company with negative operating cash flow because price to operating cash flow would be negative and thus very low in the ranking. In both cases, the analyst can add additional screening criteria to avoid unintentional selection (e.g., criteria requiring positive shareholders' equity and operating cash flow).

> Second, the inputs to ratio analysis are derived from financial statements, and companies may differ in the financial standards applied (e.g., IFRS versus U.S. GAAP); the specific accounting method chosen within those allowed under any body of reporting standards; and/or the estimates made in applying an accounting method.
>
> Third, backtesting may not provide a reliable indication of future performance because of survivorship bias, look-ahead bias, or data snooping; furthermore, as suggested by finance theory and by common sense, the past is not necessarily indicative of the future. Fourth, implementation decisions can crucially affect returns. For example, decisions about frequency and timing of portfolio selection and reevaluation affect transaction costs and taxes paid out of the portfolio.

6 ANALYST ADJUSTMENTS TO REPORTED FINANCIALS

When comparing companies that use different accounting methods or estimate key accounting inputs in different ways, analysts frequently adjust a company's financials. In this section, we first provide a framework for considering potential analyst adjustments to facilitate such comparisons and then provide examples of such adjustments. In practice, required adjustments vary widely. The examples presented here are not intended to be comprehensive, but rather to illustrate the use of adjustments to facilitate comparison.

6.1 A Framework for Analyst Adjustments

In this discussion of potential analyst adjustments to a company's financial statements, we employ a balance sheet focused framework. Of course, because the financial statements are interrelated, adjustments to items reported on one statement must also be reflected in adjustments to items on another statement. For example, an analyst adjustment to the balance sheet item inventory affects the income statement item cost of goods sold; and the owners' equity amount is affected by analyst adjustments relating to expense or revenue recognition.

Regardless of the particular order in which an analyst considers the items that may require adjustment for comparability, the following considerations are appropriate:

▶ *Importance.* Is an adjustment to this item likely to affect my conclusions? In other words, does it matter? For example, in an industry where companies require minimal inventory, does it matter that two companies use different inventory accounting methods?

▶ *Body of standards.* Is there a difference in the body of standards being used (U.S. GAAP versus IFRS)? If so, in which areas is the difference likely to affect a comparison?

▶ *Methods.* Is there a difference in methods?

▶ *Estimates.* Is there a difference in important estimates?

The following sections illustrate analyst adjustments—first those relating to the asset side of the balance sheet and then those relating to the liability side.

6.2 Analyst Adjustments Related to Investments

Accounting for investments in the debt and equity securities of other companies (other than investments accounted for under the equity method and investments in consolidated subsidiaries) depends on management's intention (i.e., to actively trade the securities, make them available for sale, or, in the case of debt securities, to hold them to maturity). When securities are classified as "trading" securities, unrealized gains and losses are reported in the income statement. When securities are classified as "available-for-sale" securities, unrealized gains and losses are not reported in the income statement and instead are recognized in equity. If two otherwise comparable companies have significant differences in the classification of investments, analyst adjustments may be useful to facilitate comparison.

Also, IFRS requires that those unrealized gains and losses on available-for-sale debt securities that arise due to exchange rate movements be recognized in the income statement, whereas U.S. GAAP does not. To facilitate comparison across companies, increases (decreases) in the value of available-for-sale debt securities arising from exchange rate movements can be deducted from (added to) the amount of income reported by the IFRS-reporting company.

6.3 Analyst Adjustments Related to Inventory

With inventory, adjustments may be required for different accounting methods. As described in previous readings, a company's decision about the inventory method will affect the value of inventory shown on the balance sheet as well as the value of inventory that is sold (cost of goods sold). If one company, not reporting under IFRS,[14] uses LIFO (last in, first out) and another uses FIFO (first in, first out), comparison of the two companies may be difficult. However, companies that use the LIFO method must also disclose the value of their inventory under the FIFO method. To place inventory values for a company using LIFO reporting on a FIFO basis, the analyst would add the ending balance of the LIFO reserve to the ending value of inventory under LIFO accounting; to adjust cost of goods sold to a FIFO basis, the analyst would subtract the change in the LIFO reserve from the reported cost of goods sold under LIFO accounting. Example 10 illustrates the use of a disclosure of the value of inventory under the FIFO method to make a valid current ratio comparison between companies reporting on a LIFO and FIFO basis.

EXAMPLE 10

Adjustment for a Company Using LIFO Method of Accounting for Inventories

An analyst is comparing the financial performance of SL Industries (AMEX: SLI), a U.S. company operating in the electric lighting and wiring industry, with a company that reports using IFRS. The IFRS company uses the FIFO method of inventory accounting, and you therefore must convert SLI's results to a comparable basis.

---

[14] IAS No. 2 does not permit the use of LIFO.

EXHIBIT 5	Data for SL Industries	

	31 December	
	2005	**2004**
Total current assets	$44,194,000	$37,990,000
Total current liabilities	18,387,000	18,494,000

NOTE 6. INVENTORIES

Inventories consist of the following ($ in thousands):

	31 December	
	2005	**2004**
Raw materials	$ 9,774	$ 9,669
Work in process	4,699	5,000
Finished goods	1,926	3,633
	16,399	18,302
Less: Allowances	(1,829)	(2,463)
	$14,570	$15,839

The above includes certain inventories that are valued using the LIFO method, which aggregated $4,746,000 and $3,832,000 as of December 31, 2005 and December 31, 2004, respectively. The excess of FIFO cost over LIFO cost as of December 31, 2005 and December 31, 2004 was approximately $502,000 and $565,000, respectively.

Source: 10-K for SL Industries, Inc. for the year ended 31 December 2005; filed with the SEC 24 March 2006.

---

1. Based on the information in Exhibit 5, calculate SLI's current ratio under FIFO and LIFO for 2004 and 2005.

2. Interpret the results of adjusting the current ratio to be consistent with inventory on a FIFO basis.

Solution to 1: The calculations of SLI's current ratio (current assets divided by current liabilities) are given below.

	2005	2004
I. Current Ratio (Unadjusted)		
Total current assets	$44,194,000	$37,990,000
Total current liabilities	18,387,000	18,494,000
Current ratio (unadjusted)	2.40	2.05

	2005	2004
II. Current Ratio (Adjusted)		
Adjust the inventory to FIFO, add	502,000	565,000
Total current assets (adjusted)	$44,696,000	$38,555,000
Total current liabilities	18,387,000	18,494,000
Current ratio (adjusted)	2.43	2.08

To adjust the LIFO inventory to FIFO, the excess amounts of FIFO cost over LIFO cost are added to LIFO inventory, increasing current assets by an equal amount. The effect of adjusting inventory on the current ratio is to increase it from 2.05 to 2.08 in 2004 and from 2.40 to 2.43 in 2005.

Solution to 2: SLI appears to be somewhat more liquid based on the adjusted current ratio. However, the year-over-year improvement in the current ratio on an adjusted basis at 16.8 percent $(2.43/2.08 - 1)$ was slightly less favorable than the improvement of 17.1 percent $(2.40/2.05 - 1)$ on an unadjusted basis.

In summary, the information disclosed by companies using LIFO allows an analyst to calculate the value of the company's inventory as if it were using the FIFO method. In the example above, the portion of inventory valued using the LIFO method was a relatively small portion of total inventory, and the LIFO reserve (excess of FIFO cost over LIFO) was also relatively small. However, if the LIFO method is used for a substantial part of a company's inventory and the LIFO reserve is large relative to reported inventory, the adjustment to a FIFO basis can be important for comparison of the LIFO-reporting company with another company that uses the FIFO method of inventory valuation. Example 11 illustrates a case in which such an adjustment would have a major impact on an analyst's conclusions.

EXAMPLE 11

Analyst Adjustment to Inventory Value for Comparability in a Current Ratio Comparison

Company A reports under IFRS and uses the FIFO method of inventory accounting for its entire inventory. Company B reports under U.S. GAAP and uses the LIFO method. Exhibit 6 gives data pertaining to current assets, LIFO reserves, and current liabilities of these companies.

Based on the data given in Exhibit 6, compare the liquidity of the two companies as measured by the current ratio.

EXHIBIT 6	Data for Companies Accounting for Inventory on Different Bases	
	Company A (FIFO)	**Company B (LIFO)**
Current assets (includes inventory)	$ 300,000	$ 80,000
LIFO reserve	N/A	$ 20,000
Current liabilities	$ 150,000	$ 45,000

Solution: Company A's current ratio is 2.0. Based on unadjusted balance sheet data, Company B's current ratio is 1.78. Company A's higher current ratio indicates that Company A appears to be more liquid than Company B; however, the use of unadjusted data for Company B is not appropriate for making comparisons with Company A.

After adjusting Company B's inventory to a comparable basis (i.e., to a FIFO basis), the conclusion changes. The table below summarizes the results when Company B's inventory is left on a LIFO basis and when it is placed on a FIFO basis for comparability with Company A.

		Company B	
	Company A (FIFO)	**Unadjusted (LIFO Basis)**	**Adjusted (FIFO Basis)**
Current assets (includes inventory)	$ 300,000	$ 80,000	$ 100,000
Current liabilities	$ 150,000	$ 45,000	$ 45,000
Current ratio	2.00	1.78	2.22

When both companies' inventories are stated on a FIFO basis, Company B appears to be more liquid, as indicated by its current ratio of 2.22 versus Company A's ratio of 2.00. The adjustment to place Company B's inventory on a FIFO basis was significant because Company B was assumed to use LIFO for its entire inventory and its inventory reserve was $20,000/$80,000 = 0.25, or 25 percent of its reported inventory.

As mentioned earlier, an analyst can also adjust the cost of goods sold for a company using LIFO to a FIFO basis by subtracting the change in the amount of the LIFO reserve from cost of goods sold. Such an adjustment would be appropriate for making profitability comparisons with a company reporting on a FIFO basis and would be important to make when the impact of the adjustment would be material.

6.4 Analyst Adjustments Related to Property, Plant, and Equipment

Management generally has considerable discretion in the determination of depreciation expense. Depreciation expense affects reported net income and reported net fixed asset values. Analysts often consider management's choices related to depreciation as one qualitative factor in evaluating the quality of a company's financial reporting and, in some cases, they may adjust reported depreciation expense for a specific analytic purpose.

The amount of depreciation expense depends on both the accounting method and the estimates used in the calculations. Companies can depreciate fixed assets (other than land) using the straight-line method, an accelerated method, or a usage method. The straight-line method reports an equal amount of depreciation expense each period, computed as the depreciable cost divided by the estimated useful life of the asset (when acquired, an asset's depreciable cost is calculated as its total cost minus its estimated salvage value). Accelerated methods depreciate the asset more quickly, apportioning a greater amount of the depreciable cost to depreciation expense in the earlier periods. Usage-based methods depreciate an asset in proportion to its usage. Apart from selecting a depreciation method, companies must estimate an asset's salvage value and useful life to compute depreciation.

Disclosures required for depreciation often do not facilitate specific adjustments, so comparisons across companies concerning their decisions in depreciating assets are often qualitative and general. The accounts that are associated with depreciation include the balance sheet accounts for gross property, plant, and equipment (gross PPE); accumulated depreciation; the income statement account for depreciation expense; and the statement of cash flows disclosure of capital expenditure (capex) and asset disposals. The relationships between these items can reveal various pieces of information:

▶ accumulated depreciation divided by gross PPE, from the balance sheet, suggests how much of its useful life the company's overall asset base has passed;

▶ accumulated depreciation divided by depreciation expense suggests how many years' worth of depreciation expense has already been recognized (i.e., the average age of the asset base);

▶ net PPE (net of accumulated depreciation) divided by deprecation expense is an approximate indicator of how many years of useful life remain for the company's overall asset base;

▶ gross PPE divided by depreciation expense can suggest the average life of the assets at installation;

▶ capex divided by the sum of gross PPE plus capex can suggest what percentage of the asset base is being renewed through new capital investment; and

▶ capex in relation to asset disposal provides information on growth of the asset base.

These relationships can be evaluated across companies in an industry to suggest differences in strategies for asset utilization or areas for further investigation.

EXAMPLE 12

Differences in Depreciation

An analyst is evaluating the financial statements for two companies in the same industry. The companies have similar strategies with respect to the use of equipment in manufacturing their products. The following information is provided (amounts in millions):

	Company A ($)	Company B ($)
Net PPE	1,200	750
Depreciation expense	120	50

1. Based on the information given, estimate the average remaining useful lives of the asset bases of Company A and Company B.

2. Suppose that, based on a physical inspection of the companies' plants and other industry information, the analyst believes that the actual remaining useful lives of Company A's and Company B's assets is roughly equal at 10 years. Based only on the facts given, what might the analyst conclude concerning Company B's reported net income?

Solution to 1: The estimated average remaining useful life of Company A's asset base, calculated as net PPE divided by depreciation expense, is $1,200/$120 = 10 years. For Company B, the average remaining useful life of the asset base appears to be far longer at 15 years ($750/$50).

Solution to 2: If Company B's depreciation expense were calculated using 10 years, it would be $75 million (i.e., $25 million higher than reported) and higher depreciation expense would decrease net income. The analyst might conclude that Company B's reported net income reflects relatively aggressive accounting estimates compared with Company A's reported net income.

6.5 Analyst Adjustments Related to Goodwill

Goodwill is an example of an intangible asset (i.e., one without physical substance). Goodwill arises when one company purchases another for a price that exceeds the fair value of the assets acquired. Goodwill is recorded as an asset. For example, assume ParentCo purchases TargetCo for a purchase price of $400 million, the fair value of TargetCo's identifiable assets is $300 million, and the excess of the purchase price is attributed to TargetCo's valuable brands and well-trained workforce. ParentCo will record total assets of $400 million, consisting of $300 million in identifiable assets and $100 million of goodwill. The goodwill is tested annually for impairment, and if its value has declined, ParentCo will reduce the amount of the asset and report a write-off due to impairment.

One of the conceptual difficulties with goodwill arises in comparative financial statement analysis. Consider, for example, two hypothetical U.S. companies, one of which has grown by making an acquisition and the other one of which has grown internally. Assume that the economic value of the two companies is identical: Each has an identically valuable branded product, well-trained workforce, and proprietary technology. The company that has grown by acquisition will incur a related expenditure and will report assets on its balance sheet equal to the amount of the expenditure (assuming no write-offs). The company that has grown internally will have done so by incurring expenditures for advertising, staff training, and research, all of which are expensed as incurred under U.S. GAAP and are thus not directly reflected on the company's balance sheet. Ratios based on asset values and/or income, including profitability ratios such as return on assets and MV/BV, will generally differ for the two companies because of differences in the accounting values of assets and income related to goodwill, although by assumption the economic value of the companies is identical.

EXAMPLE 13

Ratio Comparisons for Goodwill

Miano Marseglia is an analyst who is evaluating the relative valuation of two footwear manufacturing companies: Phoenix Footwear Group (AMEX: PXG) and Rocky Brands (NASDAQ: RCKY). As one part of an overall analysis, Marseglia would like to see how the two companies compare with each other and with the industry based on price/book (P/B) ratios.[15] Because both companies are nondiversified, are small, and have high risk relative to larger, more diversified companies in the industry, Marseglia expects them to sell at a lower P/B ratio than the industry average of 3.68. Marseglia collects the following data on the two companies.

	PXG ($)	RCKY ($)
Market capitalization at 11 October 2006 (Market price per share times the number of shares outstanding)	37.22 million	67.57 million
Total shareholders' equity as of the most recent quarter (MRQ)	54.99 million	100.35 million
Goodwill	33.67 million	24.87 million
Other intangible assets	33.22 million	38.09 million

Marseglia computes the P/B ratios as follows:

PXG $37.22/$54.99   =   0.68

RCKY $67.57/$100.35   =   0.67

The companies have similar P/B ratios (i.e., they are approximately equally valued relative to MRQ shareholders' equity). As expected, each company also appears to be selling at a significant discount to the industry average P/B multiple of 3.68. Marseglia is concerned, however, because he notes that both companies have significant intangible assets, particularly goodwill. He wonders what the relative value would be if the P/B ratio were computed after adjusting book value first to remove goodwill and then to remove all intangible assets. Book value reduced by all intangible assets is known as "tangible book value." The average price/tangible book value for the industry is 4.19.

1. Compute the P/B ratio adjusted for goodwill and the price/tangible book value ratio for each company.

---

[15] Price/book, or P/B, is the price per share divided by stockholders' equity per share. It is also referred to as a market/book, or MV/BV, ratio because it can also be calculated as total market value of the stock (market capitalization) divided by total stockholders' equity.

2. Which company appears to be a better value based *solely* on this data? (Note that the P/B ratio is only one part of a broader analysis. Much more evidence on the valuation and the comparability of the companies would be required to reach a conclusion about whether one company is a better value.)

Solution to 1:

	PXG ($)	RCKY ($)
Total stockholders' equity	54.99 million	100.35 million
Less: Goodwill	33.67 million	24.87 million
Book value, adjusted	21.32 million	75.48 million
Adjusted P/B ratio	37.22/21.32 = 1.75	67.57/75.48 = 0.90

	PXG ($)	RCKY ($)
Total stockholders' equity	54.99 million	100.35 million
Less: Goodwill	33.67 million	24.87 million
Less: Other intangible assets	33.22 million	38.09 million
Tangible book value	(11.90) million	37.39 million
Price/tangible book value ratio	NM (not meaningful)	67.57/37.39 = 1.81

Solution to 2: Based on an adjustment for goodwill accumulated in acquisitions, RCKY appears to be selling for a lower price relative to book value than PXG (0.90 versus 1.75). Both companies are selling at a significant discount to the industry, even after adjusting for goodwill.

Based on price/tangible book value, RCKY is also selling for a lower multiple than the industry (1.81 versus 4.19). PXG has a negative tangible book value, and its price/tangible book value ratio is not meaningful with a negative denominator. Based on this interpretation and based *solely* on this information, PXG appears relatively expensive compared with RCKY.

6.6 Analyst Adjustments Related to Off-Balance Sheet Financing

A number of business activities give rise to obligations which, although they are economically liabilities of a company, are not required to be reported on a company's balance sheet. Including such off-balance sheet obligations in a company's liabilities can affect ratios and conclusions based on such ratios. In this section, we describe adjustments to financial statements related to one type of off-balance sheet obligation, the operating lease.

The rights of a lessee (the party that is leasing some asset) may be very similar to the rights of an owner, but if the terms of the lease can be structured so it can be accounted for as an operating lease, the lease is treated like a rental contract, and neither the leased asset nor the associated liability is reported on the balance sheet.[16] The lessee simply records the periodic lease payment as a rental expense in its income statement. In contrast, when a company actually owns an asset, the asset is shown on the balance sheet along with any corresponding liability, such as financing for the asset. Similarly, if a lease is accounted for as a capital lease—essentially equivalent to ownership—the leased asset and associated liability appear on the lessee's balance sheet. The issue of concern to analysts arises when a lease conveys to the lessee most of the benefits and risks of ownership, but the lease is accounted for as an operating lease—the case of off-balance sheet financing. International accounting standard setters have stated that the entities should not avoid balance sheet recording of leases through artificial leasing structures, seeking to avoid the substance of the transaction.

A 2005 report by the U.S. SEC on off-balance sheet financing estimates that more than 63 percent of companies in the United States report having an operating lease. The SEC estimate of total future lease payments under operating leases was $1.2 trillion.

Because companies are required to disclose in their financial statements the amount and timing of lease payments, an analyst can use this information to answer the question: How would a company's financial position look if operating lease obligations were included in its total liabilities?

Exhibit 7 presents selected items from the balance sheet of AMR Corporation (the parent of American Airlines) and the text of the footnote from the financial statements about the company's leases. We can use the information in this exhibit to illustrate analyst adjustments:

EXHIBIT 7	Lease Arrangements of AMR Corporation (NYSE: AMR) Selected Items from Balance Sheet ($ Millions)	
	31 December	
	2005	**2004**
Total Assets	**$29,495**	**$28,773**
Current maturities of long-term debt	$ 1,077	$ 659
Long-term debt, less current maturities	12,530	12,436
Total long-term debt	13,607	13,095
Current obligations under capital leases	162	147
Obligations under capital leases, less current obligations	926	1,088
Total long-term debt and capital leases	$14,695	$14,330

From Footnote 5. Leases

AMR's subsidiaries lease various types of equipment and property, primarily aircraft and airport facilities. The future minimum lease payments required under capital leases, together with the present value of such payments, and future minimum lease payments required under operating leases that have initial or

(Exhibit continued on next page . . .)

---

[16] A lessee classifies a lease as an operating lease if certain guidelines concerning the term of the lease, the present value of the lease payments, and the ownership of the asset at the end of the lease term are satisfied. Under U.S. GAAP, FAS No. 13 specifies the criteria for classification.

EXHIBIT 7	(continued)

remaining non-cancelable lease terms in excess of one year as of December 31, 2005, were (in millions):

Year Ending December 31	Capital Leases	Operating Leases
2006	$263	$1,065
2007	196	1,039
2008	236	973
2009	175	872
2010	140	815
2011 and thereafter	794	7,453
	$1,804	$12,217[a]
Less amount representing interest	716	
Present value of net minimum lease payments	$1,088	

[a] As of December 31, 2005, included in Accrued liabilities and Other liabilities and deferred credits on the accompanying consolidated balance sheet is approximately $1.4 billion relating to rent expense being recorded in advance of future operating lease payments.

Source: AMR Corporation's Form 10-K for period ending 31 December 2005, filed 24 February 2006.

To evaluate the company's solvency position, we can calculate the debt-to-assets ratio, defined in the reading on financial analysis techniques as the ratio of total debt to total assets. Excluding obligations under capital leases (amounting to $1,088 in 2005) from the definition of total debt, we would calculate the ratio for 2005 as 46.1 percent (total long-term debt/total assets = $13,607/$29,495). Properly including obligations under capital leases in the definition of total debt, we would calculate the ratio as 49.8 percent ($14,695/$29,495).

The company's footnote on leases discloses a total of $12.2 billion of future payments for operating leases on an undiscounted basis. The footnote also indicates that, of this amount, only $1.4 billion is shown on the balance sheet. To determine the impact of including operating lease obligations in the total liabilities, we will calculate the present value of the future operating lease payments. Calculating the present value of the future operating lease payments requires a discount rate. We can estimate an appropriate discount rate from the information about the present value of the capital lease payments. The discount rate is the internal rate of return implied by the stream of lease payments and their present value.

For AMR, the present value of the capital lease payments is $1,088 million. Using the stream of payments shown in the footnote and assuming that all of the $794 million payments are made in the year 2011 would give an internal rate of return of 13.7 percent. However, based on the schedule of payments shown, a better assumption is that the $794 million payments do not all occur in a single year. One approach to estimating the timing of these payments is to assume that the payments in 2011 and subsequent years equal the average annual payments in years 2006 to 2010 of $202 = ($263 + $196 + $236 + $175 + $140)/5. Using this approach, there are four annual payments in 2011 and thereafter, and the internal rate of return of the capital lease is 12.1 percent. Given that lease payments have been generally declining over 2006 to 2010, another approach resulting in lower lease payments after 2010 would be to assume that the $794 million is paid equally over some longer time span, such as 10 years. Using this assumption, the internal rate of return of the capital lease payments is 10.0 percent.[17]

EXHIBIT 8	Present Value of Operating Lease Payments Using Discount Rate Derived from Present Value of Capital Lease Payments ($Millions)				
	Capital Lease			**Operating Lease**	
	Payments (as Given)	Payments Incl. Estimated Annual Payments for 2011 and Thereafter	Payments Incl. Estimated Annual Payments for 2011 and Thereafter	Payments (as Given)	Payments Incl. Estimated Annual Payments for 2011 and Thereafter
Present value, *given*	−$1,088	−$1,088	−$1,088		
Year 2006	$263	$263	$263	$1,065	$1,065
2007	$196	$196	$196	$1,039	$1,039
2008	$236	$236	$236	$973	$973
2009	$175	$175	$175	$872	$872
2010	$140	$140	$140	$815	$815
2011 and thereafter	$794	$202	$79	$7,453	$953
		$202	$79		$953
		$202	$79		$953
		$188	$79		$953
			$79		$953
			$79		$953
			$79		$953
			$79		$782
			$79		
			$79		
Internal rate of return	13.7%	12.1%	10.0%		
Present value of operating lease payments using a 13.7% discount rate:					$5,671
Present value of operating lease payments using a 12.1% discount rate:					$6,106
Present value of operating lease payments using a 10.0% discount rate:					$6,767

---

[17] If the term structure of the capital and operating leases can be assumed to be similar, an alternative, shortcut, way to estimate the present value of future operating lease payments that do not appear on the balance sheet is to assume that the relationship between the discounted and undiscounted operating lease payments is approximately the same as the relationship between the discounted and undiscounted capital lease payments. The discounted capital lease payments of $926 million as reported on the balance sheet are 56.4 percent of the undiscounted noncurrent capital lease payments of $1,642 million ($1,804 million total minus $162 million current payments). Applying the same relationship to operating lease payments, 56.4 percent of the undiscounted noncurrent operating lease payments of $10,817 million ($12,217 million total minus $1,400 million current) equals $6.1 billion, yielding $7.5 billion as the present value of operating lease payments including the current obligation of $1.4 billion.

Having estimated an appropriate discount rate, we can calculate the present value of the future operating lease payments. Exhibit 8 presents the results of these calculations and illustrates the sensitivity of the analysis to assumptions about the timing of cash flows. We developed discount rate estimates of 12.1 percent and 10 percent. Using a discount rate of 12.1 percent, the present value of future operating lease payments would be roughly $6.1 billion, and using a discount rate of 10.0 percent, the present value would be around $6.8 billion. Because $1.4 billion of the amounts related to operating leases already appear on the balance sheet (as disclosed in the company's lease footnote), the value of the future operating lease payments that do not appear on the balance sheet are estimated to be in the range of $6,106 million − $1,400 million = $4,706 million, or about $4.7 billion, to $6,767 million − $1,400 million = $5,367 million, or about $5.4 billion. The lower the assumed discount rate, the higher the present value of the lease payments.

We now add the present value of the off-balance sheet future operating lease payments to the company's total assets and total debt. Making this adjustment increases the debt-to-assets ratio to an amount between ($14,695 + $4,706)/($29,495 + $4,706) = 56.7 percent and ($14,695 + $5,367)/($29,495 + $5,367) = 57.5 percent. If a point estimate of the debt-to-assets ratio were needed, in this case, the analyst might select the 57.5 percent estimate based on the lower discount rate because that discount rate is more consistent with yields on investment-grade bonds as of the date of the example.

EXAMPLE 14

Analyst Adjustment to Debt for Operating Lease Payments

An analyst is evaluating the capital structure of two (hypothetical) companies, Koller Semiconductor and MacRae Manufacturing, as of the beginning of 2006. Koller Semiconductor makes somewhat less use of operating leases than MacRae Manufacturing. The analyst has the following additional information:

	Koller Semiconductor	MacRae Manufacturing
Total debt	$1,200	$2,400
Total equity	$2,000	$4,000
Average interest rate on debt	10%	8%
Lease payments on operating leases:		
2006	10	90
2007	18	105
2008	22	115
2009	25	128
2010 and thereafter	75	384

Based on the information given, discuss how adjusting for operating leases affects the companies' solvency based on their debt to debt-plus-equity ratios, assuming no adjustment to equity. (Assume payments after 2009 occur at the same rate as for 2009. For example, for Koller Semiconductor, the payments for 2010 through 2012 are assumed to be $25 each year.)

Solution: Before making the adjustment, the companies' debt to debt-plus-equity ratios are identical, both at 37.5 percent. To make the adjustment for operating leases, the first step is to calculate the present value of the operating lease payments. Assuming that payments after 2009 occur at the same rate as for 2009, Koller's payment would be $25 in 2010, 2011, and 2012. The present value of $25 discounted for five years at 10 percent is $15.52. MacRae's payment is assumed to be $128 in each of 2010, 2011, and 2012. The present value of $128 discounted for five years at 8 percent is $87.11. Calculations for the following two years are made in the same manner, resulting in the present values shown in the following table:

	Koller Semiconductor ($)	MacRae Manufacturing ($)
2006	9.09	83.33
2007	14.88	90.02
2008	16.53	91.29
2009	17.08	94.08
2010	15.52	87.11
2011	14.11	80.66
2012	12.83	74.69
Total present value (PV)	100.04	601.18

After adding the present value of capitalized lease obligations to total debt, MacRae Manufacturing's debt to debt-plus-equity ratio is significantly higher, at 42.9 percent, as shown in the following table. The higher ratio reflects the impact of lease obligations on MacRae's solvency:

	Koller Semiconductor		MacRae Manufacturing	
	Before Capitalizing	After Capitalizing	Before Capitalizing	After Capitalizing
Total debt	$1,200	$1,300	$2,400	$3,001
Total equity	$2,000	$2,000	$4,000	$4,000
Debt/ (Debt + Equity)	37.5%	39.4%	37.5%	42.9%

The adjustment for operating leases essentially treats the transaction as if the asset had been purchased rather than leased. The present value of the capitalized lease obligations is the amount owed and the amount at which the asset is valued. Further adjustments reflect the reduction of rent expenses (if the asset is owned, rent would not be paid), the related interest expense on the amount owed, and a depreciation expense for the asset. The reduction of rent expense can be estimated as the average of two years of rent expense. Interest expense is estimated as the interest rate times the PV of the lease payments. Depreciation is estimated on a straight-line basis based on the number of years of future lease payments.

EXAMPLE 15

Stylized Example of Effect on Coverage Ratio for Operating Lease Adjustment

The analyst is also evaluating the interest coverage ratio of the companies in the previous example, Koller Semiconductor and MacRae Manufacturing.

	Koller Semiconductor ($)	MacRae Manufacturing ($)
EBIT before adjustment	850	1,350
Interest expense before adjustment	120	192

The prior-year (2005) rent expense was $11 for Koller Semiconductor and $90 for MacRae Manufacturing.

Using the information in Example 14 and the additional information given above, discuss how adjustment for operating leases affects the companies' solvency as measured by their coverage ratios.

Solution: Interest coverage is calculated as EBIT divided by interest. For the adjustments, rent expense is the average of two years' rent. For Koller Semiconductor, rent expense is calculated as ($11 + $10)/2. The cost of interest on lease obligations is estimated as the interest rate multiplied by the present value of the lease payments. For Koller Semiconductor, this interest expense is calculated as 10% × $100.04, and for MacRae Manufacturing, it is calculated as 8% × $601.18. Depreciation is estimated on a straight-line basis by dividing the PV of lease payments by the number of years of lease payments (seven years). After the adjustment, both companies show a decline in interest coverage ratio, reflecting the increased obligation associated with the operating lease obligations. There is also a larger apparent difference in the coverage between the two companies.

	Koller Semiconductor	MacRae Manufacturing
Interest coverage before adjustment	**7.1**	**7.0**
EBIT before adjustment	**850**	**1,350**
Rent expense; an add-back to EBIT	10.5	90.0
Depreciation; a deduction from EBIT	(14.3)	(85.9)
EBIT after adjustment	846.2	1354.1
Interest expense before adjustment	120	192
Assumed cost of interest on lease obligation (to add to interest)	10.0	48.1
Interest expense after adjustment	130.0	240.1
Interest coverage after adjustment	**6.5**	**5.6**

In summary, adjusting a company's financial statements to include amounts of lease payments gives a more complete picture of the company's financial condition and enables the comparison of companies with varying arrangements for financing assets. It may additionally be necessary to adjust for amounts associated with other off-balance sheet financing arrangements.

SUMMARY

This reading described selected applications of financial statement analysis, including the evaluation of past financial performance, the projection of future financial performance, the assessment of credit risk, and the screening of potential equity investments. In addition, the reading introduced analyst adjustments to reported financials. In all cases, the analyst needs to have a good understanding of the financial reporting standards under which financial statements are prepared. Because standards evolve over time, analysts must stay current in order to make good investment decisions. The main points in the reading include the following:

▶ Evaluating a company's historical performance addresses not only what happened but also the causes behind the company's performance and how the performance reflects the company's strategy.

▶ The projection of a company's future net income and cash flow often begins with a top-down sales forecast in which the analyst forecasts industry sales and the company's market share. By projecting profit margins or expenses and the level of investment in working and fixed capital needed to support projected sales, the analyst can forecast net income and cash flow.

▶ Projections of future performance are needed for discounted cash flow valuation of equity and are often needed in credit analysis to assess a borrower's ability to repay interest and principal of a debt obligation.

▶ Credit analysis uses financial statement analysis to evaluate credit-relevant factors, including tolerance for leverage, operational efficiency, and margin stability.

▶ When ratios using financial statement data and market data are used to screen for potential equity investments, fundamental decisions include which metrics to use as screens, how many metrics to include, what values of those metrics to use as cutoff points, and what weighting to give each metric.

▶ Analyst adjustments to a company's reported financial statements are sometimes necessary (e.g., when comparing companies that use different accounting methods or assumptions). Adjustments include those related to investments; inventory; property, plant, and equipment; goodwill; and off-balance sheet financing.

PRACTICE PROBLEMS FOR READING 42

1. Projecting profit margins into the future on the basis of past results would be *most* reliable when the company:

   A. is a large, diversified company operating in mature industries.

   B. is in the commodities business.

   C. operates in a single business segment.

2. Galambos Corporation had an average receivable collection period of 19 days in 2003. Galambos has stated that it wants to decrease its collection period in 2004 to match the industry average of 15 days. Credit sales in 2003 were $300 million, and analysts expect credit sales to increase to $400 million in 2004. To achieve the company's goal of decreasing the collection period, the change in the average accounts receivable balance from 2003 to 2004 that must occur is *closest* to:

   A. −$420,000.

   B. $420,000.

   C. $836,000.

3. Credit analysts are likely to consider which of the following in making a rating recommendation?

   A. Business risk, but not financial risk.

   B. Financial risk, but not business risk.

   C. Both business risk and financial risk.

4. When screening for potential equity investments based on return on equity, to control risk an analyst would be *most likely* to include a criterion that requires:

   A. positive net income.

   B. negative net income.

   C. negative shareholders' equity.

5. One concern when screening for low price-to-earnings stocks is that companies with low price-to-earnings ratios may be financially weak. What criteria might an analyst include to avoid inadvertently selecting weak companies?

   A. Current-year sales growth lower than prior-year sales growth.

   B. Net income less than zero.

   C. Debt-to-total assets ratio below a certain cutoff point.

6. When a database eliminates companies that cease to exist because of a merger or bankruptcy, this can result in:

   A. look-ahead bias.

   B. backtesting bias.

   C. survivorship bias.

7. In a comprehensive financial analysis, financial statements should be:

   A. used as reported without adjustment.

   B. adjusted after completing ratio analysis.

   C. adjusted for differences in accounting standards, such as international financial reporting standards and U.S. generally accepted accounting principles.

8. When comparing financial statements prepared under IFRS with those prepared under U.S. generally accepted accounting principles, analysts may need to make adjustments related to:

   A. realized losses.

   B. unrealized gains and losses for trading securities.

   C. unrealized gains and losses for available-for-sale securities.

9. When comparing a U.S. company using the last in, first out (LIFO) method of inventory to companies preparing their financial statements under international financial reporting standards (IFRS), analysts should be aware that according to IFRS, the LIFO method of inventory:

   A. is never acceptable.

   B. is always acceptable.

   C. is acceptable when applied to finished goods inventory only.

10. An analyst is evaluating the balance sheet of a U.S. company that uses last in, first out (LIFO) accounting for inventory. The analyst collects the following data:

	31 Dec 05	31 Dec 06
Inventory reported on balance sheet	$500,000	$600,000
LIFO reserve	$50,000	$70,000
Average tax rate	30%	30%

After adjustment to convert to first in, first out (FIFO), inventory at 31 December 2006 would be closest to:

   A. $600,000.

   B. $620,000.

   C. $670,000.

11. An analyst gathered the following data for a company ($ in millions):

	31 Dec 2000	31 Dec 2001
Gross investment in fixed assets	$2.8	$2.8
Accumulated depreciation	$1.2	$1.6

The average age and average depreciable life, respectively, of the company's fixed assets at the end of 2001 are *closest* to:

	Average Age	Average Depreciable Life
A.	1.75 years	7 years
B.	1.75 years	14 years
C.	4.00 years	7 years

12. To compute tangible book value, an analyst would:

   A. add goodwill to stockholders' equity.

   B. add all intangible assets to stockholders' equity.

   C. subtract all intangible assets from stockholders' equity.

13. Which of the following is an off-balance sheet financing technique?
The use of:

   A. the LIFO inventory method.

   B. capital leases.

   C. operating leases.

14. To better evaluate the solvency of a company, an analyst would most likely add to total liabilities:

   A. the present value of future capital lease payments.

   B. the total amount of future operating lease payments.

   C. the present value of future operating lease payments.

SOLUTIONS FOR READING 42

1. A is correct. For a large, diversified company, margin changes in different business segments may offset each other. Furthermore, margins are most likely to be stable in mature industries.

2. C is correct. Accounts receivable turnover is equal to 365/19 (collection period in days) = 19.2 for 2003 and needs to equal 365/15 = 24.3 in 2004 for Galambos to meet its goal. Sales/turnover equals the accounts receivable balance. For 2003, $300,000,000/19.2 = $15,625,000, and for 2004, $400,000,000/24.3 = $16,460,905. The difference of $835,905 is the increase in receivables needed for Galambos to achieve its goal.

3. C is correct. Credit analysts consider both business risk and financial risk.

4. A is correct. Requiring that net income be positive would avoid selecting companies that report positive return on equity because both net income and shareholders' equity are negative.

5. C is correct. A lower debt-to-total assets ratio indicates greater financial strength. Requiring that a company's debt-to-total assets ratio be below a certain cutoff point would allow the analyst to screen out highly leveraged and, therefore, potentially financially weak companies. Requiring declining sales growth (answer A) or negative income (answer B) would not be appropriate for screening out financially weak companies.

6. C is correct. Survivorship bias exists when companies that merge or go bankrupt are dropped from the database and only surviving companies remain. Look-ahead bias involves using updated financial information in backtesting that would not have been available at the time the decision was made. Backtesting involves testing models in prior periods and is not a bias itself.

7. C is correct. Financial statements should be adjusted for differences in accounting standards (as well as accounting and operating choices). These adjustments should be made prior to ratio analysis.

8. C is correct. IFRS makes a distinction between unrealized gains and losses on available-for-sale debt securities that arise due to exchange rate movements and requires these changes in value to be recognized in the income statement, whereas U.S. GAAP does not make this distinction.

9. A is correct. LIFO is not permitted under international financial reporting standards.

10. C is correct. To convert LIFO inventory to FIFO inventory, the entire LIFO reserve must be added back: $600,000 + $70,000 = $670,000.

11. C is correct. There were no additions or deletions to the fixed asset account during the year, so depreciation expense is equal to the difference in accumulated depreciation at the beginning of the year and the end of the year, or 0.4 million. Average age is equal to accumulated depreciation/depreciation expense, or 1.6/0.4 = 4 years. Average depreciable life is equal to ending gross investment/depreciation expense = 2.8/0.4 = 7 years.

12. C is correct. Tangible book value removes all intangible assets, including goodwill, from the balance sheet.

13. C is correct. Operating leases can be used as an off-balance sheet financing technique because neither the asset nor liability appears on the balance sheet. Inventory and capital leases are reported on the balance sheet.

14. C is correct. The present value of future operating lease payments would be added to total assets and total liabilities.

4⅝ 4¹¹⁄₁₆ ³⁄₈
5½ 5½ −
5½ 21³⁄₁₆ − ¼₆
20⅝ 21³⁄₁₆ − ¼₆
17⅜ 18⅛ + ⅞
9½ 6½ −
6½ 6½ − ½
7¼ 31⁄₃₂ − ⅜
15⁄₁₆ 9⁄₁₆
9⁄₁₆
9⁄₃₂ 7¹³⁄₁₆ 7¹⁵⁄₁₆
7¹⁵⁄₁₆ 7¹³⁄₁₆
2⅝ 2¹¹⁄₃₂ 2½ +
2¾ 2¼ 2¼
6½ 12¹⁄₁₆ 11⅜ 11¼ +
87 33¾ 33 33⅛ −
502 25⅝ 24⁹⁄₁₆ 25⅝ +
833 12 11⅝ 11⅞ +
16 10½ 10½ 10⅝ −
78 15⅞ 15¹³⁄₁₆ 15⅞ −
4508 9¹⁄₁₆ 8¼ 8⅞ +
430 11¼ 10⅞ 10⅞

INTERNATIONAL STANDARDS CONVERGENCE

by Thomas R. Robinson, CFA, Jan Hendrik van Greuning, CFA, R. Elaine Henry, CFA, and Michael A. Broihahn, CFA

LEARNING OUTCOMES

The candidate should be able to:	Mastery
a. identify and explain the major international accounting standards for each asset and liability category on the balance sheet and the key differences from U.S. generally accepted accounting principles (GAAP);	☐
b. identify and explain the major international accounting standards for major revenue and expense categories on the income statement and the key differences from U.S. GAAP;	☐
c. identify and explain the major differences between international and U.S. GAAP accounting standards concerning the treatment of interest and dividends on the statement of cash flows;	☐
d. interpret the effect of differences between international and U.S. GAAP accounting standards on the balance sheet, income statement, and the statement of changes in equity for some commonly used financial ratios.	☐

THEME

The momentum for the convergence between international financial reporting standards (IFRS) and U.S. generally accepted accounting principles has increased significantly over the past few years. The two bodies now issue joint exposure drafts for a number of standards. Around the world, many national accounting standard setters have adopted, or are in the process of adopting, IFRS.

This reading describes the context within which IFRS are issued and objectives for their application in various financial statements. However, the fact that convergence is ongoing implies that standards are frequently changing. Although this text presents basic principles and issues, analysts should also be aware of available resources to find the timeliest information on IFRS.

International Financial Statement Analysis, by Thomas R. Robinson, CFA, Jan Hendrik van Greuning, CFA, R. Elaine Henry, CFA, and Michael A. Broihahn, CFA. Copyright © 2007 by CFA Institute. Reprinted with permission.

1

INTRODUCTION

The International Accounting Standards Board (IASB) is the standard-setting body of the International Accounting Standards Committee (IASC) Foundation. The objectives of the IASC Foundation are to develop a single set of global financial reporting standards and to promote the use of those standards. In accomplishing these objectives, the IASC Foundation explicitly aims to bring about convergence between national standards and international standards.

Around the world, many national accounting standard setters have adopted, or are in the process of adopting, the standards issued by the IASB: International Financial Reporting Standards, or IFRS.[1]

Over the past few years, convergence between IFRS and U.S. generally accepted accounting principles (U.S. GAAP), which are issued by the Financial Accounting Standards Board (FASB), has increased significantly. The two accounting standards boards now issue joint exposure drafts for a number of standards. In February 2006, the FASB and IASB published a memorandum of understanding outlining a "roadmap for convergence" over the next several years.

The IFRS *Framework for the Preparation and Presentation of Financial Statements* (referred to here as the "Framework") was introduced in the reading on financial reporting standards. In this reading, we review certain key aspects of the *Framework*. Section 2 provides an overview of the *Framework*. Sections 3, 4, and 5 provide additional descriptions of the IFRS relevant to each of the financial statements, noting some of the differences currently remaining between IFRS and U.S. GAAP. Section 6 summarizes the standard setters' agenda for convergence. Section 7 describes the effect on selected financial ratios of current differences between U.S. and international standards. A summary of key points and practice problems in the CFA Institute multiple-choice format conclude the reading.

A note of caution: The stated objective of the IASB/FASB convergence project is to eliminate differences between IFRS and U.S. GAAP. The convergence project implies that frequent changes to accounting standards are bound to continue for a number of years. Because a detailed comparison of current differences between IFRS and U.S. GAAP would be of limited practical value, this reading aims to present basic principles and issues. Analysts should be aware of resources available to find the timeliest information on IFRS, including the website of the IASB (www.iasb.org) and the website of the FASB (www.fasb.org).

---

[1] International accounting standards also include standards with a numbering system identified as "IAS" (international accounting standards), which were issued by the board of the IASC prior to the formation of the IASB in 2001 and the hand-over of standard-setting functions from the IASC's board to the IASB.

THE IFRS *FRAMEWORK*   2

The IFRS *Framework*, which is currently being re-examined as part of the international convergence project, was originally published in 1989 and was designed to assist the IASB in developing standards as well as to assist users of financial statements in interpreting the information contained therein. The *Framework* sets forth the concepts that underlie the preparation and presentation of financial statements and provides guidance on the definition, recognition, and measurement of the elements from which financial statements are constructed. In addition, the *Framework* discusses the concepts of capital and capital maintenance.

2.1 Key Aspects of the IFRS *Framework*

The objectives of financial statements, as stated in the *Framework*, are "to provide information about the financial position, performance, and changes in financial position of an entity; this information should be useful to a wide range of users for the purpose of making economic decisions."[2] The definition, therefore, covers the balance sheet (including the statement of changes in equity), income statement, and statement of cash flows.

To achieve the objective of providing useful information, financial statements should have certain characteristics. Recent IASB updates emphasize the following qualitative characteristics related to the usefulness of information in financial statements:

► relevance;

► predictive value;

► faithful representation (an emphasis on economic substance over form, reliability, and completeness);

► neutrality (absence of bias);

► verifiability.

Financial statements provide information on the financial position and performance of an entity by grouping the effects of transactions and other events into the following five broad classes or elements:

Balance Sheet Elements (Financial Position):

► Assets. Resources controlled by an entity as a result of past events and from which future economic benefits are expected to flow to the entity.

► Liabilities. Present obligations of an entity arising from past events, the settlement of which is expected to result in an outflow of resources from the entity.

► Equity. Assets less liabilities (for companies, shareholders' equity), which is the residual interest in the assets of the entity.

---

[2] *Framework for the Preparation and Presentation of Financial Statements*, IASC, 1989, adopted by IASB 2001, paragraph 12.

Income Statement Elements (Performance):

▶ Income. Increases in economic benefits that result in an increase in equity, other than increases resulting from contributions by owners. The increases in economic benefits may be in the form of inflows of assets, enhancements to assets, or decreases in liabilities. Income includes both revenues and gains. Revenues are income from the ordinary activities of the entity (e.g., the sale of products). Gains result from activities other than ordinary activities (e.g., the sale of equipment no longer needed).

▶ Expenses. Decreases in economic benefits that result in decreases in equity, other than decreases because of distributions to owners. The decreases in economic benefits may be in the form of outflows of assets, depletions of assets, or increases in liabilities. (Expenses include losses as well as those items normally thought of as expenses, such as the cost of goods sold or wages.)

Changes in these five basic elements are portrayed in the statement of cash flow and the statement of changes in equity.

2.2 Challenges in Financial Statement Preparation: Timing and Amounts

Two key challenges for preparers of financial statements are determining when to recognize financial events and how to measure the financial effect of these events.

Recognition is the process of incorporating into the financial statement an item that meets the definition of a financial statement element (i.e., assets, liabilities, equity, income, and expenses) and satisfies the criteria for recognition. The IFRS criteria for recognition of an item are that it should be recognized in the financial statements if:

▶ it is *probable* that any future economic benefit associated with the item will flow to or from the entity, and

▶ the item has a cost or value that can be *measured with reliability*.

Measurement is the process of determining the monetary effect of financial events and thus the amounts that are to be recognized and presented in the financial statements.

In meeting the challenges of recognition and measurement, financial statement preparers employ judgment about appropriate methods—many of which are constrained by IFRS requirements to use specific methods—and the estimation of relevant parameters. Such judgments and estimates can vary across companies and across time; therefore, analysts should develop awareness of the potential effect of these variations on financial statements.

3   THE BALANCE SHEET

A number of standards, including the *Framework* described above, apply to the majority of the components of the balance sheet. These include standards describing requirements for companies adopting international financial standards for the first time,[3] requirements for presenting financial statements under international financial standards,[4] and accounting for changes in accounting principles and estimates.[5]

Other standards apply more directly to specific components of the balance sheet. The sections below describe the key aspects of the standards relevant to each component of the balance sheet.

3.1 Marketable Securities

The international standards of accounting for marketable securities, contained in IAS No. 39, require that companies recognize securities initially at fair market value; for investments in marketable securities, this is typically the cost to acquire securities.

The fair market value of securities changes over time, and the central issue in accounting for securities is: Should securities continue to be presented at cost or adjusted as changes occur in their fair market value? Under the accounting standards, the answer depends on how the security is categorized.

Securities with fixed maturities and payments (e.g., bonds) that the company intends to hold until maturity (and has the ability to do so) can be categorized as "held to maturity." Held-to-maturity securities are presented at their original cost, updated for any amortization of discount or premium. A debt security purchased for an amount greater than its principal value is said to have been purchased at a premium; if purchased for an amount less than its principal value, it is said to have been purchased at a discount. Any premium or discount is amortized (i.e., reduced) over the remaining life of the security so that at maturity, the value of the security in the accounting records equals the principal value.

Securities that do not have fixed maturities (e.g., equity) and bonds that a company does not intend to hold until maturity are presented at their fair market value, and the reported value continues to be adjusted as changes occur in the fair market value. Such changes in a security's fair market value during an accounting period, assuming the security is not sold, give rise to unrealized gains or losses. An unrealized gain results from an increase in a security's value over the accounting period, and an unrealized loss results from a decrease in a security's value. If the security is sold, the gain or loss is said to be realized. When securities are sold, a company realizes a gain (loss) if the sale price is greater than (less than) the value of the security in the company's books.

The accounting for unrealized holding gains or losses differs for **held-for-trading securities** (trading securities) versus available-for-sale securities. Trading securities are simply those securities that the company intends to trade, and available-for-sale securities are those that do not fall into any other category. The category "trading securities" also includes derivatives.

Unrealized holding gains or losses on trading securities are recorded in the income statement. Unrealized holding gains or losses on available-for-sale securities are recorded in equity (as part of other comprehensive income) until the securities are sold. So, both trading and available-for-sale securities are valued at market value, but only the unrealized holding gains or losses on trading securities flow directly through the income statement. As a result, the performance of trading securities portfolios is more transparently reflected in the financial statements.

---

[3] IFRS No. 1.

[4] IAS No. 1.

[5] IAS No. 8.

Exhibit 1 summarizes the different categories of marketable securities and their accounting treatment.

EXHIBIT 1	Categories of Marketable Securities and Accounting Treatment		
Category	**How Measured**	**Unrealized and Realized Gains and Losses**	**Income (Interest and Dividends) Reported**
Held to maturity	Amortized cost	Unrealized: not reported Realized: reported in income statement	In income statement
Trading	Fair value	Unrealized: reported in income statement Realized: reported in income statement	In income statement
Available for sale	Fair value	Unrealized: reported in equity Realized: reported in income statement	In income statement

EXAMPLE 1

Accounting for Marketable Securities

Assume a company has the following portfolio of marketable securities:

Category	Value at Fiscal Year End 2005 ($)	Value at Fiscal Year End 2006 ($)
Held to maturity	10,000,000	10,000,000
Held for trading	5,000,000	5,500,000
Available for sale	8,000,000	7,000,000

1. What amount of unrealized holding gains or losses would the company report in total?

2. How much unrealized holding gains or losses would the company report in its income statement?

Solution to 1: The total amount of unrealized holding gains or losses that the company would report is determined by comparing the end-of-period value of held-for-trading and available-for-sale securities with their values as reported at the end of the previous period. In this example, the company would report a total of $500,000 as unrealized holding *losses*, calculated as the value of the held-for-trading and available-for-sale securities at the end of the period ($12,500,000) minus their value at the beginning of the period ($13,000,000).

Solution to 2: The company would report an unrealized holding *gain* of $500,000 in its income statement. The change in the market value of the available-for-sale securities (the unrealized loss of $1,000,000) would not be reported in the income statement. Instead, it would be shown as part of comprehensive income.

An analyst should obtain an understanding of management's rationale for categorizing securities as "trading securities" or as "available for sale." The performance of trading securities portfolios is more transparently reflected in the financial statements because the income statement shows both income (interest and dividends) and changes in value, whether realized or unrealized. In contrast, with available-for-sale securities, there is an asymmetrical treatment of income and changes in value. This asymmetrical treatment can cause an unsophisticated user of financial statements to misinterpret the performance of a company's marketable securities portfolio. It is possible, for example, that unrealized losses could accumulate in equity without affecting the income statement.

An additional standard relevant to marketable securities is the requirement that risk exposures arising from financial instruments be disclosed; requirements include specified minimum qualitative and quantitative disclosures about credit risk, liquidity risk, and market risk.[6] Qualitative disclosures require a description of management's objectives, policies, and processes for managing those risks. Quantitative disclosures refer to the provision of information regarding the *extent* to which an entity is exposed to risk. Together, these disclosures provide an overview of the entity's use of financial instruments and the resulting risk exposures.

3.2 Inventories

The reading on balance sheets describes various methods by which companies determine the cost of goods in inventory. Unlike U.S. GAAP, international accounting standards[7] require that the choice of the accounting method used to value inventories should be based upon the order in which products are sold, relative to when they are put into inventory. Therefore, whenever possible, the cost of a unit of inventory should be assigned by specific identification of the unit's costs. In many cases, however, it is necessary to use a formula to calculate inventory costs.

International standards permit the use of two alternative formulas for assigning the cost of inventory: 1) weighted average cost, in which the cost per unit of inventory is determined as a weighted average of the cost of all units of inventory, and 2) first in, first out (FIFO), in which it is assumed that the costs associated with the first units purchased (first in) are considered to be the cost of the first units sold (first out).

---

[6] IFRS No. 7.

[7] IAS No. 2.

Unlike U.S. GAAP, international standards do not allow the use of the LIFO (last in, first out) method to calculate the cost of inventory because the method is not considered a faithful model of inventory flows. The IASB has noted that the use of LIFO is often tax driven because this method results in lower taxable income during periods of rising prices; however, they concluded that tax considerations do not provide a conceptual basis for selecting an appropriate treatment.

Like U.S. GAAP, international standards require inventory to be reported at the lower of cost or net realizable value. However, IFRS permits the reversal of inventory write-downs, but no such provision exists in U.S. GAAP.

3.3 Property, Plant, and Equipment

The international standards of accounting for property, plant, and equipment, contained in IAS No. 16, require companies to recognize these assets initially at cost.

Like U.S. GAAP, international standards allow property, plant, and equipment to be reported in the financial statements at cost less accumulated depreciation. "Depreciation" is the systematic allocation of the cost of the asset over its useful life, and "accumulated depreciation" is the cumulative amount of depreciation expense recorded in relation to the asset.

Unlike U.S. GAAP, international accounting standards allow another alternative: reporting property, plant, and equipment at a revalued amount. When property, plant, and equipment are revalued, they are reported in the financial statements at fair value as of the revaluation date, less accumulated depreciation subsequent to the revaluation. Any revaluation increase is reported as part of equity, unless it is reversing a previous revaluation decrease. (The reason for this is that the previous decrease was reported as a reduction in the company's net income.) Any revaluation decrease is reported in profit and loss unless it is reversing a previous revaluation increase.

3.4 Long-Term Investments

The overall IFRS *Framework* for accounting for a company's investments in the securities of another company is based on the extent of control that the investing company has on the investee company. In the discussion of marketable securities above, it was assumed that the equity investment gave the investing company no control over the investee. As discussed, in such cases, the investments are designated as "trading" or "available for sale" and reflected at fair value.

If, however, an equity investment *did* give the investing company some control over the investee, the accounting standards require a different treatment. The specific treatment depends on the amount of control. If an investor owns 20 percent or more of the voting power of an investee, such an ownership stake would provide significant influence, where significant influence is defined as "power to participate in financial and operating policy decisions of the investee but is not control or joint control over those policies."[8] When an investor has significant influence, international standards require that the investment be reported using the equity method of accounting. The equity method of accounting means that the investor reports its pro rata share of the investee's profits as an increase in the amount of investment.

---

[8] IAS No. 28.

If an investor owns more than 50 percent of the voting power of the investee, such an ownership stake would provide significant control and the investee's financial statements would be consolidated with those of the investor. Consolidation roughly means that the investee's assets, liabilities, and income are combined into those of the investor. *Note*: The IFRS standard on business combinations is an active agenda item of the convergence project and is, therefore, subject to change during coming years.

When an investor shares the ownership of an investee, as in a joint venture, control is shared and the investor would account for the investment using either the proportionate consolidation method or the equity method. Proportionate consolidation roughly means that the investor's financial statements include its proportionate share of the investee's assets, liabilities, and income.

Exhibit 2 summarizes the different levels of control associated with each level of ownership and the accounting treatment used in each situation.

EXHIBIT 2	Accounting Treatment for Different Levels of an Investor's Percentage Ownership in an Investee and Related Extent of Control		
Extent of Control	Percent Ownership	Accounting Treatment	IFRS Reference
Significant influence	Between 20–50%	Equity accounting	IAS No. 28
Control	More than 50%	Business combinations/ consolidation	IAS No. 27/IFRS No. 3/SIC 12
Joint control	Shared	Joint ventures/ proportionate consolidation or equity accounting	IAS No. 31/ SIC 13

Note: SIC = Standing Interpretations Committee.

Like U.S. GAAP, international standards use extent of control as a factor determining whether an investee should be consolidated. U.S. GAAP differs from IFRS in that it allows a dual model: one model based on extent of voting control and one model based on an alternative assessment of economic control. The model based on economic control depends first on the economic substance of the investee and second on the investor's economic interests in the investee (liability for the investee's losses and opportunity to benefit from the investee's gains).

Unlike U.S. GAAP, international standards permit that interests in joint ventures may be accounted for using the proportionate consolidation method or the equity method,[9] whereas U.S. GAAP requires the equity method of accounting.

3.5 Goodwill

IFRS defines **goodwill** as the amount an acquirer pays to buy another company, minus the fair value of the net identifiable assets acquired. Goodwill is intended to represent future economic benefits arising from assets that are not capable of

---

[9] IAS No. 31.

being individually identified and separately recognized. Goodwill is considered an **intangible asset** (i.e., an asset without physical substance). Whereas some intangible assets—so-called identifiable intangible assets, such as patents and trademarks—can be bought and sold individually, goodwill cannot. Goodwill is an **unidentifiable intangible**.

Under IFRS No. 3, goodwill is capitalized as an asset and tested for impairment annually. **Impairment** means diminishment in value. Impairment of goodwill is a noncash expense; however, the impairment of goodwill does affect reported net income. When impairment of goodwill is charged against income in the current period, current reported income decreases. This charge against income also leads to reduced net assets and reduced shareholders' equity, but potentially improved return on assets, asset turnover ratios, return on equity, and equity turnover ratios because equity, the denominator in these ratios, is smaller. Even if the market reacts indifferently to an impairment write-off, an analyst should understand the implications of a goodwill write-off and, more generally, evaluate whether reported goodwill has been impaired. Example 2 presents a partial goodwill impairment footnote for Prudential PLC.

EXAMPLE 2

Goodwill Impairment Testing

Susan Lee is examining the financial statements of Prudential PLC and notes that the income statement shows a goodwill impairment charge of £120 million. Lee finds the following footnote to Prudential's financial statements.

Prudential PLC
2005 Annual Report Footnote H1

Impairment Testing

Goodwill does not generate cash flows independently of other groups of assets and thus is assigned to cash generating units (CGUs) for the purposes of impairment testing. These CGUs are based upon how management monitors the business and represent the lowest level to which goodwill can be allocated on a reasonable basis. An allocation of the Group's goodwill to CGUs is shown below:

	2005 £Millions	2004 £Millions
M&G	1,153	1,153
Japan life company	—	120
Venture investment subsidiaries of the PAC with-profits fund	607	784
Other	188	188
	1,948	2,245

'Other' represents goodwill amounts allocated across cash generating units in Asia and U.S. operations. These goodwill amounts are not individually material. There are no other intangible assets with indefinite useful lives other than goodwill.

Assessment of Whether Goodwill May Be Impaired

With the exception of M&G and venture investment subsidiaries of the PAC with-profits fund, the goodwill in the balance sheet relates to acquired life businesses. The Company routinely compares the aggregate of net asset value and acquired goodwill on an IFRS basis of acquired life business with the value of the business as determined using the EEV methodology, as described in section D1. Any excess of IFRS over EEV carrying value is then compared with EEV basis value of current and projected future new business to determine whether there is any indication that the goodwill in the IFRS balance sheet may be impaired.

Goodwill is tested for impairment by comparing the CGUs carrying amount, excluding any goodwill, with its recoverable amount.

M&G

The recoverable amount for the M&G CGU has been determined by calculating its value in use. This has been calculated by aggregating the present value of future cash flows expected to be derived from the component businesses of M&G (based upon management projections) and its current surplus capital.

The discounted cash flow valuation has been based on a three-year plan prepared by M&G, and approved by the directors of Prudential plc, and cash flow projections for later years.

As a cross check to the discounted cash flow analysis, a review was undertaken of publicly available information for companies engaged in businesses comparable to the component businesses, including reported market prices for such companies' shares. In addition, a review was undertaken of publicly available terms of transactions involving companies comparable to the component businesses. In particular, comparison has been made of the valuation multiples implied by the discounted cash flow analysis to current trading multiples of companies comparable to the component businesses, as well as to multiples achieved in precedent transactions.

The value in use is particularly sensitive to a number of key assumptions, as follows:

  i. The assumed growth rate on forecast cash flows beyond the terminal year of the budget. A growth rate of 2.5 percent has been used to extrapolate beyond the plan period.

  ii. The risk discount rate. Differing discount rates have been applied in accordance with the nature of the individual component businesses. For retail and institutional business a risk discount rate of 12 percent has been applied. This represents the average implied discount rate for comparable UK listed asset managers calculated by reference to risk-free rates, equity risk premiums of 5 percent and an average 'beta' factor for relative market risk of comparable UK listed asset managers. A similarly granular approach has been applied for the other component businesses of M&G.

  iii. That asset management contracts continue on similar terms.

Management believes that any reasonable change in the key assumptions would not cause the carrying amount of M&G to exceed its recoverable amount.

Japanese Life Company

As noted above, the entire goodwill relating to the Japanese life operation of £120 million has been deemed to be impaired following impairment testing carried out in 2005. This testing was based on a recoverable amount for the Japanese company that was determined by calculating its value in use based on net present value cash flow projections. Such projections reflected existing business over the expected duration of the contracts and expected new business. A risk discount rate of 5 percent was applied to the projected cash flows. On the basis of the results of this exercise it was determined that all goodwill held in relation to the Japanese business should be written off in 2005.

PAC With-Profits Fund Venture Investment Subsidiaries

The recoverable amount for the ventures entities controlled by the Group through PPM Capital has been determined on a portfolio CGU basis by aggregating fair values calculated for each entity less costs to sell these entities.

The fair value of each entity is calculated by PPM Capital in accordance with the International Private Equity and Venture Capital Valuation Guidelines which set out industry best practice for determining the fair value of private equity investments. The guidelines require that an enterprise value is calculated for each investment, typically using an appropriate multiple applied to the Company's maintainable earnings. All amounts relating to financial instruments ranking higher in a liquidation than those controlled by PPM Capital are then deducted from the enterprise value and a marketability discount applied to the result to give a fair value attributable to the instruments controlled by PPM Capital. The marketability discount ranges from 10 percent to 30 percent, depending on PPM Capital's level of control over a realization process.

Management believes that any reasonable change in the key assumptions would not give rise to an impairment charge.

---

1. What operating unit resulted in a goodwill impairment charge, and how was the charge computed?

2. For the operating unit identified in Part 1, would an analyst anticipate subsequent goodwill impairments?

Solution to 1: The entire impairment charge for 2005 was related to the Japanese life company operating unit. The loss was determined by projecting future cash flows for this unit and discounting them at a rate of 5 percent.

Solution to 2: Because the impairment charge for 2005 represented all of the goodwill of the Japanese life company operating unit, subsequent goodwill impairments for this operating unit should not occur.

Because goodwill can significantly influence the comparability of financial statements between companies using different accounting methods, analysts sometimes make certain goodwill-related adjustments to a company's financial statements. The objective of such adjustments is to remove any distortion that goodwill and its recognition, amortization, and impairment might create. Adjustments include the following:

► subtracting goodwill from assets and use of this adjusted data to compute financial ratios;

► excluding goodwill impairment charges from income and use of this adjusted data when reviewing operating trends; and

► evaluating future business acquisitions by taking into account the purchase price paid relative to the net assets and earnings prospects of the acquired company.

If the amount an acquirer pays to buy another company is less than the fair value of the net identifiable assets acquired, it is not recognized as "negative goodwill." Instead, a gain is recognized. However, before any gain is recognized, the acquirer should reassess the cost of acquisition and the fair values attributed to the acquiree's identifiable assets, liabilities, and contingent liabilities.

As noted, goodwill arises in connection with acquisitions. Several other aspects of international accounting for acquisitions may be noted. Under the purchase method of accounting,[10] the acquisition price must be allocated to all of the acquired company's identifiable tangible and intangible assets, liabilities, and contingent liabilities. The assets and liabilities of the acquired entity are combined into the financial statements of the acquiring company at their fair values on the acquisition date. Because the acquirer's assets and liabilities, measured at their historical costs, are combined with the acquired company's assets and liabilities, measured at their fair market value on the acquisition date, the acquirer's pre- and post-merger balance sheets are often not easily compared.

Furthermore, under the purchase method, the income statement and the statement of cash flows include the operating performance of the acquiree from the date of the acquisition forward. Operating results prior to the acquisition are not restated and remain the same as historically reported by the acquirer. Consequently, although the financial statements of the acquirer will reflect the reality of the acquisition, they will not be comparable before and after the acquisition.

3.6 Intangible Assets Other than Goodwill

IAS No. 38 includes standards for reporting certain intangible assets other than goodwill. These intangible assets are referred to as "identifiable intangible assets." Identifiable intangible assets arise either from contractual or other legal rights, or must be capable of being separated from the company and sold, transferred, licensed, rented, or exchanged.

The standards for reporting identifiable intangible assets, contained in IAS No. 38, provide that an intangible asset is recognized—at cost—if it is probable

---

[10] IFRS No. 3.

that the future economic benefits attributable to the asset will flow to the company and if the cost of the asset can be measured reliably. Only those intangibles that have been purchased or manufactured (in limited instances) may be recognized as assets. Internally produced items, such as customer lists, are not recognized as assets.

Given that it meets the criteria for recognition, an intangible asset with a finite useful life is amortized on a systematic basis over the best estimate of its useful life. In other words, the cost of the identifiable intangible asset is allocated systematically over the asset's useful life. If the identifiable intangible asset does not have a finite useful life, it is not amortized. Instead, the asset is tested at least annually for impairment as with goodwill. Testing for impairment involves evaluating whether the current value of an asset is materially lower than its carrying value.

Like U.S. GAAP, international standards allow identifiable intangibles to be reported in the financial statements at cost less amortization and less any impairment charges.

Unlike U.S. GAAP, international accounting standards allow another alternative: reporting identifiable intangible assets at a revalued amount. When identifiable intangible assets are revalued, they are reported in the financial statements at fair value as of the revaluation date, less accumulated amortization subsequent to the revaluation. Any revaluation increase is reported as part of equity, unless it is reversing a previous revaluation decrease. Any revaluation decrease is reported in profit and loss unless it is reversing a previous revaluation increase. U.S. GAAP prohibits revaluations.

Companies also have intangible assets that accounting rules do not include as items that can be recorded in financial statements; these intangible assets include management skill, a positive corporate culture, trademarks, name recognition, a good reputation, proprietary products, and so forth. However, the costs related to these intangible assets—such as training, advertising, and research—must be expensed. An analyst must be aware of the potential value of such unrecorded assets.

3.7 Provisions (Nonfinancial Liabilities)

Nonfinancial liabilities include **provisions**, which are liabilities of uncertain timing or amount, such as warranty obligations, and contingent liabilities, which are liabilities contingent on the occurrence of some event. The standards for reporting nonfinancial liabilities, contained in IAS No. 37, provide that a company should recognize nonfinancial liabilities when it has a present obligation as a result of a past event and the company can reliably estimate the cost to settle the obligation.

The amount recognized as a nonfinancial liability should be the best estimate, as of the balance sheet date, of the cost that will be required to settle the obligation.

4   THE INCOME STATEMENT

A number of standards, including the *Framework* (described above), apply to the majority of the components of the income statement. These include standards describing requirements for companies adopting international financial standards for the first time, requirements for presenting financial statements under international financial standards, and accounting for changes in accounting principles and estimates.[11]

Other standards apply more directly to specific components of the income statement. The sections below describe the key aspects of the standards relevant to each component in the same order as the components described in the reading discussing the income statement.

4.1 Revenue Recognition: General

The IASB *Framework* defines income as including both revenue and gains. In IAS No. 18, revenue is defined as the gross inflow of economic benefits during the period, arising in the ordinary course of activities, or resulting in increases in equity other than contributions by equity participants.

IAS No. 18 addresses how revenue is to be measured, namely, at the fair value of consideration received. The standard also addresses the timing of revenue recognition.

Some criteria for recognizing revenue are common to both the sale of goods and the provision of services: It must be possible to reliably measure the amount of revenue and costs of the transaction, and it must be probable that economic benefits of the transaction will flow to the seller. In addition, to recognize revenue from the sale of goods, it is necessary that the risks and rewards of ownership pass to the buyer and that the seller not have continued control over the goods sold. To recognize revenue from the provision of services, it is necessary that the stage of completion of the service can be measured reliably.

U.S. GAAP defines revenue in terms of actual or expected cash flows, and, for revenue recognition, U.S. GAAP focuses extensively on realization and earned status. U.S. GAAP also provides more extensive guidance than IFRS regarding industry-specific issues. Despite such differences, the key principles are similar in U.S. GAAP and IFRS.

4.2 Revenue Recognition for Construction Contracts

IAS No. 11 deals with the recognition of construction contract revenue and costs—in particular, the allocation of contract revenue and costs to the accounting periods in which construction work is performed. The standard applies to the accounting for construction contracts in the financial statements of contractors.

A construction contract is a contract specifically negotiated for the construction of an asset or a combination of assets that are closely interrelated or interdependent in terms of their design, technology, and function, or their ultimate purpose or use. Construction contracts include those for the construction or restoration of assets and the restoration of the environment.

When the outcome of a construction contract can be estimated reliably, revenue and costs (and, therefore, profit) should be recognized based on the stage of completion (percentage of completion method). When the outcome of a contract *cannot* be reliably estimated, revenue should be recognized to the extent that it is probable to recover contract costs. This requirement differs from U.S. GAAP, which requires that the completed contract method be used in such cases.

---

[11] IFRS No. 1, IAS No. 1, and IAS No. 8, respectively.

4.3 Cost of Sales

Two international accounting standards, IAS No. 2 (accounting for the cost of inventories) and IAS No. 18 (revenue recognition), have an effect on cost of sales. As noted, under international standards, LIFO is not an acceptable method for the valuation of inventory. Consequently, financial statements prepared according to U.S. GAAP may differ significantly from those prepared under IFRS.

U.S. GAAP does, however, require that companies using LIFO disclose the information required to enable a user of financial statements to adjust the inventory and cost of sales figures to a basis comparable with financial statements prepared using IFRS.

4.4 Administrative Expenses (Including Employee Benefits)

Administrative (or operating) expenses typically include overheads related to employee costs. The IASB *Framework* defines expenses to include losses because expenses are decreases in economic benefits that result in a decrease in equity. The inclusion of losses as expenses contrasts with U.S. GAAP, which differentiates expenses from losses by restricting the term "expenses" to refer to those outflows (of cash or the equivalent) that relate to the entity's ongoing primary business operations.

One type of administrative expense with specific international accounting principles is the expense related to employee benefits, such as salaries, bonuses, post-employment benefits, and termination benefits. Recognition and measurement principles, as well as the disclosure requirements, are provided in IAS No. 19. IFRS No. 2 deals with equity compensation benefits, such as share options.

4.5 Depreciation Expenses

As discussed above, depreciation is the process of recognizing the costs of fixed assets over time by systematically decreasing the assets' value and reporting a commensurate expense on the income statement. The term "depletion" is used for this process when the asset is a natural resource, and the term "amortization" is used for this process when the asset is an intangible asset. The cost of acquiring land is not depreciated.

International standards require companies to review the depreciation method applied to an asset at least at each financial year-end. If there has been a significant change in the expected pattern of consumption of the future economic benefits embodied in the asset, companies must change the depreciation method to reflect the changed pattern. Similar to U.S. GAAP, such a change is accounted for as a change in accounting estimate[12] and thus reflected on future financial statements.

Various depreciation methods exist, including the straight-line method (which allocates evenly the cost of a long-lived asset over its estimated useful life) and accelerated methods (which allocate a greater proportion of the

---

[12] IAS No. 8.

asset's cost in the earlier years of its useful life, thus accelerating the timing of the depreciation expense). In choosing the appropriate depreciation method, IFRS requires:

▶ the depreciable amount is allocated on a *systematic* basis over the useful life, and

▶ the method used must reflect the pattern of expected *consumption*.

Whether the straight-line depreciation method or an accelerated method is used, the method complies with IFRS *only* if it reflects the pattern of the expected consumption of the assets.

4.6 Finance Costs

In general, borrowing costs—defined as interest and other costs incurred by an entity in connection with the borrowing of funds—are expensed in the period incurred.

IFRS offers an alternative to expensing borrowing costs immediately. When borrowing costs are incurred in connection with the acquisition, construction, or production of an asset that takes a long time to be ready for its intended use, such borrowing costs can be added to the total cost of the asset.[13] In other words, rather than expensing these costs immediately, a company has the alternative to capitalize these borrowing costs and depreciate them over time. This topic is an item on the list of IASB's short-term convergence projects as of December 2006.

U.S. GAAP requires the capitalization of interest costs for assets that take a substantial time to complete.

4.7 Income Tax Expense

IAS No. 12 prescribes the accounting treatment for income taxes and specifically addresses issues relating to the carrying amount of assets as well as transactions and other events of the current period, which are recognized in the entity's financial statements.

As with U.S. GAAP, international standards provide for the accounting treatment when differences exist between accounting methods allowed by the relevant taxing authority and accounting methods allowed for financial statement reporting (i.e., IFRS). Where differences exist between methods allowable by taxing authorities and by IFRS, differences will exist between taxable profit and financial statement pretax profit (also referred to as "accounting profit"). Such differences give rise to differences in the value of a company's assets and liabilities recorded in its financial statements (balance sheet) and the tax bases of those assets and liabilities. In turn, these differences can result in future taxes payable or receivable, so-called deferred tax liabilities and deferred tax assets.

The primary differences between U.S. GAAP and IFRS are attributable to differences in exceptions to the application of the principles (i.e., differences in the scope of coverage of the principles).

---

[13] IAS No. 23.

4.8 Nonrecurring Items

Nonrecurring items generally include discontinued operations, accounting changes, and unusual or infrequent items. As noted, analysts typically find it useful to break reported earnings down into recurring and nonrecurring components. Recurring earnings are viewed as permanent or sustainable, whereas nonrecurring earnings are considered to be somewhat random and unsustainable. Therefore, analysts often exclude the effects of nonrecurring items when performing a short-term analysis of an entity (e.g., estimating next year's earnings). However, even so-called nonrecurring events, such as sales of a part of a business, tend to recur from time to time, so analysts may include some average (per year) amount of nonrecurring items for longer-term analyses.

IFRS and U.S. GAAP differ in their treatment of these issues, although as with other areas, convergence is occurring.[14]

For discontinued operations, IFRS changed to align with U.S. GAAP. IFRS No. 5 generally converges with SFAS No. 144. The new international guidance, like the U.S. standards, requires that discontinued operations be reported when a company disposes of one of its business components (or when the component is being held for sale) and will no longer have management involvement.

For accounting changes, U.S. GAAP changed to align with IFRS. SFAS No. 154, issued in June 2005, generally converges with IAS No. 8. Changes in accounting principles are accounted for retrospectively, and changes in accounting estimates are accounted for prospectively.

For extraordinary items, convergence has not yet been achieved. U.S. GAAP continues to allow extraordinary items (i.e., items that are both unusual in nature and infrequent in occurrence) to be reported separately from net income.

Unlike U.S. GAAP, IFRS do not distinguish between items that are and are not likely to recur. Furthermore, IFRS do not permit any items to be classified as "extraordinary items." However, IFRS do require the disclosure of all material information that is relevant to understanding a company's performance. The analyst generally can use this information, together with information from outside sources, to estimate amounts of recurring and nonrecurring items.

5   THE STATEMENT OF CASH FLOWS

Both international standards and U.S. GAAP require that a statement of cash flows be included among a company's full set of financial statements (FASB Statement No. 95, *Statement of Cash Flows*, and IAS No. 7, *Cash Flow Statements*) showing the changes in cash and cash equivalents over an accounting period.

Both sets of standards require that the statement of cash flows include sections covering operating, investing, and financing activities of the company. The differences between international and U.S. standards arise in the classification of certain cash flows.

International standards allow companies to report cash inflows from interest and dividends as either operating or investing activities and cash outflows for interest and dividends as either operating or financing activities (see Exhibit 3).

---

[14] This topic is discussed in "Convergence: In Search of the Best," D. Herrmann and I.P.N. Hauge, *Journal of Accountancy* online edition, January 2006: www.aicpa.org/PUBS/JOFA/jan2006/herrmann.htm.

In contrast, U.S. standards require the following: Interest and dividends received are classified as inflows from operating activities; interest paid is classified as an outflow for operating activities; and dividends paid are classified as financing activities.

EXHIBIT 3	Statement of Cash Flows

Classification of Interest and Dividends under International and U.S. Standards

Category	Classification in IFRS vs. U.S. GAAP

Cash Flows from *Operating* Activities

Cash from principal revenue-producing activities of the entity (i.e., cash receipts from customers less cash payments to suppliers and employees).

Interest received	IFRS alternatives: operating or investing section
	U.S. GAAP: mandated operating section
Dividends received	IFRS alternatives: operating or investing section
	U.S. GAAP: mandated operating section
Interest paid	IFRS alternatives: operating or financing section
	U.S. GAAP: mandated operating section
Dividends paid (IFRS only)	IFRS alternatives: operating or financing section

Cash Flows from *Investing* Activities

Purchases of long-term assets and other investments not included in cash equivalents; proceeds on sale.

Interest received (IFRS only)	IFRS alternatives: operating or investing section
Dividends received (IFRS only)	IFRS alternatives: operating or investing section

Cash Flows from *Financing* Activities

Cash from issuance or repayment of equity capital and/or long-term debt.

Dividends paid	IFRS alternatives: operating or financing section
	U.S. GAAP: mandated financing section
Interest paid	IFRS alternatives: operating or financing section

6   STANDARD SETTERS' AGENDA FOR CONVERGENCE

As noted in the introduction to this reading, in February 2006, the FASB and IASB published a memorandum of understanding outlining a "roadmap for convergence" over the next several years. This section summarizes the standard setters' agenda for convergence over the period 2006 to 2008.

By 2008, the IASB and FASB aim to conclude whether any major differences should be eliminated in the following topics for short-term convergence, and if so, to complete the work to do so: fair value option (allow companies to report financial assets and liabilities at fair value on a contract-by-contract basis, converging to IFRS); borrowing costs (eliminate alternative to expense immediately when in connection with longer-term projects, converging to U.S. GAAP); research and development; impairment; segment reporting; subsequent events; and income taxes.

Topics that are already on an active agenda for IASB and/or FASB include business combinations, consolidations, fair value measurement guidance, liabilities and equity distinctions, performance reporting, post-retirement benefits (including pensions), and revenue recognition. Joint IASB and FASB goals for 2008 have been established for each of these topics.

7   EFFECT OF DIFFERENCES BETWEEN ACCOUNTING STANDARDS

As we note throughout this reading, differences between international and U.S. accounting standards are decreasing as convergence between the two sets of standards occurs. Differences that do exist have an effect on commonly used financial ratios. We discuss several major differences here.

If comparing a U.S. company that uses LIFO accounting with an international company for whom this method is not allowable, an analyst will make adjustments. Specifically, using financial statement note disclosures, the analyst will adjust the U.S. company's profits (gross, operating, and net), ending inventory, and total assets. These adjustments will affect certain profitability, solvency, liquidity, and activity ratios. For comparison purposes, inventory is adjusted from LIFO to FIFO by adding the LIFO reserve to the LIFO inventory value on the balance sheet. Under U.S. GAAP, a company must disclose the LIFO reserve amount in the financial statement notes if the LIFO method is followed. In addition, cost of goods sold is adjusted from LIFO to FIFO by subtracting the net increase in the LIFO reserve that occurred during the fiscal year. Example 3 illustrates a LIFO to FIFO conversion.

EXAMPLE 3

LIFO Effects on Financial Statements and Ratios

Buccaneer Corporation prepares its financial statements (Exhibits 4 and 5) in accordance with U.S. GAAP and uses the LIFO inventory method. During the year, Buccaneer's LIFO reserve increased from $40 million to $64 million. The income tax rate is 30 percent.

EXHIBIT 4	Income Statement and Balance Sheet under LIFO and FIFO Inventory Accounting ($ Millions)		
Account	LIFO Method	LIFO to FIFO Adjustment	FIFO Method
Sales	1,800.0	—	1,800.0
Cost of sales	1,060.0	(24.0)	1,036.0
Gross profit	740.0	24.0	764.0
Operating expenses	534.0	—	534.0
Income before taxes	206.0	24.0	230.0
Income taxes	61.8	(7.2)	69.0
Net income	144.2	(16.8)	161.0
Cash	80.0	—	80.0
Inventory	356.0	64.0	420.0
Other current assets	344.0	—	344.0
Fixed assets, net	1,120.0	—	1,120.0
Total assets	1,900.0	64.0	1,964.0
Current liabilities	200.0	—	200.0
Noncurrent liabilities	424.0	19.2	443.2
Common stock	840.0	—	840.0
Retained earnings	436.0	44.8	480.8
Total liabilities and equity	1,900.0	64.0	1,964.0

The net increase in Buccaneer's LIFO reserve during the fiscal year was $24 million ($64 million − $40 million). To adjust from LIFO to FIFO, the net increase in the LIFO reserve must be subtracted from the LIFO reported cost of sales. (A net decrease in the LIFO reserve during the year would be added to LIFO reported cost of sales in a LIFO to FIFO conversion.) Accordingly, because reported gross profits are $24 million higher after the FIFO conversion, income tax expense will increase by $7.2 million ($24 million × 30% income tax rate), resulting in an increase to net income of $16.8 million. For the balance sheet conversion, the year-end LIFO reserve of $64 million is added to the LIFO reported inventory, resulting in an increase of $64 million to both inventory and total assets under FIFO. In addition, the deferred income tax liabilities will increase by $19.2 million ($64 million × 30% income tax rate), and retained earnings will increase by $44.8 million ($64 million × 70% after-tax retention).

Comparative selected profitability, solvency, liquidity, and activity ratios for Buccaneer Corporation under the two inventory methods are given in Exhibit 5.

EXHIBIT 5	Financial Ratios under LIFO and FIFO Inventory Accounting		
Ratio	Formula	LIFO Method	FIFO Method
Net profit margin	Net income ÷ Net sales	8.01%	8.94%
Financial leverage	Total assets ÷ Total equity	1.489	1.487
Current ratio	Current assets ÷ Current liabilities	3.90	4.22
Inventory turnover	Cost of sales ÷ Ending inventory	2.98 turns	2.47 turns

If comparing an IFRS company with a U.S. company that reports extraordinary items separately from net income but which reports certain unusual items as part of operating income, an analyst will examine the financial statement notes to identify similar items that have received different reporting treatment.

If comparing an IFRS company, which has written up the value of its intangible or tangible long-term assets, with a U.S. company, an analyst will eliminate the effect of the write-ups in calculating asset-based ratios. Example 4 illustrates a revaluation adjustment conversion.

EXAMPLE 4

Analyst Adjustments to Revaluations in IFRS/U.S. GAAP Comparisons

Aramis Ltd. prepares its financial statements in accordance with IFRS. During the current year, Aramis revalued its fixed assets upward by a total of €75 million to better reflect its present fair market value.

The analyst must reverse the revaluation adjustments that Aramis has made if Aramis is to be compared with a company that complies with U.S. GAAP. For Aramis, the analyst will reduce both fixed assets and other equity by the upward revaluation of €75 million. Exhibit 6 shows these adjustments.

EXHIBIT 6	Analyst Adjustments to Revaluation (€ Millions)		
Account	Unadjusted	Reversal of Revaluation	Post-Adjustment
Sales	1,700.0	—	1,700.0
Cost of sales	1,040.0	—	1,040.0
Gross profit	660.0	—	660.0
Operating expenses	475.0	—	475.0
Income before taxes	185.0	—	185.0
Income taxes	74.0	—	74.0
Net income	111.0	—	111.0

(Exhibit continued on next page . . .)

	EXHIBIT 6	(continued)	

Account	Unadjusted	Reversal of Revaluation	Post-Adjustment
Fixed assets, net	1,150.0	(75.0)	1,075.0
Inventory	310.0	—	310.0
Other current assets	120.0	—	120.0
Cash	20.0	—	20.0
Total assets	1,600.0	(75.0)	1,525.0
Noncurrent liabilities	370.0	—	370.0
Current liabilities	225.0	—	225.0
Contributed capital	550.0	—	550.0
Earned and other equity	455.0	(75.0)	380.0
Total liabilities and equity	1,600.0	(75.0)	1,525.0

Selected comparative performance ratios for Aramis under the two approaches are given in Exhibit 7.

	EXHIBIT 7	Financial Ratios Pre- and Post-Adjustment	

Ratio	Formula	Unadjusted	Post-Adjustment
Return on assets	Net income ÷ Total assets	6.94%	7.28%
Return on equity	Net income ÷ Total equity	11.04%	11.94%
Asset turnover	Net sales ÷ Total assets	1.063 turns	1.115 turns
Equity turnover	Net sales ÷ Total equity	1.692 turns	1.828 turns
Financial leverage	Total assets ÷ Total equity	1.592	1.640

SUMMARY

The IASB is the standard-setting body of the IASC Foundation. The objectives of the IASC Foundation are to develop a single set of global financial reporting standards and to promote the use of those standards. In accomplishing these objectives, the IASC Foundation explicitly aims to bring about convergence between national standards and international standards. Many national accounting standard setters have adopted, or are in the process of adopting, the IFRS.

This reading discussed both the IFRS *Framework* and the IFRS standards for reporting accounting items on the balance sheet, income statement, and cash flow statement. Key points include the following:

▶ The objectives of financial statements, as stated in the *Framework*, are "to provide information about the financial position, performance, and changes in financial position of an entity; this information should be useful to a wide range of users for the purpose of making economic decisions."

▶ To achieve the objective of providing useful information, financial statements should have the following qualitative characteristics: relevance, predictive value, faithful representation, neutrality, and verifiability.

▶ Financial statements provide information on the financial position and performance of an entity by grouping the effects of transactions and other events into the following five broad elements: assets, liabilities, equity, income, and expenses.

▶ Both IFRS and U.S. GAAP require companies to present basic financial statements: balance sheet, income statement, statement of cash flows, and statement of changes in equity.

▶ One major difference between IFRS and U.S. GAAP affecting all three statements involves inventories: U.S. GAAP allows the LIFO method for inventory costing, whereas IFRS does not.

▶ Another major balance sheet difference between IFRS and U.S. GAAP is that IFRS allows companies to revalue property, plant, and equipment as well as intangible assets.

▶ Accounting for investments is another area of difference: IFRS uses a voting control model to determine need for consolidation, whereas U.S. GAAP uses a dual model based on voting control and economic control.

▶ An important difference between IFRS and U.S. GAAP is the treatment of some nonrecurring items. IFRS does not permit any items to be classified as "extraordinary items."

▶ International standards allow companies to report cash inflows from interest and dividends as relating to either "operating" or "investing activities," and cash outflows for interest and dividends as relating to either "operating" or "financing activities."

▶ Convergence between IFRS and U.S. GAAP has increased significantly over the past few years and is continuing.

▶ Analysts should know how to make financial statement adjustments to better compare IFRS reporting companies with those companies reporting under U.S. GAAP.

PRACTICE PROBLEMS FOR READING 43

1. According to the IFRS *Framework*, which of the following is a qualitative characteristic related to the usefulness of information in financial statements?

   A. Neutrality.

   B. Timeliness.

   C. Accrual basis.

2. Under the IFRS *Framework*, changes in the elements of financial statements are *most likely* portrayed in the:

   A. balance sheet.

   B. income statement.

   C. statement of cash flows.

3. Under IASB standards, which of the following categories of marketable securities is *most likely* to incur an asymmetrical treatment of income and changes in value?

   A. Held for trading.

   B. Held to maturity.

   C. Available for sale.

4. According to IASB standards, which of the following inventory methods is *most preferred*?

   A. Specific identification.

   B. Weighted average cost.

   C. First in, first out (FIFO).

5. According to IASB standards, which of the following inventory methods is not acceptable?

   A. Weighted average cost.

   B. First in, first out (FIFO).

   C. Last in, first out (LIFO).

6. Under IASB standards, inventory write-downs are:

   A. not allowed.

   B. allowed but not reversible.

   C. allowed and subject to reversal.

7. According to IASB standards, property, plant, and equipment revaluations are:

   A. not allowed.

   B. allowed for decreases only.

   C. allowed for both increases and decreases.

8. Under IASB standards, a joint venture interest is accounted for by using:

   A. consolidation.

   B. the equity method or consolidation.

   C. the equity method or proportionate consolidation.

9. Under IASB standards, goodwill:

   A. may be written off when acquired.

   B. is subject to an annual impairment test.

   C. is amortized over its expected useful life.

10. Under IASB standards, negative goodwill:

   A. must be recorded as a gain.

   B. is prorated to the noncurrent assets.

   C. is accounted for as an extraordinary item.

11. Under IASB standards, an identifiable intangible asset with an indefinite life:

   A. may be written off when acquired.

   B. is amortized over a 20-year period.

   C. is accounted for in the same manner as goodwill.

12. Under IASB standards, identifiable intangible assets are:

   A. only revalued downward, with the decrease reported to profit and loss.

   B. revalued upward and reported to equity when reversing a previous revaluation decrease.

   C. revalued upward and reported to profit and loss when reversing a previous revaluation decrease.

13. Under IASB standards, when the outcome of a construction contract cannot be estimated reliably, revenue and costs should be:

   A. recognized by using the completed contract method.

   B. recognized by using the percentage of completion contract method.

   C. recognized to the extent that it is probable to recover contract costs.

14. Under IASB standards, fixed asset depreciation methods must be:

   A. rational and systematic.

   B. rational and reviewed at least annually.

   C. systematic and reflect the pattern of expected consumption.

15. Under IASB standards, cash inflows for the receipt of interest and dividends are:

   A. operating cash flows.

   B. either operating or investing cash flows.

   C. either investing or financing cash flows.

16. Under IASB standards, cash outflows for the payment of interest are:

   A. operating cash flows.

   B. either investing or financing cash flows.

   C. either operating or financing cash flows.

17. Under IASB standards, cash outflows for the payment of dividends are:

   A. financing cash flows.

   B. either operating or investing cash flows.

   C. either operating or financing cash flows.

18. When comparing a U.S. company that uses LIFO accounting with an IFRS company that uses FIFO accounting, an analyst will:

   A. make no adjustment if the adjustment data are unavailable.

   B. adjust either company to achieve comparability with the other.

   C. adjust the U.S. company to achieve comparability with the IFRS company.

19. When comparing an IFRS company that has written up the value of its intangible assets with a U.S. company, an analyst will eliminate the effect of the write-ups in calculating the:

   A. gross margin.

   B. earnings per share.

   C. financial leverage multiplier.

SOLUTIONS FOR READING 43

1. A is correct. Neutrality is a qualitative characteristic. (Timeliness is a constraint and accrual basis is an assumption.)

2. C is correct. Changes in the five basic elements (assets, liabilities, equity, income, and expenses) are portrayed in the statement of cash flows and the statement of changes in equity.

3. C is correct. For available-for-sale securities, there is an asymmetrical treatment of income and changes in value. Under this classification, unrealized gains and losses can accumulate in equity without affecting the income statement.

4. A is correct. Whenever possible, the cost of inventory should be assigned by specific identification of the unit's costs. Two alternative formulas for assigning the cost of inventory are weighted average cost and FIFO.

5. C is correct. LIFO is not an acceptable inventory costing method.

6. C is correct. Like U.S. GAAP, international standards require inventory to be reported at the lower of cost or net realizable value. However, IFRS permit the reversal of inventory write-downs, but no such provision exists in U.S. GAAP.

7. C is correct. Unlike U.S. GAAP, international accounting standards allow revaluations (both increases and decreases) for property, plant, and equipment.

8. C is correct. When an investor shares the ownership of an investee, as in a joint venture, control is shared and the investor would account for the investment using a proportionate consolidation method, with the equity method as an alternative.

9. B is correct. Under IFRS No. 3, goodwill is capitalized and tested for impairment annually.

10. A is correct. A gain is recognized if the amount an acquirer pays to buy another company is less than the fair value of the identifiable net assets acquired. Extraordinary gains are not allowed under IASB.

11. C is correct. If an intangible asset does not have a finite life, it is not amortized. Instead, the asset is tested at least annually for impairment (like goodwill).

12. C is correct. Any upward revaluation is reported as part of equity, unless it is reversing a previous revaluation decrease.

13. C is correct. When the outcome of a contract cannot be reliably estimated, revenue should be recognized to the extent that it is probable to recover contract costs. This differs from U.S. GAAP, which requires that the completed contract method be used in such cases.

14. C is correct. In choosing the appropriate depreciation method, IFRS requires that 1) the depreciable amount is allocated on a systematic basis over the useful life, and 2) the method used must reflect the pattern of expected consumption.

15. B is correct. IASB allows cash flows from interest and dividends to be reported as either "operating" or "investing cash inflows." Under U.S. GAAP, these must be reported as "operating cash inflows."

International Financial Statement Analysis, by Thomas R. Robinson, CFA, Jan Hendrik van Greuning, CFA, R. Elaine Henry, CFA, and Michael A. Broihahn, CFA. Copyright © 2007 by CFA Institute. Reprinted with permission.

16. C is correct. IASB allows cash payments for interest to be reported as either "operating" or "financing cash outflows." Under U.S. GAAP, these must be reported as "operating cash outflows."

17. C is correct. IASB allows cash payments for dividends to be reported as either "operating" or "financing cash outflows." Under U.S. GAAP, these must be reported as "financing cash outflows."

18. C is correct. If comparing a U.S. company that uses LIFO accounting with an international company for whom this method is not allowable, an analyst will make adjustments. Specifically, using LIFO reserve note disclosures, the analyst will adjust the U.S. company's profits, ending inventory, and total assets.

19. C is correct. If comparing an IFRS company, which has written up the value of its intangible assets, with a U.S. company, an analyst will eliminate the effect of the write-ups in calculating any affected asset-based ratios, which, in this case, includes the financial leverage multiplier (Total assets ÷ Total common equity).

A priori probability A probability based on logical analysis rather than on observation or personal judgment.

Abandonment option The ability to terminate a project at some future time if the financial results are disappointing.

Abnormal rate of return The amount by which a security's actual return differs from its expected rate of return which is based on the market's rate of return and the security's relationship with the market.

Above full-employment equilibrium A macroeconomic equilibrium in which real GDP exceeds potential GDP.

Absolute dispersion The amount of variability present without comparison to any reference point or benchmark.

Absolute frequency The number of observations in a given interval (for grouped data).

Accelerated methods of depreciation Depreciation methods that allocate a relatively large proportion of the cost of an asset to the early years of the asset's useful life.

Account With the accounting systems, a formal record of increases and decreases in a specific asset, liability, component of owners' equity, revenue, or expense.

Account format A method of presentation of accounting transactions in which effects on assets appear at the left and effects on liabilities and equity appear at the right of a central dividing line; also known as T-account format.

Accounting profit (income before taxes or pretax income) Income as reported on the income statement, in accordance with prevailing accounting standards, before the provisions for income tax expense.

Accounting risk The risk associated with accounting standards that vary from country to country or with any uncertainty about how certain transactions should be recorded.

Accounts payable Amounts that a business owes to its vendors for goods and services that were purchased from them but which have not yet been paid.

Accounts receivable turnover Ratio of sales on credit to the average balance in accounts receivable.

Accrual basis Method of accounting in which the effect of transactions on financial condition and income are recorded when they occur, not when they are settled in cash.

Accrued expenses (accrued liabilities) Liabilities related to expenses that have been incurred but not yet paid as of the end of an accounting period—an example of an accrued expense is rent that has been incurred but not yet paid, resulting in a liability "rent payable."

Accrued interest Interest earned but not yet paid.

Accumulated benefit obligation Under U.S. GAAP, a measure used in estimating a defined-benefit pension plan's liabilities, defined as "the actuarial present value of benefits (whether vested or non-vested) attributed by the pension benefit formula to employee service rendered before a specified date and based on employee service and compensation (if applicable) prior to that date."

Accumulated depreciation An offset to property, plant, and equipment (PPE) reflecting the amount of the cost of PPE that has been allocated to current and previous accounting periods.

Accumulation phase Phase in the investment life cycle during which individuals in the early-to-middle years of their working career attempt to accumulate assets to satisfy short-term needs and longer-term goals.

Acquiring company, or acquirer The company in a merger or acquisition that is acquiring the target.

Acquisition The purchase of some portion of one company by another; the purchase may be for assets, a definable segment of another entity, or the purchase of an entire company.

Acquisition method A method of accounting for a business combination where the acquirer is required to measure each identifiable asset and liability at fair value. This method was the result of a joint project of the IASB and FASB aiming at convergence in standards for the accounting of business combinations.

Active factor risk The contribution to active risk squared resulting from the portfolio's different-than-benchmark exposures relative to factors specified in the risk model.

Active return The return on a portfolio minus the return on the portfolio's benchmark.

Active risk The standard deviation of active returns.

Active risk squared The variance of active returns; active risk raised to the second power.

Active specific risk or asset selection risk The contribution to active risk squared resulting from the portfolio's active weights on individual assets as those weights interact with assets' residual risk.

G-1

Active strategy In reference to short-term cash management, an investment strategy characterized by monitoring and attempting to capitalize on market conditions to optimize the risk and return relationship of short-term investments.

Activity ratios (asset utilization or operating efficiency ratios) Ratios that measure how efficiently a company performs day-to-day tasks, such as the collection of receivables and management of inventory.

Addition rule for probabilities A principle stating that the probability that A or B occurs (both occur) equals the probability that A occurs, plus the probability that B occurs, minus the probability that both A and B occur.

Add-on interest A procedure for determining the interest on a bond or loan in which the interest is added onto the face value of a contract.

Adjusted beta Historical beta adjusted to reflect the tendency of beta to be mean reverting.

Adjusted R^2 A measure of goodness-of-fit of a regression that is adjusted for degrees of freedom and hence does not automatically increase when another independent variable is added to a regression.

Agency costs Costs associated with the conflict of interest present when a company is managed by non-owners. Agency costs result from the inherent conflicts of interest between managers and equity owners.

Agency costs of equity The smaller the stake that managers have in the company, the less is their share in bearing the cost of excessive perquisite consumption or not giving their best efforts in running the company.

Agency problem, or principal-agent problem A conflict of interest that arises when the agent in an agency relationship has goals and incentives that differ from the principal to whom the agent owes a fiduciary duty.

Agency relationships An arrangement whereby someone, an agent, acts on behalf of another person, the principal.

Aggregate demand The relationship between the quantity of real GDP demanded and the price level.

Aggregate hours The total number of hours worked by all the people employed, both full time and part time, during a year.

Aging schedule Λ breakdown of accounts into categories of days outstanding.

Allowance for bad debts An offset to accounts receivable for the amount of accounts receivable that are estimated to be uncollectible.

Alternative hypothesis The hypothesis accepted when the null hypothesis is rejected.

American option An option contract that can be exercised at any time until its expiration date.

Amortization The process of allocating the cost of intangible long-term assets having a finite useful life to accounting periods; the allocation of the amount of a bond premium or discount to the periods remaining until bond maturity.

Amortizing and accreting swaps A swap in which the notional principal changes according to a formula related to changes in the underlying.

Analysis of variance (ANOVA) The analysis of the total variability of a dataset (such as observations on the dependent variable in a regression) into components representing different sources of variation; with reference to regression, ANOVA provides the inputs for an F-test of the significance of the regression as a whole.

Annual percentage rate The cost of borrowing expressed as a yearly rate.

Annuity A finite set of level sequential cash flows.

Annuity due An annuity having a first cash flow that is paid immediately.

Anomalies Security price relationships that appear to contradict a well-regarded hypothesis; in this case, the efficient market hypothesis.

Anticipation stock Excess inventory that is held in anticipation of increased demand, often because of seasonal patterns of demand.

Antidilutive With reference to a transaction or a security, one that would increase earnings per share (EPS) or result in EPS higher than the company's basic EPS—antidilutive securities are not included in the calculation of diluted EPS.

Arbitrage 1) The simultaneous purchase of an undervalued asset or portfolio and sale of an overvalued but equivalent asset or portfolio, in order to obtain a riskless profit on the price differential. Taking advantage of a market inefficiency in a risk-free manner. 2) A trading strategy designed to generate a guaranteed profit from a transaction that requires no capital commitment or risk bearing on the part of the trader. A simple example of an arbitrage trade would be the simultaneous purchase and sale of the same security in different markets at different prices. 3) The condition in a financial market in which equivalent assets or combinations of assets sell for two different prices, creating an opportunity to profit at no risk with no commitment of money. In a well-functioning financial market, few arbitrage opportunities are possible. 4) A risk-free operation that earns an expected positive net profit but requires no net investment of money.

Arbitrage opportunity An opportunity to conduct an arbitrage; an opportunity to earn an expected positive net profit without risk and with no net investment of money.

Arbitrage portfolio The portfolio that exploits an arbitrage opportunity.

Arithmetic mean The sum of the observations divided by the number of observations.

Arrears swap A type of interest rate swap in which the floating payment is set at the end of the period and the interest is paid at that same time.

Asian call option A European-style option with a value at maturity equal to the difference between the stock price at maturity and the average stock price during the life of the option, or $0, whichever is greater.

Asset allocation The process of deciding how to distribute an investor's wealth among different asset classes for investment purposes.

Asset beta The unlevered beta; reflects the business risk of the assets; the asset's systematic risk.

Asset class Securities that have similar characteristics, attributes, and risk/return relationships.

Asset purchase An acquisition in which the acquirer purchases the target company's assets and payment is made directly to the target company.

Asset retirement obligations (AROs) The fair value of the estimated costs to be incurred at the end of a tangible asset's service life. The fair value of the liability is determined on the basis of discounted cash flows.

Asset-based loan A loan that is secured with company assets.

Assets Resources controlled by an enterprise as a result of past events and from which future economic benefits to the enterprise are expected to flow.

Assignment of accounts receivable The use of accounts receivable as collateral for a loan.

Asymmetric information The differential of information between corporate insiders and outsiders regarding the company's performance and prospects. Managers typically have more information about the company's performance and prospects than owners and creditors.

At the money An option in which the underlying value equals the exercise price.

Autocorrelation The correlation of a time series with its own past values.

Autocorrelation test A test of the efficient market hypothesis that compares security price changes over time to check for predictable correlation patterns.

Automated Clearing House An electronic payment network available to businesses, individuals, and financial institutions in the United States, U.S. Territories, and Canada.

Automatic fiscal policy A fiscal policy action that is triggered by the state of the economy.

Automatic stabilizers Mechanisms that stabilize real GDP without explicit action by the government.

Autonomous tax multiplier The magnification effect of a change in taxes on aggregate demand.

Autoregressive (AR) model A time series regressed on its own past values, in which the independent variable is a lagged value of the dependent variable.

Available-for-sale investments Debt and equity securities not classified as either held-to-maturity or held-for-trading securities. The investor is willing to sell but not actively planning to sell. In general, available-for-sale securities are reported at fair value on the balance sheet.

Average cost pricing rule A rule that sets price to cover cost including normal profit, which means setting the price equal to average total cost.

Average fixed cost Total fixed cost per unit of output.

Average product The average product of a factor of production. It equals total product divided by the quantity of the factor employed.

Average tax rate A person's total tax payment divided by his or her total income.

Average total cost Total cost per unit of output.

Average variable cost Total variable cost per unit of output.

Backtesting With reference to portfolio strategies, the application of a strategy's portfolio selection rules to historical data to assess what would have been the strategy's historical performance.

Backward integration A merger involving the purchase of a target ahead of the acquirer in the value or production chain; for example, to acquire a supplier.

Backwardation A condition in the futures markets in which the benefits of holding an asset exceed the costs, leaving the futures price less than the spot price.

Balance sheet (statement of financial position or statement of financial condition) The financial statement that presents an entity's current financial position by disclosing resources the entity controls (its assets) and the claims on those resources (its liabilities and equity claims), as of a particular point in time (the date of the balance sheet).

Balance sheet ratios Financial ratios involving balance sheet items only.

Balanced budget A government budget in which tax revenues and outlays are equal.

Balanced budget multiplier The magnification effect on aggregate demand of a simultaneous change in government expenditure and taxes that leaves the budget balanced.

Balance-sheet-based accruals ratio The difference between net operating assets at the end and the beginning of the period compared to the average net operating assets over the period.

Balance-sheet-based aggregate accruals The difference between net operating assets at the end and the beginning of the period.

Bank discount basis A quoting convention that annualizes, on a 360-day year, the discount as a percentage of face value.

Bargain purchase When a company is acquired and the purchase price is less than the fair value of the net assets. The current treatment of the excess of fair value over the purchase price is different under IFRS and U.S. GAAP. The excess is never accounted for as negative goodwill.

Barriers to entry Legal or natural constraints that protect a firm from potential competitors.

Barter The direct exchange of one good or service for other goods and services.

Basic EPS Net earnings available to common shareholders (i.e., net income minus preferred dividends) divided by the weighted average number of common shares outstanding.

Basis The difference between the spot price of the underlying asset and the futures contract price at any point in time (e.g., the *initial* basis at the time of contract origination, the *cover* basis at the time of contract termination).

Basis point value (BPV) Also called *present value of a basis point* or *price value of a basis point* (PVBP), the change in the bond price for a 1 basis point change in yield.

Basis swap 1) An interest rate swap involving two floating rates. 2) A swap in which both parties pay a floating rate.

Bayes' formula A method for updating probabilities based on new information.

Bear hug A tactic used by acquirers to circumvent target management's objections to a proposed merger by submitting the proposal directly to the target company's board of directors.

Bear spread An option strategy that involves selling a put with a lower exercise price and buying a put with a higher exercise price. It can also be executed with calls.

Behavioral finance Involves the analysis of various psychological traits of individuals and how these traits affect how they act as investors, analysts, and portfolio managers.

Below full-employment equilibrium A macroeconomic equilibrium in which potential GDP exceeds real GDP.

Benchmark A comparison portfolio; a point of reference or comparison.

Benchmark error Situation where an inappropriate or incorrect benchmark is used to compare and assess portfolio returns and management.

Benchmark portfolio A comparison standard of risk and assets included in the policy statement and similar to the investor's risk preference and investment needs, which can be used to evaluate the investment performance of the portfolio manager.

Bernoulli random variable A random variable having the outcomes 0 and 1.

Bernoulli trial An experiment that can produce one of two outcomes.

Beta A standardized measure of systematic risk based upon an asset's covariance with the market portfolio.

Big tradeoff The conflict between equality and efficiency.

Bilateral monopoly A situation in which a single seller (a monopoly) faces a single buyer (a monopsony).

Binomial model A model for pricing options in which the underlying price can move to only one of two possible new prices.

Binomial random variable The number of successes in n Bernoulli trials for which the probability of success is constant for all trials and the trials are independent.

Binomial tree The graphical representation of a model of asset price dynamics in which, at each period, the asset moves up with probability p or down with probability $(1 - p)$.

Black market An illegal market in which the price exceeds the legally imposed price ceiling.

Block Orders to buy or sell that are too large for the liquidity ordinarily available in dealer networks or stock exchanges.

Bond equivalent yield A calculation of yield that is annualized using the ratio of 365 to the number of days to maturity. Bond equivalent yield allows for the restatement and comparison of securities with different compounding periods.

Bond option An option in which the underlying is a bond; primarily traded in over-the-counter markets.

Bond yield plus risk premium approach An estimate of the cost of common equity that is produced by summing the before-tax cost of debt and a risk premium that captures the additional yield on a company's stock relative to its bonds. The additional yield is often estimated using historical spreads between bond yields and stock yields.

Bond-equivalent basis A basis for stating an annual yield that annualizes a semiannual yield by doubling it.

Bond-equivalent yield The yield to maturity on a basis that ignores compounding.

Bonding costs Costs borne by management to assure owners that they are working in the owners' best interest (e.g., implicit cost of non-compete agreements).

Book value equity per share The amount of book value (also called carrying value) of common equity per share of common stock, calculated by dividing the book value of shareholders' equity by the number of shares of common stock outstanding.

Bootstrapping earnings An increase in a company's earnings that results as a consequence of the idiosyncrasies of a merger transaction itself rather than because of resulting economic benefits of the combination.

Bottom-up analysis With reference to investment selection processes, an approach that involves selection from all securities within a specified investment universe, i.e., without prior narrowing of the universe on the basis of macroeconomic or overall market considerations.

Box spread An option strategy that combines a bull spread and a bear spread having two different exercise prices, which produces a risk-free payoff of the difference in the exercise prices.

Break point In the context of the weighted average cost of capital (WACC), a break point is the amount of capital at which the cost of one or more of the sources of capital changes, leading to a change in the WACC.

Breakeven point The number of units produced and sold at which the company's net income is zero (revenues = total costs).

Breakup value The value that can be achieved if a company's assets are divided and sold separately.

Breusch–Pagan test A test for conditional heteroskedasticity in the error term of a regression.

Broker 1) An agent who executes orders to buy or sell securities on behalf of a client in exchange for a commission. 2) *See* Futures commission merchants.

Budget deficit A government's budget balance that is negative—outlays exceed tax revenues.

Budget surplus A government's budget balance that is positive—tax revenues exceed outlays.

Bull spread An option strategy that involves buying a call with a lower exercise price and selling a call with a higher exercise price. It can also be executed with puts.

Business risk The risk associated with operating earnings. Operating earnings are uncertain because total revenues and many of the expenditures contributed to produce those revenues are uncertain.

Butterfly spread An option strategy that combines two bull or bear spreads and has three exercise prices.

Call An option that gives the holder the right to buy an underlying asset from another party at a fixed price over a specific period of time.

Call market A market in which trading for individual stocks only takes place at specified times. All the bids and asks available at the time are combined and the market administrators specify a single price that will possibly clear the market at that time.

Cannibalization Cannibalization occurs when an investment takes customers and sales away from another part of the company.

Cap 1) A contract on an interest rate, whereby at periodic payment dates, the writer of the cap pays the difference between the market interest rate and a specified cap rate if, and only if, this difference is positive. This is equivalent to a stream of call options on the interest rate. 2) A combination of interest rate call options designed to hedge a borrower against rate increases on a floating-rate loan.

Capital allocation line (CAL) A graph line that describes the combinations of expected return and standard deviation of return available to an investor from combining the optimal portfolio of risky assets with the risk-free asset.

Capital appreciation A return objective in which the investor seeks to increase the portfolio value, primarily through capital gains, over time to meet a future need rather than dividend yield.

Capital asset pricing model (CAPM) An equation describing the expected return on any asset (or portfolio) as a linear function of its beta relative to the market portfolio.

Capital budgeting The allocation of funds to relatively long-range projects or investments.

Capital market line (CML) The line with an intercept point equal to the risk-free rate that is tangent to the efficient frontier of risky assets; represents the efficient frontier when a risk-free asset is available for investment.

Capital preservation A return objective in which the investor seeks to minimize the risk of loss; generally a goal of the risk-averse investor.

Capital rationing A capital rationing environment assumes that the company has a fixed amount of funds to invest.

Capital structure The mix of debt and equity that a company uses to finance its business; a company's specific mixture of long-term financing.

Capitalized inventory costs Costs of inventories including costs of purchase, costs of conversion, other costs to bring the inventories to their present location and condition, and the allocated portion of fixed production overhead costs.

Caplet Each component call option in a cap.

Capped swap A swap in which the floating payments have an upper limit.

Captive finance subsidiary A wholly-owned subsidiary of a company that is established to provide financing of the sales of the parent company.

Carrying amount (book value) The amount at which an asset or liability is valued according to accounting principles.

Cartel A group of firms that has entered into a collusive agreement to restrict output and increase prices and profits.

Cash In accounting contexts, cash on hand (e.g., petty cash and cash not yet deposited to the bank) and demand deposits held in banks and similar accounts that can be used in payment of obligations.

Cash basis Accounting method in which the only relevant transactions for the financial statements are those that involve cash.

Cash conversion cycle (net operating cycle) A financial metric that measures the length of time required for a company to convert cash invested in its operations to cash received as a result of its operations; equal to days of inventory on hand + days of sales outstanding – number of days of payables.

Cash equivalents Very liquid short-term investments, usually maturing in 90 days or less.

Cash flow additivity principle The principle that dollar amounts indexed at the same point in time are additive.

Cash flow at risk (CFAR) A variation of VAR that reflects the risk of a company's cash flow instead of its market value.

Cash flow from operations (cash flow from operating activities or operating cash flow) The net amount of cash provided from operating activities.

Cash flow statement (statement of cash flows) A financial statement that reconciles beginning-of-period and end-of-period balance sheet values of cash; consists of three parts: cash flows from operating activities, cash flows from investing activities, and cash flows from financing activities.

Cash offering A merger or acquisition that is to be paid for with cash; the cash for the merger might come from the acquiring company's existing assets or from a debt issue.

Cash price or spot price The price for immediate purchase of the underlying asset.

Cash ratio A liquidity ratio calculated as (cash + short-term marketable investments) divided by current liabilities; measures a company's ability to meet its current obligations with just the cash and cash equivalents on hand.

Cash settlement A procedure used in certain derivative transactions that specifies that the long and short parties engage in the equivalent cash value of a delivery transaction.

Cash-flow-statement-based accruals ratio The difference between reported net income on an accrual basis and the cash flows from operating and investing activities compared to the average net operating assets over the period.

Cash-flow-statement-based aggregate accruals The difference between reported net income on an accrual basis and the cash flows from operating and investing activities.

Central bank A bank's bank and a public authority that regulates the nation's depository institutions and controls the quantity of money.

Central limit theorem A result in statistics that states that the sample mean computed from large samples of size n from a population with finite variance will follow an approximate normal distribution with a mean equal to the population mean and a variance equal to the population variance divided by n.

Centralized risk management or companywide risk management When a company has a single risk management group that monitors and controls all of the risk-taking activities of the organization. Centralization permits economies of scale and allows a company to use some of its risks to offset other risks. See also *enterprise risk management*.

Chain rule of forecasting A forecasting process in which the next period's value as predicted by the forecasting equation is substituted into the right-hand side of the equation to give a predicted value two periods ahead.

Characteristic line Regression line that indicates the systematic risk (beta) of a risky asset.

Chart of accounts A list of accounts used in an entity's accounting system.

Cheapest to deliver A bond in which the amount received for delivering the bond is largest compared with the amount paid in the market for the bond.

Cherry-picking When a bankrupt company is allowed to enforce contracts that are favorable to it while walking away from contracts that are unfavorable to it.

Classical A macroeconomist who believes that the economy is self-regulating and that it is always at full employment.

Classified balance sheet A balance sheet organized so as to group together the various assets and liabilities into subcategories (e.g., current and noncurrent).

Clean-surplus accounting The bottom-line income reflects all changes in shareholders' equity arising from other than owner transactions. In the absence of owner transactions, the change in shareholders' equity should equal net income. No adjustments such as translation adjustments bypass the income statement and go directly to shareholders equity.

Clearinghouse An entity associated with a futures market that acts as middleman between the contracting parties and guarantees to each party the performance of the other.

Clientele effect The preference some investors have for shares that exhibit certain characteristics.

Closeout netting Netting the market values of *all* derivative contracts between two parties to determine one overall value owed by one party to another in the event of bankruptcy.

Coefficient of variation (CV) The ratio of a set of observations' standard deviation to the observations' mean value.

Cointegrated Describes two time series that have a long-term financial or economic relationship such that they do not diverge from each other without bound in the long run.

Collar An option strategy involving the purchase of a put and sale of a call in which the holder of an asset gains protection below a certain level, the exercise price of the put, and pays for it by giving up gains above a certain level, the exercise price of the call. Collars also can be used to provide protection against rising interest rates on a floating-rate loan by giving up gains from lower interest rates.

Collusive agreement An agreement between two (or more) producers to restrict output, raise the price, and increase profits.

Combination A listing in which the order of the listed items does not matter.

Command system A method of allocating resources by the order (command) of someone in authority. In a firm a managerial hierarchy organizes production.

Commercial paper Unsecured short-term corporate debt that is characterized by a single payment at maturity.

Commission brokers Employees of a member firm who buy or sell securities for the customers of the firm.

Committed lines of credit A bank commitment to extend credit up to a pre-specified amount; the commitment is considered a short-term liability and is usually in effect for 364 days (one day short of a full year).

Commodity forward A contract in which the underlying asset is oil, a precious metal, or some other commodity.

Commodity futures Futures contracts in which the underlying is a traditional agricultural, metal, or petroleum product.

Commodity option An option in which the asset underlying the futures is a commodity, such as oil, gold, wheat, or soybeans.

Commodity swap A swap in which the underlying is a commodity such as oil, gold, or an agricultural product.

Common size statements Financial statements in which all elements (accounts) are stated as a percentage of a key figure such as revenue for an income statement or total assets for a balance sheet.

Common-size analysis The restatement of financial statement items using a common denominator or reference item that allows one to identify trends and major differences; an example is an income statement in which all items are expressed as a percent of revenue.

Company fundamental factors Factors related to the company's internal performance, such as factors relating to earnings growth, earnings variability, earnings momentum, and financial leverage.

Company share-related factors Valuation measures and other factors related to share price or the trading characteristics of the shares, such as earnings yield, dividend yield, and book-to-market value.

Comparable company A company that has similar business risk; usually in the same industry and preferably with a single line of business.

Competitive bid An underwriting alternative wherein an issuing entity (governmental body or a corporation) specifies the type of security to be offered (bonds or stocks) and the general characteristics of the issue, and the issuer solicits bids from competing investment banking firms with the understanding that the issuer will accept the highest bid from the bankers.

Complement In probability, with reference to an event *S*, the event that *S* does not occur; in economics, a good that is used in conjunction with another good.

Completed contract A method of revenue recognition in which the company does not recognize any revenue until the contract is completed; used particularly in long-term construction contracts.

Completely diversified portfolio A portfolio in which all unsystematic risk has been eliminated by diversification.

Component cost of capital The rate of return required by suppliers of capital for an individual source of a company's funding, such as debt or equity.

Compounding The process of accumulating interest on interest.

Comprehensive income The change in equity of a business enterprise during a period from nonowner sources; includes all changes in equity during a period except those resulting from investments by owners and distributions to owners; comprehensive income equals net income plus other comprehensive income.

Conditional expected value The expected value of a stated event given that another event has occurred.

Conditional heteroskedasticity Heteroskedasticity in the error variance that is correlated with the values of the independent variable(s) in the regression.

Conditional probability The probability of an event given (conditioned on) another event.

Conditional variances The variance of one variable, given the outcome of another.

Confidence interval A range that has a given probability that it will contain the population parameter it is intended to estimate.

Conglomerate merger A merger involving companies that are in unrelated businesses.

Consistency A desirable property of estimators; a consistent estimator is one for which the probabil-ity of estimates close to the value of the population parameter increases as sample size increases.

Consistent With reference to estimators, describes an estimator for which the probability of estimates close to the value of the population parameter increases as sample size increases.

Consolidation The combining of the results of operations of subsidiaries with the parent company to present financial statements as if they were a single economic unit. The asset, liabilities, revenues and expenses of the subsidiaries are combined with those of the parent company, eliminating intercompany transactions.

Consolidation phase Phase in the investment life cycle during which individuals who are typically past the midpoint of their career have earnings that exceed expenses and invest them for future retirement or estate planning needs.

Constant maturity swap or CMT swap A swap in which the floating rate is the rate on a security known as a constant maturity treasury or CMT security.

Constant maturity treasury or CMT A hypothetical U.S. Treasury note with a constant maturity. A CMT exists for various years in the range of 2 to 10.

Constant returns to scale Features of a firm's technology that lead to constant long-run average cost as output increases. When constant returns to scale are present, the *LRAC* curve is horizontal.

Construct the portfolio Given the strategy and economic outlook, what specific stocks and/or bonds will be put into the portfolio at the present time that are consistent with the client's policy statement.

Consumer Price Index (CPI) An index that measures the average of the prices paid by urban consumers for a fixed "basket" of the consumer goods and services.

Consumer surplus The value (or marginal benefit) of a good minus the price paid for it, summed over the quantity bought.

Contango A situation in a futures market where the current futures price is greater than the current spot price for the underlying asset.

Contestable market A market in which firms can enter and leave so easily that firms in the market face competition from potential entrants.

Contingent claims Derivatives in which the payoffs occur if a specific event occurs; generally referred to as options.

Continual monitoring The constant evaluation of the economic environment, the policy statement, and the portfolio to ensure that it is consistent with the policy statement. Also involves evaluating performance to determine if changes are required in the portfolio, the strategy, or the policy statement.

Continuous market   A market where stocks are priced and traded continuously by an auction process or by dealers when the market is open.

Continuous random variable   A random variable for which the range of possible outcomes is the real line (all real numbers between $-\infty$ and $+\infty$ or some subset of the real line.

Continuous time   Time thought of as advancing in extremely small increments.

Continuously compounded return   The natural logarithm of 1 plus the holding period return, or equivalently, the natural logarithm of the ending price over the beginning price.

Contra account   An account that offsets another account.

Contribution margin   The amount available for fixed costs and profit after paying variable costs; revenue minus variable costs.

Controlling interest   An investment where the investor exerts control over the investee, typically by having a greater than 50 percent ownership in the investee.

Convenience yield   The nonmonetary return offered by an asset when the asset is in short supply, often associated with assets with seasonal production processes.

Conventional cash flow   A conventional cash flow pattern is one with an initial outflow followed by a series of inflows.

Conversion factor   An adjustment used to facilitate delivery on bond futures contracts in which any of a number of bonds with different characteristics are eligible for delivery.

Convertible debt   Debt with the added feature that the bondholder has the option to exchange the debt for equity at prespecified terms.

Cooperative equilibrium   The outcome of a game in which the players make and share the monopoly profit.

Core inflation rate   A measure of inflation based on the core CPI—the CPI excluding food and fuel.

Corporate governance   The system of principles, policies, procedures, and clearly defined responsibilities and accountabilities used by stakeholders to overcome the conflicts of interest inherent in the corporate form.

Corporate raider   A person or organization seeking to profit by acquiring a company and reselling it, or seeking to profit from the takeover attempt itself (e.g. greenmail).

Corporation   A legal entity with rights similar to those of a person. The chief officers, executives, or top managers act as agents for the firm and are legally entitled to authorize corporate activities and to enter into contracts on behalf of the business.

Correlation   A number between -1 and $+1$ that measures the co-movement (linear association) between two random variables.

Correlation analysis   The analysis of the strength of the linear relationship between two data series.

Correlation coefficient   A standardized measure of the relationship between two variables that ranges from -1.00 to $+1.00$.

Cost averaging   The periodic investment of a fixed amount of money.

Cost of capital   The rate of return that suppliers of capital require as compensation for their contribution of capital.

Cost of carry   The cost associated with holding some asset, including financing, storage, and insurance costs. Any yield received on the asset is treated as a negative carrying cost.

Cost of carry model   A model for pricing futures contracts in which the futures price is determined by adding the cost of carry to the spot price.

Cost of debt   The cost of debt financing to a company, such as when it issues a bond or takes out a bank loan.

Cost of goods sold   For a given period, equal to beginning inventory minus ending inventory plus the cost of goods acquired or produced during the period.

Cost of preferred stock   The cost to a company of issuing preferred stock; the dividend yield that a company must commit to pay preferred stockholders.

Cost recovery method   A method of revenue recognition in which the seller does not report any profit until the cash amounts paid by the buyer—including principal and interest on any financing from the seller—are greater than all the seller's costs for the merchandise sold.

Cost structure   The mix of a company's variable costs and fixed costs.

Cost-push inflation   An inflation that results from an initial increase in costs.

Council of Economic Advisers   The President's council whose main work is to monitor the economy and keep the President and the public well informed about the current state of the economy and the best available forecasts of where it is heading.

Covariance A measure of the co-movement (linear association) between two random variables.

Covariance matrix A matrix or square array whose entries are covariances; also known as a variance–covariance matrix.

Covariance stationary Describes a time series when its expected value and variance are constant and finite in all periods and when its covariance with itself for a fixed number of periods in the past or future is constant and finite in all periods.

Covered call An option strategy involving the holding of an asset and sale of a call on the asset.

Covered interest arbitrage A transaction executed in the foreign exchange market in which a currency is purchased (sold) and a forward contract is sold (purchased) to lock in the exchange rate for future delivery of the currency. This transaction should earn the risk-free rate of the investor's home country.

Credit With respect to double-entry accounting, a credit records increases in liability, owners' equity, and revenue accounts or decreases in asset accounts; with respect to borrowing, the willingness and ability of the borrower to make promised payments on the borrowing.

Credit analysis The evaluation of credit risk; the evaluation of the creditworthiness of a borrower or counterparty.

Credit derivatives A contract in which one party has the right to claim a payment from another party in the event that a specific credit event occurs over the life of the contract.

Credit risk or default risk The risk of loss caused by a counterparty's or debtor's failure to make a promised payment.

Credit scoring model A statistical model used to classify borrowers according to creditworthiness.

Credit spread option An option on the yield spread on a bond.

Credit swap A type of swap transaction used as a credit derivative in which one party makes periodic payments to the other and receives the promise of a payoff if a third party defaults.

Credit VAR, Default VAR, or Credit at Risk A variation of VAR that reflects credit risk.

Credit-linked notes Fixed-income securities in which the holder of the security has the right to withhold payment of the full amount due at maturity if a credit event occurs.

Creditworthiness The perceived ability of the borrower to pay what is owed on the borrowing in a timely manner; it represents the ability of a company to withstand adverse impacts on its cash flows.

Cross elasticity of demand The responsiveness of the demand for a good to a change in the price of a substitute or complement, other things remaining the same. It is calculated as the percentage change in the quantity demanded of the good divided by the percentage change in the price of the substitute or complement.

Cross-product netting Netting the market values of all contracts, not just derivatives, between parties.

Cross-sectional analysis Analysis that involves comparisons across individuals in a group over a given time period or at a given point in time.

Cross-sectional data Observations over individual units at a point in time, as opposed to time-series data.

Crowding-out effect The tendency for a government budget deficit to decrease investment.

Cumulative distribution function A function giving the probability that a random variable is less than or equal to a specified value.

Cumulative relative frequency For data grouped into intervals, the fraction of total observations that are less than the value of the upper limit of a stated interval.

Currency The notes and coins held by individuals and businesses.

Currency drain ratio The ratio of currency to deposits.

Currency forward A forward contract in which the underlying is a foreign currency.

Currency option An option that allows the holder to buy (if a call) or sell (if a put) an underlying currency at a fixed exercise rate, expressed as an exchange rate.

Currency swap A swap in which each party makes interest payments to the other in different currencies.

Current assets, or liquid assets Assets that are expected to be consumed or converted into cash in the near future, typically one year or less.

Current cost With reference to assets, the amount of cash or cash equivalents that would have to be paid to buy the same or an equivalent asset today; with reference to liabilities, the undiscounted amount of cash or cash equivalents that would be required to settle the obligation today.

Current credit risk The risk associated with the possibility that a payment currently due will not be made.

Current exchange rate For accounting purposes, the spot exchange rate on the balance sheet date.

Current income A return objective in which the investor seeks to generate income rather than capital gains; generally a goal of an investor who wants to supplement earnings with income to meet living expenses.

Current liabilities Short-term obligations, such as accounts payable, wages payable, or accrued liabilities, that are expected to be settled in the near future, typically one year or less.

Current rate method Approach to translating foreign currency financial statements for consolidation in which all assets and liabilities are translated at the current exchange rate. The current rate method is the prevalent method of translation.

Current ratio A liquidity ratio calculated as current assets divided by current liabilities.

Current taxes payable Tax expenses that have been recognized and recorded on a company's income statement but which have not yet been paid.

Cyclical change An economic trend arising from the ups and downs of the business cycle.

Cyclical company A firm whose earnings rise and fall with general economic activity.

Cyclical stock A stock with a high beta; its gains typically exceed those of a rising market and its losses typically exceed those of a falling market.

Cyclical surplus or deficit The actual surplus or deficit minus the structural surplus or deficit.

Cyclical unemployment The fluctuating unemployment over the business cycle.

Daily settlement See *marking to market.*

Data mining The practice of determining a model by extensive searching through a dataset for statistically significant patterns.

Day trader A trader holding a position open somewhat longer than a scalper but closing all positions at the end of the day.

Days of inventory on hand (DOH) An activity ratio equal to the number of days in the period divided by inventory turnover over the period.

Days of sales outstanding (DSO) An activity ratio equal to the number of days in the period divided by receivables turnover.

Dead-hand provision A poison pill provision that allows for the redemption or cancellation of a poison pill provision only by a vote of continuing directors (generally directors who were on the target company's board prior to the takeover attempt).

Deadweight loss A measure of inefficiency. It is equal to the decrease in total surplus that results from an inefficient level of production.

Dealing securities Securities held by banks or other financial intermediaries for trading purposes.

Debit With respect to double-entry accounting, a debit records increases of asset and expense accounts or decreases in liability and owners' equity accounts.

Debt covenants Agreements between the company as borrower and its creditors.

Debt incurrence test A financial covenant made in conjunction with existing debt that restricts a company's ability to incur additional debt at the same seniority based on one or more financial tests or conditions.

Debt rating approach A method for estimating a company's before-tax cost of debt based upon the yield on comparably rated bonds for maturities that closely match that of the company's existing debt.

Debt ratings An objective measure of the quality and safety of a company's debt based upon an analysis of the company's ability to pay the promised cash flows, as well as an analysis of any indentures.

Debt with warrants Debt issued with warrants that give the bondholder the right to purchase equity at prespecified terms.

Debt-to-assets ratio A solvency ratio calculated as total debt divided by total assets.

Debt-to-capital ratio A solvency ratio calculated as total debt divided by total debt plus total shareholders' equity.

Debt-to-equity ratio A solvency ratio calculated as total debt divided by total shareholders' equity.

Decentralized risk management A system that allows individual units within an organization to manage risk. Decentralization results in duplication of effort but has the advantage of having people closer to the risk be more directly involved in its management.

Deciles Quantiles that divide a distribution into 10 equal parts.

Decision rule With respect to hypothesis testing, the rule according to which the null hypothesis will be rejected or not rejected; involves the comparison of the test statistic to rejection point(s).

Declaration date The day that the corporation issues a statement declaring a specific dividend.

Declining trend channel The range defined by security prices as they move progressively lower.

Deductible temporary differences Temporary differences that result in a reduction of or deduction from taxable income in a future period when the balance sheet item is recovered or settled.

Deep in the money Options that are far in-the-money.

Deep out of the money Options that are far out-of-the-money.

Default risk premium An extra return that compensates investors for the possibility that the borrower will fail to make a promised payment at the contracted time and in the contracted amount.

Defensive company   Firms whose future earnings are likely to withstand an economic downturn.

Defensive interval ratio   A liquidity ratio that estimates the number of days that an entity could meet cash needs from liquid assets; calculated as (cash + short-term marketable investments + receivables) divided by daily cash expenditures.

Defensive stock   A stock whose return is not expected to decline as much as that of the overall market during a bear market (a beta less than one).

Deferred tax assets   A balance sheet asset that arises when an excess amount is paid for income taxes relative to accounting profit. The taxable income is higher than accounting profit and income tax payable exceeds tax expense. The company expects to recover the difference during the course of future operations when tax expense exceeds income tax payable.

Deferred tax liabilities   A balance sheet liability that arises when a deficit amount is paid for income taxes relative to accounting profit. The taxable income is less than the accounting profit and income tax payable is less than tax expense. The company expects to eliminate the liability over the course of future operations when income tax payable exceeds tax expense.

Defined-benefit pension plans   Plan in which the company promises to pay a certain annual amount (defined benefit) to the employee after retirement. The company bears the investment risk of the plan assets.

Defined-contribution pension plans   Individual accounts to which an employee and typically the employer makes contributions, generally on a tax-advantaged basis. The amounts of contributions are defined at the outset, but the future value of the benefit is unknown. The employee bears the investment risk of the plan assets.

Definitive merger agreement   A contract signed by both parties to a merger that clarifies the details of the transaction, including the terms, warranties, conditions, termination details, and the rights of all parties.

Degree of confidence   The probability that a confidence interval includes the unknown population parameter.

Degree of financial leverage (DFL)   The ratio of the percentage change in net income to the percentage change in operating income; the sensitivity of the cash flows available to owners when operating income changes.

Degree of operating leverage (DOL)   The ratio of the percentage change in operating income to the percentage change in units sold; the sensitivity of operating income to changes in units sold.

Degree of total leverage   The ratio of the percentage change in net income to the percentage change in units sold; the sensitivity of the cash flows to owners to changes in the number of units produced and sold.

Degrees of freedom (df)   The number of independent observations used.

Delivery   A process used in a deliverable forward contract in which the long pays the agreed-upon price to the short, which in turn delivers the underlying asset to the long.

Delivery option   The feature of a futures contract giving the short the right to make decisions about what, when, and where to deliver.

Delta   The relationship between the option price and the underlying price, which reflects the sensitivity of the price of the option to changes in the price of the underlying.

Delta hedge   An option strategy in which a position in an asset is converted to a risk-free position with a position in a specific number of options. The number of options per unit of the underlying changes through time, and the position must be revised to maintain the hedge.

Delta-normal method   A measure of VAR equivalent to the analytical method but that refers to the use of delta to estimate the option's price sensitivity.

Demand for money   The relationship between the quantity of money demanded and the interest rate when all other influences on the amount of money that people wish to hold remain the same.

Demand-pull inflation   An inflation that results from an initial increase in aggregate demand.

Dependent   With reference to events, the property that the probability of one event occurring depends on (is related to) the occurrence of another event.

Dependent variable   The variable whose variation about its mean is to be explained by the regression; the left-hand-side variable in a regression equation.

Depository institution   A firm that takes deposits from households and firms and makes loans to other households and firms.

Depreciation   The process of systematically allocating the cost of long-lived (tangible) assets to the periods during which the assets are expected to provide economic benefits.

Derivative   A financial instrument whose value depends on the value of some underlying asset or factor (e.g., a stock price, an interest rate, or exchange rate).

Derivatives dealers Commercial and investment banks that make markets in derivatives.

Derived demand Demand for a factor of production, which is derived from the demand for the goods and services produced by that factor.

Descriptive statistics The study of how data can be summarized effectively.

Designated fair value instruments Financial instruments that an entity chooses to measure at fair value per IAS 39 or SFAS 159. Generally, the election to use the fair value option is irrevocable.

Desired reserve ratio The ratio of reserves to deposits that banks want to hold.

Diff swaps A swap in which the payments are based on the difference between interest rates in two countries but payments are made in only a single currency.

Diffuse prior The assumption of equal prior probabilities.

Diluted EPS The EPS that would result if all dilutive securities were converted into common shares.

Diluted shares The number of shares that would be outstanding if all potentially dilutive claims on common shares (e.g., convertible debt, convertible preferred stock, and employee stock options) were exercised.

Diminishing balance method An accelerated depreciation method, i.e., one that allocates a relatively large proportion of the cost of an asset to the early years of the asset's useful life.

Diminishing marginal returns The tendency for the marginal product of an additional unit of a factor of production to be less than the marginal product of the previous unit of the factor.

Direct debit program An arrangement whereby a customer authorizes a debit to a demand account; typically used by companies to collect routine payments for services.

Direct financing lease A type of finance lease, from a lessor perspective, where the present value of the lease payments (lease receivable) equals the carrying value of the leased asset. The revenues earned by the lessor are financing in nature.

Direct format (direct method) With reference to the cash flow statement, a format for the presentation of the statement in which cash flow from operating activities is shown as operating cash receipts less operating cash disbursements.

Direct write-off method An approach to recognizing credit losses on customer receivables in which the company waits until such time as a customer has defaulted and only then recognizes the loss.

Dirty-surplus accounting Accounting in which some income items are reported as part of stockholders' equity rather than as gains and losses on the income statement; certain items of comprehensive income bypass the income statement and appear as direct adjustments to shareholders' equity.

Dirty-surplus items Direct adjustments to shareholders' equity that bypass the income statement.

Disbursement float The amount of time between check issuance and a check's clearing back against the company's account.

Discount To reduce the value of a future payment in allowance for how far away it is in time; to calculate the present value of some future amount. Also, the amount by which an instrument is priced below its face value.

Discount interest A procedure for determining the interest on a loan or bond in which the interest is deducted from the face value in advance.

Discount rate The interest rate at which the Fed stands ready to lend reserves to depository institutions.

Discounted cash flow analysis In the context of merger analysis, it is an estimate of a target company's value found by discounting the company's expected future free cash flows to the present.

Discouraged workers People who are available and willing to work but have not made specific effort to find a job in the previous four weeks.

Discrete random variable A random variable that can take on at most a countable number of possible values.

Discrete time Time thought of as advancing in distinct finite increments.

Discretionary fiscal policy A fiscal action that is initiated by an act of Congress.

Discriminant analysis A multivariate classification technique used to discriminate between groups, such as companies that either will or will not become bankrupt during some time frame.

Diseconomies of scale Features of a firm's technology that lead to rising long-run average cost as output increases.

Dispersion The variability around the central tendency.

Disposable income Aggregate income minus taxes plus transfer payments.

Divestiture The sale, liquidation, or spin-off of a division or subsidiary.

Dividend discount model (DDM) A technique for estimating the value of a stock issue as the present value of all future dividends.

Dividend discount model based approach An approach for estimating a country's equity risk premium. The market rate of return is estimated as the sum of the dividend yield and the growth rate in dividends for a market index. Subtracting the risk-free rate of return from the estimated market return produces an estimate for the equity risk premium.

Dividend payout policy The strategy a company follows with regard to the amount and timing of dividend payments.

Dividend payout ratio The ratio of cash dividends paid to earnings for a period.

Dividends per share The dollar amount of cash dividends paid during a period per share of common stock.

Dominant strategy equilibrium A Nash equilibrium in which the best strategy for each player is to cheat (deny) regardless of the strategy of the other player.

Double declining balance depreciation An accelerated depreciation method that involves depreciating the asset at double the straight-line rate. This rate is multiplied by the book value of the asset at the beginning of the period (a declining balance) to calculate depreciation expense.

Double taxation Corporate earnings are taxed twice when paid out as dividends. First, corporate earnings are taxed regardless of whether they will be distributed as dividends or retained at the corporate level, and second, dividends are taxed again at the individual shareholder level.

Double-entry accounting The accounting system of recording transactions in which every recorded transaction affects at least two accounts so as to keep the basic accounting equation (assets = liabilities + owners' equity) in balance.

Down transition probability The probability that an asset's value moves down in a model of asset price dynamics.

Downstream A transaction between two affiliates, an investor company and an associate company such that the investor company records a profit on its income statement. An example is a sale of inventory by the investor company to the associate.

Drag on liquidity When receipts lag, creating pressure from the decreased available funds.

Dummy variable A type of qualitative variable that takes on a value of 1 if a particular condition is true and 0 if that condition is false.

Duopoly A market structure in which two producers of a good or service compete.

DuPont analysis An approach to decomposing return on investment, e.g., return on equity, as the product of other financial ratios.

Duration A measure of an option-free bond's average maturity. Specifically, the weighted average maturity of all future cash flows paid by a security, in which the weights are the present value of these cash flows as a fraction of the bond's price. A measure of a bond's price sensitivity to interest rate movements.

Dutch Book theorem A result in probability theory stating that inconsistent probabilities create profit opportunities.

Dynamic hedging A strategy in which a position is hedged by making frequent adjustments to the quantity of the instrument used for hedging in relation to the instrument being hedged.

Earnings at risk (EAR) A variation of VAR that reflects the risk of a company's earnings instead of its market value.

Earnings expectation management Attempts by management to influence analysts' earnings forecasts.

Earnings game Management's focus on reporting earnings that meet consensus estimates.

Earnings management activity Deliberate activity aimed at influencing reporting earnings numbers, often with the goal of placing management in a favorable light; the opportunistic use of accruals to manage earnings.

Earnings multiplier model A technique for estimating the value of a stock issue as a multiple of its future earnings per share.

Earnings per share The amount of income earned during a period per share of common stock.

Earnings surprise A company announcement of earnings that differ from analysts' prevailing expectations.

Economic depreciation The change in the market value of capital over a given period.

Economic efficiency A situation that occurs when the firm produces a given output at the least cost.

Economic exposure The risk associated with changes in the relative attractiveness of products and services offered for sale, arising out of the competitive effects of changes in exchange rates.

Economic order quantity–reorder point An approach to managing inventory based on expected demand and the predictability of demand; the ordering point for new inventory is determined based on the costs of ordering and carrying inventory, such that the total cost associated with inventory is minimized.

Economic profit A firm's total revenue minus its total cost.

Economic rent Any surplus—consumer surplus, producer surplus or economic profit. The income received by the owner of a factor of production over and above the amount required to induce that owner to offer the factor for use.

Economies of scale Features of a firm's technology that lead to a falling long-run average cost as output increases. In reference to mergers, it is the savings achieved through the consolidation of operations and elimination of duplicate resources.

Economies of scope Decreases in average total cost that occur when a firm uses specialized resources to produce a range of goods and services.

Effective annual rate The amount by which a unit of currency will grow in a year with interest on interest included.

Effective annual yield (EAY) An annualized return that accounts for the effect of interest on interest; EAY is computed by compounding 1 plus the holding period yield forward to one year, then subtracting 1.

Efficiency In statistics, a desirable property of estimators; an efficient estimator is the unbiased estimator with the smallest variance among unbiased estimators of the same parameter.

Efficiency wage A real wage rate that is set above the equilibrium wage rate and that balances the costs and benefits of this higher wage rate to maximize the firm's profit.

Efficient capital market A market in which security prices rapidly reflect all information about securities.

Efficient frontier The portion of the minimum-variance frontier beginning with the global minimum-variance portfolio and continuing above it; the graph of the set of portfolios offering the maximum expected return for their level of variance of return.

Efficient portfolio A portfolio offering the highest expected return for a given level of risk as measured by variance or standard deviation of return.

Elastic demand Demand with a price elasticity greater than 1; other things remaining the same, the percentage change in the quantity demanded exceeds the percentage change in price.

Elasticity A measure of sensitivity; the incremental change in one variable with respect to an incremental change in another variable.

Elasticity of supply The responsiveness of the quantity supplied of a good to a change in its price, other things remaining the same.

Electronic funds transfer The use of computer networks to conduct financial transactions electronically.

Empirical probability The probability of an event estimated as a relative frequency of occurrence.

Employment Act of 1946 A landmark Congressional act that recognizes a role for government actions to keep unemployment low, the economy expanding, and inflation in check.

Employment-to-population ratio The percentage of people of working age who have jobs.

Enhanced derivatives products companies (EDPC) A type of subsidiary engaged in derivatives transactions that is separated from the parent company in order to have a higher credit rating than the parent company.

Enterprise risk management A form of *centralized risk management* that typically encompasses the management of a broad variety of risks, including insurance risk.

Equitizing cash A strategy used to replicate an index. It is also used to take a given amount of cash and turn it into an equity position while maintaining the liquidity provided by the cash.

Equity Assets less liabilities; the residual interest in the assets after subtracting the liabilities.

Equity carve-out A form of restructuring that involves the creation of a new legal entity and the sale of equity in it to outsiders.

Equity forward A contract calling for the purchase of an individual stock, a stock portfolio, or a stock index at a later date at an agreed-upon price.

Equity method A basis for reporting investment income in which the investing entity recognizes a share of income as earned rather than as dividends when received. These transactions are typically reflected in Investments in Associates or Equity Method Investments.

Equity options Options on individual stocks; also known as stock options.

Equity risk premium The expected return on equities minus the risk-free rate; the premium that investors demand for investing in equities.

Equity swap A swap transaction in which at least one cash flow is tied to the return to an equity portfolio position, often an equity index.

Error autocorrelation The autocorrelation of the error term.

Error term The portion of the dependent variable that is not explained by the independent variable(s) in the regression.

Estimate The particular value calculated from sample observations using an estimator.

Estimated (or fitted) parameters With reference to regression analysis, the estimated values of the population intercept and population slope coefficient(s) in a regression.

Estimated rate of return The rate of return an investor anticipates earning from a specific investment over a particular future holding period.

Estimation With reference to statistical inference, the subdivision dealing with estimating the value of a population parameter.

Estimator An estimation formula; the formula used to compute the sample mean and other sample statistics are examples of estimators.

Eurodollar A dollar deposited outside the United States.

European-style option or European option An option contract that can only be exercised on its expiration date.

Event Any outcome or specified set of outcomes of a random variable.

Event study Research that examines the reaction of a security's price to a specific company, world event, or news announcement.

Excess kurtosis Degree of peakedness (fatness of tails) in excess of the peakedness of the normal distribution.

Excess reserves A bank's actual reserves minus its desired reserves.

Exchange for physicals (EFP) A permissible delivery procedure used by futures market participants, in which the long and short arrange a delivery procedure other than the normal procedures stipulated by the futures exchange.

Exchange ratio The number of shares that target stockholders are to receive in exchange for each of their shares in the target company.

Ex-dividend Trading ex-dividend refers to shares that no longer carry the right to the next dividend payment.

Ex-dividend date The first date that a share trades without (i.e. "ex") the dividend.

Exercise or exercising the option The process of using an option to buy or sell the underlying.

Exercise date The day that employees actually exercise the options and convert them to stock.

Exercise price (strike price, striking price, or strike) The fixed price at which an option holder can buy or sell the underlying.

Exercise rate or strike rate The fixed rate at which the holder of an interest rate option can buy or sell the underlying.

Exhaustive Covering or containing all possible outcomes.

Expected rate of return The return that analysts' calculations suggest a security should provide, based on the market's rate of return during the period and the security's relationship to the market.

Expected value The probability-weighted average of the possible outcomes of a random variable.

Expensed Taken as a deduction in arriving at net income.

Expenses Outflows of economic resources or increases in liabilities that result in decreases in equity (other than decreases because of distributions to owners); reductions in net assets associated with the creation of revenues.

Expiration date The date on which a derivative contract expires.

Exposure to foreign exchange risk The risk of a change in value of an asset or liability denominated in a foreign currency due to a change in exchange rates.

External diseconomies Factors outside the control of a firm that raise the firm's costs as the industry produces a larger output.

External economies Factors beyond the control of a firm that lower the firm's costs as the industry produces a larger output.

External efficiency A market in which prices adjust quickly to new information regarding supply or demand. Also referred to as *informational efficiency*.

External growth Company growth in output or sales that is achieved by buying the necessary resources externally (i.e., achieved through mergers and acquisitions).

Externality The effect of an investment on other things besides the investment itself.

Face value (also principal, par value, stated value, or maturity value) The amount of cash payable by a company to the bondholders when the bonds mature; the promised payment at maturity separate from any coupon payment.

Factor A common or underlying element with which several variables are correlated.

Factor risk premium (or factor price) The expected return in excess of the risk-free rate for a portfolio with a sensitivity of 1 to one factor and a sensitivity of 0 to all other factors.

Factor sensitivity (also factor betas or factor loadings) A measure of the response of return to each unit of increase in a factor, holding all other factors constant.

Fair market value The market price of an asset or liability that trades regularly.

Fair value The amount at which an asset could be exchanged, or a liability settled, between knowledgeable, willing parties in an arm's-length transaction; the price that would be received to sell an asset or paid to transfer a liability in an orderly transaction between market participants.

Federal budget The annual statement of the outlays and tax revenues of the government of the United States, together with the laws and regulations that approve and support those outlays and taxes.

Federal funds rate The interest rate that the banks charge each other on overnight loans.

Federal Open Market Committee The main policy-making organ of the Federal Reserve System.

Federal Reserve System (the Fed) The central bank of the United States.

Fiduciary call A combination of a European call and a risk-free bond that matures on the option expiration day and has a face value equal to the exercise price of the call.

FIFO method The first in, first out, method of accounting for inventory, which matches sales against the costs of items of inventory in the order in which they were placed in inventory.

Filter rule A trading rule that recommends security transactions when price changes exceed a previously determined percentage.

Finance lease (capital lease) Essentially, the purchase of some asset by the buyer (lessee) that is directly financed by the seller (lessor).

Financial analysis The process of selecting, evaluating, and interpreting financial data in order to formulate an assessment of a company's present and future financial condition and performance.

Financial distress Heightened uncertainty regarding a company's ability to meet its various obligations because of lower or negative earnings.

Financial flexibility The ability to react and adapt to financial adversities and opportunities.

Financial futures Futures contracts in which the underlying is a stock, bond, or currency.

Financial leverage The extent to which a company can effect, through the use of debt, a proportional change in the return on common equity that is greater than a given proportional change in operating income; also, short for the financial leverage ratio.

Financial leverage ratio A measure of financial leverage calculated as average total assets divided by average total equity.

Financial reporting quality The accuracy with which a company's reported financials reflect its operating performance and their usefulness for forecasting future cash flows.

Financial risk The risk that environmental, social, or governance risk factors will result in significant costs or other losses to a company and its shareholders; the risk arising from a company's obligation to meet required payments under its financing agreements.

Financing activities Activities related to obtaining or repaying capital to be used in the business (e.g., equity and long-term debt).

Firm An economic unit that hires factors of production and organizes those factors to produce and sell goods and services.

First-differencing A transformation that subtracts the value of the time series in period $t-1$ from its value in period t.

First-order serial correlation Correlation between adjacent observations in a time series.

Fiscal imbalance The present value of the government's commitments to pay benefits minus the present value of its tax revenues.

Fiscal policy The government's attempt to achieve macroeconomic objectives such as full employment, sustained long-term economic growth, and price level stability by setting and changing tax rates, making transfer payments, and purchasing goods and services.

Fixed asset turnover An activity ratio calculated as total revenue divided by average net fixed assets.

Fixed charge coverage A solvency ratio measuring the number of times interest and lease payments are covered by operating income, calculated as (EBIT + lease payments) divided by (interest payments + lease payments).

Fixed costs Costs that remain at the same level regardless of a company's level of production and sales.

Fixed rate perpetual preferred stock Nonconvertible, noncallable preferred stock that has a fixed dividend rate and no maturity date.

Fixed-income forward A forward contract in which the underlying is a bond.

Flat trend channel The range defined by security prices as they maintain a relatively steady level.

Flip-in pill A poison pill takeover defense that dilutes an acquirer's ownership in a target by giving other existing target company shareholders the right to buy additional target company shares at a discount.

Flip-over pill A poison pill takeover defense that gives target company shareholders the right to purchase shares of the acquirer at a significant discount to the market price, which has the effect of causing dilution to all existing acquiring company shareholders.

Float In the context of customer receipts, the amount of money that is in transit between payments made by customers and the funds that are usable by the company.

Float factor An estimate of the average number of days it takes deposited checks to clear; average daily float divided by average daily deposit.

Floating-rate loan A loan in which the interest rate is reset at least once after the starting date.

Floor A combination of interest rate put options designed to hedge a lender against lower rates on a floating-rate loan.

Floor brokers Independent members of an exchange who act as brokers for other members.

Floor traders or locals Market makers that buy and sell by quoting a bid and an ask price. They are the primary providers of liquidity to the market.

Floored swap A swap in which the floating payments have a lower limit.

Floorlet Each component put option in a floor.

Flotation cost Fees charged to companies by investment bankers and other costs associated with raising new capital.

Foreign currency transactions Transactions that are denominated in a currency other than a company's functional currency.

Forward contract An agreement between two parties in which one party, the buyer, agrees to buy from the other party, the seller, an underlying asset at a later date for a price established at the start of the contract.

Forward integration A merger involving the purchase of a target that is farther along the value or production chain; for example, to acquire a distributor.

Forward price or forward rate The fixed price or rate at which the transaction scheduled to occur at the expiration of a forward contract will take place. This price is agreed on at the initiation date of the contract.

Forward rate agreement (FRA) A forward contract calling for one party to make a fixed interest payment and the other to make an interest payment at a rate to be determined at the contract expiration.

Forward swap A forward contract to enter into a swap.

Four-firm concentration ratio A measure of market power that is calculated as the percentage of the value of sales accounted for by the four largest firms in an industry.

Free cash flow The actual cash that would be available to the company's investors after making all investments necessary to maintain the company as an ongoing enterprise (also referred to as free cash flow to the firm); the internally generated funds that can be distributed to the company's investors (e.g., shareholders and bondholders) without impairing the value of the company.

Free cash flow hypothesis The hypothesis that higher debt levels discipline managers by forcing them to make fixed debt service payments and by reducing the company's free cash flow.

Free cash flow to equity The cash flow available to a company's common shareholders after all operating expenses, interest, and principal payments have been made, and necessary investments in working and fixed capital have been made.

Free cash flow to the firm The cash flow available to the company's suppliers of capital after all operating expenses have been paid and necessary investments in working capital and fixed capital have been made.

Frequency distribution A tabular display of data summarized into a relatively small number of intervals.

Frequency polygon A graph of a frequency distribution obtained by drawing straight lines joining successive points representing the class frequencies.

Frictional unemployment The unemployment that arises from normal labor turnover—from people entering and leaving the labor force and from the ongoing creation and destruction of jobs.

Friendly transaction A potential business combination that is endorsed by the managers of both companies.

Full employment A situation in which the quantity of labor demanded equals the quantity supplied. At full employment, there is no cyclical unemployment—all unemployment is frictional and structural.

Full-employment equilibrium A macroeconomic equilibrium in which real GDP equals potential GDP.

Full price The price of a security with accrued interest.

Functional currency The currency of the primary economic environment in which an entity operates.

Fundamental beta A beta that is based at least in part on fundamental data for a company.

Fundamental factor models A multifactor model in which the factors are attributes of stocks or companies that are important in explaining cross-sectional differences in stock prices.

Future value (FV) The amount to which a payment or series of payments will grow by a stated future date.

Futures commission merchants (FCMs) Individuals or companies that execute futures transactions for other parties off the exchange.

Futures contract A variation of a forward contract that has essentially the same basic definition but with some additional features, such as a clearinghouse guarantee against credit losses, a daily settlement of gains and losses, and an organized electronic or floor trading facility.

Futures exchange A legal corporate entity whose shareholders are its members. The members of the exchange have the privilege of executing transactions directly on the exchange.

Gains Asset inflows not directly related to the ordinary activities of the business.

Game theory A tool that economists use to analyze strategic behavior—behavior that takes into account the expected behavior of others and the recognition of mutual interdependence.

Gamma A numerical measure of how sensitive an option's delta is to a change in the underlying.

Generalized least squares A regression estimation technique that addresses heteroskedasticity of the error term.

Generational accounting An accounting system that measures the lifetime tax burden and benefits of each generation.

Generational imbalance The division of the fiscal imbalance between the current and future generations, assuming that the current generation will enjoy the existing levels of taxes and benefits.

Geometric mean A measure of central tendency computed by taking the nth root of the product of n non-negative values.

Gifting phase Phase in the investment life cycle during which individuals use excess assets to financially assist relatives or friends, establish charitable trusts, or construct trusts to minimize estate taxes.

Giro system An electronic payment system used widely in Europe and Japan.

Goodwill An intangible asset that represents the excess of the purchase price of an acquired company over the value of the net assets acquired.

Government debt The total amount that the government has borrowed. It equals the sum of past budget deficits minus the sum of past budget surpluses.

Government expenditure multiplier The magnification effect of a change in government expenditure on goods and services on equilibrium expenditure and real GDP.

Grant date The day that options are granted to employees; usually the date that compensation expense is measured if both the number of shares and option price are known.

Greenmail The purchase of the accumulated shares of a hostile investor by a company that is targeted for takeover by that investor, usually at a substantial premium over market price.

Gross profit (gross margin) Sales minus the cost of sales (i.e., the cost of goods sold for a manufacturing company).

Gross profit margin The ratio of gross profit to revenues.

Grouping by function With reference to the presentation of expenses in an income statement, the grouping together of expenses serving the same function, e.g. all items that are costs of goods sold.

Grouping by nature With reference to the presentation of expenses in an income statement, the grouping together of expenses by similar nature, e.g., all depreciation expenses.

Growth company A company that consistently has the opportunities and ability to invest in projects that provide rates of return that exceed the firm's cost of capital. Because of these investment opportunities, it retains a high proportion of earnings, and its earnings grow faster than those of average firms.

Growth investors With reference to equity investors, investors who seek to invest in high-earnings-growth companies.

Growth option or expansion option The ability to make additional investments in a project at some future time if the financial results are strong.

Growth stock A stock issue that generates a higher rate of return than other stocks in the market with similar risk characteristics.

Harmonic mean A type of weighted mean computed by averaging the reciprocals of the observations, then taking the reciprocal of that average.

Hedge ratio The relationship of the quantity of an asset being hedged to the quantity of the derivative used for hedging.

Hedging A general strategy usually thought of as reducing, if not eliminating, risk.

Held-for-trading securities (trading securities) Debt or equity financial assets bought with the intention to sell them in the near term, usually less than three months; securities that a company intends to trade.

Held-to-maturity investments Debt (fixed-income) securities that a company intends to hold to maturity; these are presented at their original cost, updated for any amortization of discounts or premiums.

Herfindahl–Hirschman Index A measure of market concentration that is calculated by summing the squared market shares for competing companies in an industry; high HHI readings or mergers that would result in large HHI increases are more likely to result in regulatory challenges.

Heteroskedastic With reference to the error term of a regression, having a variance that differs across observations.

Heteroskedasticity The property of having a non-constant variance; refers to an error term with the property that its variance differs across observations.

Heteroskedasticity-consistent standard errors Standard errors of the estimated parameters of a regression that correct for the presence of heteroskedasticity in the regression's error term.

Histogram A bar chart of data that have been grouped into a frequency distribution.

Historical cost In reference to assets, the amount paid to purchase an asset, including any costs of acquisition and/or preparation; with reference to liabilities, the amount of proceeds received in exchange in issuing the liability.

Historical equity risk premium approach An estimate of a country's equity risk premium that is based upon the historical averages of the risk-free rate and the rate of return on the market portfolio.

Historical exchange rates For accounting purposes, the exchange rates that existed when the assets and liabilities were initially recorded.

Historical method A method of estimating VAR that uses data from the returns of the portfolio over a recent past period and compiles this data in the form of a histogram.

Historical simulation (or back simulation) Another term for the historical method of estimating VAR. This term is somewhat misleading in that the method involves not a *simulation* of the past but rather what *actually happened* in the past, sometimes adjusted to reflect the fact that a different portfolio may have existed in the past than is planned for the future.

Holder-of-record date The date that a shareholder listed on the corporation's books will be deemed to have ownership of the shares for purposes of receiving an upcoming dividend; two business days after the ex-dividend date.

Holding period return The return that an investor earns during a specified holding period; a synonym for total return.

Holding period yield (HPY) The return that an investor earns during a specified holding period; holding period return with reference to a fixed-income instrument.

Homogenization Creating a contract with standard and generally accepted terms, which makes it more acceptable to a broader group of participants.

Homoskedasticity The property of having a constant variance; refers to an error term that is constant across observations.

Horizontal analysis Common-size analysis that involves comparing a specific financial statement with that statement in prior or future time periods; also, cross-sectional analysis of one company with another.

Horizontal common-size analysis A form of common-size analysis in which the accounts in a given period are used as the benchmark or base period, and every account is restated in subsequent periods as a percentage of the base period's same account.

Horizontal merger A merger involving companies in the same line of business, usually as competitors.

Hostile transaction An attempt to acquire a company against the wishes of the target's managers.

Hurdle rate The rate of return that must be met for a project to be accepted.

Hypothesis With reference to statistical inference, a statement about one or more populations.

Hypothesis testing With reference to statistical inference, the subdivision dealing with the testing of hypotheses about one or more populations.

Identifiable intangible An intangible that can be acquired singly and is typically linked to specific rights or privileges having finite benefit periods (e.g., a patent or trademark).

If-converted method A method for accounting for the effect of convertible securities on earnings per share (EPS) that specifies what EPS would have been if the convertible securities had been converted at the beginning of the period, taking account of the effects of conversion on net income and the weighted average number of shares outstanding.

Impairment Diminishment in value as a result of carrying (book) value exceeding fair value and/or recoverable value.

Impairment of capital rule A legal restriction that dividends cannot exceed retained earnings.

Implicit rental rate The firm's opportunity cost of using its own capital.

Implied repo rate The rate of return from a cash-and-carry transaction implied by the futures price relative to the spot price.

Implied volatility The volatility that option traders use to price an option, implied by the price of the option and a particular option-pricing model.

Implied yield A measure of the yield on the underlying bond of a futures contract implied by pricing it as though the underlying will be delivered at the futures expiration.

Imputation In reference to corporate taxes, a system that imputes, or attributes, taxes at only one level of taxation. For countries using an imputation tax system, taxes on dividends are effectively levied only at the shareholder rate. Taxes are paid at the corporate level but they are *attributed* to the shareholder. Shareholders deduct from their tax bill their portion of taxes paid by the company.

Incentive system A method of organizing production that uses a market-like mechanism inside the firm.

Income Increases in economic benefits in the form of inflows or enhancements of assets, or decreases of liabilities that result in an increase in equity (other than increases resulting from contributions by owners).

Income elasticity of demand The responsiveness of demand to a change in income, other things remaining the same. It is calculated as the percentage change in the quantity demanded divided by the percentage change in income.

Income statement (statement of operations or profit and loss statement) A financial statement that provides information about a company's profitability over a stated period of time.

Income tax paid The actual amount paid for income taxes in the period; not a provision, but the actual cash outflow.

Income tax payable The income tax owed by the company on the basis of taxable income.

Income tax recoverable The income tax expected to be recovered, from the taxing authority, on the basis of taxable income. It is a recovery of previously remitted taxes or future taxes owed by the company.

Incremental cash flow The cash flow that is realized because of a decision; the changes or increments to cash flows resulting from a decision or action.

Independent With reference to events, the property that the occurrence of one event does not affect the probability of another event occurring.

Independent and identically distributed (IID) With respect to random variables, the property of random variables that are independent of each other but follow the identical probability distribution.

Independent projects Independent projects are projects whose cash flows are independent of each other.

Independent variable A variable used to explain the dependent variable in a regression; a right-hand-side variable in a regression equation.

Index amortizing swap An interest rate swap in which the notional principal is indexed to the level of interest rates and declines with the level of interest rates according to a predefined schedule. This type of swap is frequently used to hedge securities that are prepaid as interest rates decline, such as mortgage-backed securities.

Index option An option in which the underlying is a stock index.

Indexing An investment strategy in which an investor constructs a portfolio to mirror the performance of a specified index.

Indirect format (indirect method) With reference to cash flow statements, a format for the presentation of the statement which, in the operating cash flow section, begins with net income then shows additions and subtractions to arrive at operating cash flow.

Induced taxes Taxes that vary with real GDP.

Inelastic demand A demand with a price elasticity between 0 and 1; the percentage change in the quantity demanded is less than the percentage change in price.

Inflation premium An extra return that compensates investors for expected inflation.

Inflation rate The annual percentage change in the price level.

Inflation rate targeting A monetary policy strategy in which the central bank makes a public commitment to achieve an explicit inflation rate and to explain how its policy actions will achieve that target.

Inflationary gap The amount by which real GDP exceeds potential GDP.

Information An attribute of a good market that includes providing buyers and sellers with timely, accurate information on the volume and prices of past transactions and on all currently outstanding bids and offers.

Information ratio (IR) Mean active return divided by active risk.

Informationally efficient market A more technical term for an efficient capital market that emphasizes the role of information in setting the market price.

Initial margin requirement The margin requirement on the first day of a transaction as well as on any day in which additional margin funds must be deposited.

Initial public offering (IPO)　A new issue by a firm that has no existing public market.

In-sample forecast errors　The residuals from a fitted time-series model within the sample period used to fit the model.

Instability in the minimum-variance frontier　The characteristic of minimum-variance frontiers that they are sensitive to small changes in inputs.

Installment　Said of a sale in which proceeds are to be paid in installments over an extended period of time.

Installment method (installment-sales method)　With respect to revenue recognition, a method that specifies that the portion of the total profit of the sale that is recognized in each period is determined by the percentage of the total sales price for which the seller has received cash.

Instrument rule　A decision rule for monetary policy that sets the policy instrument at a level that is based on the current state of the economy.

Intangible assets　Assets lacking physical substance, such as patents and trademarks.

Interest coverage　A solvency ratio calculated as EBIT divided by interest payments.

Interest rate　A rate of return that reflects the relationship between differently dated cash flows; a discount rate.

Interest rate call　An option in which the holder has the right to make a known interest payment and receive an unknown interest payment.

Interest rate cap or cap　A series of call options on an interest rate, with each option expiring at the date on which the floating loan rate will be reset, and with each option having the same exercise rate. A cap in general can have an underlying other than an interest rate.

Interest rate collar　A combination of a long cap and a short floor, or a short cap and a long floor. A collar in general can have an underlying other than an interest rate.

Interest rate floor or floor　A series of put options on an interest rate, with each option expiring at the date on which the floating loan rate will be reset, and with each option having the same exercise rate. A floor in general can have an underlying other than the interest rate.

Interest rate forward　(See *forward rate agreement*)

Interest rate option　An option in which the underlying is an interest rate.

Interest rate parity　A formula that expresses the equivalence or parity of spot and forward rates, after adjusting for differences in the interest rates.

Interest rate put　An option in which the holder has the right to make an unknown interest payment and receive a known interest payment.

Interest rate swap　A swap in which the underlying is an interest rate. Can be viewed as a currency swap in which both currencies are the same and can be created as a combination of currency swaps.

Intergenerational data mining　A form of data mining that applies information developed by previous researchers using a dataset to guide current research using the same or a related dataset.

Internal rate of return (IRR)　The discount rate that makes net present value equal 0; the discount rate that makes the present value of an investment's costs (outflows) equal to the present value of the investment's benefits (inflows).

Interquartile range　The difference between the third and first quartiles of a dataset.

Interval　With reference to grouped data, a set of values within which an observation falls.

Interval scale　A measurement scale that not only ranks data but also gives assurance that the differences between scale values are equal.

In-the-money　Options that, if exercised, would result in the value received being worth more than the payment required to exercise.

Intrinsic value or exercise value　The value obtained if an option is exercised based on current conditions.

Inventory　The unsold units of product on hand.

Inventory blanket lien　The use of inventory as collateral for a loan. Though the lender has claim to some or all of the company's inventory, the company may still sell or use the inventory in the ordinary course of business.

Inventory turnover　An activity ratio calculated as cost of goods sold divided by average inventory.

Inverse floater　A floating-rate note or bond in which the coupon is adjusted to move opposite to a benchmark interest rate.

Investing activities　Activities which are associated with the acquisition and disposal of property, plant, and equipment; intangible assets; other long-term assets; and both long-term and short-term investments in the equity and debt (bonds and loans) issued by other companies.

Investment decision process　Estimation of intrinsic value for comparison with market price to determine whether or not to invest.

Investment opportunity schedule　A graphical depiction of a company's investment opportunities ordered from highest to lowest expected return. A company's optimal capital budget is found where the investment opportunity schedule intersects with the company's marginal cost of capital.

Investment strategy A decision by a portfolio manager regarding how he or she will manage the portfolio to meet the goals and objectives of the client. This will include either active or passive management and, if active, what style in terms of top-down or bottom-up or fundamental versus technical.

IRR rule An investment decision rule that accepts projects or investments for which the IRR is greater than the opportunity cost of capital.

Joint probability The probability of the joint occurrence of stated events.

Joint probability function A function giving the probability of joint occurrences of values of stated random variables.

Joint venture An entity (partnership, corporation, or other legal form) where control is shared by two or more entities called venturers.

Just-in-time method Method of managing inventory that minimizes in-process inventory stocks.

Keynesian A macroeconomist who believes that left alone, the economy would rarely operate at full employment and that to achieve full employment, active help from fiscal policy and monetary policy is required.

Keynesian cycle theory A theory that fluctuations in investment driven by fluctuations in business confidence—summarized in the phrase "animal spirits"—are the main source of fluctuations in aggregate demand.

k-percent rule A rule that makes the quantity of money grow at a rate of k percent a year, where k equals the growth rate of potential GDP.

kth Order autocorrelation The correlation between observations in a time series separated by k periods.

Kurtosis The statistical measure that indicates the peakedness of a distribution.

Labor force The sum of the people who are employed and who are unemployed.

Labor force participation rate The percentage of the working-age population who are members of the labor force.

Labor union An organized group of workers whose purpose is to increase wages and to influence other job conditions.

Laddering strategy A form of active strategy which entails scheduling maturities on a systematic basis within the investment portfolio such that investments are spread out equally over the term of the ladder.

Laffer curve The relationship between the tax rate and the amount of tax revenue collected.

Law of diminishing returns As a firm uses more of a variable input, with a given quantity of other inputs (fixed inputs), the marginal product of the variable input eventually diminishes.

Law of one price The condition in a financial market in which two equivalent financial instruments or combinations of financial instruments can sell for only one price. Equivalent to the principle that no arbitrage opportunities are possible.

Legal monopoly A market structure in which there is one firm and entry is restricted by the granting of a public franchise, government license, patent, or copyright.

Legal risk The risk that failures by company managers to effectively manage a company's environmental, social, and governance risk exposures will lead to lawsuits and other judicial remedies, resulting in potentially catastrophic losses for the company; the risk that the legal system will not enforce a contract in case of dispute or fraud.

Legislative and regulatory risk The risk that governmental laws and regulations directly or indirectly affecting a company's operations will change with potentially severe adverse effects on the company's continued profitability and even its long-term sustainability.

Leptokurtic Describes a distribution that is more peaked than a normal distribution.

Lessee The party obtaining the use of an asset through a lease.

Lessor The owner of an asset that grants the right to use the asset to another party.

Level of significance The probability of a Type I error in testing a hypothesis.

Leverage In the context of corporate finance, leverage refers to the use of fixed costs within a company's cost structure. Fixed costs that are operating costs (such as depreciation or rent) create operating leverage. Fixed costs that are financial costs (such as interest expense) create financial leverage.

Leveraged buyout (LBO) A transaction whereby the target company management team converts the target to a privately held company by using heavy borrowing to finance the purchase of the target company's outstanding shares.

Leveraged floating-rate note or leveraged floater A floating-rate note or bond in which the coupon is adjusted at a multiple of a benchmark interest rate.

Leveraged recapitalization A post-offer takeover defense mechanism that involves the assumption of a large amount of debt that is then used to finance share repurchases; the effect is to dramatically change the company's capital structure while attempting to deliver a value to target shareholders in excess of a hostile bid.

Liabilities   Present obligations of an enterprise arising from past events, the settlement of which is expected to result in an outflow of resources embodying economic benefits; creditors' claims on the resources of a company.

LIFO layer liquidation (LIFO liquidation)   With respect to the application of the LIFO inventory method, the liquidation of old, relatively low-priced inventory; happens when the volume of sales rises above the volume of recent purchases so that some sales are made from relatively old, low-priced inventory.

LIFO method   The last in, first out, method of accounting for inventory, which matches sales against the costs of items of inventory in the reverse order the items were placed in inventory (i.e., inventory produced or acquired last are assumed to be sold first).

LIFO reserve   The difference between inventory reported at FIFO and inventory reported at LIFO (FIFO inventory value less LIFO inventory value).

Likelihood   The probability of an observation, given a particular set of conditions.

Limit down   A limit move in the futures market in which the price at which a transaction would be made is at or below the lower limit.

Limit move   A condition in the futures markets in which the price at which a transaction would be made is at or beyond the price limits.

Limit order   An order that lasts for a specified time to buy or sell a security when and if it trades at a specified price.

Limit pricing   The practice of setting the price at the highest level that inflicts a loss on an entrant.

Limit up   A limit move in the futures market in which the price at which a transaction would be made is at or above the upper limit.

Linear association   A straight-line relationship, as opposed to a relationship that cannot be graphed as a straight line.

Linear interpolation   The estimation of an unknown value on the basis of two known values that bracket it, using a straight line between the two known values.

Linear regression   Regression that models the straight-line relationship between the dependent and independent variable(s).

Linear trend   A trend in which the dependent variable changes at a constant rate with time.

Liquid   Term used to describe an asset that can be quickly converted to cash at a price close to fair market value.

Liquidation   To sell the assets of a company, division, or subsidiary piecemeal, typically because of bankruptcy; the form of bankruptcy that allows for the orderly satisfaction of creditors' claims after which the company ceases to exist.

Liquidity   The ability to buy or sell an asset quickly and at a reasonable price based on information. A company's ability to satisfy its short-term obligations using assets that are most readily converted into cash; the ability to trade a futures contract, either selling a previously purchased contract or purchasing a previously sold contract.

Liquidity premium   An extra return that compensates investors for the risk of loss relative to an investment's fair value if the investment needs to be converted to cash quickly.

Liquidity ratios   Financial ratios measuring the company's ability to meet its short-term obligations.

Liquidity risk   The risk that a financial instrument cannot be purchased or sold without a significant concession in price due to the size of the market.

Living wage   An hourly wage rate that enables a person who works a 40-hour work week to rent adequate housing for not more than 30 percent of the amount earned.

Local currency   The currency of the country where a company is located.

Lockbox system   A payment system in which customer payments are mailed to a post office box and the banking institution retrieves and deposits these payments several times a day, enabling the company to have use of the fund sooner than in a centralized system in which customer payments are sent to the company.

Locked limit   A condition in the futures markets in which a transaction cannot take place because the price would be beyond the limits.

Logit model   A qualitative-dependent-variable multiple regression model based on the logistic probability distribution.

Log-linear model   With reference to time-series models, a model in which the growth rate of the time series as a function of time is constant.

Log-log regression model   A regression that expresses the dependent and independent variables as natural logarithms.

London Interbank Offer Rate (LIBOR)   The Eurodollar rate at which London banks lend dollars to other London banks; considered to be the best representative rate on a dollar borrowed by a private, high-quality borrower.

Long The buyer of a derivative contract. Also refers to the position of owning a derivative.

Long run A period of time in which the quantities of all resources can be varied.

Longitudinal data Observations on characteristic(s) of the same observational unit through time.

Long-lived assets (or long-term assets) Assets that are expected to provide economic benefits over a future period of time, typically greater than one year.

Long-run aggregate supply The relationship between the quantity of real GDP supplied and the price level in the long run when real GDP equals potential GDP.

Long-run average cost curve The relationship between the lowest attainable average total cost and output when both plant size and labor are varied.

Long-run industry supply curve A curve that shows how the quantity supplied by an industry varies as the market price varies after all the possible adjustments have been made, including changes in plant size and the number of firms in the industry.

Long-run macroeconomic equilibrium A situation that occurs when real GDP equals potential GDP—the economy is on its long-run aggregate supply curve.

Long-run Phillips curve A curve that shows the relationship between inflation and unemployment when the actual inflation rate equals the expected inflation rate.

Long-term contract A contract that spans a number of accounting periods.

Long-term debt-to-assets ratio The proportion of a company's assets that is financed with long-term debt.

Long-term equity anticipatory securities (LEAPS) Options originally created with expirations of several years.

Long-term liability An obligation that is expected to be settled, with the outflow of resources embodying economic benefits, over a future period generally greater than one year.

Long-term, high-priority goal A long-term financial investment goal of personal importance that typically includes achieving financial independence, such as being able to retire at a certain age.

Look-ahead bias A bias caused by using information that was unavailable on the test date.

Losses Asset outflows not directly related to the ordinary activities of the business.

Lower bound The lowest possible value of an option.

Lower-priority goal A financial investment goal of lesser personal importance, such as taking a luxurious vacation or buying a car every few years.

M1 A measure of money that consists of currency and traveler's checks plus checking deposits owned by individuals and businesses.

M2 A measure of money that consists of M1 plus time deposits, savings deposits, and money market mutual funds, and other deposits.

Macaulay duration The duration without dividing by 1 plus the bond's yield to maturity. The term, named for one of the economists who first derived it, is used to distinguish the calculation from modified duration. See also *modified duration.*

Macroeconomic factor A factor related to the economy, such as the inflation rate, industrial production, or economic sector membership.

Macroeconomic factor model A multifactor model in which the factors are surprises in macroeconomic variables that significantly explain equity returns.

Macroeconomic long run A time frame that is sufficiently long for the real wage rate to have adjusted to achieve full employment: real GDP equal to potential GDP, unemployment equal to the natural unemployment rate, the price level is proportional to the quantity of money, and the inflation rate equal to the money growth rate minus the real GDP growth rate.

Macroeconomic short run A period during which some money prices are sticky and real GDP might be below, above, or at potential GDP and unemployment might be above, below, or at the natural rate of unemployment.

Maintenance margin The required proportion that the investor's equity value must be to the total market value of the stock. If the proportion drops below this percent, the investor will receive a margin call.

Maintenance margin requirement The margin requirement on any day other than the first day of a transaction.

Managerialism theories Theories that posit that corporate executives are motivated to engage in mergers to maximize the size of their company rather than shareholder value.

Manufacturing resource planning (MRP) The incorporation of production planning into inventory management. A MRP analysis provides both a materials acquisition schedule and a production schedule.

Margin The percent of cost a buyer pays in cash for a security, borrowing the balance from the broker. This introduces leverage, which increases the risk of the transaction. Also the amount of money that a trader deposits in a margin account. In futures markets, there is no borrowing so the margin is more of a down payment or performance bond.

Margin call   A request by an investor's broker for additional capital for a security bought on margin if the investor's equity value declines below the required maintenance margin.

Marginal cost   The opportunity cost of producing one more unit of a good or service. It is the best alternative forgone. It is calculated as the increase in total cost divided by the increase in output.

Marginal cost pricing rule   A rule that sets the price of a good or service equal to the marginal cost of producing it.

Marginal product   The increase in total product that results from a one-unit increase in the variable input, with all other inputs remaining the same. It is calculated as the increase in total product divided by the increase in the variable input employed, when the quantities of all other inputs are constant.

Marginal revenue   The change in total revenue that results from a one-unit increase in the quantity sold. It is calculated as the change in total revenue divided by the change in quantity sold.

Marginal revenue product   The change in total revenue that results from employing one more unit of a factor of production (labor) while the quantity of all other factors remains the same. It is calculated as the increase in total revenue divided by the increase in the quantity of the factor (labor).

Marginal tax rate   The part of each additional dollar in income that is paid as tax.

Market   The means through which buyers and sellers are brought together to aid in the transfer of goods and/or services.

Market order   An order to buy or sell a security immediately at the best price available.

Market portfolio   The portfolio that includes all risky assets with relative weights equal to their proportional market values.

Market power   The ability to influence the market, and in particular the market price, by influencing the total quantity offered for sale.

Market price of risk   The slope of the capital market line, indicating the market risk premium for each unit of market risk.

Market rate   The rate demanded by purchasers of bonds, given the risks associated with future cash payment obligations of the particular bond issue.

Market risk   The risk associated with interest rates, exchange rates, and equity prices.

Market risk premium   The expected excess return on the market over the risk-free rate.

Market-oriented investors   With reference to equity investors, investors whose investment disciplines cannot be clearly categorized as value or growth.

Marking to market   A procedure used primarily in futures markets in which the parties to a contract settle the amount owed daily. Also known as the *daily settlement.*

Markowitz decision rule   A decision rule for choosing between two investments based on their means and variances.

Mark-to-market   The revaluation of a financial asset or liability to its current market value or fair value.

Matching principle   The accounting principle that expenses should be recognized when the associated revenue is recognized.

Matching strategy   An active investment strategy that includes intentional matching of the timing of cash outflows with investment maturities.

Materiality   The condition of being of sufficient importance so that omission or misstatement of the item in a financial report could make a difference to users' decisions.

Matrix pricing   In the fixed income markets, to price a security on the basis of valuation-relevant characteristics (e.g. debt-rating approach).

Maturity premium   An extra return that compensates investors for the increased sensitivity of the market value of debt to a change in market interest rates as maturity is extended.

McCallum rule   A rule that makes the growth rate of the monetary base respond to the long-term average growth rate of real GDP and medium-term changes in the velocity of circulation of the monetary base.

Mean   The sum of all values in a distribution or dataset, divided by the number of values summed; a synonym of arithmetic mean.

Mean absolute deviation   With reference to a sample, the mean of the absolute values of deviations from the sample mean.

Mean excess return   The average rate of return in excess of the risk-free rate.

Mean rates of return   The average of an investment's returns over an extended period of time.

Mean reversion   The tendency of a time series to fall when its level is above its mean and rise when its level is below its mean; a mean-reverting time series tends to return to its long-term mean.

Mean–variance analysis   An approach to portfolio analysis using expected means, variances, and covariances of asset returns.

Means of payment   A method of settling a debt.

Measure of central tendency A quantitative measure that specifies where data are centered.

Measure of location A quantitative measure that describes the location or distribution of data; includes not only measures of central tendency but also other measures such as percentiles.

Measurement scales A scheme of measuring differences. The four types of measurement scales are nominal, ordinal, interval, and ratio.

Median The value of the middle item of a set of items that has been sorted into ascending or descending order; the 50th percentile.

Merger The absorption of one company by another; that is, two companies become one entity and one or both of the pre-merger companies ceases to exist as a separate entity.

Mesokurtic Describes a distribution with kurtosis identical to that of the normal distribution.

Minimum efficient scale The smallest quantity of output at which the long-run average cost curve reaches its lowest level.

Minimum wage A regulation that makes the hiring of labor below a specified wage rate illegal. The lowest wage at which a firm may legally hire labor.

Minimum-variance frontier The graph of the set of portfolios that have minimum variance for their level of expected return.

Minimum-variance portfolio The portfolio with the minimum variance for each given level of expected return.

Minority active investments Investments in which investors exert significant influence, but not control, over the investee. Typically, the investor has 20 to 50% ownership in the investee.

Minority interest (noncontrolling interest) The proportion of the ownership of a subsidiary not held by the parent (controlling) company.

Minority passive investments (passive investments) Investments in which the investor has no significant influence or control over the operations of the investee.

Mismatching strategy An active investment strategy whereby the timing of cash outflows is not matched with investment maturities.

Mixed factor models Factor models that combine features of more than one type of factor model.

Mixed offering A merger or acquisition that is to be paid for with cash, securities, or some combination of the two.

Modal interval With reference to grouped data, the most frequently occurring interval.

Mode The most frequently occurring value in a set of observations.

Model risk The use of an inaccurate pricing model for a particular investment, or the improper use of the right model.

Model specification With reference to regression, the set of variables included in the regression and the regression equation's functional form.

Modified duration A measure of a bond's price sensitivity to interest rate movements. Equal to the Macaulay duration of a bond divided by one plus its yield to maturity.

Monetarist A macroeconomist who believes that the economy is self-regulating and that it will normally operate at full employment, provided that monetary policy is not erratic and that the pace of money growth is kept steady.

Monetarist cycle theory A theory that fluctuations in both investment and consumption expenditure, driven by fluctuations in the growth rate of the quantity of money, are the main source of fluctuations in aggregate demand.

Monetary assets and liabilities Assets and liabilities with value equal to the amount of currency contracted for, a fixed amount of currency. Examples are cash, accounts receivable, mortgages receivable, accounts payable, bonds payable, and mortgages payable. Inventory is not a monetary asset. Most liabilities are monetary.

Monetary base The sum of Federal Reserve notes, coins and banks' deposits at the Fed.

Monetary policy The Fed conducts the nation's monetary policy by changing interest rates and adjusting the quantity of money.

Monetary policy instrument A variable that the Fed can control directly or closely target.

Monetary/nonmonetary method Approach to translating foreign currency financial statements for consolidation in which monetary assets and liabilities are translated at the current exchange rate. Nonmonetary assets and liabilities are translated at historical exchange rates (the exchange rates that existed when the assets and liabilities were acquired).

Money Any commodity or token that is generally acceptable as the means of payment.

Money market The market for short-term debt instruments (one-year maturity or less).

Money market yield (or CD equivalent yield) A yield on a basis comparable to the quoted yield on an interest-bearing money market instrument that pays interest on a 360-day basis; the annualized holding period yield, assuming a 360-day year.

Money multiplier The ratio of the change in the quantity of money to the change in the monetary base.

Moneyness The relationship between the price of the underlying and an option's exercise price.

Money-weighted rate of return The internal rate of return on a portfolio, taking account of all cash flows.

Monitoring costs Costs borne by owners to monitor the management of the company (e.g., board of director expenses).

Monopolistic competition A market structure in which a large number of firms compete by making similar but slightly different products.

Monopoly A market structure in which there is one firm, which produces a good or service that has no close substitutes and in which the firm is protected from competition by a barrier preventing the entry of new firms.

Monopsony A market in which there is a single buyer.

Monte Carlo simulation method An approach to estimating a probability distribution of outcomes to examine what might happen if particular risks are faced. This method is widely used in the sciences as well as in business to study a variety of problems.

Moving average The continually recalculating average of security prices for a period, often 200 days, to serve as an indication of the general trend of prices and also as a benchmark price.

Multicollinearity A regression assumption violation that occurs when two or more independent variables (or combinations of independent variables) are highly but not perfectly correlated with each other.

Multiple linear regression model A linear regression model with two or more independent variables.

Multiple _R_ The correlation between the actual and forecasted values of the dependent variable in a regression.

Multiplication rule for probabilities The rule that the joint probability of events _A_ and _B_ equals the probability of _A_ given _B_ times the probability of _B_.

Multi-step format With respect to the format of the income statement, a format that presents a subtotal for gross profit (revenue minus cost of goods sold).

Multivariate distribution A probability distribution that specifies the probabilities for a group of related random variables.

Multivariate normal distribution A probability distribution for a group of random variables that is completely defined by the means and variances of the variables plus all the correlations between pairs of the variables.

Mutually exclusive events Events such that only one can occur at a time.

Mutually exclusive projects Mutually exclusive projects compete directly with each other. For example, if Projects A and B are mutually exclusive, you can choose A or B, but you cannot choose both.

_n_ Factorial For a positive integer _n_, the product of the first _n_ positive integers; 0 factorial equals 1 by definition. _n_ factorial is written as _n_!.

Nash equilibrium The outcome of a game that occurs when player A takes the best possible action given the action of player B and player B takes the best possible action given the action of player A.

Natural monopoly A monopoly that occurs when one firm can supply the entire market at a lower price than two or more firms can.

Natural unemployment rate The unemployment rate when the economy is at full employment. There is no cyclical unemployment; all unemployment is frictional, structural, and seasonal.

Near-term, high-priority goal A short-term financial investment goal of personal importance, such as accumulating funds for making a house down payment or buying a car.

Needs-tested spending Government spending on programs that pay benefits to suitably qualified people and businesses.

Negative serial correlation Serial correlation in which a positive error for one observation increases the chance of a negative error for another observation, and vice versa.

Negotiated sales An underwriting arrangement wherein the sale of a security issue by an issuing entity (governmental body or a corporation) is done using an investment banking firm that maintains an ongoing relationship with the issuer. The characteristics of the security issue are determined by the issuer in consultation with the investment banker.

Net asset balance sheet exposure When assets translated at the current exchange rate are greater in amount than liabilities translated at the current exchange rate. Assets exposed to translation gains or losses exceed the exposed liabilities.

Net book value The remaining (undepreciated) balance of an asset's purchase cost. For liabilities, the face value of a bond minus any unamortized discount, or plus any unamortized premium.

Net income (loss) The difference between revenue and expenses; what remains after subtracting all expenses (including depreciation, interest, and taxes) from revenue.

Net liability balance sheet exposure When liabilities translated at the current exchange rate are greater than assets translated at the current exchange rate. Liabilities exposed to translation gains or losses exceed the exposed assets.

Net operating assets The difference between operating assets (total assets less cash) and operating liabilities (total liabilities less total debt).

Net operating cycle An estimate of the average time that elapses between paying suppliers for materials and collecting cash from the subsequent sale of goods produced.

Net operating profit less adjusted taxes, or NOPLAT A company's operating profit with adjustments to normalize the effects of capital structure.

Net present value (NPV) The present value of an investment's cash inflows (benefits) minus the present value of its cash outflows (costs).

Net profit margin (profit margin or return on sales) An indicator of profitability, calculated as net income divided by revenue; indicates how much of each dollar of revenues is left after all costs and expenses.

Net realizable value Estimated selling price in the ordinary course of business less the estimated costs necessary to make the sale.

Net revenue Revenue after adjustments (e.g., for estimated returns or for amounts unlikely to be collected).

Netting When parties agree to exchange only the net amount owed from one party to the other.

New classical A macroeconomist who holds the view that business cycle fluctuations are the efficient responses of a well-functioning market economy bombarded by shocks that arise from the uneven pace of technological change.

New classical cycle theory A rational expectations theory of the business cycle that regards unexpected fluctuations in aggregate demand as the main source of fluctuations of real GDP around potential GDP.

New issue Common stocks or bonds offered by companies for public sale.

New Keynesian A macroeconomist who holds the view that not only is the money wage rate sticky but also that the prices of goods and services are sticky.

New Keynesian cycle theory A rational expectations theory of the business cycle that regards unexpected and currently expected fluctuations in aggregate demand as the main source of fluctuations of real GDP around potential GDP.

Node Each value on a binomial tree from which successive moves or outcomes branch.

Nominal rate A rate of interest based on the security's face value.

Nominal risk-free interest rate The sum of the real risk-free interest rate and the inflation premium.

Nominal scale A measurement scale that categorizes data but does not rank them.

Nonconventional cash flow In a nonconventional cash flow pattern, the initial outflow is not followed by inflows only, but the cash flows can flip from positive (inflows) to negative (outflows) again (or even change signs several times).

Noncurrent Not due to be consumed, converted into cash, or settled within one year after the balance sheet date.

Noncurrent assets Assets that are expected to benefit the company over an extended period of time (usually more than one year).

Nondeliverable forwards (NDFs) Cash-settled forward contracts, used predominately with respect to foreign exchange forwards.

Nonlinear relation An association or relationship between variables that cannot be graphed as a straight line.

Nonmonetary assets and liabilities Assets and liabilities that are not monetary assets and liabilities. Nonmonetary assets include inventory, fixed assets, and intangibles, and nonmonetary liabilities include deferred revenue.

Nonparametric test A test that is not concerned with a parameter, or that makes minimal assumptions about the population from which a sample comes.

Nonrenewable natural resources Natural resources that can be used only once and that cannot be replaced once they have been used.

Nonstationarity With reference to a random variable, the property of having characteristics such as mean and variance that are not constant through time.

Normal backwardation The condition in futures markets in which futures prices are lower than expected spot prices.

Normal contango The condition in futures markets in which futures prices are higher than expected spot prices.

Normal distribution A continuous, symmetric probability distribution that is completely described by its mean and its variance.

Normal profit The return that an entrepreneur can expect to receive on the average.

Notes payable Amounts owed by a business to creditors as a result of borrowings that are evidenced by (short-term) loan agreements.

***n*-Period moving average**   The average of the current and immediately prior $n - 1$ values of a time series.

NPV rule   An investment decision rule that states that an investment should be undertaken if its NPV is positive but not undertaken if its NPV is negative.

Null hypothesis   The hypothesis to be tested.

Number of days of inventory   An activity ratio equal to the number of days in a period divided by the inventory ratio for the period; an indication of the number of days a company ties up funds in inventory.

Number of days of payables   An activity ratio equal to the number of days in a period divided by the payables turnover ratio for the period; an estimate of the average number of days it takes a company to pay its suppliers.

Number of days of receivables   Estimate of the average number of days it takes to collect on credit accounts.

Objective probabilities   Probabilities that generally do not vary from person to person; includes a priori and objective probabilities.

Objectives   The investor's goals expressed in terms of risk and return and included in the policy statement.

Off-balance sheet financing   Arrangements that do not result in additional liabilities on the balance sheet but nonetheless create economic obligations.

Off-market FRA   A contract in which the initial value is intentionally set at a value other than zero and therefore requires a cash payment at the start from one party to the other.

Offsetting   A transaction in exchange-listed derivative markets in which a party re-enters the market to close out a position.

Oligopoly   A market structure in which a small number of firms compete.

One-sided hypothesis test (or one-tailed hypothesis test)   A test in which the null hypothesis is rejected only if the evidence indicates that the population parameter is greater than (smaller than) θ_0. The alternative hypothesis also has one side.

Open market operation   The purchase or sale of government securities—U.S. Treasury bills and bonds—by the Federal Reserve in the open market.

Operating activities   Activities that are part of the day-to-day business functioning of an entity, such as selling inventory and providing services.

Operating breakeven   The number of units produced and sold at which the company's operating profit is zero (revenues = operating costs).

Operating cycle   A measure of the time needed to convert raw materials into cash from a sale; it consists of the number of days of inventory and the number of days of receivables.

Operating lease   An agreement allowing the lessee to use some asset for a period of time; essentially a rental.

Operating leverage   The use of fixed costs in operations.

Operating profit (operating income)   A company's profits on its usual business activities before deducting taxes.

Operating profit margin (operating margin)   A profitability ratio calculated as operating income (i.e., income before interest and taxes) divided by revenue.

Operating return on assets (operating ROA)   A profitability ratio calculated as operating income divided by average total assets.

Operating risk   The risk attributed to the operating cost structure, in particular the use of fixed costs in operations; the risk arising from the mix of fixed and variable costs; the risk that a company's operations may be severely affected by environmental, social, and governance risk factors.

Operations risk or operational risk   The risk of loss from failures in a company's systems and procedures (for example, due to computer failures or human failures) or events completely outside of the control of organizations (which would include "acts of God" and terrorist actions).

Opportunity cost   The value that investors forgo by choosing a particular course of action; the value of something in its best alternative use.

Opportunity set   The set of assets available for investment.

Optimal capital structure   The capital structure at which the value of the company is maximized.

Optimal portfolio   The portfolio on the efficient frontier that has the highest utility for a given investor. It lies at the point of tangency between the efficient frontier and the curve with the investor's highest possible utility.

Optimizer   A specialized computer program or a spreadsheet that solves for the portfolio weights that will result in the lowest risk for a specified level of expected return.

Option   A financial instrument that gives one party the right, but not the obligation, to buy or sell an underlying asset from or to another party at a fixed price over a specific period of time. Also referred to as contingent claims.

Option price, option premium, or premium The amount of money a buyer pays and seller receives to engage in an option transaction.

Ordinal scale A measurement scale that sorts data into categories that are ordered (ranked) with respect to some characteristic.

Ordinary annuity An annuity with a first cash flow that is paid one period from the present.

Ordinary least squares (OLS) An estimation method based on the criterion of minimizing the sum of the squared residuals of a regression.

Ordinary shares (**common stock or common shares**) Equity shares that are subordinate to all other types of equity (e.g., preferred equity).

Organic growth Company growth in output or sales that is achieved by making investments internally (i.e., excludes growth achieved through mergers and acquisitions).

Orthogonal Uncorrelated; at a right angle.

Other comprehensive income Items of comprehensive income that are not reported on the income statement; comprehensive income minus net income.

Other post-retirement benefits Promises by the company to pay benefits in the future, other than pension benefits, such as life insurance premiums and all or part of health care insurance for its retirees.

Other receivables Amounts owed to the company from parties other than customers.

Outcome A possible value of a random variable.

Outliers Small numbers of observations at either extreme (small or large) of a sample.

Out-of-sample forecast errors The differences between actual and predicted value of time series outside the sample period used to fit the model.

Out-of-sample test A test of a strategy or model using a sample outside the time period on which the strategy or model was developed.

Out-of-the-money Options that, if exercised, would require the payment of more money than the value received and therefore would not be currently exercised.

Output gap Real GDP minus potential GDP.

Overnight index swap (OIS) A swap in which the floating rate is the cumulative value of a single unit of currency invested at an overnight rate during the settlement period.

Overweighted A condition in which a portfolio, for whatever reason, includes more of a class of securities than the relative market value alone would justify.

Owners' equity The excess of assets over liabilities; the residual interest of shareholders in the assets of an entity after deducting the entity's liabilities.

Paired comparisons test A statistical test for differences based on paired observations drawn from samples that are dependent on each other.

Paired observations Observations that are dependent on each other.

Pairs arbitrage trade A trade in two closely related stocks involving the short sale of one and the purchase of the other.

Panel data Observations through time on a single characteristic of multiple observational units.

Parameter A descriptive measure computed from or used to describe a population of data, conventionally represented by Greek letters.

Parameter instability The problem or issue of population regression parameters that have changed over time.

Parametric test Any test (or procedure) concerned with parameters or whose validity depends on assumptions concerning the population generating the sample.

Partial regression coefficients or partial slope coefficients The slope coefficients in a multiple regression.

Partnership A business owned and operated by more than one individual.

Passive strategy In reference to short-term cash management, it is an investment strategy characterized by simple decision rules for making daily investments.

Payables turnover An activity ratio calculated as purchases divided by average trade payables.

Payer swaption A swaption that allows the holder to enter into a swap as the fixed-rate payer and floating-rate receiver.

Payment date The day that the company actually mails out (or electronically transfers) a dividend payment.

Payment netting A means of settling payments in which the amount owed by the first party to the second is netted with the amount owed by the second party to the first; only the net difference is paid.

Payoff The value of an option at expiration.

Payoff matrix A table that shows the payoffs for every possible action by each player for every possible action by each other player.

Payout ratio The percentage of total earnings paid out in dividends in any given year (in per-share terms, DPS/EPS).

Peak The culmination of a bull market when prices stop rising and begin declining.

Pecking order theory The theory that managers take into account how their actions might be interpreted by outsiders and thus order their preferences for various forms of corporate financing. Forms of financing that are least visible to outsiders (e.g., internally generated funds) are most preferable to managers and those that are most visible (e.g., equity) are least preferable.

Per unit contribution margin The amount that each unit sold contributes to covering fixed costs—that is, the difference between the price per unit and the variable cost per unit.

Percentage-of-completion A method of revenue recognition in which, in each accounting period, the company estimates what percentage of the contract is complete and then reports that percentage of the total contract revenue in its income statement.

Percentiles Quantiles that divide a distribution into 100 equal parts.

Perfect collinearity The existence of an exact linear relation between two or more independent variables or combinations of independent variables.

Perfect competition A market in which there are many firms each selling an identical product; there are many buyers; there are no restrictions on entry into the industry; firms in the industry have no advantage over potential new entrants; and firms and buyers are well informed about the price of each firm's product.

Perfect price discrimination Price discrimination that extracts the entire consumer surplus.

Perfectly elastic demand Demand with an infinite price elasticity; the quantity demanded changes by an infinitely large percentage in response to a tiny price change.

Perfectly inelastic demand Demand with a price elasticity of zero; the quantity demanded remains constant when the price changes.

Performance appraisal The evaluation of risk-adjusted performance; the evaluation of investment skill.

Performance guarantee A guarantee from the clearinghouse that if one party makes money on a transaction, the clearinghouse ensures it will be paid.

Performance measurement The calculation of returns in a logical and consistent manner.

Period costs Costs (e.g., executives' salaries) that cannot be directly matched with the timing of revenues and which are thus expensed immediately.

Periodic rate The quoted interest rate per period; the stated annual interest rate divided by the number of compounding periods per year.

Permanent differences Differences between tax and financial reporting of revenue (expenses) that will not be reversed at some future date. These result in a difference between the company's effective tax rate and statutory tax rate and do not result in a deferred tax item.

Permutation An ordered listing.

Perpetuity A perpetual annuity, or a set of never-ending level sequential cash flows, with the first cash flow occurring one period from now.

Pet projects Projects in which influential managers want the corporation to invest. Often, unfortunately, pet projects are selected without undergoing normal capital budgeting analysis.

Phillips curve A curve that shows a relationship between inflation and unemployment.

Plain vanilla swap An interest rate swap in which one party pays a fixed rate and the other pays a floating rate, with both sets of payments in the same currency.

Platykurtic Describes a distribution that is less peaked than the normal distribution.

Point estimate A single numerical estimate of an unknown quantity, such as a population parameter.

Point of sale Systems that capture transaction data at the physical location in which the sale is made.

Poison pill A pre-offer takeover defense mechanism that makes it prohibitively costly for an acquirer to take control of a target without the prior approval of the target's board of directors.

Poison puts A pre-offer takeover defense mechanism that gives target company bondholders the right to sell their bonds back to the target at a pre-specified redemption price, typically at or above par value; this defense increases the need for cash and raises the cost of the acquisition.

Policy statement A statement in which the investor specifies investment goals, constraints, and risk preferences.

Pooled estimate An estimate of a parameter that involves combining (pooling) observations from two or more samples.

Pooling of interests accounting method A method of accounting in which combined companies were portrayed as if they had always operated as a single economic entity. Called pooling of interests under U.S. GAAP and uniting of interests under IFRS. (No longer allowed under U.S. GAAP or IFRS.)

Population All members of a specified group.

Population mean The arithmetic mean value of a population; the arithmetic mean of all the observations or values in the population.

Population standard deviation A measure of dispersion relating to a population in the same unit of measurement as the observations, calculated as the positive square root of the population variance.

Population variance A measure of dispersion relating to a population, calculated as the mean of the squared deviations around the population mean.

Portfolio performance attribution The analysis of portfolio performance in terms of the contributions from various sources of risk.

Portfolio possibilities curve A graphical representation of the expected return and risk of all portfolios that can be formed using two assets.

Position trader A trader who typically holds positions open overnight.

Positive serial correlation Serial correlation in which a positive error for one observation increases the chance of a positive error for another observation, and a negative error for one observation increases the chance of a negative error for another observation.

Posterior probability An updated probability that reflects or comes after new information.

Potential credit risk The risk associated with the possibility that a payment due at a later date will not be made.

Potential GDP The value of production when all the economy's labor, capital, land, and entrepreneurial ability are fully employed; the quantity of real GDP at full employment.

Power of a test The probability of correctly rejecting the null—that is, rejecting the null hypothesis when it is false.

Precautionary stocks A level of inventory beyond anticipated needs that provides a cushion in the event that it takes longer to replenish inventory than expected or in the case of greater than expected demand.

Pre-investing The strategy of using futures contracts to enter the market without an immediate outlay of cash.

Prepaid expense A normal operating expense that has been paid in advance of when it is due.

Present (price) value of a basis point (PVBP) The change in the bond price for a 1 basis point change in yield. Also called *basis point value* (BPV).

Present value (PV) The present discounted value of future cash flows: For assets, the present discounted value of the future net cash inflows that the asset is expected to generate; for liabilities, the present discounted value of the future net cash outflows that are expected to be required to settle the liabilities.

Presentation currency The currency in which financial statement amounts are presented.

Pretax margin A profitability ratio calculated as earnings before taxes divided by revenue.

Price ceiling A regulation that makes it illegal to charge a price higher than a specified level.

Price continuity A feature of a liquid market in which there are small price changes from one transaction to the next due to the depth of the market.

Price discovery A feature of futures markets in which futures prices provide valuable information about the price of the underlying asset.

Price discrimination The practice of selling different units of a good or service for different prices or of charging one customer different prices for different quantities bought.

Price elasticity of demand A units-free measure of the responsiveness of the quantity demanded of a good to a change in its price, when all other influences on buyers' plans remain the same.

Price floor A regulation that makes it illegal to trade at a price lower than a specified level.

Price limits Limits imposed by a futures exchange on the price change that can occur from one day to the next.

Price relative A ratio of an ending price over a beginning price; it is equal to 1 plus the holding period return on the asset.

Price taker A firm that cannot influence the price of the good or service it produces.

Price to book value A valuation ratio calculated as price per share divided by book value per share.

Price to cash flow A valuation ratio calculated as price per share divided by cash flow per share.

Price to sales A valuation ratio calculated as price per share divided by sales per share.

Price/earnings (P/E) ratio The number by which expected earnings per share is multiplied to estimate a stock's value; also called the *earnings multiplier.*

Priced risk Risk for which investors demand compensation for bearing (e.g. equity risk, company-specific factors, macroeconomic factors).

Price-setting option The operational flexibility to adjust prices when demand varies from forecast. For example, when demand exceeds capacity, the company could benefit from the excess demand by increasing prices.

Price-weighted index An index calculated as an arithmetic mean of the current prices of the sampled securities.

Primary market The market in which newly issued securities are sold by their issuers, who receive the proceeds.

Principal The amount of funds originally invested in a project or instrument; the face value to be paid at maturity.

Principal–agent problem The problem of devising compensation rules that induce an *agent* to act in the best interest of a *principal*.

Prior probabilities Probabilities reflecting beliefs prior to the arrival of new information.

Private placement A new issue sold directly to a small group of investors, usually institutions.

Probability A number between 0 and 1 describing the chance that a stated event will occur.

Probability density function A function with non-negative values such that probability can be described by areas under the curve graphing the function.

Probability distribution A distribution that specifies the probabilities of a random variable's possible outcomes.

Probability function A function that specifies the probability that the random variable takes on a specific value.

Probit model A qualitative-dependent-variable multiple regression model based on the normal distribution.

Producer surplus The price of a good minus its minimum supply-price, summed over the quantity sold.

Product differentiation Making a product slightly different from the product of a competing firm.

Production quota An upper limit to the quantity of a good that may be produced in a specified period.

Production-flexibility The operational flexibility to alter production when demand varies from forecast. For example, if demand is strong, a company may profit from employees working overtime or from adding additional shifts.

Profitability ratios Ratios that measure a company's ability to generate profitable sales from its resources (assets).

Project sequencing To defer the decision to invest in a future project until the outcome of some or all of a current project is known. Projects are sequenced through time, so that investing in a project creates the option to invest in future projects.

Projected benefit obligation Under U.S. GAAP, a measure used in estimating a defined-benefit pension plan's liabilities, defined as "the actuarial present value as of a date of all benefits attributed by the pension benefit formula to employee ser-

vice rendered prior to that date. The projected benefit obligation is measured using assumptions as to future compensation if the pension benefit formula is based on those future compensation levels."

Proportionate consolidation A method of accounting for joint ventures where the venturer's share of the assets, liabilities, income and expenses of the joint venture are combined on a line-by-line basis with similar items on the venturer's financial statements.

Protective put An option strategy in which a long position in an asset is combined with a long position in a put.

Provision In accounting, a liability of uncertain timing or amount.

Proxy fight An attempt to take control of a company through a shareholder vote.

Proxy statement A public document that provides the material facts concerning matters on which shareholders will vote.

Pseudo-random numbers Numbers produced by random number generators.

Pull on liquidity When disbursements are paid too quickly or trade credit availability is limited, requiring companies to expend funds before they receive funds from sales that could cover the liability.

Purchase method A method of accounting for a business combination where the acquiring company allocates the purchase price to each asset acquired and liability assumed at fair value. If the purchase price exceeds the allocation, the excess is recorded as goodwill.

Purchased in-process research and development costs The costs of research and development in progress at an acquired company.

Purchasing power gain A gain in value caused by changes in price levels. Monetary liabilities experience purchasing power gains during periods of inflation.

Purchasing power loss A loss in value caused by changes in price levels. Monetary assets experience purchasing power losses during periods of inflation.

Pure discount instruments Instruments that pay interest as the difference between the amount borrowed and the amount paid back.

Pure factor portfolio A portfolio with sensitivity of 1 to the factor in question and a sensitivity of 0 to all other factors.

Pure-play method A method for estimating the beta for a company or project; it requires using a comparable company's beta and adjusting it for financial leverage differences.

Put   An option that gives the holder the right to sell an underlying asset to another party at a fixed price over a specific period of time.

Put–call parity   An equation expressing the equivalence (parity) of a portfolio of a call and a bond with a portfolio of a put and the underlying, which leads to the relationship between put and call prices

Put–call–forward parity   The relationship among puts, calls, and forward contracts.

p-Value   The smallest level of significance at which the null hypothesis can be rejected; also called the marginal significance level.

Qualifying special purpose entities   Under U.S. GAAP, a special purpose entity structured to avoid consolidation that must meet qualification criteria.

Qualitative dependent variables   Dummy variables used as dependent variables rather than as independent variables.

Quantile (or fractile)   A value at or below which a stated fraction of the data lies.

Quantity theory of money   The proposition that in the long run, an increase in the quantity of money brings an equal percentage increase in the price level.

Quartiles   Quantiles that divide a distribution into four equal parts.

Quick assets   Assets that can be most readily converted to cash (e.g., cash, short-term marketable investments, receivables).

Quick ratio, or acid test ratio   A stringent measure of liquidity that indicates a company's ability to satisfy current liabilities with its most liquid assets, calculated as (cash + short-term marketable investments + receivables) divided by current liabilities.

Quintiles   Quantiles that divide a distribution into five equal parts.

Random number   An observation drawn from a uniform distribution.

Random number generator   An algorithm that produces uniformly distributed random numbers between 0 and 1.

Random variable   A quantity whose future outcomes are uncertain.

Random walk   A time series in which the value of the series in one period is the value of the series in the previous period plus an unpredictable random error.

Range   The difference between the maximum and minimum values in a dataset.

Ratio scales   A measurement scale that has all the characteristics of interval measurement scales as well as a true zero point as the origin.

Ratio spread   An option strategy in which a long position in a certain number of options is offset by a short position in a certain number of other options on the same underlying, resulting in a risk-free position.

Rational expectation   The most accurate forecast possible, a forecast that uses all the available information, including knowledge of the relevant economic forces that influence the variable being forecasted.

Real business cycle theory   A theory of the business cycle that regards random fluctuations in productivity as the main source of economic fluctuations.

Real exchange rate   The relative price of foreign-made goods and services to U.S.-made goods and services.

Real risk-free interest rate   The single-period interest rate for a completely risk-free security if no inflation were expected.

Real wage rate   The quantity of goods and services that an hour's work can buy. It is equal to the money wage rate divided by the price level and multiplied by 100.

Realizable value (settlement value)   With reference to assets, the amount of cash or cash equivalents that could currently be obtained by selling the asset in an orderly disposal; with reference to liabilities, the undiscounted amount of cash or cash equivalents expected to be paid to satisfy the liabilities in the normal course of business.

Realized capital gains   Capital gains that result when an appreciated asset is sold; realized capital gains are taxable.

Receivables turnover   An activity ratio equal to revenue divided by average receivables.

Receiver swaption   A swaption that allows the holder to enter into a swap as the fixed-rate receiver and floating-rate payer.

Recessionary gap   The amount by which potential GDP exceeds real GDP.

Reference base period   The period in which the CPI is defined to be 100.

Regime   With reference to a time series, the underlying model generating the times series.

Registered competitive market makers (RCMMs)   Members of an exchange who are allowed to use their memberships to buy or sell for their own account within the specific trading obligations set down by the exchange.

Registered traders   Members of the stock exchange who are allowed to use their memberships to buy and sell for their own account, which means they save commissions on their trading but they provide liquidity to the market, and they abide by exchange regulations on how they can trade.

Regression coefficients   The intercept and slope coefficient(s) of a regression.

Regulatory risk   The risk associated with the uncertainty of how derivative transactions will be regulated or with changes in regulations.

Rejection point (or critical value)   A value against which a computed test statistic is compared to decide whether to reject or not reject the null hypothesis.

Relative dispersion   The amount of dispersion relative to a reference value or benchmark.

Relative frequency   With reference to an interval of grouped data, the number of observations in the interval divided by the total number of observations in the sample.

Relative-strength (RS) ratio   The ratio of a stock price or an industry index value to a market indicator series, indicating the stock's or the industry's performance relative to the overall market.

Renewable natural resources   Natural resources that can be used repeatedly without depleting what is available for future use.

Rent ceiling   A regulation that makes it illegal to charge a rent higher than a specified level.

Rent seeking   The pursuit of wealth by capturing economic rent—consumer surplus, producer surplus, or economic profit.

Reorganization   Agreements made by a company in bankruptcy under which a company's capital structure is altered and/or alternative arrangements are made for debt repayment; U.S. Chapter 11 bankruptcy. The company emerges from bankruptcy as a going concern.

Replacement value   The market value of a swap.

Report format   With respect to the format of a balance sheet, a format in which assets, liabilities, and equity are listed in a single column.

Reputational risk   The risk that a company will suffer an extended diminution in market value relative to other companies in the same industry due to a demonstrated lack of concern for environmental, social, and governance risk factors.

Required reserve ratio   The minimum percentage of deposits that banks are required to hold as reserves.

Reserve ratio   The fraction of a bank's total deposits that are held in reserves.

Reserves   A bank's reserves consist of notes and coins in its vaults plus its deposit at the Federal Reserve.

Residual autocorrelations   The sample autocorrelations of the residuals.

Residual claim   The owners' remaining claim on the company's assets after the liabilities are deducted.

Residual dividend approach   A dividend payout policy under which earnings in excess of the funds necessary to finance the equity portion of company's capital budget are paid out in dividends.

Residual loss   Agency costs that are incurred despite adequate monitoring and bonding of management.

Resistance level   A price at which a technician would expect a substantial increase in the supply of a stock to reverse a rising trend.

Retail method   An inventory accounting method in which the sales value of an item is reduced by the gross margin to calculate the item's cost.

Return on assets (ROA)   A profitability ratio calculated as net income divided by average total assets; indicates a company's net profit generated per dollar invested in total assets.

Return on common equity (ROCE)   A profitability ratio calculated as (net income − preferred dividends) divided by average common equity; equal to the return on equity ratio when no preferred equity is outstanding.

Return on equity (ROE)   A profitability ratio calculated as net income divided by average shareholders' equity.

Return on total capital   A profitability ratio calculated as EBIT divided by the sum of short- and long-term debt and equity.

Return prediction studies   Studies wherein investigations attempt to predict the time series of future rates of return using public information. An example would be predicting above-average returns for the stock market based on the aggregate dividend yield—e.g., high dividend yield indicates above average future market returns.

Revaluation   The process of valuing long-lived assets at fair value, rather than at cost less accumulated depreciation. Any resulting profit or loss is either reported on the income statement and/or through equity under revaluation surplus.

Revenue   The amount charged for the delivery of goods or services in the ordinary activities of a business over a stated period; the inflows of economic resources to a company over a stated period.

Reverse stock split   A reduction in the number of shares outstanding with a corresponding increase in share price, but no change to the company's underlying fundamentals.

Revolving credit agreements The strongest form of short-term bank borrowing facilities; they are in effect for multiple years (e.g., 3–5 years) and may have optional medium-term loan features.

Rho The sensitivity of the option price to the risk-free rate.

Ricardo-Barro equivalence The proposition that taxes and government borrowing are equivalent—a budget deficit has no effect on the real interest rate or investment.

Rising trend channel The range defined by security prices as they move progressively higher.

Risk averse The assumption about investors that they will choose the least risky alternative, all else being equal.

Risk budgeting The establishment of objectives for individuals, groups, or divisions of an organization that takes into account the allocation of an acceptable level of risk.

Risk governance The setting of overall policies and standards in risk management

Risk management The process of identifying the level of risk an entity wants, measuring the level of risk the entity currently has, taking actions that bring the actual level of risk to the desired level of risk, and monitoring the new actual level of risk so that it continues to be aligned with the desired level of risk.

Risk premium The expected return on an investment minus the risk-free rate.

Risk-free asset An asset with returns that exhibit zero variance.

Risk-neutral probabilities Weights that are used to compute a binomial option price. They are the probabilities that would apply if a risk-neutral investor valued an option.

Risk-neutral valuation The process by which options and other derivatives are priced by treating investors as though they were risk neutral.

Risky asset An asset with uncertain future returns.

Robust The quality of being relatively unaffected by a violation of assumptions.

Robust standard errors Standard errors of the estimated parameters of a regression that correct for the presence of heteroskedasticity in the regression's error term.

Root mean squared error (RMSE) The square root of the average squared forecast error; used to compare the out-of-sample forecasting performance of forecasting models.

Roy's safety first criterion A criterion asserting that the optimal portfolio is the one that minimizes the probability that portfolio return falls below a threshold level.

Rule of 72 The principle that the approximate number of years necessary for an investment to double is 72 divided by the stated interest rate.

Runs test A test of the weak-form efficient market hypothesis that checks for trends that persist longer in terms of positive or negative price changes than one would expect for a random series.

Safety stock A level of inventory beyond anticipated needs that provides a cushion in the event that it takes longer to replenish inventory than expected or in the case of greater than expected demand.

Safety-first rules Rules for portfolio selection that focus on the risk that portfolio value will fall below some minimum acceptable level over some time horizon.

Sales Generally, a synonym for revenue; "sales" is generally understood to refer to the sale of goods, whereas "revenue" is understood to include the sale of goods or services.

Sales returns and allowances An offset to revenue reflecting any cash refunds, credits on account, and discounts from sales prices given to customers who purchased defective or unsatisfactory items.

Sales risk Uncertainty with respect to the quantity of goods and services that a company is able to sell and the price it is able to achieve; the risk related to the uncertainty of revenues.

Sales-type lease A type of finance lease, from a lessor perspective, where the present value of the lease payments (lease receivable) exceeds the carrying value of the leased asset. The revenues earned by the lessor are operating (the profit on the sale) and financing (interest) in nature.

Salvage value The amount the company estimates that it can sell the asset for at the end of its useful life.

Sample A subset of a population.

Sample excess kurtosis A sample measure of the degree of a distribution's peakedness in excess of the normal distribution's peakedness.

Sample kurtosis A sample measure of the degree of a distribution's peakedness.

Sample mean The sum of the sample observations, divided by the sample size.

Sample selection bias Bias introduced by systematically excluding some members of the population according to a particular attribute—for example, the bias introduced when data availability leads to certain observations being excluded from the analysis.

Sample skewness A sample measure of degree of asymmetry of a distribution.

Sample standard deviation   The positive square root of the sample variance.

Sample statistic or statistic   A quantity computed from or used to describe a sample.

Sample variance   A sample measure of the degree of dispersion of a distribution, calculated by dividing the sum of the squared deviations from the sample mean by the sample size (n) minus 1.

Sampling   The process of obtaining a sample.

Sampling distribution   The distribution of all distinct possible values that a statistic can assume when computed from samples of the same size randomly drawn from the same population.

Sampling error   The difference between the observed value of a statistic and the quantity it is intended to estimate.

Sampling plan   The set of rules used to select a sample.

Sandwich spread   An option strategy that is equivalent to a short butterfly spread.

Sarbanes–Oxley Act   An act passed by the U.S. Congress in 2002 that created the Public Company Accounting Oversight Board (PCAOB) to oversee auditors.

Scalper   A trader who offers to buy or sell futures contracts, holding the position for only a brief period of time. Scalpers attempt to profit by buying at the bid price and selling at the higher ask price.

Scatter plot   A two-dimensional plot of pairs of observations on two data series.

Scenario analysis   Analysis that shows the changes in key financial quantities that result from given (economic) events, such as the loss of customers, the loss of a supply source, or a catastrophic event; a risk management technique involving examination of the performance of a portfolio under specified situations. Closely related to stress testing.

Screening   The application of a set of criteria to reduce a set of potential investments to a smaller set having certain desired characteristics.

Search activity   The time spent looking for someone with whom to do business.

Seasoned equity issues   New equity shares offered by firms that already have stock outstanding.

Seats   Memberships in a derivatives exchange.

Secondary market   The market in which outstanding securities are bought and sold by owners other than the issuers. Purpose is to provide liquidity for investors.

Sector neutralizing   Measure of financial reporting quality by subtracting the mean or median ratio for a given sector group from a given company's ratio.

Securities Act of 1933   An act passed by the U.S. Congress in 1933 that specifies the financial and other significant information that investors must receive when securities are sold, prohibits misrepresentations, and requires initial registration of all public issuances of securities.

Securities Exchange Act of 1934   An act passed by the U.S. Congress in 1934 that created the Securities and Exchange Commission (SEC), gave the SEC authority over all aspects of the securities industry, and empowered the SEC to require periodic reporting by companies with publicly traded securities.

Securities offering   A merger or acquisition in which target shareholders are to receive shares of the acquirer's common stock as compensation.

Security market index   An index created as a statistical measure of the performance of an entire market or segment of a market based on a sample of securities from the market or segment of a market.

Security market line (SML)   The graph of the capital asset pricing model.

Segment debt ratio   Segment liabilities divided by segment assets.

Segment margin   Segment profit (loss) divided by segment revenue.

Segment ROA   Segment profit (loss) divided by segment assets.

Segment turnover   Segment revenue divided by segment assets.

Semideviation   The positive square root of semivariance (sometimes called semistandard deviation).

Semilogarithmic   Describes a scale constructed so that equal intervals on the vertical scale represent equal rates of change, and equal intervals on the horizontal scale represent equal amounts of change.

Semistrong-form efficient market hypothesis   The belief that security prices fully reflect all publicly available information, including information from security transactions and company, economic, and political news.

Semivariance   The average squared deviation below the mean.

Sensitivity analysis   Analysis that shows the range of possible outcomes as specific assumptions are changed.

Separation theorem   The proposition that the investment decision, which involves investing in the market portfolio on the capital market line, is separate from the financing decision, which targets a specific point on the CML based on the investor's risk preference.

Serially correlated   With reference to regression errors, errors that are correlated across observations.

Service period   The period benefited by the employee's service, usually the period between the grant date and the vesting date.

Settlement date or payment date   The date on which the parties to a swap make payments.

Settlement period   The time between settlement dates.

Settlement price   The official price, designated by the clearinghouse, from which daily gains and losses will be determined and marked to market.

Settlement risk   When settling a contract, the risk that one party could be in the process of paying the counterparty while the counterparty is declaring bankruptcy.

Share repurchase   A transaction in which a company buys back its own shares. Unlike stock dividends and stock splits, share repurchases use corporate cash.

Shark repellents   A pre-offer takeover defense mechanism involving the corporate charter (e.g., staggered boards of directors and supermajority provisions).

Sharpe ratio   The average return in excess of the risk-free rate divided by the standard deviation of return; a measure of the average excess return earned per unit of standard deviation of return.

Short   The seller of a derivative contract. Also refers to the position of being short a derivative.

Short run   The period of time in which the quantity of at least one factor of production is fixed and the quantities of the other factors can be varied. The fixed factor is usually capital—that is, the firm has a given plant size.

Shortfall risk   The risk that portfolio value will fall below some minimum acceptable level over some time horizon.

Short-run aggregate supply   The relationship between the quantity of real GDP supplied and the price level when the money wage rate, the prices of other resources, and potential GDP remain constant.

Short-run industry supply curve   A curve that shows the quantity supplied by the industry at each price when the plant size of each firm and the number of firms in the industry remain the same.

Short-run macroeconomic equilibrium   A situation that occurs when the quantity of real GDP demanded equals the quantity of real GDP supplied—at the point of intersection of the *AD* curve and the *SAS* curve.

Short-run Phillips curve   A curve that shows the tradeoff between inflation and unemployment, when the expected inflation rate and the natural unemployment rate remain the same.

Short sale   The sale of borrowed securities with the intention of repurchasing them later at a lower price and earning the difference.

Shutdown point   The output and price at which the firm just covers its total variable cost. In the short run, the firm is indifferent between producing the profit-maximizing output and shutting down temporarily.

Signal   An action taken by an informed person (or firm) to send a message to uninformed people or an action taken outside a market that conveys information that can be used by the market.

Simple interest   The interest earned each period on the original investment; interest calculated on the principal only.

Simple random sample   A subset of a larger population created in such a way that each element of the population has an equal probability of being selected to the subset.

Simple random sampling   The procedure of drawing a sample to satisfy the definition of a simple random sample.

Simulation   Computer-generated sensitivity or scenario analysis that is based on probability models for the factors that drive outcomes.

Simulation trial   A complete pass through the steps of a simulation.

Single-payment loan   A loan in which the borrower receives a sum of money at the start and pays back the entire amount with interest in a single payment at maturity.

Single-price monopoly   A monopoly that must sell each unit of its output for the same price to all its customers.

Single-step format   With respect to the format of the income statement, a format that does not subtotal for gross profit (revenue minus cost of goods sold).

Skewed   Not symmetrical.

Skewness   A quantitative measure of skew (lack of symmetry); a synonym of skew.

Sole proprietorship   A business owned and operated by a single person.

Solvency   With respect to financial statement analysis, the ability of a company to fulfill its long-term obligations.

Solvency ratios   Ratios that measure a company's ability to meet its long-term obligations.

Sovereign yield spread   An estimate of the country spread (country equity premium) for a developing nation that is based on a comparison of bonds yields in country being analyzed and a developed country. The sovereign yield spread is the difference between a government bond yield in the country being analyzed, denominated in the currency of the developed country, and the Treasury bond yield on a similar maturity bond in the developed country.

Spearman rank correlation coefficient A measure of correlation applied to ranked data.

Special purpose entity (special purpose vehicle or variable interest entity) A non-operating entity created to carry out a specified purpose, such as leasing assets or securitizing receivables; can be a corporation, partnership, trust, limited liability, or partnership formed to facilitate a specific type of business activity.

Specialist The major market maker on U.S. stock exchanges who acts as a broker or dealer to ensure the liquidity and smooth functions of the secondary stock market.

Specific identification method An inventory accounting method that identifies which specific inventory items were sold and which remained in inventory to be carried over to later periods.

Speculative company A firm with a great degree of business and/or financial risk, with commensurate high earnings potential.

Speculative stock A stock that appears to be highly overpriced compared to its intrinsic valuation.

Spending phase Phase in the investment life cycle during which individuals' earning years end as they retire. They pay for expenses with income from social security and returns from prior investments and invest to protect against inflation.

Spin-off A form of restructuring in which shareholders of the parent company receive a proportional number of shares in a new, separate entity; shareholders end up owning stock in two different companies where there used to be one.

Split-off A form of restructuring in which shareholders of the parent company are given shares in a newly created entity in exchange for their shares of the parent company.

Split-rate In reference to corporate taxes, a split-rate system taxes earnings to be distributed as dividends at a different rate than earnings to be retained. Corporate profits distributed as dividends are taxed at a lower rate than those retained in the business.

Spread An option strategy involving the purchase of one option and sale of another option that is identical to the first in all respects except either exercise price or expiration.

Spurious correlation A correlation that misleadingly points towards associations between variables.

Stagflation The combination of inflation and recession.

Standard cost With respect to inventory accounting, the planned or target unit cost of inventory items or services.

Standard deviation The positive square root of the variance; a measure of dispersion in the same units as the original data.

Standard normal distribution (or unit normal distribution) The normal density with mean (μ) equal to 0 and standard deviation (σ) equal to 1.

Standardized beta With reference to fundamental factor models, the value of the attribute for an asset minus the average value of the attribute across all stocks, divided by the standard deviation of the attribute across all stocks.

Standardizing A transformation that involves subtracting the mean and dividing the result by the standard deviation.

Stated annual interest rate or quoted interest rate A quoted interest rate that does not account for compounding within the year.

Stated rate (nominal rate or coupon rate) The rate at which periodic interest payments are calculated.

Statement of cash flows (cash flow statement) A financial statement that reconciles beginning-of-period and end-of-period balance sheet values of cash; provides information about an entity's cash inflows and cash outflows as they pertain to operating, investing, and financing activities.

Statement of changes in shareholders' equity (statement of owners' equity) A financial statement that reconciles the beginning-of-period and end-of-period balance sheet values of shareholders' equity; provides information about all factors affecting shareholders' equity.

Statement of retained earnings A financial statement that reconciles beginning-of-period and end-of-period balance sheet values of retained income; shows the linkage between the balance sheet and income statement.

Static trade-off theory of capital structure A theory pertaining to a company's optimal capital structure; the optimal level of debt is found at the point where additional debt would cause the costs of financial distress to increase by a greater amount than the benefit of the additional tax shield.

Statistic A quantity computed from or used to describe a sample of data.

Statistical factor models A multifactor model in which statistical methods are applied to a set of historical returns to determine portfolios that best explain either historical return covariances or variances.

Statistical inference Making forecasts, estimates, or judgments about a larger group from a smaller group actually observed; using a sample statistic to infer the value of an unknown population parameter.

Statistically significant A result indicating that the null hypothesis can be rejected; with reference to an estimated regression coefficient, frequently understood to mean a result indicating that the corresponding population regression coefficient is different from 0.

Statistics The science of describing, analyzing, and drawing conclusions from data; also, a collection of numerical data.

Statutory merger A merger in which one company ceases to exist as an identifiable entity and all its assets and liabilities become part of a purchasing company.

Stock grants The granting of stock to employees as a form of compensation.

Stock options (stock option grants) The granting of stock options to employees as a form of compensation.

Stock purchase An acquisition in which the acquirer gives the target company's shareholders some combination of cash and securities in exchange for shares of the target company's stock.

Stock-out losses Profits lost from not having sufficient inventory on hand to satisfy demand.

Storage costs or carrying costs The costs of holding an asset, generally a function of the physical characteristics of the underlying asset.

Straddle An option strategy involving the purchase of a put and a call with the same exercise price. A straddle is based on the expectation of high volatility of the underlying.

Straight-line method A depreciation method that allocates evenly the cost of a long-lived asset less its estimated residual value over the estimated useful life of the asset.

Strangle A variation of a straddle in which the put and call have different exercise prices.

Strap An option strategy involving the purchase of two calls and one put.

Strategies All the possible actions of each player in a game.

Stratified random sampling A procedure by which a population is divided into subpopulations (strata) based on one or more classification criteria. Simple random samples are then drawn from each stratum in sizes proportional to the relative size of

each stratum in the population. These samples are then pooled.

Stress testing A set of techniques for estimating losses in extremely unfavorable combinations of events or scenarios.

Strip An option strategy involving the purchase of two puts and one call.

Strong-form efficient market hypothesis The belief that security prices fully reflect all information from both public and private sources.

Structural change Economic trend occurring when the economy is undergoing a major change in organization or in how it functions.

Structural surplus or deficit The budget balance that would occur if the economy were at full employment and real GDP were equal to potential GDP.

Structural unemployment The unemployment that arises when changes in technology or international competition change the skills needed to perform jobs or change the locations of jobs.

Structured note A variation of a floating-rate note that has some type of unusual characteristic such as a leverage factor or in which the rate moves opposite to interest rates.

Subjective probability A probability drawing on personal or subjective judgment.

Subsidiary merger A merger in which the company being purchased becomes a subsidiary of the purchaser.

Subsidy A payment made by the government to a producer.

Sunk cost A cost that has already been incurred.

Supply-side effects The effects of fiscal policy on employment, potential GDP, and aggregate supply.

Support level A price at which a technician would expect a substantial increase in price and volume for a stock to reverse a declining trend that was due to profit taking.

Surprise The actual value of a variable minus its predicted (or expected) value.

Survey approach An estimate of the equity risk premium that is based upon estimates provided by a panel of finance experts.

Survivorship bias The bias resulting from a test design that fails to account for companies that have gone bankrupt, merged, or are otherwise no longer reported in a database.

Sustainable growth rate The rate of dividend (and earnings) growth that can be sustained over time for a given level of return on equity, keeping the capital structure constant and without issuing additional common stock.

Swap An agreement between two parties to exchange a series of future cash flows.

Swap spread The difference between the fixed rate on an interest rate swap and the rate on a Treasury note with equivalent maturity; it reflects the general level of credit risk in the market.

Swaption An option to enter into a swap.

Symmetry principle A requirement that people in similar situations be treated similarly.

Synthetic call The combination of puts, the underlying, and risk-free bonds that replicates a call option.

Synthetic forward contract The combination of the underlying, puts, calls, and risk-free bonds that replicates a forward contract.

Synthetic index fund An index fund position created by combining risk-free bonds and futures on the desired index.

Synthetic put The combination of calls, the underlying, and risk-free bonds that replicates a put option.

Systematic factors Factors that affect the average returns of a large number of different assets.

Systematic risk The variability of returns that is due to macroeconomic factors that affect all risky assets. Because it affects all risky assets, it cannot be eliminated by diversification.

Systematic sampling A procedure of selecting every kth member until reaching a sample of the desired size. The sample that results from this procedure should be approximately random.

Takeover A merger; the term may be applied to any transaction, but is often used in reference to hostile transactions.

Takeover premium The amount by which the takeover price for each share of stock must exceed the current stock price in order to entice shareholders to relinquish control of the company to an acquirer.

Tangible assets Long-term assets with physical substance that are used in company operations, such as land (property), plant, and equipment.

Target balance A minimum level of cash to be held available—estimated in advance and adjusted for known funds transfers, seasonality, or other factors.

Target capital structure A company's chosen proportions of debt and equity.

Target company, or target The company in a merger or acquisition that is being acquired.

Target payout ratio A strategic corporate goal representing the long-term proportion of earnings that the company intends to distribute to shareholders as dividends.

Target semideviation The positive square root of target semivariance.

Target semivariance The average squared deviation below a target value.

Targeting rule A decision rule for monetary policy that sets the policy instrument at a level that makes the forecast of the ultimate policy target equal to the target.

Tax base (tax basis) The amount at which an asset or liability is valued for tax purposes.

Tax expense An aggregate of an entity's income tax payable (or recoverable in the case of a tax benefit) and any changes in deferred tax assets and liabilities. It is essentially the income tax payable or recoverable if these had been determined based on accounting profit rather than taxable income.

Tax incidence The division of the burden of the tax between the buyer and the seller.

Tax loss carry forward A taxable loss in the current period that may be used to reduce future taxable income.

Tax risk The uncertainty associated with tax laws.

Tax wedge The gap between the before-tax and after-tax wage rates.

Taxable income The portion of an entity's income that is subject to income taxes under the tax laws of its jurisdiction.

Taxable temporary differences Temporary differences that result in a taxable amount in a future period when determining the taxable profit as the balance sheet item is recovered or settled.

Taylor rule A rule that sets the federal funds rate at the equilibrium real interest rate (which Taylor says is 2 percent a year) plus amounts based on the inflation rate and the output gap.

***t*-Distribution** A symmetrical distribution defined by a single parameter, degrees of freedom, that is largely used to make inferences concerning the mean of a normal distribution whose variance is unknown.

Technical analysis Estimation of future security price movements based on past price and volume movements.

Technological efficiency A situation that occurs when the firm produces a given output by using the least amount of inputs.

Technology Any method of producing a good or service.

Temporal method A variation of the monetary/nonmonetary translation method that requires not only monetary assets and liabilities, but also nonmonetary assets and liabilities that are measured at their current value on the balance sheet date to be translated at the current exchange rate. Assets and liabilities are translated at rates consistent with the timing of their measurement value. This method is typically used when the functional currency is other than the local currency.

Tender offer A public offer whereby the acquirer invites target shareholders to submit ("tender") their shares in return for the proposed payment.

Tenor The original time to maturity on a swap.

Termination date The date of the final payment on a swap; also, the swap's expiration date.

Test statistic A quantity, calculated based on a sample, whose value is the basis for deciding whether or not to reject the null hypothesis.

Theta The rate at which an option's time value decays.

Third market Over-the-counter trading of securities listed on an exchange.

Time series A set of observations on a variable's outcomes in different time periods.

Time to expiration The time remaining in the life of a derivative, typically expressed in years.

Time value or speculative value The difference between the market price of the option and its intrinsic value, determined by the uncertainty of the underlying over the remaining life of the option.

Time value decay The loss in the value of an option resulting from movement of the option price toward its payoff value as the expiration day approaches.

Time value of money The principles governing equivalence relationships between cash flows with different dates.

Time-period bias The possibility that when we use a time-series sample, our statistical conclusion may be sensitive to the starting and ending dates of the sample.

Time-series analysis An examination of a firm's performance data over a period of time.

Time-series data Observations of a variable over time.

Time-weighted rate of return The compound rate of growth of one unit of currency invested in a portfolio during a stated measurement period; a measure of investment performance that is not sensitive to the timing and amount of withdrawals or additions to the portfolio.

Top-down analysis With reference to investment selection processes, an approach that starts with macro selection (i.e., identifying attractive geographic segments and/or industry segments) and then addresses selection of the most attractive investments within those segments.

Total asset turnover An activity ratio calculated as revenue divided by average total assets.

Total cost The cost of all the productive resources that a firm uses.

Total fixed cost The cost of the firm's fixed inputs.

Total invested capital The sum of market value of common equity, book value of preferred equity, and face value of debt.

Total probability rule A rule explaining the unconditional probability of an event in terms of probabilities of the event conditional on mutually exclusive and exhaustive scenarios.

Total probability rule for expected value A rule explaining the expected value of a random variable in terms of expected values of the random variable conditional on mutually exclusive and exhaustive scenarios.

Total product The total output produced by a firm in a given period of time.

Total return A return objective in which the investor wants to increase the portfolio value to meet a future need by both capital gains and current income reinvestment.

Total return swap A swap in which one party agrees to pay the total return on a security. Often used as a credit derivative, in which the underlying is a bond.

Total revenue The value of a firm's sales. It is calculated as the price of the good multiplied by the quantity sold.

Total revenue test A method of estimating the price elasticity of demand by observing the change in total revenue that results from a change in the price, when all other influences on the quantity sold remain the same.

Total variable cost The cost of all the firm's variable inputs.

Tracking error The standard deviation of the difference in returns between an active investment portfolio and its benchmark portfolio; also called tracking error volatility, tracking risk, and active risk.

Tracking portfolio A portfolio having factor sensitivities that are matched to those of a benchmark or other portfolio.

Tracking risk The standard deviation of the differences between a portfolio's returns and its benchmark's returns; a synonym of active risk.

Trade credit A spontaneous form of credit in which a purchaser of the goods or service is financing its purchase by delaying the date on which payment is made.

Trade receivables (commercial receivables or accounts receivable) Amounts customers owe the company for products that have been sold as well as amounts that may be due from suppliers (such as for returns of merchandise).

Trading securities (held-for-trading securities) Securities held by a company with the intent to trade them.

Transaction cost The cost of executing a trade. Low costs characterize an operationally efficient market.

Transaction exposure The risk of a change in value between the transaction date and the settlement date of an asset or liability denominated in a foreign currency.

Transactions motive In the context of inventory management, the need for inventory as part of the routine production–sales cycle.

Translation exposure The risk associated with the conversion of foreign financial statements into domestic currency.

Treasury bill A negotiable U.S. government security with a maturity of less than one year that pays no periodic interest but yields the difference between its par value and its discounted purchase price.

Treasury bond A U.S. government security with a maturity of more than 10 years that pays interest periodically.

Treasury note A U.S. government security with maturities of 1 to 10 years that pays interest periodically.

Treasury shares Shares that were issued and subsequently repurchased by the company.

Treasury stock method A method for accounting for the effect of options (and warrants) on earnings per share (EPS) that specifies what EPS would have been if the options and warrants had been exercised and the company had used the proceeds to repurchase common stock.

Tree diagram A diagram with branches emanating from nodes representing either mutually exclusive chance events or mutually exclusive decisions.

Trend A long-term pattern of movement in a particular direction.

Trimmed mean A mean computed after excluding a stated small percentage of the lowest and highest observations.

Trough The culmination of a bear market at which prices stop declining and begin rising.

Trust receipt arrangement The use of inventory as collateral for a loan. The inventory is segregated and held in trust, and the proceeds of any sale must be remitted to the lender immediately.

***t*-Test** A hypothesis test using a statistic (*t*-statistic) that follows a *t*-distribution.

Two-sided hypothesis test (or two-tailed hypothesis test) A test in which the null hypothesis is rejected in favor of the alternative hypothesis if the evidence indicates that the population parameter is either smaller or larger than a hypothesized value.

Type I error The error of rejecting a true null hypothesis.

Type II error The error of not rejecting a false null hypothesis.

Unbiasedness Lack of bias. A desirable property of estimators, an unbiased estimator is one whose expected value (the mean of its sampling distribution) equals the parameter it is intended to estimate.

Unbilled revenue (accrued revenue) Revenue that has been earned but not yet billed to customers as of the end of an accounting period.

Unclassified balance sheet A balance sheet that does not show subtotals for current assets and current liabilities.

Unconditional heteroskedasticity Heteroskedasticity of the error term that is not correlated with the values of the independent variable(s) in the regression.

Unconditional probability (or marginal probability) The probability of an event *not* conditioned on another event.

Underlying An asset that trades in a market in which buyers and sellers meet, decide on a price, and the seller then delivers the asset to the buyer and receives payment. The underlying is the asset or other derivative on which a particular derivative is based. The market for the underlying is also referred to as the spot market.

Underweighted A condition in which a portfolio, for whatever reason, includes less of a class of securities than the relative market value alone would justify.

Unearned fees Unearned fees are recognized when a company receives cash payment for fees prior to earning them.

Unearned revenue (deferred revenue) A liability account for money that has been collected for goods or services that have not yet been delivered; payment received in advance of providing a good or service.

Unemployment rate The number of unemployed people expressed as a percentage of all the people who have jobs or are looking for one. It is the percentage of the labor force who are unemployed.

Unidentifiable intangible An intangible that cannot be acquired singly and that typically possesses an indefinite benefit period; an example is accounting goodwill.

Unit elastic demand   Demand with a price elasticity of 1; the percentage change in the quantity demanded equals the percentage change in price.

Unit root   A time series that is not covariance stationary is said to have a unit root.

Uniting of interests method   A method of accounting in which combined companies were portrayed as if they had always operated as a single economic entity. Called pooling of interests under U.S. GAAP and uniting of interests under IFRS. (No longer allowed under U.S. GAAP or IFRS.)

Units-of-production method   A depreciation method that allocates the cost of a long-lived asset based on actual usage during the period.

Univariate distribution   A distribution that specifies the probabilities for a single random variable.

Unlimited funds   An unlimited funds environment assumes that the company can raise the funds it wants for all profitable projects simply by paying the required rate of return.

Unrealized capital gains   Capital gains that reflect the price appreciation of currently held unsold assets.

Unsystematic risk   Risk that is unique to an asset, derived from its particular characteristics. It can be eliminated in a diversified portfolio.

Unweighted index   An indicator series affected equally by the performance of each security in the sample regardless of price or market value. Also referred to as an *equal-weighted series*.

Up transition probability   The probability that an asset's value moves up.

Upstream   A transaction between two affiliates, an investor company and an associate company such that the associate company records a profit on its income statement. An example is a sale of inventory by the associate to the investor company.

Utilitarianism   A principle that states that we should strive to achieve "the greatest happiness for the greatest number of people."

Valuation   The process of determining the value of an asset or service.

Valuation allowance   A reserve created against deferred tax assets, based on the likelihood of realizing the deferred tax assets in future accounting periods.

Valuation process   Part of the investment decision process in which you estimate the value of a security.

Valuation ratios   Ratios that measure the quantity of an asset or flow (e.g., earnings) in relation to the

price associated with a specified claim (e.g., a share or ownership of the enterprise).

Value   The amount for which one can sell something, or the amount one must pay to acquire something.

Value at risk (VAR)   A money measure of the minimum value of losses expected during a specified time period at a given level of probability.

Value investors   With reference to equity investors, investors who are focused on paying a relatively low share price in relation to earnings or assets per share.

Value stocks   Stocks that appear to be undervalued for reasons besides earnings growth potential. These stocks are usually identified based on high dividend yields, low *P/E* ratios, or low price-to-book ratios.

Value-weighted index   An index calculated as the total market value of the securities in the sample. Market value is equal to the number of shares or bonds outstanding times the market price of the security.

Variable costs   Costs that fluctuate with the level of production and sales.

Variance   The expected value (the probability-weighted average) of squared deviations from a random variable's expected value.

Variation margin   Additional margin that must be deposited in an amount sufficient to bring the balance up to the initial margin requirement.

Vega   The relationship between option price and volatility.

Velocity of circulation   The average number of times a dollar of money is used annually to buy the goods and services that make up GDP.

Venturers   The owners of a joint venture. Each is active in the management and shares control of the joint venture.

Vertical analysis   Common-size analysis using only one reporting period or one base financial statement; for example, an income statement in which all items are stated as percentages of sales.

Vertical common-size analysis   The most common type of common-size analysis, in which the accounts in a given period are compared to a benchmark item in that same year.

Vertical merger   A merger involving companies at different positions of the same production chain; for example, a supplier or a distributor.

Vested benefit obligation   Under U.S. GAAP, a measure used in estimating a defined-benefit pension plan's liabilities, defined as the "actuarial present value of vested benefits."

Vested benefits   Future benefits promised to the employee regardless of continuing service. Benefits typically vest after a specified period of service or a specified period of service combined with age.

Vesting date The date that employees can first exercise stock options; vesting can be immediate or over a future period.

Volatility As used in option pricing, the standard deviation of the continuously compounded returns on the underlying asset.

Warehouse receipt arrangement The use of inventory as collateral for a loan; similar to a trust receipt arrangement except there is a third party (i.e., a warehouse company) that supervises the inventory.

Weak-form efficient market hypothesis The belief that security prices fully reflect all security market information.

Weighted average cost method An inventory accounting method that averages the total cost of available inventory items over the total units available for sale.

Weighted mean An average in which each observation is weighted by an index of its relative importance.

Weighted-average cost of capital A weighted average of the after-tax required rates of return on a company's common stock, preferred stock, and long-term debt, where the weights are the fraction of each source of financing in the company's target capital structure.

White knight A third party that is sought out by the target company's board to purchase the target in lieu of a hostile bidder.

White squire A third party that is sought out by the target company's board to purchase a substantial minority stake in the target—enough to block a hostile takeover without selling the entire company.

White-corrected standard errors A synonym for robust standard errors.

Winner's curse The tendency for the winner in certain competitive bidding situations to overpay, whether because of overestimation of intrinsic value, emotion, or information asymmetries.

Winsorized mean A mean computed after assigning a stated percent of the lowest values equal to one specified low value, and a stated percent of the highest values equal to one specified high value.

Working capital The difference between current assets and current liabilities.

Working capital management The management of a company's short-term assets (such as inventory) and short-term liabilities (such as money owed to suppliers).

Working capital turnover A comparison of revenues with working capital to produce a measure that shows how efficiently working capital is employed.

Working-age population The total number of people aged 15 years and over.

Yield The actual return on a debt security if it is held to maturity.

Yield beta A measure of the sensitivity of a bond's yield to a general measure of bond yields in the market that is used to refine the hedge ratio.

Yield spread The difference between the yield on a bond and the yield on a default-free security, usually a government note, of the same maturity. The yield spread is primarily determined by the market's perception of the credit risk on the bond.

Yield to maturity The annual return that an investor earns on a bond if the investor purchases the bond today and holds it until maturity.

Zero-cost collar A transaction in which a position in the underlying is protected by buying a put and selling a call with the premium from the sale of the call offsetting the premium from the purchase of the put. It can also be used to protect a floating-rate borrower against interest rate increases with the premium on a long cap offsetting the premium on a short floor.

INDEX

I-1

corporations, V2: 110–112
defined, V2: 100
demand for labor, V2: 272
departmental separation, V1: 40
dominant firm oligopoly, V2: 236–237
economic accounting by, V2: 102–103
economic efficiency, V2: 105–107, 180–181
economic problems of, V2: 100–104
economic profit, V2: 102
economies of scale/scope/team production, V2: 120–121
efficiency wages of, V2: 283
employee resignation procedures, V1: 70–71
entry and exit effects, V2: 171–173, 180–181, 222, 226
frictional unemployment and, V2: 312
GIPS and
    benefits of, V1: 130, 136, 138
    compliance guidelines, V1: 143
    definition of, V1: 137, 142–143
    fundamental responsibilities of, V1: 143
    policies and procedures, V1: 143, 156
    requirements, V1: 137, 139, 141
    verification requirements, V1: 144, 154–158
goals of, V2: 100
historical performance record, V1: 138, 150
incentive systems, V2: 108
independence and objectivity of, V1: 22, 23–24
information and organization, V2: 107–112
innovation in, V2: 208–209, 228–229
labor unions and, V2: 277–282
liability of, V1: 41
loyalty to, V1: 69
number of, in monopolistic competition, V2: 220–221
opportunity cost, V2: 101–102
partnerships, V2: 110–112
perfect competition decisions, V2: 163–169
price takers, V2: 161
principal-agent problem, V2: 108–109
procedures/policies for, V1: 26, 97
profit maximization decisions, V2: 102–103
profit measurement, V2: 100–101
proprietorships, V2: 109–112
range of goods/services, V2: 120, 209
in short-run/long-run, V2: 163

size, and survival of, V2: 131–132
supply curve, V2: 167–169
technology effects, V2: 104–105, 163, 178–179
transactions costs, V2: 119–120
types of, V2: 109–112
wage constraints, V2: 72–73
first call date, V5: 243
First Call/Thomson Financial, V1: 284
first derivative: as interpretation of duration, V5: 542
first in, first out (FIFO) methods
    accounting changes for inventory, V5: 84
    financial statements, V3: 405
    IFRS *Framework*, V3: 653
    inventory cost accounting, V3: 158–159, 213, 382–384, 395–403
    LIFO method vs., V3: 625–628, 666–668
first mortgage bonds, V5: 327
first par call date, V5: 245, 247
first refunding mortgage bonds, V5: 327
first-come, first-served, V2: 39, 56
first-stage financing in venture capital investing, V6: 214
fiscal imbalance, V2: 445–446
fiscal policy
    aggregate demand, V2: 338
    analysis of, V2: 455–457
    automatic, V2: 447
    business cycle stabilization, V2: 447–454
    defined, V2: 338, 426
    discretionary, V2: 447, 448–450
    Employment Act (1946), V2: 427
    expansionary fiscal policy, V2: 449
    federal budget, V2: 426–434
    generational effects, V2: 443–447
    goals of, V2: 357
    Keynesian view and, V2: 349
    supply side
        employment and GDP, V2: 434–438
        savings and investment, V2: 439–443
    valuation influence of, V5: 128
fiscal year, V2: 427
Fisher, Irving, V4: 45n2
Fisher, Kenneth, V5: 152
Fisher, Philip, V5: 152
Fitch ratings, V3: 9; V5: 278
five-component model: financial statement analysis, V4: 147–149
fixed assets
    disclosures to compare average age of depreciable assets, V3: 438–442
    turnover of
        calculating, V3: 322–324

defined, V3: 322
interpreting, V3: 326
fixed burden estimates: financial statement, V4: 155
fixed charges coverage, V3: 333, 334
fixed costs. See also average fixed cost (AFC); total fixed cost (TFC)
    leverage, V3: 332
fixed-income securities. See also debt securities
    arbitrage funds, V6: 221–223
    categories of, V5: 234
    exchange traded funds (ETFs), V6: 198
fixed-principal Treasury securities, V5: 307
fixed-rate debt. See also long-term liabilities (debt)
    floating-rate debt vs., V4: 49
fixed-rate payer, V5: 380
fixed-rate perpetual preferred stock, V4: 50
fixed-rate receiver, V5: 380
fixed-rate swaps
    defined, V6: 9
    interest rate swap, V6: 141
    termination, V6: 133–134
flat interest rate term structure, V5: 365–366
flat trend channels, V1: 576–577, 583
flat yield curve, V5: 363, 476
flexibility
    short-term borrowing options, V4: 131
    in standards, V3: 18
float
    cost of, V4: 70–72
    defined, V4: 117
    disbursement float, V4: 125–126
    float factor, V4: 117–118
floating-rate debt. See long-term liabilities (debt)
floating-rate securities (floaters)
    in cash flow estimation, V5: 400
    coupon payments, V5: 238–242
    deleveraged, V5: 332
    dual-indexed, V5: 332
    fixed-rate debt securities vs., V4: 49
    interest rate risk for, V5: 268–269
    interest rate swaps as, V5: 380–381
    medium-term notes, V5: 331
    spread/margin measures for, V5: 461–464
    swaps, V6: 9, 133–134, 141–144
floor
    coupon rate, V5: 239, 249
    interest rate options, V6: 94–95
floor brokers, V5: 24
floor traders, V6: 62–63